MOON HANDBOOKS

D0388720

ISTANBUL
& THE TURKISH COAST

JESSICA TAMTÜRK

ISTANBUL & THE TURKISH COAST

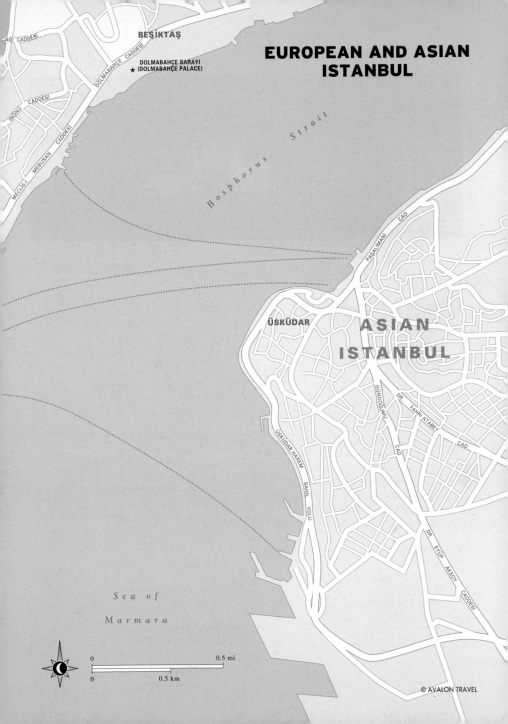

Contents

Discover Istanbul & the Turkish Coast

Istanbul not only delineates the continental divide between Asia and Europe, but serves as a meeting point of occidental, oriental, and Middle Eastern cultures. Turkey's crown jewel, known as the "muse of history," is the only city in the world to occupy two continents, and was so desirable that it bore three names and won the heart of as many empires.

Soak up the magic of Istanbul and enjoy the contradictions of its daily life. Muezzins call the faithful to prayer from minarets atop basilicas that were built by Christianity's forebears. In the streets, fashion battles are waged with hijabs and designer miniskirts. And nowhere is the synergy more apparent than on the table, where spice-infused kebabs are served alongside Greek *mezes* (appetizers) and, of course, the ubiquitous western cola.

This rich historical, cultural, and spiritual melting pot extends to the water-lapped lands just beyond Istanbul as well. Steeped in a past spanning over 10 millennia, the history of this fertile land is as layered as baklava. More than a dozen distinct peoples rose and fell during their time in the region, each fighting to gain or retain their wedge of this surreal geography. In Turkey's interior, between the sun-kissed, rambling Aegean coast in the west and the glistening waters of the Turkish riviera in

Planning Your Trip

▶ WHERE TO GO

Istanbul

Istanbul's endless variety of venues tickle the senses, offer an intimate view of civilizations past, and quicken the heart with its fast-paced metropolitan beat. Old town Sultanahmet's sights include Topkapı Palace; 1,500-year-old Byzantine basilica Ayasofya; the scintillating Blue Mosque; and the original enclosed mall—the Grand Bazaar. Cross the Golden Horn for Taksim's belle-époque architecture, cross the Bosphorus into Asia, or sail to the Princes' Islands.

IF YOU HAVE . . .

- **ONE WEEK:** Visit Istanbul and Cappadocia.
- **TWO WEEKS:** Add a cruise through the Turquoise Coast's half dozen resorts.
- **THREE WEEKS:** Add the Southern Aegean cities of Kuşadası, Pamukkale, and Selçuk.
- **FOUR WEEKS:** Add the Northern Aegean Coast, Ankara, and Konya.

Thrace and the Sea of Marmara

This little-known slice of Turkey is gaining popularity due to places like Gökçeada island. Windsurfing, diving among antique amphorae, and biking draw visitors to its shores. The Dardanelles Strait, gateway to inland Anatolia, bears the scars of lengthy battles at Gallipoli National Park. Other highlights of the region are Kırkpınar Oil Wrestling Festival and Selimiye Mosque in Edirne; Ottoman landmarks in Bursa; and Iznik, where Christianity's First Ecumenical Council met in A.D. 325.

The Northern Aegean Coast

At the tip of Anatolia, this region unfurls like an archaeological dig in progress, heightened by history's major capitals Pergamum and King Croesus's Sardis. Catapult back 5,000 years by visiting Troy. Sample Turkey's best vintages in the rustic B&Bs on the island of Bozcaada. Visit Izmir's metropolitan and Levantine haunts and explore Alaçatı's windsurfing and spa-hopping potential in Çeşme.

Cappadocia's fairy chimneys

The Southern Aegean Coast

Hugged by gorgeous beaches and 17 bygone cities, this coast lures sun worshippers and history buffs. Kuşadası entices with modern hotels, sandy beaches, and water sports. Ephesus, once home to the Temple of

the south, there are more than 150,000 square miles of rugged mountain ranges and cultivated plains, peppered with countless remnants of erstwhile civilizations.

Perhaps the most bizarre geography in the country lies in Cappadocia. The region is home to centuries-old cave dwellings and chapels carved inside majestic fairy chimneys, eroded from volcanic tuff accumulation. Explore this intense and unbelievable landscape from above in a hot-air balloon, the preferred method of sightseeing in Cappadocia. Rides dip low enough for passengers to pick lusciously ripe apricots from high branches.

Come, sail off on the dreamy Blue Voyage along the Turquoise Coast's scintillating waters. Feed loggerhead turtles by hand in Dalyan. Trek the 500-kilometer Lycian Way along the pine-clad mountains that jut into the Med. Mull over matters of mysticism at the Mevlâna Museum and Mosque in Konya. As dazzling and mysterious as its landscape and history are, Istanbul is also amazing because of the people who live here. Meet the locals and see for yourself what Turkish hospitality is all about.

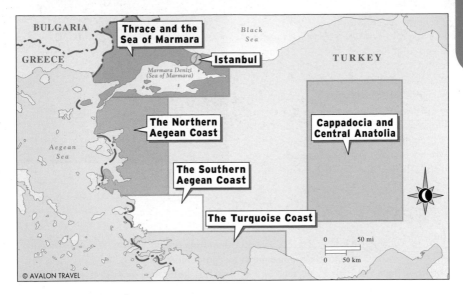

Artemis, is Turkey's largest ancient city. Another crowd-pleaser, Meryemana is believed to be the final resting place of the Virgin Mary. Turkey's interior beckons with dizzying petrified waterfalls, terraced basins at Pamukkale, and Greco-Roman ruins at the 2,300-year-old spa Hierapolis.

The Turquoise Coast

The idyllic Blue Voyage cruises along 1,000 kilometers of coastline, set against vertiginous cliffs, luxuriant forests, ancient cities, and the azure Mediterranean Sea. The region features Fethiye's ghost town, Kayaköy; hedonist resort Bodrum; natural Blue Lagoon near Ölüdeniz; and Dalyan's river-hugging mountains. Coastal resorts Kaş and Kalkan

give way to Kaleköy, with its Crusader fortress and sunken city. En route to historical and modern Antalya is Demre's Byzantine church of Santa Claus.

Cappadocia and Central Anatolia

Turkish capital Ankara was settled over 3,000 years ago. Its Citadel district boasts the Museum of Anatolian Civilizations. To the west, Konya awaits with spectacular Seljuk mosques, the Mevlana Shrine, and its whirling dervish order. East of Ankara lies Hattuşaş, whose 4,000-year-old Lion's Gate is impressive. Inland, fairy chimneys, underground cities, rock-hewn chapels, and five-star cave hotels and restaurants roused Cappadocia's global appeal.

▶ WHEN TO GO

The country's most visited destinations remain the coastal provinces, with a high tourist season in June–early September. Istanbul's heat and long lines can be overwhelming in July and August. The western and southern coasts benefit from a seasonal Mediterranean climate, with hot summers and chilly winters. Turkey's Anatolian plateau is dry and cold in winter.

The shoulder seasons, early April–late May and mid-September–mid-November, offer milder weather, sparser crowds, and better deals on airfares and hotels. Spring heralds Istanbul's annual tulip celebration and the city's world-renowned annual arts festival. Wine aesthetes uncork their passion in Thrace, Çeşme, or Cappadocia at the tail end of September, just in time for the grape harvest. To get the most for your buck consider visiting Turkey in the spring or fall.

The month of April heralds Istanbul's venerated tulip season.

► BEFORE YOU GO

Prior to visiting Turkey, you need a valid passport and a visa. However, don't spend time securing a visa with a consulate or embassy; three-month, single- or multiple-entry visas can be obtained at every entry point in Turkey, including airports. There are no medical requirements to enter Turkey.

What to Take

Packing for your trip is simple because clothing in Turkey is inexpensive enough to allow purchases on the go without breaking the bank. A medium-sized wheeled suitcase carrying just the bare necessities is all that you'll need. Backpacks, on the other hand, are easy bait for lurking pickpockets and thieves and can be too bulky for public transportation.

As with all travel, try to limit clothing to versatile, wrinkle-free pieces that can be mixed and matched. While most hotels have laundry services—not inexpensive—small village inns may not. Fashion trends are closely followed in Turkish society and, as in the West, anything is fair game, from t-shirts, jeans, and sneakers to heels, chiffon, and a handbag. Dining at a five-star restaurant may require more formal attire: a tie, dress shirt, and slacks for men and a dressy ensemble for women. Bar and nightclub attire is pretty much on par with the United States.

While the headscarf does exist in Turkey in various incarnations, visitors to Turkey are not required to don one, except when visiting Islamic places of. As coastal weather in winter can often change quickly, sweaters, light jackets, and pashminas come in handy. July and August call for t-shirts and shorts.

If you bring appliances like hairdryers or electronic devices like laptops and digital cameras, a 220-volt converter is necessary. It is also a good idea to purchase a cheap cell phone line and prepaid minutes, which should not set you back more than US$100. It will allow you to call out at anytime from even the most remote parts of the country without incurring huge charges. Finally, a money belt is essential to stash important items such as a copy of your passport, credit cards, transportation tickets, trip itineraries, currency, driver's license, and critical medical information.

Explore Istanbul & the Turkish Coast

▶ THE BEST OF ISTANBUL AND THE TURKISH COAST

With such a dizzying array of natural attractions, peppered with the remnants of 13 civilizations, selecting exactly where to go, what to do, and what to see can be a challenge, particularly if you have less than two weeks. This itinerary quickly transforms you from being a newbie to a die-hard fan—by way of grand Istanbul, antique Ephesus, the snowy white travertines of Pamukkale, sun-kissed Antalya, spiritual Konya, and the moonscape of Cappadocia—in just 13 jam-packed days!

Day 1

Arrive in Istanbul, find your hotel and your bearings . . . and rest. If time or energy allows, head to Sultanahmet Square to acclimate to the beat of this modern antique city. Once there, the Ayasofya beckons. Take an hour, or more, to visit this holy museum that's withstood the whim of several empires over nearly 1,500 years. After rotating your thumb inside the Stele of Saint Gregory Thaumaturgus for luck, turn your sights to any of the fabulous eateries around for a quick bite of *köfte* (meatball), such as Tarihi Sultanahmet Köfteci or the traditional meze table at the renowned Balıkcı Sabahattin.

Day 2

After rising to the sound of the muezzin, head to Topkapı Palace, Istanbul's top tourist draw, for a long stroll through the hundreds of rooms, its harem, and Seraglio Point. After lunch, visit the underground Basilica Cistern, and the enclosed antique shopping structure of the Grand Bazaar. In the evening, take the metro to Taksim, where an Ottoman feast awaits at Haci Abdüllah restaurant. After, have a drink at 360° for, well, a 360-degree view of the city by night.

Day 3

Fly early to Izmir, where an abundance of food and sights await. From Izmir, hop on a bus to the resort town of Kuşadası and book a hotel room. Have lunch at the nearby

the lush gardens of Sultanahmet, with the Ayasofya's minarets and dome soaring in the background

ancient Ephesus's most stunning relic, the iconic Library of Celsus

Day 5

Join a pre-reserved bus tour to Pamukkale's cascading travertine pools and healing thermal waters. For lunch, try Ünal Restaurant for the owner's famed tzatziki dip and kebabs accompanied by homemade red wine. After lunch, check out the remains of the antique Roman resort city Hierapolis, or go for another therapeutic dip. Enjoy a traditional Turkish folkore show at Kuşadası's Club Caravanserail in the evening.

Day 6

If you can avoid the urge to charter your own yacht and set sail on the unforgettable escapade of a Blue Cruise, hop on a bus to Antalya for more fun in the sun. Once there, stay at the historic and centrally located Tuvana Hotel and dine there, or head out to one of old town Kaleiçi's eateries and to Kale Bar for an after-dinner drink with unbeatable harbor views.

picturesque village of Şirince, accompanied with a glass of the region's famed home-concocted wine. Then off to Ephesus, the best preserved antique city of its kind. Explore the Grotto of the Seven Sleepers and visit the House of the Virgin Mary. For dinner, head to Kuşadası's Pigeon Island for a relaxed evening along the calm, glittery waters of the Aegean Sea.

Day 4

Ride a bus to the Ionian valley, where Priene, Miletus, and Didyma fill up a full day of archaeological pleasure. Or, stay in Priene for a hike along its cliffs and then on to the outlet shopping centers and eateries of Söke, for indigenous çöp shish kebab. If you're up for it, take the 20-mile bus ride to Dilek Peninsula National Park to discover hidden coves, protected clans of wild pigs, and colorful indigenous flora.

Day 7

Start off the day with a trip to Aspendos to see the best-preserved Roman amphitheater of its kind (particularly enjoyable during the summer concert season); on the return, check out the 3,500-year-old antique Pamphylian city Perge and its stadium and fine marble carvings. Back in Antalya, opt for more historical treasures at the archaeological museum or enjoy a scuba diving session among the sunken WWII ships and vibrant undersea flora right off the shore.

Day 8

Konya's Jelaleddin Rumî Mausoleum and Mevlâna Museum are a five-hour bus ride from Antalya. When you arrive in Konya, check into the Dedeman Konya hotel and then see the sights. The nearby 13th-century *medrese* (Islamic seminary), now the Karatay Museum, and the Selemiye Mosque exemplify the best of Seljuk and Ottoman architecture. End the day with a classic Turkish feast and a *sema* (Whirling Dervish nightly show) at Mevlevi Sofrası.

Day 9

Take a three-hour coach ride to eerie Cappadocia. Upon arrival, check in to your cave room at the Serinn House, and proceed for the house's light meal or opt for Ziggy's Shoppe and Café's culture-blending Pastırma fettuccine dish. When you're delightedly full, head out to Turasan Şarapevi (winery), perhaps the world's only underground vineyard, for a taste of its full-bodied wine. Next, cast your luck at the nearby Temenni "Wishing" Hill prior to turning in early for the next day's pre-sunset wake-up call.

Day 10

Armed with a camera, go to the adjoining village of Göreme to meet your pre-reserved hot-air Kapadokya Balloons tour for a three-hour mind-bending, heart-stopping, once-in-a-lifetime flight over the valley's tufa landscape. Back on solid ground, grab lunch. Thereafter, the magic of Göreme's Open-Air Museum provides an afternoon spent in the grandest of outdoors. Come evening, claim your seat at A'laturca for a meal so sumptuous it rivals Istanbul's five-star headliners.

Day 11

If you pass on the recommended guided trip, head to Avanos's Akhal-Teke Horse Riding Center to meet your equestrian riding companion. Hop on and trot off to the rock-carved Zelve Open-Air Museum, and explore the monastery complex, various churches, and long-deserted abodes carved entirely of volcanic ash. Continue on horseback from Çavuşin to Ortahısar, admiring rock formations and rock-cut chapels along the way. Make a short trip to the hillside parish of Üçhısar to discover Pigeon Valley and the Ottoman castle, amid fields of grapevines. After returning your four-hoofed riding partner, check out Avanos's Yellow Caravansary and try your hand at potting at the various pottery workshops. Dinner at the marble-roofed Şömine Café & Restaurant in Ürgüp is a must; try the delicious *saç tava* (baked eggplant purée and bite-size beef morsels).

Day 12

After bidding a warm *alasmaladık* (farewell) to this surreal moonscape, head off to Kayseri to fly back to sensual Istanbul. Drop your bags at the Empress Zoe and take a taxi to the decadent imperial Dolmabahçe Palace along the European shore of the Bosphorus. Catch another taxi ride to the modern-yet-classic Ortaköy to check out the breathtaking sunset along the shore of the straits, and the nearby neo-baroque Ortaköy Mosque, before heading to Anjelique , an exclusive restaurant and bar that caters to Istanbul's elite with superb haute cuisine and sumptuous cocktails.

Day 13

Ah…. the last day may just prove to be the best. Head out mid-morning to the embarcadero at Eminönü for a continental-hopping cruise along the majestic straits. Stopping at various villages, the 90-minute trip takes you to Anadolu Kavağı, the last port-of-call on the Bosphorus. From there, hike up to the Yoros Castle for incredible views of the seemingly untouched Black Sea. Quayside, Yosun Restaurant's fried mussels and calamari will be the reward after the walk back down. Head to the top of the Galata Tower for an evening of authentic cuisine, music, and dance.

TURKISH DELIGHT

Turkish cuisine has long been eclipsed by the veritable crock pot of Italian and French succulence, and unfairly stuffed in the catchall Mediterranean category. Its delectable array of exotic cuisines is at best little known. The specialties that make Turkey's tables so unique are easily found in culinary-rich Istanbul, but foodies and travel buffs should aim their forks to western and central Turkey's inner realms for a perfect mélange of palatable travels. *Afiyet olsun* (bon appétit)!

ANATOLIAN CUISINE

A mix of cuisines either indigenous to the steppe region or derived from Turkey's neighbors, Anatolian cuisine rarely gets the praise it deserves. For a real Anatolian treat, check out anthropologist Musa Dağdeviren's **Çiya** restaurant in Kadıköy. A visit here isn't complete without trying the deliciously varied soups, perfectly-herbed pilafs, tender kebabs and veggie stews, ambrosial sherbets, and exotic desserts concocted in the open kitchen daily. The day's specialties are created from long-lost recipes retrieved by the master chef himself through decades of research. That je ne sais quoi, either spice or herb, elevates the blue-collar smorgasbord of feasts that garnered the talented Dağdeviren international accolades from food critics. Being partial to eggplant in all of its forms, I love the *alinazık* – grilled morsels of lamb or chicken atop a roasted eggplant, pureed with garlic and yogurt. Or try the loquat stuffed with lamb, before finishing off with a piping hot portion of *künefe* (sweet, cheesy, shredded pastry dish). And Çiya also boasts one of the meanest *lahmacun* (thin-crusted meaty pizza) in town.

BAKLAVA AND TURKISH DELIGHT

If layers of flaky phyllo dough delicately stuffed with toasted nut morsels and sweetened to perfection with syrup elicit pangs of yearning, then head to the original **Güllüoğlu Baklava & Café** in Istanbul's Karaköy neighborhood. There are many contenders for Baklava mastery, but this one remains the top.

The other sweet indigenous to Istanbul is *lokum* (Turkish Delight), a nougat-like confection created by Ali Muhiddin Hacı Bekir in 1777 to meet the fickle taste of Topkapı Palace's concubines who thought regular candy just too hard for their palate. **Ali Muhiddin Hacı Bekir** boasts 27 varieties of *lokum* from its original location in Istanbul's Bahçekapı quarter, but the twice-roasted pistachio *lokum* remains the bestseller at its other branches in Eminönü and Kadıköy.

FISH

Wherever you choose to stay along the coast, chances are a great fish restaurant is nearby. But my fave in Istanbul remains **Çengelköy Iskele Restaurant,** in the Çengelköy neighborhood, for its grilled *levrek* (seabass) and the dish called Atom – a stew of seafood plucked from the waters of the Bosphorus just outside.

Along the Aegean coast, **Deniz Restaurant** has remained Turkey's "Best Of" contender since its opening in 1981; try any of its lauded calamari dishes and the grilled *çipura* (gilthead sea bream).

If in Bodrum, fishtail it to **Hasan'in Yeri** for the sole shish kebabs, followed by an unreal dessert platter of baklava and clotted cream-stuffed apricots and figs. Did I mention that all of these locations have to-die-for seaside scenery?

MEYHANE (TURKISH TAVERN)

Traditional Turkish taverns are proof that *rakı* (Turkish aperitif), mezes (appetizers) and grilled fish plus a handful of close friends equals bliss. Any fish restaurant that serves the anise-flavored liquor *rakı* is worth a try, especially along the coast. But since the practice actually originated in Istanbul, a *meyhane* ex-

lokum (Turkish Delight)

perience isn't the same outside the city. By far the best is **Refik** in Beyoğlu.

OTTOMAN CUISINE

The culinary tradition of the ancient Ottomans is still alive and kicking on dinner tables throughout the nation with unique dishes like dolmas and *zeytinyağlıs*, fresh veggies sauteed ever-so-slowly in olive oil. A good example is *imam bayıldı*, a concoction of onion, garlic, and tomato stuffed inside an eggplant and cooked to such perfection it made an "imam swoon" (the literal translation) centuries ago.

To experience firsthand the mortar-and-pestle ateliers of the master chefs of the Ottoman sultans, one must head to the fabulously grand kitchens of Topkapı Palace and taste their handed-down artistry – like the eggplant-lamb concoction of *hünkar beğendi* (Sultan's Delight) – onsite at the regally-decorated **Konyalı Topkapı Sarayı Lokantası.**

If time allows, learn the secrets of Ottoman and Turkish cuisine at **Cooking Alaturca,** a refreshingly unique restaurant/cooking studio in Sultanahmet.

TURKISH COFFEE

Nowadays, the number of custom coffee houses has eclipsed that of traditional Turkish coffee joints in Turkey's largest metropolises, but the café culture still remains. Join the Turks in one of their favorite pastimes – *kahve muhabbeti* (coffee chat) – at **Pierre Loti** café in Fatih for supreme views of the Golden Horn or at the terrace overlooking the exotic Seraglio Point at Topkapı Palace's **Konyalı Topkapı Sarayı Lokantası.**

▶ TOP 10 BEST BEACHES

Turkey's sandy expanses are aplenty and do not disappoint. With a coastline extending more than 4,200 miles, finding the "best" stretch is at best a personal choice. But I'll let you be the judge of my own top 10 (appearing in alphabetical order).

Alaçatı

For fun in the sun, this beach is unbeatable. From people-watching to surfing of all kinds, Alaçatı's atmosphere oozes youth. Gusty winds, considerable waves, and heady currents consistently pound the shore. But it's the crystalline waters that have transformed this once-shunned seaboard into a funfest May–October. On the northern flank of the Çeşme Peninsula, Alaçati is a resort with a couple of good hotels. The beach can be reached by *dolmuş* (communal taxi) from Çeşme's town center.

Altınkum

With a name that translates into "golden sands," this remote spot's cooler waters and

DIVING DISCOVERIES

Here's an intrepid holiday idea that'll tickle sea enthusiasts. Imagine exploring Turkey's western coast through its wreck-littered seabed; technicolor, undersea flora and fauna; and its myriad of mysterious submarine caves and walls. Newbies to the sport can earn their underwater wings through dozens of certified outfits, while die-hard divers can enjoy the challenge of the more arduous sea outings. The dive sites are organized from north to south, starting at the Aegean Sea's northeastern tip with the boat wrecks near Çanakkale, through the surreal undersea landscapes of its sister cities along the littoral, and ending at the Mediterranean port city of Antalya.

ÇANAKKALE

During the ill-planned 1915 Gallipoli campaigns, some Allied warships landed way off base, while others never made it to shore and sank before arrival. Remains of the British **HMS Majestic, Triumph, Irresistible,** and **Goliath,** as well as the Turkish battleship **Messudiah** and several German torpedo ships, litter the seabed at a maximum depth of 42 meters.

The lobster-filled reefs of **Saros Bay** and the colorful, gigantic sea sponges of **Cape Toplar** add to the diving sites available near this slice of the coast. Highly recommended for its fully-certified diving guides and instructors, **Argos**

Underwater Diving Center (Binevler K:2, D:3, Edirne, 0284/235-8588, www.diveargos.net) provides daily outings in the summer and a three-day CMAS training course.

AYVALIK

The shores of Ayvalık are rumored to hold the **lost city of Atlantis.** Try your luck at discovering its remains or at least have fun exploring the 15 underwater isles with one of the few certified dive operators in the region, such as **Körfez Diving Center** (Atatürk bulvarı Özaral pasajı 617a-30, 0266/312-4996, www.korfezdiving.com, 50–500TL). They offer everything from a one-day dip and dive to a full-fledged three-day course for new divers.

BODRUM

As the Aegean Sea port where undersea archaeology got its start, Bodrum boasts rugged, volcanic offshore islands and long underwater reefs and mysterious caves amid its translucent, calm seas. **Aşkın Diving Center** is *the* diving provider of choice. The center's owner, Aşkın Canbazoğlu, is an archaeologist who was affiliated with the Bodrum's Underwater Archaeology Museum for eight years before going commercial. Aşkın leads divers to Bodrum's offshore archeological sites, while snorkelers are free to explore the surface.

wide-open seas primarily attract twenty-something Turks and covert nudists. Relatively unknown a few years ago, the beach park is climbing up the holiday resort charts, thanks perhaps to its well-deserved moniker. Developers, however, are closely heeding the trend. Getting to Altınkum, on Çeşme's south coast, is as easy as hopping on a southbound *dolmuş* from Çeşme's town center on the Çeşme Peninsula.

Butterfly Valley

Barely a half-hour from Fethiye, the only access to this secluded beach is by boat. It's reputed as a backpacker's heaven, thanks to tents and tepees available onsite. Only a few sunbathers grace this cove: those who stop for lunch and a dip during a Blue Cruise layover; or trail-weary Lycian Way hikers ambling down the cliffs for a refreshing swim.

İztuzu

Popular among endangered loggerhead turtles, İztuzu's 2.5-mile stretch of pale sands is just minutes away from Dalyan. While certain areas are strictly protected during reptilian egg-laying and hatching season May—September, the lush hilly backdrop and lack of concrete

The Aegean waters off of Ayvalık – rumor has it, they hold the lost city of Atlantis.

KAŞ
As tiny as Kaş may be, its offshore diving potential is astounding with no less than 19 unique underwater sites. Spots like **Stonehenge** and **İnce Boğaz,** both close to the port, provide a unique opportunity to swim with endangered loggerhead turtles. A 400-year-old Ottoman shipwreck near a spectacular reef highlight the **Lighthouse dive,** while the stingrays lying on the sea floor near **Hidayet Bay,** further north, provide a challenge at a depth of 35 meters. Of the dozen dive operators in Kaş, **Nautilus Diving** (Uzun Çarşı Cad. Kaş, 0242/836-2580, www.nautilusdiving. org) offers PADI and CMAS diving courses, as well as two diving tours daily, year-round.

MARMARIS
Diving takes on a whole different meaning in Marmaris's splendid underwater landscape. The tiny isles surrounding this resort are home to schools of groupers and sea breams, large octopuses, and shapely sea sponges. The island of **Bedir Ada** boasts the remains of an Ottoman ship (at a depth of 24 meters) that capsized during Sultan Mehmet II's naval envoy to conquer Rhodes in 1480. **Paradise Diving Center** (Namik Kemal Cad. 25, 0252/417-6366, www.paradisediving.net) provides qualified instructors, diving equipment rental, and evening dives.

ANTALYA
A couple of WWII Allied shipwrecks and seemingly millions of whole and broken amphorae litter the bay near Antalya. Its seabed, pocked by refreshingly-frigid water springs, provides a unique slant to the area. And so do the magnificent caves and undersea caverns of **Sican Island,** whose western rock cliff dips down 22 meters. Antalya's outfitter and instruction facility of choice is **Yunus Diving School** (Konyaaltı Beachpark 5-6, 0242/238-4486). Led by Cumhur Tuğ, the founder of the Antalya Underwater Sports Association, Yunus offers two-hour dives and week-long certification programs.

here offer a nice respite from the urban hustle of the neighboring resort cities. Also, the proximity of the Dalyan River is great for rapids enthusiasts. The nearby Lycian ruins only add to the beauty of this area. Getting to Dalyan is a snap from Dalaman Airport, which is just 16 miles away.

Kaleköy

Called Simena by the ancient Greeks, this charming little peninsula doesn't offer a beach per se, but the crystalline waters that lap sunken ruins and a Lycian tomb are glorious. A handful of excellent restaurants, a medieval castle, warm waters, and the lack of crowds are always pluses in my book. This place is accessible only by boat from Demre or Üçağız.

Kaputaş

It's not so much the beach that's surreal here, but the nearby phosphorescent caves. A path down a rocky gorge leads straight to a small shingle cove. Mostly accessed from the sea, this small sandy stretch is a 10-minute *dolmuş* (communal taxi) ride on the windy picturesque road that leads to Kalkan, a less touristy Mediterranean resort that has been compared to the Italian Riviera. Kaputaş is 2.5 hours from Antalya Airport and 3 hours from Dalaman Airport. A long way perhaps, but the lush forests that hug this serpentine road on one side and the wave-lapped cliffs on the other are must-see sights unto themselves.

Patara

Usually sharing top billing with Ölüdeniz among international tourists, the 12-mile-long beach at Patara is protected from the current wave of development, thanks to the crumbling Lycian ruins, just steps away. The nearby sleepy Patara Village is famous for being the birthplace of Saint Nicholas, the good Samaritan and former bishop who was the inspiration for the white-bearded Santa in a red suit. Patara is an 80-minute ride south of Dalaman Airport.

Pırlanta

Meaning "diamond," this beach's long and broad white sandy shore on the coast of the Çeşme Peninsula aptly deserves its title. Typically attracting surfing enthusiasts, this spot is wide open to the Aegean Sea and can get gusty. Pırlanta is just a short ride from Çeşme's town center, located on the westernmost tip of the Çeşme Peninsula, which is a 90-minute ride from Izmir's Adnan Menderes Airport.

Ölüdeniz

Touted nationally as the best seashore in the country for sunbathers and flying fanatics, it's minutes away from Fethiye. With warm and still turquoise waters, creamy fine sand, and lush vegetation, Belcekiz Beach lies on the tip of a long skinny peninsula protected as a national park and therefore off-limits to developers. An about-face will reveal Babadağ, a lofty mount that translates into paradise for paragliders, trekkers, and mountain bikers. Numerous resorts are located nine miles away in the nearest town of Fethiye, which is served by the Dalaman Airport, some 31 miles further.

Türkbükü

The peninsula that's been referred to as the Turkish French Riviera, Bodrum, has more than a dozen beaches that adorn its circuitous coastline. But there's none like Türkbükü. It's not really a beach by definition, but more of a string of high-price clubs built on pillars. With million-dollar vessels anchored just beyond the shore, the only access to the water is by paying a lofty ransom at one of the trendy cafés or posh beach clubs. Located on the northern flank of the Bodrum Peninsula, Türkbükü is less than a half hour from the Bodrum Airport.

▶ FOLLOWING ALEXANDER THE GREAT

Exploring Turkey is like taking a crash course in history, only a lot more fun than sitting in a classroom. This itinerary retraces the steps of Macedonian King Alexander the Great's conquests in 334 B.C. Starting and finishing in Istanbul, this ten-day trip snakes along the Aegean and Mediterranean. It's best accomplished in a rented vehicle from Istanbul. Traveling by bus is also an option; it takes more time, but is more economical in the long run.

Day 1

Arrive in Istanbul, check into the Armada Istanbul City Hotel. If time allows, explore the artisans open market at Arasta Bazaar on the way to the grand basilica of Ayasofya. Pick up your rental vehicle and have a dinner of mezes and the catch of the day at Balıkcı Sabahattin.

Day 2

Head for the port of Yenikapı and board the 7 A.M. ferry to Bandırma. Disembark and travel west to Çanakkale, stopping on the way at Biga Çayı (Granicus River), the brook where Alexander defeated the Persian satraps in 334 B.C. In Çanakkale, go for an incredibly tasty and fresh seafood lunch at Liman Yalova Restaurant. Homer's Troy awaits 50 miles to the west. For dinner, dine over regional fish fare and award-winning mezes at Biberevi Restaurant. Overnight just down hill at Assos Kervansaray.

Day 3

Today you will follow Alexander's conquest of the North Aegean. Get an early start and head east to Kaz Mountain National Park, also known as Mount Ida, the lofty inspiration of Greek mythologists and from whence

tourist replica of the infamous Trojan Horse in Troy

THE SEVEN CHURCHES OF THE REVELATION

For thematically- and spiritually-driven travelers, the proximity of the Seven Churches of the Revelation – discussed in the New Testament's *Book of Revelation* – offers a great opportunity to retrace Christianity's early footsteps in Antiquity's Asia Minor and discover their ruins along the sinuous Aegean Coast of present day Turkey. Writer John, believed to be Saint John the Apostle, received visions in which he was instructed to pen and send what would later be considered apocalyptic messages to the church of each of seven major cultural centers, famed for either reasons of commerce, trade, military, or pure hedonism. Just want to visit one? Then head to Ephesus. To see them all, allow 2-3 days.

Ephesus's amphitheater

EPHESUS

Early Christianity's most important center was heralded in its time, but was condemned in prose for "forsaking its first love" (Revelation 2:1-7). Ancient Ephesus was one of Asia Minor's prominent capitals; in fact, it was the Roman Empire's second largest city. Today it's the world's best preserved ancient site, replete with a hub of ancient streets, arches, temples, and monuments, including its spectacular fu-

neral library and a whopping 25,000-person amphitheater.

SMYRNA

Just north of Ephesus, the port city of Izmir has been an important trading center since time immemorial. Turkey's third largest city, with a population nearing three million, is known domestically as the "Pearl City of the Aegean" and remains a Western-looking cultural melt-

---

the Trojan Wars were launched. Hike in the park's pine landscape among its trails and waterfalls to Şarlak for great views of the Aegean Sea from the tea garden there.

Back on the road, make a beeline to ancient Pergamum to visit the abundant Greco-Roman ruins, in particular the Acropolis and Asclepion (Temple of Healing Arts).

Head south towards Izmir for about 50 kilometers and hang a right at the Foça intersection. Drive another 36 kilometers to the quaint fishing village of Foça, where you'll overnight at the brick Foçantique Hotel Hotel and dine at one of the delectable fish restaurants along the pier.

Day 4

Head south past Izmir to the village of Sartmahmut—or Sardes, which was liberated from the Persians by Alexander in 340 B.C.—and its impressive Temple of Artemis and gymnasium.

Continue south 65 kilometers to the quaint village of Şirince and check into the cute boutique Şirince Terrace Houses. For dinner, sample the fruity local red wines and the mouthwatering *keşkek* (red pepper, barley, and lamb stew) at Arşipel Greek Café and Restaurant.

Day 5

After the generous Şirince Terrace breakfast,

ing pot, but its biblical message warned of "false Jews and impending persecution," while encouraging "perseverance which will be rewarded" (Rev. 2:8-11).

PERGAMUM
Forget mincing words, this materialistic city was encouraged to repent for preaching mixed doctrines (Rev. 2:12-17). Pergamum was a major metropolis in Asia Minor since the 3rd century B.C. and its temples became influential centers of worship for Greeks and Romans. Today's Bergama is an increasingly influential city in terms of regional politics, mining, and agriculture.

THYATIRA
While the locals were commended for their increasing faith, Thyatira's church was reprimanded for also following the seductive prophetess Jezebel (Rev. 2:18-29). The ruins of Thyatira, once known for its textile and dye trade, are situated about 65 kilometers from the Aegean Sea in the modern city of Akhisar.

SARDIS
This "dead" church was told to wake up from its long sleep and that some of its parishioners were "worthy" for they had not yet "soiled their clothes" (Rev. 3:1-6). Located near the modern village of Sart, about 96 kilometers east of Izmir, Sardis is strictly an archaeological site with spectacular temples and bath house complexes.

PHILADELPHIA
This church of fraternal love is applauded for its perseverance, but told of a pending judgment of the false Jews who, in fact, represented the "Synagogue of Satan" (Rev. 3:7-13). Located about 20 kilometers east of Izmir in the modern city of Alaşehir, Philadelphia's scant remains still boast the status of one of Asia Minor's largest centers of temple worship.

LAEODICEA
Criticized as a church of "lukewarm" faith, Laeodicea's wealthy church is told to forgo adoration of worldly goods to focus on its spirituality (Rev. 3:14-22). The ruins of Laeodicea, which was once an important stop on the East-West trade route just north of modern-day Denizli, still pend archaeological excavation.

visit the nearby ruins at Ephesus, which Alexander liberated along with most cities in Asia Minor after defeating the Persians in the Battle of the Granicus. After ambling through the phenomenal Library of Celsus and the ornate Temple of Hadrian, among other ruins, visit the House of the Virgin Mary. It is believed that Saint John brought Mary here to live out her life. In the Seljuk hills, check out Saint John's Basilica, where the apostle is said to be buried, and the Isabey Mosque, one of the oldest and most impressive architectural gifts in this Anatolian principality.

Day 6
Drive south to Priene, once a leading member of the Ionian League, where Alexander constructed the Temple of Athena to gaze down on the winding path of the Menderes River and the lush agricultural valley. Twenty-two km south, the ruins—like the Ionic Stoa on the Sacred Way—at the ancient city of Miletus await. The Siege of Miletus was Alexander the Great's first naval encounter with the Achaemenid Empire. Next up is Didim. Once an oracle city, Didim's Temple of Apollo, where mortals once sought and received advice from the god through the assistance of antiquity's very first family of Branchidae priests, was partly rebuilt by Alexander after its destruction at the hands of the Persians.

the early–17th-century Blue Mosque in Istanbul

On the return to the hotel, stop at Artemis wine house to sample the local fruity wine and fab *gözleme*-a browned lavash filled with cheese, meat or herbs.

Day 7

Check out and head east for 120 kilometers on Highway O32 to Aphrodisias, a city named after the Greek goddess of love. Its temple and monumental gate are among nine focal points. This ancient city became an artistic center shortly after Alexander's conquest.

Have lunch in Aphrodisias and then drive southwest for 172 kilometers to Kalkan and check in to the small Villa Mahal, where sumptuous Turkish and Mediterranean gourmet dining awaits at the Rooftop Restaurant.

Day 8

Head out early for the 150-kilometer drive to Antalya on Highway D400, by way of Xanthos, the Lycian League capital, and Myra, the birthplace of St. Nicholas and home to ornate Lycian rock tombs. The next town is Phaselis, the famed Lycian port that Alexander captured from the Persians. The Lycians were so fed up with the ruthless rule of the Carian Satrapy that they actually welcomed Alexander as their deliverer. Once in Antalya, check into Tuvana Hotel and dine in, or head out to one of old town Kaleici's eateries and to Kale Bar for an after-dinner drink with unbeatable harbor views.

Day 9

Drive 20 kilometers east to Aspendos to discover the best-preserved Roman amphitheater of its kind, particularly enjoyable during the summer concert season. Spectators shook in their sandals when Alexander appeared on stage one evening during his layover on the way to Antioch. On the return, stop at the nearby 3,500-year-old antique Pamphylian city of Perge. Once back in Antalya, opt for more historical treasures at the archeological museum or enjoy a scuba diving session among the sunken WWII ships and vibrant undersea flora right off the shore.

Day 10

Get a very early start on the long drive back to Istanbul. Once there, stretch your legs by taking a stroll to At Meydanı, a great square and former home of the Byzantine Hippodrome. If time allows, head off to the majestic Blue Mosque and the eerie Basilica Cistern. Alternatively, shopaholics should definitely not miss the Grand Bazaar.

ISTANBUL

Blending the lines between East and West, modernism and antiquity, secularism and piety, Istanbul brims with diversity, complexity, and some 8,000 years of history. Lulled by the call of the muezzin, walking through the streets of Sultanahmet is like being sent back in time. At least up until the baristas at the Western-style cafés on virtually every corner ask, "Blended or on ice?"

Sultanahmet, Istanbul's oldest hub, is located on one of seven hills the city originally occupied. It boasts two UNESCO World Heritage sites in less than a square mile, along with three other must-see sights. Also, beyond the rails of a 21st-century tramway are dozens of street merchants selling their wares as their precursors did 500 years ago.

With an official 12 million residents—some claim more like 17—Istanbul is abuzz with activity day and night. Its main streets are no different than their European counterparts, with tree-lined boulevards filled with posh eateries, cafés, and young fashionistas showing off their designer duds. In the back streets, just steps away, shoeshine boys and garbage collectors reside among the cacophony of street vendors, seagulls, and inescapable traffic.

From almost any point in the greater city, the calm azure waters of the Bosphorus Strait, Marmara Sea, or Black Sea are visible and attainable. Infinitely more than just a pretty landscape, the city's geographic location and the abundance that it brings have for millennia been Istanbul's claim to fame. It is at once the world's busiest maritime strait and home to nature's richest underwater bounty. Come

COURTESY OF REPUBLIC OF TURKEY CULTURE AND TOURISM MINISTRY

HIGHLIGHTS

◖ Ayasofya (Saint Sophia Church): The mid-6th-century Byzantine sanctuary is both a UNESCO World Heritage Site and a recent contender for the New Seven Wonders of the World (page 30).

◖ Sultanahmet Camii (Blue Mosque): Light reflects through hundreds of glass windows onto blue tiles, casting a blue haze within the mosque's main hall (page 36).

◖ Topkapı Sarayı (Topkapı Palace): As the vanguard of all imperial palaces, the royal residence houses one of the rarest collections of porcelain, as well as the mythic 86-carat Spoonmaker's Diamond and a world-famous harem (page 37).

◖ Yerebatan Sarayı (Basilica Cistern): Used as one of the film locations for James Bond's *From Russia with Love*, this surreal, 6th-century underground cistern mystifies with hundreds of columns that lead to its innermost sanctum, the Medusa pillars (page 39).

◖ Kapalı Çarşı (Grand Bazaar): Haggle like a pro, sip Turkish coffee, or just take in the Grand Bazaar's historical splendor. Window-

shop along its 4,000 boutiques to find out why it has remained a shopper's dream for more than half a millennium (page 43).

◖ Beyoğlu: Hop on the antique tram that crisscrosses this belle époque district's pint-sized neighborhoods, where modern shops, consulates, fish mongers, and off-the-beaten-path churches await discovery (page 53).

◖ Dolmabahçe Sarayı (Dolmabahçe Palace): Offering a glimpse of Ottoman decadence at its best, this mid-19th-century imperial structure has a crystal staircase and a bed made of pure silver, among other things, in Sultan Abdülmecid's living quarters (page 57).

◖ Bosphorus Cruise: Perhaps the pièce de résistance of a journey to Istanbul, this cruise boasts myriad historical sights that truly convey the value of these straits (page 60).

◖ Kariye Müzesi (Chora Museum): This museum boasts over 6,000 square feet of not-to-be-missed mosaics and frescoes. So beautiful was its iconography that even Constantinople's Islamic conquerors could not bring themselves to whitewash its gilded treasures (page 72).

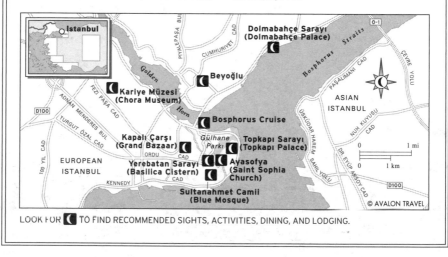

LOOK FOR **◖** TO FIND RECOMMENDED SIGHTS, ACTIVITIES, DINING, AND LODGING.

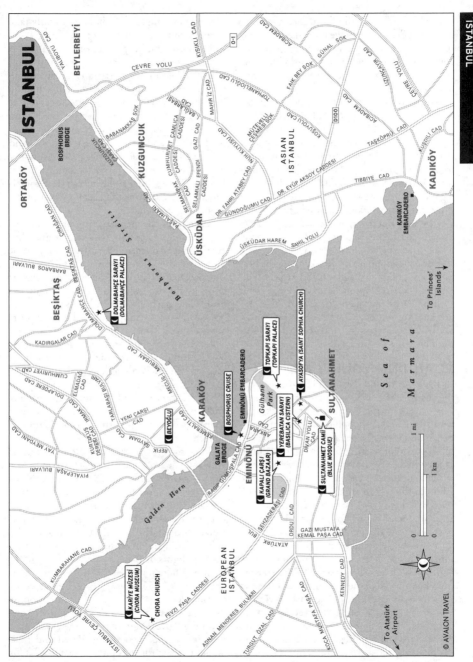

© AVALON TRAVEL

winter, fish from small gild-headed bream to nine-pounder turbot all vie for real estate along these precious waters. The waters' edge also becomes the playground for well-to-do fun-seekers, who flock in droves to the many trendy hangouts.

As the only city in the world to spread over two continents, Istanbul also comprises a history-filled Anatolian side just across the Bosphorus Strait. Its name was once Chalcedon, an Asian outpost that dates back to at least 3,000 B.C. The water-lapped quarter of Kuzguncuk in Üsküdar exemplifies this legacy with the centuries-old sanctuaries of three different religions dwelling uneventfully side-by-side. But if you expected sleepy villages on this coast, the diversity will surprise you. The district of Kadıköy boasts modernity, with world class shopping and dining along the hectic thoroughfare of Bağdat Caddesi, whose illustrious destinations include Gucci and Louis Vuitton. With so much diversity to offer, it's not hard to find out why Istanbul was chosen as the European Capital of Culture in 2010 by the European Union Council.

PLANNING YOUR TIME

In three whirlwind days you could check out the charm of the city, learn to feast the Turkish way, set sail on the Bosphorus and click heels with *Istanbullus* at shopping and partying meccas around town. To get a real grasp of the city in all of its contrasting beauty, plan to spend at least five days. This will allow for a couple of trips: a cruise to the nearby Prince Islands; a hop to the city's various Asian draws. With five days there's also time to explore the city at night, including its boisterous cabarets and posh waterside nightclubs.

If Istanbul is your first stop in Turkey en route to other destinations, plan an extra 24 hours on both legs to visit sights. Try to refrain from lumping all of the museum trips on either stop to avoid overkill, particularly trying to jam in the sights at **Sultanahmet Square** all in one day. For a more enjoyable journey, vary destinations and activities: take in a museum in the morning and a cruise and shopping trip in

the early evening. After all, one can only take in so much history in one go!

The best time to plan a trip to Istanbul is April, when the city's tulip commemoration is in full bloom and virtually every square inch of earth seems to be covered with the indigenous flower in all of its spectacular glory. Spring also announces the beginning of Istanbul's popular arts festival season, from modern arts and film, to classical music, and the city's famed concert series. While summer is still the busiest tourist season countrywide, Istanbul's late spring and early fall now constitute shoulder seasons that herald lower prices than June–September.

Aside from cheaper accommodations, visiting Istanbul in late fall guarantees availability at the better hotels and practically no lines at museums. Fall also calls for Turkey's **Republic Day** on October 29, when *Istanbullus* flock outdoors by the thousands to show their national pride. The celebration culminates with an exquisite fireworks show along the Bosphorus come evening.

During the summer, the weather is at its hottest and stickiest and there are lines at most tourist venues. If possible, avoid a visit during this time of year. The upside to this season is that June and July feature excellent rock and jazz shows that are jam-packed and offer a chance to see famous performers at their most relaxed.

For some locals, winter is the best time of year and the occasional snow flurry gives the city an entirely different feel. Christmas is not celebrated in most households, as Turkey is a predominantly Muslim nation, but New Year's Eve is a time when gifts are exchanged and stores throughout the city capitalize on the holiday by luring in customers with their best seasonal lights display.

Also of note to travelers is Ramadan, which occurs every 355 days. This religious commemoration falls during the summer months through at least the next decade, and will undoubtedly affect tourists in some small way. Adherers begin their fast at dawn and rush home at sunset for the opulent feast of *Iftar* for

30 consecutive days. In Istanbul, the practice is widely observed and its repercussions might translate into cranky cabbies weathering sugar lows and difficulty in finding a ride come *Iftar* time. But this period also presents an occasion to partake in the breaking of bread over the lengthy, lavish *Iftar* menus proffered by many eateries throughout the city.

As the fourth largest city in the world, sprawling over some 27 districts, picking the ideal place to stay during your Istanbul whirl can be daunting. Base yourself in the midst of the "old town" of Sultanahmet, where public transportation is plentiful and proximity to sights and other noteworthy boroughs is guaranteed. The only caveat when booking in Sultanahmet is to reserve well ahead of time to secure availability and cheaper accommodations.

HISTORY

The emergence of the land that straddles the strategic Bosphorus Strait is the stuff of legends. But a chance discovery of four human skeletons some four miles beneath Yenikapı in mid-2008 confirmed that the city was inhabited during the Neolithic Age, an estimated 8,000 years ago. Up until that point, the Thracians were thought to have settled the Seraglio—the tip of the Sultanahmet peninsula—at Lygos between the 13th and 11th centuries B.C. Winding forward four centuries, King Byzas was actually the first to colonize it. He was the ruler of the Greek town of Megara who, after consulting with the Oracle at Delphi as to where to found a new city, was told to look "opposite the blind." Byzas reached the settlement of Chalcedon—today's Kadıköy—and thought that Chalcedonians must have been "blind" for not realizing the much finer land that lay just across the Bosphorus Strait. Byzas settled the territory in the 7th century B.C. and called it Byzantion after himself. Later the colony took on a Latin name: Byzantium. It became a part of the Roman Empire in the 1st century B.C., and by A.D. 306 it was assigned the status of capital by Emperor Constantine, who thought it wise to redub the city Constantinople.

The 5th century proved tempestuous and fractious for the Roman Empire. The west was conquered by Barbarians, and the Eastern Roman Empire—a.k.a. the Byzantine Empire—remained centralized in Constantinople. In A.D. 532, the Nika Revolts fanned the flames of a brewing discord among the city's two political factions. After a week of incessant fires and pillage that reduced the Sultanahmet and its environs to rubble, some 30,000 rioters were slaughtered in the Hippodrome. But from the ruins, structures such as Ayasofya and the Great Palace of Constantinople were entirely rebuilt—the former to such grandeur that it remains a symbol of the Byzantine Empire's architectural and cultural prowess to this day.

What made the city so desirable—mainly its straits—continued to be the Achilles' heel for its occupiers *du jour*, as Persians, Arabs, and nomadic tribes each tried their luck at conquering the city. That is, until the Fourth Crusade, when the Catholic Latin Empire replaced its Orthodox Byzantine namesake in 1204. Their rule would last slightly more than 50 years under various diminutive emperors until its previous Byzantine rulers recaptured Constantinople in 1261. By then, the city was in ruins and its population had dwindled to a mere 30,000—less than 10 percent of what it had been under Justinian, the Eastern Roman emperor. The state of Constantinople at this time provided an opportune moment for yet another takeover. The advancing Ottoman Turks led by Mehmet the Conqueror II ascended the peninsula from the northeast and gained control of the city. The Turks thought it wise to change the name once again; this time it would be called Istanbul—the seat of the Islamic Caliphate, and the head of an empire that would become one of the 10 largest in history.

In just six decades, Istanbul's multi-cultural population under the Turks exploded ten-fold, as the reigning sultan offered Istanbul as a refuge to Jews and Muslims fleeing the Iberian peninsula during the late 15th-century Spanish Inquisition. The city became a cultural, political, and commercial center under the Ottomans, with opulent palaces and spiritual sanctuaries. This lasted until their demise at the hands of the Allied forces during World War I.

After a bloody four-year war of independence, Mustafa Kemal Atatürk—known nationally as the father of Turks—moved the governmental seat of the newly formed Turkish nation to Ankara in 1923. Despite its loss of capital status, Istanbul has always remained the cultural heart of Turkey.

Sights

Flying into the city, you may be disheartened to realize that Istanbul's sheer size proves too big for one visit. It's true that you could spend years trying to conquer its every fishing village, cultural sight, and historical cranny. But do not despair, it may be big, but its boroughs are easy to navigate, at least when the traffic is agreeable.

Istanbul is bisected by the Bosphorus Strait, a 19-mile natural channel that links the Black Sea in the northeast to the Sea of Marmara in the southwest, and serves as a natural continental divide between Europe and Asia. The major attractions, such as the modern "old town" of Sultanahmet, crowded Beyoğlu, dizzying Istiklal Caddesi, effervescent Taksim, as well as posh Nişantaşı and Akaretler are all located on the European flank. These locations are close to the Golden Horn, an inlet of the Bosphorus that forms a natural harbor. Destinations lying on the periphery, like the sleepy retreats of the Prince Islands, the busy working-class district of Kadıköy and the Rumeli and Anatolian Fortresses, can be reached effortlessly and explored in a half-day or full-day excursion. The point is: Don't be afraid to walk, ride the tramway, or get around the city by funicular, *dolmuş* (communal taxi), bus, or taxi. Armed with a map and a couple of Turkish words, getting around Istanbul is a snap.

SULTANAHMET AND VICINITY

Containing by far the most popular sights, Sultanahmet Square and Kapalı Çarşı are the meat and potatoes of your journey here. Along with the museums of Topkapı Sarayı and Ayasofya, a dozen sights virtually piled atop each other await the curious.

Classified as a UNESCO World Heritage site since 1985, the urban historical park of Sultanahmet graces one of Istanbul's seven hills. It boasts relics of several bygone civilizations in a jumble of attractions jam-packed around a hectic plaza. Jutting off from this main square are narrow, cobble-stoned streets housing hotels, shops, and eateries. Starting at Ayasofya and ending at the University of Marmara, alongside the Blue Mosque, the square once housed the Byzantine Hippodrome—a sprawling stage where more than 80,000 people took part in chariot and horse races, riots, and political events that ruled the day some 1,800 years ago. Getting a good grasp of the timeline of the "old city" can be quite helpful in understanding the various layers of history wrapped around the Golden Horn.

While modern Istanbul sprawled to become the world's fourth largest city in terms of population, the ancient lure of today's Sultanahmet Square remains, even with the rapid tramway that whips past its dizzying variety of layered ruins, notable museums, popular eateries, and boutique hotels. The square encompasses 15 streets, most of which are for pedestrian use only, and is a virtual open-air museum that offers affordable and extravagant accommodations and dining options.

◀ Ayasofya (Saint Sophia Church)

The Ayasofya (Sultanahmet Square, 0212/528-4500, 9 A.M.–5 P.M. Tues.–Sun. Sept.–May, until 7 P.M. June–Oct., upper

COURTESY OF REPUBLIC OF TURKEY CULTURE AND TOURISM MINISTRY

The Ayasofya was commissioned as a basilica by Emperor Justinian in the sixth century, became a mosque 900 years later, and finally was converted into a museum.

gallery closes at 4 P.M. Sept.–May and 6 P.M. June–Oct., 15TL) was a New Seven Wonders of the World contender in 2007. Commissioned by Emperor Justinian I as a means to establish his claim to the imperial throne of Byzantium, this basilica remains to this day one of the largest testaments of faith and architectural might on the globe. It was inaugurated in A.D. 537 as Hagia Sophia—Greek for Holy Wisdom— and remained the largest Christian cathedral for more than 1,000 years. So enthralled was Justinian by its magnificence and opulent interior, replete with glittering mosaics and sleek marble pillars, that he proclaimed: "Solomon, I have surpassed Thee."

Justinian employed the architect Antheius of Tralles and the mathematician Isidorus of Miletus to design a plan to place a circular dome on a rectangular floor plan—a structural exploit that had never been done before. With the empire's treasury at their disposal, the duo devised the basilica with a perimeter of 300 by 210 feet, topped by a gigantic dome of just over 100 feet in diameter and a central height of 185

feet, supported by four massive pillars. Eight gigantic Corinthian columns imported from Lebanon support the structure's center. Using only the choicest material mined from the best quarries throughout the empire, it took more than 10,000 workers five years to craft this truly extraordinary Great Church. Incidentally, today's Ayasofya is the third church on site; the previous two were burned down.

A series of earthquakes shook Hagia Sophia's structure. The main dome collapsed twice; both times requiring immediate reconstruction. When the Byzantines reclaimed Constantinople in 1261, decades of sieges and tremors had taken their toll on the basilica. And another major retrofit was undertaken, with the addition of the four buttresses on its flank. The interior hall was in a state of disrepair by the time the Ottomans arrived in the mid-15th century. Sultan Mehmet II ordered the third major overhaul, which included its conversion into a mosque. A century later, Sultan Selim II commissioned the famed Ottoman architect Sinan to retrofit the

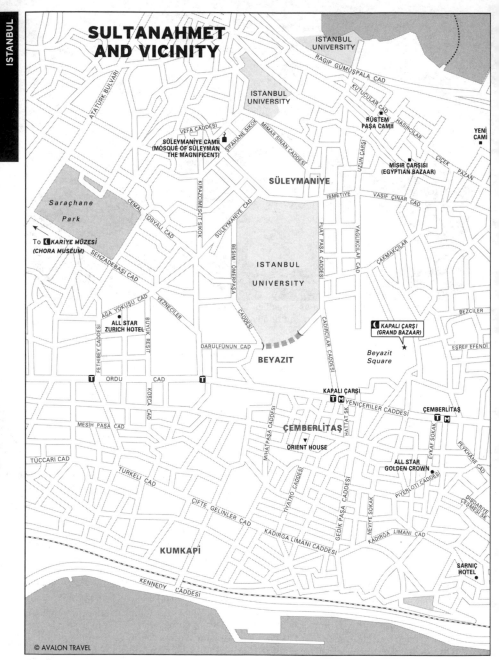

SULTANAHMET AND VICINITY

ISTANBUL UNIVERSITY

RAGIP GÜMÜŞPALA CAD

ISTANBUL UNIVERSITY

KUTUCULAR CAD

HASIRCILAR

VEFA CADDESI

SÜLEYMANIYE CAMİİ (MOSQUE OF SÜLEYMAN THE MAGNIFICENT)

ŞİFAHANE SOKAK

MİMAR SİNAN CADDESİ

RÜSTEM PAŞA CAMİİ

UZUN ÇARŞI

ÇİÇEK

YENİ CAMİİ

PAZAR

MISIR ÇARŞISI (EGYPTIAN BAZAAR)

SÜLEYMANİYE

İSMETİYE

VASİF ÇINAR CAD

KIRAZCI MESCIT SIKOK

CEMAL TOSYALI CAD

Saraçhane Park

SÜLEYMANİYE CAD

BEŞİM ÖMERPAŞA

FUAT PAŞA CADDESİ

YAĞLIKCILAR CAD

ÇAKMAKCILAR

To KARİYE MÜZESİ (CHORA MUSEUM)

ŞEHZADEBAŞI CAD

ISTANBUL UNIVERSITY

BEZCILER

CADDESİ

AĞA YOKUŞU CAD

VEZNECİLER

ALL STAR ZURICH HOTEL

BÜYÜK REŞİT

FETHİBEY CADDESİ

DARÜLFÜNUN CAD

CADIRCILAR CADDESİ

KAPALI ÇARŞI (GRAND BAZAAR)

EŞREF EFENDİ

Beyazit Square

BEYAZIT

ORDU CAD

KOSKA CAD

KAPALI ÇARŞI

YENİÇERİLER CADDESİ

ÇEMBERLİTAŞ

HATTAT SK

EVKAF SOKAK

PEYKHANE CAD

MESİH PAŞA CAD

MHATPAŞA CADDESİ

ÇEMBERLİTAŞ

ORIENT HOUSE

ALL STAR GOLDEN CROWN

PİYERLOTİ CADDESİ

TÜCCARİ CAD

TURKELİ CAD

TİYATRO CADDESİ

GEDİK PAŞA CADDESİ

NEVİYE SOKAK

DİSDARİYE ÇEŞMESİ SK

ÇİFTE GELİNLER CAD

KADIRGA LİMANI CADDESİ

KADIRGA LİMANI CAD

KUMKAPİ

SARNIÇ HOTEL

KENNEDY CADDESİ

© AVALON TRAVEL

ISTANBUL

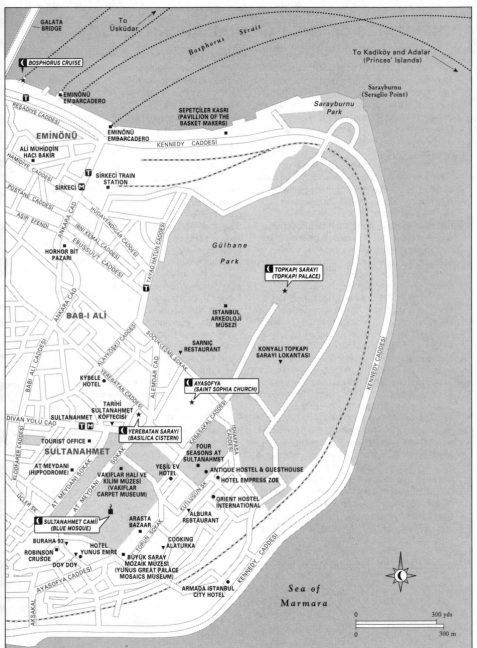

GALATA BRIDGE

To Üsküdar

Bosphorus Strait

BOSPHORUS CRUISE

To Kadiköy and Adalar (Princes' Islands)

EMINÖNÜ EMBARCADERO

Sarayburnu (Seraglio Point)

SEPETÇİLER KASRI (PAVILLION OF THE BASKET MAKERS)

Sarayburnu Park

EMINÖNÜ EMBARCADERO

REŞADIYE CADDESİ

KENNEDY CADDESİ

EMİNÖNÜ

ALİ MUHİDDİN HACI BAKIR

HAMIDIYE CADDESİ

SİRKECİ TRAIN STATION

SİRKECİ

POSTANE CADDESİ

ANKARA CAD

AŞİR EFENDI

İBNİ KEMAL CADDESİ

EBUSSUUT CADDESİ

HÜDAVENDIGAR CADDESİ

HORHOR BİT PAZARI

TAYAO HATUN CADDESİ

Gülhane Park

TOPKAPI SARAYI (TOPKAPI PALACE)

ANKARA CAD

BAB-I ALİ

İSTANBUL ARKEOLOJİ MÜZEZİ

ALAYKÖŞKU CADDESİ

YEREBATAN CADDESİ

ALEMDAR CAD

SOCÜKÇEŞME SOKAK

SARNIÇ RESTAURANT

KONYALI TOPKAPI SARAYI LOKANTASI

KENNEDY CADDESİ

BABI ALİ CADDESİ

KYBELE HOTEL

TARİHİ SULTANAHMET KÖFTECİSİ

AYASOFYA (SAINT SOPHIA CHURCH)

SULTANAHMET

DİVAN YOLU CAD

YEREBATAN SARAYI (BASILICA CISTERN)

TOURIST OFFICE

SULTANAHMET

FOUR SEASONS AT SULTANAHMET

KABASAKAL CADDESİ

İSHAKPAŞA CADDESİ

KLODFARER CADDESİ

AT MEYDANI (HIPPODROME)

AT MEYDANI SOKAK

VAKIFLAR HALI VE KİLİM MÜZESİ (VAKIFLAR CARPET MUSEUM)

SOKAK

YEŞİL EV HOTEL

ANTIQUE HOSTEL & GUESTHOUSE

HOTEL EMPRESS ZOE

KUTLUGÜN SK.

ÜÇLER SK.

SULTANAHMET CAMİİ (BLUE MOSQUE)

AT MEYDANI SOKAK

ARASTA BAZAAR

ALBURA RESTAURANT

ORIENT HOSTEL INTERNATIONAL

BURAHA 93

HOTEL YUNUS EMRE

ROBINSON CRUSOE

DOY DOY

TORUN SOKAK

COOKING ALATURKA

BÜYÜK SARAY MOZAİK MÜZESİ (YUNUS GREAT PALACE MOSAICS MUSEUM)

KENNEDY CADDESİ

AYASOFYA CADDESİ

ARMADA İSTANBUL CİTY HOTEL

AKSAKAL

Sea of Marmara

0   300 yds
0   300 m

THE GENIUS OF THE IMPERIAL ARCHITECTS

Nearly five centuries of Ottoman rule gave Istanbul its dramatic cachet. From the grand spired mosques in the Sultanahmet quarter to the posh palaces lining the Bosphorus, these ornate buildings attest to the grandeur of their imperial commissioners. This impressive architecture is the amalgam of a variety of styles, each stamped by a master builder handpicked from within the imperial realm or invited from Europe's posh capitals by the ruler himself. But the brick-and-mortar testaments to spectacular or not-so-memorable reigns didn't start with the Ottomans. In fact, the Greeks, Romans, and even the Persians had done so long before. What makes Ottoman architecture unique, however, is the almost unlimited creative autonomy imperial architects enjoyed, the variety of building styles typical of the era, and the sheer decadence of the exteriors and interiors of the structures.

Historically, **Ottoman architecture** emerged in Bursa at the turn of the 14th century during the reign of the dynasty's founder, Osman I (1258-1324). From a base rooted deeply in Selçuk architecture, a mixture of Byzantine and Persian ornamentation was incorporated as the style evolved. Bursa's Ulu Mosque, for example, exemplifies the budding movement. It's fashioned in the traditionally modest Selçukian architectural style – characterized by large, dark praying halls, forested with columns holding massive ceilings. But its exterior was later amended to portray the grander Ottoman style with the addition of domes and gilded calligraphy. Buildings grew bigger and more lavish when the Ottomans named Edirne (1365) and later Istanbul (1453) their capital. The many-domed Topkapı Palace (1465) reflects that era. More sweeping innovations were introduced with the construction of Istanbul's Fatih Mosque (1470); the first of its

kind to include a *külliye* (the social/religious complex) on its grounds.

The **Classical Period** (1437-1703) ensued, highlighted by the mastery of Mimar Sinan, whose lauded for having greatly advanced global architecture during his lifetime. He conceived vast interiors enclosed by seemingly weightless yet massive domes, introduced harmony between inner and outer spaces, and played with light and shadow throughout his grand designs. During his time, mosques went from being somber and confined caverns embellished by Islamic calligraphy to artistically and technically complex sanctuaries. Süleymaniye Camii, in Istanbul, and Edirne's Selimiye are considered the movement's most exquisite examples.

By the turn of the 18th century, the **Westernization Period** was in full swing. Thanks to a political rapprochement between the western European nation and the empire, foreign emissaries and artists on both sides exchanged ideas. Baroque and Rococo styles found in France were introduced in the Ottoman Empire, while the French were lured by tales of Seraglios and the exotic pull of Orientalism. The **Tulip Period** (1730-1757) ensued, marking the launch of an era when the introverted Ottoman elite began to explore the outdoors. Public places became the focal point and lavish fountains, waterside residences, and large outdoor recreational spaces were all the rage. The curved lines of the **Baroque Period** (1757-1808), exemplified by the Selimiye Barracks on Istanbul's Asian side, preceded the memorable **Empire Period** (1808-1876). Much like the Classical Period is synonymous with Mimar Sinan, the Balyan family of architects highlights the Empire Period. The spectacular Dolmabahçe and Beylerbeyi Palaces, as well as the petite yet fabulous Ortaköy Mosque, high-

© JESSICA TAMTÜRK

The Sirkeci Tren Istasyonu (Sirkeci Train Station) is a blend of Ottoman and Beaux Arts styles.

light their achievements in Istanbul. During the 18th and 19th centuries and the reign of six consecutive sultans, nine Balyans from this Armenian family integrated western design elements in Istanbul's imperial and religious architecture. As a result of this aesthetic rapprochement to the west, minorities like Greeks and Armenians were accepted top artisans. Later Balyans incorporated techniques and design elements studied in the west without omitting traditional Ottoman building characteristics.

The **Late Period** (1876-1922) culminates Ottoman architecture style with the contributions of no less than eight master builders, whose slants tended toward the popular art nouveau, Vienna Secession, and Revivalism of the period. Two architects, Raimondo D'Aronco and Alexandre Vallaury, in particular, impacted the imperial building trove. The former's greatest contributions are the massive Haydarpaşa School of Medicine campus (Marmara University, 1883) on Istanbul's Asian shores and the chalet-like compound of Yıldız Palace in Beşıktaş (1893). While the latter, a Levantine of French parentage, is remembered as the founder of Neo-Ottoman style. Vallaury's melding of classical Ottoman and Beaux Arts building styles is best evidenced in buildings like Sirkeci Train Station, Istanbul Archaeological Museum, and the famed Pera Palace Hotel.

building by adding structural supports. He also commissioned the two larger minarets located on its western flank, the original sultan's loge, and the mausoleum of Selim II. In 1739, Sultan Mahmud I ordered yet another restructure, adding a *medrese* (Islamic seminary), library, soup kitchen, and a fountain. In the mid-19th century however, architectural aesthete Sultan Abdülmecid ordered the most complete renovation yet. Under the watchful eye of two Italian architects, it took more than two years to refurbish the structure. In 1935, Turkish President Mustafa Kemal Atatürk converted the sanctuary into a museum, an act that began the painstaking process of restoring the basilica to its original state. Restoration currently taking place is slowly uncovering the basilica's original mosaics, a process that's been somewhat controversial since the sanctuary has served both as a mosque and a church. Removing the plaster and tiles to reveal the Christian iconography beneath would destroy significant Islamic art, such as the calligraphy that covers what is thought to be a mosaic of *Christ Pantocrator* on the dome.

From afar, the sheer size of the building is astounding. The inner grounds are filled with stone remains of the two previous churches that stood on the site before Ayasofya; marble blocks from the second church are strewn on either sides of the path leading to the structure's heart. Once inside, the marble inner narthex reveals the mosaic of *Christ Pantocrator,* just above the massive Imperial Door. The Imperial Door, which was reserved for the Emperor, is the largest of three entrances. The calm interior beyond beckons, with the famous dome towering over a dark marble expanse. The genius behind this circular, seemingly floating structure lies in the innovative use of four pendentives— hollow triangular sections of stonework that allowed for the placement of the huge circular element on the rectangular structure. The pendentives transfer the dome's colossal weight to four massive piers at each corner of the basilica. The Ottoman imperial architect Sinan reinforced the scheme by using buttresses. At both western and eastern ends, half domes were added to create an oblong-ish interior. Carved from a single marble slab during the Hellenistic period, the 500-year-old marble jar to the right of the entrance originates from Pergamon. Opposite, the copper-covered marble Stele of Saint Gregory Thaumaturgus—the miracle worker—is believed to bring good luck. Just stick your thumb in the central recess and rotate it counterclockwise. If it comes out moist, good fortune will surely follow. Sultan Ahmet III devised the lofty and semi-private Sultan's Loge in order to use the sanctuary surreptitiously. The apse mosaic represents the Virgin and Child, which was the first post-iconoclastic of its kind in 944; she sits on a backless throne with Christ the child sitting comfortably on her lap. Mostly hidden by scaffolding, the large platform to the southeast of the apse is the largest *müezzin mahfili*—a raised dais where the Koran was read during services. Ayasofya's three other smaller *mahfilis* also date from the reign of Sultan Murat III (1574–1595). Also concealed under the scaffolding is the Byzantine coronation square—a collection of colored marble inlays—where the emperor's throne is presumed to have stood. Upon exiting the structure, turn around and look up at what is perhaps the grandest mosaic in the entire museum. The mosaic shows the Virgin Mary with Child Christ, flanked on one side by Justinian I offering the pair the Ayasofya, and on the other by Constantine I offering the city of Constantinople. Before leaving though, know that the majority of the basilica's mosaics are in the Upper Gallery, accessed by a steep, narrow walkway to the left of the inner-narthex's entrance.

The EU is pressuring Turkey to restore the structure to its original status of Orthodox Church before granting the country's accession to the economic bloc.

◖ Sultanahmet Camii (Blue Mosque)

Completed in 1617, the Sultan Ahmet Mosque (Sultanahmet Square, www.sultanahmetcami.com/hakkinda_eg.php, closed during prayer time, free) was commissioned by Sultan Ahmet as a means to outdo what was at the time the most lavish sanctuary in the world—the Ayasofya. Ahmet, left raw from a peace deal with Persia, and thus with no spoils of war, veered heavily from tradition by dipping into state coffers to fund his project.

The Sultan Ahmet Mosque indeed towers over the Ayasofya, and in fact, is the last grand mosque built in the classical style, widely considered to be the epitome of Byzantine and Ottoman mixed architecture. Its crown is a jumble of full and half domes, topped by a massive central dome, which soars at about 130 feet at its center and measures almost 90 feet in diameter. Upon completion, the mosque had six minarets, and was one of only two that had as many. Ahmet's audacity was criticized for constructing an edifice with the same amount of lanky spires as Mecca's Sacred Mosque. To resolve this issue, Ahmet ordered the addition of a seventh minaret to the latter.

Today, light from the 260 glass windows still floods the cavernous, carpeted space and bounces off the more than 21,000 hand-painted blue Iznik tiles to create a bluish haze, hence its nickname, the Blue Mosque. Almost as large as the mosque, the forecourt is defined by a continuing archway on its perimeter, with a central fountain some consider too cautious in size for the sheer dimension of the courtyard. Women are expected to cover their heads with scarves provided at the entrance. Individuals bearing too much skin are also asked to cover their legs. Visiting the grounds shouldn't take more than 30 minutes.

Ⓒ Topkapı Sarayı (Topkapı Palace)

Serving as the seat of the Ottoman government, the imperial residence, and as the location of the Sultan's legendary harem, Topkapı Sarayı (Sultanahmet, Eminönü, 0212/512-0480, www.topkapisarayi.gov.tr/eng/indexalt.html, 9 A.M.–7 P.M. Wed.–Mon., until 5 P.M. Nov.–May, adults 20TL) housed more than 4,000 people and regaled many a visiting dignitary in its heyday. Sultan Mehmet II (1432–1481) ordered its construction right atop the ruins of

The harem of Topkapı Palace was built in the mid-16th century.

the Acropolis of Byzantium. The New Palace opened its doors in 1465; its name changed to Topkapı Palace in the 19th century. Vastly improved from the Old Palace, the New Palace is situated atop Seraglio Point, overlooking the Sea of Marmara, the Golden Horn, and the Bosphorus Strait. The site's structures were built originally around a variety of ruins, including the mid-6th century Aya Eirene church, an underground Byzantine cistern, and four main courtyards. But subsequent sultans added their flair to create what resulted in an asymmetrical exterior layout. To the south and west of the palace is Gülhane Park; the north and east sides directly face the Sea of Marmara. Much larger than the 173-acre complex seen today, the palace was once home to mosques, schools, dormitories, a mint, a treasury, the location where the Ottoman archives were stored, and even kiosks and pavilions. This palace deteriorated after Abdülmecid (1823–1861) decided to move his court to the opulent Dolmabahçe Palace in 1853. Converted by Atatürk into a museum in 1923, Topkapı remains the largest and oldest palace in the world.

The Imperial Gate, or Gate of the Sultan, was built along with the palace, but its marble overlay was added in the late 19th century. With gilded calligraphy and a Sultan's seal embellishing the upper portion, verses from the Koran appear on either side of the entrance. Only viziers and foreign diplomats were allowed to cross to the **First Courtyard.** This garden currently houses, among others structures, the former 170,000 square-foot imperial mint, the 6th-century Church of Aya Eirene, the Fountain of the Executioner, and the tiled Ceremonial Pavilion. Accessible through the Gate of Salutation, the **Second Courtyard** is the actual and sole entrance to the museum. It opens onto a square that was once utilized as the administrative center of the Ottoman government. Only citizens with official business, janissaries on payday, or foreign diplomats were allowed here. Ceremonies, sometimes attended by thousands, were held in the courtyard, with the sultan sitting atop his throne by the gate. Only accessible from the harem, the building's only tower—the Tower of Justice—is located here. It's a high dungeon from which the city, the straits, and nearby Marmara could be espied.

Sprawling over 60 percent of the property, the **harem** became the residence of the sultan and his court—his immediate family, as well as concubines and the eunuchs, who were charged with their safety—by the mid-1500s. Enhanced and enlarged by various sultans, the 400 or so rooms are connected by narrow hallways. It's an area so secretive it became the stuff of legends.

The separate, guided tour of the harem (10TL, box office at harem entrance, varying times) starts through the 40 ornate rooms reserved for the Valide Sultan, ensued by the spacious marbled hammam, and finally the sultan's domed grand hall. Queuing through leads visitors past lavish spaces adorned with ornate fireplaces and relaxing fountains until the large hall where an astounding tiled pool awaits. The tour ends with two 16th-century rooms, outfitted by large stained-glass windows, from which the sultan-in-waiting would gaze out, undoubtedly biding his time for the throne.

The surrounding structures offer an intimate view of the history, wealth, breadth, and power of the once mighty Ottoman rule. Particularly impressive is the Armory and Council Hall, housed in the former realm's Council of State, where viziers and secretaries would meet on affairs of state chaired by the Grand Vizier, as the Sultan took note from a window carved high in a wall. An extensive collection of weapons and fatigues are displayed chronologically. Long, curved gilded sabers give way to intricately inlaid 19th-century firearms. Some utilized by sultans; others from conquered nations. The Kitchen and Porcelain Collection has, among others, a priceless array of some 12,000 gifted Chinese and Japanese pieces, including a large 15th-century Ming vase with Ottoman gold mounts displayed along with another 2,500 pieces in a separate room. The Third Courtyard, the private domain of the Sultan, was guarded by white eunuchs. The imperial university, treasury, and the Sacred Relics building are here. Guarded by a hand-picked selection of deaf and mute young men, the sultans heard foreign ambassadors and high officials in the throne room also located in this square. In its center, the 18th-century library commissioned by Ahmet III defines the epoch's popular blend of baroque and Turkish architectural styles. Along the remaining buildings that boast the luxurious, ankle-length silk kaftans of the sultans, perhaps the most remarkable is the Treasury Hall. A collection of thrones, like the golden throne which was used for coronations and holidays, and of course the 86-carat Spoonmaker's Diamond, one of the biggest bling in the world, await amongst the world's largest—and most expensive—jewelry stashes. To view Topkapı, get there bright and early, as crowds start flocking by mid-morning. Start with the harem, obviously the most popular section, and plan at least a half day to view the palace. If you don't have that much time, do the 30-minute tour of the harem and move on to the crown jewels.

◀ Yerebatan Sarayı (Basilica Cistern)

The largest underground structure of its kind, the Yerebatan Sarayı (Yerebatan Cad. 13, 212/522-1259, www.yerebatan.com/english/index.html, 9 A.M.–6:30 P.M. daily Apr.–Sept., until 5:30 P.M. Oct.–Mar., adults 10TL), is a refreshing experience, particularly when the thermometer hovers above 100° Fahrenheit in the climatic throes of summer. Also known as the Sunken Palace Cistern—a direct translation from *Yerebatan Sarayı Sarnıçı*—the cistern is a surreal, wide colonnaded space that is capable of holding over 21 million gallons of water. The mid-6th-century cistern was another of Emperor Justinian I's schemes and it bears the name of the grand basilica that had preceded it.

The idea behind building the cistern was to collect water for local use from the Valens Aqueduct in the Belgrade Forest, some 12 miles away. The cistern was constructed with 15-foot-thick brick walls and 336 Doric and Corinthian columns standing 9-feet tall and just 15 feet apart. Seven thousand slaves are thought to have built the formidable structure, whose ceiling is entirely supported by the 12 rows of 28 marble and granite cylindrical columns. Be sure not to miss the two Medusa heads used as pedestals for two of the columns; one lies sideways and the other upside down in the cistern's northwest corner.

Today, the shallow waters of the cistern are home to koi fish bopping above a veritable fortune in coins of every perceivable currency. Strolling through Yerebatan takes about 30 minutes, and is one of the most memorable sights Sultanahmet has to offer.

Haseki Hürrem Sultan Hamami (Baths of Roxelana)

The Haseki Hürrem Sultan Hamami (Aya Sofya Meydanı 4, 0212/638-0035, 9 A.M–5:30 P.M. Tues.–Sun. Nov.–May, until 6:30 P.M. June–Oct.) is a lavish, marble 16th-century hamam built by the great architect Mimar Sinan. Sultan Süleyman the Magnificent commissioned the double-hammam—one for each gender—in honor of his wife Lady Hürrem, better known as Roxelana. The interior of the structure is typical of many Turkish baths and provides an ideal glimpse of a hamam without having to participate in the bathing ritual. Composed of three rooms on either side (a dressing facility, washing quarters, and the sweating and scrubbing rooms), the building is crowned by two impressive domes, effortlessly blending with nearby monuments. Closed for ablutions for about a century, it's now a state-run carpet shop. Alas, the majority of the foot traffic ambling through this structure is more interested in its historical interior than in haggling over its contents.

At Meydanı (Hippodrome)

What was once the Hippodrome is now a municipal park and pedestrian thoroughfare known as At Meydani (Sultanahmet Square, adjacent to the Blue Mosque). The ancient Hippodrome precedes many of the top sights in the city, however it is buried just 12 feet under the current promenade, with only its tall obelisks to mark its presence. In its heyday 100,000 spectators would fill its stands, cheering for one of four teams, each team bankrolled by different political parties.

This site is where the Nika Riots of A.D. 532 took place, as dissent between the two major factions of the day—the Blues and the Greens—led to a tense six-day siege of the city. It ended when Emperor Justinian ordered the massacre of some 30,000 rioters in the Hippodrome.

The Hippodrome was built by Septimius Severus to echo Rome's Circus Maximus in A.D. 203, and later enlarged and strengthened at its Sphendome by Constantine. The racetrack would be abandoned as early as the 13th century with the arrival of the Fourth Crusade. It even served as a quarry under the Ottomans. Today, the Sphendome—the Hippodrome's 180-degree curve and retaining wall—is located directly under Marmara University. Its remnants were discovered just recently; it's accessible through a three-foot hole located behind the Sultanahmet's Technical High School. Those daring a foray in its vicinity will, in the company of a guide, discover an underground system of stables and an amazing view of a 90-foot drop into the sea.

The columns that once embellished the Hippodrome and marked its center were brought from the furthest reaches of the Roman Empire. One of the remaining columns is the original **Serpent Column** from the Temple of Apollo at Delphi, which Constantine had removed and transferred to the Hippodrome. The Serpent Column was placed in the dead center of the Hippodrome. Originally, the three entwining serpents peaked into three golden serpent heads that supported a golden bowl. The bowl was either destroyed or stolen by knights of the Fourth Crusade.

The second column was a gift from Theodosius the Great. In A.D. 390, Theodosius ordered the 60-ton, pink granite obelisk, that had graced Luxor's Temple of Karnak since the late 15th century, to be cut into three pieces and shipped to Constantinople. Two of the pieces were lost in transit from Egypt, but the remaining third piece was placed on a marble pedestal in the Hippodrome. The surviving piece is etched with depictions of Theodosius' clan, racing scenes, and hieroglyphics attesting to the greatness of the God Horus and the Pharaoh, which run along the 65-feet height of the pillar's four surfaces.

A third surviving column is the **Walled Obelisk,** which was originally commissioned by Emperor Constantine Porphyrogenitus in the 10th century A.D. The Walled Obelisk is located at the southern end of the Hippodrome, near the Sphendome. The obelisk was used to secure a pulley system that would raise awnings to shade spectators from the sun. Its original gold-plated bronze plaques were removed by knights of the Fourth Crusade to be minted into coins.

At the northern end of the square lies the octagonal, domed Fountain of Wilhelm II, right in front of the Sultanahmet Camii. The initials of both Sultan Abdülhamid (1842–1918) and the Kaiser attest to a long-standing chumminess between the two empires. Brought in pieces from Germany, it was assembled here in 1895 to commemorate the Kaiser's visit.

Büyük Saray Mozaik Müzesi (Great Palace Mosaics Museum)

It wasn't until the late 1930s that the amazing mosaics of the peristyle courtyard (an open court with porticos) of Constantine's Great Palace were discovered. Led by a team of Scottish archaeologists from the University of Saint Andrews, the dig took place right under the Arasta Bazaar, an early 17th-century "row of shops" built by Sultan Ahmet I (1590–1617) that ironically protected the ceramic cache from the elements. Returning two decades later, the British team excavated a pavement consisting of hunting and mythological scenes near the rear of Sultanahmet Camii. By then, Turkish authorities realized the momentous find and sacrificed the more than dozen shops to open Büyük Saray Mozaik Müzesi (Torun Sok. Arasta Çarşısı, 0212/518-1205, 9 A.M.–4:30 P.M. Tues.–Sun. Nov.–May, until 6:30 P.M. June–Oct., 5TL) to the public. If you have an hour to spare, preferably in the morning, plan to stroll along this structure's galleries to look at the remains of what is perhaps the only Byzantine mosaics collection in the entire city, sans religious depictions.

Türk ve Islam Eserleri Müzesi (Museum of Turkish and Islamic Arts)

Inaugurated in 1984, Türk ve Islam Eserleri Müzesi (At Meydanı 46, Sultanahmet, 0212/518-1805, 9 A.M.–4:30 P.M. Tues.–Sun. until 6:30 P.M. June–Oct., 10TL) lies on the Hippodrome's western flank. A visit to view floor-to-ceiling Uşak carpets, the ethnographic collection, and the historical Korans are well worth a half-hour stroll. Its lesser-known tea garden in the former palace's lush central court is the ideal resting space on a hot summer day.

Also known as the Ibrahim Paşa Palace Museum, Atmeydanı Palace, Mehterhane Summer Pavilion, and Hiyamite Summer

Pavilion, the building has had just as many incarnations as it has names. Its most renowned owner, Ibrahim Paşa, was a close friend and the brother-in-law of Süleyman the Magnificent. He was captured as a child in Greece and brought into the imperial court as a slave. He trained as a page, all the while befriending the young Prince Süleyman. Ibrahim was appointed grand vizier when the latter became sultan, and received this palace after accepting the hand of Süleyman's sister, Hadice. But Ibrahim's growing wealth and influence over state affairs riled many in the court, including the cunning Roxelana. And after being accused of disloyalty by one of his peers, she convinced her husband Süleyman that his best friend could no longer be trusted. Ibrahim was strangled in 1536 and his assets reverted to the state. In the late 18th century, the palace, by then dilapidated, housed the official registry and functioned as the headquarters of the royal band. A mental hospital ensued, then a lion den, a textile workshop, and finally slums, before it was partially razed in 1939 to accommodate a modern courthouse. The museum today is the result of a 15-year restoration that began in 1966.

Vakıflar Halı ve Kilim Müzesi (Vakıflar Carpet Museum)
The collection of antique carpets and kilims that once graced the floors of mosques throughout the Ottoman Empire have recently found a home at the Vakıflar Halı ve Kilim Müzesi (Sultanahmet Mosque, Sultanahmet, 0212/518-1330, 9 A.M.–noon and 1–4 P.M. Tues.–Sat., 3TL). The former Imperial Pavilion of Sultanahmet Camii—a place utilized by sultans during their prayer time—is a fitting setting for the display of these 14th–20th-century rugs. The good half-hour tour takes tourists past carpets exhibited next to the sultan's loge and kilims in the vaulted galleries right beneath the mosque. Once short on funds, this museum lacked the proper lighting to display its then threadbare assortment. But renewed efforts have remedied the situation, rendering this collection a must for carpet enthusiasts.

When out on a stroll along Sultanahmet's back streets, don't miss out on the beautifully refurbished **Soğukçeşme Sokak.** It's part of a sweeping, decades-long project undertaken by Turkey's Touring and Automobile Club to restore historical landmarks. Celik Gülersoy, the visionary at the helm of the club, saw a diamond in the rough when ambling along the string of greasy automotive repair shops that backed Topkapı some 30 years ago. Through a love-hate relationship with the municipality, Gülersoy labored to convince the city's leadership of his grand plan to erect a row of houses reminiscent of Istanbul's late 19th-century architectural wealth. His vision and dedication for his native city continue today, albeit posthumously, with an award-winning hotel, street-side cafés, and internationally acclaimed restaurants.

BAZAAR QUARTERS
Istanbul's Bazaar quarters slopes from the Kapalı Çarşı (Grand Bazaar), which crowns the city's second hill, through a jumble of narrow streets to its end near the large port of Eminönü. Along the massively populated squares and back alleys, one gets the sense that they're in for yet another history lesson. True to form, this is Sinan country, where two of his greatest architectural accomplishments—the mid-16th-century Mosques of Süleyman and Rüstem Paşa—are located. Also in the vicinity is the complex of the Armenian Orthodox Patriarchate, which is a highly guarded fully functioning complex unfortunately not open for public viewing. Just outside the Kapalı Çarşı is the hectic, historical center of Beyazit, where Istanbul University's colossal gate looms over the square. Just as the road's slant tapers, the organized chaos of the Mısır Çarşısı (Egyptian Bazaar), near the just recently renovated Yeni Cami, is a web of narrow, packed alleys full of tiny, over-stocked shops, relentless peddlers, and avid shoppers. Pencil in a full day at the very least; two days are ideal. You'll be rewarded at the end with a glass of steaming tea at the waterside cafés along the Galata Bridge's lower level.

BUYING AN AUTHENTIC RUG

Exactly when Turkish nomads began weaving animal hair to create their yurts is unknown, but it's safe to assume that the practice dates well before the 5th century B.C. That's according to the carbon dating of the oldest knotted-pile carpet ever found – an impressive 3.5-square-meters rug that belonged to a Scythian prince and features the famed Turkish double knots, some 347,000 of them per square meter to be exact. By then, the practice of weaving had already evolved from a need basis to an artful pursuit. Rug-making was introduced to Anatolia by the Selçuk Turks sometime in the 11th century, and from there nomadic *Yörük* tribes throughout the country advanced their craft by introducing fine silks, elaborate colors made form vegetable dyes, and innumerable weaving forms. Today, there are 18 succinct rug-making centers, which boast their own colors and motifs. The rise of Ottoman aestheticism demanded the production of fine palatial-size rugs – mostly made of silk – to be used in imperial residences. For that, sultans conferred with the master artisans of Hereke, an area that has continued to produce some of the world's finest (and priciest) woven floor coverings.

While searching for that perfect piece, know that each color has a meaning. Red, for instance, is the dominant hue in Turkish rug-weaving and symbolizes wealth, joy, and happiness. Green represents heaven; blue stands for nobility and grandeur; yellow keeps evil away; while black keeps worries at bay. The assigned meanings to colors and motifs date back to paganism. The scorpion symbolizes pride and liberty. Weavers use images of the ram's horn (fertility, heroism, and power) and evil eye to convey their happiness and piety.

Finding an original, one-of-a-kind rug – knotted-pile carpet or woven, flat kilim – depends largely on three things: taste, budget, and, of course, the right seller. Taste is easy: you like it, you buy it. From the heavy floral patterns and deep hues used in Bergama to the fine silks and wools used to create the tiniest of blooms on a Hereke, more than a dozen styles and a variety of sizes are available. Budget, however, is a little more difficult: Original pieces run the gamut from $80 to $80,000, or more, depending on size, age, condition, and quality of materials. Prices also increase according to sheen, depth of hues, and complexity of design. Shops sell antiques and new rugs, as well as replicas of historical rugs. Note that if a seller is trying to pass off an antique that seems in mint condition, meaning no signs of wear and tear or repair, you may be dealing with a new rug that has been artificially aged to look like the real McCoy.

If you're wondering whether to buy a less expensive machine-made rug versus a hand-woven one, consider that the former is typically created with synthetic or inferior fabrics. Machine-made rugs have poor stain resistance and low structural integrity, requiring more maintenance than their handwoven counterparts. So owning a mechanically-made rug will cost more in the long run. To add insult to injury, machine-made carpets have virtually no resale value. A superior quality, hand-knotted carpet, on the other hand, retains its market price well.

The rules of engagement are pretty simple. Expect glasses of tea while the owner's staff unfurls his wear. Keep the ones that appeal to you and send the rest back. If you're in the mood to buy, start the haggling process. The shopowner's starting quote may be anywhere from 30-50 percent above his intended selling price. If you're not buying, tell him you'll return and thank him for his time and effort. Remember to stick to a pre-determined budget.

For more background information on Turkish carpets, peruse Jon Thompson's *Oriental Carpets: From the Tents, Cottages and Workshops of Asia* or Oktay Aslanapa's *One Thousand Years of Turkish Carpets*. To receive an onsite lesson on the art of handwoven carpets or to purchase from a reputable dealer, head to **Sude Old Rugs and Antique Textiles** in Sultanahmet or **Kemal Erol** in the Grand Bazaar.

ISTANBUL

COURTESY OF REPUBLIC OF TURKEY CULTURE AND TOURISM MINISTRY

More than 4,000 shops make up the Grand Bazaar, the world's oldest shopping mall.

◖ Kapalı Çarşı (Grand Bazaar)

A must on a first or repeat visit to Istanbul, the Kapalı Çarşı (near Beyazit, Sirkeci, or Üniversite tram stops, www.grandbazaaristanbul.org, 9 A.M.–7 P.M. Mon.–Sat.) is a mind-boggling collection of over 4,000 businesses. Souvenirs, leather, jewelry, clothing, carpets, copper, and anything else that might interest tourists can be found here. Roughly 65 pedestrian streets traverse this domed structure, which is accessed through 22 gates. There are also 24 *hans* that now function more as markets than the combination market and inn of old, as well as two enclosed *bedestens* (marketplaces).

Kapalı Çarşı has been the ideal place to bargain for centuries, though nowadays most salespersons won't budge on items they've hiked up as much as 300 percent. A knock-off designer bag priced at more than 200TL, for instance, can be bought elsewhere for a third of the price. These exorbitant prices are paid by affluent tourists, who are either above haggling or just too embarrassed to quibble over a couple of liras.

The shops' sky-high rates have become too steep for locals. That is, except for the haunts of a select few, who can afford some of the famed artisans' more opulent, custom jewelry. Merchants, like sharks smelling blood, have this innate ability to sniff out the unseasoned shopper. Largely left to the owners' guise, prices fluctuate from shop to shop and from customer to customer. That said, there still exist some incredible vendors who are open to negotiation. Bargaining is easy once you get the hang of it. Offer cash right off the bat and the price will go down. The rules of engagement here state that once a deal is reached it's in bad taste to back out.

Entering from the **Çarşı Kapısı** (Bazaar Gate), located across the eponymous tramway stop on Ordu Caddesi, is highly recommended for its convenience. Or, follow the facade to the right until **Nuruosmaniye Kapısı,** which actually boasts a mosque noted for being the prototype for Istanbul's Baroque architectural era. Once inside, the structure's largest street—**Kapakçılar Caddesi**—unfolds right before your eyes. The astounding displays of gold and the heady smell emanating from the myriad leather shops captivate the senses, but the real treasure of this place lies in its back alleys, where the deals worth haggling over and a great cup of tea can be found. Alas, toting antiques onto a plane will be out of the question, but do head to the **İç Bedesten** (Inner Bazaar) by hanging a right on Kolancılar Caddesi. Aside from exquisite copperware, really intricate pipes and boxes of indigenous meerschaum are found here. In addition to the *hans* worth visiting inside, the ones just outside—like **Mercan Han**—are where you can check out unique artistry, with pieces available for a fraction of the price charged inside Kapalı Çarşı.

Historically, the structure was Mehmet the Conqueror's first order of business to reinvigorate trade after conquering Constantinople. Mehmet commissioned the construction of the İç Bedesten in the mid-15th century. But in the midst of burning down twice, prior to being reconstructed of block stone, the **Sandal Bedesten** (Silk Bazaar) was built and is considered today to be the oldest structure. Other markets, like the jewelry-focused **Zincirli Han**—a quaint, open-air haven from the crowds inside—are more recent additions. You can spend days roaming through every cranny of this place, but do earmark at least four hours for a good self-guided tour. Beware of pickpockets: they prowl the alleys looking for ambling tourists prone to moments of inattention.

Beyazit Meydanı (Beyazit Square)

Officially called Freedom Square, but not even the government uses that name, Beyazit Meydanı is flanked to the east by Beyazit Camii. The monumental portal is that of Istanbul University, which was also built by Mehmet in 1453 and is considered one of the oldest colleges in the world. On Sunday, the hectic atmosphere here sizzles even more with the city's largest combo flea and farmer's market. Immediately west of the Grand Bazaar, on

Çadırcilar Caddesi, the **Sahaflar Çarsısı** (Old Book Bazaar) is the place to buy books, used or new. Even out-of-print English titles, if you look hard enough.

The paved, landscaped entrance of the university bears a few marble blocks of the triumphal arch that graced the original Byzantine plaza known as Forum of Theodosius, after the 4th-century emperor. It was the largest forum of antiquity, and was patterned after Rome's Forum of Trajan, with a gigantic arch crowned by bullheads. Perhaps that's how it earned its other moniker, the Forum of Tauri (Bulls). The other possibility could be that Theodosius was paying homage to the Roman cattle market that had been there before this colossal architectural scheme. We may never know. The grand Mosque of Sultan Süleyman the Magnificent is just behind the campus.

Süleymaniye Camii (Mosque of Süleyman the Magnificent)

By far the finest sanctuary of its kind in the city, the Süleymaniye Camii (Prof. Siddik Sami Onar Cad., 0212/514-0139, 9 A.M.–4:30 P.M. daily except prayer times, donations accepted) towers over the Golden Horn, eclipsing all other structures on the peninsula's northeastern flank. It not only crowns Istanbul's second hill, but the complex's strategic placement seems to organically extend the promontory rather than overwhelm it. Both its intricate facade and interior attest to the immaculate and complex workmanship that propelled Mimar Sinan to be recognized as the ablest of all imperial architects.

It also symbolizes the military and reigning prowess of its benefactor Sultan Süleyman, under whose reign the Ottoman Empire expanded to encircle the Mediterranean and even went as far as knocking on Vienna's door. Commissioned in 1550, the mosque is second in size after Sultan Ahmet, but its interior and exterior designs outshine those of the former. What makes Süleymaniye's architecture unique for its time is the location of its minarets, in which the spires delineate the courtyard rather than the mosque. This innovative concept filled the negative space created by the low-lying complex adjacent to the towering building. Sinan followed the dome design of Ayasofya, adding buttresses to strengthen the building in an area he knew was prone to seismic activity.

The surrounding grounds were planned to function as a *külliye*, a semi-autonomous complex with a *medrese*, infirmaries, caravanserais, hammams, schools of Tradition, a hospital, as well as lodging and bathing facilities. The courtyard is filled with columns of the finest crystalline rock known as porphyry, as well as marble and granite. One towering minaret rises to the sky from each corner of the property to indicate that Süleyman was the fourth sultan to rule in Istanbul; the 10 balconies attest to his place in the Ottoman Dynasty. Sinan's tomb can be found in a walled plot north of the mosque, while Süleymaniye's southeastern corner is home to a cemetery where the elaborately tiled tomb of Süleyman the Magnificent can be found, alongside that of his wife Hürrem (Roxelana).

The mosque's interior is nothing short of splendid in its simplicity. The light hue of its inner walls refracts the sunlight flooding in from hundreds of windows, rendering Süleymaniye's inner sanctum bright and cheery, unlike the often cavernous feel of other mosques. Both the *minbar* and *mihrab*—the Imam's pulpit and a niche indicating the direction of Mecca, respectively—are crafted of a fine indigenous Proconessian marble. Heralded imperial calligraphers Ahmet Karahisarı and Hasan Celebi also beautifully inscribed their creative involvement. Do take an hour to linger in this complex, stopping to absorb its unique charm and sanctity over tea and a snack in the courtyard's Darüzziyafe Restaurant.

Mısır Çarşısı (Egyptian Spice Bazaar)

A rambling expanse of back alleys, Mısır Çarşısı (8:30 A.M.–6:30 P.M. Mon.–Sat.) is across the Eminönü Embarcadero and slightly to the right of Yeni Cami. Here you'll find the freshest condiments just beyond its gate; for the finest of fabrics, school supplies, or anything else of interest shop the side alleys. Mısır Çarşısı's much smaller than the Grand Bazaar. It was built in 1660 to support the maintenance of Yeni Cami, and as a sale point of exotic spices arriving from the then newly-conquered state of Egypt. The spectral colors of herb and spice stands, as well as tea baskets are mesmerizing. So is the sheer selection of Turkish delicacies, such as *lokum*, baklava, and dried fruits. Merchants braying to attract their next sale may appear intimidating, but most will gladly let you sample their offering, if you just ask. *Kuruyemiş* (dry foodstuff) stands make a great stop for caked olive soap, as well as inexpensive bath accessories like loofah and indigenous sea sponges. Try the rumored aphrodisiac of honey-soaked pistachios, olives of every color and size, succulent dried figs, and Turkey's reputable cheeses. While most of the stands sell loose spices, you may inquire about the possibility of vacuum-sealing your selections to ensure their scent doesn't alert the attention of canine officers on the way home. Note: Entering the U.S. with walnut-based products may be an issue.

Rüstem Paşa Camii (Mosque of Rüstem Paşa)

Fresh from the architectural triumph of Süleymaniye, Sinan went right to work on the rarely-visited marvel Rüstem Paşa Camii (Hasırcılar Cad., open daily outside of prayer times, donation suggested). It may just be a fraction of its predecessor, but what this mosque lacks in size it oozes in prime Ottoman artistry. An octagonal thimble-sized design gives rise to just one minaret, replete with doors crafted in the three-dimensional, wood crafting art of *kündekâri,* which involves the mind-boggling, painstaking task of placing pieces of wood of various geometric shapes decorated with vegetal motifs side by side. The intricate interior boasts finely gilded minutiae high up on its entrance walls; its inner sanctum amazes with

© ZEYNEP GÖZEN

the Galata Bridge, with the port of Eminönü beyond, from high atop Beyoğlu

what is perhaps the finest in the art of tile making. The red on white as primary colors, as opposed to the easily blended tints of blue, green, and yellow prevalent in the 1560s, and the faience depicting flowers throughout epitomizes Iznik tile mastery. These pricey decorative ceramics show yet again the power and wealth of its egotistical owner, Rüstem Paşa.

As Süleyman's Grand Vizier and son-in-law, Rüstem was a Bosnian who attained the highest seat in government through manipulation, greed, and cunning. He fell into the graces of Süleyman's wife, the pretty Roxelana, and the two schemed to convince the sultan that his son, Prince Mustafa, was himself devising a military coup to dethrone him. Süleyman fell for the ruse and Mustafa's beheading guaranteed Roxelana's son Selim's ascension to the throne. Ironically, Selim was a womanizing drunkard who became known as Selim the Sot, and his pitiful reign signified the start of the empire's 200-year decline. Facing the Egyptian Bazaar, the Rüstem Paşa Camii is located to the right, opposite the municipal bus depot.

Yeni Cami (New Mosque)

Only Turks, who live among some of the oldest monuments on the planet, refer to a building erected 300-plus years ago as new. The Yeni Cami (Yenicami Meydanı Sok., dawn–dusk daily, donation suggested) is actually the Mosque of Valide Sultan (Queen Mother), after Sultan Mehmet III's mom, Safiye. Commissioned in 1597, the construction was halted for more than five decades after Safiye lost her powers and royal purse strings when her son passed away. Incidentally, her ruthless son Mehmet is rumored to have ordered the strangulation of over 36 of his siblings in order to secure his accession to the throne and her undivided love. The mosque was completed in 1657, thanks to its new benefactor Turhan Hatice, the mother of Sultan Mehmet IV. Though large, Yeni Cami pales in comparison to Istanbul's other mosques. It's crafted in true Ottoman style with a series of domes crowned by a large dome; the sanctuary features a wealth of gold, meticulously crafted tiles, and carved marble. Turhan Hatice's tomb is located here;

ISTANBUL

© FUAT TAMTÜRK

The New Mosque and the Mosque of Süleyman the Magnificent (rear) are the backdrop to the harried transportation hub of Eminönü.

her son Mehmet and some five other sultans were laid alongside her tomb.

Galata Köprusu (Galata Bridge)

While only a fraction in size of the two massive suspension bridges that span the Bosphorus, Galata Köprusu is pure Istanbul—a successful mix of modern and old. Its center lane accommodates a rapid tramway that whooshes along just as hundreds of anglers lazily line its edges waiting for their next catch. Professionals and homemakers alike scurry across to their destinations as peddlers push socks, sesame-crusted tea rings, and even hunting knives. About 20 waterside cafés, fish restaurants, and narghile joints line the bridge's lower terrace; it's an ideal spot to experience the city's rhythm, particularly at prayer time when the call of the muezzins from the nearby mosques simultaneously beckon the faithful over a backdrop of screeching seagulls.

The bridge links the frantic ports of Karaköy and Eminönü, and extends over the Golden Horn—the natural estuary that flows from the

Sea of Marmara. Built in 1994, today's Galata Bridge modernized a nostalgic pontoon bridge that seductively swayed along with the currents beneath it. While feasibility studies are underway to build a practical footbridge, according to a design presented to Sultan Beyazit II by Leonardo da Vinci in 1502, overpasses spanning the waterway such as Galata have been around since Constantine's time.

EMINÖNÜ AND VICINITY

A stroll down Ankara Caddesi, the street that leads northeast of Sultanahmet Square to the busy port of Eminönü, will snake past facades of Tophane's modern shops and boutique hotels interspersed by antique Ottoman buildings. Just a 10-minute brisk walk away from Ayasofya, the neighborhood of Gülhane offers a rambling park that was once part of Topkapı Palace. It's now home to the entrance of Istanbul's archaeology museum, where more than one million relics are on display, as well as a variety of sly felines waiting for softhearted western tourists. Also of note, is the nearby

Sirkeci Train Station—the famed terminus for the Orient Express.

Istanbul Arkeoloji Müzesi (Istanbul Archaeological Museum)

The impressive artifact collections displayed at Istanbul Arkeoloji Müzesi (behind Topkapı Palace in Gülhane Park, 0212/520-7740, 9 A.M.–5 P.M. Tues.–Sun., 15TL) comprise one of the most extensive in the world. If time is of the essence, take 90 minutes to view the following not-to-miss pieces: the 18 ornate battles scene carvings on the 4th-century B.C. sarcophagi; the 13th-century B.C. remains of the sphinx from the Yarkapı Gate at Hattusas; and, one of three known tablets of the Treaty of Kadesh, the first recorded peace treaty signed between Ramses II and the Hittites, inscribed in Akkadian, the vernacular of the time. The chronological compilation of local artifacts help viewers trace the lengthy history of the city from its infancy; this alone is worth the trip! Add to this the most recent 8,000-year-old finds at Yenikapı and other archaeological finds and you'll realize just how deep this city's roots are.

A lion statue originating from the Mausoleum of Halicarnassus, one of the Seven Ancient Wonders of the World, tips off visitors to the magnitude of the museum's contents right from the get-go. Nearby, a series of sarcophagi found at the ancient city of Sidon, today's Syria, are displayed in the halls. Demonstrating superb Roman stone artistry influenced by the ancient Mediterranean cultures, the pieces are highlighted by the Alexander Sarcophagus, with carvings relating to his battles and life. Ironically, this tomb was long thought to be the emperor's, but later investigation revealed that it was actually that of Sidonian King Abdalonymos. The Sarcophagus of the Mourning Women, which was found in the same Sidonian necropolis, boasts 18 panels of complex carvings depicting women in mourning. Next is a 14th-century bell from the Galata Tower and one of the three snake's heads from the Hippodrome's Serpentine Column.

The museum's mezzanine level houses the "Istanbul Through the Ages" exhibit, which received the Council of Europe Museum Award in 1993. Adeptly presented, this section's maps and diagrams effectively give a bird's eye view into the city's past, from pre-historical remains found on Istanbul's Asian flank to mid-15th Byzantine artistry. Aside from a library that boasts more than 70,000 titles, the upper floor consists of smaller items, like terracotta statuettes, cooking implements, a collection of 800,000 Ottoman coins, medals, and seals. The upper floors are home to the Troy exhibit, the halls containing Syrian and Palestinian sculptures and the history of Anatolia.

Once a fine arts school, the building commissioned by Osman Hamdi Bey in 1883 now houses the Ancient Eastern Works Museum. Recently reopened after lengthy restorations, the museum displays an exceptionally abundant array of artifacts from the earliest civilizations of Anatolia, the Arab continent, Egypt, and Mesopotamia. Along with a small collection of Egyptian artifacts, pagan divinities originating from the Al-Ula temple are on display.

Built in the late 19th-century by imperial architect Alexandre Vallaury, the facade of the museum, which was commissioned by Osman Hamdi Bey in 1881, was inspired by both the Sarcophagi Alexander and the Sarcophagus of the Mourning Women. History aesthetes can revel in the richness of this museum for days, but for the rest of us three hours at opening time should suffice.

Gülhane Parkı (Gülhane Park)

Once the gardens of sultans and concubines, today's sprawling 40-acre park is by far Istanbul's largest and oldest. Gülhane (adjacent to Topkapı Palace) is a meticulously landscaped hangout for sunflower seed-gnawers, picnickers, and runners. A tea garden, set high up on a slope opposite the end of the park's Ankara Caddesi entrance, affords fantastic views of the Bosphorus. Spreading along the rear of Topkapı Palace to Seraglio Point, panoramic terraces and benches are scattered throughout to offer visitors a place from which to enjoy the park's lush atmosphere. The fragrance that emanated from the millions of rose buds planted here during the sultanate was replaced by the stench—and cacophony—caused by dozens of animals during the park's short stint as a municipal zoo. Today, whistle sounds warning that the grass is off limits and the passing of the occasional municipal vehicle break the serenity of this green enclave.

Historically, the space Gülhane occupies served as military depots during the Byzantine era. By the late 11th century it was home to the Mangana Palace, Hagios Georgios Monastery, and Sacred Panagia Fountain. When Mehmet the Conqueror claimed Sarayburnu (the tip of Seraglio Point) in 1453, he ordered the construction of lavish city walls encompassing the land. A series of pavilions and mansions were later built by his successors in and around these lush gardens.

Getting past the touting vendors just outside the entrance is always tricky for visitors who out of politeness offer replies to their advances. But walking past them resolutely and without engaging in conversation always does the trick. Following the ample footpath will take you directly to the coastal road that borders the Sea of Marmara, not far from the Sepetçiler Kasrı (Basket weavers Mansion)—a late 16th-century imperial embarcadero and ceremonial pavilion that now serves as the Foreign Press Center and as banquet facilities for Swissôtel.

Sirkeci Tren Istasyonu (Sirkeci Train Station)

The famed terminus of the Orient Express, Sirkeci Tren Istasyonu (near Seraglio Point) welcomes tourists with a renewed vigor. The station was once the terminus of the Simplon Line, which transported passengers to seductive Istanbul from Paris' Gare de L'Est in utter luxury. It saw its literal end of the line in 1977; a similar service was reinstated in 2007 with much fanfare. What that meant for Sirkeci was a renovation to highlight its early 20th-century mystique, while modernizing its services and facilities to accommodate well-heeled travelers.

A far cry from the importance of its European peers, Sirkeci is small. What it lacks in size it makes up for with a grand facade and strategic location. Situated just a traffic-jammed, 10-minute walk west of Gülhane Park, it's smack in the middle of the south easternmost European hub of Eminönu, right where the Sea of Marmara meets the Bosphorus Strait. Today, Sirkeci operates as the terminus for trains coming from the Thracian peninsula and Eastern Europe. As posh as the Simplon line was, today's mundane connections are just the opposite—slow, dreary, and somewhat unsafe. So don't expect a red carpet here on most days, as it is just a working rail terminal.

At 1,200 square meters, the terminal is pure European Orientalism in architecture. Stylishly bold at the time of its inauguration in 1890; its unique design was replicated across the continent. An exact turret-less replica can be found in Varna, Bulgaria. The building sprawls on either side of a soaring turreted entrance that boasts geometrical detail extending to a series of circular oriels and lofty bay windows. The Station Restaurant inside became a hub for elite members of the media and writers, such as Graham Greene and Agatha Christie, in the mid-20th century. Agatha Christie is said to have researched the classic *Murder on the Orient Express* here. Today, the colorful quayside eatery pulls out all the stops with white linens and vested-waiters, and is aptly called the Orient Express Restaurant. To the right of the restaurant, the station also boasts the often-missed pint-size **Turkish Railroad Museum** (9 A.M.–5 P.M., free admission), which displays Turkish State Railways memorabilia. The splendidly renovated hall between the restaurant and the museum welcomes the traditional Whirling Dervish ceremony of *sema* (7:30 P.M. Tues. and Sat., about 20TL).

BEYOĞLU AND ŞIŞLI

Abutting the tiny neighborhood of Galata, with its looming Genoese tower, the district of Beyoğlu winds vertiginously from the busy port of Karaköy, through the cobbled back streets of artisans. Further up, it opens

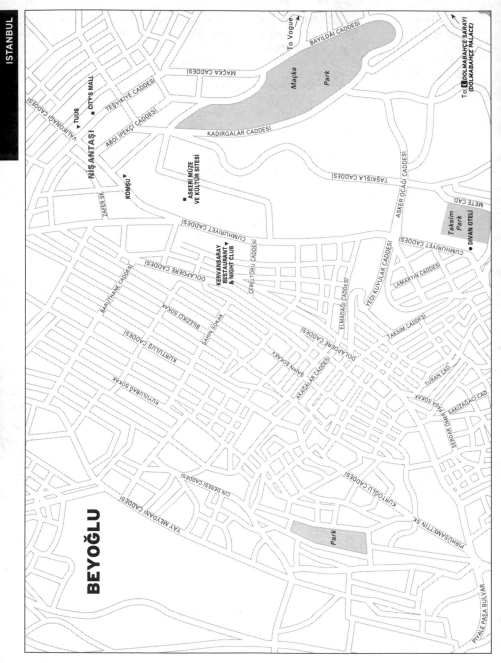

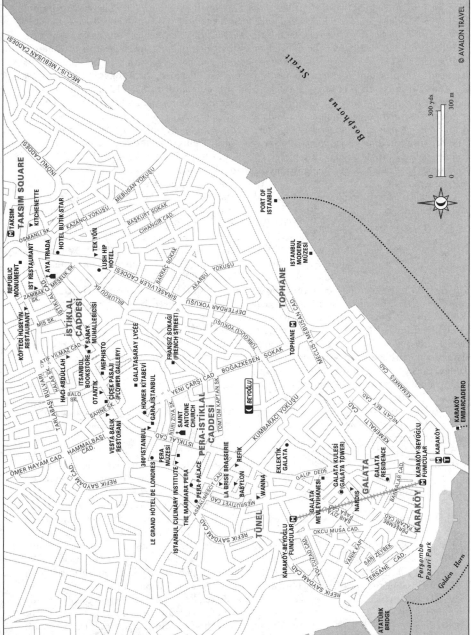

straight into the super-crowded pedestrian avenue of Istiklal Caddesi, which itself ends in Taksim—the heart of modern Istanbul. Taksim flows northeast into the district of Şişli, where the prized enclave of Nişantaşı—Istanbul's smaller but just as posh version of New York's Fifth Avenue—draws the nation's elite.

By foot or by tram, jaunting across Galata Bridge is like zapping back to the belle époque. The rich minorities that once worked, played, and resided in Beyoğlu have been replaced by legions of expats and a bustling nighttime entertainment center.

Once called Péra, Beyoğlu was the financial and diplomatic center in the 19th and early 20th century. Furriers, cafés, and grand hotels catered to foreign attachés, the literati, and all the trade that went along with it. When Turkey's capital was moved to Ankara in the mid-1920s, foreign embassies followed suit, leaving their lavish townhouses to function as consular offices. Beyoğlu's mystique spiraled downwards, and became known for its back alleys where drug dealers and prostitutes thrived. By the early 1990s, the smaller neighborhoods that comprise this district were reenergized. Today, the construction of a large shopping mall is underway, as more brand name boutiques and rooftop bars and swanky restaurants pop up along this stretch.

Beyoğlu's also renowned for its centuries-old Jewish synagogues, as well as Greek and Armenian Orthodox sanctuaries. In fact, Karaköy owes its name to a small, albeit still thriving, Jewish colony of Karaites, whose ancestors escaped the Spanish Inquisition in the late 15th century.

Moving quickly, these districts can be experienced in one day by riding the city's tramway to Karaköy, climbing Galata's backstreets to Istiklal Caddesi, and ambling along the thoroughfare to Taksim Meydanı. Once there, the Military Museum and Nişantaşı are both at an easy walking distance.

Galata

A wealth of Jewish sanctuaries abound in this small neighborhood. The **Neve Shalom Synagogue** (Büyük Hendek Cad. 61, 0212/292-0386, nevesalom@nevesalom.org, email or call for tour) was built by Galata's conservative congregation in 1951. Just above Bankalar Caddesi, the **Ashkenazi Synagogue** (Yüksek Kaldırım 37, 212/243-6909, open mornings Mon.–Fri. and Sabbath services on Sat. morning) remains the only active synagogue of Ashkenazi Jews in Istanbul. The nearby **Italian Synagogue** (Laleli Çeşme Sok. 8, 0212/293-7784, open mornings Mon.–Fri. and Sabbath services on Sat. morning) was founded in the late 19th century after turf disputes led Beyoğlu's Jewish population to seek protection from the Italian Embassy. Entering through the front reveals the sanctuary's Gothic facade and lovely marble staircase. The mid-17th-century **Zülfaris Synagogue** (Haracci Ali Sok., towards the square of Karaköy, 0212/244-4474) houses the Museum of Turkish Jews, which covers Sephardic Jewish life in Turkey over the past 500 years.

Galata Kulesi (Galata Tower)

For the ultimate view of Istanbul, the Galata Kulesi (Galata Meydanı, Karaköy, 0212/293-8180, www.galatatower.net/english, 9 A.M.–5 P.M. Nov.–May, until 7 P.M. June–Oct., 10TL) can't be beaten. The 210-foot citadel's upper terrace is just a short ride by elevator, followed by a climb up a spiraling staircase. Opening up to a circular expanse pocked with watch windows, this was, and remains, the best vantage point to keep tabs on the sprawling city.

The tower was commemorated as the Tower of Christ in the mid-14th century by the Genoese. It was renamed Galata Kulesi after the Ottoman conquest of Istanbul. Looming over the walled enclave of Galata, sentries would utilize its lofty location until well after the mid-1950s to monitor the vulnerable straits and Sea of Marmara, as well as to get an early call on recurrent fires that then afflicted the city. Checking out the panorama that extends well beyond the Princes Islands and the hilly

Asian banks of the Bosphorus is well worth a half-hour. Unless, of course, opting to linger over the views over moderately priced tea or beer at the café is de rigueur.

Tünel

Tünel is home to Istanbul's original cable car, or funicular. It connects Karaköy and Istiklal Caddesi's southern end at Tünel Meydanı through a 1,500-foot-long, 90-second ride. Such a short hop may seem pointless, but it's ideal for those not wishing to scale or seesaw down the cobbled back streets that link the two spots. Inaugurated in 1875, the single car was originally powered by horses. It wasn't until 1910 that the wooden cable cars were outfitted for electrical power. Tünel is the oldest subway in the world after the London Underground. Renovated in 1971 with spiffy metal cars, the connector was most recently upgraded with a silent car in 2007. The lower station's late-19th-century European Orientalism, with multi-colored tiles and yellow walls, was unfortunately replaced to accommodate modern tastes. Today, hopping to or fro costs less than a Turkish lira, and is well worth the two-minute wait for the next car, particularly with tots in tow.

Galata Mevlevihanesi (Galata Mevlevi Monastery)

Experiencing a *sema*—or Whirling Dervish ceremony—is a must on any trip to Turkey; attending one in Istanbul rates second best to actually visiting the lavish performance hall in Konya, where the ritual originated. The Galata Mevlevihanesi (Galıpdede Cad. 15, 0212/245-4141, 9:30 A.M.–4:30 P.M. Wed.–Mon., free) was refurbished in 2007, and welcomes tourists once again for their 5 P.M. Sunday evening performances (25TL), with shows scheduled on some Saturdays. While the new hall offers a cleaner look, the regularly sold-out shows tend to be uncomfortably packed. Since times and dates can change on a moment's notice, securing tickets from your hotel's concierge the day of your arrival in Istanbul will save you the trouble of having

to wait several hours in line at the box office. If tickets prove elusive, there are still evening performances held at the quaint, albeit less authentic, hall at the Sirkeci Train Station.

The Dervish hall was founded by an Ottoman aristocrat of Sultan Beyazid II's court in the late 15th century. Its first leader was Sheik Muhammed Semaî Sultan Divanî, a direct descendant of Mevlâna Jelaleddin Rumî. The street on which the structure lies was named after Galıp Dede (Grandfather Galıp), who was a respected leader of the order; his tomb is located to the left of the entrance. Kumbaracıbaşı Ahmet Paşa, a French count who converted to Islam and served in the imperial army, is also buried here alongside the remains of Ibrahim Müteferrika, who introduced the first printing press in the empire in the 17th century. Unless attending the show, the Galata Mevlevihanesi is a bit lackluster and truly doesn't warrant a special trip.

C Beyoğlu

Hectic **Istiklal Caddesi** (Independence Avenue) exudes old European flair and style. Apart from the arabesque or traditional *fasıl* music drifting from restaurants, you could be in any European capital. And, while on this side of town, you are. A contradiction in spades: the tall buildings that line this mile-long avenue may be categorized as historical by Turkish government standards, but the shops at street level are anything but historical. For decades, Beyoğlu's been the cultural center of town and Istiklal, as its respective core, has been its muse. From Tünel all the way to Taksim Square, this is where to find artists seeking inspiration, foreign journalists filing their stories in a string of western-style coffee shops, and diplomats being carried away in their convoys. The main drag's couturiers of yesteryear have been replaced by brand name shops, the musty bookstores by high-speed Internet cafés, and the five-starred eateries by jazzy rooftop bars. Some of its back streets, however, are still home to the marginalized: from transvestites, whose lifestyles have been made popular by the likes of the nationally beloved singer Bülent Ersöy, to drug pushers, prostitutes, and thieves. For a good sense of what lays ahead along this street, hop on the nostalgic **tram** that links Tünel to Taksim Square, and walk back. Word to the wise: Remain alert, keep all valuables tucked closely under clothing, and avoid quiet side streets after dark.

Situated across Tünel's upper station is **Tünel Pasajı**—a gallery of tiny shops selling nostalgic items and musical instruments. To the left of Tünel Square is the *Tepebaşı* district, home to **Pera Palace Hotel** (Meşrutiyet Cad. 98–100 Beyoğlu, 0212/251-4560, www. perapalas.com). This hotel was the famed pied á terre of such notables as Agatha Christie, Ernest Hemingway, and the irresistible WWII spy Mata Hari.

Just up the Meşrutiyet Caddesi is **Pera Müzesi** (Pera Museum, Meşrutiyet Cad. 141, Beyoğlu, 0212/334-9900, www.peramuzesi. org.tr/index_en.html, 10 A.M.–7 P.M. Tues.– Sat., noon–6 P.M. Sun., 7 TL). The splendid colonnaded mansion was inaugurated in 2005 as a museum of Turkish Arts. The museum boasts its benefactors' extensive collections, including: priceless Kütahya tiles, some dating back to 1377; 18th–20th-century original paintings of the Imperial Ottoman Court; and, the vast, must-see array of Anatolian weights and measures, including bronze balance pans and a cylindrical seal impression used by Assyrian traders 4,000 years ago.

Doubling back on Istiklal Caddesi, the gilded, monumental gate arising on the right is the entrance to **Galatasaray Lycée.** The high school was built by imperial edict in 1481; it remained the first of its kind in Istanbul until a transformation some four centuries later propelled it to exemplary status for its superb blend of European Oriental architecture, rigorous French curriculum, and for being one of modern Turkey's most prestigious scholastic establishments.

Following the school's southern perimeter wall leads to **Fransız Sokağı** (French Street). It's Istanbul's tribute to Paris's belle époque. In pure Toulouse Lautrec fashion, the facades on either side of the back alley's steep flight of stairs are rose-colored, with blooming planters gracing their myriad forged iron balconies. The sounds of Edith Piaf and the aroma of French-press coffee served at a handful of cafés fill the air. Enjoy lunch or dinner at one of the cafés' 2nd- or 3rd-floor balconies, overlooking this nostalgic street. This collaborative effort between the municipality and a group of creatives highlights centuries of French influence on Beyoğlu's architecture and arts. The French introduced the area's first movie theater and café in the 19th century.

Just north is Istiklal's **Çiçek Pasajı** (Flower Gallery), an arched, L-shaped arcade comprised of lofty early 19th-century facades. This was the Cité de Péra—the hobnobbing heart of erstwhile fashionistas. It was refurbished in the early 1990s after decades of neglect. The mundane beer joints and *köftecis* (small eateries specializing in grilled meat patties) that lined its sides were transplanted to side streets to make way for poshier yet reasonably-priced fish restaurants. Just outside, **Balık Pazarı** (Fish Market) is a noisy hodge-podge of fishmongers and delis, interspersed with side streets replete with estate jewelry dealers and souvenir shops.

Almost a dozen Catholic and Orthodox churches, as well as synagogues, can be found in Pera. Istiklal's prime example is **Saint Antoine** (a.k.a. San Antonio di Padova, Istiklal Cad. 325, Beyoğlu, 0212/244-0635, Catholic Mass in Italian on Sun., donations suggested), which is on the avenue's right-hand side, before the bend that houses Galatasaray Lycée. Since its inauguration in 1912, Saint Antoine has remained Istanbul's largest church and congregation. The church is one of the few open to the public; others like **Aya Triada** (Holy Trinity, Meşelik Sok. 11/1, Taksim, 0212/244-1358, donations suggested) are more often than not closed. If the gates are closed, knock; the warm Turkish caretaker will most likely comply with a gentle plea. Aya Triada's one of Beyoğlu's hidden jewels. This Greek Orthodox church, with its adjoining school, was founded in 1882. Newly refurbished, the inner sanctum reflects the benevolence of its wealthy congregation with massive crystal chandeliers, ornate walnut pews, and exquisite iconographical artwork on panels that open to secret loges. Don't forget to sweeten the tour with Beyoğlu's decadent, nut-filled chocolate bars available at the corner vendor— **Nostalji** (Istiklal Cad. 69–A, Beyoğlu).

Taksim

The transportation hub and heart of the city, Taksim sprawls from a hectic square, lined with high-class hotels and restaurants, into wide boulevards and cobbled side streets. Its square is flanked to the east by the lofty **Atatürk Kültür Merkezi** (Atatürk Cultural Center), home to the State Symphony Orchestra and Choir, Modern Folk Music Ensemble, and Classical Turkish Music Choir. The Republic Monument, which was built in 1928 to commemorate the founding of the Turkish Republic, is in the center of the square. Taksim's underbelly boasts a metro and funicular station, which was inaugurated in mid-2006 to connect the port of Kabataş and the financial center of Levent.

Taksim Square remains heavily guarded in an attempt to deter political rallies and marches, such as the Taksim Square Massacre, where more than 30 left-wing protestants were shot by alleged right-wing supporters. But the area is best known for its New Year's gala, where in 2006, more than one million bopped to their favorite Turkish pop-star crooning from a stage built right below the mega screen.

Originating from the Arabic *taqsīm,* meaning division, Taksim Square was baptized by Sultan Mahmud I (1696–1754) after an underground stone reservoir that collected water from Istanbul's aqueducts.

Askeri Müze ve Kültür Sitesi (Military Museum)

With conquests encompassing the Arabian Peninsula, Eastern Europe, North Africa, and a variety of Turkic states, the Ottoman—and later Turkish—military might and its more than 1,000-year history is proudly displayed at the celebrated Askeri Müze ve Kültür Sitesi Komutanlığı (Valı Konağı Sok., Harbiye–Şişli, 0212/233-2720, 9 A.M.–5 P.M. Wed.–Sun.,

7 TL). This must-do museum displays some 9,000 pieces out of an inventory of 55,000, ranging from massive cannons and mortars on the museum's extensive lawns to Ottoman uniforms and weapons in some 22 rooms. But the pièce de résistance has to be the chain the Byzantines stretched across the Golden Horn to block the sultan's navy from entering Constantinople. And so is the imperial *sayeban*—a jewel-encrusted campaign pavilion in which the sultan received foreign emissaries. This military facility once housed the Ottoman Imperial Military Academy, similar to the U.S.'s West Point. It also served as a military reserve until 1993, when the grounds opened as a museum.

Time the roughly 45 minutes it'll take to tour the museum in the late afternoon so that you can experience the performances (3–4 P.M.) of the traditionally-garbed Janissary Band, the world's oldest military band. The Ottomans were the first to integrate live music in military life and during campaigns. The soldiers fought to the tune of the janissaries. The band also joined the commander in a slow march to the beat laggard and somber cadence of oboes and the native cymbals, as well as kettledrums, in and around newly conquered lands to inform its populace of their victory. The museum is about a 15-minute walk due north from Taksim Square.

Nişantaşı

Less than a mile, but an entire world, away from the Military Museum, at the intersection of Valı Konağı Sokak and Rumeli Caddesi, is the shopping paradise of Nişantaşı. Foodies and the well-clod rejoice in this old affluent neighborhood. The few streets here are where names like Dior and Van Cleef & Arpels cater to Istanbul's super rich. Inaugurated in early 2008, the **City's** (Teşvikiye Cad. 162, 0212/373-3300, www.citysnisantasi.com) mall on Teşvikiye Caddesi is also a hotspot for brand names and swanky eateries. You'll have to search hard for Turkish culinary delights here, dishes like veal piccata, California rolls, and *steak au poivre* are the fave fares at

NOVEL CITY TOURS

Istanbul's incredible breadth and diversity remains unmatched in the world. But if the idea of conquering its every facet by public transportation or by cab is less than alluring, then ditch the crowded metros, boats, and taxis. There are other options. Experience this imperial city from the sky, on a sultan's *caïque* (boat), on a double-decker bus, or aboard a 1950s Chevrolet *dolmuş* (communal taxi). Splurge a little and enjoy the ride.

BY HELICOPTER

Discover Istanbul's sexy curves from the sky in a 25-minute helicopter sightseeing tour that features imperial Sultanahmet, the Golden Horn, the majestic Bosphorus, and the Black Sea. Contact **All Istanbul Tours** (Binbirdirek Mahallesi; Klodfarer Cad. 3/36, Sultanahmet, 0212/458-2191, www.allistanbultours.com, US$230 pp) to arrange this sky-bound escapade. Note that the tour requires a minimum of four people.

BY *CAÏQUE* (ROWBOAT)

For a truly regal tour of the Bosphorus that's somehow simultaneously historic and innovative, why not try an imperial *caïque?* In the past, Ottoman sultans and their posses checked on their realm by traveling Istanbul's waterways aboard an elongated gondola. These seaworthy vessels were plush to say the least, with solid gold gilding embellished with precious jewels. Today much of the pompous glitter has gone the way of the dodo, but the style remains. In fact, these are so elegant that Elizabeth Hurley chose to celebrate her 39th birthday on one of these in 2004, and Naomi Campbell just had to see what all the fuss was

about. To discover it for yourself, contact **Sultan Kayıkları** (0212/268-0299, www.sultankayiklari.com) for more information.

BY DOUBLE-DECKER BUS

Experiencing the city's major landmarks in a double-decker bus can be a hoot. The ride lasts almost two hours and travels to 64 sites. A day-long ticket allows passengers to hop on and off at five official stops (Dolmabahçe Palace, Sultanahmet, Taksim Square, Edirnekapı, and Kumkapı). The buses feature top decks that are open to maximize the sightseeing experience, and are rigged with a sound system that pipes in historical info about Istanbul and its monuments. Buses depart hourly on the hour from Sultanahmet Square, across from Ayasofya. Tickets and can be purchased at hotels, at **City Sightseeing** (0212/458-1800, www.city-sightseeing.com, adults €20, seniors €15, families €65, children 5-15 €15) ticket booths in Taksim and Sultanahmet, or upon boarding.

BY *DOLMUŞ* (COMMUNAL TAXI)

Remember the vintage American cars of the 1950s? In the 1970s, these brightly colored Chevy and Ford behemoths, pimped out to accommodate more passengers, plied the city streets waiting for their next ride. Three of these original *dolmuşes* have been lovingly restored and brought back as tour vehicles by **Anatonina Turizm** (İstiklal Cad. 53/9, Beyoğlu, 0212/292-2874, 60TL pp). These monster sedans accommodate up to four passengers and include tours of the city's best sites and monuments. The tour cost includes chauffeur and guide fees, as well as lunch and tea.

City's. Sorry, no plastic forks here, nor trays; strictly silverware and linen. But for an irresistible meal of tender roasted lamb morsels over eggplant purée—known as *Hünkâri kebabı* (Sultan's kebab), beat the crowds and head for the southeastern Anatolian tastes of **Komşu** restaurant (Vali Konağı Cad., Işık Apt 8B, 0212/224-9666, www.komsu-kebap.com).

Spent from sightseeing and bloated on kebab, take a taxi for the narghile cafés of Tophane on the way back.

Tophane

Edging Beyoğlu on the shores of the Bosphorus and less than a mile northeast of Galata Bridge, Tophane's home to the Istanbul Museum of

Modern Art, a string of fun narghile cafés, the 19th-century Mimar Sinan University of Fine Arts, and the baroque, late-19th-century Nusretiye Clock Tower and Mosque Tophane Mosque. The modern tram that passes through Sultanahmet stops right in front of the mosque, which stands next to the row of cafés. The museum's entrance is located east of the cafés, through a barrier, then across the parking lot to the right.

Minimalist in design, **Istanbul Modern Müzesi** (Istanbul Museum of Modern Art, Meclis–i Mebusan Cad. Liman İşletmeleri Sahası Antrepo 4, 0212/334-7300, www .istanbulmodern.org, 10 A.M.–6 P.M. Tues.–Sun., 7 TL) opened its doors to international fanfare in 2004, as it blazed trails in modernism in a city known for its dead art. Aside from paintings located on the 1st floor, the basement houses carefully curated temporary exhibitions from international and Turkish masters, as well as a massive art library under a lowered ceiling composed of tomes seemingly floating in midair. The lavish views of the straits and the neo-Turkish cuisine proffered at the posh and rather pricey Istanbul Modern Café warrant a visit. Plan about 90 minutes to do this space justice, preferably on Thursdays, as the entry fee is waived until 2 P.M. and the museum extends its hours until 8 P.M.

KABATAŞ THROUGH BEBEK

Stretching just four miles along the European flank of the Bosphorus, this area simultaneously evokes the city's erstwhile splendor and its modern glitz, with opulent palaces and some of the world's most exclusive nightclubs and hotels. Brand new to the area is the revamped stretch of Akaretler. This row of houses was built in the 1870s under the orders of Sultan Abdülaziz as housing for the staff of the nearby Dolmabahçe Palace. Today it's an über exclusive thoroughfare that includes such names as Marc Jacobs and Jimmy Choo, as well astop notch eateries. Prior to reaching Bebek, the waterside enclave of Istanbul's upper crust, the road slices through the quaint, artsy village of Ortaköy.

Its fashionable bistros share space on Sundays with a trendy farmer's market.

Several ports serve this side of town, but the well-connected hubs of Kabataş and Beşiktaş bear the brunt of commuter sea traffic originating from the Asian coast. Beşiktaş is also home to the country's splendid maritime museum and the famed mausoleum of Barbarossa—a privateer so feared, Süleyman the Magnificent thought it wise to install him at the head of the mighty Ottoman navy. Imperial summer pavilions and tea gardens, as well as a sprawling open market, are also located near this port. Aside from riding a *dolmuş* (communal taxi) or hailing a cab, there are a couple of transportation options here: the fast-speed tram that serves Sultanahmet goes through to Kabataş; and a modern funicular jets down from Taksim in less than two minutes. Once there, hop on bus 25E to Ortaköy, Bebek, and beyond. If that sounds way too complicated, or time is of the essence, tour it by cab.

◖ Dolmabahçe Sarayı (Dolmabahçe Palace)

Decadent, to say the least, the Dolmabahçe Sarayı (between Besiktas and Kabatas ports, 0212/236-9000, www.dolmabahcepalace. com, 9 A.M.–4 P.M. Tues.–Wed. and Fri.–Sun., 25TL, camera 6TL, video 15TL) is the Ottomans' version of Versailles, with Rococo detailing taken to the extreme. Some 285 rooms boast floor-to-ceiling gilded mirrors, nacre-inlaid furniture, wall-to-wall carpets of the sheerest silk, and the most extravagant collection of Bohemian and Baccarat crystal chandeliers—including one that weighs 4.5 tons and is lit by some 750 lightbulbs. The highlight, however, remains the view of the Bosphorus and the building's rear facade seen from the imperial *caïque* (rowboat) dock. The addition of small tables and refreshment kiosks have heightened the experience even more, particularly in the heat of summer.

The palace is yet another signature piece of the Balyans, the Armenian family of imperial architects responsible for the construction of some of the most lavish 19th-century Ottoman

© JESSICA TAMTÜRK

Janissaries perform today as they would have centuries ago at Dolmabahçe Palace.

structures, including the spectacular Ortaköy Mosque, as well as the Çırağan and Beylerbeyi Palaces, also flanking the Bosphorus. Built on land reclaimed from the straits, Dolmabahçe (filled garden) bears meticulously landscaped flower beds and centuries-old oaks and plane trees. In another way to squander the empire's fortunes, Sultan Abdülmecid (1823–1861) called in Garabet Balyan and his son, Nikoğos, to design a regal mansion grander and bolder than any other ruler's in the world. It took nine years to create the 400,000-square foot palace that stands on 11 acres. Thanks to an unlimited budget, the pair utilized a reported dozen tons of gold to gild the expansive ceilings.

Dolmabahçe's *selamlik* (men's quarters) features a famed crystal staircase that leads to the gigantic Red Room, a hall where the sultan received visiting dignitaries. Twin bear rugs—heads and all—gifted by Tsar Nicolas the I of Russia have graced the room for more than 150 years. The harem (women's quarters) lays claim to the sultan's private quarters, including

a collection of personal tomes in a small library, a bed of pure silver in his personal boudoir, and his private marble bathing rooms with a soaking tub made of sheer alabaster. Mustafa Kemal Atatürk, Turkey's founder, spent the last years of his life in one of the rooms in Dolmabahçe Palace. His small master suite bears his passage with a bed covered with the Turkish flag and a set of toiletries in the adjoining bathroom. Grand fountains, lofty trees, a spectacular marble clock tower, and a flock of showy pheasants in an aviary fill this palace's grounds.

The Dolmabahçe Camii, commissioned in 1853 by Abdülmecid's mother, is just outside the box office. The **Clock Room** (4TL), near the aviary, features some of the palace's timepieces. They indicate 9:05, the time of Atatürk's passing. The **Crystal Palace**'s splendid chandeliers, candelabras, and even a crystal baby grand piano are free and lots of fun.

Allow at least two hours to view the palace. The harem and *selamlik* can only be visited by tour; there are several tours at varying times daily.

Deniz Müzesi (Museum of Naval History)

The three-story main exhibition building that constitutes Deniz Müzesi (Hayrettin İskelesi Sok., 0212/327-4345, www.dzkk.tsk.mil.tr/, 9 A.M.–12:30 P.M. and 1:30–5 P.M. Wed.–Sun., 5TL) explores the might of the Ottoman and Turkish navies through large collections of ensigns, early navigational instruments, and an array of maps dating back to 1461. The basement has an impressive set of antique, barnacle-crusted amphorae, and a scaphander tots will find particularly fascinating. A separate wing houses about a dozen imperial *caïques* (rowboats). Outside, campaign relics, such as an early 16th-century cannonball, propellers of every era, and fragments of a WWI German submarine found in the Black Sea, are on display. The busts of prominent Turkish admirals from the 11th century onward line the grounds.

The mausoleum of Barbaros Hayrettin Paşa

is across the square from the museum's entrance. Responsible for several successful naval campaigns as a privateer—or a legal pirate—for the Ottomans, Barbaros Hayrettin Paşa was installed as admiral-in-chief of the Ottoman Navy by Süleyman theMagnificent in 1534. He dominated the Mediterranean for decades; his successful campaigns enlarged the empire into North Africa and Western Europe. Upon his request, a tomb was built by Mimar Sinan near a *medrese* in Beşiktaş. The burial structure is crafted of ashlar (stacked stone) masonry on an octagonal base plan, and topped with a dome. It bears seven facets, each with twin windows; the eighth side serves as the porticoed entrance. Next to Paşa lie theremains of his wife and son. The tomb is only open to the public on April 4 and July 1, in commemoration of the Naval Martyrs' and National Cabotage Days, respectively.

Yıldız Parkı

Yıldız Parkı (Barbaros Bulvarı, Yıldız Parkı, 0212/258-3080, 10 A.M.–5 P.M. Tues.–Sun., 2TL) comprises the remains of palatial gardens, some old pavilions, and renowned imperial porcelain workshops. The meticulously kept gardens, alpine architecture, and priceless collection of antiques—including a large ceramic stove and grand carpets—make the **Şale Pavilion** particularly interesting, as it diverges slightly form the other garish monuments along the water. The rolling courtyards boast pavilions, greenhouses, pools, aviaries, workshops, and servants' quarters. All are separated by passageways and gates. There are also mosques outside the two main entrances.

Yıldız Parkı has an interesting history. The hill that rises from the *Beşiktaş Çarşı* (Beşiktaş Bazaar) along the traffic-jammed Barbaros Bulvarı (Barbaros Boulevard) used to be a popular imperial hunting ground and lush gardens with regal accommodations until the 18th century. When overly suspicious Sultan Abdülhamid II acceded the throne in 1876, he chose to build his own palace along this part of town, for added security. This large palace was commissioned to the Balyan

family of architects. It bears five major structures that functioned as an autonomous, well-protected imperial city where Abdülhamid II conducted both official business and the harem. Incidentally, he's remembered as the Red Sultan for the atrocities he ordered against minorities during his 33-year reign.

While the property is connected to Çırağan Palace by a footbridge, the official entrance to Yıldız Parkı is along Barbaros Bulvarı. Stroll down toward the northeast to reach the **Çadır Köşkü** (Tent Pavillion), where a stop at a relaxing café serves as the perfect transition back to Istanbul's hectic rush. Hungry? Reasonable buffet lunches are available at the splendid, neo-classic **Malta Köşkü** (Yıldız Parkı, about 25TL).

Ortaköy

Taking a trip to Ortaköy is a pleasure for sightseers, shore-lovers, trend-watchers, souvenir-seekers, or culinary aficionados; whatever its appeal, the five extra liras to hire a taxi heading northbound from Beşiktaş are well worth it. Most days are pretty busy since Ortaköy is a chic lunch and dinner destination, but Sundays take the cake because of the fantastic **Farmer's Market.** Stands filled with the freshest indigenous and exotic produce attract the hemp bag–toting upper crust. Plan a visit to coincide with the sunset for arguably the best vantage point in town for a glass of tea or a light meal, or do as the locals do, hang around and check out the people strolling by. Ortaköy's pier is also renowned as the perfect place for a quick bite before or after a jog to **Rumeli Fortress,** about two miles north.

The lure of Ortaköy, which today remains a catchall for various ethnicities, expats, and artists of all genres, was known as Damianou after a monastery built onsite in the 9th century. It became a holiday hotspot for the Ottoman aristocracy less than 600 years later. Sultan Abdülmecid selected this appealing site for his personal mosque, which he commissioned to Nikoğos Balyan in the late 19th century. Perhaps the most beautiful and most photographed building in Istanbul is the **Ortaköy**

The petite, ornate Ortaköy Mosque welcomes the faithful during *dhuhr* (noon prayer).

© ZEYNEP GÖZEN

Cami (Ortaköy Mosque, Ortaköy Pier square), which seems to cower in the shadow of the colossal Bosphorus Bridge. Pint-sized when compared to the mosques on the other side of the Golden Horn, Ortaköy Cami was crafted in a style later coined Neo-Baroque. The interior walls bear wide and high bay windows that refract daylight and its reflections on the water. This translates into an inner sanctum filled with natural and effervescent lighting. Also of note are several panels of calligraphy, produced by Sultan Abdülmecid himself.

BOSPHORUS CRUISE

One of the highlights of any trip to Istanbul is the 19-mile Bosphorus Cruise that takes off daily from the port of Eminönü (IDO dock, toll free 0212/444-4436, www.ido.com.tr, 10:35 A.M. and 1:35 P.M. daily, 12 TL). There are two additional departures (noon and 7 P.M. mid-June–Sept.); the evening cruise doesn't take off on weekends. The return leg departs from its terminus at *Anadolu Kavağı* at 3 P.M., 4:15 P.M., 5 P.M., and 10 P.M., the latter also not available on weekends. Hopping aboard in Beşiktaş is possible at 10:50 A.M. and 1:50 P.M. Plan 4.5–6 hours to really capitalize on this trip.

The boat owner's cooperative **TurYol** (Eminönü embarcadero, 0212/512-1287, 1–7 P.M., departs on the hour, 6TL) also offers a no-frills, 90-minute round-trip tour from the adjacent Eminönü embarcadero, located to the left of the IDO dock. Both have their benefits, but IDO's vessels are more nostalgic, roomier, and by far quieter. TurYol's boats are modern and glide closer to the shores, but they only take passengers up to the Bosphorus's second bridge, or only about two-thirds up the straits. Opting for the shorter cruise will save time but most of the fun at Anadolu Kavağı (Anatolian Poplar) will be missed.

Taking off from the Golden Horn, with Seraglio Point—Sultanahmet's westernmost point—as a backdrop, the ferry hugs the European coast up to the embarcadero of Beşiktaş. From there it crisscrosses the strait, making three additional stops before arriving at Anadolu Kavağı (Anatolian Poplar). In late spring to early fall, keep an eye on the waters along the way for a glimpse of a playful dolphin. To avoid whiplash from the myriad sites on either side, focus on the European coast's landmarks, located portside. A panoramic view of the Bosphorus's mouth to the Black

STRAIT FACTS

WHAT'S IN A NAME

The channel owes its name of Bosphorus, which translates into "ford of the calf," to an ancient Greek love triangle pitting Zeus between his bespoken Hera and his true love, Io. Seeking her beloved Zeus' undivided attention and fearing the jealous wrath of his Hera, the seductive Io transformed herself into a heifer. When sly Hera demanded that Zeus turn over the beast, he complied. She then called on the 100-eyed Argus to watch Io. Hermes killed Argus at Zeus' request, thusly freeing Io. A raging Hera then sent a gadfly to torment her nemesis, causing Io to hop from coast to coast along the strait.

CRUNCH THE NUMBERS

- Maritime toll: 0; since the Bosphorus is a natural strait, no toll is levied.

- Width: varies between 0.5 and 1.5 miles

- Number of currents: 2; the swift and simultaneously opposing currents make navigation tricky.

- Average depth: 164 feet

- Number of ships that pass through the strait annually: 38,000

© JESSICA TAMTÜRK

a trio of wooden mansions lining the Bosphorus Strait with the late 14th-century Anatolian Fortress in the background

Sea from high atop a hill, where the remains of an antique Genoese fortress stand are the rewards at the terminus, as well as scores of delightful fish restaurants by the port. Most of the European sites can also be toured by taxi, or without breaking the bank by hopping on bus 25E at Kabataş.

Çırağan Palace

Right after take off, the boat enters the Bosphorus, glides by Dolmabahçe Palace, then nears another regal residence. The 19th-century Çırağan Palace (Çiragan Cad. 32, 0212/326-4646, www.kempinski.com), commissioned yet again to the illustrious imperial

MARMARAY: AN INCIDENTAL UNVEILING OF HISTORY

Ottoman Sultan Abdülmecid's lifelong dream of building a Tunnel of the Sea beneath the Bosphorus Strait is slowly becoming a reality. Almost 140 years after the original drafting of an undersea railway connector was proposed by French engineer S. Preault, a similar connector is under construction to the tune of $2.6 billion by an international engineering consortium. Feasibility reports excelled on paper until history chimed in with a slew of archaeological discoveries along the trajectory of what's being called the project of the century.

During the excavation of the connector, which aims to link Asia at Üsküdar and Europe at Yenikapı, remnants from an expected and unexpected past came to light, turning one of the largest engineering ventures of all time into a massive archaeological site. The main holdup is largely due to the excavation of the only Byzantine naval vessel ever discovered. The ship is part of the massive remains of the

4th-century port of Theodosius, which was found at the proposed site of the European tunnel terminal in 2005. The theory is that the entire port was wiped out in a massive storm or tsunami after a major earthquake hit the harbor. The discovery and excavation of Roman Emperor Theodosius's port, war ship, along with 33 other boats – some as old as 1,000 years – and thousands of clay pots has hampered construction.

And in 2006, a 400-year-old Ottoman sanctuary was discovered at the Ayrılık Fountain Station on Istanbul's Asian side. The complex's historical ablutions fountain was above ground, but the presence of the *namazgah* (an open-air Islamic sanctuary) below was unknown. Historians believe that Ottoman sultans and their armies ritually prayed at this site before military expeditions. Traditionally, Muslims visited the *Ayrılık* (separation) religious site before leaving Istanbul for the pilgrimage to Mecca. Sultan Murat IV sought

•

architect Nikoğos Balyan by Sultan Abdülaziz in 1863, was the last imperial residence to be built on the straits. The strength of the marble used in its facade proved little resistance to the fire that ravaged its interior wooden structure in 1910. It deteriorated until the 1990s, when the hotel conglomerate Kempinski purchased the land and reconstructed the palace to its former grandeur to serve as one of the world's finest five-star hotels.

Bosphorus Bridge

Just above the Ortaköy Mosque, the majestic Bosphorus Bridge looms. Fifteen years of planning led to the 1973 inauguration of this almost mile-long suspension connector that bridges Asia and Europe. The pylon structure was designed by the British civil engineer Sir Gilbert Roberts and cost 200 million dollars, a fraction of the expected 2–2.5 billion dollars a planned third bridge will entail. At night, the

connector is lit by an LED system that washes the structure, and waters below, in a spectacular rainbow of colors. The bridge gives way to Bebek Bay, one of Istanbul's most exclusive playgrounds for the rich and their wannabe counterparts.

Rumeli Hisarı (European Fortress)

The 15th-century Rumeli Hisarı (Tarabya Yeniköy Cad., north of Sarıyer, 0212/263-5305, 9 A.M.–5 P.M. Tues.–Sun., 4TL) faces **Anadolu Hisarı (Anatolian Fortress),** which was built 60 years earlier. The point between the two forts marks the Bosphorus's narrowest width of about 2,500 feet. It took three Ottoman viziers, each tasked with supervising the construction of one tower, just 4.5 months to construct this massive structure. Mehmet the Conqueror's Ottoman troops controlled the strait's north end from the forts and watchtowers, and thus

divine blessings here before launching his attack on Baghdad in 1637.

As crews continued to dig through the black clay of an ancient swamp beneath Istanbul's proposed main station at Yenikapı, the port wasn't the only thing they found. An 8,000-year-old crematorium and settlements also came to light in 2008, at a depth of 6.5 meters. This momentous find pushes Istanbul's history back by at least 5,000 years from what historians had previously believed; up till then, the city was thought to have been settled by Greek colonists in 700 B.C. A grave holding the curled-up remains of two adults and two children, also believed to be late Neolithic, were found, along with their personal belongings. Clothing, jewelry, utensils, and even the arrow the person was killed with were contained in the urn along with their owner. Housing made of tree branches, tools, and bones were also recovered from the area. Aslı Erim Özdoğan, a professor of prehistory at İstanbul Üniversity, contends that the Yenikapı settlement may date as far back as 6400 B.C. and that its Neolithic inhabitants lived on both sides of a river that at that time flowed through Yenikapı from the Sea of Marmara, which is believed to have been a small, landlocked lake long before the Bosphorus Straits were formed.

While the Marmaray project was on standby, a team of 50 archaeologists and 750 workers continued to excavate around the clock at Yenikapı. In a cordoned-off site, the size of six American football fields, lead archaeologists reported hitting bedrock in some places in early 2009. So it's doubtful further discoveries will be made there.

Preault's revolutionary design, on display at Istanbul Archaeological Museum, has stoked the imagination of many Ottomans and their Turkish progeny since 1860. In 2012, Marmaray hopes to make that dream a reality by running its first $1.5 million Hyundai unmanned metros beneath the Bosphorus Strait. This grand opening will include a new museum at the ultra-modern, underground Yenikapı Station.

isolated Byzantine Constantinople from any aid arriving from Genoese Black Sea ports. So strong are the fort's 21-foot-thick walls that they've withstood more than 500 years of considerable seismic activity, as well as the eventual fires.

Fatih Sultan Mehmet Bridge

Istanbul's second intercontinental connector, the Fatih Sultan Mehmet Bridge, not only bears the name of Constantinople's conqueror, but also the brunt of commercial traffic. It accommodates traffic from the Trans-European Motorway that links the Thracian peninsula and the capital of Ankara, and all traffic beyond those two points. Built in 1988, the FSM is a mirror copy of the Bosphorus Bridge. Incidentally, the 190-foot suspension bridge is often the spot where the down-and-out attempt to jump off. Fortunately, about 80 percent are unsuccessful.

Yalıs (Waterside Residences)

The Bosphorus's coasts are strewn with some 600 elegant *yalıs* (multi-million-dollar waterside mansions). At the going rate of US$3,000–3,500 per square foot, these wooden abodes are a restoration pastime for the rich, and constitute some of the most expensive real estate in the world. They're categorized according to their historical importance, and any renovation of the older structures must adhere to the original architectural and interior design plans. These summer homes were originally built by the high Ottoman aristocracy, with some bearing names like Crazy Ali Fuat Pasha, Snake, or Cypriot Mansion to reflect the character of their owners or architectural originality. At the height of the empire building, a *yalı*, from the Greek word *yialos* (shore), signaled societal class; the bigger the abode, the richer its owner. The *yalı* trend began in the late 17th century, as stark, wooden blocks following traditional Turkic interior design—a center room, sometimes with a fountain in its midst, that spoked out into rooms that comprised separate, gender-specific living quarters. Some of the most pivotal viziers hosted foreign dignitaries in the abodes' central *sofa* (welcoming room), in which the fate of states and alliances were invariably discussed after lavish meals. Such was the case of the Sait Halim Paşa, the grandson of a former Egyptian governor who rose to the post of minister of foreign affairs when he cemented a German-Ottoman alliance with German Envoy Baron Wangenheim in his eponymous waterside residence in 1914, leading to Ottoman involvement in WWI. Other mansions, such as today's popular Sakıp Sabancı Museum, which was transformed from a villa commissioned in 1928 by Egyptian Prince Mehmed Ali Hasan in Emirgan, later became exhibition spaces for their owners' extensive collections of Ottoman and Anatolian artifacts. But while quite a few serve as superior boutique hotels and lavish restaurants, the majority are private residences.

Kanlıca

One of the succulent surprises on this trip: a stop at Kanlıca, an Asian port village famous for its sumptuous, creamy yogurt. Luckily, there's no need to get off, as servers come aboard to sell the dairy delicacy. The yogurt's uniqueness comes from its blend of cow, sheep, and goat milk that are slowly scalded, not boiled, for 20 minutes. When the final product is mixed with powdered sugar, it results in a unique, zesty creaminess. The Asian enclave of Kanlıca is also famed for its Mecca-style coffee served in large, handle-less cups and a small, waterside mosque built by Sinan for Iskender Paşa.

Rumeli Kavağı and Anadolu Kavağı

Rumeli Kavağı is the next stop on the cruise after Kanlıca. Not much remains of the poplars that this fishing outpost was named after. Rumeli Kavağı's appeal lies mostly in fish restaurants that serve some of the finest produce from plentiful Black Sea crops. Most tourists disembark at Anadolu Kavağı, which has the added bonus of shopping and touring sites.

Finally, the boat docks at Anadolu Kavağı (Anatolian Poplar) for 90 minutes during the winter season or 3 or more hours during summertime. Lingering over fried mussels and grilled bluefish at **Yosun Restaurant** (Iskele Meydanı, 0216/320-2148, 9 A.M.–midnight, 35TL with drinks) or any of the less expensive restaurants has its merits. So does hiking up the hill to **Yoros Castle**, the 13th-century Genoese fortress that crowns the rise to the left of the dock; the fortress walls remain and visitors are free to explore on their own here. The steep climb will be rewarded with an intense bird's eye view of the Bosphorus's pristine opening to the Black Sea, and a requisite glass of tea at Yosun Restaurant's second location, whose open-air café nooks and dining patio descend over steep terraces. Reap the rewards of hearty exercise or finish off the succulent meal with a waffle cone of traditional Tia Maria or sour cherry ice cream at the stand right outside Yosun's, and head off for a stroll down Anadolu Kavağı's sleepy back streets and souvenir shops.

Kuleli Military High School

On the generally upwind return, the mid-19th-century Kuleli Military High School soars over the waters, north of Çengelköy's shores. The double-turreted structure is soaked in history. In addition to being Turkey's first military academy and high school, it served as a hospital for injured British and Turkish soldiers when war broke between the Ottoman Empire and Russia in 1875, and again during the year-long Balkan Wars of 1912. The Kuleli Barracks were a crucial element both as a weapon cache and as an infirmary.

Küçüksu Kasrı

Further along the Anatolian shores lies the lone-standing imperial hunting lodge of Küçüksu Kasrı (Küçüksu Palace, Küçüksu

Cad., 0216/332-3303, 9:30 A.M.–4:30 P.M. Tues. and Wed. and Fri.–Sun., 5TL). Its lush gardens along the tamer and warmer waters of Küçüksu were once the preferred haunt of Kaisers, who opted for this petite abode over the much more formal Topkapı Palace. This imperial playground and resting pavilion was commissioned by Sultan Abdülmecid. Within this lodge's walls, his successors rubbed elbows with their foreign contemporaries, particularly the growing entente between the powerful German and Ottoman Empires. Signed yet again by the architectural master Nikoğos Balyan, the baroque three-floored structure includes a basement filled with kitchens and storage rooms. Its charm is defined by its exquisite marble fireplaces throughout, wall-to-wall inlaid parquet, the finest of European era furnishings, and dozens of imperial crystal chandeliers. Noteworthy are the gigantic Hereke carpets, which were woven in an imperial rug workshop known to this day for some of the world's finest silk rugs. At the lodge, locals linger over a strong glass of tea and the stunning Bosphorus at a delightful tea stop and pleasant, inexpensive open-air terrace.

Beylerbeyi Sarayı (Beylerbeyi Imperial Palace)

The Beylerbeyi Sarayı (Ağa Cad., 0216/321-9320, 9 A.M.–5 P.M. Tues.–Wed. and Fri.–Sun. Apr.–Sept., to 4 P.M. Oct.–Mar., 15TL) is another early 19th-century project taken on by the illustrious Balyan family of architects. Beylerbeyi is a favorite with nationals, but not a big destination for foreigners. It has all the pomp and detailing of the grand palaces, packed in a one-hour tour. The *selamlık* and harem display the usual palatial accoutrements, like Hereke carpets, priceless crystal chandeliers, and Chinese Ming and Parisian Sèvres porcelain, as well as a fountain in the main hall. It was commissioned in 1829 by Sultan Mahmud II as a location to hold Topkapı's official affairs, and it is the first imperial structure to boast European-style architecture. Built entirely out of timber, a fire raged through it some four decades after its

inauguration, requiring Sultan Abdülaziz to order it rebuilt out of marble. What distinguishes this palace from others is its furniture, all created by Sultan Abdülaziz himself. Also worth a note is the many royalty that stayed at Beylerbeyi when it served as an imperial guesthouse. France's Empress Eugénie, the wife of Napoléon III, was so impressed with the windows of her guest room during her stay in 1869 that she had them duplicated at Paris' Tuilleries Palace. Tsars, shahs, and British dukes all overnighted here as well. Beylerbeyi served as Sultan Abdülhamid II's final residence after he was deposed and placed under house arrest by the Young Turks in 1913.

Kız Kulesi (Maiden's Tower)

Approaching Eminönü, the Maiden's Tower seemingly floats near the entrance to the Bosphorus. The story goes that it once housed a beautiful Ottoman princess whose overprotective father—a sultan who feared a curse that she would succumb to a snake bite on her 18th birthday—had her locked inside until the end of her days. But the Turkish legend that a reptilian bite would cause her death came true, as a poisonous snake hidden inside a fruit basket hand-delivered by her father bit her. During Byzantine times, the tiny islet served as a tollbooth where traders paid to make their way across the Bosphorus. It was known as Leander's Tower during antiquity, and was originally built by the Athenian general Alcibiades in the 5th century B.C in order to keep an eye on Persian ships crossing the strait. Since the Ottoman ousting of the Byzantines, it has been used as a lighthouse, and today the tower's lobby is home to a touristy café and restaurant. Beautifully lit in the evenings, the Maiden's Tower is Istanbul's best location, bar none, to watch the sun set over Sultanahmet during late summers and early falls.

ASIAN SHORE

The city's Asian shores are to Istanbul what the San Fernando Valley is to Los Angeles—a variety of underrated suburbs. Well worth a day trip, the district of **Kadıköy** is the city's oldest outpost known to date, and deserves at least a full day of exploration. Istanbul's Anatolian quarters march to the beat of a different drummer than their European counterparts, the feel is simultaneously more suburban and more industrial. Move beyond the clogged streets of well-to-do coastal enclaves and discover a forest of high-rise buildings intersected by a network of clogged modern highways that connect to the nation's heartland. Plan a visit to the distinctive strait-side village of **Beylerbeyi** and the artsy, ethnic enclave of **Kuzgunçuk** by way of the ancient port of **Üsküdar.** Or you may wish to hop on Kadıköy's historical tram, just across its feverish port, to the exclusive promontory of **Moda.** There, a tea garden offering the best view of Sultanahmet, in addition to succulent Turkish coffee, await. To the East, the elite neighborhood of **Fenerbahçe** beckons, not for its well-known soccer stadium but for its park, which boasts a large meticulously landscaped expanse replete with tea gardens, beachfront restaurants, and waterside benches to enjoy the panoramic Sea of Marmara and the Princes' Islands. And then, there is always **Bağdat Caddesi**'s fashionable boutiques and pricey eateries that rival those of any Western European capitals.

To reach Asia, it's best to embark on either the Üsküdar or Kadıköy ferries, from either the embarcadero of Eminönü or Karaköy. These depart every 20 minutes or so. Then, hop on a *dolmuş* or taxi form either port. With a reasonable fare of 4TL and a route that traverses the Bosphorus Bridge, the communal cab serving Kadıköy is also an option. Facing the building, the terminus is located to the left of Taksim's Atatürk Cultural Center (AKM).

Kadıköy

Lapped by the Sea of Marmara to the West, the port of Kadıköy is a transportation hub that connects to neighboring districts. It's also home to one of the busiest open-air markets, where eager consumers and hungry retailers vie for space in crowded back alleys. Aside form staples like bread and fish, socks, computers,

and saffron are some of the products peddled side by side in adjoining networks of related shops. In Kadıköy Valley, a take on Silicon Valley, a bootleg copy of the latest Hollywood film is sold for less than US$1.50. Just around the bend, jam-packed shopping avenues such as **Altıyol** and the increasingly hip **Bahariye** are centers for brand name products and their ridiculously cheap counterfeits. Not for those seeking quietude, the port of Kadıköy and its environs are cosmopolitan Turkey at its best: an organic disharmony of vehicular traffic, braying trade, packed real estate and sublime foodstuff. And, as with everywhere else in the larger city, the district hails back some seven centuries before the birth of Christ.

This area was a trade center when the Megarians conquered it in the Chalcolithic period (5500–3500 B.C.). They renamed it Chalcedon. And during the first five centuries after Christ, the by-then-suburb of Constantinople was host to the Chalcedon Tribunal, where Emperor Julian the Apostate condemned many of his predecessor's ministers to death. Chalcedon also hosted the Ecumenical Council of A.D. 451, in which the human and divine natures of Jesus were defined—a concept that did not fare well with the churches of the Oriental Orthodoxy. By the time the Ottomans arrived in A.D. 1353 the city was still reeling from extensive damage caused during the Fourth Crusade (A.D. 1204). The victorious Sultan Orhan Gazı renamed the outpost Kadıköy after selecting this area as the legal seat of his growing imperial empire. In peacetime or in war, Kadıköy's religious sanctuaries and monuments—mainly Marmara University, Selimiye Barracks, and the Haydarpaşa train station—boast a long tradition of serving the surrounding communities. Just miles away the neighborhoods of Fenerbahçe and Moda, as well as the 4-mile-long Bağdat Caddesi remain popular R&R destinations for Turks and expats alike.

AROUND KADIKÖY ÇARŞISI

Just across Kadıköy Haydarpaşa Rıhtım Caddesi, the hectic artery beyond the Kadıköy

© JESSICA TAMTÜRK

A nostalgic trolley chugs along Bahariye, one of Kadıköy's shopping centers.

embarcadero, is a mesh of alleys and streets that comprise the Kadıköy Çarşısı (open-air market), where you can taste head-bending chocolate bars and delicate pistachio baklava. Armed with a sugar rush, move on up the street, just along the roundabout, where to the left the just refurbished copper steeple of an Armenian Orthodox Church begs to be photographed. The alley of Muvakkıthane slants upward and leads to the busy street of Güneşli Bahçe Sokak, where, in either direction, Kadıköy's version of the Spice Bazaar unfurls. Spices, dry fruits, fish, or cheese: If it relates to food, it'll be sold here. Double back on Güneşli Bahçe Sokak to the **Osmanağa Camii** (Mosque of Osman the Landowner, Soğutlu Çeşme Cad., open for viewing outside of prayer times)— a popular early 17th-century mosque. From there, continue up the thoroughfare to reach the quarter known as **Altıyol** (the six-road intersection). Reaching the bull sculpture atop a small plaza, turn right onto the pedestrian avenue of Bahariye Caddesi and continue to climb the pedestrian avenue. It is lined with stores, cafés, and restaurants. Half a mile up Bahariye,

the just refurbished **Süreyya Operası** (Süreyya Opera and Culture Center, Bahariye Cad. 29, 0216/336-0682, 10 A.M.–6 P.M. daily) recalls the turn of the 20th century in a smart combination of art deco and Ottoman design styles. It first opened its doors in the late 1920s as Kadıköy's first opera house; its blue print was heavily influenced by German architecture and the interior decor of Paris' Champs-Elysées that its commissioner, Süreyya Paşa, so revered during his travels.

In front of the opera house is a stop of a historical tram that snakes through a one-mile ride into Moda. Ride the tram or amble back down to the port to investigate its historical monuments. On Tuesdays, Kuşdıllı Caddesi— the continuation of Soğutlu Çeşme that slants past the bull statue—welcomes **Salı pazarı** (Tuesday Farmer's Market). It's Istanbul's largest street market where hundreds of merchants vie for space and customers and peddle everything from clothing to foodstuff.

MONUMENTS

Just beyond Kadıköy's score of minibus, public

© JESSICA TAMTÜRK

Haydarpaşa is a 19th-century train station that borders the Bosphorus on Istanbul's Anatolian flank.

bus, and *dolmuş* terminuses lie a trio of historical buildings whose mundane interiors belie the majesty of their facades and historical significance. Follow the busy Haydarpaşa Kadıköy Rhıtım Caddesi, which flows into the tree-lined Tebbiye Caddesi, up to the Haydarpaşa Train Station. Its dock offers a great waterside locale for yet another tea kiosk. Then off to the other structures of interest along this stretch, which include Marmara University and the Selimiye Barracks. Consider a couple of hours to amble along the stretch, if the itinerary allows for it.

Jutting from the coastal road, the **Haydarpaşa Train Station** is set atop more than 1,000 wooden pilasters, each 69 feet in height, driven into the seabed. It looks more like a neo-renaissance palatial residence than a transport hub, but inside its main station is a real bevy of activity. Inaugurated in 1908 by the Anatolia-Baghdad Corporation as a gift to Sultan Abdülhamid II from his ally, Kaiser Wilhelm II, Haydarpaşa served as the terminus to the railways that linked Istanbul to eastern Ottoman provinces, including today's Iraqi

capital of Baghdad and Saudi Arabia's holy city of Medina. A steep pitched roof tops the station's interior, which boasts trailing foliage cartouches and garlands on its walls, and a lofty stained glass window. The handsome building is rumored to go the way of Çırağan Palace and become a luxury hotel, whose refurbished baroque decoration and balconies will surely delight future guests. **Gar Lokantası** (Haydarpaşa Tren Istatyonu, 10 A.M.–10 P.M.) offers traditional Turkish fare—and attentive service—at decent prices, as well as a nostalgic bar that has graced many of the city's top-10 lists.

The Haydarpaşa campus of **Marmara University** (Göztepe Campus, 0216/414-0545, www.marmara.edu.tr/en) is on Tebbiye Caddesi. While the university has only been open since the mid-1980s, the locale was the first nationwide to evolve from *medrese*-style medical training to the more modern medical education, on March 14, 1827, which is also the date of an annual celebration of *Tıp Bayramı* (Medicine Commemoration Day) in Turkey.

The building has seen many firsts in the development of medicine in Turkey and it treated thousands of injured during WWI in 1914 and during the National War of Independence, 1919–1923. Costing 450,000 pieces of gold in 1895, the original school's buildings encompassed 225,000 square feet in three times as much land. Late 18th-century imperial architects Alexandre Vallaury and Raimondo d'Aronco were tasked with the construction, which included garnering the best building materials from all over Europe. This includes windows and metal frames from Vienna, Austria. Today, more than 50,000 students attend the school, which is the only campus in Turkey to offer undergraduate and post-graduate curricula in four different languages: Turkish, French, English, and German.

The third major historical building in Kadıköy is **Selimiye Barracks** (Selimiye Kislasi, Haydarpaşa, 0216/343-7310, 9 A.M.–5 P.M. Mon.–Fri., appointments must be made at least 48 hours prior to visit, free admission), a gigantic building which serves as the First Army Command Post. It's heavily guarded and requires an ID to enter. The barracks were crucial as a military hospital, and within its halls walked such notables as Florence Nightingale. Along with other rooms in the building's northwest tower, Nightingale's room is now a museum marking her passage. But, during the Crimean Wars, Nightingale, with 38 other female volunteers, took care of wounded soldiers. She returned to England some three years later with a heroic welcome for having drastically curtailed the high mortality rate and improved sanitary conditions in the facility. In 1857, some 6,000 British soldiers succumbed to a cholera epidemic and were interred in an adjoining plot, which later became known as the Haydarpaşa Cemetery. Another Balyan design, the buildings—an elongated square block with two soaring towers—were constructed in the 1800s under the edict of Sultan Selim III.

MODA
With so many touristy neighborhoods to choose from, making the trip to Moda

typically doesn't score high in travel guidebooks. But its laid-back vintage feel, along with a plethora of eateries and sidewalk cafés, make this neighborhood irresistible. Moda is just a stone's throw from Kadıköy's port by foot, via the southwest seaside promenade, or nostalgic tram, along a rickety two-mile ride through Altıyol and Bahariye. Get off at Moda Caddesi before the tram snakes back down to the port. From the tram stop hang a left and walk about two-thirds of a mile to reach the enclave's center. Once there, take a right on Ferit Tek Sokak, or at the famed Ali Usta ice cream vendor. From there, go straight down until **Moda Çay Bahçe** (Moda Tea Garden, Ferit Tek Sok. 7, 0216/337-9986, 8 A.M.–midnight), just past the woodsy park on the left. There, enjoy what is arguably the best view of Sultanahmet over a cup of the house's famous Turkish Coffee; or, stroll around the lush promontory's steep promenade to the century-old Moda Embarcadero.

Little known **Ayazma**—a chapel no bigger than a broom closet—is tucked beneath the Koço restaurant (Moda Cad. 265) and accessed through a marked gate flanking the eatery. If the yummy chocolate soufflé at Koço couldn't get your attention, stroll back up to Moda's center for sour cherry, walnut, or some of the other 40 ice cream flavors peddled at **Ali Usta Dondurmacı** (Ali the Ice Cream Master, Moda Cad. 264, 0216/414-1880, 10 A.M.–midnight).

FENERBAHÇE
Known for its lighthouse and enclaves of retired military brass, Fenerbahçe is arguably one of the most exclusive waterfronts on Istanbul's Sea of Marmara coast. Come weekends, the main street is more of a show room for the latest European racer than the quiet leisure seaport it is on weekdays. Just steps away from the waterfront is the serene **Fenerbahçe Parkı** (0216/336-3828). The park is dotted with marble kiosks and their adjacent tables, which combine into open-air, makeshift cafés, all affording perfect locations to rest awhile, particularly during summer sunsets. The area

also beckons early morning joggers, moonlight strollers, or antsy toddlers. The park's lush parterres, playgrounds, and glass pergolas unite with the grounds' lofty trees to create a truly scenic experience. And for a different beach adventure, check out **True Blue** (Fener Kalamış Cad. 90, 0216/550-5195, 30TL), a hip café and restaurant in winter and snazzy beach club in summer. Take a taxi (10TL) to get to Fenerbahçe Parkı from the port of Kadıköy, four miles away.

BAĞDAT CADDESI
Demonstrative of the disparity between Turkey's social classes, Bağdat Caddesi's upmarket Suadiye stretch boasts stores like Chanel and Burberry just as errant children pander Kleenexes nearby. On weekdays homemakers congregate over coffee at the score of java joints; while on the weekends, seats at the more than five Starbucks lining the clogged four-mile stretch are hard to come by. This shopping and chill-out haven is a magnet for teenagers and shoppers alike; it offers a good view of the shopping habits of Turkey's middle and upper classes. Just beware of the weekends here: the three-lane stretch is so clogged it becomes a polluted parking lot of frustrated motorists, which makes getting in and out a hassle. Other than shopping and people-watching at sidewalk cafés, the proximity of the seaside Fenerbahçe-Bostancı promenade, parallel to the west, is just 500 feet away. The best way to get to this part of town is to hop on a *dolmuş* (2.5TL) from the port of Kadıköy or from the Bostancı embarcadero, about a mile to the southeast of the street. From Taksim, the Bostancı *dolmuş* travels alongside the shopping strip, but lets passengers off on a parallel avenue, just a block to the south. About a dozen little neighborhoods crisscross this artery, so knowing where the action is will go a long way in determining where to get off. If traveling from the west, ask the driver to let you out at Şaşkınbakkal, cross the street, and mosey on up Bağdat Caddesi, where a right turn will lead to the beginning of the artery's busier section. Coming from the east, get off at Suadiye to shop posh brand name shops,

browse trendy bookstores, and dine in some of the city's better bistros.

Kuzguncuk and Beylerbeyi
The sleepy, multi-cultural village of Kuzguncuk always appealed to artists. But in the late 1990s, galleries started popping up at the street level of the enclave's historical wooden abodes, reviving the neighborhood and ratcheting up already steep real estate prices. The arrival of the suburban upper-middle class, along with diplomats and expats of all genres, revamped lackluster residences and the surrounding landscape. Today, the village is vibrant, modern, yet rustic; its environs encapsulate an older Istanbul and serve as a spectral background for many TV shows. Icadiye Caddesi unfurls from the coastal road up along a rolling hill, lined with bright facades that offer a colorful backdrop to the scores of stalls that comprise the lively farmers' market on Thursdays.

For an enjoyable afternoon of sightseeing, start from the port of Üsküdar and travel about a mile or so north along busy Paşalimanı Caddesi by *dolmuş*. It stops right at Kuzguncuk's main road, Icadiye Caddesi, and continues on toward Beylerbeyi. Reach Üsküdar by embarking on a ferry from any of the main European coast ports.

Along with Balat on the European flank, tiny Kuzguncuk is home to two synagogues—**Merkez** (Icadiye Cad. 9, schedule a tour through www.musevicemaati.com) and **Virane** (Yakup Sok. 8); it also boasts the **Üryanizade Mescid Camii** (Paşalimanı Cad., open outside of prayer times) which abuts the Armenian **Surp Krikor Kilesi** (Church Of Saint Gregory, Çarşı Cad. 49, 0216/341-5002, schedule a visit through info@surpkrikorlusavoric.com), and the Greek Orthodox Church of **St. Panteleimon** (Tuyan Sok. 28, 0216/333-0743), all in little over a couple of square miles. According to Surp Krikor's pastor, the local Jewish minority proposed that a mosque be built on the sanctuary's large adjoining acreage to serve Kuzguncuk's growing Muslim population in 1860, a request to which the Armenians agreed by donating some of the church's land and assisting in the construction in 1860. Kuzgunçuk's heights also boast one of the oldest Jewish cemeteries in the world, with tombstones dating back to the 14th century. Still in use today, the majority of the sanctuaries are officially open to parishioners until lunch; with a little gentle nudging, most caretakers will allow visitors to view their inner sanctum. Take in the eclectic collection of modern paintings at **Harmony Art Gallery** (Icadiye Cad. 70, 0216/553-2167) and other showcases along Icadiye Caddesi in Kuzgunçuk.

GREATER ISTANBUL

Istanbul is loaded with sights just outside its central hubs: the districts of Fatih, Eyüp, and Edirnekapı are just a skip away from the Golden Horn; the Princes' Islands pepper the Sea of Marmara. All offer great destinations for day-tripping and each can be reached by public transportation. Fatih and Eyüp have incredible museums and mosques. About 90 minutes away by boat, the five Princes' Islands are an ideal escape from Istanbul's hectic pace. If there is only time for one day trip, get an early start and visit the City Fortifications and neighboring Chora Museum in Fatih in the morning, and return to the nearby port of Eminönü to hop on the cruise to the islands.

Around Fatih

Fatih is one of the city's oldest and largest districts. So old in fact that the locals call it the "real" or "first Istanbul" since it was the Ottomans' earliest conquest near Constantinople. It's a conservative bastion with five crucial religious sites, as well as garrison remnants and massive walls harking back to Byzantine times. Fevzi Paşa Caddesi is the main road that slices through this district; it originates in Beyazit, near the Grand Bazaar, and spokes out to the city walls and the amazing Chora Museum. From atop the ancient Valens Aqueduct, the 180-degree view of the waters is simply breathtaking and probably the main reason why Byzantine Emperors erected palaces in the area. Many sites have survived the passage of time, seismic activity, devastating fires, and

conquests; others, like Constantine's memorial and a church built by Justinian to commemorate the 12 disciples, did not.

The best and quickest way to get to the northern part of Fatih is from the port of Eminönü by taxi. Bus 86 also connects Eminönü to the northern quarter of Edirnekapı by way of Şezahdebaşı Caddesi.

Tour agent Başar Hol of **Team Travel Co.** (Divan Yolu Cad., Biçkiyurdu Sokak, 12, Sultanahmet, 0212/511-8600, www.tripistanbul.com) is one of the few guides to conduct daily tours of Fatih's main sites. Hol's Chora-Eyup walking tour lasts four hours and costs €40 during the high season, and €60 the rest of the year.

BOZDOĞAN KEMERI (VALENS AQUEDUCT)

How does one simultaneously connect a city of hills and channel the water that flows so amply? The answer in the 4th century A.D. was to build the Valens Aqueduct to link Istanbul's third and fourth hills. A marvel of early Roman engineering, it ran about a half-mile and transported water from the hills of Kağıthane and the Sea of Marmara into Sultanahmet for the better part of 1,500 years. Valens was only one of many endpoints in a water collection system that spanned 160 miles through hilly Thracian country; the aquaduct was also the largest of its kind in antiquity. Runoff was stored in a series of cisterns, like the Basilica Cistern, that totaled an estimated capacity of more than 250 million gallons. Beginning as Constantine's lofty project, known as the "Arcade of the Gray Falcon," it was inaugurated in A.D. 373 by Emperor Valens. Today, it not only serves as yet another benchmark of history but also as the oldest of many handsome overpasses used by motorists traveling through the city. Just up from the Golden Horn, the Valens Aqueduct spans the busy Atatürk Boulevard, which bisects Şezahdebaşı Caddesi.

FATIH CAMII (FATIH MOSQUE)

The Fatih Camii (entrance on Fevzi Paşa

Cad., Fatih, one-third of a mile northwest of Atatürk Bulvarı, no phone, open outside of prayer times, free) is both illustrious and bigger than life, just like its namesake, Sultan Mehmet II. He callously ordered the destruction of Emperor Justinian II's Church of the Holy Apostles to erect this great monument, obliterating in one swoop what was at the time perhaps Christianity's greatest monument.

The site was first built by Constantine the Great in A.D. 330 and renovated by Emperor Justinian in A.D. 550. It not only served as the burial place of Constantinople's greatest Byzantine emperors and Patriarchs (4th–11th centuries), but also housed the remains of Christian saints Luke, Andrew, Timothy, Gregory the Theologian, and John Chrysostom.

The story goes that the sultan reportedly hacked the hands of the architect who didn't quite measure up to his orders of creating a mosque that would outdo Ayasofya. The once great *külliye* (mosque complex), though, was impressively large for its time: it consisted of a caravansary, a market, a hospital, many hammams, kitchens, and *medreses* that welcomed more than 1,000 students. The tombs of Mehmet and his wife are located behind the eastern wall. Much like other 15th-century mosques, the structure bears a large central dome, supported by semi-domes on four sides. The colors and tiles gracing the mosque's interior reflect the baroque influence of an 18th-century reconstruction, ordered when a fire ravaged the building in 1771. A busy farmer's market fills the streets adjacent to the mosque on Wednesdays.

KARIYE MÜZESI (CHORA MUSEUM)

The Kariye Müzesi (Camii Sok., Kariye Meydanı, Edirnekapı, 0212/631-9241, 9:30 A.M.–4:30 P.M. Thurs.–Tues., 15TL) boasts, bar none, Istanbul's finest mosaics. Ayasofya's age and size may have earned the basilica its worldwide acclaim, but Saint Savior in Chora's array of 14th-century artwork and iconography is by far more elaborate.

Just like its larger counterpart in Sultanahmet, Chora was not treated kindly throughout history. Knights of the Fourth Crusade looted it in 1204, and some of its ornate frescoes were plastered over when Sultan Beyazit II's grand vizier ordered the sanctuary transformed into a mosque in 1511. But unlike Ayasofya's mosaics, the Ottomans barely touched the ones that had graced Chora's walls since 1310, perhaps as a testament to their sheer beauty and intricacy.

The unexciting brick facade belies the interior's astounding loftiness and scintillating walls. There are over 50 mosaics; some are barely discernible, while others are astonishing in their detail. Upon entering the museum, the first mosaics encountered depict dedication scenes to Jesus and Mary and tableaux illustrating Jesus with wealthy patron and builder Theodore Metochites. Located in the nave are three mosaics: Jesus, Mary as Teacher, and Dormition of the Virgin. The inner narthex's two small domes portray several depictions of Jesus' ancestry, including Adam. Other sets sketch the stages in Mary's life, Jesus' youth, and his teachings. Built to house the tombs of its benefactor, Metochites, and his family, the Paracclesion (mortuary chapel) aptly boasts death and resurrection frescos.

FETHIYE CAMI (VICTORY MOSQUE)

Formerly the Church of Theotokos Pammakaristos, the Fethiye Cami (Fethiyekapısı Sokak, 0212/522-1750, 9:30 A.M.–4:30 P.M. Thurs.–Tues., 5TL) is a functioning mosque adjoined by a museum. The original church ranks third in the hierarchy of Istanbul's basilicas, after Ayasofya and Kariye Chora. Lavish mosaics and frescoes fill its inner sanctum. There is also a side chapel that contains the tomb of General Michael Glabas, a nephew of Byzantine emperor Michael VIII Palaeologos who bankrolled the basilica's renovation in the 13th century. The church served as a convent after the Ottoman invasion in 1453, and two years later became the seat of the Christian Orthodox Patriarchy.

The church was converted into a mosque by Murat III, and to commemorate his successful campaigns in Azerbaijan and Georgia he had it renamed *Fethiye* for victory. While the conversion meant taking down most of the inner walls to create a larger prayer hall, the sanctuary still boasts restored remnants of spectacular Byzantine mosaic panels. These include a depiction of the Pantocrator flanked by the 12 prophets; one of Christ Hyperagathosis sided by Mary and Saint John the Baptist, in the apse; and the dazzling Baptism of Christ. It's easiest to reach Fethiye Camii from Chora Museum. Walk along Draman Caddesi, which turns into Fethiye Caddesi, and hang a left onto Fethiyekapısı Sokak.

ISTANBUL SURLARI (ISTANBUL CITY WALLS)

Extending slightly more than four miles from the Golden Horn to the Sea of Marmara, the Istanbul Surları—Constantinople's great fortifications—were virtually impregnable. That is, until the Fourth Crusade in 1204 when the Venetians, under Enrico Dandolo, successfully climbed the walls of the Phanar Gate. They were breached again by Ottoman troops in 1453, when gunpowder propelled from Ottoman cannons rendered them forever obsolete. Today, not much is left of what is perhaps one of the greatest fortification systems of antiquity.

Ever since the arrival of King Byzas in the 7th century B.C. walls have delineated Byzantium's perimeter, which then was just a trading outpost without much import. But in time, as the city gained popularity and grew, new fortifications were built and expanded. First by Constantine the Great in A.D. 364, and some 40 years later by Theodosius II, who extended the city's limit by almost a mile, from the Sea of Marmara to the Golden Horn. The crenulated, 6-foot-thick Theodosian Walls were protected by moats at half of its ten main gates, which can be seen along the four-mile-long structure. A few sections were restored in the 1980s thanks to UNESCO funding, but topical restoration may have caused the destruction

of many relics. With the city's population boom, compounded with environmental pollution, and the lack of a proper comprehensive restoration plan, the World Monuments Fund panel was prompted to include this site on its 2008 Watch List of the world's 100 Most Endangered Sites.

TEKFUR SARAYI (PALACE OF PORPHYROGENITUS)

While only a wall or two of the last and only remaining Byzantine palace still stand, that's enough to convey the scale of the former sprawling imperial Byzantine structure. It was built at the meeting point of the Theodosian Walls and the ancient holy suburbs of Blachernae in the city's northwest region. The 13th-century Tekfur Sarayı actually means *the Palace of the Christian Ruler* in Turkish. For a long time it was thought to have been the 10th-century Emperor Constantine VII Porphyrogenitus' regal abode. But the palace was actually constructed at least 200 years later. Its commissioner was in fact Constantine Palaiologos—himself, not an emperor, but the son of one. Since the mid-15th century, the locale has served as a brothel, a pottery atelier, and tenements under Ottoman rule. Tekfur Sarayı, along with the adjoining Theodosian Walls, was part of a four-year, citywide reconstruction project to take place before 2010, when Istanbul was chosen to be the European Capital of Culture. The remains of this palace are located just steps from Chora Museum, and abut the city walls.

FENER RUM PATRIKHANESI (CHURCH OF SAINT GEORGE AND THE GREEK PATRIARCHATE)

Located in the Fener district, the Fener Rum Patrikhanesi (Sadrazam Ali Paşa Cad. 35, 0212/591-3670, www.ec-patr.org, 8:30 A.M.–4 P.M. daily, free) has been home to the Greek Patriarchate—the seat of the Eastern Christian Church—since 1586. The present Ecumenical Patriarch of Constantinople, Patriarch Bartholomew, is recognized as the "first among equals" of all Orthodox spiritual leaders. This honor has been passed on continuously since Constantinople became the capital of the Roman Empire, some 1,600 years ago.

Refurbished in 1991, the architecture of the Church of Saint George pales in comparison to the city's more elaborate sanctuaries, although it's filled with the requisite ornate iconography. It does, however, contain impressive artifacts, including the Column of Flagellation, upon which Jesus was tied to and flogged; an early 5th-century patriarchal throne; relics of Saints Gregory the Theologian and John Chrysostom; the tombs of three female saints; and three antique mosaics. As the magnificent churches of Constantinople slowly transformed into the grand mosques of Istanbul, the Orthodox Patriarchate complied with the change by moving from its first home of Ayasofya to the Church of the Holy Apostles, then to Theotokos Pammacaristos Church, before calling its current location home. The adjoining buildings include the Patriarchate Library and its accounting and authorization offices. The Fener Rum Patrikhanesi is located just west of Abdülezelpaşa Caddesi, between Incebel Sokak and Yıldırım Caddesi, about a mile northwest of Atatürk Bulvarı.

YEDIKULE
(FORTRESS OF THE SEVEN TOWERS)
Yedikule, near the Sea of Marmara, was once the impressive Golden Gate of Constantinople. Flanked by four massive towers, the gates were covered in gold, hence the name, and provided a monumental portal for foreign dignitaries entering the city along the Roman road, Via Egnatia. Theodosius II inaugurated the gate in A.D. 450, and exactly a millennium later Mehmet the Conqueror re-inaugurated the monument with the addition of three towers. The whole complex became known as the *Heptapyrgion,* Greek for seven towers. Its fate would change as an Ottoman fortress. First it became the imperial treasury, and then a state prison. The 18-year-old Sultan Osman II was executed by Janissaries here in 1622, after he was incarcerated for trying to reform what he thought was a corrupt Janissary court.

Today, connected by thick Theodosian Walls, the space serves as a concert venue. To get to Yedikule, take the *Banliyö Treni* (suburban train) headed for Halkali from Sirkeci Station; it departs every 10 minutes and tickets cost less than 2TL. Get off at Yedikule, make a left turn just out of the station gate and walk a third-of-a-mile straight to the fortress.

Around Eyüp
Further down the Golden Horn, the District of Eyüp simultaneously induces reverence for the sacred sites and for the scenic beauty of the land. One of the most revered places in Islam, Eyüp features a namesake mosque and cemetery, both popular pilgrimage destinations for Muslims. And, high atop Istanbul's waters, the scenic area known as Pierre Loti, in a nod to the late 19th-century French scribe, is truly mesmerizing. Eyüp's quaint Friday bazaar is a jumble of traditional ware and trinkets from which the perfect souvenir—at a fraction of Grand Bazaar prices—may just be a foray away.

The hourly Eyüp-Üsküdar passenger ferry travels down the Golden Horn to dock at Eyüp, Hasköy, and Sütlüce. Public buses 399 B, C, or D go to Eyüp; buses 47 from Eminönü or 54HT from Taksim serve Hasköy's Rahmi Koç Museum and Sütlüce's Miniatürk, just a little further past the Halıç Bridge.

EYÜP CAMII
(MOSQUE OF EYÜP)
The oldest of its kind in Istanbul, Eyüp Camii (Eyüp Meydanı, off of Camii Kebir Cad., open outside of prayer times) was erected by Mehmet the Conqueror in 1458 on a holy site he "located" during the 1453 Siege of Constantinople. Halid bin Zeyd Ebu Eyyûb (Eyüp Sultan), the standard-bearer of the Prophet Muhammed, was slain while commanding Arab troops during an earlier Siege of Constantinople, in A.D. 668. In accordance to a peace agreement struck between the Arabs and the Byzantines, this site was selected to bury his remains. While Mehmet claimed to have discovered Eyüp Sultan's tomb—a "miracle" that rallied his troops to victory during

the dogged days of the Siege of Constantinople in 1453, the exact location of the site was discussed in texts some 300 years before his arrival. The Mosque of Eyüp bore witness to the enthronement of Ottoman princes in a ceremony celebrating the dynasty's progression and its dedication to promote Islam. So holy were the grounds, known as **Eyüp Sultan Türbesi,** that imperials and the high Ottoman aristocracy sought to be buried alongside the revered remains as a means to insure a peaceful afterlife. In fact, a pricey internment near Eyüp's grave became so popular that the few türbes (tombs) located here in the late 15th century developed into the considerable cemetery that it is today.

Aside from attracting the faithful, including ritually clad boys celebrating their circumcision, the cemetery and mosque draw sly hawkers and shady characters of all kinds.

The cemetery gives way to the famed **Pierre Loti** café and scenic area atop Eyüp's rise. It can be accessed by a steep climb or by riding the cable car that conveniently hauls sightseers to the locale's lofty position over the Golden Horn.

RAHMI KOÇ MÜZESI
(RAHMI KOÇ MUSEUM)
It's hard to believe that the Rahmi Koç Müzesi (Hasköy Cad. 27, 0212/369-6600, www.rmkmuseum.org.tr, 10 A.M.–5 P.M. Tues.–Fri., until 7 P.M. Sat.–Sun., 8TL) was once the former Ottoman Navy anchor foundry and the historic dockyard of the Ottoman Maritime Company. Call it serendipitous that both historical structures would not only be part of the museum's exhibition, but would also house an impressive museum featuring not only naval history but transportation in general. The main structure, called the *lengerhane* (anchor house), was erected atop the rubbles of a 12th-century Byzantine building during the reign of Selim III. The second building, the Hasköy Dockyards, operated as a maintenance harbor for imperial ships. When the state put both dilapidated structures up for sale in the 1990s, the sly Rahmi Koç, one of Turkey's wealthiest

industrialists, saw a potential exhibition space for his growing collection of exotic vehicles and transportation paraphernalia. The popular 100,000-square-foot museum displays an eclectic array of road, rail, marine, and aviation pieces, as well as engineering, communications, and scientific instruments. The models, toys, and loads of hands-on activities are a huge attraction for local youth. Saturday is the ideal time to view—and play—with all of the exhibits and learn about environmentally friendly transportation and industry. The museum has two diners, a bar, and, best of all, a restaurant: Café du Levant (http://cafedulevant.com, 0212/369-9450, 50 TL), a stylish French brasserie, whose *steak moutarde* is reason enough to check out the museum.

MINIATÜRK
(MINIATURE PARK OF TURKEY)
The answer to the poor man's cultural vacation, the more than 500,000-square-foot open park that is Miniatürk (Imrahor Cad., at the Borsa stop, 0212/222-2422, 9 A.M.– 6 P.M. daily, 5TL) boasts the largest collection of miniatures in the world. While it does feature some of Turkey's most renowned destinations, like Ephesus' Library of Celsus and Nemrut Dağı's venerated stone heads on a small scale, the majority of the exhibits focus on the country's famed mosques. This is not surprising since the concept was the brainchild of a conservative municipal government. Within Miniatürk, the Museum of Victory, inaugurated in 2003 to commemorate Turkey's 80th birthday, fairly depicts the War of Independence through vignettes that feature light and sound. In a nod to Atatürk, the adjoining Zafer exhibit offers some of the statesman's illustrative photos and famous quotes. The museum is worth the trip if Istanbul is the only destination on your itinerary. Otherwise, you should see Turkey's grand destinations in person rather than miniature replica.

Adalar (Princes' Islands)
Just 10 miles west of Istanbul in the Sea of Marmara, the Adalar have lured tourists and

weekenders alike for some well deserved R&R for centuries. Four of the eight islands are lush and filled with exquisite wooded villas, a good majority protected as historical structures. You'll also find relics of bygone empires, sprawling beach clubs on golden sands, great fish restaurants, and no private vehicles! Aside from weekending minorities (Jews, Armenians, and Greeks) and other wealthy *Istanbullus*, artists and retirees live in laid-back, carefree harmony. To make the most of this trip, devote an entire day to the islands, and hop on the 7 or 9 A.M. ferry from Kabataş. If time is of the essence, a quick sumptuous lunch followed by a donkey ride around Büyükada should take no more than six hours including the boat trip.

They've been home to minorities, as well as cast away princes throughout history. What Turks have called "minorities" were in fact the settlers of the archipelago in antiquity. Aristotle first spoke of these isles in the 4th century B.C. Byzantine prince Justinus Kouropalates named the largest island Prinkipo (Greek for *Prince*) in A.D. 569 at a time when he was heir apparent to the Byzantine throne. But history would dictate that the isle, today's Büyükada, live up to its name in the worst possible way: it became the home of exiled princes. Deposed Byzantine and Ottoman royalty were exiled in the confines of Aya Yorgi Monastery on the island.

BÜYÜKADA

It's easy to see why this isle was the favored retreat of Constantinople's aristocracy dating back to the first millennium. Rising steeply from the shore over two hills, each crested by celebrated monasteries, Büyükada welcomed Princess Zoe in A.D. 1012. Its most famous visitor, however, was Leon Trotsky, a Russian writer who stylishly hobnobbed with pashas and financiers in the 1930s at the **Izzet Paşa Köşkü Mansion** (Çankaya Cad. 55), while penning the *History of the Russian Revolution*. The attractive mansion is situated along the island's main street, Çankaya Caddesi.

Büyükada's southern mount, Yüce Tepe, lays claim to **Aya Yorgi Kililesi ve Manastırı** (Aya Yorgi Monastery). It's a series of chapels built on three different levels. The chapel nearest the road, which is also the oldest, bears a sacred spring where barren women have come to change their fortune for centuries. Another chapel served during Byzantine times as an insane asylum, where patients were shackled with iron restraints bolted into the sanctuary's floorboards. The main road circling the island takes visitors by Aya Yorgi; once there, climb the remainder of the hill or "borrow" one of the donkeys conveniently waiting by the roadside. The 19th-century monastery on the northern hill, Isa Tepe, is inhabited by three families, and its chapel welcomes a small congregation for mass every Sunday.

About 150 feet from the jetty lies the town square, where most of the hotels, shops, and eateries are located. Bikes can be rented from virtually anywhere around the square for about 20TL per day. Horse and carriage tours, from the **Phaeton** park on Isa Çelebi Sokak, near the mosque, can accommodate up to four people and cost 30TL for a short 45-minute tour or 45TL for a longer trip around the island. The phaeton (horse-drawn carriage) ride includes a scenic stop at a café atop Isa Tepe. Enjoy the panoramic views of the Sea of Marmara and excellent *gözleme* (Turkish pastry), served at tables set against a woodsy backdrop.

HEYBELIADA

Translated as "Island of the Saddlebag," Heybeliada conveys a feel that's simultaneously homey and academic. It's a lot less touristy than Büyükada and is a holiday escape for thousands of *Istanbullus,* including 2007 Nobel Prize laureate Orhan Pamuk. Fine sandy shores, Orhan Pamuk, and the noted water sports haven of Green Beach Club are helping the island gain popularity with a fashionable urban crowd thirsty for leisure and serenity.

Heybeliada's most noted landmark is the **Aya Triada Manastırı** (Monastery of the Holy Trinity, 0216/351-8563, call for appointment, free) on its northernmost hill. The complex lies just a 15-minute amble up from the jetty and consists of a repository for some 200,000 tomes, including significant

Byzantine texts. The manicured grounds boast a small 13th-century chapel, whose interior reveals an intricately gilded iconostasis and timeworn, dusty classrooms replete with antique desks on the periphery. While access to this literary trove is reserved to academics who can secure permission through the Greek Orthodox Patriarchate (0212/531-9670, www.ec-patr.org), touring Aya Triada's complex is by appointment only.

BURGAZADA

At slightly longer than a mile, the archipelago's third largest island, Burgazada (Fort Island), rises from a solitary hill. It was named Antigoni during classical times, after Antigonus I Monophthalmus, the father of Demetrius I of Macedon, a 4th-century B.C. king who built the bastion. The isle's main claim to fame is writer Sait Faik Abasiyanik, whose descriptive, early 20th-century prose has been likened to Mark Twain's. His immaculately preserved summer abode has been transformed into the intriguing **Sait Faik Abasiyanik Müzesi** (Sait Faik Abasiyanik Museum, Burgaz Çayırı Sok. 15, 0216/381-2132, 10 A.M.–noon and 2–4 P.M. Tues.–Fri., 10 A.M.–noon on Sat., free).

KINALIADA

Known as "Henna Island" for its red tinge arising from now defunct copper and iron mines, Kınalıada is the closest isle to Istanbul's European flank. Its proximity to Constantinople made the island the preferred location to cast off unwanted Byzantine royalty. Romanos IV Diogenes spent the rest of his days here, after his Byzantine troops were defeated in the Battle of Manzikert in A.D. 1071. Kınalıada's intrinsic lack of forestation—the archipelago's most protected commodity—has given free reign to developers who've covered virtually every square inch of the island's real estate with unimpressive housing. On the upside, its upstream location is credited for somewhat cleaner coastal waters.

ACCOMMODATIONS

The Princes' Islands are an ideal locale to stay the night, particularly in Büyükada's uptown or nostalgic digs. **{ Splendid Hotel** (23 Nisan Cad. 53, 0216/382-6950, info@splendidhotel.net, 200TL in high season) is the best on the island. The accommodations are a bit overpriced, but the sunsets, particularly seen from a top-floor room makes staying here worth every penny. Set in an art nouveau building that has hosted Edward VIII and other dignitaries, the lobby and grounds' design are an apropos mix of Greco/Ottoman touches replete with a pool. The **{ Büyükada Princess** (0216/382-1628, www.buyukadaprincess.com/en/, 250TL d) is the island's most famous and oldest hotel. At over a century old, it doesn't even list an address; a posh bar (the island's only executive bar) was added during the latest round of renovations. Its sea-facing facade features a scenic pool, wet bar, and geranium-lined balconies. Expect only the best in accommodations. **Naya Retreat** (Yılmaz Türk Cad. 96, 0216/382-4598, nayaretreats.com, 150TL rooms, 30–100TL tents and huts) is the island's newest lodgings provider. Opt for an in-house room or a bare-bones tent at this inn that doubles as Istanbul's best yoga retreat. The latest entrepreneurial venture from free-spirited expat Ludwig Lehner, Naya is set in a refurbished mansion. It, however, only accommodates yoga students.

On Heybeliada, the **Halki Palas** (Refah Sehitleri Cad. 94, Heybeliada; 0216/351-0025, www.halkipalacehotel.com, from 200TL) is a little gaudy, but still is the best option for those who wish to bask in the ultimate comfort and supreme serenity of the smaller isle.

FOOD

The archipelago's proximity to the cooler waters of the Bosphorus ensures that the straits' best fish are brought in daily and served alongside the Sea of Marmara's catch of the day. As such, the majority of the restaurants on the islands offer finned creatures for main courses, as well as some of the requisite meze. **{ Ali Baba** (Gülistan Cad. 20, 0216/382-3733, 20TL) is renowned

for its consistent quality and for not goug-
ing its foreign clientele. Mezes like octopus salad and stuffed mussels, followed by
a main course of the islands' renowned red
mullet, have been Ali Baba's forte for decades.
For those not keen on fish, a dish for every
taste can be found on Büyükada. But the recent inauguration of a franchise of **Tarihi
Sultanahmet Köftecisi** (just north of the
port, 11 A.M.–10 P.M., 15TL) ensured that its
famous juicy *köfte* (meatball) was brought to
the island in 2006. The added bonus here is
a 180-degree view of the city across the sea.
Niko the master baker has been luring main-
landers to **Büyükada Pastanesi** (Recep Koç
Cad. 18, 0216/382-4303, 6 A.M–9 P.M. daily)
since the turn of the century with his famous
local bread, delicate savories, and sweet pastries. Niko's freshly baked goodies are great
to take along on a picnic.

Heybeliada is known for its lively Greek fish
restaurants, among them is ◖ **Halki** (Ayyıldız
Cad. 24, 0216/351-0202, 20TL). Halki's

appetizer trays are as varied as their ramekin
dishes are sumptuous.

GETTING THERE AND AROUND
Sadly, the **IDO ferry** (www.ido.com.tr,
0212/444-4436 or 0212/455-6900, 5.50TL
round-trip) serving the islands no longer operates from the port of Eminönü. Embarking
from the European port of Kabataş, or Kadıköy
and Bostancı on the opposite shores, are the
only options. With a commute of about 40
minutes, the speedy hydrofoil service (12TL)
only departs from the Asian embarcadero of
Bostancı thrice 7:20–8:30 A.M. on weekdays.
There is, however, one weekend service at
10:50 A.M. from Kabataş. All boats destined
for the archipelago take off from quays called
Adalar Iskelesi. The lines at the quays are filled
to capacity during summertime, so arrive about
an hour before departure to ensure seating.
Since service and scheduling vary greatly by the
season, confirming departure times at IDO's
website is highly recommended.

Entertainment and Events

As one of the few still affordable metropolises in Europe, Istanbul brims with excitement and has plenty of venues to get your groove on. Whether it's live jazz, dancing, performing arts, or world-class bars, Istanbul's party scene has it all. The *meyhanes* (Turkish taverns) are the most popular, where the *rakı* (Turkish aperitif) flows freely over conversations that ultimately turn to politics. But jazz clubs are the new buzz among the well-heeled hipsters, largely due to Istanbul's incredibly popular annual jazz festival. Even upscale restaurants are getting into the mix by offering patrons live musical performances. Also somewhat new to the scene are *şaraphanes* (wine salons), where a newly found affinity for indigenous vintages is appreciated. These preferences in after-dark entertainment may seem odd to tourists considering that Turkey is mostly Muslim. But locals—particularly in Istanbul—are moderate in their beliefs and have adapted a personal reverence to the spiritual that doesn't always include a strict adherence to the religion's aversion to alcohol.

Time Out Istanbul magazine, available in both Turkish and English, lists all the standard hot spots, as well as the up and coming ones. It's available at newsstands throughout the city for 4TL. Online, check out www.i-gunler.com/en/istanbul_night.php for a complete listing of evening venues. For the gay and lesbian scene, visit www.istanbulgay.com/guide.html.

NIGHTLIFE

The weekend nightlife scene revolves around Ortaköy's fancy all-in-one venues—bar, restaurant, and nightclub under one roof. Posh Reina exemplifies this trend with sprawling terraces set along the waters of the Bosphorus that beckon both starlets and wealthy wannabes. Another great nighttime destination is Beyoğlu: its raving bar scene, set atop turn-of-the-century houses and in back alleys near Galata, is all the rage, particularly among expats who can afford it.

Bring along your dancing shoes because Istanbul offers great venues to cut a rug. Way more than belly dancers and the traditional *Fasıl* (Arabesque tunes), international sounds, from Salsa to techno, are popular with the city's "in" crowd. *Rakı* (Turkish aperitif) and wine are featured on bar menus alongside collections of popular beers and liqueurs from all over the world. Forget casual and go glam, and remember to bring along a well-stocked wallet, as alcoholic drinks in Turkey tend to be pricey. Earmark at least 50TL per person for the evening, sans dinner. Drink prices are around 5TL for nonalcoholic drinks and 20–30TL for premiere liqueurs. And, as in all other large metropolises, the popularity of the watering hole will greatly affect the bill's final tally.

Most locations usually open at sunset with food service, gravitate toward live entertainment around 9 or 10 P.M., and throb well into the night. In corners of town that may be more conservative, some locations restrict the sale of alcohol, but these venues are generally near mosques and tend to be more lax come tourist season. A good example is Sultanahmet, where several Muslim sanctuaries reside alongside British pubs and hotel bars. By law off-limits to minors under 18, nightclubs and bars rarely check IDs.

Although legitimate party locations reside along shady nooks throughout the city (particularly along Beyoğlu), these venues are notorious for either overcharging foreigners or attracting crooks that prey on them. While some of these dark characters specialize in picking pockets, others are more ruthless in their racket: slipping drugs into unattended drinks or tailing hotel-bound revelers only to rob them in a patch of darkness. The rule-of-thumb is to use common sense: avoid dark alleys after sunset, stick to the venues listed in this guidebook, or just hang out at hotel bars. When traveling alone, opt for taxis and refrain from using larger bank notes, such as 50s or 100s, anywhere, to avoid getting counterfeit bills in return.

Nightclubs

Still reigning supreme is **Reina** (Muallim Cad. 44, Ortaköy, 0212/259-5921, www.reina.com. tr, 30TL cover charge), with its multi-leveled restaurants featuring nouvelle cuisine and pizza, a bar set over the waters of the Bosphorus, and a nightclub. Frequented by Sting, Selma Hayek, and Uma Thurman, Reina is the place to rub elbows with Hollywood's A-list come summer, that is, if you can get in.

The newest kid on the block is **Indigo** (Istiklal Cad., Akarsu Sok., Mısı Apt. 1–5, Galatasaray, 0212/244-8567, www.livingindigo.com, 10 P.M.–5 A.M. Fri. and Sat.). Set high atop a historical building in Beyoğlu, Indigo is where Europe's best DJs flock to spin their LPs to a twenty-something crowd, bopping to the rhythm of the hypnotic light show.   Gracing the opposite coast is **Çubuklu 29** (Paşabahçe Yolu 24, 0216/322-2829, www. cubuklu29.com) in the eponymous waterside neighborhood. This outdoor nightclub is a cross between hip Rodeo Drive and exotic Marakesh. The humongous space features a restaurant/bar/pool, set under tents. Çubuklu 29 is all lit by candlelight and oil lamps to set the nocturnal mood once the sun goes down.

Niş Eaterie (Abdi Ipekci Cad. Azer Iş Merkezi, 44/3 Nişantaşı, 0212/296-9555, www.niseaterie.com) is an effort in eclecticism. Spanish tapas grace the menu and the space looks like it is straight out of SoHo. DJ Can Hatıpoğlu spins Europe's top-40 nightly. Tuesdays and Thursdays feature live music.

The best nightclub for die-hard dancers is **Sortie** (Muallim Nacı Cad 141, 0212/327-8585, www.sortie.com.tr, 40TL cover charge). This is, hands down, the place to strut your stuff. Sortie provides more than 10,000 square feet of heart-throbbing, head-bumping fun along the Bosphorus's European shores.

Bars

Pull up a stool at any of these top-notch watering holes, but only if the attire's up to snuff and the wallet's well stuffed. Noted in the press as some of Europe's top destinations for cocktails,

the following venues are run by hot hospitality groups that are painting Istanbul red with a series of multi-millionaire dollar all-in-one entertainment destinations.

Vogue (Spor Caddesi, Beşiktaş Plaza Blok A, 13th floor, 0212/227-4404, www.istanbuldoors.com, noon–3 A.M. daily) may be more than a decade old, but it still features some of the best entertainment in town. Its three terraces house a bar and two restaurants that are set high enough to offer some mind-boggling views of the straits. Its Book of Wines is another plus, with more than 200 vintages accompanied by which dish on Vogue's menu to pair them with.

Another high-class foray into Istanbul's highly competitive bar scene, Istanbul Doors Restaurant Group's **Anjélique** (Muallim Nacı Cad, Salhane Sok. 5, Ortaköy, 0212/327-2844) seems simplistic in design at first. But architect Mahmut Anlar's strategically placed angled mirrors create a magical environment that reflects the Bosphorus's shimmering waters throughout the space come nighttime. The Wolfgang Puck–like pizzeria on the 1st floor gets busy, but Anjélique's nightclub is what really draws the crowds.

Getting more international press than any of the other contenders, **360°** (Istiklal Cad. Mısır Apt. 8th floor/311, 0212/251-1042, www.360istanbul.com) is where the party is at almost every night, particularly during the summer evenings when the club's glass wall opens onto a terrace. The spacious restaurant provides spectacular 360-degree-views of the city—perfect for viewing the sunset—and has an unexpected mix of Thai and Turkish dishes on the menu. After 11 P.M. the place vibrates to the vibes of the latest tunes spun by guest DJs. The space itself may be difficult to find, as it is set atop an apartment building that blends seamlessly with its surroundings.

Live Music

The arrival of the Istanbul Modern Museum in 2004 revitalized the lower part of Beyoğlu, a strip of town that had for decades been all but forgotten. The exhibition space of the museum, along with its spiffy roof top café, brought back the crowds, including live music aficionados. This growing interest in live music has since driven up the stakes at the box office and has introduced a whole new spectrum of sound into the city. This phenomenon is undoubtedly reinforced by Istanbul's wildly popular Jazz Festival, which draws performers such as Sting and Norah Jones. There are now plenty of venues in which to see live performances. Reserving tickets in advance is highly recommended as the following venues tend to be not much more than holes in the wall.

Babylon (Seyhbender Sok. 3, 0212/292-7368, www.babylon-ist.com, 9:30 P.M.–2 A.M. Wed. and Thurs., 10:30 P.M.–3 A.M. Fri. and Sat., 30–60TL cover charge) is considered one of the world's top 100 bars for a good reason. Featuring top performers like the Latin Jazz sensation Poncho Sanchez, this hot spot hosts the best of international funk, hip-hop, and Turkish contemporary music in a chic environment.

Just down from the Galata Tower, **Nardis** (Kuledibi Sok, Galata, 0212/244-6327, www. nardisjazz.com, 9:30 P.M.–12:30 A.M. Mon.–Thurs., 10:30 P.M.–1:30 A.M. Fri.–Sat., 20TL cover charge) features mainstream jazz at its best. Set in the bowels of a brick enclave, which only enhances sound quality, Nardis gets packed quickly.

The exception to the hole-in-the-wall rule, the **Istanbul Jazz Center** (Çırağan Cad., Salhane Sok. 10, Ortaköy, 0212/327-5050, www.istanbuljazz.com, 9 P.M.–12:30 A.M. Mon.–Sat., 20–40TL cover charge) epitomizes the modern gentleman's dinner club, featuring a delectable á la carte or prix fixe Mediterranean menu served from 7 P.M. The dining tables offer the best views of the performances, which have included such extraordinary talents as Branford Marsalis and Stanley Clarke.

Cabarets

Extremely trendy with tourists, Istanbul's dinner cabarets are relegated to the European side of town. Don't expect an out-of-body dining experience, as these focus more on the whole package: an evening of traditional Turkish music and dancing combined with a variety of culinary courses, which gives the newbie a good grasp of Turkish cuisine and culture. It's wise to reserve a space online, as these venues are always packed. Dinner service typically begins at 7:30 or 8 P.M. nightly, and the prix fixe menu includes all entertainment and two drinks, but does not cover gratuities.

For more than 50 years **Kervansaray Restaurant & Night Club** (Cumhurriyet Cad. 30/5, Harbiye, 0212/247-1630, 120TL) has been thrilling guests nightly with sumptuous platters, free-flowing drinks, and at times rambunctious music and dancing. An arabesque venue, replete with tables dressed in white linen, this traditional nightclub entertains more than 150 diners with the sounds of the Alagöz siblings and the gyrations of belly dancers and folk groups. Along the same lines, the **Orient House** (Tiyatro Cad. 27, Beyazit, 0212/517-6163, www.orienthouseistanbul. com, 130TL), an all-inclusive destination, has the added bonus of whirling dervishes and an Ottoman janissary band. Reserving online will garner a 10 percent discount on the four-hour evening. The newest kid on the block is the nightly show at the **Galata Tower** (Galata Meydanı, Karaköy, 0212/293-8180, www.gal-atatower.net, 130TL). High atop the tower, the restaurant is the ideal place to experience the show while overlooking Istanbul.

The avant-garde cabaret/restaurant **Al Jamal** (Taşkışla Cad. 3, Maçka Demokrasi Parkı içi, www.cahidecabaret.com, 0212/231-0356, dinner from 50TL) offers splendid belly dancing troupes and singers belting Western pop hits in a posh 1001-Arabian-nights inspired décor, with breathtaking views of the Bosphorus. The Middle Eastern menu incorporates Turkish standbys, like *lahmacun* (thin pizza with minced meat), among its more exotic mezes. Al Jamal is trendy with international glitterati—Enrique Iglesias is a fan—and high society locals.

Gay and Lesbian

The gay and lesbian community has steadily increased in Istanbul, thanks to an influx of bisexual and homosexual expats, along with a few pop Turkish icons who have come out in drag. As a result, the gay and lesbian nightlife scene is growing. It is primarily concentrated around Beyoğlu, with more than a dozen gay and lesbian nightclubs and bars.

Renowned as a meeting place, and much tamer than the surrounding clubs, **Shake In Café and Bar** (Istiklal Cad., 25. Taksim, 0216/244-8079, 4 P.M.–1 A.M. Mon.–Thurs., until 2 A.M. Fri.–Sat.) is a relaxing space mostly patronized by the city's upscale and trendy men. A block east of Sıraselviler Caddesi, **Bar Bahçe** (Soğancı Sok. 7/1, Cihangir, 0212/256-1718, barbahce.com, 10 P.M.–4 A.M. Tues.–Thurs., until 5 A.M. Fri.–Sat.) is the weekend mecca for Istanbul's gay community. This western-style club throbs with a mix of Turkish and European techno until the wee hours of the morning. Also known for its lesbian crowd, Bar Bahçe's back room is reserved for women on Fridays and Saturdays. The cover charge is waived for students.

Hidden in the streets of Beyoğlu since 2004, **Tek Yön** (Hüseyinağa Mah. Ekrem Türk Sok. 14, 0212/252-5376, tekyonclub. com, 10:30 P.M.–4 A.M.) is mainly frequented by the local middle class and members of the bear community. On Tuesdays, friendly waiters and bar staff take part in a droll yet popular drag and male belly dancing show.

Not a lesbian bar per se, **Rocinante Café & Bar** (Sakız Ağacı Cad./Öğut Sok. 6/2, 2nd floor, Beyoğlu, 0212/244-8219, www.rocinantebar.com, 11 P.M.–2 A.M. daily) caters to a mostly female clientele.

THE ARTS

Aside from its nocturnal drinking and dancing destinations, Istanbul also has a variety of traditional shows, including ballet, folk dance, and classical music. The **Akbank Arts Foundation** runs a yearlong program of theater, classical music, and jazz at venues throughout the city; log on to www.akbanksanat.com for more information. Since 2007, **Garajistanbul** (Yeni Çarşı Cad., Kaymakan Reşat Bey Sok. 11a, Galatasaray, 0212/244-4459, info@garajistanbul.com, www.garajistanbul.com, tickets 25–35TL) has featured the most cutting-edge performing arts events every night of the week.

FESTIVALS

"Festival" has been the buzzword in Turkey since at least 2005. Now there are festivals for every art form, including wildly popular annual commemorations to music and film, and even a nod to the indigenous tulip. While festivals take place year-round, Istanbul's festival season typically runs April–July and kicks off the city's more classical programming. The best way to find out about the local and international acts is to check www.mymerhaba.com, www.istanbul.com, or *Time Out Istanbul*'s calendar section.

PIERRE LOTI IN ISTANBUL

Pierre Loti, a French naval officer turned novelist, was inspired to write his novel, *Aziyadé*, from a café situated uphill from Eyüp Camii, overlooking the Golden Horn. The breakthrough novel revealed trysts with a harem girl and a Spanish valet. It was reportedly based on personal diaries Loti kept during a three-month tour in Istanbul. The book propelled him to the top of the late 19th-century French literary scene. Described by many as a consummate Orientalist, Loti's exotic tales may have contributed to Istanbul's claim to fame in the late 1800s. Loti was infatuated with travel, and particularly with Istanbul. During his last trip to the city, in 1913, the scribe was welcomed by a cheering mob at the docks and by the sultan for a lavish dinner gala at the Topkapı Palace. On June 10, 1923, the day Loti was buried on the French island of Île d'Oléron, Istanbul's flags flew at half-mast.

Kicking of the festival season is the showy **Tulip Festival-Istanbul** in April. For two months, virtually every roadside, roundabout, and freeway median is dressed in every variety of the indigenous bloom. A little-known fact is that the tulip is not a native of Holland; rather, the tulip was brought to Western Europe by the Ottoman Empire under Suleyman the Magnificent. April is also the time when the **Istanbul International Film Festival** (various locations, 0212/334-0723, www.iksv.org) begins. The festival showcases the best of contemporary and classic films from both local and foreign filmmakers through screenings, classes, and speeches. Movie stars are known to make cameo appearances throughout the three-week long commemoration.

The Istanbul Music Festival (various locations, www.iksv.org) hosted annually in June by the Istanbul Foundation for Culture and Arts, features its acclaimed classical music concert series. The most celebrated classical etudes, performed by some of today's greatest classical talents, are paired with some of the most unforgettable venues the city has to offer. This includes the yearly rendition of Mozart's *The Abduction from the Seraglio,* staged in the forecourt of Topkapı Palace. Meanwhile, the **International Istanbul Theatre Festival** (various locations, 0212/334-0743, www.iksv.org, May and June) uses venues such as the Atatürk

Culture Center and the newly renovated Sürreyya Opera House on the Asian side.

The **Istanbul International Art and Culture Festival** (www.iksv.org, May and June) always promises about two dozen new stage acts, including workshops and conferences on the advancement of theater and dance in Turkey. But by far the most awaited festival is **Istanbul's International Music Festival** (various locations, www.iksv.org/muzik, June) due to its two-week celebration of Jazz. A bevy of top musicians and lyricists, from pop to opera, perform usually in sold-out crowds in a variety of venues citywide, including the Kuruçeşme Arena whose location abutting the straits allows for breathtaking summer sunsets. Outside of the tulip festivities, which are organized by the municipality, the remaining festivals are coordinated by the Istanbul Foundation for Culture and the Arts (www.iksv.org).

Highly anticipated each year, and attended by some 50,000 teenagers, the multiple-day outdoor **Rock 'n Coke** (www.rockncoke.com) concert highlights Billboard Magazine's chart-toppers the weekend before the academic year begins. The much tamer **Efes Pilsen Blues Festival** (www.efesblues.com, October) is a series of gigs in cities nationwide that attempt to bring the musical genre's woeful tunes to Turkey.

Shopping

Shopaholics beware! Istanbul's got the best of both worlds: tons of antiques *and* trendy names at modern multiplexes that are sprouting like wild flowers all over the city. Knowing where to go for what is the question. Without a knowledgeable roadmap, eager spenders will be remiss to locate that perfect blue eye or Kütahya ceramic plate to bring home. There's the tried-and-true **Grand Bazaar** to hone bargaining skills, while viewing one of the oldest structures of its kind. The dirt cheap catch-all of **Tahtakale,** lining the hill between the Grand

Bazaar and Eminönu, near the exotic foodstuff of the **Spice Bazaar** is also worth a look. And so are the nifty Ottoman antiques located in Beyoğlu's **Çukurcuma** neighborhood, a block behind Galatasaray High School. Further down Istiklal Caddesi is **Tünel's** old music shops, where time-worn musical sheets and instruments can be browsed. When antiquing and memento hunting has gotten old, do like Istanbul's élite and head for the brand new **Istinye Park** in its namesake neighborhood, or Nişantaşı's posh **City's** shopping complex.

ANTIQUING LIKE A NATIVE

Istanbul is a virtual trove of antiques. Collectors searching for that perfect memento, whether it be a hand-loomed carpet or antiquated ceramics, don't need to limit themselves to the Grand Bazaar. In fact, just an afternoon off the traveler's grid, in the back streets lining popular sites, you'll discover sellers peddling Turkish crafts and exquisite European furniture side-by-side in tiny little shops. While the city may be chock-full of period pieces with highly hospitable shop owners ready to elaborate on the pedigree of their wares, it always pays to be well-versed on what is an antique, a fake, or just bric-a-brac. And remember that permission is required to export Turkish antiquities and other cultural artifacts; a receipt along with an official "museum export certificate" are necessary to legally export such items abroad.

Big ticket items reside with the city's famed antique dealers, including **Portakal** (Portakal Sanat ve and Kültür EVbi, Mim Kemal Öke Caddesi, Gün Apt. 8, Nişantaşı, 0212/225-4637, www.rportakal.com/tr) and **Antik Palace** (Süleyman Seba Caddesi, Talimyeri Sok. 2, Maçka, 0212/236-2460, www.antikas.com, 9 A.M.-7 P.M. Mon.-Fri.). Silver and crystal period sets, as well as colored glass heirlooms, statuettes, gilded Korans, oil paintings, and precious estate jewelry are available for purchase in Antik Palace's Hünkar Hall. Portakal showcases about the same items, and is also open during the week. Scheduled auctions appear on their websites and are worth attending even if you don't have a million-euro bank account.

Another hotspot for collectors is Çukurcuma Square, located in the backstreets of Beyoğlu that feed into Galatasaray Square, which it-self stands midway between Karaköy and Taksim Square. You'll find antique boutiques, interspersed between a mesh of not-so-pricey shops, specializing in retro 1960s, art deco, and belle époque items, or just about any bibelot that might be deemed a collectible. Check out **Karadeniz Antik** (Çukurcuma Caddesi, Firüzağa Mah. 55, Beyoğlu, 0212/251-9605, www.karadenizantik.com), which specializes in exquisite bohemian leaded crystal lighting and carafe sets, as well as 19th century European and Russian antiques. Çukurcuma's architecture reflects the Péra epoch with Istanbul's turn-of-the century buildings.

Akin to finding the needle in the hay stack, locating **Horhor Bit Pazarı** (Horhor Flea Market, Kırık Tulumba Sokak 13, Aksaray) is a task onto itself. But once there, you'll thank yourself for the effort. This is a whopping seven-story flea market featuring 220 shops, jam-packed with antique furniture, Iznik ceramics, and collectible carpets. This is by far the city's most interesting bazaar, just steps northeast away from Sultanahmet Square. To get there from Sultanahmet's famed cistern, follow Yerebatan Caddesi and take a right on Ankara Caddesi; Horhor lies down the street on your right.

And if a trip to Istanbul's Asian side is in the cards, unbelievable 19th and early 20th century European and Ottoman finds can be had at both **Üsküdar Antikacılar Çarşısı** (Üsküdar Antique District, behind the Üsküdar municipality building on the main square) and **Kadıköy Antikacılar Çarşısı** (Moda Cad.). Kadıköy's antique dealers can be found up the streets from Kadıköy's open bazaar, along Telalzade Sokak.

Better shops will offer shipping services, so the extra purchases won't have to be packed.

BOOKS, MAPS, AND MUSIC

To browse through tomes and CDs, new and old, nothing compares to Istiklal Caddesi. There are, however, chain stores like **D&R** (www.dr.com.tr) and **Remzi** (www.remzi.com.tr) peppered throughout Istanbul, but Beyoğlu's central location enables sightseers to pop in for a quick purchase without going out of their way.

For English books, **Robinson Crusoe** (Istiklal Cad. 389, 0212/293-6968) has been the go-to shop for expats for decades. Its tall shelves have a good assortment of fiction and non-fiction, including travel guides focusing on Istanbul and Turkey. A few doors down, the municipality-owned **Istanbul Bookstore** (Istiklal Cad. 379, 0212/292-7692, www.istanbulkitapcisi.com) has a wealth of resources for both travelers and researchers. Definitely worth a trip, it's packed with rare historical tomes, maps, CDs, as well as posters and reproductions of calligraphies that can't be found elsewhere. Flanking Galatasaray High School is **Homer Kitabevi** (Yeni Çarsı Cad. 12/A, 0212/249-5902, www.homerbooks. com), where academics flock for Ottoman- or Turkish-interest titles, such as religion-centric literature, women's issues, photography, and architecture. While **Mephisto** (Istiklal Cad. 125, Beyoğlu, 0212/249-0607, www.mephisto.com. tr) is a great bookstore, its magazine stand is even better. So is its music selection, including underground jazz and techno CDs from up-and-coming talents, and more traditional Turkish sounds.

Around Sultanahmet, two bookshops share the same owner: **Galeri Kayseri** (Divan Yolu Cad. 58, 0212/512-0456) offers the expected array of tomes on everything spectacular about Turkey and Istanbul, such as the cuisine, culture, history, and architecture; the newer store, **Bookshop Istanbul** (Divanyolu Cad. 11, 0212/516-3366), offers just about the same in a less touristy location.

CERAMICS

Sultanahmet has a myriad of stores selling typical Turkish artisanal crafts, but **Caferağa Medresesi** (Caferiye Sok., Sultanahmet, 0212/513-3601, 9 A.M.–6:30 P.M. daily) has unique pieces that are perfect gifts and souvenirs. This 15th-century theological complex, one of Mimar Sinan's architectural gifts, was all but forgotten until artisans united and refurbished the structure's string of cubicles and classrooms into an exhibition and retail space.

One of the greatest places to window-shop for faience is **Tuğra Ceramic Center** (Atmeydanı Cad. 78, Sultanahmet, 0212/516-4344), where three floors of smaller items like tiles, bowls, and teapots give way to larger ornamental plates. The salespeople are very knowledgeable and not pushy. What's more, the owner Chris Kitrinos encourages the staff of artisans to create one-of-a-kind pieces for the store, in addition to traditional Kütahya and Iznik items.

When Pope Benedict XVI came to town in 2006, he received a departing gift commissioned by Tahir Eğinci, owner of **Iznik Classics** (Arasta Bazaar, 67 and 73, Sultanahmet, 212/517-1705, www.iznikclassics.com, 9 A.M.–8 P.M. daily). His creations, along with piles of more affordable yet beautifully mass-produced items, are just superb. And with four floors to stroll, there's bound to be something for every taste and wallet. Visit Iznik Classics at their other locations (Iç Bedesten, Serifağa Sok. 18/21, Grand Bazaar, 0212/520-2568; or, Utangaç Sok. 17, Sultanahmet, 0212/516-8874).

At the Grand Bazaar, **Deli Kızın Yeri** (Halcılar Cad. 82, Grand Bazaar, 0212/526-1251, www.delikiz.com, 8:30 A.M.–7 P.M. Mon.–Sat.) is chock-full of hand-made items Linda Caldwell and her staff of three produces, as well as *oya* (needle lace) and dolls crafted by villagers from the Tarsus Mountains and Iznik. A New York resident, Caldwell, who may not be as nutty as her shop's name "The Crazy Lady's Place" states, does appear to be the first foreign woman to own one of the thousands of shops in the Bazaar.

JEWELRY

Goldsmiths from the Grand Bazaar and Sultanahmet to chain stores peddle unique pieces, from the cutting-edge in new design to *nazar boncuk* (Turkish evil eyes), set amidst diamonds or strung on simple 22-karat gold chains. Turkey, particularly Istanbul, has a long tradition of jewelry artistry. If you can't find what you're looking for, Murat Ismailli (better known as the Jewelry Magician) follows in his family tradition and custom crafts pieces to order. Ismailli's shop **Dilara Kuyumculuk** (Içbedesten 28 & 30, Grand Bazaar, 0212/512-8364, www.dilarajewellery. com) offers a wide variety of gilded opulence and irresistible trinkets. Requesting prices for items along Bazaar's Nuruosmaniye Caddesi, where some of the more flamboyant and generally more expensive gemologists are, is a good way to compare prices. For custom-yet-strictly-Turkish baubles, head east a couple of blocks from the Grand Bazaar's Kilitçiler Gate to **DesignZone** (Ali Baba Türbe Sok. 21/4 Nuruosmaniye, 0212/527-9285, www.designzone.com.tr), where artist-turned-entrepreneur Özlem Tuna displays her tulip-inspired collection, as well as busts, earthly ceramics, and her alaTurka candle series.

In up-market Nişantaşı, diamonds may be king, but novel **Rumî** (Şakayık Sok., Ihlamur Palas Apt. 40/4, 0212/240-4360, www.rumi-jewelry.com), headed by designer Erdal Tekisalp, embraces simple styles reflecting authentic Turkic and Anatolian epochs. Some pieces are inspired by Neolithic artifacts, while others evoke more recent examples of Hittite embellishments. Also in Nişantaşı, the **Zen Diamonds** (Rumeli Cad. 4, Nişantaşı, 0212/240-1911, 9 A.M.–8 P.M. Mon.–Sat.) chain is known for its whimsical animal collection, commissioned by National Geographic, and its latest, wildly popular Ottoman-inspired trinket series. Finally, there's the Turkish gone-global manufacturer **Altınbaş** (Divanyolu Cad. 80, Sultanahmet, 0212/513-9288, www.altinbas.com), respected nationally for some of the finest rocks, particularly in solitary settings, as well as earrings and necklace sets.

MALLS

Istanbul is the mecca of megaplexes. Not just a compilation of stores, these shopping centers are floors upon floors of mammoth brands, swanky couture, beckoning cafés, and spiffy eateries under one roof, all appealing to the fickle upper middle-class Turk. Malls sit at virtually every cardinal point, but do check out the gargantuan **Istinye Park** (Istinye Bayiri Cad., 0212/345-5555, www.istinyepark.com, 10 A.M.–10 P.M.), towering over its namesake neighborhood over the Bosphorus's northeastern flank. Buy Sony's latest plasma screen, a diamond-studded Rolex, or a just-flown-in Mexican guava all in one go. Nişantaşı's **City's** (Teşvikiye Cad. 162, 0212/373-3300, www.citysnisantasi.com) is the *crème de la crème*. No plastic cutlery or trays here; forgo

the burger and opt for a steak au poivre at L'Entrecôte de Paris, a bistro restaurant that has won the hearts of well-heeled foodies. While fashion rules in this neighborhood, little did the developers know that the big-name restaurateurs they tried to lure would overshadow City's world-class boutiques, such as Jean Paul Gaultier's first ever shop.

Smack in the center of the business district of Levent is **Kanyon** (Büyükdere Cad. 185, Levent, 0212/281-0800, www.kanyon.com. tr), an open-air shopping complex designed to resemble, well, a canyon flanked by some 160 retailers, including the British flagship department store of Harvey Nichols. A nine-screen theater and tons of parking are Kanyon's greatest assets. Kanyon is truly an architectural feat worth seeing. But make sure to visit in the summer, as the structure's design only accentuates Istanbul's polar weather in winter.

SWEETS

"Eat sweet, talk sweet" goes the popular Turkish saying. And indeed, after trying some sugary, nutty concoctions such as flaky baklava, hard candy, or the famed *rahat lokum* (Turkish confection known as Turkish Delight), it's easy to understand why. Historic candy maker **Ali Muhiddin Hacı Bekir** (Ali Muhiddin Hacı Bekir, Hamidiye Cad. 83, Eminönü, 0212/522-0666, www.hacibekir. com.tr, 9 A.M.–8 P.M.) set up shop upon his arrival in Istanbul from his Black Sea hometown of Kastamonu more than 230 years ago. Hacı Bekir—a title afforded to those who've completed the *Hac* (pilgrimage) to Mecca—created a softer chew that bowled over the harem, and started a tradition that's been practiced under the same roof for longer than any other business in town. These sumptuous morsels can also be purchased in Beyoğlu (Istiklal Cad. 83, 0212/244 2804) or in Kadıköy (Muvakıthane Cad. 14 & 16, 0216/336-1519).

For a heavenly bit of a different texture, **Güllüoğlu Baklava & Café** (Mumhane Cad. 171, Karaköy, 0212/249-9680) offers baklava in no less than 12 varieties for about 5TL apiece. Stumped? Try the *çam fıstık* (pistachio) baklava made from nuts imported from Barak. It compiles about 30 pastry sheets, so thin they're transparent, and milk culled from sheep and goats bred in Urfa's Sihan Plateau. For a smorgasbord of purely Turkish desserts, **Saray Muhallebicisi** (Istiklal Cad. 23, Beyoğlu, 0212/292-3434, www.saraymuhallebicisi.com, 6 A.M.–11 P.M.) has been offering flaky pastry and creamy dairy desserts for more than seven decades. Sample the *tavuk göğsü* (chicken breast)—a rice pudding made with finely chopped chicken breast. Saray is also known for its *Ekmek Kadayıfı* (bread morsels baked in syrup), served with a heaping dollop of thick clotted cream.

TEXTILES, LEATHER, AND CARPETS

For Istanbul's in-crowd, it doesn't get any better than **Sivaslı İstanbul Yazmacısı**'s store (Yağlıkçılar Cad. 57, 212/526-7748, Grand Bazaar). This is where fashion icons like Rifat Özbek, Hussein Chalayan, and Dolce & Gabbana come to purchase fabrics. Intricate needlework, pricey antique lacework, and newer lace tatted by women deep within the Anatolian hinterland hang side by side in this small atelier.

Doğan & Özgür Bilgili (Takkeciler Sok 93–95, Grand Bazaar, 0212/527-6359, www.bilgili.info) is where the Clintons drop by for well-tailored, fine leather jackets and full-length coats, starting at about 150TL. For innovative purses, slippers, and Western-style boots crafted out of kilim, from 25–250TL, Ercan May's **Ercan Hediyelik Eşya** (Kolancılar Sok 7, 0212/522-5361) is the place to go. For the softest Turkish cotton bathrobes and towels, you can't go wrong with **Abdulla Natural Products** (Halıcılar Cad. 62, Grand Bazaar, 0212/527-3684, www.abdulla.com). For a versatile pashmina (20–40TL), **Igüs Eşarp** (Yağlıkçılar Cad. 80, Grand Bazaar, 0212/512-2538, www.igustekstil.com) has every possible shawl imaginable, from premium silk, wool, and velvet to viscose. Rugs are the mainstay at **Şişko Osman** (Zincirli Han 15, 0212/528-3548, www.siskoosman.com), a decades-old, well-respected institution. Looking for silk? Head to **Ipek** (Istiklal Cad. 120, Beyoğlu, 0212/249-8207) for scarves (12–95TL) so luxurious they should be framed, not worn. Men will also find silken ties and cravats starting at 17TL. Owners Selim and Işmail will be pleased to unravel their entire collection.

Sports and Recreation

For a long time, athletics—and exercise in general—were relegated to professionals or the youth, but now a visiting jogger or swimmer will find that he or she doesn't have to go it alone while in Turkey. Jogging is an increasingly popular activity. So are trendy body workouts, like calisthenics and yoga, along with the more traditional tennis and sailing. Istanbul is peppered with arenas devoted to well-being, in addition to gyms and spas provided by the better hotels in town. For those wishing to exercise on weekends, head out early to beat the crowds and traffic.

WALKING AND BIKING TRAILS

A marked two-kilometer stretch along the Sea of Marmara, the **Dalyan-Bostancı** is a paved

route along Istanbul's Anatolian shore that beckons hundreds come the weekend. Lapped by seawaters below, the elevated path features outdoor training areas with rudimentary exercise machinery, parks for children, tiny cafés, and acres of landscaped lawns. To get there, ride the Eminönü ferry to Kadıköy and hop on a *dolmuş* headed for Bostancı. Also hugging the Sea of Marmara is **Fenerbahçe Park** (0216/336-3828, 6 A.M.–midnight, daily), a small woodsy retreat that offers a cobbled route that's about two-thirds of a mile around. Gracing a small promontory, the protected park is replete with cafés and many opportunities to rest—or stretch—on one of the benches overlooking the waters.

For serious joggers, hikers, or bikers,

HAMMAM: THE GREAT RUBDOWN

When the world-renowned Turco-Welsh photographer team of Mert Alas and Marcus Piggot searched for the ideal photo location to shoot a pictorial featuring fashion icon Kate Moss for *W* magazine in 2008, they knew it had to be sexy and steamy to match their subject. Nothing is sultrier than a hammam (Turkish bath), so the duo chose the Cağaloğlu Hamamı, which incidentally is included in Patricia Schultz's *1,000 Places to See Before You Die* (#1 on the New York Times Bestseller list). This centuries-old marble den has become one of Istanbul's notorious places to visit for those heavy into pop culture. If you're not into A-list haunts, but would like that perfect steam bath while in town, here's a list of more centrally-located, less-hyped, and altogether more reasonable hammams. These baths will get your temperature up, take off pounds of dead skin, and give you that new lease on life you've been looking for.

Cemberlitaş Hamamı (Divan Yolu, Vezirhan Cad. 8, Cemberlitaş, 0212/522-7974, www.cemberlitashamami.com.tr, 6 A.M.-midnight daily) is just steps west of Sultanahmet on the way to the Grand Bazaar. One of Istanbul's most historic hammams, Cemberlitaş was designed by imperial architect Mimar Sinan in the mid-16th century. A bath will set you back 35TL; a massage and *kese* (vigorous scrubbing session) is about 20TL. There's a section for each gender.

Tarihi Galatasaray Hamamı (Turnacıbaşı Sok. 24, Beyoğlu; men's section 0212/252-4242, 5 A.M.-midnight daily; women's section 0212/249-4342, 8 A.M.-8 P.M. daily; www.galatasarayhamami.com) was commissioned by Sultan Beyazit II in the early 16th century, as an addition to the famed Galatasaray Lisesi. Both its women's and men's sections are a favorite of Beyoğlu's upper-crust and the locale's historical exoticism and its staff's no-nonsense cordiality have also lured Hollywood's elite. Take it from John Travolta; he flew in personally just for their Pasha treatment. There is an all-inclusive package (115TL) which includes a couple of steams, soap and exotic oil scrubs, as well as a wash that, when done sequentially,

Büyükada is unrivaled. The nine-mile trail circles the island and offers serious sports enthusiasts a run for their money, while a shorter five-mile path crisscrosses the isle. Accessed by riding the ferry, the idyllic island offers steep inclines through woods that give way to the flat, seaside road called *Büyük Tur Yolu*. Best of all, aside from the haphazard clip-clopping phaeton traffic, hikers will find themselves alone along this route. The halfway is marked with a café overlooking the Sea of Marmara's horizon.

On the European side, the **Belgrade Forest** (0212/559-2549, adult 1TL/vehicle 4TL) long an imperial hunting venue, now welcomes hikers and cyclists along its four-mile-long walking path, aptly named the "Live Young Route." Seventeen fitness stations and several heart rate checkpoints dot this pastoral path that passes by a lovely lake. The Route is about 13 miles from Taksim, so taking a taxi or a rental car is recommended. Alternatively, Bus 42T stops at Bahçeköy, which is just a short walk from the park's entrance.

Circling Sultanahmet to the north is **Gülhane Park** (0212/455-5900, 6 A.M.–midnight), a great getaway in the midst of the city's bustle. At about a kilometer, the paved pedestrian route bisects what once was the rose-filled imperial garden of Topkapı Palace. The path may be short, but its proximity to most sights and hotels is convenient for those aching for a quick jog.

SAILING

The city's largest leisure marina sprawls along the Sea of Marmara at Kalamış/Fenerbahçe, on Istanbul's Asian shores. With offices at Kalamış (Münir Nurettin Selçuk Caddesi, 0216/346-2346, kalamis@seturmarinas.com, www.seturmarinas.com), the main pier is replete with stores and restaurants. Don't want to drive there? There is an air taxi and helicopter service for those wanting to avoid the

detoxes the system and alleviates rheumatism. A simple bath costs around 30TL. **Cağaloğlu Hamamı** (Yerebatan Caddesi, Ankara Caddesi, 0212/522-2424, www.cagalogluhamami.com.tr; men's section 7 A.M.-7 P.M. daily; women's section 8 A.M.-8 P.M. daily) may only date back to the mid-18th century but it has remained the bath of choice for visiting glitterati since British King Edward VIII and Florence Nightingale took it all off back in the day. The scrub costs about 50TL; the bath runs about 35TL. The structure was a gift to the city from Sultan Mehmet I.

Süleymaniye Hamamı (Mimar Sinan Cad. 20, Süleymaniye, 0212/519-5569, www.suleymaniyehamami.com.tr) was built for the sultan Süleyman the Great in the mid-16th century by imperial architect and friend Mimar Sinan. Here, you'll get the full package for €35, which includes a wash, scrub and soap massage, the use of a lockable changing room, the traditional *peştemal* (wrap), and *takunya* (slippers).

Üsküdar Çinili Hamamı (Murat Reis Mahallesi Cavusdere Cad., 0216/553-1593; men's section 7 A.M.-10 P.M. daily; women's section 8 A.M.-6 P.M. daily; entrance 15TL) is a gorgeous set of authentic Turkish baths, which were commissioned by Sultan Ahmed I in 1648 for his Bosnian wife, Köşem Sultan. It's one of the few that has withstood the test of time and remains much as it did 360 years ago when it first opened. Like most other hammams listed here, Çinili features separate women and men sections. The latter boasts the rare addition of a sauna. Since this hammam is run by the municipality, expect a little less pomp and much lower prices.

Want to visit a hammam, but don't care much for the bath? The impressive **Haseki Sultan Hamamı** in Sultanahmet will give you that option. Built in 1557 by Sinan for the infamous Lady Roxelana, the structure no longer serves its original purpose. Instead it houses a carpet and textile flea market run by the municipality. Visitors may still visit the twin-domed halls − which once housed a bath for each gender − that made this facility so spectacular.

city's horrendous traffic. For beginners, the nearby **Istanbul Sailing Club** (İstanbul Yelken Kulubu, Fenerbahçe Cape; 0216/336-0633, www.istanbulyelken.org.tr in Turkish) will help in setting sail towards a new hobby. Along the European shores, the **Ataköy Marina** (Sahilyolu, Ataköy, 0212/560-4270, www.atakoymarina.com.tr) provides mooring space, sailing lessons, and a great meal in the club-like eatery whose dining room overlooks the Sea of Marmara. Kartal's **Marina Dragos Charter & Beneteau Sailing School** (Mutlu Sok. 11, Dragos, 0216/370-7898, marinadragosgroup.com) offers sailing courses for all levels, from beginners to the highly experienced. The outfit also charters a full range of yachts, starting at €150 per day or €1,200 for the week.

SWIMMING

Istanbullus love water activities, from swimming, water surfing, and sailing to sunbathing poolside or on the city's golden beaches. Traditionally, city denizens have flocked to Turkey's southern and western beaches in June, but as more women join the workforce, families increasingly remain in the city for the summer. This development led to the inauguration of more beach and urban country clubs. Swimming pools are relegated to hotels; the better the hotel, the finer the facilities. Along with pay-per-use of their services, like saunas and gyms, most hotels allow walk-ins the use of their pool. On the weekends, beaches and beach clubs are the places to be.

Beaches

If the itinerary doesn't call for a stopover on Turkey's Aegean or Mediterranean coasts, don't fret! Located at opposite ends, either on the Sea of Marmara or the Black Sea, beaches abound in Istanbul. Starting with the warmer and calmer waters of the Sea of Marmara, the Princes'

Islands offer not only an idyllic escape for tired sightseers, but also some great seaside lounging options. The quality of the water is questionable; that's what the locals say. But the recent return of indigenous dolphins proves that the municipality cleaned the shores to some extent. Unlike American beaches, guards are not lifeguards, but hired hands who collect usage fees for parasols and chaises lounges. So, swim with care, particularly around the shores of the Black Sea.

In the Marmara, the Princes' Islands' Büyükada has a nice array of public beaches, including **Yörük Ali, Princess, Kumsal,** and **Nakibey.** Since it is after all an island, if there's a piece of sandy real estate you'd like to try, by all means do so. Some of the beach clubs, like **Yaman Beach Club** (Prenses Köyu, Büyükada, 0216/382-8111), lay right by the pier. There, you can bask in the serenity of the archipelago while gazing at the concrete jungle across the Marmara. Heybeliada's cove is open to the public, and its **Green Beach Club** (0216/351-1600, www.clubgreenbeach.com) is the Turks' fun retreat, filled with banana floaties, tons of swimming, waterskiing lessons, and other activities. The beaches of **Caddebostan, Suadiye,** and **Bostancı,** hugging the coast of their eponymous Asian boroughs along the Sea of Marmara, get crowded once school is out. Their proximity to the shopping mecca of Bağdat Caddesi offers the exhausted shopper a much needed respite.

Along the northeastern Asian shores of the Bosphorus, the small beach at **Küçüksu** reopened in 2005 to great fanfare. The currents can get tricky here and are best left to experienced swimmers. The upside is that a dip in Küçüksu's cooler waters might involve dolphins!

The Black Sea resort city of Kylyos is well worth the 24-mile road trip from Taksim. Always refreshing, the Black Sea's cooler waters have an occasional undertow that swimmers should be aware of. This seashore's beach club of note is **Nonstop Beach** (Turban Yolu, 4, Kilyos, 0212/201-2305, www.nonstopbeach.com).

Pools

The pool at **Çırağan Kempinski Hotel** (Çırağan Cad. 32, Beşiktaş, 0212/326-4646,

www.kempinski-istanbul.com, 7 A.M.–11 P.M. daily, 120TL Mon.–Fri., 200TL Sat.–Sun.) is at sea level, just steps away from the Bosphorus. In addition to the sublimely thick towels of the finest Turkish cotton, the cuisine at the poolside gazebo is also on par with the Kempinski's renowned luxury.

Just down the street, **Hôtel Les Ottomans** (Muallim Naci Cad. 68, Kuruçeşme, 0212/359-1500, www.lesottomans.com, 9 A.M.–7 P.M., 100TL), in the historic Muhsinzade Waterside Mansion, boasts a pool fit for the late-18th-century pasha who commissioned the beautiful structure. This pool is so close to the straits, it's like swimming in it sans currents.

For the best in woodsy yet still urban retreats, the pool at **Parkorman** (Büyükdere Cad., Maslak, 0212/328-2000, www.parkorman.com.tr, 9 A.M.– 6 P.M. daily, 35TL Mon.–Fri., 50TL Sat.–Sun.) is nothing short of humongous. A variety of restaurants, outdoor activities, along with festivals and concerts, await kids and adults in a park-like atmosphere, just minutes away from the city's financial center.

SPECTATOR SPORTS

Aside from the much-awaited Istanbul Grand Prix, a leg of the annual F1 competition, there are myriad annual sporting events hosted by the city, from sailing to the increasingly popular Bosphorus swimming race. The events generally occur around the same time every year; the programming, location, and tickets for each event are available online.

The most popular events, drawing in millions of spectators every year, span various sporting activities. For long distance runners, the **Intercontinental Eurasia Istanbul Marathon** (www.istanbulmarathon.org) takes place each October and has attracted international runners for about three decades. With prize monies totaling over one million dollars, participants in a variety of categories, including a 15K race, compete in this event that stretches across the Bosphorus Bridge. Another event that draws crowds is the **Red Bull Air**

Race (www.redbullairrace.com), which features amazing aerial acrobatics every June. The race consists of an aerial racetrack in which daredevil pilots fly through a course. The tour hits 12 cities each year; the Istanbul leg of the tour is set above the Golden Horn between the Galata and Atatürk Bridges. Truly a dazzling air show, smoke trails and roaring engines complete the experience. Held in September, the **Istanbul Formula 1 Grand Prix** (www.formula1-istanbul.com) is a magnet for the rich and famous, as well as auto racing fanatics. Unless booked way ahead of time, there are few affordable tickets for the Istanbul race, one of the most recently added cities to this famous worldwide circuit. Also among the big spectator events is the **World Tennis Association's Istanbul Tennis Cup** (mid-May, www.istanbulcup.com, tickets 15–270TL), pitting tennis starlets to the joy of international fans.

Other distinctive spectator sporting events include dressage (competitive horse training), water sports, and extreme sports. The **International Istanbul Horse Show** (http://www.kg-cc.com/banner/horsephoto/index.htm), held at the prestigious Kemer Country

Club in Kemerburgaz, a woodsy outpost 20 minutes outside Istanbul proper, lures jumping and dressage enthusiasts every July. During the last week of July, the **World Kiteboard Cup Istanbul** brings together young talent at Burç Beach in Kilyos, on the Black Sea. Sponsored by Jim Beam, other exclusive venues for this tournament include the Kuruçeşme Arena, along the Bosphorus, and Dragos, an enclave along the Sea of Marmara coast. Also for water fanatics, the **Eurasian Swimming-Sailing-Rowing Competition** (www.olimpiyatkomitesi.org.tr), organized by the National Olympic Committee of Turkey every July, remains the only event of its kind where swimmers cross continents to complete the race. Finally, the **International Sailing Week of Istanbul** (www.istanbulyelken.org.tr/sailweek) commences every third week of August from the Istanbul Sailing Club's Fenerbahçe marina, with a lavish opening ceremony. For spectators, the regatta is a dazzling site of ballooning sails set against the ice blue waters of the Sea of Marmara; for sailors, the thrill of comparing skills with some of the best seafarers in the world is alluring.

Accommodations

As in every major city, the quality and rates of Istanbul's hotel rooms run the gamut, from the most expensive room in the world at the Çırağan Kempinski at a whopping €35,000 a night to youth hostels at about 35TL. There is a large section of smaller boutique inns that are just as charming as they are easy on the wallet. Best of all, these alternative B&B's will add a custom touch to any trip to ensure that guests are pleased, thusly guaranteeing that sought after word-of-mouth recommendation. Throughout the book, and particularly in Istanbul, special attention has been given to these upcoming stars in the hospitality industry. Budget rooms are also listed along with the expensive digs.

Hostels and pensions are the least expensive

accommodations. Some feature a variety of options, from en-suite family rooms to multi-bed dormitories with common facilities, just a breakfast room, or a bar/restaurant combination. A few make extra money as makeshift travel agencies, offering economical tour packages and other related services. Turks are generally sticklers for cleanliness, so expect the majority of lodgings to be pristine.

Booking early is highly recommended, as the popularity of Istanbul with tourists increases yearly. Finding accommodations once onsite is not impossible, but why chance having to settle for a less-than-adequate room for a higher rate? Aside from booking early, one thing to remember is that lodgings typically include breakfast. If the establishment does not include a morning meal, forgo its typically more expensive á la carte fare and head out to find a nearby café. Alternatively, ask for directions to the neighborhood *fırın* (bakery) to select a variety of *poğaca* (savory rolls) or *açma* (flaky, buttery Danishes), prior to heading to the neighborhood's tea garden.

Beware of hotels that do not offer rates online. Request a rate via email and claim the room with a printout of the reply to ensure quoted tariffs. To check out the city's exhaustive list of accommodations, log on to www.istanbulhotelreservations.com. Hotel charges, which are traditionally listed in euros, generally include the Value Added Tax (VAT); if the online brochure doesn't guarantee that it does, do inquire, as the extra fee can total up to 20 percent of the cost of an entire stay. Another good rule of thumb is to ask about air-conditioning, as Istanbul's summers can be torrid. While better hotels today provide it, older, smaller B&B's may not. Noise can also be a factor, particularly in quarters like Taksim and Sultanahmet. Short of bringing earplugs, restful nights can be assured by booking a room away from the main drag. While exotic to most, the crack-of-dawn call of the muezzin is sure to rouse unaccustomed tourists. Securing lodgings away from these sanctuaries might also be a consideration.

Finally, where to book is always the inevitable question, whose reply always relies on personal preferences and budget. Lodging in the thick of the action involves selecting hotels around Taksim or Sultanahmet. But for a stay to remember, nothing beats a room by the straits at one of the newer boutique hotels. And while the lowest peak season rates are listed, knock off at least 10 percent during the off-season months November–March. Keep in mind that some places might even offer discounts if you pay in cash.

SULTANAHMET
Under €75
The best for the buck is **[(Antique Hostel & Guesthouse** (Kutlugün Sok. 51, 0212/638-1637, www.antiquehostel.com,

from €13). Known for its lavish complimentary breakfasts, Antique has redefined the hostel experience to include satellite TVs, Wi-Fi access, and air-conditioning in all its sparkling clean dormitory-style rooms, singles and doubles. Preferred by young adults, it gets loud, particularly in the early evenings. But at €70, the rates for the triples that overlook the Sea of Marmara cannot be beat. Another good option for the budget traveler is **[(Hotel Yunus Emre** (Şifa Hamamı Sok. 30, 0212/638-4562, www.yunusemrehotel.com, from €50). All the comforts of home: satellite TV, wireless Internet access, air-conditioning, hair dryers, and breakfast for about €65 per double room. Under the attentive management of Maria and Bülent Irem, pleasantly pastel, pristine rooms and ample bathrooms await guests, as well as a rooftop terrace facing the grand Blue Mosque.

For backpackers, the **Orient Hostel International** (Akbiyik Cad. 13, 0212/517-9493, www.orienthostel.com, from €18) is a good base for an inexpensive Istanbul stay. Groups of guests can participate in the Orient's popular four-day tours (120TL) to the southern Aegean region of Ephesus or to the battlefields of Çanakkale. The place is best known for its Terrace Café & Restaurant, great views, tours, belly dancers, boisterous bar, and large collection of hookah pipes. Internet access and a travel agency are also on-hand.

Towering over the ancient Greek water cistern it's named after, **Sarnıç Hotel** (Küçük Ayasofya Cad. 26, 0212/518-2323, www.sarnichotel.com, from €60) is an economical solution that packs a bunch of services and accommodations. Early Eastern European chic furnishings and modern fixtures grace spacious guest rooms and public spaces. Amenities include color cable TV; minibar; tiled bathroom; an underground cistern open to the public; cooking lessons; free Internet access; and, a terrace with a view so incredible you'll want to stay in for the evening. If booking for more than three nights, request the Sarnıç's complimentary airport transfer.

€75-150
The **Armada Istanbul City Hotel** (Ahırkapı

Sok. 24, 0212/455-4455, www.armadahotel. com.tr, from €80) gets terrific deals, some as low as €80 in July. Just south of Seraglio Point overlooking the Sea of Marmara, this hotel is huge with the national press both for its five highly superior restaurants and its special packages, including Istanbul Old City Special, which features a full day of sightseeing through Sultanahmet. Another package, its three-day Formula One Special deal, boasts two-way transfers from Atatürk Airport and one dinner. The style is Istanbul classic with dazzling views of the entire historic peninsula and the added bonuses of bathtubs and wireless Internet access throughout.

(Hotel Empress Zoe (Adliye Sok. 10, 0212/518-2504, www.emzoe.com, from €75), a fully renovated mid-15th-century bathhouse, has a lobby that exudes historical charm, with ancient walls and barrel Byzantine vaulted passages. If the lush patio reminds of the beauty of California's meticulously landscaped gardens, that's because EmZoe's owner, Ann Nevens, is a San Franciscan who hasn't felt the urge to leave the old peninsula for three decades. Filled top to bottom with frescoes, the rooms are adorned in traditional Anatolian furnishings, some even boast hammam-like marbled bathrooms. At €135, EmZoe's best room is its small garden suite with adjoining terrace that features the area's stunning scenery.

For a room possibly more exotic than the surrounding neighborhood, **Kybele Hotel** (Yerebatan Cad. 35, 0212/511-7766, www. kybelehotel.com, €100) fits the bill with glass lamps hanging from every ceiling, including more than a thousand lamps in Kybele's lobby. A bit quirky at best, the veritable treasure trove inside is the accumulation of a trio of antiquing brothers whose Ottoman doors, calligraphic works, and other objets d'art are just a few items in a sometimes stuffy collection. Sprawling over two adjoining townhouses, the hotel reminds of the cavernous Basilica Cistern it sits above.

Over €150

Rated Europe's best hotel by *Travel + Leisure* in 2007 and second in the glossy's

best overall value rating, the **Four Seasons at Sultanahmet** (Tevkifhane Sok. 1, 0212/638-8200 or 800/332-3442, www. fourseasons.com/istanbul, nightly packages from €460) was refurbished from the rubbles of a prison and galvanized in celluloid by the hit movie *Midnight Express*. This 65-room neoclassical hotel offers, bar none, the most luxurious accommodations around the tourist magnets of Ayasofya and the Grand Bazaar, just a 15-minute dash away. True to form, the service at this location is immaculate.

For old world accommodations, nothing beats **(Yeşil Ev** (Kabasakal Cad. 5, 0212/517-6785, www.istanbulyesilev.com, from €180). Set along picturesque Kabasakal, abutting the Topkapı Palace's perimeter, the "Green House" is appropriated with turn-of-the-19th-century furnishings that never fail to transplant guests to the decadence of the Ottoman Empire. It was once an aristocratic abode, and its 19 rooms, layout, and facade have been flawlessly recreated with 21st-century comforts.

BAZAAR QUARTERS

For the dependable comfort of hotel chains and for lodging near the Grand Bazaar, the **(All Star Zurich Hotel** (Harikzadeler Sok. 37, 0212/512-2350, www.hotelzurichistanbul. com, from €110) fits the bill with its sumptuously modern rooms. Overwrought sightseers will also enjoy the Zurich's noted facilities, including an ample hammam, a rooftop terrace that doubles as the ideal tanning deck, throbbing nightclub, and fully appointed fitness center. Best of all, it is located right between the Bazaar and the historic Sultanahmet. Also to consider, the **All Star Golden Crown** (Piyerloti Cad. 40, Cemberlitaş, 0212/225-4204, www. allstarhotels.com, from €50) may be inexpensive, but it packs full amenities in all of its 35 rooms. Book rooms up high for great views of the Sea of Marmara and ask for the complimentary airport transfers.

BEYOĞLU AND TAKSIM

The District of Beyoğlu consists of about a dozen neighborhoods all sharing mid-19th-

ISTANBUL

century architecture in a modern hub of foot and vehicular traffic. Whether opting for the storied grand hotels of Tepebaşı (hilltop), a neighborhood undergoing a culinary renaissance; the chain lodgings over the bustle of Taksim Square, minutes away from posh Nişantaşı; or any of the smaller boutique hotels along narrow side streets, you'll be pleased if you like action.

€75-150

The pleasant surprise in Beyoğlu is **€ Galata Residence** (Bankalar Cad. & Hacı Ali Sok., Galata, 0212/292-4841, www.galataresidence. com, from €75). Its apart/hotel mini suites can easily accommodate smaller families for about €120. Designed with frugal adjoining kitchens, some of the top-floor two-bedroom apartments have views onto the Bosphorus, but the brouhaha emanating from the top-floor Ege & Rum Greek restaurant may not gel with those seeking serenity. With a quaint decor and not many extra frills, each room has a study with a convenient sofa bed. Built in 1881, this is Istanbul's first apartment building. Underground, the vaulted Café Mahzen's catacomb-y feel is a perfect place for tea.

For the swankiest of boutique hotels tucked in a Taksim side street, **€ Lush Hip Hotel** (Siraselviler Cad. 50, 0212/292-9566, www. lushhiphotel.com, from €125) is all about the trends. Its mundane facade belies the all-encompassing richness of its interior decor, with each room offering a different vibe from classic Ottoman to Warhol-*esque* pop art. With just 22 rooms, this is the national press' sweetheart, raking in more rosy reviews than it truly deserves. Though fascinating and easy on the wallet, its all-the-rage Brasserie proves a little noisy for overnight guests. The sometimes–snobby atmosphere may have you gasping for a breath of fresh air. On the upside, the hotel offers relaxing spa services starting at 60TL; all-inclusive packages for romantics, racing fans, or visiting weekenders; and modern theater Tuesdays, staged in one of Lush's bedrooms.

Le Grand Hôtel de Londres (Meşrutiyet Cad. 117, 0212/245-0670, www.londrahotel.

net, from €70) oozes with oddball, somewhat Gothic charm throughout its lobby and dining room, which have remained untouched since the early 1890s. The expected touches of the era, bold velvet curtains, gilded design, and grand piano bar delight guests seeking old "Stamboul" charm. The hotel is undergoing a haphazard, lengthy renovation, with about a dozen rooms refurbished and the rest decrepit at best. Ask to check out a few rooms before committing.

Tucked in a dead-end side street is Beyoğlu's most recent hotel addition: **Eklektik Galata** (Serdari Ekrem Cad. & Kadribey Cıkmazı 4, 0212/243-7446, www.eklektikgalata.com, from €95). Managed by owners Jeffrey Tucker and Can Petruzelli, the four-level brick townhouse boasts eight simple rooms, each either an experiment in color—like the eccentric Red Room, scarlet all the way to the rotary telephone; or outfitted in epoch-style—like the Sultan Room, which boasts a marble shower tub just inches away from a queen bed. Centrally located, the hotel is a brisk five-minute walk away from the tram to Taksim, the tramway to Sultanahmet Square, or the Karaköy embarcadero. A vanguard of the cultural revival of Beyoğlu, Eklektik is a stone's throw away from thimble-sized brasseries, underground, and music bars.

Hotel Butik Star (Sıraselviler Cad. 71, 0212/293-8080, www.butikstar.com, from €85) packs a punch, and may be the best refurbished townhouse to hang one's hat while in Istanbul. Expect tons of personal touches, such as a complimentary fruit basket upon arrival, an unrivaled breakfast bar, and five-star amenities, like sauna, indoor pool, and whirlpool tub. Best of all, it's a step away from busy Istiklal Caddesi and, with a beautifully-classic triple room that boasts views of the straits from an attached balcony (€125), it's not hard to see why this is Taksim's gem.

Over €150

Close to Taksim Square, the **Divan Oteli** (Cumhurriyet Cad. 2, 0212/315-5500, www. divan.com.tr, from €160) is a gem for chocolate lovers, made apparent through the aromas of freshly blended concoctions wafting from the patisserie just behind the hotel's entrance. The Divan brand equates to excellence in hospitality that extends to dozens of upscale restaurants, brasseries, and hotels throughout Turkey. And that's exactly what is to be expected at their flagship business in Istanbul, the first to boast five-star accommodations. The lobby is pure contemporary: sleek elegance peppered with colossal vases and planters filled with exotic floral bouquets. Albeit a bit tame on the decor and lacking a complimentary breakfast, the ample rooms do not disappoint with a collection of indigenous art.

Undergoing a major restoration, swanky (**Pera Palace Hotel** (Meşrutiyet Cad. 52, 0212/243-0737, www.perapalas.com, from €250) is being redefined thanks to a collection of Europe's best architects. Built in 1894 as the first European hotel in Turkey, the hotel once served as a chic terminus for distinguished Orient Express guests like Greta Garbo and Alfred Hitchcock. With the renovation, Pera emphasizes its historical significance in a semi-museum atmosphere that may prove too busy for those seeking respite. The Grand Hall and regal touches like the red-carpeted floor, crystal chandeliers, and thick marble columns throughout still greet guests. The rickety, gilded cage elevator remains for display purposes only, alongside newer versions. Opt for accommodations on the 2nd floor or higher for a view of the Golden Horn and beyond. Gastronomes enjoy Tepebaşı's top ranking brasseries and cafés.

BOSPHORUS

Refurbishing Istanbul's *yalı*'s (the waterside wooden mansions gracing the shores of the Bosphorus) has been a hobby for the very rich for more than 150 years. Some have done this elegantly. Others have gaudily splattered their wealth to impress the Joneses. But less than a handful were able to recreate the atmosphere that led to 19th-century French scribe Lamartine's eloquent prose: "The Bosphorus can be described as an avenue of water surrounded by mansions one more beautiful than the other. Believe me, if fate had granted you one of these, you would never think of leaving to your last day." Spending the night in one of these mansions is integral to the Istanbul experience, one that can be easier on the wallet than expected. An online search should reveal some advantageous packages to snatch that piece of Bosphorus real estate, just for a night or weekend. Most waterside hotels offer guests boat or car service to facilitate travel across the straits. Most of these boutique hotels start at €350.

European Shore

For secluded luxury, nothing beats (**Hôtel Les Ottomans** (Muallim Naci Cad. 68, Kuruçeşme, 0212/359-1500, www.lesottomans.com, from €800). Socialite Ahu Aysal dished out some €65 million of her family's fortune to turn the eyesore that was once the 19th-century Muhsinzade Paşa Waterside Mansion into the most exclusive and unique property. Epitomizing traditional Ottoman decor with handpicked antiques and luscious fabrics, 10 rooms, each a haven of serenity within itself, are packed with luxurious touches, like the latest in technology throughout. Astounding to the say the least, the Ottomans experience is heightened with the award-winning Claudalie Vinotherapie Spa, a 21,000-square-foot facility earmarked to allay the stresses of hours of sightseeing through individualized treatments. From butler to yacht services, and Chef Robyn Cooper's masterful tweaking of local gastronomy with international accents, the Ottomans is an unforgettable experience.

Not exactly on the water, but a location that hovers sublimely close to it, is the **W Istanbul** (Suleyman Seba Cad. 22, Beşiktaş, 0212/381-2121, www.whotels.com, from €340). It is the Starwood Hotels & Resorts' first foray into the fickle European market with their heavily branded hotel replication concept. That means that guest services (like the Sweat Fitness Centers and Whatever/Whenever concierge service) and accommodations have been streamlined worldwide to produce an identical experience from, say, New York to Doha. Totally neo-Zen, with a slate of lip-smacking colors, serenity rules supreme on the upper floors, while grooviness governs the ground floor with W's Living Room model, which boasts a library of flicks and tunes on demand, international noshes, and vibrant cocktails. Browse extensively online through hospitality wholesalers like Expedia and Travelocity, as W is one of the only hotels in town to extend an additional 10 percent discount if a lower room tariff on accommodations is found up to 24 hours prior to arrival.

If Dolmabahçe is the *Valide Sultan* (imperial mum) of the shores, then **Çırağan Kempinski Hotel** (Çırağan Cad. 32, Beşiktaş, 0212/326-4646, www.kempinski-istnabul.com, from €357) is the lady-in-waiting. Renovated in 2008 to enhance the palace's original oriental decor and peppered with the eclecticism so fashionable in the late 18th century, this is the real deal for those seeking imperial digs while in town. For the extremely wealthy, there is the ridiculously lavish 5,500-square-foot Grande Sultan Suite (€27,000 per night!), where the 24-hour butler and chef service cater to your every whim. But don't let that be a deterrent from enjoying one of the smaller rooms, all offering video and music on demand, as well as luxurious bathrooms. With the exception of the Park View room, all accommodations come with a view. Private cabanas on the lawn surrounding the hotel's pool, one of the largest in town, come with complimentary fresh fruit, bottled water, and even an assistant to wipe your sunglasses!

Also inaugurated in mid-2008, the decade-in-the-making **Four Seasons Istanbul at the Bosphorus** (Çırağan Cad. 268, Beşiktaş, 0212/381-4000, www.fourseasons.com/bosphorus, from €400) is the second luxury hotel chain to refurbish a colossal 19th-century waterside palace into a chic urban destination after Kempinski. Boasting a 10-room spa facility and quayside pools overlooking Asia's western edge, Istanbul's second Four Seasons location offers the spotless service that garnered its sister location in Sultanahmet the best

European hotel award from *Travel+Leisure*. The hotel's least expensive offering, the almost 500-square-foot Superior Room, may house a 42-inch LCD television, but what makes it unique is its luxurious floor-to-ceiling marble and ensuite bathroom with a soaking tub and separate glass-enclosed shower space.

Asian Shore

With a modern minimalist interior decor that belies its historic facade, the lobby of **A'jia Hotel** (Çubuklu Cad. 27, Kanlıca, 0216/413-9300, www.ajiahotel.com, from €255) welcomes guests with a cool white and beige palette. This is Istanbul's truly first high-class boutique hotel. The water views from 11 of A'jia's rooms are particularly superb due to the slight elevation the building enjoys. Guests are pampered with bathrobes, towels, and slippers of chunky Turkish cotton and goose-feather down comforters covering king size beds. Internet access and LCD flat television screens are some of the location's amenities, along with the property's small commuter boat.

The **Sumahan On The Water** (Kuleli Cad. 51, Çengelköy, 0216/422-8000, www.sumahan.com, from €280) is the only hotel of its kind refurbished from the rubble of a *rakı* (Turkish aperitif) refinery. Darker tones with contemporary architecture—think of a loft by the water—and dazzling views from every room were conceived by the architects, the Turco-American couple Nedret and Mark Butler, who incidentally also own the spectacular property. The reflection of the sun's rays bouncing from the water creates an ever-changing atmosphere within the Sumahan. Staying the night near the historic village of Çengelköy is an added bonus. Also opened in 2005, the Sumahan's incredibly popular Kordon restaurant is where Istanbul's elite gather to savor delectable fish and meze.   Situated in a refurbished aristocratic residence is the **Bosphorus Palace Hotel** (Yalıboyu Cad. 64, Beylerbeyi, 0216/422-0003, www.bosphoruspalace.com, from €250). Seemingly stuck in time, the neo-Ottoman residence offers 14 opulent guest rooms, dressed in the rich fabrics and antique furnishings reminiscent of the residence's heyday. Near Beylerbeyi Palace, this boutique hotel may be a continent away, but it does offer guests the option of a chauffeured boat or car service. Complimentary Internet connections, satellite television, secretarial services, and bathrooms equipped with robes of the thickest Turkish cotton, separate showers, and hair dryers, the Bosphorus is one of the most affordable hotels along the straits, and in this case, right below its majestic bridge.

ASIAN SIDE

Preferred for their proximity to Istanbul's Formula One race track and Sabiha Gökcen Airport, as well as the area's generally more suburban feel, the hotels on the city's Asian side offer a variety of accommodations. From five-star luxury to boutique and pensions, there are choices, albeit limited when compared to those on the European flank. Aside from the bragging rights of having stayed in an entirely different continent, do consider sojourning in the greener, slower-paced Asian flank, where culinary and shopping expeditions are on par with those on the opposite shores. Getting to the sights of Sultanahmet and Beyoğlu is just a very enjoyable, half-hour ferry ride away.

Under €125

Since its 2006 renovation, **Hotel My Dora** (Rhıtım Cad. & Recaizade Sok., Kadıköy; 0216/414-8350, www.hotelmydora.com, from €65) has been a breath of fresh air to the transportation hub of Kadıköy. Its relatively small, with just about three dozen rooms. Epitomizing quirkiness, each room boasts a different style of decor—from quirky industrialism with red splashes to classic furnishing replete with wooden accents throughout. Featuring spotless bathrooms, My Dora is a smart choice for discriminating travelers and those abiding to a strict budget. Choose a front-facing room on one of the top floors for stunning views of Sultanahmet and Haydarpaşa.

Steps away from Kadıköy's hectic open-air market, **Zumrut Hotel** (Rhıtım Cad. and Reşitefendi Sok., Kadıköy, 0216/450-0454,

www.kadikoyzumrutotel.com, from €55) is an economical solution for the travel savvy. With just two stars, it packs bare-bone accommodations with the necessities, like air-conditioning, satellite TV, and Wi-Fi access. Expect clean accommodations and a copious complimentary breakfast buffet.

Over €125

Nestled along what was once one of Istanbul's prized holiday resorts, **Hotel Suadiye** (Plaj Yolu 25, Suadiye, 0216/ 445-8424, info@hotelsuadiye.com, www.hotelsuadiye.com, from €170) is a hybrid of boutique charm with all the expected comforts of a hotel chain. Overlooking the Sea of Marmara and the picturesque Princes' Islands, the Suadiye offers quiet accommodations just steps away from the shopping and dining haven of Bağdat Caddesi. Spacious bedrooms, with a decor bordering on the gaudy, have large, tiled baths and direct-dial telephones. Aside from Wi-Fi, a myriad of business services and facilities are also offered.

About 15 miles from Istanbul's Sabiha Gökçen Airport, the **Prenses Hotel Bostancı** (Bostancı Değirmenyolu 24, Bostancı, 0216/577-2600, www.hotelbostanciprenses. com, from €140) offers five-star amenities, including a slew of wellness options—a hammam, sauna, Finnish bath, as well as an adjoining fitness center, indoor swimming pool, and whirlpool tub. For an additional boost, try the Vitamin Bar's refreshing juices or enjoy the spa's popular deep-tissue massage. Aside from complimentary Internet access, the Prenses is equally geared toward business as it is toward leisure. About 160 large, pristine rooms feature air-conditioning and satellite TV, as well as fully equipped bathrooms. Some of the upper suites peek out at the Sea of Marmara.

The Green Park Hotel Bostancı (Ali Nihat Tarlan Cad., Ertas Sok. 16, Içerenköy, 0212/444-7275, www.thegreenpark.com, from €125) is the first five-star hotel to open on Istanbul's Asian side. Bulging with amenities, the location is renowned for its lavish catered weddings, business conferences, and wellness facilities. Relaxing at The Green Park is easy with a fitness center that includes a sauna, hammam, whirlpool tub, massage services, and beauty centers. Picking up a game of table tennis is also an option, and so is a dip in the rooftop swimming pool. Vitas Restaurant quells even the biggest of appetites with its superb open buffet breakfast.

AIRPORT HOTELS

Attracting a large business clientele, airport accommodations are typically large international chains that provide streamlined and replicated rooms and facilities. If opting to stay in one of these hotels, check for conventions occurring during your stay, which may raise the price of rooms and the noise level of the hotel's public facilities. On the plus side, the commute to and from the airport is a snap. Also, American hotel chains like Marriott will honor AAA discounts, as well as those for seniors and military and government personnel, along with mileage or usage points accumulated with airlines or credit card companies.

For a no-brainer, stay at **(€ Istanbul International Airport Hotel** (International Terminal, Atatürk International Airport, 0212/465 4030, www.airporthotelistanbul.com, from €177) without even leaving the terminal. Awesome for in-transit passengers requiring a couple hours of rest, it's 51 "air side" guest rooms are within the airport's security zone, meaning no traffic hassles and international travelers only. Rented in two-hour increments, the accommodations are ideal to complete work, get a nap (lying down!), or shower away the stresses of a long transcontinental flight. The remaining 34 "land side" rooms serve the general public with the same

two-hour deal as well as overnight and extended stays. The hotel's fitness center also offers a popular 30-minute foot or body massage (60TL). Overlooking the tarmac, the Sky Restaurant's Turkish specialties are great for hotel guests, or travelers seeking a more serene dining environment than the airport's food court.

The **(€ Renaissance Polat** (Sahil Cad. 2, Yeşilyurt, 0212/414-1800, 800/219-1007, www.marriott.com, from €200) is a block of mirrored concrete, towering over the Sea of Marmara. All rooms and public spaces offer wireless, high-speed Internet and entertainment options. Although a bit stark, rooms are spacious and most offer floor-to-ceiling windows that provide uninterrupted sea views. Pick from five international dining and bar options, including the Champions American Sport Bar & Restaurant, which serves a typically American menu and has the necessary wide-screen TV to watch sports live. The Bierstube Restaurant boasts strictly German fare, the Daphne specializes in Mediterranean dishes, and the Royal China Chinese Restaurant caters to guests desiring Szechwan cuisine.

Istanbul's mainstay, the **Çınar Hotel** (Fener Mevkii, Yeşilköy, 0212/663-2900, www.cinarhotel.com.tr, from €195) was one of the first local hotels to combine luxury accommodations and superior catering in 1958. Ask to check accommodations prior to your stay to make sure the room meets your standards. The hotel may have gone down hill recently, but it redeems itself with its 2.5-mile-proximity to the airport, seaside views from most guest rooms, a pool and restaurant by the Sea of Marmara, and rare facilities, like a sandy beach and tennis courts.

Food

Eating in Turkey is half the fun of traveling through it. In cosmopolitan Istanbul, the national Anatolian cuisine, influenced by Arabic, Armenian, Georgian, Russian, Greek, and Mediterranean flavors, is only enhanced by the seafood that regional waters provide.

When in town, don't pass up the savors of Istanbul's renowned Ottoman cuisine or you will be denying yourself the rich and complex compilation of tastes and textures that emerged from the imperial kitchens of the Ottoman Palaces lining the Bosphorus. Istanbul's street fare is also peppered with interesting finds. One of them is the *balık ekmeği* (fish sandwich), found near the embarcaderos at Eminönü. The ubiquitous grilled-cheese toast, best with a steaming cup of fresh tea or a cold glass of *ayran* (yogurt drink), is another popular alternative. Ditto for the simple *simit* (a sesame encrusted tea ring). But the *dürüm* (think lavash bread filled with thin slices of lamb or chicken roasted on a spit) remains the crowd favorite for a quick and filling bite to eat. A midday stop at any busy diner around town reveals a menu chockfull of interesting dishes, flavors, and smells.

Primarily due to its location, Istanbul also offers eclectic fusions of various cuisines, as well as a myriad of fine restaurants specializing in classical European gastronomy or cutting-edge cuisine. If visitors crave the comfort food of home, typical American fast food chains, like McDonald's, Burger King, and KFC, are never too far from busy street corners.

Aside from the quick bite to eat, the historical peninsula of Sultanahmet is rather low on foodie destinations. Beyoğlu and areas beyond are where diners go for a feast, whether at a simple restaurant or a finer eatery. For the latest in cutting-edge gastronomy, head out in your best designer duds to Şişli's Nişantaşı or the Bosphorus's shores. There you'll find some of the world's best culinary destinations. Another good option is Bağdat Caddesi on the city's Anatolian side, where most bistros cluster on the drag's eastern end, toward Suadiye and Bostancı. The bottom line is that Istanbul is meant to be enjoyed one bite at a time. And with so many dining options, the only question will be what to try next.

For the rules of engagement: retailers and restaurateurs are required to post prices by law, however some eateries just list their dishes and not much else. If this is the case, do ask before ordering and ensure that the bill gels with previously quoted tariffs.

English and other languages may be spoken at upscale establishments, where reservations are helpful in securing space for that perfect table. Hotel concierges can be helpful in making reservations and suggesting where to dine. Fine-dining restaurants may impose a per person fee called a *kuver* (cover), which is basically a service fee that includes bottled water and bread. These fees are 3–10TL per head and are typically not listed on the menu, just on the final bill. Tips are included in the tab, but adding at least another five percent of the check, particularly if the service was attentive, guarantees a choice of seating or a table without reservations on the next trip, or even freebies after the meal. Tipping extra works every time, especially in Turkey.

Most fish restaurants and *meyhanes* (traditional taverns that dish out ample meze and *raki*) do not provide menus. Diners select cold or hot meze from enormous trays presented at tables, and their entrée from a refrigerated display case located at the entrance. Unless otherwise stated, upscale restaurants, which are generally located in hotels, serve food noon to 3 P.M. and 5 P.M. until at least 11 P.M. In contrast most eateries continue their service throughout the day. The average cost of a meal with alcohol is listed for fine dining establishments in this guide, while the rest of the suggestions throughout this book include the median price of an entrée.

Lastly, a good rule of thumb is not to feed the multitude of cats begging for scraps along terraces. Just throwing a piece of fish or even bread will summon felines and irk managers who try to stave them off.

SULTANAHMET AND VICINITY
Fusion

Sarnıç Restaurant (Soğukçeşme Sokak, 0212/512-4291, www.ayasofyakonaklari.com, 80TL) is set in a 1,500-year-old Roman cistern that flanks Topkapı Palace. It's striking, a bit Las Vegas-ish, with a roaring fire in a large rock chimney, backed by soaring colonnades with humongous domes aloft and hundreds of candle-lit tables that all combine to raise the expectancy of great things to come. The large space can get cantankerous, but the menu is above average. It proposes a meaty fusion of French and Turkish cuisines.

Abutting the lobby of the eponymous hotel, **Yeşil Ev** (Kabasakal Cad. 5, 0212/517-6785, www.istanbulyesilev.com, 50TL) appeals to a classy clientele seeking a romantic location and a serenity that's frankly hard to find in Sultanahmet. Marrying classical Turkish fare with the French touch that was all the hype in late 1980s Istanbul, main dishes like the duck á l'orange are a bit worn but pleasant. The atmosphere is a throwback to the city's near-orientalism heyday in the 19th century, with the sounds of contemporary Mendelssohn and Liszt piped in for added flair. The rear garden, with an ornate marble fountain, shady trees, and showy planters, makes for one of the loveliest settings in Sultanahmet.

Always a hit with returning tourists and locals in the know, **Albura Restaurant** (Yeni Akbiyik Cad. 26, 0212/517-9031, 30TL) offers a range of appetizing, reasonably priced mixed fare in a busy bistro-like atmosphere. The wooden ceiling, pocked with iron fixtures, and floor counterbalance a mixture of brick and ochre walls, creating the quirky and homey feel the managing owner, Bülent Yeter, was going for. The menu is as varied as the decor itself, from ample spinach crepes to kebabs and, for those who might be a bit homesick, yummy, tall brownies served with ice cream. Crowds tend to gather after 8:30 P.M., so be sure to arrive early.

Seafood

Compared with Istanbul's many neighborhoods, Sultanahmet is rather low on better dining options. There is, however, an exception to the rule: **(Balıkcı Sabahattin** (Seit Hasan Koyu Sok. 1, Cankurtaran, 0212/458-1824, www.armadahotel.com.tr/pg_en/restaurants5.asp, 50TL, reservations strongly recommended). This crowd favorite is tucked at the end of a dark, narrow street in the historic peninsula. It's reminiscent of a bistro in Provence with tables so close they almost touch; the energy, though, is truly Turkish. A darling of the international press, Sabahattin has galvanized a reputation among tourists and Istanbul's élite for well-prepared fish. The meze, however, are just decent. Their delectable *tahin* (sesame paste) ice cream simply must be sampled. Reserve a patio table and expect fastidious service with a smile.

Turkish

Konyalı Topkapı Sarayı Lokantası (Topkapı Palace, Sultanahmet, 0212/513-9696, www.konyalilokantasi.com, 60TL) has remained the gathering place for international heads of state since the days in the early 1970s when Richard Nixon, Queen Elizabeth II, and the late Benazir Bhutto supped here. Its authentic Ottoman cuisine, which includes lots of pricey kebabs, is prepared just steps away from the imperial kitchens from which it originated. The main dining room is elegantly, and fancily, tailored. The adjoining bistro, however, offers similar fare at a fraction of the price, as well as great sea views.

The four-course daily menu at **(Cooking Alaturka** (Akbiyik Caddesi 72a, Sultanahmet, www.cookingalaturka.com, 0212/458-5919, 50–70TL) offers foreigners a succulent overview of Turkish cuisine. Grand chef and expat owner Eveline Zoutendijk has created the pint-size, airy restaurant that features three set menus with limited á la carte options. There's also a collection of strictly Turkish foodstuff available for purchase, like red pepper flakes and pomegranate extract.

Quick and Inexpensive

Mention Sultanahmet to locals and the first topic of conversation will be *köfte* (meatball), but only those served at **Tarihi Sultanahmet Köfteci** (Divanyolu Cad. 12, 0212/520-0566, www.sultanahmetkoftesi. com, 15TL, no credit cards) are worth mentioning. Packed everyday noon–10 P.M., the restaurant has a slim menu—but who needs selection when the main draw is so sumptuous? Who knew ground lamb with breadcrumbs could be blended to a pulp, then grilled to such perfection? Obviously Selim Usta did when he began serving those walnut-sized patties more than a century ago. Try the *bir büçük porsyon* (one-and-a-half portions) with a mouth-watering white bean salad, best enjoyed with *limon* rather than vinegar, and the watered down yogurt drink of *ayran*. Top it all off with a hefty slice of delicious *irmik helvası* (sweetened semolina with pine nuts). The food is definitely worth the wait.

Tucked behind Sultanahmet Camii are two notable restaurants. The first is **Doy Doy** (Şifa Hamamı Sok. 13, 0212/517-5188, 10–15TL), which features inexpensive classical Turkish home food. Known for its kebab, Doy Doy stands out with its lamb moussaka, served with loads of fresh bread. The homemade baklava, not overly sweetened, and *lokum* (Turkish Delight) are also on the menu. Typically reserved for heavy smokers, the bottom floor tends to get noisy; opt instead for Doy Doy's rooftop terrace for uninterrupted views of the entire promontory. The other restaurant is **Buraha 93** (Şifa Hamamı Sok. 13, 0212/518-1511, 15TL). Buraha 93 is known for its eponymous special kebab of grilled lamb morsels, served with bread baked fresh on the premises. There's also salads, pizzas and *pides* (oval shaped dough slathered with cheese, meat, or sausage and eggs baked). Dervish shows or live music most summer evenings are the added bonus.

AROUND BEYOĞLU

Cafés

Executives and diplomats often frequent **Ist** (Istiklal Cad. 10/12, Taksim, 0212/251-7944, www.istcafé.com, 15TL) for its 25 breakfast entrées and great coffee. Its refreshing homemade lemonade in several flavors, such as mint, guava, and blackberry, and the iced rosehip juice are great reasons to make a pit stop after hours of sightseeing.

Fusion

For a smart, mid-priced restaurant, try **Kitchenette** (ground floor of The Marmara Istanbul, Tak-I Zafer Sok., Taksim Meydanı, 0212/292-6862, 20TL) in the heart of Taksim. It's been packed daily since its opening in Spring 2008. Try their avant-garde hamburger, which consists of a grilled patty of ground lamb and beef, served on buttered homemade bread, packed high with sautéed spinach, cinnamon onions, Kars gruyere, tomatoes, and pickles. The hamburger comes with a side of coleslaw, French fries, and an impressively delicious leek sauce. Kitchenette is the seventh location opened by the Istanbul Doors Restaurant group, Turkey's premiere entertainment concept chain. Kitchenette outdoes its counterparts by consistently providing attentive service and a fresh menu. This is a great breakfast, lunch, or dinner alternative as well as a great spot to experience Taksim Square's happy hour buzz. There are truly no favorites here; the salads, sandwiches, and seafood have yet to disappoint. The side terrace on Meşelik Sokak is a great place to people-watch over coffee and a slice of chestnut cheesecake.

On a side street, **Tuus** (Teşvikiye Cad. 123, 0212/224-8181, closed Sun., 50TL) has remained one of the "in" eateries for more than two years—quite an accomplishment considering that six months is the average. Among its mainly Mediterranean menu, the fish served with eggplant and beef ribs is unusual and awakens the taste buds. Call a few days ahead to reserve a terrace table for an alfresco dinner under and among the stars.

International

Tired of Turkish food? Gather your chopsticks and try the Japanese, Vietnamese, and Thai influenced Asian spread at ◖ **Wanna** (Meşrutiyet Cad. 151, Tepebaşı, 0212/243-1794, closed Mon., 80TL). Truly the place to be seen, Wanna started the culinary revival of Tepebaşı and for good reason. The food is just marvelous, and so is the decor. With conceptual neon lighting over the tables and video art projections splashing the walls, the restaurant is a new concept that attracts Istanbul's well-to-do without being too snooty. Come 11 P.M., the bar is roaring (it's open untill 4 A.M.). On weekends, the venue welcomes DJ's of international fame.

Gracing a corner in busy Beyoğlu, the new **La Brise Brasserie** (Asmalı Mescid Cad. 28, 0212/244-4846, 60TL) combines the cuisine of Alsace-Lorraine in a Parisian bistro atmosphere. A meal of steak and *pommes frites,* among tablecloths, cherry-wood and brass appointed decor, and the sounds of Edith Piaf, will help those who've overdosed on Turkish culture.

Ottoman

A fixture in Taksim since 1888 for some of the most sumptuous Ottoman and Turkish fare in town, **Haci Abdüllah** (Istiklal Cad. and Sakızağacı Sok. 17, 0212/293-8561, www.haci-abdullah.com.tr, 40TL) is filled with shelves of homemade fruit compotes that make their way into the house's desserts. The *Húnkar beğendi* (tender chunks of lamb roasted with tomatoes and served over eggplant purée) is one of the best in town. And so is the traditional *turşu* (crisp and slightly garlicky pickled vegetables). Usually hard to find, the sun-dried eggplant *dolma* will have you begging for seconds.

Regional Turkish

In Nişantaşı, ◖ **Komşu** (Vali Konağı Cad., Işık Apt 8B, 0212/224-9666, www.komsu-kebap.com, 18TL) serves truly authentic Adana cuisine, which is not the spin on classical Turkish cuisine that impresses the local fickle socialites. Try the southeastern specialty

of *şalgam,* a concoction of juices of root vegetables touted as a great blood cleanser, with the *acılı kebab,* another Adana specialty of grilled oh-so spicy ground lamb kebabs. Request a rear window table or one at the hip and lush terrace below.

With more traditional entrées to choose from than any other restaurant on the strip, ◖ **Otantık** (Istiklal Cad. 170, 0212/293-8451, www.otantikay.com, until 4 P.M., 10TL) is renowned for its homemade *yufkas* (paper-thin dough rolled and cooked by local women right at the entrance). Filled with kilims and pillow-backed banquettes, Otantık's window tables on the upper floors are ideal for watching hectic Istiklal below. The thick lentil soup is a mainstay and warming during Istanbul's chilly season. Follow it up with a *gözleme* (thick crepe filled with a choice of lamb, feta, or spinach) and a crisp shepherd's salad (tomato, cucumbers, onions, and parsley).

The new kid on the block in Tepebaşı, the **Istanbul Culinary Institute** (Meşrutiyet Cad. 59, Tepebaşı, 0212/251-2214, www.istanbulculinary.com, 12TL) is part school, part Turkish gastronomical diplomat, and part restaurant. What owner Hande Bozdogan has done superbly, though, is reawaken local taste buds to the incredible richness of Anatolian cuisine. The atmosphere is of a simple bistro with a clean and minimalist Nordic décor. The hit on any day in this charming eatery is the *table d'hôte*—French for the day's prix-fixe menu. Visit their website for the daily offering, or simply show up. One thing not to miss is ICI's light and creamy yogurt and their semolina dessert of *irmik helvasi.*

Dirt cheap and always good, **Köfteci Hüseyin** (Kurabiye Sok. 7/A, 0212/243-7637, 15TL) is a hole in the wall that caters to blue collar workers in a back street of Beyoğlu. Since Hüseyin's untimely passing in 2005, his progeny carry on his vision of good *köftes* (meatballs) at a reasonable price. A limited, but delicious menu of *köfte,* white bean salad, and shepherd salad are served here, a part of town that recently saw only daytime pedestrian traffic. Beyoğlu's revival has extended to Kurabiye

Sokak, and with it outside seating has appeared at various eateries on this strip.

Seafood

Touted in the press as the pearl of the Fish Bazaar, **Vesta Balık Restorani** (Balık Pazarı and Sahne Sok. 17, 0212/252-1073, www.vestabalik.com, 40TL) lures diners away from La Rue de Péra's average fish restaurants. With a fresco overlooking the few interior tables of this tiny eatery, the atmosphere is pure Mediterranean and somewhat serene, except for the braying of vendors and the incessant foot traffic on this 150-year-old shopping artery. With more than 30 meze choices, including the tasty Armenian appetizer of *topik* (a mixture of chick peas, currants, onions, and tahini spiced with cumin), owner Bünyamin Bardak ensures that only the best catch of the day will grace his customers' plates. Vesta also offers a large selection of grilled meats, as well as a crisp Mediterranean salad for vegetarians.

For a traditional *meyhane* (Turkish tavern) experience, **◖ Refik** (Aşmalımescit Cad. Sofyalı Sok.10/1, Tunel, 0212/243-2834, 50TL) is an institution. Nestled along one of lower Beyoğlu's winding streets, Refik specializes in the Black Sea's finned bounty, such as succulent anchovies, floured and deep-fried. (By the way, they're best eaten whole, heads and all.) In addition, this place turns out a great *lakerda* (salted tuna, sliced thin) and *pilaki* (a broad bean and olive oil concoction to die for). Get there by 7 P.M. and ask for an outside table if you'd like to avoid the smoke-filled indoor dining room.

ALONG THE SHORES OF THE BOSPHORUS
Fusion

The restaurant at **Hôtel Les Ottomans** (Muallim Naci Cad. 68, 0212/359-1500, www.lesottomans.com, 100–150TL) offers, bar none, one of the ultimate gastronomical experiences along the Bosphorus. Where most of Istanbul's finer dining establishments look to the East for inspiration, Australian chef Robyn Cooper combines Western and Turkish influences to prepare fish she handpicks daily. Imbuing the palate with an explosion of texture and flavors, the duck liver terrine—suffused with apple jelly, red onion preserve, and port—is to die for. The popular cold starter of salmon and sea bass carpaccio is sliced so thin it melts in your mouth.

If *Sex in the City* were to be filmed in Istanbul, the long-awaited **◖ Zuma London** (Salhane Sok. 7, Ortaköy, 0212/236-2296, www.zumarestaurant.com, 180TL) would be the perfect hangout for Carrie Bradshaw and her gal pals. A neo-Zen inspired lounge and bar grace the upper floor, while the restaurant boasts a stylish, neon-bathed Sushi Bar and Robata Grill. Zuma's forte is their presentation of the informal Japanese culinary experience of Izakaya, in which a series of small plates are served for all to try. The Istanbul location, in the opinion of the local clientele, surpasses the original location in London, thanks to the wonderful scenery afforded by the straits below. Try their signature dish, spicy barbecued beef tenderloin, with Sakura (a raspberry infused sake mixed with cucumber, vodka, and lime).

Ottoman

Armed with a credit card, head for **Tuğra** (Çırağan Cad. 32, Beşiktaş, 0212/236-4646, 7–11 P.M., 100–150TL) for what is arguably the best fine dining Ottoman cuisine—and views—in town. Taste the dishes that made sultans in this very palace swoon, like *kabuni* (sweet cinnamon-y Albanian rice pilaf with raisins) and *Mahmudiye* (chicken baked with almonds, apricots, and black pepper). To complete the over-the-top experience, savor a candy stick rolled at the table from the *macun,* an authentic sweets trolley that winds through the tables of this gastronome's paradise of opulence.

Seafood

Popular **Garaj** (Yeniköy Cad. 30, Tarabya, 0212/262-0032, www.garajrestaurant.com, 60TL) is located in a bay on the Bosphorus's northern European shores. Packed daily since 1962—my mom still swoons over the grilled swordfish kebab she had here in 1974—Garaj is the place for delicate *ciroz* (salted, dried mackerel) and octopus salad in olive oil. Once the faraway playground for the rich, this place in Tarabya is well worth the 30-minute drive from Taksim.

Real *Istanbullus* know where to eat their fish, and those who can afford the time travel to the adjoining Asian outposts of Beylerbeyi and Çengelköy, both noted for their superior catch, particularly *palamut* (a tender tuna), and the meaty mussels that line their banks. Aside from a plethora of popular fish stands, there are two eateries, run by the same owners, that consistently lure the illustrious and off-the-clock food critics with simple, yet delicious versions of the local catch. Occupying part of the lobby of Sumahan on the Water, (**Kordon Balık** (Kuleli Sok. 51, Çengelköy, 0216/321-0473, www.kordonbalik.com, 80TL) serves up enticing appetizers like a chunky *paçanga börek* (fried wrap filled with cured pastrami and melted cheese) and what is arguably the best fried calamari in town. It all takes place in a modern Turkish-style, parquet-floor bistro, boasting a fair wine list of national vintages. Call ahead to reserve a waterfront table from which to view the sunset over the Golden Horn or the spectacular nocturnal lightshow of the Bosphorus Bridge. Kordon has excellent service, as does its sister restaurant **Çengelköy Iskele Restaurant** (Çengelgöy Iskelesi Meydanı 10A, 0216/321-5505, www.cengelkoyiskelerestaurant.com, 50TL). A toned down version of Kordon, this fish eatery offers a rooftop balcony that's literally over the straits. You may find yourself seated next to a Koç or a Sabancı, Turkey's top two industrialist families whose members reside nearby. Do head out to Çengelköy Iskele Restaurant for lunch if time allows; weekend evenings tend to be packed and rather loud at this location. Also, stick with Kordon if you dig wine.

KUZGUNÇUK AND BEYLERBEYI
Seafood
The waters around Beylerbeyi, and its neighboring fishing village of Çengelköy, are famous for the abundance of mussels that crowd the canal wall. Restaurateurs for decades have battered and deep-fried the mollusk to perfection. Sample the *midiye dolma*—an herby and nutty rice concoction piled high on the mussel still in its shell. Either way, both are a great starter to a grilled bonito or a pan-fried serving of the enormous turbots or bluefin tuna at **Villa Bosphorus** (Iskele Cad. 14, 0216/318-6810, www.beylerbeyivillabosphorus.com, 35–50TL with drinks). From there, visit the tiny souvenir shops by the port or take 90 minutes to stroll **Beylerbeyi Palace** (Cayirbasi Cad., 0216/321-9320, 9 A.M.–4 P.M. daily, 5TL).

Cafés
Enjoy the relaxing rhythm of the Bosphorus's flow over aromatic Turkish coffee served in a traditional, tiny copper pot at **Çınaraltı Kahve** (at the crossing of Paşalimanı and Icadiye Caddesis, 0216/422-1036, 6 A.M.–11 P.M.). It's rated the second best coffeehouse in Turkey, according to the national media.

ASIAN SIDE
Ottoman
For authentic classic dishes, **Eski Osmanlı Mutfağı** (Bağdat Cad. 340, Şaşkinbakkal, 0216/358-8545, 30TL) offers about 36 original choices that include succulent Swiss chard dolma and a finger-licking, oven-baked chicken and eggplant dish.

Quick and Inexpensive
A favorite of the international press, (**Çiya** (Güneşlibahçe Sok. 48B, Kadıköy, 0216/336-3013, www.ciya.com.tr, 20TL) boasts hundreds of Turkish specialties. More of a food anthropologist than a chef per se, Gaziantep-born owner Musa Dağdeviren continues to add to Çiya's culinary anthology. It not only translates into good home-cooked fare in a chic bistro atmosphere, but also a tantalizing taste-bud trip into Turkey's nether regions. There are no recommendations, as the daily menus, like fruit-based meat stews and freshly-made baklava, continue to astound.

In Üsküdar, **Kanaat Lokantası** (Selmanipak Cad. 25, 0216/341-5444, www.kannatlokantasi.com, 15TL) has dedicated itself to *ev yemekleri* (or good ole heart-warming home food) since 1933. Turkey's national dish of white beans stewed in tomato sauce with sporadic lamb chunks, in addition to another dozen of the chef's daily specialties, is found here. Don't expect much, aside from fast, friendly service and crowds.

Specializing in slices of tender spit-roasted lamb, served with tomato sauce and melted butter over chunks of fresh pita bread, **Niyazibey** (Ahmediye Meydanı 1, Üsküdar, 0216/310-4821, www.niyazibey.com.tr, 15TL) never disappoints. Also great here is *perde pilavı*, a complex dish traditionally served at weddings throughout Anatolia. The dish is decorated with a crust that symbolizes a new couple's house: nuts represent the couple themselves; and currants, all their future progeny. And a kebab house would be remiss without a *küneyfe*, a baked dessert consisting of kashkaval cheese wrapped in hair-thin pastry dough and sweetened with sugar.

Seafood

A great place for meze, **Ⓒ Foça** (Turgut Özal Bulvarı 110, Küçükyalı, 0216/519-8686, www.focarestaurant.com, 50TL) is reminiscent of the battery of boats that bop atop the waves just across the way from the restaurant itself. A walk inside the main cabin of this pseudo ship reveals both interior seating and a large terrace. Opt for the latter, as the rear of this eatery flanks a railway that rattles noisily with the passage of each train. No one does *lakerda* (thick chunks of fried calamari) like Foça, and no fish has ever disappointed. But, unless you're into chocolate omelets, stay away from their soufflé.

For the feel and spread of an authentic

meyhane (Turkish tavern), head to **Ⓒ Koço** (Moda Cad. 265, Moda, 0216/336-0795, 50TL). The chef in attendance, Muharrem Usta, is famous for turning out an Albanian liver—a meze that is first floured, then sautéed and served with sliced onions with sumac. Most fish on offer is good, but they excel at preparing the smaller ones, like anchovies. For a divine sweet, try their chocolate soufflé, slathered with fresh cream and powdered sugar. And don't forget to light a candle for luck at the small Orthodox sanctuary below the restaurant.

Turkish

For those who've developed a hankering for Anatolian meat concoctions and *lahmacuns* (ground lamb appetizers), there is **Ⓒ Develi Kebap** (Münir Nurettin Selçuk Caddesi, 216/418-9400, www.develikebap.com, 40TL), which packs its clientele like sardines on weekends. Set along the docks of Istanbul's most luxurious marina, its location doesn't hurt either. There's a dressy casual atmosphere here, which can get cankerous on Friday nights. The hectic kitchen, edged by a kiddy playroom, produces an amazing *içli köfte* (deliciously stuffed bulgur meatball) and *fındık lahmacun* (small version of the tasty, pizza-like ground lamb appetizer).

A block north of Bağdat Avenue in Göztepe, **Adana Yüzevler** (Göztepe Istasyon Cad. 17, Göztepe, 0216/355-1880, www.yuzevler.com, 40TL) serves the best of Adana in Istanbul. The meze options feature tons of herb dishes dressed with refreshingly sweet pomegranate concentrate and olive oil, as well as a garlicky tehina dip. Order a *karışık porsyion* for a sample platter of meat. Be forewarned, though, the food concocted by the Aydoğdu's—the team of siblings that own and run this busiest of three locations—is on the spicy side.

Information and Services

TOURIST AND TRAVEL INFORMATION

While there are loads of tourist offices throughout town, the most helpful ones, aside from the locations at Atatürk International and Sabiha Gökçen Airports, are in the heart of Sultanahmet (Divanyolu Caddesi, 0212/518-1802), steps away from the Hippodrome, and the Taksim branch (Taksim Meydanı, 0212/245-6876). There are also smaller offices in Beyazit Meydanı (near the Grand Bazaar, 0212/522-4902); Karaköy Seaport (0212/249-5776); and the one run out of the Hilton Hotel Arcade (0212/233-0592). For emergencies or any pressing issue, the **Tourism Police** (0212/527-4503) can be of some assistance. Most offices are open 9 A.M.–5 P.M. daily, but the hours are often extended depending on foot traffic. In true Turkish hospitality, staffers assist with most requests; maps and general information are also available. A good resource before departure is the American version of the Turkish Ministry's website (www.tourismturkey.org), but its British version (www.goturkey.com) is infinitely more comprehensive.

There are a couple of magazines that list events around town. *Time Out Istanbul* is a trendy monthly catering to Istanbul's expatriate community with listings on popular dining and entertainment establishments of all genres, from art to alternative lifestyles. The other, *The Guide: Istanbul* is a bimonthly that provides extensive restaurant listings and critiques, as well as art reviews and interesting articles.

Several online resources, including the exhaustive **www.mymerhaba.com,** are recommended reading before departure. Register for their weekly newsletter for the latest announcements, from arts and movies to concerts, art exhibitions, and popular festivals. Geared more toward travelers, **www.istanbulcityguide. com** frequently updates its thorough schedule of events occurring in town around the year. For those who prefer to discover the city by clicking through websites rather than leafing through a guidebook, there's **http://english. istanbul.com.**

To get a grasp of the lay of the land, check out Google's interactive maps online for arguably the most thorough layout. Saving a file on a desktop and transferring it to a smart phone or portable media player, such as an iPod, allows for quick reference. Once in town, paper maps can be purchased at either information kiosks or bookstores listed in the text.

Luggage Storage

Better lodgings allow for safe luggage storage and so do most transportation hubs. Located in the international arrival terminal of **Atatürk International Airport,** the check-in **Emanet Bagaj** facility holds lost luggage in addition to storing it—ensure that it's locked—for a daily fee ranging from 6–12TL. Its smaller counterpart on the Asian side, **Sabiha Gökçen International Airport** also provides the same services. **Haydarpaşa Train Station** offers automatic lockers for up to 36 hours, and for as little as 3–14TL.

Laundry

Most hotels have laundry services. Attendants at **Star Laundry** (Yeni Akbiyik Cad. 18, Sultanahmet, 0212/638-2302, 3TL/kilo) are very helpful. Good dry cleaners are very expensive; should you need one, stick with your hotel if possible—it probably offers lower rates.

MONEY
Currency Exchange and Banks

Both Atatürk International and Sabiha Gökçen Airports have several Automated Teller Machines (ATMs) and exchange bureaus, where most currencies can be converted into Turkish liras (TL). Some may even assist travelers in borrowing cash from credit cards.

One of Turkey's booming sectors, banking, rebounded with revenge since the post-2001 market crash. Particularly in Istanbul, streets are teeming with banks and ATMs. During banking hours (9 A.M.–5 P.M. Mon.–Sat.), ensure safety by using ATMs located inside most banks. Be wary of any loitering pickpockets if using the facility's outside withdrawal machines and try to restrict transactions to your card's issuer, like HSBC or ING, to avoid hefty non-customer fees and double charges. Aside from keeping all receipts, try to limit cash withdrawals from credit cards to **Turkiye Iş Bankası** (Beyoğlu Branch, on Istiklal Cad. 298, 0212/251-8129, www.isbank.com.tr, 9 A.M.–12:30 P.M. and 1:30–5:30 P.M.). The largest and most reliable bank in Turkey, Iş Bankası, maintains broad agreements with most international banks, and with Bank of America in particular. Banking in Sultanahmet can be tricky, as most facilities are located outside the historical peninsula and will require some transit time to get to. Also, try to remove your card as soon as possible from ATMs, as some machines are notorious for swallowing cards after five seconds to protect their clientele from loss or theft.

In a country where most real estate is listed in either dollars or euros, changing currency is prevalent. Exchange bureaus charge little commission, if any, to compete for both tourist and local funds. To exchange foreign notes, head to any of the *döviz bürosu* (9 A.M.–7 P.M. daily, open later during peak season), found in Sultanahmet, Taksim, Karaköy, Eminönü, and along the major thoroughfares. Also, kiosks can be found at Atatürk International Airport (24 hours daily); Esenler Otogar (8:30 A.M.–11 P.M. daily); and Sirkeci Train Station (9 A.M.–5 P.M. daily, travelers' checks accepted). Keeping in mind that bank and hotel exchange rates are so steep in comparison that even with a small cut or a slightly higher exchange rate you'll lose in *kuruş* (pennies) rather than in Turkish liras by swapping your dollars at an exchange bureau. As a rule, keep in mind that the more touristy the area, the greater the commission. Most post offices—**PTT's**—also convert foreign cash at a fee; there's one located next to Sultanahmet Camii (Topkapı Place, 0212/513-3958, 9 A.M.–5 P.M. daily, April–Sept.) with a convenient ATM located next door.

For wire transfers, **Western Union** operates through 3,046 locations in Turkey, among which are Ziraat Bank, Finansbank, MNG Bank, Oyak Bank, Fortis Bank, Deniz Bank, and all PTT offices. Respecting the 9-to-5 schedule, with the exception of Sunday, services at any of one of these firms' branches should be textbook, and so should be finding English-speaking staff.

Traveler's checks are a thing of the past, and are more of a hassle and certainly more expensive to convert when traveling through Turkey. Few banks will honor travelers' checks; those who do may end up referring the bearer to another branch. Once there, don't be surprised if a fee of up to $20, or as much as 20 percent of the check, and a passport—not a photocopy—is required to redeem the note's face value.

Credit Cards
As is the case throughout Turkey's larger cities and popular coastlines, Istanbul shop owners accept all forms of Visa and MasterCard for credit or debit transactions. American Express is honored only at upscale hotels and eateries. Cashiers may request that you punch in a pin when charging, as demands traditional usage in Turkey, but just inform them that the card is *şifresiz* (without a code) to complete the transaction. Try to restrict credit card usage to hotels, transportation, and entertainment, such as fine dining and theater tickets, and keep all receipts in the event that a surcharge or double charge occur. If a credit card receipt is misplaced, there's no need to worry since its digits, except for the last four, are blurred, as is customary in the U.S. For purchases, remember that cash enables bargaining.

Theft and Money Scams
Airport taxis usually carry more change than those crisscrossing the city, but make sure that your pocket is stocked with at least a couple of 20-lira notes, just in case. Passing fake currency, mostly larger bills, is one of the latest frauds perpetrated by cabbies, and other ruthless business owners. The scam goes something

like this: You offer a 50-lira note to pay for the fare and the shady cab-driver hands back a counterfeit 50-lira bill, claiming that he doesn't have change after leafing through a large stack of money. So authentic are the forgeries that the unknowing traveler can be duped out of several notes at a time.

Thorough door checks at all entrances of Istanbul's Atatürk International Airport deter somewhat scrupulous characters from entering the building, but luggage snatching is not unheard of. Neophytes to Turkey should practice extreme caution when stepping out of the airport, as vehicular traffic can be overwhelming.

COMMUNICATIONS
Mail
To purchase stamps, send mail, make calls, or receive telegrams, the main post office, **PTT** (Yeni Posthane Cad., 8 A.M.–5:30 P.M. daily) is located in Sirkeci on Yeni Posthane Caddesi. Other main branches are open fewer hours (8:30 A.M.–12:30 P.M. and 1:30–5 P.M.) and are located in Taksim (Cumhuriyet Caddesi, Gezi Dükkanları 2, 0212/292-3650); Kadıköy (Caferağ Mah., Damga Sok. 1, 0216/377-4410); Üsküdar (Hakimiyeti Milliye Cad.); and Beşiktaş (Ortabahçe Cad. 26/B, 0212/236-9870). There are also smaller branches throughout the city that typically open 8:30 A.M.–3 P.M. Monday–Friday.

Internet Access
Aside from providing telephone and fax services, most hotels will provide free usage of the Internet from a desktop, located either in a lobby or lounge. If traveling with a laptop, surfing the Internet is as easy as requesting the password (*şifre*) in most small and medium-sized hotels and in some restaurants and cafés. Around Sultanahmet, you'll find the **Istanbul Cyber Café** (Cayiroğlu Sok. 9; 0212/516-5528) adjacent to Sultan Ahmet Mosque. Most American-style coffee shops, like Starbucks, have Wi-Fi access through Türk Telekom, which charges an hourly fee of 6TL after the initial registration.

Telephones
A new **cell phone** and **SIM card**—if your phone happens to be unlocked and can operate in 900–1800 Mhz bands—can be purchased at a competitive price upon arrival at either the Vodafone or Avea kiosks along the exit gate of the international arrival terminal at Atatürk International Airport. For a no-frill or used cell phone, there are loads of merchants around city centers like those along Ankara Caddesi, just north of Sultanahmet towards the port of Eminönü. The underground marketplace of Karaköy, alongside the port in Beyoğlu, also has merchants that sell phones. Purchase a prepaid starter pack from Vodafone, Avea, or TurkCell. The pack consists of a phone number, SIM card, and a slew of services and instructions on how to use them. There are also shops that specialize in unlocking locked GSM phones for as little as 15TL. Reach a land telephone line on the European side of Istanbul by dialing 0212; call a number located on the Asian shores by dialing 0216.

EMERGENCY SERVICES
For urgent ambulatory services, dial 112; law enforcement, 115; or the gendarmerie, 156. The fire department can be reached at 110. All emergency numbers provide English-speaking staff, and may also have operators conversant in other languages. If a crime has been committed against your person, such as theft, make a report at the local *karakol* (police station). The law enforcement branch dedicated to serve foreigners in Istanbul is the **Turizm Polisi** (Yerebatan Cad. 6, Sultanahmet, 0212/528-5369). Other police stations that may be helpful depending on your location are: Beyoğlu (Karaköy Polis Merkezi, 0212/292-5758) and Kadıköy (Iskele Polis Merkezi, 0216/336-4339).

If dialing 112 for ambulatory services, the request will be handled on a first-come first-served basis. To avoid a potential wait, the private company **Medline** (0212/282-0000) responds to emergencies with fully equipped and certified medical personnel. Medline transfers and care start at 120TL. Hospitals treat emergencies in the order of how critical they are. The U.S. Department of State recommends the following centers: **Koç American Hospital** (Güzelbahçe Sokak, Nişantaşı, 0212/311-2000) and **Metropolitan Florence Nightingale Hospital** (Cemil Aslan Güder Sok. 8, Gayrettepe, 0212/288-3400). For clinical services, the state-run **Taksim First Aid Hospital** (Sıraselviler Cad. 112, Taksim, 0212/252-4300) deals with emergencies and refers patients to hospitals for continued care. In Beyoğlu, the **German Hospital** (Sıraselviler Cad. 119, 0212/293-2150) is not only geared to resolve most emergencies, but also excels as a dental and eye clinic. On the Asian side, **Acıbadem Hospital** (Tekin Sok. 18, Kadıköy, 0216/544-4444) is also suggested by the American Embassy. All of these facilities are open 24 hours a day and, aside from Taksim First Aid Hospital, expect first-rate care, equipment, and facilities. If carrying the recommended traveler's health insurance, the bills are forwarded to the carrier for processing. If uninsured, the hospitals listed here bill emergencies at about 150TL.

Aside from filling prescriptions, pharmacies throughout Turkey can provide a range of medical services, such as topical treatment of cuts and burns as well as injections. Pharmacies throughout the city are required to post the address of the *nöbetçi eczane* (24-hour pharmacy) on their front door. You can also call the **Association of Pharmacists** (0212/6336-9964 or 118) for this information. To purchase medication in Beyoğlu, head to **Yeşilcam Eczanesi** (Istiklal Caddesi, Ayhan Işık Sok. 7/A, 0212/292-0888).

The **American Consulate** (Kaplıcalar Mavkii 2, Istiniye, 0212/335-9000, amcongen1@tnn.net, 8–11:30 A.M. and 1:30–3 P.M.) assists with a variety of issues. Visit their website at istanbul.usconsulate.gov and click on the U.S. Citizen Services tab. An attendant on duty answers calls after business hours.

Getting There

AIR
Atatürk International Airport
Istanbul's Atatürk International Airport (0212/465-5555, www.ataturkairport.com) is situated in Yeşilköy, about 17 miles west of the city center. Turkey's largest air transportation hub and Europe's 11th most important, it accommodates two large terminals: one for international flights, with a level for arrivals and another for departures; the other is earmarked for both incoming and departing domestic flights. With more than 20 million passengers landing on an annual basis, the international terminal, inaugurated in 2001, is highly efficient and relieved the once-solitary, crowded terminal that previously handled all air traffic. Unlike other European airports, the luggage carts are not free, and require the insertion of one Turkish lira. So, head straight for the exchange booth in the baggage claims hall before retrieving your luggage. Along with the expected restaurants, cafés, and executive lounges, services like car rental companies, a florist, currency exchange kiosks, banks and ATMs, a photographer, hairdresser, travel agent, and even a hotel within the airport's security zone are available for passengers.

There are various options for transferring to the city centers. Some hotels provide convenient free transfers for guests who book three or more nights. By far the most convenient and least expensive solution to reaching any destination in Istanbul is hailing one of the myriad orange taxis waiting by the passenger unloading zone outside the airport terminals. Relatively inexpensive compared to other fares across the continents, the ride to Sultanahmet shouldn't cost more than 30TL, add another 10TL for Beyoğlu, and double the rate for a ride to the Asian shores, depending on traffic. The departure fee is about 2TL, with a charge of 1.20TL for ever kilometer traveled;

the nighttime rate increases by 50 percent midnight–6 A.M. Turkish cabbies rarely receive tips, nor do they often pay attention to the *kuruş* (pennies), so the rate typically gets rounded off to the nearest half-lira. The ride to Sultanahmet can take anywhere from 20 minutes to more than an hour, depending on the congestion.

The comfortable, white minibus of the **Havaş Shuttle Service** (Atatürk Airport Shuttle Bus Service, 0212/444-0487, www.havas.com.tr, 4 A.M.–1 A.M. every half-hour daily, 10TL) departs from the airport for the 40-minute ride to Taksim. Unlike similar services in the U.S., which drop passengers at their desired destinations along the route, there are just two stops on Havaş's Taksim route. One is in Aksaray—the nearest stop to Sultanahmet; a cab will get you there in less than 10 minutes. The second Havaş stop is in Tepebaşı. Another service runs to the Bakırköy ferry docks (15-minute ride, 5TL), where travelers can ride the Bostancı catamaran to Istanbul's Asian neighborhoods for 3TL. Weekend service to and from the port of Bakırköy is hourly.

If your baggage is not too obtrusive and your adventurous side has gotten the best of you, why not give the **tramway** a whirl. Ascend the long, covered passageway that connects the domestic and international terminals and the Hafif Metro (light rail system), to the left of the arrival hall. Follow the metro signs to the quay, where a 2TL token or an AKBIL can be purchased. Ride the service until Zeytinburnu, where a transfer onto the Zeytinburnu-Kabataş tramway is required to travel to Sultanahmet, Sirkeci Train Station, and Eminönü and Karaköy embarcaderos, as well as to the transportation hub of Kabataş, from which point a funicular heads to Taksim Square. Allow 90 minutes for a ride that should set you back about 3TL.

Sabiha Gökçen International Airport

Sabiha Gökçen International Airport (0216/585-5000, www.sgairport.com) is located in the Asian town of Pendik, some 20 miles southeast of—and a good hour's travel time from—the Golden Horn. Mostly charter flights by low-cost European and national airlines, as well as some domestic routes by Turkish Airlines and Pegasus Airlines, are operated from Sabiha Gökçen's airstrips. Jam-packed around the clock, Istanbul's second airport is a popular departure spot for *Istanbullus* heading out on vacation or business.

Aside from taxis, Sabiha Gökçen International Airport is served by the **Haydarpaşa-Gebze Express train** (www.tcdd.gov.tr, 1.50TL) from the Pendik Train Station, or Haydarpaşa on the Asian side. This railway shuttle departs from either terminal every 15 minutes on average, from 5 A.M.–11:30 P.M. There are also public buses heading for the business center of Levent on the European side, departing every 20 minutes. **Havaş Shuttle Service** (0212/444-0487, www.havas.com.tr) picks up passengers en route to Taksim from the airport's loading zone every hour for the 60-minute ride (4 A.M.–1 A.M. daily, 10TL). Also, consider arranging a transfer available through most airlines, such as Pegasus, for 7–20TL. Various small and medium-sized hotels offer a transfer service for free as a bonus for staying at least three nights. A cab ride from Taksim to Sabiha Gökçen costs about 70TL.

TRAIN

Istanbul has two major train stations, Sirkeci and Haydarpaşa. Trains crisscrossing the country and heading into Europe are operated by **Turkish State Railways** (Türkiye Cumhuriyeti Demiryolları, 444-8233, www.tcdd.gov.tr) and may offer the best travel solution when heading across the country. Sirkeci is served by the Zeytinburnu-Kabataş tramway line that zips through Sultanahmet, as well as public buses and *dolmuş*. The best way of getting to Haydarpaşa, near Kadıköy, is either by *dolmuş* or ferry.

Situated at the tip of the Golden Horn, **Sirkeci** (near Seraglio Point, main office: 0212/527-0050, 7 A.M.–11 P.M. daily; reservations: 0212/520-6575 8 A.M.–6 P.M. daily) serves both domestic routes as well as those extending into Europe. When you call for

© ZEYNEP GÖZEN

a transcontinental ferryboat

Otogar (0212/658-0505, www.otogaristan-bul.com) is the main terminal; **Harem Otogar** (0216/333-3763, 24 hours a day) is on the city's Asian side. There are a host of smaller bus stations dispersed in between.

Six miles northwest of Sultanahmet, near the district of Esenler, the Büyük Istanbul Otogar serves hundreds of small and large companies with thousands of lines, connecting points throughout Turkey, into Greece, Bulgaria, as well as Central and Eastern Europe. Travel with **Ulusoy** (444-1888, www.ulusoy.com.tr) or **Varan** (0212/658-0279, www.varan.com.tr), the largest, safest, and most dependable coach companies in Turkey. Both phone numbers are available 24 hours a day.

CAR

Driving in Istanbul, particularly for first timers, is not advisable. If you are arriving by car from Ankara, any other Turkish city, or neighboring European countries, you'll find road signage ample, but posted very close to the exits or areas they signal. For this reason, it is advisable to remain in the right lane. And forget chatting on your Blackberry or sipping that caramel macchiato, you'll need both hands on the wheel and both eyes on the road. The rules of road engagement respected in the U.S. are rarely valued here. Getting to Istanbul from Europe is simple by following the E80 Trans–European Motorway (TEM), which becomes Highway O2 six miles north of the city. From there, take the Fatih Sultan Mehmet Bridge, or the Bosphorus Bridge, to travel eastward into Istanbul's Asian territories.

Once in the city, avoid rush hour traffic between the hours of 7–9 A.M. and 3–8 P.M. Monday–Friday, unless sitting in the car listening to traditional Turkish music for hours on end is on your itinerary. On weekends, streets near the major centers are heavily congested. Leaving the car in the hotel's parking lot and traveling instead by *dolmuş*, tramway, or taxi is recommended.

If you plan to drive cross-country, rent a vehicle at the end of your Istanbul stay so you won't have to worry about its safe-keeping while

reservations, the automated answering system does not offer options in English, so you may be better off reserving or seeking information online. Aside from lines serving the Thracian peninsula, regular routes go through Sofia, Bulgaria and Thessaloniki, Greece.

On the Asian shores, **Haydarpaşa** (Tebbiye Cad., train schedule: 0216/348-8020, 7 A.M.–midnight; reservations: 0216/336-4470, 8 A.M.–6 P.M. daily) links Istanbul to the rest of Anatolia Teheran, Iran, and Damascus, Syria. There are several ways to get to the station, either by taxi, *dolmuş*, or ferry.

Both stations have food stands and cafés, as well as newsstands, in and around their perimeter. Arrive early for international lines, also know as the tongue-in-cheek "visa run"—lines filled with expats wishing to hop over the border to renew temporary residence permits.

BUS

Bus travel is the most popular, easiest, and most affordable method of travel in Turkey. Although once outrageously expensive, domestic routes are quickly gaining ground with dirt-cheap runs. There are two major bus stations in Istanbul: **Büyük Istanbul**

in town. Recommended car rental agencies at Atatürk International Airport include **Avis** (0212/663-0646, www.avis.com.tr/english); **Hertz** (0212/465-5999, www.hertz.com.tr); **Budget** (0212/663-0858, www.budget.com); and, **National Car Rental** (0212/663-7119, www.nationalcar.com).

BOAT

Cruise ships arriving in Istanbul dock at Karaköy's **International Maritime Passenger Terminal** (0212/249-5776), just northwest of the mouth of the Bosphorus.

The **IDO** (Istanbul Deniz Otobüsleri, 0212/444-4436, www.ido.com.tr) car ferries and fast passenger boats crossing the Sea of Marmara from Bandırma, Yalova, and Mudanya arrive at Yenikapı. From there, taxis, *dolmuş*'s, and the train into Sirkeci are all viable options to reach the city center. An IDO fast-ferry service to Yalova is also available from Kabataş.

Getting Around

If it weren't for its manic traffic, Istanbul would be idyllic. But what has now become the fourth largest city in the world, with an official 15 million residents—add at least two more for a realistic count—is also one of the worst when it comes to commuting. In the future, a third bridge, in addition to the gutsy Marmaray project that aims to run a metro under the Bosphorus, will relieve some of the stress caused by vehicular traffic. When in Istanbul, do as most of the locals do and opt for public transportation.

DOLMUŞ (COMMUNAL TAXI)

Depending on the itinerary, a visitor may find the *dolmuş* extremely useful. The hubs of Taksim and Kadıköy are served by several *dolmuş* services that crisscross the city through a defined route at a set price. With a load of eight passengers, vans linking Bostancı, Beşiktaş, or Sarıyer depart from various points around Taksim Square, and charge 1.20–4.80TL one way. In Kadıköy, *dolmuş*'s are located to the west of the Beşiktaş embarcadero. These minibuses become convenient after at 11 P.M. when the IDO ferries that serve ports along the Bosphorus stop running.

TAXI

Taxi service is popular and inexpensive in Istanbul. There are tons of these yellow vehicles, which operate on two tariffs: *gündüz*

(daytime) and *gece* (nighttime). The *gece* rate, running midnight–6 A.M., is 50 percent higher than the daytime fare. Most cabbies are decent individuals, but quite a few take tourists for a ride, literally and figuratively. Things to watch out for when stepping into one of these vehicles is the LCD display. Along with the flashing fare, *gündüz* or *gece* is shown, signaling which rate the driver has engaged. Watch out for the nighttime rates in the middle of the day, and ensure not to exchange too many bills or notes larger than 10TL to prevent getting counterfeits in return or falling prey to any other scam.

Some cabbies are notorious for hanging out outside the five star hotels and charging a set fee for a destination. Avoid those who propose to drive you to a popular tourist destination, say, Dolmabahce from Taksim for 20TL. That's a 300 percent rip-off. To reiterate, the meter should start ticking at about 2TL and increase by a 1.50TL at the most for every kilometer increment. Any tolls incurred along freeways or along the Bosphorus Bridge is the passenger's responsibility. Cabbies do not expect gratuities, but locals typically round off the fare to the next lira.

TRAMWAY

Istanbul's tramway (0212/245-0720, www.iett.gov.tr/en) is an asset for visitors: it zips from Kabataş, along the Bosphorus through Karaköy, crossing the Galata Bridge to Eminönü and Sirkeci. Once there it climbs the hill into Sultanahmet, then follows Divan Yolu into Beyazit—the stop for the Grand Bazaar. Then through Aksaray—by Istanbul's main coach station, followed by the City Walls, to finally reach its last stop of Zeytinburnu, near Atatürk International Airport. The entire trip can take up to an hour. The service runs every 10 minutes, 6 A.M.–midnight, and costs 1.30TL.

A historic tram of **Nostalgic Tramway** (0212/245-0720, www.iett.gov.tr/en) noisily clatters the length of Istiklal Caddesi every 10 minutes, from Taksim Square to the entrance of the funicular station at Tünel. Another loops through the shopping strip of Bahariye and the enclave of Moda, from the port of Kadıköy on the Asian side. Extending about a mile, both nostalgic tram routes will save quite a considerable amount of walking. The fare is 0.90TL and requires either a token or an Akbil (a transit magnetized keychain).

BUS
Istanbul's public bus system, **IETT** (0800/211-6068, www.iett.gov.tr) is extremely reliable and inexpensive. Each ride costs 1.30TL and can be deducted from the balance on an Akbil or through the use of tickets, which can be purchased from the white booths at all IETT centers, in Aksaray, Beşiktaş, Eminönü, Kadıköy, Taksim, and Üsküdar. Note that the **Akbil**—the advantageous magnetized keychain—is accepted on all public transport; and passengers get a reduction of 5–10 *kuruş* (pennies) just for using it. Do check out the bus schedules online; busy routes run on average every 15 minutes. Some buses popular with tourists include: 25E, which hugs the European coast of the Bosphorus from Kabataş to Sarıyer; and TZK1, from Sultanahmet to the Kabataş funicular.

The smaller blue buses—or **Özel Halk Otobüsü**—are cooperatively owned, but regulated by the municipality. Their service is just as frequent, but their drivers are known for their recklessness. Until the city fulfills its plan to take them off the streets by doubling

the IETT service, they will remain popular commuting options. Use an Akbil or purchase a ticket onboard.

FUNICULAR
Two funiculars climb either side of the steep hill, crossed by Istiklal Caddesi, from the shores of the Bosphorus. The first, Tünel, which is the second oldest of its kind in Europe, was renovated in 2007. Its newer, silent version saves passengers the steep climb through the back streets of Galata, en route to the popular business artery. Running about every five minutes, a ride on the funicular costs 0.90TL. Use an Akbil or a token available at booths along both entrances. The second and newer funicular, built in 2005, bypasses the hectic traffic from Kabataş to Taksim Square with an underground ride that takes less than two minutes. The fare and payment is the same as its counterpart in Beyoğlu. Funicular service runs 7 A.M.–12:30 A.M. daily. Log onto IETT's website (www.iett.gov.tr) for more information.

METRO AND LIGHT RAIL
Istanbul's **metro** (0212/245-0720, www.iett.gov.tr/en), inaugurated in 2000, runs from Taksim Square to the Fourth Levent in 10 minutes, through Osmanbey, Şişli, Mecidiyeköy, Gayrettepe, Levent, and Maslak. Running roughly every 5 minutes, a token costs 1.35TL or you can use a trusty Akbil; log onto IETT's website for more information.

The light rail system, called **Hafif Metro** (0212/245-0720, www.iett.gov.tr/en), links Aksaray with Atatürk International Airport and Istanbul's Coach Station, and some 14 other stops. A metro runs every 10 minutes; the fare is 1.30TL. It operates 6 A.M.–12:30 A.M. daily.

BOAT
The ferries that zigzag the Bosphorus are operated by **IDO** (Istanbul Deniz Otobüsleri, 0212/444-4436, www.ido.com). Tourists and locals alike find this mode of transportation pleasurable, particularly sitting atop the deck

sipping tea, and a timesaver. The main embarcaderos are situated in Eminönü, Karaköy, Kabataş, Beşiktaş, Üsküdar, and Kadıköy. The ride cost 1.30TL, upwards of 3TL for those headed for the Princes' islands. Tokens are available at booths along the embarcaderos; or you can use an Akbil. For an updated list of routes, fares and schedules, check the IDO website or pick up a timetable at any of the ports listed. Fast boats, known as *hızlı feribot,* are catamarans that traverse the longer routes, between Kadıköy and Bakırköy, Bostancı and Kabataş, in addition to a few others, for a few liras more.

TRAIN

Istanbul's trans-city trains—or *banlyö tren*— are operated along two lines: the first leaves from Sirkeci and runs along the Sea of Marmara to well beyond Atatürk International Airport. Stops include Seraglio Point, Cankurtaran, Kumkapı, the port Yenikapı. The second city train takes departs from Haydarpaşa and runs to Gebze, stopping through a variety of points along the Asian coast of the Sea of Marmara. Both have a railway shuttle service that departs every 15 minutes on average from 5 A.M. to 11:30 P.M. The ride costs 1.50 TL, regardless of whether the trip lasts one mile or ten. For more information, contact the **Sirkeci Train Station** (0212/527-0050) or the Haydarpaşa Train Station (0216/348-8020), or log on to **Turkish Railways** (www.tcdd.gov.tr in Turkish).

CAR

Driving through Istanbul is a nightmare; parking is even worse. But if you must, take a deep breath and prepare for hectic traffic, double- or triple-parking, disrespect for most traffic signs, angry drivers at every corner, and a price of gas that's almost three times greater than the already expensive gallon in the U.S. Again, if you arrive to the city with a vehicle, seriously consider parking it in the hotel's underground or a municipal parking facility for a small fee. Generally staffed by an attendant hired by the municipality, street parking is inexpensive, as little as 2TL per hour or as much as 15TL for a 24-hour period. You may also consider parking at either airport for about 90TL per week.

There are tricks to navigating the city's thoroughfares, however, that a newbie driver would be remiss not to heed. Take a deep breath and, while there are street signs, remember that they're mere suggestions that often go unheeded. Some streets are one-way, with alternates going in the opposite direction. But even those are fair game. If caught bumper to bumper with an incoming vehicle, be the wise one and backup. Bus drivers pull out into lanes without checking their rearview mirrors. Expect the unexpected and leave more than ample distance between vehicles.

THRACE AND THE SEA OF MARMARA

After an eyeful of Istanbul, the majority of visitors head for the irresistible golden sands of Southwestern Anatolia. Few foray into the farther reaches of the Marmara Denizi (Sea of Marmara) or even north into Trakya (Thrace). What they miss is the area's unique mix of Balkan and Greek origins, a trove of stunning early Ottoman architecture, the rejuvenating thermal springs of emperors, and a string of fishing villages that have barely changed over the centuries.

Geographically speaking, the Sea of Marmara is bound to the north by Thrace and to the south by northwestern Anatolia. Its western reaches bottleneck into the strategic Dardanelles Strait, the maritime channel where Alexander the Great conquered the Persians in the 4th century B.C. Thrace's

craggy southwestern tip is known as Gelibolu Yarımadası (Gallipoli Peninsula). Its lush national park commemorates the thousands of ill-fated Allied, Australian, New Zealand, and Ottoman troops who lost their lives in the prolonged bloody conflicts of World War I. To the east, the Sea of Marmara flows between low coastal crags into the Bosphorus Straits.

Much like an appendage jutting from Turkey's somewhat rectangular borders, Thrace is bound by Greece and Bulgaria and by the Black, Aegean, and Marmara Seas. Its countryside boasts miles of sunflowers—cultivated mostly for their oil—that bloom into an endless yellow blanket come summer. The pine forests that once cloaked Thrace's southern flank have given way to the more lucrative real-estate industry. Like the proverbial cherry, the Ottoman

THRACE

HIGHLIGHTS

◖ **Yeşil Cami (Green Mosque):** Day-trip to Bursa to bask in the beauty of the Green Mosque, an early-Ottoman architectural gem. Best time to visit is June, when gatherers of the finest silk flock en masse to the former Ottoman capital's impressive bazaar (page 122).

◖ **Çekirge:** De-stress sultan-style in the tepid effervescence of these thermal baths, made famous by the Romans (page 126).

◖ **Iznik Şehir Surları (City Walls):** Climb Iznik's 1,900-year-old city ramparts, near the town's majestic Istanbul Gate, and peer at the sleepy lake just to the west and the verdant surrounding valley (page 134).

◖ **Gelibolu Yarımadası Tarihi Milli Parkı (Gallipoli National Park):** At

Gallipoli National Park, pay homage to the thousands of fallen heroes who gave their lives to gain the strategic Dardanelles and breathe in the serenity of this sprawling memorial to both friend and foe (page 137).

◖ **Gökçeada:** Drink wine and recline on this picturesque isle, steeped in Greek history and just off Thrace's coast (page 142).

◖ **Selimiye Camii:** Architecture devotees will fall in love with Selim's Mosque, considered Mimar Sinan's pious masterpiece (page 148).

◖ **Kırkpınar Yağı Güreşleri (Kırkpınar Oil Wrestling Festival):** In this centuries-old annual Oil Wrestling Festival, grown men, with bodies oiled, wrestle to win the golden belt award. Come in July and sit back and watch the festivities (page 151).

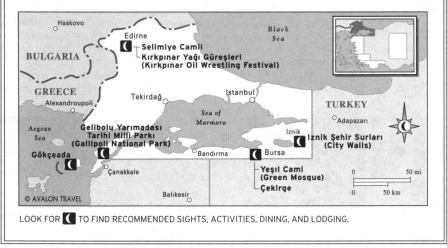

LOOK FOR ◖ TO FIND RECOMMENDED SIGHTS, ACTIVITIES, DINING, AND LODGING.

capital of Edirne is the main highlight of Thrace. It's also its largest city, a living museum of sorts, with pristinely preserved Ottoman sites, like antique bridges, Ottoman mosques, and caravanserais. Aside from Selimiye Camii (Selimiye Mosque)—considered to be Ottoman master architect Mimar Sinan's greatest feat— Edirne's tourism draw remains the Kırkpınar Yağı Güreşleri (Kırkpınar Oil Wrestling

Festival). Thousands of visitors flock to the annual event to see who will win the Golden Belt through a series of free-for-all, eliminatory bouts. Edirne also makes for a quick getaway into neighboring Greece, Bulgaria, or Eastern Europe. In contrast, the coast to the west brags that the Turkish isle of Gökçeada, one of two Turkish islands in the Aegean Sea, has remained free of international tourism.

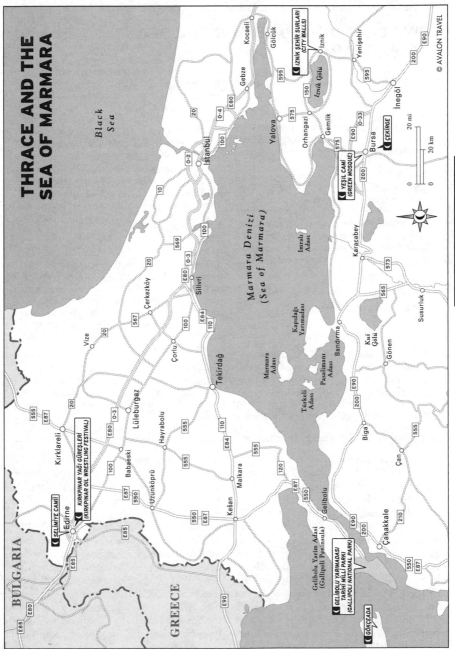

THRACE AND THE SEA OF MARMARA

© AVALON TRAVEL

THRACE

FIVE DAYS IN THRACE AND THE SEA OF MARMARA

The best way to cover this large area is to rent a vehicle for a whirlwind five-day car trip and the best time to go is in July.

DAY 1

From Istanbul, drive north to Edirne to take in the splendor of the Selimiye Mosque and the fun of the Kırkpınar Oil Wrestling Festival.

DAY 2

Zip down the E87 through the Gallipoli Peninsula en route to the fields and rolling mountains of the memorial park of Gallipoli. From the cape's Kabatepe port, hop on the nightly car ferry to cross the 14-mile Aegean channel to the idyllic isle of Gökçeada, where the road-weary can lounge and enjoy the serenity of this isle.

DAY 3

Spend the day on the little-known Gökçeada and check out its winemaking facilities and water sports.

DAY 4

Catch the 8 A.M. ferry back through the entrance of the Dardanelles to the port of Çanakkale. Once back on the mainland of Anatolia, drive along the Sea of Marmara's southern coastal regions through the barren Biga Peninsula – where Alexander the Great fought off the Persians – to the port city of Bandırma. Break for lunch at one of the many waterside eateries on the picturesque Erdek Peninsula. If time allows, wander north to the prosaic, lackluster Marmara Islands or opt instead for a southward push toward the majesty of Kuş Gölü, a watery expanse that serves as a pit stop for thousands of vivid migratory birds. Drive eastward on the E90 toward the former Ottoman stronghold of Bursa. Here, sports enthusiasts can hike the mount of Uludağ and those in need of relaxation can set the compass for Çekirge's famed springs.

DAY 5

On your last day, aim for Iznik to survey the remnants of Christianity's early beginnings and even older Neolithic ruins as you search for that perfect faience to take home. Then, make a beeline for the lush greenery that abounds in the spa resort of Termal, before heading north to Yalova's ferry station en route for Istanbul.

You can also follow this itinerary in the opposite direction, from Yalova to Edirne. For the Çanakkale/Gallipoli/Gökçeada region, www .anzachotel.com has exhaustive resources for travelers.

The southern edge of this area hugs the Sea of Marmara and is noted for its thermal activity and some less-than-stellar beaches packed in summer with Istanbul's lower middle class. Its bucolic countryside unfurls along a series of hills that give way to Bursa. Another of the Ottomans' erstwhile capitals, Bursa is now a progressive city teeming with industry and artists. And, there's also Iznik, a sleepy lake town where organized Christianity essentially got under way and where the art of intricate faience was mastered. To the west, the bird paradise of Kuş Gölü is a popular rest stop for hundreds of migratory bird species, including the graceful flamingo. The southern region's backstreets, with their prolific agriculture and abundant heritage, offer a glimpse of the Anatolian richness that awaits the traveler as they go deeper into the backcountry.

This region delights foodies. A trip to Bursa wouldn't be complete without lunching over its famed Iskender Kebab—slices of tender lamb drenched in tomato sauce and melted better. Tekirdağ offers up its namesake köfte (meatball) and Edirne features its popular fried liver. Bounded by the warmer waters of the Sea of Marmara, a handful of fishing villages boast delicate fish, like gilthead bream and red mullet.

Thrace and the Sea of Marmara regions provide a stunning array of destinations and a unique history travelers would be remiss not to discover.

PLANNING YOUR TIME

Visiting each of the destinations featured along the Sea of Marmara and Thrace region can be easily completed through one- or two-day–long trips from Istanbul, via bus or boat service. To really tour the region, a five-day trip is recommended.

The climate of the Sea of Marmara and Thrace is quite seasonal much like Istanbul. Winters can get bitterly cold, however, with storms thrashing the western coast of the Gallipoli Peninsula and Çanakkale, rendering boat transport obsolete for the duration. A fun one-day trip to Gökçeada in late October–early April may very well leave you stranded if the weather is bad. Conversely, summers can be torrid, but remain incomparable to the broiling heat of the Southern Aegean or Mediterranean coasts. The proximity of the water, however, offers a pleasing antidote to the sun's relentless lashing.

Outside of Bursa and the massive crowds visiting Gallipoli on Anzac Day, this territory remains somewhat undisturbed by tourism. Late spring and early fall are perhaps the best time to visit its cities. The months of July and August remain best suited for beachcombers wishing to spread their towels on the tawny sands of Gökçeada, which also features wind sailors on its northern flank. Also amazing in summer are the humongous sunflower meadows, providing a splash of yellow on the otherwise monotonous agricultural landscape. Come winter, goat shepherds, garbed in sheepskin, steer their herd over a land left bare by the annual tobacco and wheat harvest.

Expect lower prices for accommodations and meals than in Istanbul, with rates peaking during the summer months. During the shoulder seasons of May and October, you'll find lower prices on fares and lodging; fair weather; doting hotel owners and restaurateurs; and no lines at monuments and parks. Once again, Anzac Day—the biggest tourist draw of the entire region—is commemorated on April 25, and the Kırkpınar Oil Wrestling Festival occurs in July.

Marmara Denizi (Sea of Marmara)

Extending west from its easternmost Bay of Izmit, the Sea of Marmara is sprinkled with hidden natural delights and relics spanning several millennia. Known as *Propontis* throughout antiquity, the Sea of Marmara separates the Black and Aegean Seas. The once fertile plains just beyond the low verdant crags that cordon off the Marmara's southern coast have given way to the nation's industrial backbone, thanks to the area's proximity to Istanbul. It has become one of Eastern Europe's manufacturing powerhouses, primarily in the automotive sector. But agriculture remains the primary focus of this area, with independent farmers and food processing giants alike. The olive, in particular, is still the region's most prominent product. In Bursa, an architectural trove awaits with ornate mosques, *hans,* and *medreses.* Food is also

a highlight, especially with the phenomenal dish of Iskender kebab, tender slices of spit-roasted lamb slathered with tomato sauce and butter—by itself reason enough to visit. After heightening your sensual experiences with natural Thelasso therapy at Termal or Çekirge, you'll realize that Anatolia's western tip mirrors the boundless pleasures to be had inland.

BURSA

Bursa is synonymous with affluence. Bursa's modern periphery sprawls out from the lush, green slopes of the Uludağ Mountain to incorporate an industrial center. It was once nicknamed *Yeşil* (Green) Bursa. But more than three decades of industrialization and growth have replaced a good portion of the fields and woods that inspired its moniker. Its insatiable

THRACE

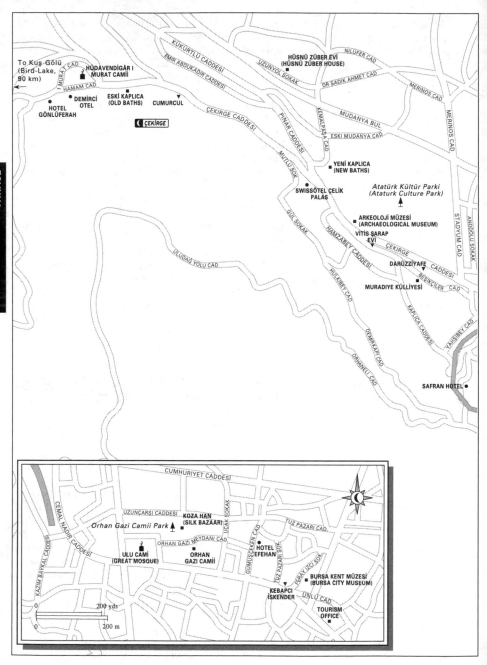

To Kuş Gölü
(Bird-Lake,
90 km)

HÜDAVENDİGÂR I
MURAT CAMİİ

HOTEL
GÖNLÜFERAH

DEMİRCİ
OTEL

ESKİ KAPLICA
(OLD BATHS)

CUMURCUL

ÇEKİRGE

KÜKÜRTLÜ CADDESİ

EMİR ABDÜKADIR CADDESİ

NİLÜFER CAD

HÜSNÜ ZÜBER EVİ
(HÜSNÜ ZÜBER HOUSE)

UZUNYOL SOKAK

DR SADIK AHMET CAD

MERİNOS CAD

MERİNOS CAD

MUDANYA BUL

ESKİ MUDANYA CAD

ÇEKİRGE CADDESİ

PINAR CADDESİ

KEMALPAŞA CAD

MUTLU SOK

YENİ KAPLICA
(NEW BATHS)

SWISSOTEL ÇELİK
PALAS

Atatürk Kültür Parki
(Ataturk Culture Park)

GÜL SOKAK

HAMZABEY CADDESİ

ARKEOLOJİ MÜZESİ
(ARCHAEOLOGICAL MUSEUM)

VİTİS ŞARAP
EVİ

ÇEKİRGE

STADYUM CAD

ANDOLU SOKAK

ULUDAĞ YOLU CAD

HÜLKİBEY CAD

DARÜZZİYAFE CADDESİ

BEŞİKÇİLER CAD

MURADİYE KÜLLİYESİ

KAPLICA CADDESİ

YAHŞİBEY CAD

DEMİRKAPI CAD

ORHANELİ CAD

SAFRAN HOTEL

CUMHURİYET CADDESİ

CEMAL NADİR CADDESİ

KAZIM BAYKAL CADDESİ

UZUNÇARŞI CADDESİ

KOZA HAN
(SILK BAZAAR)

UÇAK SOKAK

TUZ PAZARI CAD.

Orhan Gazi Camii Park

ORHAN GAZİ MEYDANI CAD

GÜMÜŞÇEKEN CAD

HOTEL
EFEHAN

TUZ PAZARI SOK

ERAY İKCİ SOK.

ULU CAMİ
(GREAT MOSQUE)

ORHAN
GAZİ CAMİİ

BURSA KENT MÜZESİ
(BURSA CITY MUSEUM)

KEBAPCI
İSKENDER

ÜNLÜ CAD.

TOURISM
OFFICE

0   200 yds

0   200 m

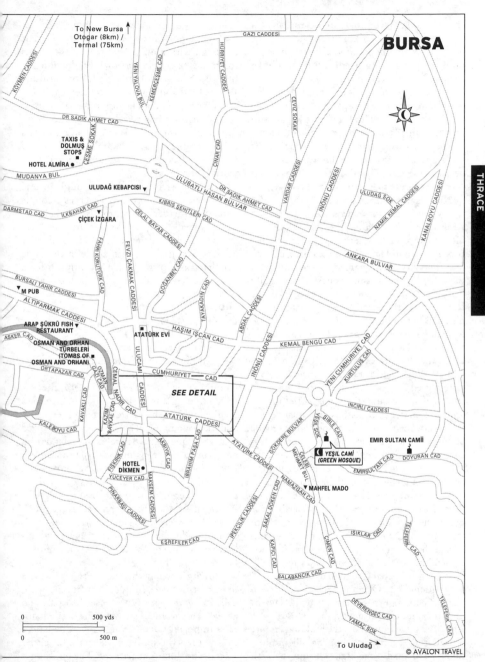

THRACE

BURSA

To New Bursa
Otogar (8km) /
Termal (75km)

GAZI CADDESI

KÖYMEN CADDESI

HÜRRIYET CADDESI

KEMERÇEŞME CAD

YENI YALOVA BUL

CEVIZ SOKAK

DR SADIK AHMET CAD

TAXIS &
DOLMUŞ
STOPS
HOTEL ALMİRA ●

ÇEŞME SOKAK

CINAR CAD

VARDAR CADDESI

İNÖNÜ CADDESI

ULUDAĞ SOK

NAMIK KEMAL CADDESI

KANALBOYU CADDESI

MUDANYA BUL

ULUDAĞ KEBAPCISI ▼

ULUBATLI HASAN BULVAR

DR SADIK AHMET CAD

KIBRIS ŞEHITLERI CAD

DARMSTAD CAD   İLKBAHAR CAD
ÇİÇEK İZGARA ▼

CELAL BAYAR CADDESI

FAHRI KORUTÜRK CAD

FEVZI ÇAKMAK CADDESI

DOSABEY CAD

TAYAKADIN CAD

ABDAL CADDESI

ANKARA BULVAR

BURSALI TAHIR CADDESI
▼ M PUB

ALTIPARMAK CADDESI

ASKER CAD

ARAP ŞÜKRÜ FISH ▼
RESTAURANT

OSMAN AND ORHAN
TÜRBELERI
(TOMBS OF ■
OSMAN AND ORHAN)

ORTAPAZAR CAD

ULUCAMI

■ ATATÜRK EVI

HAŞIM İŞCAN CAD

İNÖNÜ CADDESI

KEMAL BENGÜ CAD

YENI CUMHURIYET CAD

KURTULUŞ CAD

OZANLAR
GAZI CAD
KAZIM
BAYKAL CAD

CEMAL NADIR CAD

CADDESI

CUMHURIYET   CAD

KAVAKLI CAD

SEE DETAIL

İNCİRLİ CADDESI

KALE BOYU CAD

ATATÜRK   CADDESI

GÖKDERE BULVAR

YEŞIL SOK

SIBLE CAD

EMIR SULTAN CAMİİ

FESTIRIK CAD
HOTEL ●
DİKMEN
YÜCEYER CAD
AKBIYIK CAD

İBRAHIM PAŞA CAD

MAKSEM CADDESI

ATATÜRK CADDESI

CELEBI
MEHME BUL

NAMAZGAH CAD

☾ YEŞIL CAMİ
(GREEN MOSQUE)

DOYURAN CAD

EMIRSULTAN CAD

▼ MAHFEL MADO

PINARBAŞI CADDESI

PEYÇILIK CADDESI

SAKAL DÖKEN CAD

KAPICI CAD

CMEN CAD

IŞIKLAR CAD

TELEFERIK CAD

EŞREFILER CAD

BALABANCIK CAD

DEVERENGEÇ CAD

YAMAÇ SOK

TELEFERIK CAD

0   500 yds
0   500 m

To Uludağ ↘

© AVALON TRAVEL

appetite for labor continues to beckon migrant workers from rural and eastern Anatolia by the busload. With a population at more than 1.9 million, and growing steadily, Bursa is one of the country's largest cities. However, unlike Istanbul and Ankara, it is not frenzied and disorderly. In fact, its noted spa hamlet of Çekirge and its ski resort of Uludağ (Great Mountain) inspire both relaxation and excitement. Home to a bevy of artists, from silk weavers to painters and singers, Bursa is known for its progressiveness and a sense of liberalism that stands out in Turkey's increasingly conservative climate.

Historically, Bursa traces its origins to 202 B.C., when its territory was gifted to Bythinian King Prusias I by Philip V of Macedonia for his assistance in conquering Pergamon on the Aegean Sea and Heraclea Pontica on the Black Sea. The city was renamed Prusa, and soon thereafter became an important stop on the Silk Road. But it really wasn't until the arrival of the Romans that the therapeutic powers of its indigenous hot springs in Çekirge were exploited. Roman emperors constructed edifices and attractive marble bathhouses around the gushers. Later, the Byzantines introduced silk production. As the Byzantine Empire withered, Bursa's claims lured the Selçuks of Rûm, the Crusaders, and a few marauding tribes into battles for the 13th and better part of the early 14th centuries. Following the decline of the highly mobile Selçuk Sultanate of Rûm, small emirates or principalities—known as *beylik*'s—fought for control of the Anatolian plateau. Leading from the chief city of Soğut, Ertuğrul Gazı launched the first attacks of a decade-long battle to conquer Prusa. In 1326, after a year-long siege against the Byzantines, his son Osman Bey—after whom the Osmanlı (Ottoman) Empire is named—conquered the city. This crucial event transformed the semi-itinerant Osman tribe into what would become the imperial Ottoman dynasty.

Unquenched, Osman Bey's son, Orhan Gazı, set his sights to the west while lavishing his capital of Bursa with the spoils of war. The city's trade flourished; the budding empire minted its first coins; and, imperial silk production rose to an all time high. During the 17th

century, Bursa became renowned for carriage-making. The industry continues to this day, although with more modern vehicles, thanks to Oyak-Renault's large vehicle production line here. Both Coca Cola and Pepsi Cola headline Bursa's food and beverage producers.

Despite its modern factories, Bursa is chock-full of historic relics and architecture, from mosques to the Byzantine baths. The city's other notable delights include *kestane şekeri* (candied chestnut sweets) and perhaps the world's best peaches.

While most tours breeze through in one long afternoon, Bursa truly deserves a couple of days. Earmark a full day to leisurely sightsee, haggle for silk in the old bazaar, attend a local puppet show, and relax in Çekirge's balmy springs. Top it all off with a ride in the cable car that zips up the Uludağ Mountain for a bird's eye view of Bursa's magnificent wealth.

Sights
◖ YEŞIL CAMI (GREEN MOSQUE)
Yeşil Cami (east on Atatürk Caddesi, North on Yeşil Sokak, sunrise to sunset daily, free) is one of the country's more ornate mosques. Commissioned in 1412 by Mehmet I, the emerald building was the foundation of Ottoman architecture. Its showy arched marble entrance and the flagrant use of color throughout proved that a mosque could be architecturally daring and a bona fide religious sanctuary simultaneously—a far cry from the rather atonal and austere Persian and Selçuk styles of architecture that were previously utilized throughout Anatolia. Aside from its architectural significance, Yeşil Cami also glorifies Mehmet I's triumph in a decade-long power struggle with his brothers for ascension after the passing of their father Beyazit I.

Moving beyond the elaborate archway, a mammoth, 45-foot-high niche in the wall, called *mihrab,* points to Mecca. Just past and above the entrance is the ornately tiled sultan's **Imperial Loge** private suite. The harem in tow used the more subtle space on either sides of the sultan's apartment. The building is

The early 15th-century Yeşil Cami (Green Mosque) may no longer bear its namesake color on the outside, but the interior faience does in every shade.

named after the green faience located throughout the space. The free use of ceramics was a new trend, which became all the rage in later religious monuments and propelled Iznik tile mastery to the cultural forefront.

Outside, the **Yeşil Türbe** (Green Tomb, 8 A.M.–noon, 1–5 P.M. daily, free) holds the remains of Mehmet I. Built on an octagonal floor plan, the burial place bore the brunt of the massive earthquake of 1855. The namesake green faience was replaced by turquoise tiles from Kütahya in a later renovation. Before stepping through the embellished wooden portal, stroll around the tomb to check out the superb Koranic calligraphy above the perimeter windows. The interior tile-work is original and is echoed on the largest of the tombs, which encases the sultan. The other coffins belong to his immediate descendants, each with a tiled *mihrab* (niche) pointing to Mecca.

BURSA BAZAAR

Just north of Atatürk Caddesi, Bursa's downtown is a beguiling beehive of trade that still attracts as much commerce as it did centuries

ago. Unlike Istanbul's version, Bursa's bazaar (enter on Borsa, Uçak or Ulucami Cadde; 9 A.M.–7 P.M. daily)is airy, with plenty of courtyards doubling as open tea gardens that offer ample opportunities to relax. The bazaar is located just north of Gazı Orhan Park, which itself abuts Atatürk Caddesi to the North. Its girded by Cemal Nadir Caddesi to the west; Cumhuriyet Caddesi to the north; and, İnönü Caddesi to the east.

The first structure across from Orhan Gazı Camii Park is the **Eski Aynalı Çarşı** (Old Mirrored Market). Prior to welcoming trade, it served as the Orhan Gazı Hamamı (baths). Built in 1339, it's the first Turkish bath built by the Ottomans. Today, it's a covered passage filled with merchants selling the famed Karagöz and Hacıvat shadow puppets. Across Arakcıler Sokak, today's **Emir Hanı** (courtyard) offers an arena to discuss politics over tea; its burbling fountain brings respite from an arduous day's labor. Come July, silk auctioneers fill the space with the year's yield: worms and weaves. Centuries ago, caravans traveling along the arduous Silk Road stopped here. The camels brayed in the courtyard, as trade was conducted with the locals.

To the west lies **Kapalı Çarşı** (Covered Market), a labyrinthine vaulted market which is geared towards locals rather than tourists. This translates into lower prices and a pretty good chance to get your haggling groove on. Now a hit with westerners, thick Turkish cotton goods can be had for dimes on the dollar. If you're interested in purchasing towels or bathrobes, see if shipping can be arranged rather than schlepping the goods back in a suitcase.

At the northernmost point of the Bursa Bazaar is a 14th-century *bedesten* (marketplace). Built by Beyazit I, it's the oldest part of the open-air market. It was partly leveled during the 1885 earthquake and by a fire seven decades later. It was rebuilt each time to exceed its preceding form in area and strength. Today, it's known as the **Kuyumcular Çarşısı** (Jeweler's Market).

Doubling back east through the Emir Hanı and Eski Aynalı Çarşısı, the **Koza Han**

THRACE

(Cocoon Market) is a five-centuries-old, two-story, brick building crested with a series of chimneys. Built by Beyazit II, this cocoon-trading structure was beautifully revamped thanks to funds donated by the Ağa Khan Foundation in 1985. Encompassing a large courtyard shaded by plane trees is an octagonal *mescit* (prayer hall). Farmers of old gathered annually to peddle the silk cocoons that brought Bursa its textile fame. Today's satiny fabric is sold in the finished form, mostly on this *han's* (caravansary) second floor. Further east, the **Çiçek Pazarı** (Flower Market) is a fragrant spectral spray of blooms, whose final scent leads through to the **Tuz Pazarı** (Salt Market), on the right-hand side. Across Inönü Caddesi is the **Demirciler Çarşısı**, (Blacksmith's bazaar) where welders still practice their trade.

ULU CAMI
(GREAT MOSQUE)

Serving as a beacon to the faithful, the Ulu Cami (north of Atatürk Caddesi, just east of Ulucami Caddesi, sunrise to sunset daily, free) was commissioned by Beyazit I in 1396. It rises as an immense rectangular brick heap, crafted from stone quarried from nearby Uludağ Mountain. It is topped by 20 domes and a massive solitary minaret. An example of Selçuk architecture, square columns support the mosque's domed roof and break the vastness of the interior hall. The burbling **şardivan** (a fountain for ritual cleansing), smack in the hall's center, is really interesting. Recently added, the domed glass above allows much needed light to penetrate the otherwise dark sanctuary. The *minbar* (pulpit) is elegantly carved out of walnut and exemplifies the artistry of early Ottoman wood crafters.

ORHAN GAZI CAMII
(ORHAN GAZI MOSQUE)

Abutting the Koza Han to the south, the Orhan Gazı Mosque (north of Atatürk Caddesi, 200 m East of Ulu Cami, north on Yeşil Sokak, sunrise to sunset daily, free) was commissioned in 1339 by the warlord of the same name. Instead of the traditional square floor plan, this

sanctuary retained the T-shaped structure of the *zaviye* (Dervish hall) it replaced. Despite the natural calamities that befell this mosque, various restructuring efforts have maintained the original layout, with cubicles lining the main prayer hall.

EMIR SULTAN CAMII
(EMIR SULTAN MOSQUE)

Slightly out of the way, but well worth the trip, the Emir Sultan Mosque marks a spot once popular with early dervishes. Pious locals visit the tombs on site. Built in the late 14th century, the structure underwent a couple of renovations, resulting in a more elaborate interior and exterior that mirrors the ornate styles of a late 19th-century restoration. Towering over the city, amidst large plane trees and a nearby cemetery, the complex makes for a serene excursion. Its showy grounds reveal a diminutive fountain of scalloped marble and exotic arches that give way to a rather bland white prayer hall, pleasantly broken up by the liberal use of dark wood.

For those fond of the region's famous lamb dish, Kebapçı Iskender, the genius who created the original dish is interred in the burial ground just outside of the mosque.

MURADIYE KÜLLIYESI
(MURADIYE COMPLEX)

On the opposite end of central Bursa, Muradiye Külliyesi (a block south of Bursa Atatürk Stadium at the entrance of Çekirge in Muradiye, 8:30 A.M.–noon, 1–5 P.M. daily, free), theological complex, marks the last imperial structure to grace Bursa. Built in 1426 for Sultan Murat II, the mosque, with its burst of color and intricate *mihrab*, is reminiscent of Yeşil Camion on the city's opposite hill. The old seminary on the grounds doubles as a clinic today, and the original soup kitchen is now a restaurant that serves exceptional Ottoman cuisine.

Situated in a fragrant rose garden shaded by tall cypress trees behind the mosque is a burial ground with 12 tombs. The largest is that of **Sultan Murat II.** Interestingly, he requested that his mausoleum remain open so that the rains prevalent in the region fall over his tomb—perhaps as regular ablutions in an eternal state of piety. His imperial sons, slain by their stronger brother in a race for the throne, are also buried here. Alongside them are tombs of imperial descendants who suffered a similar fate decades later. Unlike other Islamic chieftains, the heir to the Ottoman dynasty was not designated before a sultan's death, making the post fair game for the slew of able-bodied male progenitors who arose from a crowded harem. Son of Beyazit II, Sultan Selim, a.k.a. The Grim, is a prime example of the brutality prevalent among the heirs. The remains of his older brother are interred in the **Şehzade Ahmet Türbesi.** The bloody sultan insured his supremacy by erasing three of his own sons, another brother, and a half a dozen nephews. If closed, request the assistance of the groundskeeper.

OSMAN AND ORHAN TÜRBELERI (TOMBS OF OSMAN AND ORHAN)

At the westernmost point of Atatürk Caddesi, the remains of a *hısar* (fortress)—also referred to as Tophane—mark Bursa's oldest relic. Dating back to Roman Prusa, the last vestige of a thick city wall, surrounding what was once an acropolis, is still visible. The arrival of the Ottomans signaled Bursa's expansion into the valley, keeping the hillside for more posh architecture, including the few remaining *konaks* (residences) that grace this lofty part of town.

Climbing Orhan Gazı Caddesi, turn right into the Timurtaş Paşa Park to gain access to the Osman and Orhan Türbeleri (9 A.M.–noon and 1–5 P.M. Tues.–Wed. and Fri.–Sun., donation recommended). The tombs enclose the father and son pair that took most of Anatolia and Thrace from the Byzantines and founded the Ottoman Empire. The beautiful baroque structure that houses both tombs was Sultan Abdül Aziz's contribution to his forebears, after the earthquake of 1855 leveled the original building. Inside, beautiful crystal chandeliers embellish the space. Outside, one of three 19th-century clock towers, that once doubled as fire alarms, graces a peaceful park filled with tea gardens. This is a nice spot to rest and view the bustling city below.

YENI KAPLICA (NEW BATHS)

Just northwest of Kültür Parkı, the Yeni Kaplıca (Mudanya Cad. 10, 0224/233-6955, 6 A.M.–11 P.M. daily, up to 30TL for full scrub) actually dates back to Byzantine emperor Justinian I. It probably owes its name to a floor-to-ceiling renovation commissioned by the lice-ridden and gout-inflicted Rüstem Paşa—Sultan Süleyman the Magnificent's grand vizier. Great for a relaxing immersion or as a treatment for rheumatism, the hot springs' temperature is at a blistering temperature of 122°F. The adjoining **Karamustafa Çamur Banyosu** offers mud bathing, communal baths, and rudimentary lodgings for about 60TL.

MUSEUMS

The ultra modern **Bursa Kent Müzesi** (Bursa City Museum, Atatürk Cad. 8, Heykel, 0224/220-2626, www.bursakentmuzesi.gov.tr, 9:30 A.M.–6 P.M. Mon.–Fri., 10 A.M.–6:30 P.M. Sat.–Sun., 3TL) is housed in Bursa's old courthouse. Three floors relay local history, starting with the reconstruction of more than a dozen various workshops and a short history of the area's silk production in the basement. The city's 7,000-year history, along with its conquering warlords, is recounted in the ground floor. The upper floor details Bursa's recent history and the artists it bred.

The living museum of **Hüsnü Züber Evi** (Hüsnü Züber House, Uzunyol Sok. 3, 0224/221-3542, 10 A.M.–noon and 1–5 P.M. Tues.–Sun., 5TL) is an authentic 1836 *konak* (residence) painstakingly restored by local artist Hüsnü Züber in 1988. Originally a guesthouse, it later housed the Russian consulate. Though it is now owned by the municipality, the original proprietor Hüsnü Bey still guides visitors through the ground floor. There's a large collection of wooden implements, such as an array of spoons amassed from various regions in Anatolia.

THRACE

North of the Muradiye Complex and set amidst the tea gardens and playgrounds of the just re-landscaped Küktür Parkı, the **Arkeoloji Müzesi** (Archaeological Museum, 8:30 A.M.– noon and 1–5:30 P.M. Tues.–Sun., 3TL) boasts a fine collection of Byzantine and Roman stone relics, such as sarcophagi and statues found locally, as well as glassware and jewelry collected throughout Anatolia.

Amid immaculately landscaped gardens, the **Atatürk Evi** (Atatürk House, 8:30 A.M.–noon and 1–5:30 P.M. Tues.–Sun., free) was the father of modern Turkey's seat during his 13 visits to Bursa. Built in 1895, the residence offers a glimpse of this statesman's inner sanctum, replete with personal effects found on two of the three floors open to the public.

Day Trips
ÇEKIRGE

About two miles west of Bursa's center, Çekirge sprawls along a foothill of lush Uludağ Mountain. Its baths date back to the Romans. Here, both old posh residences and better hotels feature in-house thermal baths.

Built by luxury-seekers Byzantine Emperor Justinian I and his wife Theodora in the mid-6th century, **Eski Kaplıca** (Old Baths, Çekirge Meydanı, 0224/233-9300, 7 A.M.–10:30 P.M., 25–75TL) is a grand marble structure in which both dawdlers and the infirm, who seek the thermal baths' therapeutic benefits, loll away the hours. It was renovated by the adjacent Kervansaray Termal Hotel, which is conveniently and hideously connected by a modern walkway. The old baths feature separate opalescent marble pools for men and women, hammams, and adjacent cool pools.

Located just up the hill from the Old Baths, **Hüdavendigâr I Murat Camii** (east on Çekirge Caddesi to Murat Caddesi, and left onto Cami Sokak, sunrise to sunset daily, free) took over two decades to build, perhaps because its commissioner, Sultan Murat, was constantly waging war against the irreverent in the Balkans. Incidentally, the appellation *Hüdavendigâr* (Creator of the Universe) was humbly affixed by Murat himself. The mosque has a unique inverse-T shape and features a *medrese* (Islamic seminary) on the ground level, along its two barrel-roofed wings. The *medrese* was used by traveling dervishes. Inaugurated in 1385, the complex features a rather bland prayer hall, highlighted only by an ornate *mihrab* (niche in the wall pointing to Mecca). Just across the street, the huge tomb of Murat I was built after he was slain in Kosova in 1389 during a Serbian-led upheaval to free Balkan territories from Ottoman rule.

I Murat Caddesi is Çekirge's main drag, from which frequent *dolmuş* (communal taxi) service and Bus 96, headed for either Heykel or Atatürk Caddesi, are available. Coming from Bursa, hop on a *dolmuş* en route to Çekirge or SSK Hastanesi (Public Hospital).

ULUDAĞ

Translated in English as "Great Mountain," Uludağ is Turkey's preferred ski resort, 36 kilometers south of Bursa. The massif's flanks make up the **Uludağ Milliyet Parkı** (3TL for driver and vehicle, 1TL for every additional passenger) a national park of towering conifers and wildlife, interspersed by trails that wind up to the 7,700-foot-tall giant. Come summer, legions of cars filled to the brim with picnickers sputter up Uludağ to claim their piece of meadow. For those not keen on physical exertion, there is a *teleferik* (cable car) that seesaws the five-mile stretch between Uludağ and its main ski resort of **Sarıalan.**

Featuring 13 lifts, Uludağ is ideal for beginners and intermediate skiers. Its expansive meadows appeal to cross-country skiers as well. Come in late January or early February to avoid the packed winter break season. Skiing gear is available onsite for less than 30TL per day. Operated by each resort, the majority of lifts are modern, with tickets sold at their respective hotels.

Throughout summer, Uludağ provides spectacular scenery and newly-marked trails for avid trekkers. But do not dismiss the unpredictable weather—summer wind storms are not unheard of—and bring the necessary gear, including a cell phone, even if setting out for only a couple of hours.

the popular alpine playground of Uludağ, near Bursa

While more frequent in November–April, *dolmuş* service is reduced to a handful of daily departures during the summer. Communal taxis marked for Uludağ (6TL) and Sarıalan (9TL) pick up passengers along their route. Return before dark in the summer to ensure transportation back to the city center. Chains, which may be purchased at inflated prices from sly entrepreneurs along the roadside, are required during the winter season. A taxi costs up to 50TL, but a return may be negotiated as drivers are reluctant to come back empty.

To reach the must-do *teleferik* (cable car) ride, hop on a *dolmuş* marked *teleferik* at the stop on Orhan Gazı Caddesi in the west, or behind the Bursa City Museum (1.50TL) across town. Keep in mind that a wait is possible as the vehicle only takes off for the 15-minute ride when the car is full. Departing approximately every half-hour, the 40-person *teleferik* (Teleferik Caddesi, 8 A.M.–10 P.M. summer, until 5 P.M. in winter, 8TL) takes about 30 minutes to complete its scenic trajectory to the top of expansive Bursa, if weather permits. The *teleferik* stops in Kadıyayla,

where a lift change is necessary for the final climb to Sarıalan.

TERMAL

Just south of the Yalova port, Termal (Yalova Thermal Hot Springs Resort, 0226/675-7400, bath and spa facilities 8 A.M.–10 P.M. daily) is a massive complex of geothermal activity. Roman emperors were first to lay claim to the warm waters spewing from underground some 17 centuries ago. Justinian I commissioned large marble baths for his personal use, but years of fierce battle and strong earthquakes ravaged the structures. Rediscovered under a pile of earth in 1900, Sultan Abdülmecid commissioned a major renovation of additions to the imperial facilities. Republic founder and leader Mustafa Kemal Atatürk was one of the area's most noted guests. He so enjoyed Termal's restorative powers that he had an elegant series of pavilions, surrounded by exotic landscaping, built in 1929. This estate overlooks the complex. While the area's population swells during the summer from 45 to 500, the resort, with its surrounding web of trails and

BIRDS OF PARADISE

Manyas Lake, just 16 kilometers south of Bandırma on the Bandirma-Balikesir Highway, is the richest habitat for local and migratory birds in Turkey. Some 239 species of birds feed, rest, and breed here in May and June on their way to Europe and in September and October on their return trip to the warmer climate of Africa. Declared a conservation area in 1959, the 158-acre Bird Paradise National Park, adjoining Manyas Lake, is a veritable ornithological heaven come spring and fall.

A reported three million feathered friends gather here twice annually. Hundreds of graceful posers, like tufted herons, large spoonbills, glossy ibises, black cormorants, and leggy storks, nest in the willow copses along the banks of the lake. The area is generally calm and outfitted with observation towers to sneak a close look at some rare species. The endangered yellow-beaked Dalmatian pelicans gather by the dozen on specially-built platforms in May and June.

Most species of large birds return to the same nesting spot, often times conveniently utilizing last year's aerie. While the lake and its levees are typically quiet, eventual arguments over territory do arise. Once settled, birds repair any damages caused by wintry storms and move right back in to lay and hatch their eggs in tandem. Moorhens, ducks, coots, and geese nest in reeds and rushes, while egrets, night and purple herons, glossy ibises, and pelicans arrive in early March to nest on higher platforms.

Manyas' **Kuşcenneti Millî Parkı** (Bird Paradise National Park, 7 A.M.-5:30 P.M., 3TL) is the smallest of Turkey's national parks, with a square area comprising about 0.25 percent of the adjacent Manyas Lake. The lake provides the birds with plenty of fish, particularly in spring when the placid waters around the reeds teem with 23 species of spawning finned creatures. The habitat, comprised of a rich vegetation which grows on bird droppings, is ideal for the growth of larva.

Despite its small size, Kuşcenneti's unique natural features lure tens of thousands of bird aficionados. The observation towers, lakeside restaurants, and picnic areas make this an excellent destination for locals and tourists visiting Bursa and the northwestern coast of Turkey.

streams, beckons anglers, hikers, and bathers year-round.

Across the parking lot at the entrance of Termal, the **Atatürk Evi** (Atatürk House, 0226/675-7400, 9:30 A.M.–5 P.M.) lies at the end of a wooded path on the left. Beyond the exotic landscaping, the quaint museum provides an intimate look at this very public figure's inner sanctum. The first and most popular bath is **Kurşunlu Banyo** (0226/675-7400), named after its lead-covered dome. Head to its outdoor facilities (10TL per hour), which are perfect for families. Or, follow in Emperor Justinian's stead and opt for the indoor pool and sauna (8TL per hour). Private booths are also available for 10–15TL. The superior **Sultan Banyo** (0226/675-7400, 3TL per hour) offers separate bathing sections for women and men. These baths are typically frequented by more conservative users. The 26 private bathing rooms at the **Valide Banyo** (0226/675-7400, 15–20TL per hour) are the more comfortable options. Massage and acupuncture services are also available.

Awakening to the potential of health-oriented tourism, the entire complex has been revamped by the onsite office of the Ministry of Health (0226/675-7400). They also manage Termal's five hotels. Once drab and threadbare, these lodgings have been whipped into appealing lodging and dining facilities. **[** **Çınar** and **Çamlık** hotels (0226/675-7400, 50–90TL) together offer 100 alluring rooms. Inspired by two centenarian sycamore trees in its yard, the Çınar surrounds a large welcoming courtyard with a bustling café. Çamlık's bar and restaurant may be a better bet for grown-ups. A third property, the **Apart Hotel** (0226/675-7400, from 100TL) is specifically intended for large groups with six rustic, air-conditioned apartments. Booking accommodations in any of these hotels secures unlimited free access to the baths. Located just eight miles from the port of Yalova, Termal is accessible through *dolmuş* service (3TL) that shuttles passengers straight to the Termal parking lot within 30 minutes. IDO (Istanbul Deniz Otobüsleri, 0212/444-4436, www.ido.com.tr) has fast ferries from Yenikapı, Bostancı, and Pendik to Yalova. Termal provides is an ideal pit stop on either leg of an itinerary revolving around Bursa.

KUŞ GÖLÜ
The southern coast of the Sea of Marmara is mostly blue-collar and virtually devoid of any tourist destinations, with the exception of the Marmara Islands and a splendid bird paradise. The region is usually missed entirely by foreigners outside of avian buffs, professional photographers, and truckers making their way from Yalova to Çanakkale.

Just 10 miles south of Bandırma, **Kuşcenneti Milli Parkı** (Bird Paradise National Park, 0266/735-5422, 7 A.M.–5:30 P.M., 3TL) is located two miles south of the turnoff along the Bandırma-Balıkesir Highway. It's a 128-acre wetland reserve on the banks of Kuş Gölü (formerly Manyas Gölü) that serves as roosting grounds and annual migratory stop for some 270 species of birds. The best time to see feathered species in transit—like showy pelicans and graceful storks—is April–June and September–November.

From Bursa's *otogar* (bus station), take a two-hour bus ride to Bandırma, which is also connected by ferry from Istanbul's Yenikapı port. From Bandırma, a cab is the best method to travel the ten miles to Kuş Gölü.

Festivals
For three weeks starting in mid-June, Bursa's **Uluslararası Festival** (0224/220-8848, www.bursafestivali.org) is the annual tribute to the city's performing arts. Organized by master puppeteer Şinasi Çelikkol, the five-day **International Golden Karagöz**

Dance Competition (Bursa Kültür Sanat ve Turizm Vakfı, Kültürpark İçi, Osmangazi; 0224/234-4912, altinkaragoz.org, in Turkish) is staged annually in Bursa's open air culture park during the first half of July.

Nightlife
As soon as the sun sets, Bursa's throbbing nightlife gives Istanbul a run for its money, thanks in part to the legions of youths attending Uludağ University nearby. From information on some 30 after-dark venues, from classic pubs to state-of-the-art bars and thumping nightclubs, check out www.lifeinbursa.com/mekan.

Wine lovers flock to Ali Ataş's **Vitis Şarap Evi** (Çekirge Cad. 69, Osmangazı, 0224/234-2444, www.vitis.com.tr) to savor a variety of vintages. Sip velvety reds produced from the regional Muscadine grape in vaulted, brick rooms or on a terrace, amid green conifers. Vitis also cooks up a full Turkish menu, including mixed kebabs served hanging from a trundle over marble.

If you're in Uludağ with no where to go, head to what could be a grown-up Barbie's haunt, **St. Bernard** (Oteller Bölgesi, Uludağ, 0224/285-2359, 10 P.M.–2 A.M.). Eerily blending pinks and beads in a chalet atmosphere, replete with the crackle of a roaring fireplace, the café/club caters to Istanbul's blinged and botoxed crowds, with prices to match.

Calling all revelers, **Kat 3 Bar** (Emek Caddesi, Basın ve Kültür Sarayı, 19 2nd floor, 0224/443-2272, kat3.com.tr, 5 P.M.–5 A.M. daily, live music 11 P.M.–3 A.M., 10–20TL entrance fee Wed., Fri., and Sat.) is a British pub, disco, and restaurant all in one. There's a different theme every night; Latin Beat Tuesdays are by far the busiest. For another all-inclusive location, **Club Vici** (Mudanya Yolu 7, 0224/244-7373, www.clubvici.com, 11 P.M.–5 A.M.) boasts both sizzling outdoor and indoor dance floors, as well as a 600-guest bar and restaurant that opens its doors at 7 P.M. The unassuming, but always fun, **M Pub** (Altıparmak Cad. 9D, 0224/220-9428, noon–3 A.M.) is where locals hang out over a

THRACE

couple of beers during the week. Live DJs work their magic on Fridays and Saturdays.

Accommodations

The best hotels can be found in Çekirge, just two miles west of Bursa's center. Typically, accommodations in Bursa's chaotic Merkez (center) are geared to serve businesspeople, while the neighborhoods of Soğanlı and Çekirge offer a more relaxing atmosphere. Those headed for the slopes will find Uludağ has a slew of hotels that cater to Istanbul's in-crowd during the winter, at very inflated prices. The rest of the year they'll charge a fraction of their winter—or semester—rates. For a more exhaustive list, log onto to www.bursahotels.net.

UNDER 100TL

For an inexpensive option smack in the center of the action, the **Hotel Efehan** (Gümüşçeken Cad. 34, Merkez, 0224/225-2260, www.efehan.net.tr, from 75TL) can't be beat. It may be the best all-around value with its large, classic rooms and attached baths. Gazing at the sunset from the spacious, rooftop terrace café and restaurant could end up being the highlight of your trip to the former Ottoman capital.

Hotel Dikmen (Maksem Cad. 78, Ozmangazı, 0224/224-1840, www.dikmenotel.com, from 65TL) offers consistently clean and pleasant rooms. The complimentary breakfast is served in the sumptuously landscaped courtyard downstairs. Serving à la Turca fare, the quaint terrace of Dikmen's top-floor restaurant offers views of Ulucami and the valley beyond, if smog allows.

A restored townhouse on the outskirts of town, the **Safran Hotel** (Ortapazar Cad., Arka Sok. 4, Tophane, 0224/224-7216, http://site.mynet.com/safranhotel, 65–120TL) cheers up its guests with a saffron-hued facade and modern amenities throughout. Though rooms are a bit bare. There's a live *fasıl* music band playing on most nights in its ground-level restaurant, which serves a typical and delectable array of meze. The **Demirci Otel** (Hammamlar Cad. 33, Çekirge, 0224/236-5104, from 40TL) may be humble, but it's always a good

bet for the cleanest, most inexpensive lodgings in pricey Çekirge.

OVER 100TL

In Çekirge, **Hotel Gönlüferah** (I Murat Cad. 24, Çekirge, 0224/233-9210, www.gonluferahhotel.com, from 200TL) achieves utter luxury with a captivating mix of Ottoman classic furnishings and modern design in a spectrum of dazzling color. Canopied beds and plush carpets can be found throughout; its Zoe Spa offers 12 custom massages. Valley views abound. Plasma screens and the divine haute cuisine at the posh A La Carte restaurant top off the exquisite experience.

The **Swissôtel Çelik Palas** (Çekirge Cad. 79, Çekirge, 0224/233-3800, www.hotelcelikpalas.com.tr, from 190TL) mixes colorful luxury with its illustrious history. In the late 1920s, premier Atatürk commissioned this hotel to provide space for his esteemed guests. The grand house he utilized during his sojourn in Bursa is now a 38-room annex to the hotel. The Çelik also features one of Çekirge's most beautiful marble thermal spas.

For top-notch accommodations in downtown Bursa, the five-star **Hotel Almira** (Ulubatlı Hasan Bulvarı 5, Merkez, 0224/250-2020, www.almira.com.tr, from 140TL) has perhaps the most elegant and modern rooms. While the Almira excels at taking care of Bursa's business guests, those here for pleasure will not be short-changed. Onsite facilities include a full-service spa, salon, hammam, gaming arcades, and boutiques.

The 29 pricey rooms at the special-class **Authentique Club Hotel** (Botanik Parkı, Soğanlı, 0224/211-3280, www.otantikclubhotel.com, from 175TL) boast classic Ottoman decor that makes its highbrow guests feel like sultans. Expect modern amenities, including Internet, satellite television, air-conditioning, and a large pool. Its top-notch restaurant, Authentique, serves superb fish fare. The nearby botanical gardens and zoo make for a great after-dinner stroll.

In Uludağ, towering amid an expansive meadow is the **Monte Baia Hotel** (2. Gelişim

Oteller Bölgesi, 0224/285-2383, www.baia hotels.com, from 200TL in high-season). It offers a ton of amenities, including babysitting services for parents wishing to hit the slopes on their own. At over 180 rooms, the Monte is part of the Baia chain, renowned for their attentive service and cleanliness in ultra modern semi-luxury. Also atop the massif, **Hotel Genç Yazıcı** (1. Gelişim Oteller Bölgesi, Uludağ, 0224/285-2040, www.yazicihotel.com, from 100TL off-season) runs the most ski trails from its location. Its ski school and family-oriented amenities add up to an unparalleled ski experience. A bit bare, the spacious comfortable rooms come in a lip-smacking pastel palette. This all-inclusive winter resort features a heated pool with whirlpool tub overlooking the slopes, along with an adjoining Turkish bath.

Food

Bursa is hailed for its kebab, in particular the authentic, ubiquitous spit-roasted, tomato sauce–slathered Iskender Kebab (10TL). However, a burgeoning haute cuisine—typically offered in upscale hotels—is getting nods from gastronomes west of the Bosphorus. Of course, fine dining requires dressy attire and is not cheap. If you're traveling during the month of July, you'd be remiss not to try the local peach that's sold by local farmers along the roadside.

CAFÉS

OD'ed on local cuisine? Then opt for the predictable, **Mahfel Mado** (Namazgah Cad. 2, 0224/326-8888, www.mahfelmado.com, 8TL). This eatery unites the menu of the country-wide Mado franchise with Bursa's first café-style diner. The chain is known for serving breakfast anytime. Try their Turkish pastry- or dairy-based desserts, which accompany mid-afternoon tea to a tee. But unlike its scores of sister restaurants throughout Turkey, this location offers live music on the patio during the summer and a small art gallery buried in the basement.

FISH

The first fish restaurant to open its doors in Bursa, **Arap Şükrü** (Sakarya Cad. 4, 0224/220-6716, 11 A.M.–11 P.M., 18TL) is so famous with locals that its name is used as a location marker in the city's former Jewish enclave. While there's a host of similar diners crowding Sakarya Street, Arap Şükrü is the original whose long-standing consistent popularity speaks volumes for its quality. Summertime is particularly delightful when the sidewalks offer added seating and people-watching. Not into fish! Don't fret, there are plenty of meat specialties as well.

FUSION

The only eatery outside of hotel diners worth a try in Çekirge is **Cumurcul** (Kükürtlü Mah., Çekirge Cad., Çekirge, 0224/235-3707, 20TL). Owned and operated by a Turkish chef trained in Europe, Cumurcul's menu features regional fish and meat prepared with an unexpected continental twist. With small rooms serving as private alcoves with one or two tables, the exclusive Ottoman mansion in which the restaurant is located is extremely appealing to its highbrow clientele. The ambience ratchets up a notch after 11 P.M., when the restaurant turns into a swanky nightclub.

LOCAL FARE

Kebapcı Iskender (Ünlü Cad. 7, 0224/221-4615, kebapciiskender.com.tr, 10 A.M.–10 P.M., 13TL) has been in business and serving its patented recipe of sliced pit-roasted lamb since 1867. What started as Mehmet Efendi's restaurant, serving food to tradesmen in the local bazaar in 1850, grew into a brand that extends throughout the continent. Even the popular vertical revolving spit was invented here as a way to provide a more hygienic method, rather than rotating the circular slab of meat over a fire in the ground.

Ask a local where to eat meat in Bursa and **Çiçek Izgara** (Belediye Cad. 15, 2nd floor, 0224/221-6526, 6TL) will inevitably score high on the list. It's casual, yet somewhat refined for a *köfte* (meatball) dive, with white tablecloths throughout. The restaurant turns into a noisy cafeteria-style diner come lunchtime.

THRACE

Accompany a meal of *kabak dolması* (stuffed zucchini) with çaçık (cold, garlicky yogurt soup) for a light summer repast. The Iskender Kebab at the blue-collar **Uludağ Kebapcısı** (Uluyol Şirin Sok. 12, 0224/251-4551, 11 A.M.–9 P.M., 10TL) far outdo Iskender's version, or anybody else's, for that matter. Cemal and Cemil Usta, the diner's managing owners for over four decades, recently added another location right in the Bursa City Square Shopping Center. The meat and creamy yogurt served onsite is farm fresh. Top it all off with a dessert of *sütlü irmik helva* (sweetened milk and semolina concoction).

OTTOMAN

For Ottoman fare in a historically Ottoman location, head out to **(Darüzziyafe** (II Murat Cad. 36, Muradiye, 0224/224-6439, www.daruzziyafe.com, 20TL) in the restored soup kitchen of the 15th-century Muradiye Complex. Ponder what to order from the 400 different dishes the rustic restaurant features. Dine in one of the rows of red-clothed tables that pack an antique hall. In summertime, outside seating provides the perfect setting from which to savor an *Ali Nazık Kebabı* (morsels of stewed lamb wrapped in thin strips of sautéed eggplant).

Information and Services

Like Istanbul, Bursa is a large city filled with modern conveniences. Banks and ATMs are located along Atatürk Caddesi and Namazgah Caddesi. Most businesses accept credit cards; but for bargaining, cash still rules. Currency exchange booths are located in the Bazaar and at the bus and airline terminals.

The **Turizm Ofisi** (Orhan Gazı Altgeçidi, Koza Parkı, 0224/220-1848, 8 A.M.–noon and 1–5 P.M. Mon.–Fri.) is located along the shops in the arcade beneath Atatürk Caddesi. It provides a host of information regarding hotels, spas, restaurants, and other local tourist destinations.

Available through most hotels, **Internet services** are also on hand at **Café Enigma** (Zafer Sok. 1/A, Osmangazı, 0224/262-1196, 9 A.M.–midnight, 2TL/hour).

Getting There

The best way to get to Bursa is by riding the recently added **IDO** (Istanbul Deniz Otobüsleri, 0212/444-4436, www.ido.com.tr, 20TL) fast ferry line from Yenikapı (80 minutes) straight into Bursa's port, then hopping on a *dolmuş* (communal taxi) labeled *Merkez* for another 10-minute ride. This ferry also accommodates vehicles (75TL, plus 20TL for the driver).

Bus service to Bursa either crosses the Sea of Marmara—labeled *feribot ile* (by ferry)—with the IDO ferry at Topçular, or goes *karayolu ile* (by road) on a five-hour route around the Bay of Izmit. Five miles north from the center, the **Otogar** (Yeni Yalova Yolu, 0224/261-5400, www.bursaterminali.com in Turkish) houses all passenger bus companies.

Getting Around

The best way to travel within Bursa is to use the *dolmuş* (communal taxi). The main terminal is located just south of Heykel Square behind the governmental building, with a service heading to Çekirge (1.5TL) and another for Teleferik, among several others. **Taxi** service is also possible; a ride across town from Heykel to Çekirge shouldn't set you back more than 12TL.

Municipal buses crisscross the town and operate solely on a prepaid system, with tickets (1–2TL) that can be purchased at either booths or shops that display the BursaKart logo near bus stops. With destinations marked curbside or on the front of the yellow vehicles, the buses run from the major terminal at Koza Parkı on Atatürk Caddesi. Line 1 goes through Emir Sultan Mosque and Teleferik; Line 2 for Muradiye; and Line 3 serves the Kültür Parkı.

IZNIK

A momentous city, sprawling through an abundant valley formed by the Bithynian peaks, Iznik is set amidst olive and peach orchards, punctuated by soaring cypress and a serene lake. Its agricultural trove is not unlike so many of its sister cities throughout the Aegean. However, its past unveils a long history of faith

and capitulation to countless tribes, kingdoms, and empires.

After viewing many of Istanbul's monuments, visitors head to Iznik primarily for its faience. Once there, they get sideswept by its momentous significance in the birth of organized Christianity. In fact, Christians considered Nicaea (Iznik's Roman name) the third among holy cities, after Jerusalem and the Vatican. Little remains of its early history except for a scattering of city walls and a few lackluster monuments. But thanks to national and local efforts to reinvigorate its artistic legacy and to lure tourism, the rural town's easy-going atmosphere has become a weekend destination for local and faith-based tourism. Its lake is a bird-lover's paradise. Earmark a half-day to visit the sights and lunch at a café by the lake.

Following an original Hellenic city plan, Iznik is basically a square surrounded by fortifications. Most sights are within the city walls, which have four cardinal gates: Göl Kapıları (Lake Gate), Yenişhir, Istanbul, and Lefke.

Atatürk Caddesi connects the gates from north to south and Kılıçaşlan Caddesi, from east to west, with Ayasofya right in the middle.

History

Iznik was a stomping ground for many ancient Greek kingdoms. It was rebuilt in 316 B.C. as Antigoneia in honor of the one-eyed Macedonian King Antigonus, who claimed the city several years after the death of his commander, Alexander the Great. But conspiracy among the ranks led to his demise and one of the scheming generals, Lysimachus, became Iznik's new ruler. The former general renamed the city Nicaea, as a token of affection to his wife. For the next two centuries, the city served as the center of the Bithynian realm and a bastion of trade, thanks to its location between Galatia and Phrygia. And in 74 B.C., its title along with ownership of its sister cities throughout the region was transferred to the Romans. The rise of nearby Nicomedia—today's Izmit—produced a vehement battle for supremacy between the two cities. It was eventually settled by the reading of an official decree entitling the latter the status of metropolis. After temporary invasions from the Goths of the West and the Persians from the East, Nicaea surpassed its previous grandeur under the Byzantines.

The 4th and 8th centuries A.D. proved fortuitous for the city and a budding Christianity, as two church meetings would cement the religion's foundation and its principles. The first, convened by Constantine the Great in A.D. 325, saw the creation of the Nicene Creed, a document establishing the divinity of Christ. The second, held in Nicaea's Hagia Sophia (Ayasofya) Church in A.D. 787, settled the Iconoclastic Controversy. This raging dispute over the depiction and veneration of holy figures ended in the rift between the Orthodox and Roman Catholic Churches.

After serving as a Byzantine buttress against the advancing Turks in the Middle Ages, Nicaea reclaimed its prosperity and was lavished with majestic edifications and fortifications by Justinian I during the 6th century A.D.

In 1078, it took the Selçuk Turks an entire year to break through these thick walls and conquer the city within. Crusaders would come knocking at the behest of Byzantium less than 20 years later. But, during an overnight strategic sleight, the Byzantines, who had arrived moments before Europe's army, raided the city and reaped its riches. When the Venetians took Byzantium in 1204, Emperor Theodore I retreated to Nicaea and affirmed it the capital of the Byzantine Empire.

The advancing Ottomans conquered Nicaea on March 2, 1331. Sultan Orhan I ordered the destruction of its buildings, with the remaining rubble to be used in the construction of mosques and the first Islamic theological school. After the conquest of Constantinople in 1453, Iznik lost its importance. It would soon regain some of it back—at least artistically—however, when Sultan Selim I ordered all of the ceramics artisans from the newly conquered Persian city of Tabriz to move west to Iznik. Inspired by ornate Chinese porcelain and Islamic motifs, the tile makers created impressive faience—tin-glazed pottery. By the 1700s, the city's artistic renown and the art form declined, leaving behind agriculture as its main export. Thanks to demand from the tourism sector, Iznik's ceramics is back into contention.

Sights

◖ IZNIK ŞEHIR SURLARI (CITY WALLS)

Spanning some 2.7 miles in length, the Iznik Şehir Surları didn't fare too well. The majority of the more than 100 watchtowers that soared from the fortifications lay mostly in rubble. What remains intact, though, are three of the original four monumental gates, plus a few smaller gates. The **Istanbul Gate,** reached from the north, boasts a triumphant arch honoring Hadrian, between its inner and outer gateways. The **Lefke Gate,** to the east, is similarly stunning and actually comprises a central gateway with two side portals. Built by Proconsul Plancius Varus to honor Hadrian's visit in A.D. 123, the main gate's outside facade is replete with ornate scenes of warfare etched into its stonework. Climb through the gate for spectacular city views. Selçuks, Ottomans, and Byzantines repeatedly breached the fortifications through the **Yenişehir Gate** to the south. Less than a 1,000 feet due east from this entry, you'll reach the small **Horoz Gate.** Just inside this door, a scattering of stones are the vestiges of the imperial **Church of Koimesis.** It was built for Byzantine emperor Theodore I, who fled Constantinople after the Venetian crusaders overtook the city. The leafy path nearby winds by a ruined 15,000-seat **Roman theater** and the smaller **Saray Gate,** which led to Sultan Orhan's palace. The **Göl Kapıları** (Lake Gate) is little more than an opening through the walls. The two main streets in town connect the cardinal gates: Atatürk Caddesi runs north-south between Istanbul and Yenişehir Gates; Kılıçaşlan Caddesi runs east-west between Lefke and Lake Gates.

AYASOFYA
(CHURCH OF THE HOLY WISDOM)

Not much more than a roofless shell, what remains of Ayasofya (Atatürk Cad., 0224/757-1027, 9 A.M.–noon and 1–5:30 P.M. Tues.–Sun.) is an accumulation of three massive renovations. Set amidst a fragrant sunken rose garden, the seemingly freestanding structure offers little for the visitor except a discolored fresco of Mary, Jesus, and John the Baptist in an area once used as the nave. There are also portions of an 11th-century mosaic floor protected under glass sheathing. Constantine commissioned the original building. It succumbed to a massive earthquake and then was rebuilt entirely by the culturally-inclined Justinian I. In 1331, the church was converted into the Ulu Mosque. It was brutally damaged by a Mongol invasion in the early 14th century, and by fire some 200 years later. The ill-fated structure's last renovation fell into the able hands of Mimar Sinan, who lavished the building with Iznik tiles. Fierce fighting between Greek and Turkish troops in 1922 severely damaged the sanctuary. As in most churches, if the gate is locked during

opening hours, proceed to the groundskeeper's residence and politely ask for the key.

MOSQUES

Crouching amid lawns and sporadic firs, the **Yeşil Cami** (Green Mosque, Müze Sok., no phone, open daily outside of prayer times) provides a splash of color in Iznik's prevailing dowdiness. Its petite single minaret, tiled in red, white, and turquoise, replaced the emerald hue the monument was named after. Its colorful spire tips off visitors to the wealth of faience within the thick brick walls it towers over. The ornate etchings on the marble portico lead into a sanctuary that was custom-built in 1378 for Çandarlı Kara Halil Hayrettin Paşa, a commander who led Sultan Orhan I's army and later served as grand vizier under the subsequent emperor, Murat I. Like the minaret, the inner sanctum's red, blue, and white faience challenge the mosque's green moniker.

Further west, the **Hacı Özbek Camii** (just north of Kılıçarslan Caddesi, between Mevlana and Eşrefoğlu Sokak, no phone, sunrise to sunset, free) is the town's oldest mosque, one that has been the target of inept re-beautification schemes. And just to its north, the **Eşrezade Abdullah Rumi Tomb** (located behind Hacı Özbek Camii) encases the remains of a noted Sufi mystic. Adjacent, is a solitary minaret bearing the torch for a mosque that was wiped out during the conflicts of 1922.

IZNIK ARKEOLOJI MÜZESI
(IZNIK ARCHAEOLOGICAL MUSEUM)

Across the street from the Green Mosque, Iznik Arkeoloji Müzesi (Müze Sok., 0224/754-1027, 9 A.M.–noon and 1–5:30 P.M. daily, 3TL) is housed in the Nilüfer Hatun Imareti, the shelter built by Murat I in 1388 in tribute to his mother. She was a smart and artistically gifted Byzantine blue-blood, who, through a twist of fate, was snatched by Sultan Osman the day she was to marry the Greek Prince of Bilecik. Her father, the Prince of Yarhısar, had lured Osman to the wedding ceremony to assassinate him. Aware of the scheme, Osman stole the soon-to-be princess. She went on to marry his son, Orhan, and subsequently controlled the Ottoman State during her husband's many conquests. The building was used as a hospice for the Ahi Brotherhood of skilled artisans long before it was re-dedicated to Nilüfer.

The grounds are a catchall for tombs and statues dating back to the Romans, the town's stint as a capital, and the early Ottoman era. On display are samples of original Iznik tile work, such as the complex red faience; ceramic artifacts from the mid-1500s; an intact Roman sarcophagus; and samples of Ottoman craftsmanship, like weaponry, weaving, and kitchenware.

OTHER HISTORICAL BUILDINGS

The **Süleyman Paşa Medresesi** is located on the eponymous street. This chimneyed structure was built by Sultan Orhan as the first theological school in the empire, right after he conquered Nicaea in 1313. While it's still functioning after almost 700 years, the *medrese* (Islamic seminary) also houses a few tile ateliers and shops.

Just southeast of the central square lies the 15th-century **II Murat Hamamı** (one block south of Ayasofya, 0224/757-1459, 6 A.M.–midnight daily, 1–5 P.M. daily for women). What was once the women's section now serves as a showroom for dazzling ceramics.

Accommodations and Food

Iznik is short on upscale hotels. The few that are here are jam-packed during the holidays and summer. For the pick of the litter, book way ahead or opt to stay in Bursa's myriad of no-frill lodgings and boutique hotels. The 🄲 **Çamlık Motel** (Sahil Yolu, 0224/757-1362, www.iznik-camlikmotel.com, from 60TL) remains the best and most reliable place to spend the night. Right on the lake, the hotel has bright, minimalist rooms with air-conditioning, Internet access, balconies, and attached baths. The facility's rustic restaurant surpasses any other diner in town. Samples of Iznik Lake fish and seafood—like crayfish—are served under plane trees by the placid lake.

The quaint **Iznik Vakıf Konukevi** (Sahil Yolu, Vakıf Sokak 13, 0224/757-6025, info@iznik.com, from 75TL) is strictly a boutique hotel with miles of tiles and classic, yet refined, comfort. Personal touches, such as dazzling faience creamers at the breakfast table, add to the ambience. This gem of a hotel doubles as a convenient stop to buy colorful ceramic mementos. Email early for a reservation, as the establishment is gathering international media coverage and popularity by the day.

Five miles southeast of Iznik, up on a hill overlooking the city, are three far-off cabins at **Salıcı Evi** (7 km southeast of Iznik in Çamoluk Köyü, 0532/315-4536, www.salicievi.com, 150–200TL). Owner Zeki and Filiz Salice's trio of wooden lodges sleep up to six people in an atmosphere that appeals to cosmopolitan hunter-gatherers.

For an economical solution, **Cem Hotel** (Sahil Yolu 34, 0224/757-1687, www.cemotel.com, 50–75TL) has a variety of accommodations, from pension-style to more luxurious. Newly refurbished, it features air-conditioning, wireless Internet access throughout, and large bathrooms with tubs. Reserve a suite and enjoy the complimentary farm-fresh breakfast served on the lakeside balcony. Its restaurant offers a delectable selection of locally grown produce.

Also a good bet, **Kaynarca Pansiyon** (Gündem Sok 1, 0224/757-1723, from 20TL) is a favorite with backpackers. Here you'll find free maps, satellite TV, and an adjoining Internet café. Since no advanced booking is allowed, you'll have to take your chances.

Being a guest of Serdar Aydın at **Hotel Aydın** (Kılıçaslan Cad. 64, 0224/757-7650, www.iznikhotelaydin.com, 80–120TL) may add inches to your waist. It's known locally for its patisserie, which serves food onsite and for takeout. Right in the center of town, Hotel Aydın has three floors of pastel-hued, clean rooms with all the expected necessities, in addition to wireless Internet, satellite TV, and air-conditioning.

Iznik's find-dining restaurants are located at the Çamlık or Cem Hotels, whose lakeside eateries provide a mesmerizing location to break bread. For finer digs and a bigger buzz after dark, one should aim their fork for Bursa. But, **Konya Etli Pide Salonu** (Atatürk Cad. 75, 8 A.M.–9 P.M., 10TL) provides a tantalizing *pide* (pita bread) and *lahmacun* (thin pizza with minced meat crust). Every town has a *köfte* (meatball) dive popular with the workforce and **Kenan Çorba and Izgara** (Atatürk Cad. across from Ayasofya, 0224/757-0235) is it for Iznik. Savor their Inegöl version of the meaty bite and succulent soups in a clean and modern environment.

Information and Services

Near the *otogar* (bus station) in the town's center, you'll find plenty of ATMs and the **turism ofisi** (Kılınçaslan Cad. 130, 0224/757-1933, 9 A.M.–noon and 1–5 P.M. daily).

Getting There

Bus service linking Iznik to Bursa (7TL, 90-minute ride) departs every 30 minutes from the *otogar* (bus station, 0224/757-1418). Another bus service connects to Yalova (8TL, 60-minute ride), departing every hour.

Gelibolu Yarımadası (Gallipoli Peninsula)

Every year on April 25, Australians and New Zealanders flock in droves to the cemeteries and the memorialized combat zone of Gelibolu Yarımadası Tarihi Milli Parkı (Gallipoli National Park) for a dawn ceremony marking the anniversary of the Allied landings during WWI. Outside of this date, only weekending Turkish families visit the rolling plains and undeveloped beaches of this pristine peninsula, north of the strategic Dardanelles. Perhaps left unspoiled as a giant reminder of the tens of thousands who perished trying to breach or defend the straits, Gallipoli Peninsula inspires serene contemplation of the region.

GELIBOLU YARIMADASI TARIHI MILLI PARKI (GALLIPOLI NATIONAL PARK)
Tips Before You Go

The park is quiet year-round, except on ANZAC (Australian and New Zealand Army Corps) Day. The event has ballooned in popularity during the last decade, particularly with young Kiwis and Aussies. To avoid inflated rates for everything from flights to hotel rooms, as well as dense crowds, avoid the second half of April altogether. Otherwise, join the ceremonies.

One could spend days visiting the 20 or so main sites that comprise the park. If exploring on your own at a leisurely pace, the best

plan of attack is to divide the park into two fronts: the Northern Battlefields, where the Anzac forces landed; and, the southern section, or Cape Helles, where the allied French and British troops were positioned. For the northern section, begin at the Kabatepe Information Center. This location is served by an inconsistent *dolmuş* service from Eceabat. A more regular *dolmuş* service crisscrosses the southern section, picking up passengers arriving from Çanakkale at the port of Kilitbahir and subsequently making its way through the main sites in about 2.5 hours. Visitors in search of a tour guide onsite should look around Eceabat, Çanakkale, or Kilitbahir; remember that daily and hourly rates are set high in order to be negotiated down.

Tours

Since the park is such a big draw, buses depart almost hourly for Çanakkale from Istanbul. Myriad packages, even private tours of the memorial, are available through a variety of tour operators. The best all around package is run by the **Anzac House** (Akbiyik Cad. 10, Sultanahmet, 0212/458-9500, www.anzachouse.com), which specializes in Gallipoli National Park and is the affordable guide of choice for international, military, and diplomatic personnel visiting the memorial. Another great choice for the roughly six-hour tour

THRACE

(lunch included) is the dependable **Crowded House** (0286/814-1565, www.crowdedhouse-gallipoli.com, 50TL). Touring the park, which spans some 23 miles of rough backcountry from top to bottom, is nearly impossible without a vehicle. This is another reason to opt for a guided outing. If departing from Istanbul, plan a full two days for the trip. If joining in Çanakkale, it can take up to 10 hours to visit the entire site; keep in mind that most tours focus on the northern section of the site. For trekkers, walking is feasible with the right gear: hiking boots, long pants, sun hat, good map, and plenty of bottled water. For more detailed historical information, log onto the exhaustive site maintained by the Australian government at www.anzacsite.gov.au, or view the documentary *Gallipoli,* directed in 2005 by Tolga Örnek.

History

In August of 1914, Enver Paşa, the Supreme Commander of Turkish Forces, signed a secret alliance with German pal Kaiser Wilhelm II with the aim of regaining the Eastern province of Kars, which was ceded to Russia during the Russo Turkish Wars of 1877. Or so he thought. This deal provided the Ottomans much needed weaponry from Germany, and in return allowed Germans to maneuver two warships through the Dardanelles to escape British pursuit. A couple of months later, all hell broke loose when this newfound military alliance used the same two ships, backed by the Ottoman Navy, to raid a handful of Russian ports. Russia was forced to declare war on the Ottoman Empire and the British saw an opportunity to take Ottomans out of the conflict by launching a strategic attack on the capital city of Istanbul.

The game plan, organized and coordinated by then First Lord of the Admiralty Winston Churchill, was two-pronged: to destabilize the Ottoman batteries guarding the Aegean coast, followed by an allied French and British naval push through the Dardanelles. So, on March 18, 1915, under the command of Admiral de Roebeck, a seven-hour sea offensive transpired.

Allied warships penetrated some seven miles through the straits before being forced to retreat. This single event cost the lives of more than 20,000 people. The Allies later realized that their Turkish opponents had been on the verge of capitalizing on that fateful day, for they had all but exhausted their ammunition. Retreating to the Greek Island of Limnos in the Aegean Sea, the Allies took roughly a month to prepare a ground offensive to secure the Gallipoli Peninsula, Dardanelles, and the Asian coastal region to the south. Then, on April 14, the strategy was implemented. British and French troops were to land near Cape Helles on the peninsula's southern tip, while Anzac forces aimed for the isthmus's western flank. The plan was for these two flanks to rejoin somewhere in between.

Little did they know that the Turks had also regrouped. With the Ottoman army's ninth infantry division showing impossible resolve, the Anglo-Franco offensive only succeeded in gaining a single beach and little scrubland after months of warfare. The Anzacs were not as lucky. They botched their landing: the troops reached Arıburnu's massive cliffs miles north of their intended target of Kabatepe's wide-open beach. And then, not only would the precipitous terrain impede their inland progress, but so would the resilient counter-offensive commanded by none other than Ottoman Lieutenant Colonel Mustafa Kemal Atatürk. Led by the future founder of Turkey, the Turks pushed the Anzacs back over the crags and, in doing so, strengthened their lines over the next few months. Some of WWI's goriest trench warfare ensued between the Johnnies (Anzacs) and Mehmets (Turks). Out of human respect, both sides cleared the other's fallen, despite frostbite in the winter and widespread epidemics of enteric fever and dysentery. Turks and Anzacs, some entrenched just 25 feet apart, engaged each other in conversation once the bell signifying the end of combat for the day would ring. So close was their proximity that a despondent Atatürk led his men into battle with these words: "I am not asking you to attack, I am ordering you to die. For in the time it takes for us to die other soldiers and commanders will arrive to take our place."

It wasn't until December of 1916, after a handful of ineffective campaigns, that the Allies issued the first order to withdraw. With losses estimated at well over 130,000, more than 70 percent of which were Turks, one of WWI's goriest conflicts lasted nine months. The blame of the botched offensive was laid squarely on British command, with repercussions including Churchill's demotion to Minister of Munitions and a loss of faith in British prime minister Herbert Asquith's single-party Liberal Government. For the Aussies: Gallipoli was their first conflict after gaining their independence from Britain, a turning point for the then fledgling state. For the Turks: Little was said, except that they maintained their reputation for fierceness and bravery in battle, gained centuries before. And, for Atatürk: His military success at Gallipoli cost him dearly some five years later when he rallied just a handful of Turks into the War of Independence. Following the 1918 Armistice, the French and British returned to Gallipoli to officially bury their fallen men.

© JESSICA TAMTÜRK

THRACE

The Unknown Soldier Monument, at Gallipoli National Park, commemorates the Turkish soldier who carried an injured Anzac across enemy lines during a nightly cease-fire.

Northern Battlefields

With a wide collection of dusty uniforms and weaponry collected from the fields, **Kabatepe Tanıtma Merkezi Müzesi** (Kabatepe Information Center, 8 A.M.–noon and 1–5 P.M., 3TL) is a good place to begin the tour. Housed in a bunker near Kabatepe, the museum offers a photographic recount of Gallipoli's horrid timeline, as well as images of recent commemorations held on the peninsula. There is a poignant display of a Turk's bullet-pierced skull.

Heading westward, a 2,000-foot uphill climb leads to the camping grounds and ferry docks of **Kabatepe.** Following the coastal road for a couple of miles north leads through the cemeteries of **Shrapnel Valley, Beach,** and **Shell Green.** There's also **Anzac Cove,** the Aussies and Kiwis' ill-fated landing site. Down the cliffs, and slightly to the left, is where Anzac forces were ordered to climb over the crag with lines of Turkish infantry guns pointed at them from the ledge above. Atatürk commanded the Ottoman troops to that very spot, ignoring his orders to station his men at Cape Helles. Failing miserably to gain the cliffs, the remains of thousands of doomed Anzacs are buried in rows of graves. Atatürk's stirring 1934 tribute to the enemy is memorialized in marble nearby:

*"[T]hose heroes that shed their blood
And lost their lives . . .
You are now lying in the soil of a friendly country.
Therefore, rest in peace
There is no difference between the Johnnies
And the Mehmets to us where they lie side by side,
Here in this country of ours.
You, the mothers, who sent their sons from far away countries . . .*

Wipe away your tears.
Your sons are now lying in our bosom
And are in peace.
After having lost their lives on this land,
they have
Become our sons as well."

Just north of Anzac Cove, the cemeteries of **Arıburnu** and **Canterbury** center around the **Anzac Commemorative Site,** where the annual memorial ceremonies of April 25th are held. Two-thirds of a mile north are two more stark graveyards, **No. 2 Outpost** and **Embarkation Pier.**

A few hundred feet ahead, take a left at the junction to climb circuitously toward the largest cluster of memorials located on this route. The first monument is the **Mehmet Çavuş Monument,** which commemorates the *Mehmetçiks* (Turkish soldiers) who fatally defended their native soil. This stretch marks the site where arguably the bloodiest warfare occurred. Next is the cemetery at **Lone Pine,** *(Kanlı Sırt),* where Aussies mounted a large offensive the evening of August 6 to divert the Turks away from Suvla Bay, where the Brits were landing. That attack alone took more than 6,000 lives. But again, the Anzacs gained little ground. The present road delineates roughly the line of battle, with each shoulder containing the trench of the enemy. Beneath, a large system of tunnels was dug to provide a supply line. Above, several cemeteries, including **Johnston's Jolly** and **Quinn's Post,** grimly observe the sheer amount of lives lost along this path. Along the way there's the **Unknown Soldier Monument,** depicting a Turkish soldier carrying a wounded Brit back across enemy lines. This poignant memorial was inspired by Australian Governor General Lord Casey during a visit to the peninsula in 1967. While serving as a lieutenant during the campaign, Casey witnessed a Mehmet carry a wounded British soldier from a Turkish position, where the latter had fallen, back to his comrades in Allied trenches, just feet away.

Five miles south of Kabatepe, **Kum Limanı** boasts a good beach for the road-weary.

Southern Battlefields

Largely skipped over by tourists, but not forgotten, the region southwest of Kilitbahir is known as Cape Helles, where the Franco-Anglo offensive was launched. Near the main intersection in Alcıtepe village, ten miles from Kilitbahir, is a privately owned **war museum** (9 A.M.–5 P.M., donations accepted). Proprietor Salim Mutlu has amassed a small but interesting collection of war memorabilia, such as artillery, medals, and letters laboriously handwritten by the soldiers to their families waiting for their return. Past the village, the road continues to several cemeteries and monuments along the tip of the peninsula.

The southernmost farming village of **Seddülbahir** contains, aside from a beach, a port, and bland pensions, the remains of an **Ottoman fortress.** Less than a mile to the west is the stark **Cape Helles Memorial Center,** a tall obelisk honoring the 20,000 British who fought during the arduous nine-month campaign. This monument provides an ideal place from which to watch cargo ships lazily pass through the straits. But on August 15, 1915, just past 6 A.M., the Brits landed at the mouth of the straits, barely a thousand feet to the west, producing a hailstorm of bullets at **"V" Beach.** Thousands of lives were lost as the Brits tried to press their ships through the channel and force the greatly outnumbered Turkish line into retreat. There is a memorial, displaying models of trenches dedicated to Yahya Çavuş, the sergeant who commanded the initial defense of the peninsula, between Helles and "V" Beach, and there are British cemeteries.

Five miles northeast of Seddülbahir, there's the **French War Memorial and Cemetery.** The moving monument contains a handful of ossuaries and endless rows of metal crosses. In March of 1915, 10,000 French troops, including those of the country's colonies, mainly North Africans, descended on the Asian shores at Kumkale and had no problem claiming the outpost. They then joined the British front, where they suffered a near annihilation. Just east, the 145-foot tall **Abide Memorial** honors the martyrs of Çanakkale, all the Turks who

COURTESY OF REPUBLIC OF TURKEY CULTURE AND TOURISM MINISTRY

THRACE

The French War Memorial and Cemetery commemorates the 10,000 French nationals who perished at Cape Helles during World War I's Gallipoli campaign.

bravely gave their lives during the Gallipoli campaign.

Accommodations and Food

If you plan to stay overnight in the region, there are several options. Modern hotels are available in Çanakkale, just across the straits. Eceabat, on the other hand, offers quaint, serene pensions, with affordable rooms that are well worth a look. That is, if the bare minimum of a clean bed and running water sounds acceptable. The outposts of Seddülbahir and Kum Limanı also boast a number of small motels, but their isolation makes them almost inaccessible during the evenings, unless you have your own transportation.

In Eceabat, the **(Aqua Hotel** (Istiklal Caddesi, 0286/814-2864, www.heyboss.com, 50–140TL) is birthed from a dilapidated canning factory right on the waterfront. It quirkily has extended its cobblestone exterior to its rooms' decor. But while the building appears like a squat industrial factory from the outside, every touch inside has been modernized in

full spectral color. The patio along the water's edge is a meeting point—and popular drinking spot—for visitors the area. Expect satellite TV, air-conditioning, and a private beach.

The **Eceabat Hotel** (Cumhurriyet Cad. 5, 0286/814-3121, www.anzacgallipolitours. com, 40–120TL) offers lodging for every budget, from bunks to air-conditioned rooms with balconies, smack in the fishing town's main square. Owned and operated by the Turkish-Australian couple Bernina and Ihlami Gezici (a.k.a. TJ), who guided Prince Andrew through the Gallipoli Memorial in 1998, this hotel boasts a roof-top bar, Ottoman-style lobby, and a tourism agency.

For the best in inexpensive and pristine lodgings, the brand new **Crowded House** (Huseyin Avni Sok. 4, 0286/814-1565, www.crowdedhousegallipoli.com, 20TL/dorm bed, 70TL/room with A/C) offers 24 en suite rooms, and some dorms, with complimentary breakfast. Both family- and backpacker-oriented, the hotel is owned by amicable owner/manager Ziya Artman, who's always happy to share his extensive knowledge of the peninsula, assist with tours, and offer a host of fun activities. For out-of-the-way rustic accommodations, **◖ The Gallipoli Houses** (Kocadere Village, 0286/814-2640, www.gallipoli.com.tr, 130TL) offer renowned complimentary breakfasts and dinners, home-cooked by owner and tourism specialist Özlem Gündüz. With her significant other, Belgian historian Eric Goosens, the duo have provided an unequaled experience, merging European elegance and Turkish hospitality in this idyllic, traditional stone B&B.

Hotel Kum (Kum Limanı, 0286/814-1455, www.hotelkum.com, 75–120TL) is a resort destination on the Bay of Saros, just three miles from the port of Kabatepe. With beach clubs, nightclubs, and bars, the facility, which also includes a large camping site, is geared for the young in all of us. With beach volleyball, a soccer field, large swimming pools, scuba-diving and windsurfing center, as well as a computer arcade, the hotel is the best option in the area for families with children. Although spotless, the air-conditioned, balconied rooms are very basic.

In Seddülbahir, **Pansiyon Helles Panorama** (atop Seddülbahir Hill, 0286/862-0035, 35–70TL) is a gem of a boutique that stares straight at the colossal Abide monument. Superior in service and lodgings, the only downside here is that the bathrooms are shared.

Outside of the decent restaurants in some of the hotels, fish lovers will revel in Eceabat. Along the harbor are a variety of fish restaurants, but none equal **◖ Liman Balık Restoran** (Istiklal Cad. 67, 0286/814-2755, www.limanrestaurant.net, 14TL). There are great views of the straits and about eight prix-fixe specials (10 25TL) that'll please carnivores and vegetarians alike. The set menus include five dishes. Another sensational choice by the port is **Maydos Restaurant** (Yalı Cad. 12, 0286/217-4090, www.maydos.com.tr, 15TL), which also doubles as a hotel. The newest on the peninsula's hospitality scene, its scrumptious breakfast buffet is also served to walk-ins—not staying in the

hotel. Pull up a chair by the window overlooking the port and enjoy typical Aegean seafood meze followed by traditional Turkish dishes or grilled local fish. For typical Turkish fare, head to **Zubeyde Lokantası** (Zubeyde Hanım Meydanı, 0286/814-1357, www.meydanlokantasi.com) for a variety of Turkish home foods, as well as tons of grills and a variety of flour-based desserts.

◖ GÖKÇEADA

Ancient logic must have dictated that whoever ruled this island reigned over the nearby Dardanelles because Gökçeada has been invaded by so many nations and tribes that its history is hard to follow. But aside from what's been discovered in chronicles, few relics remain on this isle, the largest of two islands awarded to Turkey in the post-WWI Lausanne Treaty.

Gökçeada stretches some 20 miles from west to east and 13 miles from north to south. The isle's 8,600 inhabitants on nine villages and one town center have farmed the olive and *suma* (Mediterranean grape) orchards on the hilly land since time immemorial. Even Homer wrote about the inebriation of gods on Imvroz—its Greek name—centuries before the ancient Athenians colonized it. In 1915, the Anglo-French navies commandeered the island as a base for the allied Gallipoli Campaign, led by General Sir Ian Hamilton. Incidentally, most villages were settled far inland and built on hillsides rather than in the valleys, for fear of the constant pirate invasions of old.

Mostly inhabited by Greeks until the first part of the 20th century, Gökçeada's seen its numbers of indigenes decline steadily due to tensions between Greece and Turkey. The last blow came during the tense tug-of-war between the two neighbors over the island of Cyprus in 1963, when natives of Greek descent throughout the country were asked to leave. Thanks in part to the less than 250 who ignored the warning, the island maintains some ethnic diversity today.

In addition to fine sandy beaches, wine's recent popularity with Turks is bringing Gökçeada to the limelight. So is its near remoteness. It's far away from the concrete jungles to the east and yet so close that it can be reached in a couple of hours by boat, making this floating landmass the ideal unwinding and water sports paradise.

Sights

After landing at the port of Kuzulimanı, most visitors opt for the three-mile *dolmuş* ride headed northwest to the small fishing village of **Kaleköy.** En route lies the **Sualtı Milli Parkı,** a protected coastal strip filled with colorful underwater mollusks and starfish. Next to it is **Kaşkaval Burnu,** an interesting outcrop of rocks stacked like the wheels of Kaşkaval cheese it's named after. Lying in ruins on the village's north shore is the 16th-century Ottoman castle, after which the town derives its Turkish and Greek name of Kasro. A ten-minute climb up the barren hill to **Kaleköy Üstü** reveals the island's oldest church, which could be very well omitted, but the sumptuous meze made of local produce at Güzelyalı restaurant (0286/232-8332) would be a shame to miss.

Go southward past the municipal seat of Gökçeada, head another two miles due west to **Zeytinli,** where most of the island's Greek Orthodox reside. About five miles further west is the village of **Tepeköy,** whose purely Hellenistic architecture looks like a television ad sponsored by the Greek Tourism Board. Back on the road, rural **Dereköy** is straight ahead, followed by **Uğurlu,** which is just a few minutes' walk from the wind-battered beaches of the island's southwestern coast.

Pristine sandy shores abound on Gökçeada. **Aydıncık Sahil,** nine miles south of the town center, gets crowded come summer, particularly with windsurfing enthusiasts or those wishing to learn at the onsite surf school. Right next to it is **Salt Lake,** which, aside from drying up to a black muck said to be therapeutic for skin and joint ailments, doubles as a late winter stop for dozens of migratory species, including the majestic pelicans and flamingos. If you're bold enough, the tried-and-true method of ridding the skin of the ebony mud

is to run back to the sea as quickly as possible before it dries up to a cakey crust. The beach at **Aydıncık** also has a surf school. And, near the sandy shore at **Kokina,** there's a **tomb** carved into the rock face. Believed to date back to the Roman era, the tomb is about 300 feet to the right of the road.

There are two annual events held on Gökçeada in August: the first celebrates the Virgin Mary in the village of Dereköy on August 15; the other is the island's decade-old **Film Festival,** which is held throughout the month. Right by the dock, the **tourizm ofisi** (Barbaros Cad. 56, Kaleköy, 0286/887-4642, www.gokceada.com) offers information on island tour operators and decent maps, but you may find more luck contacting them through their website.

Accommodations and Food

As more entrepreneurs lay stake to Gökçeada's booming tourism growth and the forthcoming yacht marina is set to be inaugurated in Kaleköy, more resort-type accommodations will become available. Ask hotel proprietors about the availability of air-conditioned rooms and private tours of the island. Check out the room or apartment before cinching the deal in smaller hotels.

Steps away from the port, the pristine **Zeus Bungalow Hotel** (Kuzu Limanı, 0286/887-3332, www.zeusotel.com, 50–90TL) consists of a set of ochre-hued chalets in a lush meadow. One of two sites on the island to offer a pool, Zeus boasts the quietest of rooms, bathed in sunshine throughout the day. The complimentary, farm-fresh breakfast is served poolside overlooking the turquoise Aegean Sea. The establishment's homemade cheese, just-picked olives, and thyme-flavored honey are worth the trip to the island alone.

One of the isle's most famous residents is Yorgo Zarbozan, a retired *Istanbullu* whose migration back to Gökçeada after retirement led to the creation of an overwhelmingly popular tavern and hotel. The **Barba Yorgo** (Tepeköy, 0286/887-4247, www.barbayorgo. com, 40–80TL) offers five bare pension-type rooms and six apartment units, often crammed in the summer with returning Greeks. Guests and walk-ins revel rambunctiously to live music as soon as the sun sets.

For a full-amenity seaside resort, the only game in town is **Gökçeada Resort Hotel** (Barbaros Cad. 16, Kaleköy, 0286/887-4040, www.gokceadaresort.com, 110–200TL). Individual air-conditioned units, as well as an onsite billiards room and gym, may justify the hefty price of this property's 62 rooms.

The decor of the dozen hotels that pepper the island is so curiously similar that their owners obviously hold regular meetings to select bed linens. Apart from cleanliness, price, and location, little truly sets them apart. Among these, the **Kalimerhaba Hotel** (Barbaros Cad. 33, Kaleköy, 0286/0286/887-3648, www.gokceada.com/kalimerhaba, 50–80TL) offers a serene courtyard restaurant and individual bathrooms. Only six of its rooms have air-conditioning. There are dazzling views of the Aegean up front or a backdrop of lush hills in the rear of the property.

Gökçeadans are known for their wine, a battered calamari served with a walnut and garlic dip, and of course their veggie salads and meze served à la Grecque and ideal as accompaniments to fish and meat grills. Included here are hotels that rate highly not only for their lodging but also for their culinary spread. Aside from the diner/pension combos, there are plenty of picture-perfect options for the hungry. **C Çakır'ın Yeri** (Gökçeada, 0286/887-2393) is set in the back of a dark terrace in the island's business center. Strictly indigenous, with fishing nets hanging ubiquitously, Çakır's place provides a party atmosphere most summer evenings. It's clear that owner Çakır created this environment to share in the authenticity and wealth of his native island. Ask to try the amazing *zeytin reçeli* (olive jam). Another tempting choice is **Ada Sofrasi** (Kadrı Üçok Cad., across from Türkiye İş Bankası, 0286/887-2125). Try the grilled gilt-headed bream (10TL), the most expensive dish on the menu, and the *çoban salata* (farmer salad), with Turkey's best tomatoes brought in from Çanakkale.

Getting There and Around

Gökçeada is served through **ferry service** (www.canakkaletravel.com/feribot.htm for tickets and schedules) from either the port of Kabatepe (3TL/person, 17.50TL/vehicle) or Çanakkale (5TL/person, 28TL/vehicle) on the southern flank of the Dardanelles. The 75-minute route from Kabatepe is more reliable year-round, with the following schedule: departs Kabatepe 11 A.M. and 6 P.M., with returning service at 7 A.M. and 4 P.M. Departing on weekdays only, the Çanakkale ferry takes off at 5 P.M., with the return from Gökçeada at 8 A.M. The trip lasts about 2.5 hours. There are more boat departures scheduled throughout summer, while the high winds prevalent throughout the winter season cause all services to cease. Do check with the tourism office online for service and weather information before departure.

Dolmuş service to the town center of Gökçeada (2TL) and Kaleköy (4TL) is available from the Kuzulimanı port. Hiring a **Taxi** is about the only way to get to Uğurlu or Aydıncık (25TL/one-way trip).

TEKIRDAĞ

On the northern flank of the Sea of Marmara, the town of Tekirdağ's claim to fame is its eponymous *rakı* (potent anise-flavored drink) and pinky-sized, juicy *köfte* (meatball). With Istanbul and Edirne's historical treasures in such close proximity, this water-lapped town has operated under the radar for millennia. Most who do stop by, however, will find a small archaeological and historical trove to fill a couple of hours between sumptuous meals. With large fields rolling seemingly into the warm waters of the Marmara Sea, Tekirdağ's coastal atmosphere is pastoral and laid back. That is, if you steer clear from the tourist clatter of the larger bus stops and its growing center.

Sights

The first stop in town is the **promenade** *(sahıl)* that loops around an elongated bay filled with cafés and seaside restaurants. Start on the eastern end of the esplanade at the **Rustem Paşa Complex** (Ertuğrul Mahallesi, Mimar Sinan Caddesi, no phone, sunset to sunrise daily, free admission) This magnificent mid-16th-century building was built by the great Mimar Sinan for the lice-ridden Rustem Paşa, the grand vizier of Süleyman the Magnificent. The mosque is flanked by two seminaries and three hammams.

Past the square and up along Mimar Sinan Caddesi, the **Namık Kemal Evi** (Namık Kemal Cad. 7, 9 A.M.–5 P.M. Mon.–Sat.) commemorates the mid-19th-century poet. Namık Kemal was an early vociferous nationalist and steadfast Freemason, whose strong ideologies later inspired Atatürk.

Moving west to Barbaros Caddesi, the **Arkeoloji ve Etnografi Müzesi** (Archaeology and Ethnography Museum, Valı Konağı Cad. 21, 0282/261-2082, 9 A.M.–5 P.M. Tues.–Sun., 3TL) is yet another amazing collection that retraces the area's history from its ancient Greek colonizers to the Ottomans. Relics unearthed from locally found *tumuli* (burial mounds) date back to the 7th century B.C. and are all tucked inside this beautiful Ottoman mansion. Among the slabs of marbles, the finds made at Perinthos in Marmara Hereclea, an ancient Greek town 20 miles due east of Tekirdağ, are particularly dazzling.

Further down the street, the impressive array of artifacts and rooms at the **Rakoczy Museum** (Barbaros Cad. 32, 0282/263-8577, 9 A.M.–5 P.M. Tues.–Sun., 3TL) are reconstructed meticulously, including the stately dining room and artistic snippets hanging on the walls. The museum is located in an abode built by Ferenc II Rákóczi. A Transylvanian prince considered a national hero in Hungary, Rákóczi led an ultimately unsuccessful uprising against the Austrian Habsburgs at the turn of the 18th century. He fled to Poland in 1711 and was offered the Polish Crown by Russian tsar Peter I. He refused and bounced around Europe before accepting Sultan Ahmet II's invitation for residency in the Ottoman Empire. A few feet downhill, the road leads back to the promenade and the beautiful wooden library

built in Namık Kemal's honor. Ambling east along the boardwalk, a **tourizm ofisi** (Atatürk Bulvarı 65, 0282/261-1698, 9 A.M.–5 P.M. Mon.–Fri.) provides area maps and exhaustive information about the town and its coastline to the west.

Accommodations and Food

The only lodging worth recommending in Tekirdağ is **Rodosto Hotel** (Iskele Cad. 34, 0282/263-3701, 75–140TL). Not necessarily economical, but definitely worth every *kuruş*, the seaside rooms are right above the promenade. Plush touches include whirlpool tubs, an onsite restaurant, and an attention to detail that's frankly hard to find outside of Turkey's larger cities.

For dining, (**Ali Usta Köfteci** (Atatürk Bulvarı, 0282/261-1621, www.meshurkoftecialiusta.com, 12TL) is synonymous with the succulent Tekirdağ *köfte* (meatball). Its cafeteria-style interior is immense and needs to be since it gets filled to capacity most evenings. Next door and owned by the same family, **Özdörtler Fish Restaurant** fries the local red mullet to perfection for bus-loads of national tourists.

Getting There and Around

Bus service between Tekirdağ and Istanbul (16TL) is available hourly through several companies. The **Tekirdağ Otogarı** (just north of Atatürk Caddesi on Yüzbaşı Mayadağlı Caddesi, 0282/261-7748) services **Metro Turizm** (444-3455, www.metroturizm.com. tr), which runs a regular service between both cities. Service to Çanakkale and throughout the Thracian peninsula is also possible through a variety of private bus and minibus service providers operating through Tekirdağ's bus terminal.

Getting around Tekirdağ on foot is highly doable. But should you need transportation, dolmuş and taxi services are also available just outside the Otogar. An **Avis** (Atatürk Blv. 59030 Merkez Tekirdağ, 0282/261-6831) branch is located one-half kilometer west of the Otogar.

THRACE

THRACE

GELIBOLU

Bearing the same name as the surrounding peninsula, Gelibolu is arguably the peninsula's most attractive fishing town. The smell of fish emanating from the harbor's busy canneries steers many tourists subconsciously toward the rows of restaurants lining its central pier. The iodine-laden air wafts all the way up Liman Caddesi, the outpost's main street which ascends eastward away from the harbor. This is the location of the ferry to the summer hub of Lapseki.

Since time immemorial Gelibolu has been the front door Western invaders seeking Istanbul were forced to unlock prior to reaching the wealth of the golden city. Today, many active military outposts continue to attest to the strategic importance of the location.

Sights

Housed in a small tower built by the Byzantines in the 12th century, along fortification walls that predate it by six centuries, the **Piri Reis Müzesi** (Piri Reis Museum, adjacent to the Gelibolu port to the east on the 17-01 country road, 8:30 A.M.–6 P.M. Tues.–Sun., donations welcome) showcases a small collection of historical artifacts relating to the Gallipoli battles. The cartographer after which the museum is named was the first to fully map the American continents; reproductions of these maps and others are exhibited here.

Up Fener Yolu, by the lighthouse overlooking the Dardanelles, lies a small, almost all marble prayer hall of **Azebler Namazgah** (located in Fener Parkı in Hoca Hamza at the tip of the peninsula, open-air site, no phone). It's one of a few remaining outdoor mosques. It was built by Architect Aşık bin Süleyman in 1407 and hardly ever welcomes visitors. This type of open-air mosque was traditionally built along city outskirts and was used by the faithful during torrid summers to bid farewell to soldiers and pilgrims, to pray for rain during droughts, or to break up a particularly long journey. The Azebler's intricate design and pricey material makes it one of the most stunning of the few remaining *namazgahs* (prayer places) in Anatolia.

An ossuary built to honor the slain Senegalese who fought for the French during the Gallipoli campaign is located along the main thoroughfare. At a ten-minute walk northeast of the town's center, the resort of **Hamzaköy** boasts a fine sandy beach and seaside restaurants. It's an ideal spot to relax before leaving town.

Accommodations and Food

Aside from a handful of traditional Turkish pensions, there are a couple of noted four-star hotels in Gelibolu. The first is the rose-tinted (**Otel Hamzaköy** (Hamzaköy Bay, 0286/566-8080, www.hamzakoyotel.com, from 80TL). As Gelibolu's sole resort accommodations, you'll find an indoor bar, beach terrace, and a restaurant whose pink interior doubles as a dining room, serving an exceptional buffet-style breakfast. For a more economical option, the friendly staff at **Hotel Oya** (Miralay Şefik Aker Caddesi 7, 0286/556-0392, from 30TL) make this location a great base from which to visit the peninsula. As added bonuses, most rooms include private bathrooms, some with bathtubs, and cable television.

Gelibolu's best diners are situated along its harbor, and get packed on most summer evenings. The town's main draw is its sardines, coupled with the region's tasty squid—fried or grilled.

(**Gelibolu Cafeteria & Restaurant** (Iskele Meydanıl, 0286/566-1227, gelibolurestaurant.com, 15TL) can serve up to 700 people in their indoor dining room and outdoor terrace. Featuring inexpensive, yet succulently fresh, prix fixe menus for all tastes, owner Ismet Tan highlights local catch you'd be remiss not to try—like the local calamari accompanied by an entrée of grilled sardines. Head to **Boğaz** (12TL) up the boardwalk for ridiculously inexpensive and good sardines and *mevsim salatası* (fresh seasonal veggies dressed with lemon juice and olive oil).

Getting Around

Gelibolu is a minor transportation hub to Çanakkale and the summer resort town of Lapseki, directly across the Dardanelles. Both,

KARAGÖZ-HACIVAT: TURKEY'S BELOVED SHADOW PUPPETS

Of the four traditional Turkish theatrical arts – folk, court, Western, and popular – the latter has held a special place in the national culture ever since the Ottomans popularized Karagöz (blackeye) and Hacivat. The two lead characters represent the class struggle still present in modern Turkey. Often deceitful and lewd, Karagöz personifies the uneducated public; while Hacivat epitomizes the cultivated few through his refined Ottoman-Turkish speech. The kicker is that Karagöz's street wit always trumps Hacivat's learned wisdom, although the former's harebrained schemes always backfire.

The origins of this famed duo is unclear. The 17th century travel and cultural essayist Evliya Çelebi believed that the puppets memorialize ironworker Kambur Bâli Çelebi (Karagöz) and the master mason Halil Hacı İvaz (Hacıvat). The two worked side-by-side during the construction of Ulu Cami during the reign of Sultan Orhan (1324-1362), often bantering so humorously that the hundreds of hands employed in their midst sat back and listened. Needless to say, the construction slowed down to a halt, so angering the sultan that he ordered the execution of the duo. The sultan was so inconsolably plagued by remorse that his commissioner tried to cheer him up by improvising the first ever shadow puppet performance of Karagöz and Hacıvat, using his white turban as a background and his camel hide sandals in lieu of the deceased comics. The sole historical evidence pertaining to the Karagöz plays remains a writ issued by Ottoman Grand Mufti Mehmet Ebussuud el-İmadi in the mid-16th century not only allowing, but celebrating the cultural value of the puppet show. No matter the origins, the plays still mirror the caste struggle of yesteryear, while imparting important morals in a fun manner enjoyed by legions of Turkish youth. The plays are also staple entertainment during Ramadan.

The cast of characters has grown over the centuries to reflect the various odd characters and minorities of the Ottoman Era. These include the oft tipsy Tuzsuz Deli Bekir, always toting his wine bottle; Uzun Efe, with his long neck; Kanbur Tiryaki, the opium afficionado with his pipe; the outlandish dwarf Altı Kariş Beberuhi; the dimwitted Denyo; the prodigal Civan; and the irresistible waif Nigâr. These regulars are often flanked by dancers, and the various overly-stereotyped portrayals of non-Turkish minorities.

Karagöz plays are structured in four distinct sections. The *mukaddime* (introduction), starts with Hacivat reciting a *semai* (poem), followed by a prayer. He then tells the audience that he's looking for his friend Karagöz, calling his sidekick to the stage with a monologue. A *muhavere* (dialogue) ensues between the popular duo, followed by the third part, the *fasil* (main plot). The *bitiş* (conclusion) always features an argument between Karagöz and Hacivat, in which the latter berates his sidekick for ruining the topic at hand and the former replies, "May my transgressions be forgiven."

Animators, their assistants, and the creation of the shadow puppets follow a long-standing tradition. Karagöz puppeteers are called *hayalî* (illusionist). One *hayalî* impersonates each of the shadow play's characters by performing songs and adopting dialects. An apprentice sets up and takes down stages, and hands the puppet master the puppets as required. Larger productions may involve a *sandıkkâr* (chest keeper), who's tasked with the handling of puppets; a *yardak* (back-up singer); and a *dairezen* who thumps the tambourine.

Today, the puppets have jointed limbs and are still crafted of camel hide, just like the sandals used by Sultan Orhan's assistant during the first performance almost 700 years ago. The hide is tanned and stretched to an almost paper-thin, semi-transparent consistency before being vividly colored. Finished puppets measure 35-40 centimeters in height. In the olden days, a *şem'a* (candle) was used as a light source. Oil lamps are now used to backlight the puppets and project their images onto a white muslin screen, known as an *ayna* (mirror).

THRACE

THRACE

as well as Eceabat, can be reached by minibus (4TL) at either the stop by the esplanade or at the *otogar* (bus station), located on Kore Kahramanları Caddesi—a five-minute walk southwest of the harbor. Buses from this station offer routes to Istanbul (18TL) and Edirne (15TL). The Gelibolu-Lapseki ferryboat (passengers 2TL, cars 12TL, runs hourly 9 A.M.–midnight) departs on the hour. Those heading to the Gallipoli National Park can do so by hopping on a minibus headed for Eceabat and then a *dolmuş* for Kabatepe.

Edirne

The largest city in the Thracian Peninsula, Edirne spreads along a hill above the valley where the Tunca and Meriç Rivers meet. Reputed as a trading post for ancient Romans making their way to Asia Minor, its status rose steadily with the Byzantines and was punctuated by a stint as the capital of the Ottoman Empire for less than a century. Outside of those who stop for a bathroom break en route to Greece or Bulgaria, few tourists come in early July for the city's annual Kırkpınar Oil Wrestling Festival and to get an eyeful of its exquisite Ottoman and Roman architectural relics.

Historians have pinpointed Edirne's beginnings back to the 7th century B.C., when it served as a settlement for the war-mongering Thracian tribes known as Uskadama. Forwarding the clock some nine centuries, Edirne became a bastion and pit stop on the Via Egnetia, an early road linking Byzantium to the rest of the Roman realm. This major passage to and from Asia Minor expanded and was re-founded by Roman emperor Hadrian as Hadrianopolis. Abbreviated some time later to Adrianople, the city witnessed Licinius' vicious loss against Constantine in A.D. 323, and Valens' slaughter at the hands of the bloody Visigoths some four decades later. Countless battles and sieges continued in the next millennium and Edirne grew into a fitting center for weaponry.

Aiming to encircle and starve Constantinople, Murat I's Ottoman troops finally conquered Adrianople in 1363. The city was immediately made into a capital city and renamed Edirne.

After the Turks and Allies ratified the Treaty of Sèvres in 1920—an agreement that shattered the former Ottoman empire into regions shared between the victors of WWI—Edirne fell under Greek military rule. But even that was short lived, as Mustafa Kemal Atatürk bloodily reclaimed it just months later.

Edirne is an ideal day trip from Istanbul. Leave early for the 2.5-hour coach ride and spend the rest of the morning checking out the mosques and the Edirnekâri—the city's unique Ottoman abodes—before foraging for treasures in the covered bazaar's *bedesten* (marketplace). In the afternoon, stroll down to the banks of the Meriç River to view Ottoman bridges and settle at a waterside tea garden for *çay* (tea).

SIGHTS
◖ Selimiye Camii (Selimiye Mosque)

The great Mimar Sinan considered the Selimiye Camii (Taş Odalar Sokak, Meydan, Edirne, www.selimiyecamii.com in Turkish, sunrise to sunset daily, free) to be his finest work, and pundits agreed. The mosque was commissioned by Sultan Selim II, but never welcomed its benefactor. Selim the Sot—as he was known among the ranks— died of a fever a year before the building's completion. Much smaller than Süleymaniye in Istanbul, the ornate interior of the Selimiye Mosque is what propels it to greatness. At more than 200 feet in height, the four soaring minarets also add to its majesty.

As you enter through the West gate, you encounter a spectacular dome, held by eight conspicuous columns, towering over a circular prayer hall. The *mihrab* (recess indicating the

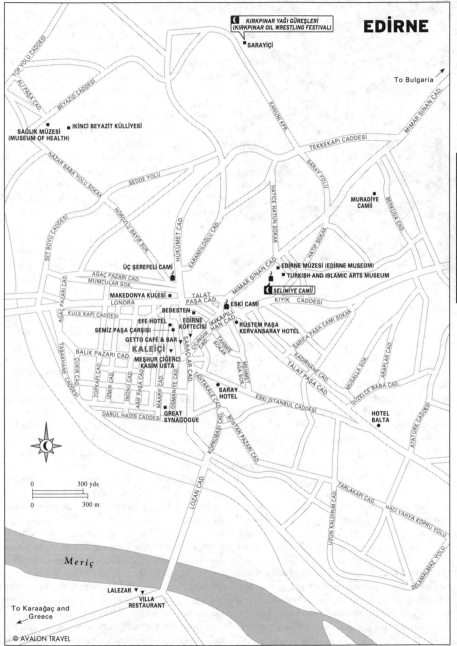

THRACE

EDİRNE

KIRKPINAR YAĞI GÜREŞLERİ
(KIRKPINAR OIL WRESTLING FESTIVAL)

SARAYİÇİ

To Bulgaria

SAĞLIK MÜZESİ
(MUSEUM OF HEALTH)

İKİNCİ BEYAZIT KÜLLİYESİ

TOP YOLU CADDESİ
ALİ PAŞA CAD.
BEYAZID CADDESİ
KANUNİ KPR.
MİMAR SİNAN CAD.
TEKKEKAPI CADDESİ
SARAY YOLU
NAZAR BABA YOLU SOKAK
SEDDE YOLU
HOROZLU BAYIR SOK.
HÜKÜMET CAD.
KARANFİLOĞLU CAD.
HATİCE HATUN SOKAK
HATİP SOKAK
BENKURA CAD.

MURADİYE
CAMİİ

ÜÇ ŞEREFELİ CAMİ

AĞAÇ PAZARI CAD.
MUMCULAR SOK.
MAKEDONYA KULESİ
LONDRA
KULE KAPI CADDESİ
AĞAÇ PAZARI CAD.
SET BOYU CADDESİ
TABAKHANE CADDESİ

EDİRNE MÜZESİ (EDIRNE MUSEUM)
TURKISH AND ISLAMIC ARTS MUSEUM
SELİMİYE CAMİİ

MİMAR SİNAN CAD.
TALAT
PAŞA CAD.
ESKİ CAMİ
KIYIK CADDESİ

BEDESTEN
EFE HOTEL
EDİRNE
KÖFTECİSİ
SEMİZ PAŞA ÇARŞISI
GETTO CAFÉ & BAR
KALEİÇİ
MEŞHUR CİĞERCİ
KASIM USTA
BALIK PAZARI CAD.
İKİKAPILI
HAN CAD.
RÜSTEM PAŞA
KERVANSARAY HOTEL

ÇELİNGİR
CAD.
TARMIŞ
SOKAK
SARAÇLAR CAD.
MEHMET
AĞA SOK.
SABICA PAŞA CAMİ SOKAK
KADİRHANE CAD.
TALAT PAŞA CAD.
MUSALLA SOK.
ARAPLAR CAD.
GÜZELCE BABA CAD.

ÇUKUR CAD.
TOPKAPI CAD.
İZMİR CAD.
İNÖNÜ CAD.
ARİF PAŞA CAD.
MAARİF CAD.
OSMANİYE CAD.
TAHTAKALE CAD.

SARAY
HOTEL
ESKİ İSTANBUL CADDESİ

HOTEL
BALTA

DARÜL HADİS CADDESİ
GREAT
SYNAGOGUE

KÖPRÜBAŞI CAD.
BOSTAN PAZARI CAD.
ATATÜRK CADDESİ

0   300 yds
0   300 m

LOZAN CAD.
UZUN KALDIRIM CAD.
TARLAKAPI CAD.
HACI YAHYA KÖPRÜ YOLU
SELİMALMAZ YOLU

Meriç

LALEZAR
VİLLA
RESTAURANT

To Karaağaç and
Greece

© AVALON TRAVEL

THRACE

Sultan Selim's mid-16th-century mosque is the finest edifice designed by Ottoman master architect Mimar Sinan.

Other Mosques

Named after the three balconies on its loftiest minaret, **Üç Şerefeli Cami** (Mosque With Three Galleries, Aℤaç Pazarı Caddesi, just east of Hükkümet Caddesi, no phone, sunrise to sunset daily, free admission) beautifully depicts the mid-15th-century transition from Selçuk architecture found in Western Anatolia to the budding complexity of Ottoman-style buildings. This is the first mosque to boast a central dome over its prayer hall and to include four subsidiary domes. Earlier structures feature a series of small domes which crown abutting, double-walled structures. This mosque's fountain appears outside, also a first of its kind. The fountain started a trend adopted by later imperial architects.

Along Talat Paşa Caddesi, **Eski Cami** (Old Mosque, adjacent the roundabout formed by Talat Paşa and Mimar Sinan Caddesi, no phon, sunrise to sunset, free) bears its name well, as it is as old. Built in 1413 for Sultan Mehmet I, this sanctuary replicates those found in the empire's former capital of Bursa. Similar to Ulu Cami across the Dardanelles, Eski Cami is a nine-domed building of cut stone, with a portico of five bays on its northern flank and a minaret gracing its northwest corner. Massive square columns, embellished with Koranic calligraphy, added in the late 19th century, break up the miles of red carpeting inside. Just across the street, the *bedesten* (marketplace, closed Sun.) is Edirne's first enclosed market. It was built by Mehmet I to generate revenue for the upkeep of the mosque. It consists of 14 vaulted chambers, fashioned after its predecessor in Bursa, that are quite banal and disorganized.

On a hill northeast of the city overlooking Sarayiçi, just a brisk ten-minute walk east of Selimiye, lies the diminutive **Muradiye Camii** (500 m northeast of Selimiye Mosque on Mimar Sinan Caddesi, no phone, sunrise to sunset daily, free). It was built in 1435 as a *tekke* (convent for the Mevlevi order), but was inaugurated as a mosque. Its construction is based on the reverse T-floor plan prevalent in that era. The Muradiye is known for its variety of hexagonal tiles—not square—that interlock

direction of Mecca) is tucked in an alcove in true Abazid-style; it's pushed back far enough to allow just enough depth for sunlight to filter through three sides, bathing the space and its miles of glittering tiles in natural light. Almost 94 feet in diameter, the interior of the dome boasts sumptuous calligraphy highlighted by the daylight shining through 45 windows at its base. The Iznik faience, including the tiles that beautify the *mihrab,* explodes in color and floral inspiration. The *minbar* (pulpit) is carved out of the finest marble.

The surrounding complex features an *arasta* (shops row) that boasts busy shops dedicated to indigenous artwork, and several seminaries. With an assortment of early Ottoman relics and a nod to the popular sport of oil wrestling, the **Turkish and Islamic Arts Museum** occupies the main *medrese* (Islamic seminary). There's also the tomb of Selim the Sot, as well as those of his three daughters, tucked into a mausoleum embellished with etched mother-of-pearl.

COURTESY OF REPUBLIC OF TURKEY CULTURE AND TOURISM MINISTRY

THRACE

Oil-slathered wrestlers vie for the title of mightiest in the land during the annual Kırkpınar Oil Wrestling Festival in July.

with triangular turquoise faience to create a unique backdrop. The tomb of Musa Kasîm Efendi, the Ottoman Empire's last Islamic judge, rests in the adjoining cemetery.

Lying on the northern end of Edirne, the immense **Ikinci Beyazit Külliyesi** (II Beyazit Caddesi, 3 km northeast of Selimiye Mosque, no phone, sunrise to sunset daily, free admission)is a feast for the eyes and a haven for the harried soul. Completed in 1488, this complex remained the largest of its kind in the Islamic world for more than a century. Along with a mosque, there are several buildings that make up the complex: a *darüşşifa* (hospital), soup kitchens, *medreses* (seminaries), hammams, a mill, depots, and even a bridge. For 200 years, the *darüşşifa* was a world-renowned hospital, particularly for treating eye diseases and mental ailments. At a time when Europe burned the mentally ill at the stake for being cohorts with the devil, at this complex, treatment for the insane included fragrance therapy. Meals prepared with exotic fowl, such as partridges and pheasants, supposedly treated certain

afflictions. Sound therapy with live music and natural running water were also popular healing methods. Today, this building serves as the not-to-be-missed **Sağlık Müzesi** (Museum of Health, 0284/224-0922, http://saglikmuzesi. trakya.edu.tr, 9 A.M.–6 P.M., 5TL), which displays original patient quarters as well as the Ottomans' innovative healing methods.

Kırkpınar Yağı Güreşleri (Kırkpınar Oil Wrestling Festival)

During the first week of July, masses descend on Sarayiçi to take part in the centuries-old Kırkpınar Oil Wrestling Festival (www.kirkpinar.com). They won't be competing—since all the fun is watching the action from the perimeter—but grown muscular men will. To make matters more slippery, literally, the wrestlers will be oiled and clad in mid-calf pants fastened tightly in strategic areas of the body. While there are many similar competitions throughout Anatolia, none compare to the Kırkpınar festival week, which welcomes national and foreign luminaries, janissary bands, folk dance

THRACE

troupes, and merchants. The festival provides a lot of activities for the entire family.

The Kırkpınar Oil Wrestling Festival may be the world's oldest wrestling contest since it has continuously been held every year since 1357 in Rumelia (modern Thrace). Believed to have originated from deep within central Asia, this ancient battle of might was brought to the Anatolian plains by Turkic nomads. And as the Ottomans conquered their way to Edirne during the mid-14th century, under the command of Süleyman Paşa, troops wrestled each other during resting periods. The myth behind Kırkpınar is that on one occasion 40 able men began wrestling each other through eliminatory bouts that finally pitted the remaining two. They battled beyond exhaustion and eventually died. The duo was buried by a fig tree near Edirne. Once the town was under Ottoman control in 1361, the remaining members of the band of 40 arrived at Ahırköy Meadow, where a clear spring gushed forth around that fig tree. The location was aptly named Kırkpınar (Forty Sources), detailing the number of wrestlers that took part in the victor-less wrestling match.

At almost 650 years old, the festival is steeped with tradition, which includes a series of rules and practices. During the Ottoman era, wrestling matches outside of palace walls were organized solely in fairgrounds, during weddings, and in the homes of notables. As master of ceremonies, the Kırkpınar Yağlı Güreş Ağası (ceremonial lord) provided guests with continuous entertainment, lodging, and sustenance, and was also responsible for calling the wrestlers to bout and ensuring that the games followed traditional rules. Today the municipality has assumed this task due to the event's popularity and rising costs. The Çazgır (emcee) introduces each wrestler by name, title, and competency to the jury and spectators. Then, the wrestlers are matched through a drawing, after which prayers and verses are recited.

The clothing abides by tradition, and so does the oiling. A participant collects dripping oil with his right hand and spreads it to his left shoulder, repeating the process with the left hand. Opponents are expected to oil each other's backs.

The longest reigning champion, Ahmet Taşcı, won the golden belt—the award given to the head wrestler—no less than nine times during the 1990s.

Edirne Müzesi (Edirne Museum)

Built around a large courtyard across the street from the Selimiye Camii, the Edirne Müzesi (Kadirpaşa Sok. 7, 0284/225-1120, www.edirnemuzesi.gov.tr/ in Turkish, 8 a.m.–noon, 1–5 p.m. Tues.–Sun., 3TL) offers a broad, jam-packed slice of Edirne's history. Rooms display early Ottoman relics, such as brass- and copper-weighing instruments and nacre-inlaid furniture, as well as reconstructed suites of Ottoman abodes that include a circumcision room. The museum's collection spans from pre-history to the Republican Era. Ancient Roman fluted-glass perfume bottles are on display in the archaeological section. The ethnography division boasts interesting early Ottoman knick-knacks.

Makedonya Kulesi (Macedonian Clock Tower)

After getting word that the Russian army was en route to capture Edirne, its governor Cemil Paşa blew up the city's large ammunition dump, eradicating in a single move Roman emperor Hadrian's magnificent, 1700-year-old Clock Tower castle (Mumcular Sokak, a block east of Hükkümet Caddesi). Only one of the four original corner towers remained standing after the four days of continuous explosions. It was restored in 1875 and renamed the Makedonya Kulesi. Continuous archaeological digs have already unearthed parts of the city walls and a Byzantine church in its vicinity.

Kaleiçi

The Kaleiçi is Edirne's Sultanahmet, with a square-like network of cobbled streets in true Roman fashion. Edirne's **Great Synagogue,** which was Europe's third largest in 1906, can be found along can be found at the end of Maarif Caddesi, just north of Darül Hadis Caddesi. Kaleiçi also has spectacular specimens of Edirne's unique wooden architecture.

Semiz Paşa Çarşısı

Less than 800 feet west of the intersection of Talat Paşa and Saraçlar Caddesi is Semiz Paşa Çarşısı, one of Edirne's covered markets. It was built in 1568 by Mimar Sinan at the request of grand vizier Semiz Ali Paşa. The structure was ravaged by a fire in 1992. Some of the 130 shops were reconstructed with great care, and so was the structure's remarkable central dome.

Bridges

Just outside the city center, Edirne's imposing bridges are the muse of many a folk song. Linking the thickly-wooded shores of the Tunca River, the most elaborate bridges are masterpieces of Mimar Sinan. The oldest example, which links both levees with 27 arches, was commissioned in the second part of the 13th century by Byzantine emperor Michael Palaelogus. It became known, however, for its restorer Gazı Mihal Bey, more than a 100 years later. The 12-arch **Şahabettin Paşa Köprüsu,** also known as the Saraçhane Köprüsü, was erected in 1451. Mehmet I's **Fatih Köprüsu** followed a year later. Mimar Sinan's **Saray Köprüsu,** which was built in 1560, honors Süleyman the Magnificent. The commission of **Ekmekçizade Ahmet Paşa Köprüsu** in 1608 and the mid-19th-century **Yeni Köprü,** at the confluence of the Meriç and Arda Rivers, are the most contemporary additions.

NIGHTLIFE

A handful of new bars and clubs are livening up Edirne's night scene. **Getto Café & Bar** (Zindanaltı Cad. 139, 0284/214-6050) sprung in modern style from a dilapidated *rakı* factory. Offering live music almost nightly, Getto boasts luscious, Western-style drink concoctions. A hangout for moneyed locals, **Paparazzi Pub** (Saraçlar Cad., next to the PTT Office, 0284/213-2200) bursts with thousands of light bulbs and jazzy Turkish music most nights. Mosey up to the bar and dare the

finned creatures staring from the aquarium underneath your cocktail to a drinking contest.

ACCOMMODATIONS AND FOOD

Don't expect much from Edirne's accommodations, but there are a couple of gems worth looking at. One of them is **Rüstem Paşa Kervansaray Hotel** (Tahmış Meydanı, 0284/212-6119, 100–250TL). It's a 76-room boutique hotel smack dab in the thick of the action. While Mimar Sinan had a hand in this structure and the rooms overlook a quiet, romantic courtyard that's flanked by a bar and terrace restaurant, the bare rooms don't justify their rates.

Ⅽ Efe Hotel (Maarif Cad. 13, Kaleiçi, 0284/213-6166, www.efehotel.com, 100–135TL) may be a two-star facility, but its location in rustic Kaleiçi, pristine and inviting environs, and its large complimentary breakfast make it an appealing option.

The towering yellow structure over Talat Paşa Caddesi is **Hotel Balta** (Talat Paşa Asfaltı 97, 0284/225-8210, www.baltahotel.com.tr, 75–175TL). The striking color doesn't end with its facade, the clean rooms and adjoining baths are a bold experiment in lime green, baby blues, and burnt amber. Kuşbakışı Restaurant, the Balta's rooftop diner, offers nice views of the city's skyline.

A smart choice all around, **Saray Hotel** (Eski Istanbul Cad. 28, 0284/212-1457, www.edirnesarayhotel.com, 40–80TL), with its checkerboard-inspired rooms, is a great deal for the buck. Rates do not include breakfast.

Leaving Edirne without tasting its homegrown delicacy of fried *çiğer* (liver) is akin to lunacy among meat-loving Turks. If the thought of eating giblets isn't appealing, there are plenty of other meat options, particularly the Edirne *köfte* (meatball)—a silver dollar-sized plump patty.

For a little ambience, head to Karaağaç Yolu to dine along the banks of the Meriç. Famed food critics, TV personalities, and politicians plan daily trips around lunch at **Ⅽ Meşhur Çiğerci Kasim Usta** (Balık Pazarı 18, 0284/214-2024, www.meshuredirneciger-cisikazimilhanusta.com, 12TL). Established in the covered bazaar, Kasım Usta relocated to a much larger three-story building near the fish market to accommodate the growing lines at the door. To avoid the intense fumes generated by the overworked fryer, upper level seating is recommended. Savor the fried spicy red pepper and lentil soup along with mounds of crusty bread.

For deliciously good and ridiculously cheap eats, no one can beat the freshness and variety at **Edirne Köftecisi** (Saraçlar Cad. 73, 0284/214-7300, www.edirnekoftesi.com, 11 A.M.–10 P.M., under 10TL). The friendly Hocaoğlu's are the rare breed that offers the more than 30 *köfte* (meatball) preparations found throughout Turkey at the adjoining deli. Where else can you get juicy lamb chops for 7TL?

Smack on the Meriç River, **Lalezar** (Karaağaç Yolu, 0284/223-2489, 11 A.M.–11 P.M., 18TL) is a fave among tourists, with a large menu featuring grilled meats and seasonal fish. Kids love Lalezar's sumptuous *köfte* (meatball) platter and playroom. Just next door, **Villa Restaurant** (Karaağaç Yolu, 0284/225-4077) is a bit larger and offers the same formula: terrace and indoor seating, in addition to an interesting floating cabana.

The name Police Station not withstanding, **Karakol Binası** (Karaağaç Yolu, under the Meriç Bridge, 0284/225-3285), is where the tea flows along a popular grassy spot right by the river. Local early birds out for a stroll head to Karakol for its typical, yet decadent, breakfast straight from the farm.

INFORMATION AND SERVICES

Edirne's exhaustive website (rehber.edirne.web.tr/) lists virtually each business and service to be found in the city, along with the popular tourist attractions. The majority of ATMs are located around Hürriyet Meydanı and along Saraçlar Caddesi, where the post office can also be found. Mostly geared for nationals, the **tourizm ofisi** (Hürriyet Square near Talat Paşa Caddesi, 0284/213-9208) provides limited information in most Western languages.

GETTING THERE AND AROUND

For an enjoyable ride to Edirne, hop on a **bus** (34TL round-trip) for a day trip from Istanbul's Grand Coach Station (İstanbul–Kapıkule Highway, 0284/225-1979) to Edirne's *otogar* (bus station), which is six miles due east of the city square. Departing roughly every 20 minutes, the 146-mile ride lasts about 2.5 hours. Passengers are taken northwest along the Trans-European Motorway (E80). Once in Edirne, a minibus service (2TL) takes passengers to Hürriyet Meydanı. A **train** also links Istanbul to Edirne. Taxis await passengers outside the station to traverse the three miles to the center of town.

By **car,** the route will be the same, but drivers tend to complete the journey within 90 minutes, with an extra toll of 10TL. Traveling into Turkey from the Bulgarian border involves taking the E80 eastbound through Kapıkule, about 12 miles from the town center. From Greece, the border town of Pazarkule is the first Turkish town, which is less than five miles from Edirne. Alternatively, the D110/E84, hugging the northern Coast of the Marmara, is a circuitous, scenic option. But the connecting routes heading north to Edirne are not much more than rough, unfrequented backcountry roads.

THE NORTHERN AEGEAN COAST

The northern Aegean has thrived for thousands of years on the fertility of its soil and the sheer beauty of its shores. Its bay of Edremit is known as the Olive Riviera. It owes this title to the miles of orchards bearing the succulent fruit and for the virtually hundreds of olive processing factories that dot the mainland and the coastal region. But there's also the verdant *Kaz Dağı* (a.k.a. Homer's Mount Ida) that slices eastward through the Bay of Edremit from its western slope on the Biga Peninsula. Its plateaus are home to *Yörüks* (local nomadic herders), who've prospered for centuries from farming and artisanship high up in the hills.

The Aegean also provides a limitless array of activities for diehard sun and sea worshippers. With a slew of boutique hotels, the water lapped resorts of Assos, Ayvalık, Foça, and Çeşme are the jewels in the region's proverbial crown. Divers will revel in the area's offshore scenery. The extremely rare Mediterranean monk seal near Foça, spectral undersea rock formations, secluded coves, and varied fauna spotted just about anywhere along the coast are just the beginning. There is also the increasingly popular island of Bozcaada—the smallest of Turkey's two remaining isles in the Aegean Sea. Just a hop away from Çanakkale, Bozcaada has been fêted since antiquity for its wine. Today, its cobblestone back streets and picturesque beaches are enjoying renewed fervor with nationals wishing to spend their holiday away from the crowded resorts to the south.

Historically, the area's natural beauty and abundance has lured civilizations from near and far for eons. Virtually every erstwhile empire

HIGHLIGHTS

(Truva (Troy): Try to keep track of the reincarnations of Homer's Troy at this ancient spot, located at the western tip of the Biga Peninsula (page 159).

(Bozcaada: Stuck in time, the smallest of two of Turkey's remaining islands is less developed than its counterpart Gökçeada. With its scenic green landscape, it's an ideal venue to frolic among the waves, catch some rays, and sip the local vintage (page 164).

(Assos: Check out what is arguably the most picturesque village on the Aegean. From its heights, the Doric Temple of Athena affords breathtaking sunset views over the Aegean Sea (page 175).

(Bergama's Acropolis: Explore the magnificent ruins and stand at the foundation of the former Altar of Zeus. From the steep terraces, look out onto the fields that comprise today's peaceful Pergamum (page 187).

(Foça: Laze through this nostalgic Greek enclave and find the perfect terrace along the city's old fishing wharf to enjoy the day's luscious catch (page 190).

(Sart (Sardis): Check out one of the richest cities of antiquities — the first to mint coins — and its ruins that span 5,000 years (page 204).

(Alaçatı: Rub elbows with the land's blinged and botoxed in this party outpost, popular for its water sports, boutique hotels, and flamboyant nightlife (page 209).

LOOK FOR **(** TO FIND RECOMMENDED SIGHTS, ACTIVITIES, DINING, AND LODGING.

of the greater Mediterranean region called this region home at one time, from the Persians and Lydians to the western Visigoths and Romans. The sheer wealth of historical sites is amazing. From the oft-visited, legendary ancient cities of Truva (Troy) and Bergama (Pergamum) to the remnants of the centuries-old synagogues and Orthodox churches of Izmir, the northern Aegean coast offers historical wonders alongside its calm, cool waters.

If that weren't enough, virtually every stop regales with tempting dishes, crafted of delectable ingredients sprouted from land so rich the very amicable locals often joke that no sowing is required. For seafood lovers, the archipelago encircling Ayvalık is filled with *papalina* (baby sardine) that's fried and served in mounds in the summer. Turks and their Hellenistic neighbors travel for miles just to gobble it whole. The region's also famed for its fabulous herbs, which make their way into lip-smackingly good appetizers. For an inside view of this

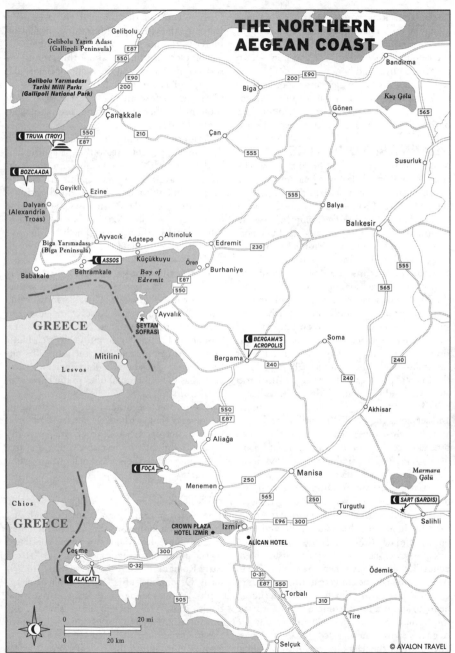

THE NORTHERN AEGEAN COAST

Gelibolu

Gelibolu Yarım Adası
(Gallipoli Peninsula) [E87]
[550]

Bandırma

Gelibolu Yarımadası [E90]
Tarihi Milli Parkı [200]
(Gallipoli National Park)

Biga

[200] [E90]

Kuş Gölü

Çanakkale

Gönen

[565]

[TRUVA (TROY)] [550]
[E87]

Çan

[210]

Susurluk

[555]

[BOZCAADA]

Geyikli Ezine

[555]

Dalyan
(Alexandria
Troas)

Balya

Balıkesir

Ayvacık Adatepe Altınoluk

Edremit

Biga Yarımadası
(Biga Peninsula)

[ASSOS] Küçükkuyu

[230]

[555]

Behramkale *Bay of* Ören Burhaniye
Edremit

Babakale

[565]

[E87]
[550]

Ayvalık

GREECE

★
ŞEYTAN
SOFRASI

[BERGAMA'S
ACROPOLIS]

Soma

Mitilini

Bergama

[240]

[240]

Lesvos

[240]

Akhisar

[550]
[E87]

Aliağa

*Marmara
Gölü*

[FOÇA]

Manisa

[SART (SARDIS)]
★

Chios

Menemen

[250]

GREECE

[565]

[250]

Turgutlu

Salihli

CROWN PLAZA
HOTEL İZMİR ●

İzmir

[E96] [300]

Çeşme

[300]

ALİCAN HOTEL

[O-32]

Ödemis

[ALAÇATI]

[O-31]

[E87] [550]

Torbalı

[310]

Tire

[505]

0   20 mi

0   20 km

Selçuk

© AVALON TRAVEL

bounty, check out a *pazar* (farmer's market) along the way. That's where the *Yörük* women, clad in traditional and colorful garb, peddle their bounty—from seaweed and home-spun carpets to olives and honey.

Ultimately, what makes this region memorable is its laid-back atmosphere and welcoming spirit. North Aegeans are known for their brand of the celebrated Turkish hospitality.

PLANNING YOUR TIME

Most tours swoop through this area in a day by coach from Çanakkale to the relics of Troy and Bergama and end in either Izmir or the overdeveloped resort of Kuşadası. Instead, take your time and discover the serene points in between. Devote the first day to touring the busy port city of Çanakkale in the morning, followed by a couple of hours in ancient Troy. From there you could either insert a day or two on the sleepy isle of Bozcaada, or head further down the Biga Peninsula to the ancient port city of Assos to climb up to the Temple of Athena for surreal sea views. Spend the evening around Assos's wharf and bed down in one of its luxurious B&Bs. On the second day, the Bay of Edremit—one of the Med's olive havens—and the bucolic parishes of Kaz Dağı Milli Parkı (Kaz Mountain National Park) await. As history's Mount Ida, this peak inspired Greek myths and served as the starting point for the Trojan assault against the Acheans. Enjoy the park's pine landscape as you follow trails that meander by waterfalls to Şarlak for great views of the Aegean Sea. Finish the tour of the bay at the once Greek enclave of Ayvalık, where a delectable repast of the area's renowned herbed mezes and strictly Aegean catch lie ahead. After overnighting in Ayvalık, head out bright and early on the third day to Şeytan Sofrası's heady views of a grassy archipelago that's set amidst resplendent turquoise waters. Then, make a beeline to Bergama to visit ancient Pergamum's abundant Greco-Roman ruins. Early in the afternoon, head to quaint Foça, some 65 miles to the south, for another memorable lunch along the Aegean's azure waters. Sated, set the compass due south for the religious treasures of biblical

Izmir—Turkey's third largest city and port. Earmark the third day for Sardis' gorgeously intact Byzantine shops and baths complex.

For a longer itinerary along this region, insert a couple of days on the island of Bozcaada. Or, opt for a boat trip to lush, green Lesvos—a Greek isle whose ancient fortifications hold monuments that retrace some three thousand years of history.

As for the prevailing climate of the Northern Aegean, the shoulder seasons, April–June and mid-September–mid-November, are the ideal time to travel. Accommodations are easy to obtain, though room rates are only slightly reduced in the popular destinations. Springtime and autumn are notorious for spectral bougainvillea shows in the villages. The buzzing olive harvest arrives in late October at the Bay of Edremit.

During the summer, the heat may top 95°F, but a dip in the typically cold coastal waters will aid in cooling off. Upscale restaurants and B&Bs get crowded. Reserve well ahead of time to ensure space and acceptable room rates. Also, most festivals in the culturally rich Izmir area occur in June and July, including the annual Bergama celebration of its ancient history as well as various annual odes to the harvest of local fruits.

Winter, on the other hand, is more temperate and cool, with some rainfall and wind gusts battering the Aegean coast. Normally vacant, lodging is inexpensive. Dine on fatty fish and explore the area's ancient ruins, free of tourists.

HISTORY

The North Aegean Coast is the top arch of a circle that encompasses the ancient Hellenes' Asia Minor realm. Major cities were populated by the prominent kingdoms of the day—from early Romans and Greeks to Persians, and finally Ottomans. This large chunk of geography retraces some of its known historical beginnings to the ancient Greek site of Troy, immortalized by Homer's hedonistic gods of the *Iliad* and *Odyssey*. It dates back to the Late Bronze Age, five million years ago. No less than 12 different sites were built on the original ruins, 9 of which are clearly detailed on-site. Its last layer is dated to a century before the birth of Christ. The region's interior may date back even further. Ruins like those found in Sart (Sardis), 65 miles east of Izmir, hold remnants attesting to the city's continuous role as a major metropolis for more than 5,000 years. Exceptionally fertile lands and a temperate climate provided endless and varied sustenance. Polytheistic kingdoms gave way to a variety of faiths—Judaism, Christianity, and Islam—that lived peacefully side-by-side for centuries.

Truva (Troy) and Çanakkale

The top of the North Aegean territory is Anatolia's westernmost point. Its low coastal crags taper off into the Dardanelles. Çanakkale sits at the narrowest distance between both the Thracian shore—across the geo-politically significant waterway—and Anatolia. The scenery boasts a land and a waterway steeped in mythology. One of the most common myths is Homer's story about Zeus' son, Dardanus, who built a city on the Asian shores of the passage and named it after himself. The name of the straits today is a corruption of that moniker. Another myth tells of young Leander, a resident of Abydus, an ancient Asian outpost along the southern shores of the straits, who swam across the treacherous straits to the town of Sestus to embrace his love Hero. One night when the torch Hero lit to guide her lover's way blew out, Leander lost his way and drowned. Among all of the stories, the latter peeked Lord Byron's interest the most and he, too, was inspired to cross the channel in 1810.

The epic ruins at Troy are situated about a half-hour west of Çanakkale. The 2004 blockbuster movie *Troy* romanticized Homer's famous accounts of the decade-long Trojan Wars. But the ruins reflect more than just the Trojans. They impart about 5,000 years of continuous history through layers upon layers of relics.

Then, just off the Aegean coast, the island of Bozcaada offers its oenological and sandy treasures. Back on the mainland, the few remaining sites near Çanakkale and Troy are a string of sleepy villages interspersed with Roman, Greek, and Ottoman relics. Along the route, rustling fields of wheat and wildflowers, olive trees, and the occasional land turtle serve as traveling companions.

◖ TRUVA (TROY)

Thought to be just a legend fabricated from Homer's active imagination, the remains of Troy weren't discovered until the late 19th century. After all, how real could the sweeping tales of demigods, epic voyages, and a wooden horse have been, except to a couple of armchair archaeologists and treasure seekers?

For one man, German-born Henrich Schliemann, the possibility of finding a cache of riches known as Priam's Treasure was too titillating. His three-year-long dig culminating in 1873 resulted in pay dirt. He discovered a collection of copper instruments and weapons, a chest of gold and silver jewelry, and a myriad of goblets made of precious metals. While a fraction remain in Turkey—thanks to a trade Schliemann made with the Ottomans to extend his permission to dig—the bulk of the precious discovery was smuggled out of the country. Most ended up at the Imperial Museum of Berlin, where it stayed until the Red Army shipped it to the former Soviet Union in 1945. After decades of a cat-and-mouse game in which the Russian government denied its presence, the treasure mysteriously appeared at Moscow's Pushkin Museum in 1993.

For some, Troy seems like just a collection of rocks; for others it stands as a concrete reminder of the grandeur of Homer's myths. For scientists, however, the ruins provide the unique chance to detail the evolution of urbanization

NORTHERN AEGEAN COAST

© JESSICA TAMTÜRK

A replica of the famed wooden Trojan horse greets visitors at Homer's legendary city of Troy.

and development at a single site over a large breadth of history. It takes about 90 minutes to stroll through Troy. For additional information on the history, as well as past and ongoing archaeological research, log onto the exhaustive Project Troia website (www.uni-tuebingen.de//troia/eng).

The site's hilly terrain warrants comfortable walking shoes. Its occasionally torrid summer weather also warrants bottled water, hat, and sunscreen. Most visitors are bused in from local or faraway places; rare are those who opt for a stay at the rudimentary pensions in the nearby farming village of Teyfikiye. Much better selections can be had from either Assos' B&Bs, about 160 kilometers south, or the modern hotels in nearby Çanakkale.

History

The self-taught archaeologist Schliemann began excavating a hill then known as Hısarlık in 1870, after securing the permission of an American consular attaché who'd just purchased the plot from the Ottomans.

There, Schliemann unearthed a knoll that in time—and several digs later—extended to almost 50 feet in depth and unveiled layers of civilizations.

The following is a short account of Schliemann's findings and later archaeological digs. At the deepest tier, **Troy I** (3000–2600 B.C.) reveals a flourishing mercantile outpost, replete with a collection of clay houses. The abodes' carbonized remains indicate their sweeping fiery end. The second layer, **Troy II** (2600–2250 B.C.), includes broad terraces and boasts a much larger and complex settlement than its predecessor. The metal coins with distinctive Mesopotamian characters found at this level indicate that trade may have been an integral part of that economy. **Priam's Treasure,** which Schliemann was so desperately seeking, was found in this section. The common villages of **Troy III–V** (2250–1800 B.C.) mark a lull in the evolution of this ancient Hellenistic settlement. The later incarnation of **Troy VI** (1800–1300 B.C.), just above, was colonized by Mycenaeans—Greeks of the Bronze Age. These settlers built 30-foot-high fortifications and a prominent acropolis, all of which were destroyed by a massive earthquake. Late-19th-century archaeologist Wilhelm Dörpfeld argued that this level—the sixth stratum—constituted the city of King Priam. But modern academia debunks this notion and deems instead that **Troy VIa** (1300–1260 B.C.) was the actual bastion that held repeated Greek attacks during the decade-long Trojan Wars, and that Homer immortalized through verse. A large cache of liquid and solid supplies stored for emergency purposes was found buried deep beneath this layer. Two subsequent incarnations, **Troy VIIb1** and **VIIb2** (1260–700 B.C.) served as humble trading posts, while **Troy VIII** (700–350 B.C.) was repopulated by Greeks from the nearby islands Lesbos and Tenedos. Lastly, **Troy IX**—or *Ilium Novum* (1st century A.D.)—was visited by Alexander the Great after he conquered the Persians at Hellespont in 334 B.C. Since Alexander considered himself a direct descendant of Achilles—the Greek hero of the

Trojan Wars—he beautified the city of his presumed heroic ancestor and swore to erect a Temple of Athena within its walls.

Troy was entirely renovated at the behest of the first Roman emperor, Augustus. Under the Byzantines, Constantine thought about endowing it with the status of capital for his fledgling Eastern Roman Empire (3rd century A.D.). But alas, the more advantageous coastal outpost of Byzantium—today's Istanbul—was found after a push eastward. Much like Efes, its larger sister to the south, the retreating seas caused Troy's decline.

Sights

Moving beyond Troy's **entrance** (0286/283-0536, 8 A.M.–7 P.M. daily, admission 15TL, 90-minute guided tour 80TL), there is the large **wooden horse** that's come to signify this historical site. It was carefully reconstructed by the Turkish Ministry of Tourism, following details found on ancient local coins. A collection of stalls selling maps and color-coded guidebooks of Troy and a **visitor's center,** which highlights the site's history and ongoing research, are near the wooden horse.

Beyond the equine plaza is a path that loops through the entirety of the site. Along its edge are copper conduits utilized by the Romans to pipe water from nearby Mount Ida. The trail leads through two facing defensive walls that ensconced the **East Gate.** Up a few steps, the first main ruins are the Greco-Roman remains of the altar of the **Temple of Athena,** which dates to *Ilium Novum* (1st century A.D.). Unfortunately, much of this monument was destroyed to allow Schliemann's men to dig a trench beneath in search of Priam's loot. The highest terrace above, once the forecourt of the temple, is where visiting dignitaries— such as Persian king Xerxes and Alexander the Great—paid homage to the deity. Linger a minute to gaze at the Dardanelles and the cultivated plains of the Scamander, over which the Aegean once extended. At the bottom of the path is a mishmash of temple remnants that reveal part of the temple's ceiling. Look closely for the small flower the temple's architect used as his signature.

Next, on the right, are the house foundations of **Troy I.** These were constructed according to the traditional Bronze Age Greek Megaron Plan—a rectangular hall, entered through an open, two-columned portico, with a central hearth. Further on the right is **Schliemann's First Trench,** the meat and butter of the site, which is laid out in wooden platforms depicting more than three millennia of ancient civilization, from the top stratum of *Ilium Novum* to Troy I in the bedrock. Beyond the steps that lead past the ongoing excavations of Project Troia—a joint American and German research project undertaken by the Universities of Cincinnati and Tübingen—the remarkable **stone ramp** was used during ceremonies and led up to **Troy II.** Just to the left, inside the walls, is where Schliemann unearthed Priam's Treasure. Just beyond is a complex believed to have held Troy IV's **Palace of Priam.** To the right is a Hellenistic **sanctuary** where ritualistic sacrifices to the deities of the era were conducted. For fans of the recent blockbuster movie *Troy,* the **Skaian gate** (South Gate) is where Hector and Achilles fought the duel the movie hinges on. The area beyond is littered with Roman monuments, including the **odion** (theater), and the **bouleuterion** (senate).

Getting There

Troy is 6 kilometers west of the Çanakkale-Izmir Highway (E87) and about 25 kilometers southwest of Çanakkale. Public transportation from Çanakkale to Troy is available via the hourly *dolmuş* service (3.50TL) that leaves on the half-hour from the station below the Sarı River Bridge. Return service departs every hour on the hour from the parking lot just outside the park. Both services run at minimum 9 A.M.–5 P.M. Transportation tariffs and schedules to and from Çanakkale—as many other services in Turkey—may change at a moment's notice. For this reason it's wise to schedule a tour with an independent travel agency in Çanakkale.

THE TRUTH ABOUT HOMER'S TROJAN WARS

Remember the beautiful Helen, whom Homer wrote about in the *Iliad* 3,000 years ago? She's said to have launched a decade-long conflict between two nations. Was it myth or fiction? Archaeologists have spent lifetimes digging for hard facts that would corroborate the Greek bard's lofty epic.

Homer's tale hinges on the drop-dead gorgeous Helen, the wife of a Greek king, who's seduced by the Trojan prince, Paris. He carries her off to the glorious city of Troy, miffing the Greeks to no end. The Greeks' fiercest king, Agamemnon, marshals an army to avenge the honor of his countrymen. A thousand ships from all over Greece convene and take off to lay siege to Troy and bring back Helen. The battle bloodily wears on for a decade. But despite all efforts, Troy's fortifications remain impregnable. So the Greeks resort to trickery and hide Greek soldiers inside a great wooden horse just outside the city. The Trojans pull it inside, unaware of the soldiers hidden within. The soldiers leap out and open the city gates.

Homer's epic poem led many a scholar to wonder if the story is true. While most academics agree that Homer composed the story in the 8th century B.C., they also concur that his prose chronicles an event which might have occurred centuries before his lifetime. This is around the late Bronze Age, when the Greeks first introduced writing, and the invention of bronze revolutionized weaponry and warfare altogether. So it's during this time, about 1200 B.C., that the story of the Trojan war is thought to have taken place. With a timeframe in place, evidence as to the actual existence of Troy had to be found. And that's what the site's first amateur excavator, Heinrich Schliemann, found in 1870.

Based on geographical clues gathered from Homer's texts, Schliemann accurately guessed Troy to be located on an ancient hillock on the northwestern tip of western Turkey's Biga Peninsula. Fifteen meters below the ground, Schliemann and his team of 200 discovered a walled palace, with a paved ramp wide enough to accommodate two chariots leading to the gate of a city – exactly matching Homer's description.

Schliemann was sure he'd found Troy, but the world was skeptical. The subsequent discovery of an amazing treasure trove of precious jewels proved the existence of prosperous and advanced people. However, as an amateur, Schliemann had been unable to date the layers of the site. The team did not account for one well-known archaeological fact: Ancient civilizations erected cities upon previous settlements, thus creating layers upon sequential layers of generations. Troy is composed of nine succinct stratum, each representing a different era in human history, totaling 4000 years of continuous inhabitation. The bottom layer is dated to 2500 B.C., a time when the Egyptians erected their pyramids. The sixth layer, for instance, represents the Exodus of the Israelites from Egypt. The top layer dates to Jesus Christ's days.

As the science of archaeology evolved, more sophisticated dating tools were used to date Schliemann's findings, which turned out to be more than a thousand years too old. Schliemann had dug down too deep, to the late Bronze Age – or the ninth layer, to be exact. Homer's Troy was higher up, around the sixth layer's fortification walls. Here, excavations revealed physical structures matching Homer's descriptions. The towers, wide streets, tall gates, and strong walls found onsite matched the myth to a tee. The regal citadel, with its impenetrable set of walls and lofty watchtowers overlooked the city, just as Homer describes. But while the city may have been wealthy and powerful, with walls that could have withstood a decade of onslaught, the site of Troy was much smaller than Homer's portrayal.

In 1988, German scientist Manfred Korfmann, along with a team of international archaeologists, turned their focus on the eight-meter-high fortification walls of the site, and discovered that while these were indeed thick defenses, the ancients had made one basic error in their construction: The gates in the walls had no closing mechanism whatsoever. The fact that fortifications of this size could have been built without any defenses perplexed Korfmann. Could it be that the city extended beyond what had already been discovered?

Almost a century after Schliemann's workers first dug, excavation resumed. Korfmann's team used magnetic imaging to explore underground, which led to an amazing discovery – a Roman city based on a grid plan, with wide streets and long avenues, was hidden beneath the fields. Korfmann spotted one feature, so faint it could easily have been overlooked. A barely-there line was located between the walls that vacillated inwards and outwards. Excavation at this spot revealed a section of a deep ditch that extended 700 meters around the mound. Korfmann believed that this was the massive defense Homer spoke of, one that was designed to stop chariots in their tracks. This marked the actual outer limit of the lower city, and carbon dating of remains found in the ditch confirmed the late Bronze Age timeframe. This sizable city of 4,000-8,000 inhabitants more closely matched the size conveyed in Homer's tale.

Korfmann's team found substantiation of violence in the lower city, in the form of arrowheads, evidence of a catastrophic fire, and skeletons, providing undeniable evidence of a city that defended itself against a considerable enemy.

With the identity and size of Troy well defined, only a couple of questions remained: Were Troy's attackers really from Greece, as Homer recited? And, if so, had they really been able to put together an armada of 1,000 war ships to avenge their honor? Well, according to historians, this slice of Greek history occurred during the Mycenean era. According to Greek archaeology professor Spyros Iakovidis, who has spent his career excavating ancient Mycenae, the capital of ancient Greece at that time was commanded from a palatial citadel, from which a web of roads unfurled to each part of its dominion. And a military attack against any enemy state of Bronze-Age Greece, say Troy, may have well been launched from here.

The legendary might of these ancient Greek warriors related by Homer was proven when a mass of graves was unearthed inside a walled cemetery within the fortifications of the Mycenaean citadel. Skeletons of men were unearthed, each wearing colossal gold death masks and ornate ceremonial armor. These Mycenaean war-rior chiefs, each buried with weapons of war, were dated to the late Bronze Age. Some were buried with as many as 40-50 swords, a collection of weapons gathered during a lifetime, each attesting to a warrior culture described by Homer.

But no shred of evidence linked these fabled combatants to Troy, nor to the myth that they had sailed en masse to recover Helen. Further excavation revealed that the Mycenaeans were in the midst of a massive rebuilding program, one that required great natural resources. So they looked east to fulfill what they lacked in their realm: tin to make bronze weapons and tools and gold. Sheer greed, not love, drove the Mycenaeans to lay siege to Troy.

A shipwreck lying along the seabed south of Troy hints that the Trojans had enough riches for the Mycenaeans to launch a massive attack. Turkish archaeologist Cemal Pulak found 11 metric tons of bronze as part of this Bronze-aged shipwreck. Ornate gold ostrich eggs from either Africa or Asia were found alongside wares from all over the known world aboard this long lost cargo ship. If this large ship had docked at Troy, then Troy may have been one of the major ports along the Aegean, a highly strategic trade position along the narrow Dardanelles Strait that links Europe and Asia.

Korfmann believed that Troy capitalized on this special geographic situation. In fact, Troy was the largest city along the Aegean littoral, and one of the wealthiest of its era. Its wealth lured the Mycenaeans, but its location was envied by another landlocked civilization: the Hittites to the east.

According to renowned Hittitologist Trevor Bryce, who has studied a large swath of the thousands of Bronze Age tablets left behind by this Anatolian civilization, references to battles over a region named Wilusha appeared in the texts. Wilusha was similar to the name Wileos, the name the ancient Greeks used for Troy. The tablets chronicled protracted conflicts involving the Mycenaeans, and showed that Mycenaean warriors had fought at Wilusha's gates.

As to the Trojan Horse, however, neither archaeological records nor clues left by Homer prove its existence outside of the Greek bard's imagination.

◖ BOZCAADA

The Greek Historian Herodotus declared that God created Bozcaada so that man could live longer. This thimble of an island is inherently Turkish yet also fundamentally Greek, combining both lineages in a smorgasbord of sites and activities that is expected of this vacation resort, yet truly unique. Beware, most visitors leave reluctantly!

This gem of an isle has been renowned for eons for its grapes, wines, and red poppies. Homer's demigods may have battled in Troy but they amused themselves on Bozcaada—or Tenedos, as the Greeks call it. Vines bearing succulent clusters of grapes grow ubiquitously, but nowhere as vibrantly as along facades of the picturesque villages that encircle this 5.5-kilometer-long island.

A foreboding fortress greets visitors upon arrival. But the sleepy Greek architecture of the backstreets of Bozcaada, the isle's main community, quickly lightens up the mood. Since antiquity to the population exchange of 1923, the island was home to an overwhelming majority of Greeks. Today, just 22 remain. Aside from its historical sites and its broad southern beaches, Bozcaada is gaining popularity with oenologists and bicyclists alike. The island's governance has tended recently to niche tourism by providing wine and bike tours—a trend that's been gathering interest from nationals and one that's extended the tourist season, outside of June–September, to include national holidays and weekends.

Just like Gökçeada, its larger counterpart to the north, Bozcaada occasionally gets battered in the winter by *poyraz* and *lodos* (northerly and southwesterly winds, respectively). These tempests cause sea traffic to cease immediately. If planning to travel to the island November–March, check the weather before departure, or you may be stranded for days during fierce windstorms. For up-to-the-minute details, log onto either www.bozcaadatenedos.com or www.bozcaadarehberi.com.

Sights

Bozcaada is rich in history. From the Persians and Greeks to the Romans and Ottomans, civilizations were quick to claim this outpost that lies at the mouth of today's strategic Dardanelles. Not much remains of their passage, except for the **Venetian Fortress** located on the northeastern cape of the island. This citadel was also used by the Genoese and Byzantines. And when the Ottomans arrived in the mid-15th century, Sultan Mehmet II ordered its complete renovation with the addition of a broad moat to separate the structure from the island. Today, its interior—much like the Venetian Fortress in Bodrum—houses the **Arkeoloji and Etnografi Müzesi** (Archaeological and Ethnographic Museum, 10 A.M.–7 P.M. Tues.–Sun., summer only) detailing Bozcaada's history.

Meryem Ana Kilisesi (Church of Mary, 8 A.M. Sun. mass only) is situated in the heart of the Greek village. While the inscription above the church's front door indicates that it was built in 1869, the local Orthodox population maintains that the Venetians were the first to construct a church on this site some four centuries before.

Wineries

According to legend, the Greek mythological hero Tenes, after which the island was originally named, found a wild Kuntra grape leaf along Poyraz Harbor and replanted it. The Greeks were avid viticulturists, as seen in Homer's *Iliad* and on ancient Tenedosian coins. With the arrival of the Turks in the early 20th century the practice was largely abandoned—outside of growing the edible varieties. Then, in 1925 Yunatçılar Şarapılık revived the industry. Later decades proved a roller-coaster ride for Bozcaadan vintners as wine trailed behind *rakı* (Turkish aperitif)—the Turk's drink of choice. But thanks to an injection of cash from the Turkish Government to modernize wine producing facilities in the late 1990s, combined with the fact that wine is now in vogue here, the area's vintners are getting the recognition they deserve.

Today, more than five million vines produce a whopping 1,600 tons of edible grapes and 3,780 tons earmarked for viniculture. Vineyards fill about a third of Bozcaada's surface and roughly 80 percent of its arable land. While indigenous grapes like Kuntra, Vasilaki, and Karalahna still produce a spectrum of strictly Turkish wines, finer and more profitable French wine grape varieties, like Chardonnay, Merlot, and Cabernet Sauvignon, were introduced in the late 1990s to supplement the crops.

The island's 3,000-year-old winemaking legacy is evident in almost every household, but can be narrowed down to just four names. The largest vintner, **Talay Şarapcılık** (Talay Winery, Lale Sok. 5, 0286/697-8080, www.talay.com.tr) peddles some 20 vintages from dry whites to dessert clarets. It boasts Bozcaada's most modern processing facilities. **Ataol Şarapcılık** (Çınarçeşme Sok. 3, 0286/697-8404, www.ataolsarapcilik.com) has been producing wines since 1927. **Corvus Vineyards** (0212/444-2787, www.corvus.com. tr) offers robust wines, such as the Corvus Aegea—a dry red wine produced with the indigenous Kuntra grape. And, the island's oldest institution, **Yunatçılar Şarapçılık** (Emniyet Sok. 24, 0286/697-8055, www.yunatcilar. com) produces eight distinct whites and reds. Visiting either of their Çamlıbağ shops in Bozcaada is well worth the trip to the island.

Bozcaadan wine can be tasted and purchased throughout the year at the **Çamlıbağ wine shops** (Demirci Sok. 4 or Sakarya Sok. 14, 0286/697-8055). For the annual grape harvest, visit the island in September. The **Vintage and Wine Tasting Tours** (0286/632-0263, info@talay.com.tr, 250TL/person) is a newly organized event by Talay, the island's largest vintner. Partake in wine-tastings, discussions, tours, and outdoor activities during this three-day tour that's held on weekends throughout the month of September. The package includes two nights' accommodations at the rustic Ataol Holiday Ranch, two wine-tastings, two breakfasts, and one picnic lunch. Of course, nothing stops the inquisitive from popping in to any of the vineyards located on Bozcaada's west coast. In pure Turkish hospitality, the management on site may just offer a private tour of the vineyards and processing plants.

Nightlife

Bozcaada's nightlife revolves around the foot of the castle. Along the water and privy to its own beach, **Barali** (Kazanlar Sokak, 0286/697-8001, 8 a.m.–4 a.m. during the high season) lures guests with the soft sounds that emanate from its rustic, brick interior. Walk through the quiet lofted bar/café to grab a cushion along the ambient beach, lit with atmospheric torches and candles. It gets packed with young locals in the hot summer months. Named after the lighthouse on the northwestern-most point of the island, **Polente Café** (Iskele Cad., 0286/697-8605, 8 a.m.–2 a.m.) is Bozcaada's busiest night haunt. It serves a wide selection of coffees and wines, and makes for the perfect hangout anytime of the day. Great tunes are piped in, from Latin Jazz to funky 1980s hits. The café also has free Internet access and a bonfire when the weather cools down.

Sports and Recreation

Bozcaada is not only a great place to kick back, catch some rays, and sip some wine, it also has the perfect geography for sport enthusiasts. Whether it's diving, hiking, cycling, or even riding a scooter, there are plenty of ways to experience the island in a novel, gung-ho, and heart-pounding way.

WATER SPORTS

The southwest coast offers scuba-diving options. **Sulu Bahçe** (Water Garden) lives up to its name. It's an underwater cliff that extends 20 meters in depth, filled with spectral corrals and finned creatures. The most diverse underwater spot, **Mermer Burnu** (Marble Cape) is home to seal caves, frisky octopi, and colorful sea sponges. The seabed here is littered with ancient artifacts, from amphorae to large ceramic slabs. But the most amazing dive remains **Kalın Burnu,** where antique clay oil and wine amphorae, as well as ship wreckage, pepper the seafloor at a depth of some 30 meters.

Boat tours are also a great way of discovering coves that are inaccessible by vehicle, make new friends, and enjoy a complimentary lunch aboard. For daily and private boat tours, as well as diving lessons, all necessary permissions, and gear rental, head to **Aganta Dalis Okulu** (Belediye Dükkanları 7, 0286/697-0569 or 0536/772-6072, www.aganta.net). They're the only folks on the isle who are fully authorized and certified to teach and guide neophytes and more experienced divers.

The extreme sport of kitesurfing has gained popularity on the isle, thanks to gusty winds and certified instructors who call Bozcaada home early June–mid-October. Bop in and out of the water at break-neck—or tamer—speeds at **Çayır Plajı,** the northernmost point on the island. Jan Aahlander and Hakan Kutlu recently launched **Bozcaada Surf Station** (Çayir Plajı, 0541/542-0075, www.bozcaadasurfstation.com) and state that they can get willing novices to fly high above the breakers after just one five-hour lesson.

BIKES AND SCOOTERS

For a wind-in-your-hair sensation, nothing beats renting a bicycle or scooter to tour the 17-kilometer Bozcaadan coastline. You'll encounter miles of beaches and coves. Along the route, stop and watch the sunset at Ponente Lighthouse—this could easily be the highlight of your trip. The congenial Haluk Doğan, a fashion model–turned-entrepreneur, runs **Tenedos Bisiklet Evi** (Liman Girişi, Bozcada, 0286/697-8785, www.tenedosbisikletevi.com, 20TL/bike, 40TL/scooter, 80TL/SUV for 24 hours) and is just the person to meet. This tree-planting activist, who also launched the yearly Bozcaada Mountain Bicycle Marathon in 2005, provides tours of the island.

BEACHES

For those seeking relaxation, Bozcaada's southwestern coast is filled with picturesque sandy shores. The Aegean's waters are clean, thanks to the area's prevalent wind. The waters are also free of seaweed, but reputedly cold, even glacial at times. The most popular shore to throw down a towel has to be **Ayazma,** with its indigo waters ringed by low shrubby crags. Accessible by public transportation, this beach is long and filled with tiny coves. The other, **Habbele,** combines privacy and convenience. It's much less crowded here and waterside cafés provide chaise lounges and parasols. The sandy coastline **Ayana** to the south and **Tuz Burnu Beach** to the east are also good choices.

Accommodations

Bozcaada offers two distinct lodging options, pensions and rustic B&Bs, all with adjacent dining facilities. And as advised throughout this book, summertime generally requires arriving with reservations in hand. The high season runs June 15–September 15; most facilities close their doors November 1–April 31. Children under 6 years of age stay free of charge in most places.

For vineyard houses, **(Ada Bacchus Otel** (Sulubahçe Eski Kule Mevkii, 0286/697-8530, www.adabacchus.com, 100–210TL) blends antique furnishings with 21st-century connectivity and entertainment. It's perched high above miles of vineyards and enjoys a repeat clientele of cultured *Istanbullus,* who bask in its homey atmosphere and typical island fare. Eleven spacious, meticulously clean rooms boast balconies overlooking a pool and Ayazma Beach beyond.

Set in 3.5 acres of protected, land teeming with vineyards and sunflower fields, **Aral Tatil Çiftliği** (Aral Holiday Farm, Cayir Yolu, 2 km, Aşıklar Çeşmesi Karşısı, 0286/697-8357, www.araltatilciftligi.com, US$95–160) is a century-old Greek farmhouse that's been restored lovingly. The basic accommodations are enhanced with lots of fun activities for little ones: hiding in a tree house, picking fresh produce, and collecting fresh eggs. Parents will love the house wine, the myriad relaxing verandas, and the menu dictated by the surrounding land's bounty.

For more centrally-located lodging, the refurbished Greek townhouse of **(Kaikias** (Kale Arkası, 0286/697-0250, www.kaikias.com, 160–250TL) offers a refined, sensual ease. Originally both islanders, the husband-

and-wife team recently opened this tiny boutique hotel and are warm hosts, accustomed to pleasing the whims of the Turkish *société*. Aside from the expected cave of homemade wines and a delectable complimentary breakfast, Kaikias provides a canopied terrace that offers stunning sunsets over the nearby fortress.

Also new to the hotel scene, **Katina Otel** (Kisa Sok. 1, 0286/697-0242, www.katinaas. com, US$150) offers seven tiny, chic rooms with LCD TVs and wireless Internet in a refurbished classic Greek townhouse. The smart design extends to the well-appointed thimble-size bathrooms and sunny, white-washed breakfast room. The hotel is smaller than most single-family houses in the U.S., which means no terrace or garden.

On the budget side, **Kale Pansiyon** (Cumhurriyet Mahallesi, 0286/697-8617, www.kalepansiyon.net, 40–60TL) feels like overnighting in someone's meticulously clean spare bedroom. Enjoy a copious breakfast of farm-fresh produce and toast piled high with owner Pakize Zafer's scrumptious whole-fruit jams on an open-air terrace that affords countryside views. The rooms do boast some of the cleanest bathrooms on the island, but lack air-conditioning.

Getting a nod for its proximity to the sea and its remoteness from civilization, **C Akvaryum Pansiyon** (Mermerburun Mvk., 0532/746-4618, www.akvaryumbozcaada.com, €25–35/person) has neither electricity nor telephone lines. It's just minutes away from the most dazzling cove in the Aegean: Aquarium Cove, named for its variety of colorful marine life. Everything is ultra basic here, but the friendliness and cleanliness abound. Solar- and gas-powered appliances ensure warm showers and cold refreshments. Multi-lingual owners Berna and Deniz were so smitten with the environment that they never left. You may just follow suit!

Food
With such a long Hellenic history here, expect tantalizing Greek dishes combined with classic Turkish temptations. Indigenous grapes pop up in the most unexpected dishes, like Aegean sardines in grape leaves. Coal-grilled octopus and stuffed squid are also island specialties, which accompany the isle's excellent white wines beautifully. Succulent herbs sprout from virtually every crack on Bozcaada and often find their way into tasty omelets, *gözleme* (Turkish pastry), and mezes. Bozcaada's truly unique delicacies include red poppy liquor, olive jam, and tomato marmalade. Mostly closed during the low season, the majority of restaurants are located around the harbor and hotels and along Ayazma Beach to the southwest.

Bozcaadan cafés are an island institution. Perhaps the most sought after is **Ada Café** (Çınar Çeşme Sok. 4, 0286/697-8795, 8 A.M.–1 P.M. daily, 10TL). It's renowned for its fennel omelets, fresh olive breads, and refreshing *gelincik şerbeti* (sweet poppy-infused sorbet). A popular hangout for foreign locals and tourists is **Café at Lisa's** (Kurtuluş Sokak, 0286/697-0182, 8:30 A.M.–midnight, 8–15TL). Delight in truly international dishes like macaroni and pizza, finished off by a slice of home-baked pie. Lisa Lay is an Aussie who came to Bozcaada in the early 1980s. She renovated this once run-down bakery into a happening café. From the café, Lisa collects the local news for Bozcaada's first and only gazette, which she proudly publishes in Turkish.

Seaside restaurants are in abundance, but only a few are truly distinctive. **Sahil Restaurant** (Liman İçi 8, 0286/697-0353) serves great seafood in the shadow of the Venetian fortress, right in the harbor. This historical diner, a.k.a., the Commander's Place, served as a filming location for several Turkish movies and television series, and continues to expand from its earnest beginnings as a fishermen's teahouse. **Borusan** (Altı Boruzan Sok. 7, 0286/697-8414, www.borusanrestoran. com, from 12TL) and **Ayazma Boruzan Restaurant** (Ayazama Beach) are two upscale eateries open year round. Both restaurants have been owned and managed by seven generations of Borusans—a family name given to a forefather who served as the fortress trumpeter. The fried calamari and *torik lakerda* (salt-cured tuna slices) are house specialties that drive repeat business.

Lodos Restaurant (Çınar Çarşı Cad., behind the post office, 0286/697-0545, www.lodosbozcaada.net, from 14TL) is owned and managed by Türkan and Najat Işik. The duo revived this once colorful stretch of street to its original splendor with a busy street terrace. Their menu features more than 35 dishes, highlighted by the truly local dishes of sunflower seed rolls, melted goat cheese on grape leaves, and smoked octopus. And no list would be complete without the inclusion of **Vahit'in Yeri** (Ayazma Mevkii, Plaj Sokak, 0286/697-0130, 10 A.M.–midnight May 15–Oct., from 8TL). Vahit peddled *köftes* (meatballs) in a mobile stand, opened the first restaurant at Ayazma Beach, and now owns his share of shore beneath the trees, where he still offers some of the juiciest meatballs, along with French fries and *gözleme* (Turkish pastry).

Information and Services
For the time being there isn't a *turizm danışma* (tourism information office) on Bozcaada. The **municipality** (0286/697-8081, www.bozcaada.gov.tr) answers most inquiries, particularly if you email them. Other helpful services include the post office, **PTT** (Çınar Çeşme Sok. 4, 0286/697-8170), and bank, **Ziraat Bankası** (next to PTT on Çınar Çeşme Sokak, 0286/697-8489).

Getting There and Around
By car, bike, or foot, most visitors board the **Geyikli-Bozcaada ferry** (Gestaş, 0286/444-0752, www.gestasdenizulasim.com.tr, 2TL/passenger, 20TL/car) from Geyikli, along the coast of the Biga Peninsula south of Troy, and arrive at the Yükyeri Ferry Dock on Bozcaada. From the last week of September through mid-June, ferries depart from Geyikli at 10 A.M., 2 P.M., and 5 P.M.; and, depart from Bozcaada at 7:30 A.M., noon and 4 P.M. In the summer months, June 13–Sept. 21, boats depart Geyikli every 2 hours 9 A.M.–9 P.M., with an additional run at midnight on Friday, Saturday, and Sunday; from Bozcaada, ferry

service starts at 7:30 A.M., and runs every two hours 10 A.M.–8 P.M., with an additional service at 11 P.M. Friday, Saturday, and Sunday. Due to climate and schedule changes, check that boats are running by calling the Gestaş's **ticket office** in Geyikli (0286/632-0263) or Bozcaada (0286/697-8185). Arrive at least an hour prior to departure from Geyikli, as boats get very crowded during the summer months.

A *dolmuş* service (6TL) operates between Geyikli and the Çanakkale Otogar (bus station), a 49-kilometer trip that lasts about an hour. By car, follow Bozcaada signage on the Çanakkale-Izmir highway (E87).

Aside from renting a bike or a scooter from Tenedos Bisiklet Evi (Liman Girişi, 0286/697-8785, www.tenedosbisikletevi.com, 20TL/bike, 40TL/scooter, 80TL/SUV for 24 hours), getting around Bozcaada by riding a *dolmuş* is the way to go. From June through September, service minibuses (2TL) await passengers in front of the fortress. Departing every 15 minutes, 10 A.M.–8 P.M., the minibus makes stops along the way at the island's main beaches: Ayazma, Habbele, and Tuz Burnu.

ÇANAKKALE
A busy port town along the Dardanelles, Çanakkale serves as the typical base for tourists headed to Troy and Gallipoli National Park. Unexpected perhaps is the busy nightlife the city offers, thanks to a booming student population attending the local *Onsekiz Mart Universitesi* and the masses of Aussies who raid the scenic harbor and the bars on Fetvane Sokak in late April during Anzac Week. Aside from being Turkey's second busiest trans-continental transportation hub after Istanbul, Çanakkale's blue-collar interior abounds with food processing and manufacturing plants. The municipality is the seat of the Çanakkale province, which at last count revealed a whopping 175 archaeological sites.

Thanks to its strategic position at the narrowest point—0.75-mile across—along the 40-mile-long natural Dardanelles, the area known as Çanakkale boasts a 5,000-year-old history. This geopolitically-important location has been continually inhabited and has weathered conquests and bloodshed since antiquity. In 480 B.C., the Persian army, led by Xerxes I, crossed the channel to conquer Macedonian land. One hundred and fifty years later, Alexander the Great's Macedonian troops successfully repaid the gory visit in the opposite direction. The latter sacrificed a bull to appease the sea god Poseidon to ensure a peaceful crossing.

The channel was known as Hellespont throughout history. The name comes from the myth of Helle and Phrixus, the children of the cloud goddess Nephele and King Athamas. The king fell in love and later married Ino, leaving previous wife Nephele high and dry. Her retreat caused a great drought. One the evil Ino, ever so jealous of the children, was persuaded would end if Athamas would just pacify the gods by sacrificing Helle and Phrixus. Getting wind of this, Nephele sent her twins away, astride a flying ram with a golden fleece. While in flight over the channel, Princess Helle fell into the water and drowned.

The Dardanelles were crucial to the defense of Constantinople during Byzantine times. Knowing this, the Ottomans conquered the passage in the 14th century to control its maritime traffic, and consequently gained control of the Byzantine capital. Mehmet the Conqueror planned the construction of two bastions on either side of the channel in 1462—Kilitbahir Hısarı on the European shores and the facing Kale-I Sultaniye—to deter the eastbound passage of Christian boats and to further secure his capital seat of Istanbul.

At the turn of the 19th century, the Russian Empire set eyes on the Dardanelles. What followed is a calculated century-long tug-of-war between the flailing Ottoman Empire, the Allies, and the Russians for supremacy over the straits. And in 1915 in a push toward Istanbul, a Franco-British advance through the Dardanelles consisting of over 2,500 military personnel aboard three naval ships were stopped literally dead in their tracks by a slew of mines and artillery showers from the heavily-guarded shores.

If time allows, spend a half-day in Çanakkale along the pier and take in the importance of its geography and the succulent seafood at one of the waterside restaurants. Also, the artifacts from the campaign at Gelibolu, as well as relics from Troy and Assos, at the local museums are definitely worth checking out.

Sights

A small, landscaped park encircles **Kale-I Sultaniye and Askeri Müzesi** (Sultan's Fortress and Military Museum, 0286/217-6565, 8 A.M.–5 P.M. daily). Also known as Çimenlik Fortress, Kale-I Sultaniye citadel is comprised of a string of massive Ottoman fortifications, around which a collection of WWI cannons are displayed. Its interior serves as exhibition space for a handful of first-rate canvases detailing the Gelibolu campaign; mementos relating to Atatürk and Ottoman weapons are also here. Models of mines and anchors litter the dock, which affords great views of the straits and Kilitbahir Kalesi, amid anglers waiting for their next catch.

Nearby lies the replica of the **Nusrat** minelayer, the ship which played a crucial role in hampering the Allied attacks of March 18, 1915 by replacing mines at night on seabed that had been previously cleared by French and British minesweepers. Below deck, a series of newspaper excerpts of the period detail the campaign.

Located at the southern end of the docks, the two-story **Deniz Müzesi** (Naval Museum, 0286/217-2462, 9 A.M.–noon and 1:30–5 P.M. Tues.–Wed. and Fri.–Sun., 5TL) offers a glimpse at a collection of interesting war memorabilia and photos. Seek Atatürk's pocked pocket watch, which reportedly saved his life by diverting a bullet aimed straight for his heart.

In addition to the museums, the are four noteworthy monuments in Çanakkale: *saat kulesi* (clock tower); German Krupp gunner used during the WWI Gallipoli campaign; beautifully preserved *han* (caravansary); and Troy horse along the channel. The five-tiered, domed–clock tower, which stands across from the ferry docks, was built in 1897 by Emily Vitalis, an Italian businessman and consul who resided in this center. The giant German-made Krupp gunner lies up a ways on Cumhuriyet Bulvarı. The quaint *han* is located on Fetvane Sokak. North of the ferry docks lies the cheesy reproduction of a life-size **Trojan horse**. In his 2004 blockbuster film, *Troy*, director Wolfgang Petersen chose this massive model over the horse replica in Troy.

ARKEOLOJI MÜZESI (ARCHAEOLOGICAL MUSEUM)

Çanakkale's Arkeoloji Müzesi (0286/217-6565, 9 A.M.–5 P.M. daily, 5TL) contains an imposing display of astoundingly detailed terracotta statues, coinage, gold jewelry, and glass perfume bottles recovered from digs around the region, including those salvaged from the Dardanos tombs nearby in 1974. There's also a small array of relics unearthed by Schliemann in Troy and artifacts collected from the necropolis on Bozcaada.

To reach the museum, walk up Demircioğu Caddesi to where it meets Atatürk Caddesi. There, hail a *dolmuş* headed for Kepez or Güzelyalı, or hang a left on Atatürk Caddesi and continue walking to the Çanakkale Otogar (bus station), where the *dolmuş* terminus is located.

Events

War commemorations are held each year at two different times. The Turks celebrate **Çanakkale Deniz Zaferi** (Çanakkale Naval Victory) on March 18, the day Ottoman armed forces foiled the Allied naval push through the straits. Kiwis and Aussies honor their fallen by the thousands on Anzac Day on April 25, the day of the ill-fated Allied landings of 1915. An internationally televised ceremony at dawn is typically followed by various services throughout the historic peninsula.

Fêted in mid-August since 1963, the **International Troy Festival** (Çanakkale Municipality, 0286/217-1079, www.canakkale.bel.tr) resuscitates ancient Truva (Troy) with guided tours, reenactments, and folklore performances, in addition to a variety of art and film exhibitions.

Nightlife

The Fetvane and Yalı Sokakları area rocks after hours, with a couple of popular discos and a string of bars. Generally gathering steam at 10 P.M., the hands-down favorite among the youth hangouts is **Depo** (Fetvane Sok. 19, 0286/212-6813, 5TL cover), offering a large garden with comfy beanbags and a vast indoor space, where techno music bounces off the walls. For live-rock music **Han Bar** (Fetvane Sok. 26, 5TL cover) is the place to go. The drinking hole of the moment remains **TNT Bar** (Saat Kulesi Meydanı 6, 0286/217-0470). A favorite among the fickle collegiate crowds most nights, the vibe gets absolutely ridiculous come Anzac Week. For panoramic views of the water, the quay and coastal road, which closes to vehicular traffic in the throes of summer, hold their own with streetside terraces and a nightlife scene perfectly tailored for the more mature set.

Accommodations

As a relay city between continents, Çanakkale is filled with assorted lodging options. Again be forewarned that April's mad Anzac Week means no vacancy everywhere. So, unless you're here to honor the fallen, steer clear of the second half of April. Try to book early online, and as always come armed with a printout of the reservation to ensure room rates and stated conditions, like air-conditioning and complimentary breakfast, are met.

Packing simple beauty and classical warmth in a historical townhouse along Çanakkale's oldest and hippest drag, the ◖ **Kervansaray Hotel** (Fetvane Sok. 13, 0286/217-8192, www.otelkervansaray.com, from 100TL) is a century-old red brick pasha's mansion that packs 20 elegant rooms in Ottoman period decor. Modern amenities like Wi-Fi and satellite television are bonuses, and so is the alluringly quiet, ample garden out back where the bountiful complimentary breakfast is served.

Love Çanakkale's clock tower? Wake up right next to it from one of the 50 spacious, slightly chintzy rooms at the **Anzac Hotel** (Saat Kulesi Meydani 8, 0286/217-7777, www.anzachotel.com, from 85TL). The hotel has basic, yet comfortable, accommodations, with Internet access and an obliging staff. This establishment is geared toward foreigners; its owners are masters of hospitality and of knowledge when it comes to western Turkey.

The only five-star hotel in Çanakkale, the **Hotel Kolin—The Hellespont** (Kepez, 0286/218-0808, www.kolinhotel.com, from €85) was tailor-made for the luxurious demands of visiting dignitaries. Among the perks the likes of U.K.'s Prince Charles find appealing are the sumptuous bath options—Turkish and Finnish—indoor/outdoor pool, and a myriad of sports facilities. Banking on its peripheral amenities, the Kolin's somewhat lackluster and dated rooms don't justify their rates, except for the rooms on the upper floors, which benefit from superb views. The establishment's pièce de résistance remains the high-style Sofra Restaurant, among the nine other dining and drinking options available on the property.

For those on a tighter budget, the tiny, incredibly inexpensive **Efes Hotel** (Fetvane Sk. 5, 0286/217-3256, www.efeshotelcanakkale.com, from €20) boasts 22 rooms with air-conditioning and satellite television throughout. There's also a complimentary morning nosh right atop Çanakkale's historical drag. Its cleanliness and affordability appeals to both international backpackers and hard-to-please Turkish families. For accommodations that will save even more cash for wining and dining, the bright and airy block building that comprises **The Yellow Rose Pension** (Yeni Sok. 5, 0286/217-3343, www.yellowrose.4mg.com, 10–14€) offers a clean, bare-bones, suite with air-conditioning and a balcony. Reserve early to ensure availability. Onsite is a superior travel agency, utilized by regional tour companies.

Food

Çanakkale is a place to revel in fish, especially its ubiquitous sardines. The best dining options are among the waterside restaurants lining the wharf. Here, you'll find typical Turkish "fast food" fare, in addition to local specialties, like *peynirli helva* (concoction of sheep cheese and semolina), *şakşuka* (cacophony of Mediterranean veggies cooked in olive oil), just-picked mussels, and virtually anything else from the water.

To savor Çanakkale's bounty, aim your fork to the six-decade-old **Liman Yalova Restaurant** (Gümrük Sok., 0286/217-1045, www.yalovarest.com, 20TL). Known for its mezes, this place also serves a grilled or raw *deniz kestanesi* (supple sea urchin) as a starter. Follow it with a monkfish oven-baked with herbs and veggies. This large diner may feel cavernous on the inside. Call ahead to request a window table to watch the large car ferries dock at the port right next door. For another time-tested waterfront option, **Rihtim Cekik Restaurant** (Eski Balıkhane Sok. 7, 0286/212-5367, 10TL) offers the expected grills and appetizers, but falls victim to the raucousness of its neighboring bars and cafés. Head there early in the evening for a quieter dining experience.

Meat lovers relish the rather spicy Eastern Mediterranean cuisine of **Adana Sofrası** (Yeni Kordon Mevkii, 0286/213-9168, 13TL). Choices here include the rare and healthier chicken *lahmacun* (think pizza with minced meat), in addition to old kebab favorites and tons of herb-filled starters made popular locally by owner Halil Ibrahim Yürtsever. Murat Kanar's **Manzara Kebab II** (Inönü Cad. 203, 0286/214-2484, www.manzarakebap.com.tr, 11TL) is another mouthwatering option for tender lamb or beef. Gracing bright walls, flora emanates from the main salon by way of original artwork. Here, expect a quick meal in a diner that comes highly recommended by the municipality. One of a couple Turkish fast food branches in Çanakkale, **Meshur Sultanahmet Köftecisi** (0286/217-5844, www.sultanahmet-koftecisi.com, 8TL) is located in the Carrefour Supermarket next to the *otogar* (bus station). Not much graces the menu here except this fast food giant's branded *köfte* (meatball) and kebab.

Handan Gözleme Evi (Tarla Sok. 16, 0286/214-1143) is well-known café, just a block southeast of central Cumhuriyet Bulvarı. For those who can't get enough of the filled lavash specialty, Handan offers a cheesy mushroom or spinach combo that may just become your favorite lunch option during your stay in Çanakkale. Check out the headscarved "bakers" who prepare the flat bread to order.

For the local cheese specialties, head to **Babalik Cheese Shop** (near the clock tower) for tea with *börek* (pastry) and dazzling views of the port. This is the place to taste the sweet cheese and semolina *helva* (halvah) in the evening.

Along the glitzy waterfront, the always hip and dependable **Café Notte** (Kayserili Ahmet Paşa Cad. 40, 0286/214-9111) is not only an evening spot, infused with a chic continental feel, it's also a modern café. It features a welcoming atmosphere, chic interior, and grown-up cosmopolitan menu.

Information and Services

As the district's main city, Çanakkale's **turizm danışma** (by the jetty, 0286/217-1187) has to answer numerous inquiries and is well prepared to do so with detailed maps and brochures pertaining to the region's bigger tourism draws. Mail service and currency exchange can be done at the **PTT Office** (behind the Cumhuriyet Meydanı, 8:30 A.M.–5:30 P.M. Mon.–Sat., until 7 P.M. June–Oct.). ATMs are located throughout town; branches of national banks are located along Çarşı Caddesi. In case of emergency, contact the local office of the **Tourism Police** (0286/2175260) or the **Çanakkale State Hospital** (0286/217-1098).

Booking a two-day or longer excursion of the area through a tour provider online or through a travel agency in Istanbul is highly recommended. It not only simplifies the travel to Çanakkale, but also solves transportation to sites and such, as well as some lodging issues when in town.

Getting There

BY AIR

Since mid-2008, a daily flight has been connecting Çanakkale with Istanbul. The service is available via the Turkish airline company **Atlas Jet** (www.atlasjet.com.tr), and costs about 70TL if booked early via the Internet. The 45-minute flight departs Istanbul's Atatürk International Airport at 9:30 P.M. daily, except on Saturday. From Çanakkale Airport, planes take off at 7 A.M. daily, except on Sundays. A taxi service transports passengers across the two-mile distance between the regional airport and the city center.

BY BUS, FERRY, AND CAR

The coach companies that serve the city include **Çanakkale Truva** (0286/444-0017, www.truvaturizm.com), **Kamil Koç** (0286/444-0KOC, www.kamilkoc.com.tr), **Metro** (0286/444-3455, www.metroturizm.com.tr) and **Radar** (0286/444-2217, www.radarturizm.org). Buses arriving from Istanbul stop either near the sea terminal or at the Çanakkale Otogar (on Atatürk Caddesi), less than a third of a mile from the city's historical center. Since the websites of most carriers listed are in Turkish only, reserving through a travel agent is the simplest option. Better yet, hop on any of the 3–4 fast ferry services provided Monday–Thursday (plus 2–3 additional runs Mon.–Sun.) by **IDO** (0286/444-4436, www.ido.com.tr, 30TL/passenger) from the Yenikapı sea terminal, and take a bus to Çanakkale from there.

If driving from Istanbul, take the E6 in the direction of Edirne to the Kinali exit. Follow the Tekırdağ signage along the coastal highway toward the town of Eceabat. Once there, heed the road signs directing motorists to the Çanakkale ferryboats, which will take passengers across the Çanakkale Boğazı in 25 minutes. There's another crossing at Kilitbahir, two miles further west, where smaller ferries take ten minutes less to cross the strait. Both services are run by **Gestaş** (0286/444-0752, www.gestasdenizulasim.com.tr; passenger 2TL, car 20TL) and post schedules online and at Çanakkale's embarcaderos. Alternatively, take the IDO fast ferry at Istanbul's Yenikapı seaport in the direction of Bandırma (105 minutes, 115TL/vehicle and driver, 25TL/additional passenger). This itinerary shaves off 45 minutes from the old way of traveling the route. The remaining 100 miles westward from Bandırma to Çanakkale take about two hours.

Getting Around

Managed by the municipality and available almost from any point in the city, including the airport and *otogar* (bus station), public buses crisscross the area and connect the peripheral beaches of Güzelyalı, the fishing village of Assos, and the ruins at Troy. Working on an electronic withdrawal system—or Kent Card, much like Istanbul's Akbil—the fare is subtracted after each swipe. Purchases and credits can be performed at kiosks at the ferry port, *otogar,* or at booths or shops displaying the Kent Card logo in town.

Dolmuşes (2–4TL) to Troy and Güzelyalı leave from the station located under the Sarı Çayı Bridge. To reach Assos, hop on a minibus bound for the Ayvaçık Otogar then transfer there for Assos. Taxis are also widely available.

BIGA YARIMADASI

Looping westward from Çanakkale, the many ruins and barren coastlines of the desolate Biga Yarımadası, history's Troad, rarely get visitors but are well worth the journey. Since transportation services are rare outside of the minibuses heading for Ayvacık or Assos, driving a rental vehicle is recommended.

Dalyanköy

Originally called Alexandria Troas, Dalyan, six miles south of Deyikli, is a mere collection of what is estimated to be more than 1,000 acres of decrepit Hellenic ruins. Established in 310 B.C. as Antigonia Troas by Macedonian king Antigonus, Alexander the Great's successor, this port city fell less than a decade later to Alexander's other general Lysimachus, necessitating yet another name change to Alexandria Troas in honor of his former commander. As the main port of northwestern Asia Minor, the city gradually extended both in size and wealth to become the Troad's richest settlement. Today, the remains of its

grandeur include baths and a gymnasium dating back to A.D. 135, a two-basin harbor now almost entirely covered, vestiges of a six-mile-long strip of fortifications, and the aqueduct Trajan built almost 2,000 years ago. During the Byzantine era, Constantine weighed the merits of Alexandria Troas while searching for a capital for his fledgling empire. Much like Troy, the city began a long decline in the 3rd century A.D., mostly attributed to the diversion of marine traffic and trade to the newly established imperial seat of Constantinople. The Ottomans picked through the marble ruins in search of building material for their great mosques to the east, such as Istanbul's Sultanahmet Camii.

Just two miles south of Dalyanköy, the historical **Kestanbol Kaplıcaları** (Ezine, 0286/637-5223, 8 A.M.–10 P.M., 15–20TL/hr) spurts cool, albeit murky, water from its thermal springs, purported to be highly beneficial in the cure of nerve and muscle fatigue. Süleyman the Magnificent reportedly lulled away the pains of battles here upon his return from his push westward in the mid-15th century. Private suites with individual baths are available to kickback sultan-style, along with communal facilities for men and women.

Dalyanköy is reached by bus from Çanakkale's *otogar* (bus station), or through an inconsistent *dolmuş* service that links the site from Ezine, ten miles to the east.

Gülpınar

The expanding town of Gülpınar, a farming outpost with an illustrious past, reaps the benefits of tourism thanks to the **Apollo Smintheus Temple** (8:30 A.M.–5 P.M., 5TL), along with its small adjoining museum. The altar, set in a pastoral setting of pomegranate and olive trees on the western edge of town, was a gift to Apollo the Mouse God from the people of the Troad in appreciation of his staunch commitment to the Trojans in the decade-long war against the Acheans in the 2nd century B.C. Apollo was the king of Tenedos and the patron saint of ancient Chryse—today's Bozcaada and Gülpınar. The mouse cult associated with

NORTHERN AEGEAN COAST

Apollo arose when mythological hero Teucer, fleeing a famine on the isle of Crete, consulted an Oracle before departure for advice as to where to set up a new settlement. Teucer was told to look for a place where the "sons of the earth" would attack. Early one morning, he found that an indigenous species of white mice had gnawed at his sandals. Teucer and his Cretan followers saw this event as the long-awaited portent, and founded a colony on the spot. Impressive reliefs on marble blocks and steles depict Homer's *Iliad* in the **Gülpınar Müzesi** (Gülpınar Museum, 9 A.M.–5 P.M. June 1–Aug. 31).

Gülpınar is reached by bus from either Ezine or Çanakkale. If traveling by car, take the E87 southbound from Ezine through Ayvacık until the Highway 17-51 connector to Behramkale. Right before reaching Behramkale, you'll see the entrance of Highway 17-52, which takes motorists into Gülpınar in 32 kilometers.

Babakale (Lekton)

Babakale lies at the southwestern-most point of the Biga Peninsula. Its fishing village surrounds a large Ottoman fortress, which was entirely renovated in 2000. Sultan Ahmet III was forced to dock his armada at Babakale during a fierce storm. In gratitude to the Turcoman population who had assisted his troops during their layover, the sultan commissioned this massive citadel in 1725 to deter pirates from raiding the village. Babakale's graveyard, just off the town center, boasts the tomb of *baba*, a local dervish saint who went by the name "father." About three kilometers north of the port, a beach with rocky outcrops is a good stepping-off point to explore the vibrant marine life.

YÖRÜKS

The *Yörüks* (local nomadic herders), one of the oldest tribes of modern Anatolia, continue to add vibrancy and substance to present-day Turkey. Their colorful artisan works pepper the Aegean Coast. From beautiful carpets to simple yet fine cookery, their mastery of homemaking on the range has evolved through a thousand years of nomadic life to infuse this multi-ethnic land with a subtle authenticity.

Today just a few *Yörüks* remain migratory. But more than 1000 years ago, these nomads — one of the original tribes of Oğuz Turks — moved south from their home deep inside the Aral steppe, today's southwestern Kazakhstan. *Yörüks* inundated western Anatolia after the Selçuks conquered the Byzantines in the Battle of Manzikert in 1071. Although they're akin to the Turkmen and other Anatolian ethnic clans, the *Yörüks* boast predominantly Caucasian traits. Some settled farther west, in the Balkans, Macedonia, Thrace, and Cyprus, as the Ottoman Empire expanded.

Today *Yörüks* assimilation into the Turkish fabric is almost seamless. Their pride of heritage is palpable, and they take every opportunity to differentiate themselves from the other ethnic groups they live alongside in Turkey, like the Alevis, Turkmen, Gypsies, Kurds, Circassians, and Arabs. The "real" *Yörüks*, those deeper in Anatolia, still continue transhumance, or the act of moving livestock from one grazing ground to another in a seasonal cycle.

Their name is a phonetic take on the word *yürü*, which means *to walk; Yörük*, or *Yürük*, signifies "those who walk, walkers" and honors their nomadic existence. Today, most *Yörüks* have opted for the ease of the sedentary lifestyle, keeping the rich nomadic heritage of their forefathers alive through craft.

Their songs and crafts represent one of the last remnants of the true Turk, one whose nomadic culture has stood fiercely against Ottoman dominance. Apt at weaving *kilims* (carpets) and other crafts, *Yörük* women relate their personal heritage and mood through design, making each item as unique as the person who created it. Today, the rare nomadic *Yörük* can be found herding his stock along the Taurus Mountains in western Turkey. Just listen for their joyful song, backed by the sacred string and wind instruments they carry like amulets until their final day on earth.

Tourists flock to Babakale for its reputed seafood, which can be found in the rather inexpensive hotels that line the harbor. For a superior restaurant and traditional pension lodging, the village's best bet is Mustafa Uran's **Uran Hotel** (Babakale Köyü, 0286/747-0218, from 45TL). Enjoy the fried calamari before tucking in for the night. Buses running from Behramkale to Gülpınar, three miles north, stop at Babakale.

(ASSOS

About 25 kilometers west of the E87 and about the same distance from Ayvacık to the north, today's Assos is surrounded by the vestiges of an impressive fortification system that dates back to the Byzantines. The lure of the ancient city, which bore the same name, continues to this day with a handful of stone cottages, old warehouses reborn as pricey boutique hotels, and a harbor which remains unchanged since the 1950s, thanks to its protected historical importance and the municipality's

unwavering commitment to keep modern development on the outskirts of town. To reach the famed **Temple of Athena**—the best kept ruin and best scenery in Assos—visitors must climb a hillside. The tiny farming village of Behramkale is on the other side of the mount. And the shingle beach of Kadırga lies about four kilometers to the east.

Assos was steeped in history from the time it was founded in the 10th century B.C. by Aeolian colonists from the city of Methymna on the nearby island of Lesbos. The city prospered under the rule of Blythinian banker Eubulus during the 4th century B.C. Eubulus' former eunuch, Hermeias, who previously had studied under Plato and Aristotle in Athens, gained his freedom and rose to prominence to become Assos' next ruler. During Hermeias' reign, his former teacher Aristotle founded his—and Assos'—first school of philosophy in 348 B.C. The philosopher went on to marry Hermeias' niece, Pythia, before returning to Lesbos. Some years later, the Persians

The ruins of Assos's Temple of Athena crests a massif that has phenomenal views of the Bay of Edremit and the Greek isle of Lesbos.

invaded Assos and tortured Hermeias to death. Alexander the Great reconquered the city in 334 B.C. Saint Paul visited Assos on his way to Lesbos during his third missionary trek through Asia Minor between A.D. 53–57. Soon after, the once prosperous city dwindled into a sleepy fishing village, until its ruins attracted the young American archaeologist Francis Bacon in 1880.

Once an isolated summer hangout for a few sophisticated *Istanbullus,* Assos' up-market popularity has hit a crescendo for those wishing to escape the torrid and crowded resorts dotting the south. The city's steeper rates for lodging escalate even higher during the months of May–October and during the holidays.

Reservations must be made prior to arrival. Also, there are no banking services, post offices, or tourist information offices in Assos; most hotels do exchange currency and provide regional information to visitors.

Sights

En route from Ayvacık, look out for the pointed arches of the mid-14th-century Ottoman bridge, **Hüdavendigar Köprüsü,** built for Murad I the Master. On the approach to town, a crossroad signals the pebble beach at Kadırga to the left and Highway 17-52 to Gülpınar. Continue straight into the village of Assos until reaching its central teahouse, then hang a right past its traditional flat-top housing made out of the valuable, corrosive indigenous stone. The narrow cobblestone street leads to the ticket booth for the Temple of Athena, followed by the **Hüdavendigar Camii** on the left. Sultan Murad I, a diplomat who unabashedly nicknamed himself Hüdavendigar, meaning *master* in Persian, commissioned this mosque. A marble slab depicting a Greek inscription above the building's entrance confirms that the mosque was constructed from building blocks pilfered from the church it replaced.

Atop the hill is the 6th-century B.C. **Temple of Athena** (8 A.M.–sundown, 5TL). While tourists scramble up the mount to check out this early Doric structure, most end up baffled at the uninterrupted panorama of the isle of Lesbos, the long arch of the Bay of Edremit, and part of the Troad. Only a few of the original altar's original 44 columns remain. The rest of the structure was reconstructed with blocks of unsightly concrete.

Artifacts from the ancient city of Assos litter the hillside within the crumbling four-kilometer-long fortification system. On the way down toward the harbor, the **necropolis** and **sarcophagi** are fashioned of locally-quarried stone that's known for its caustic qualities. Interestingly enough, the term *sarcophagus* (flesh-eating) was coined in Assos. And according to Pliny the Elder's accounts (A.D. 23–79), bodies buried in the material were consumed within 40 days. Scientists later attributed the stone's corrosive property to its high alum content. Ironically, Assos' indigenous stone is impossibly difficult to hew. The towers and gates within the **city walls**—one of the best-preserved fortification systems in Turkey—are impressive. Lower still are a 2nd-century B.C. **agora** (ancient public open space), **theater,** and **gymnasium** constructed on an area that was once two terraces.

Accommodations

While Assos is reputed for its excellent, pricey boutique hotels, it offers an entire range of lodging options, from beach resorts near the stony beach of Kadırga to cozy and quieter resorts in Behramkale. The dynamic harbor and village is where the majority of tourists stake their claim. For a night under the stars, there are about a half-dozen **campsites** (tents less than 15TL/night) along the coast, just past the harbor. If you choose to stay in downtown Assos, here are a few words of advice: Reserve early and book online, either with the hotel itself or a discounter, for lower rates than those requested onsite. Most quotes are inclusive of breakfast, sometimes even dinner, but this can also be negotiated when making the reservation.

Set in a refurbished gray-stone warehouse, the town's only five-star establishment is the ◖ **Assos Kervansaray** (Assos Limanı, 0286/721-7093, www.assoskervansaray.com, from €110 high season, half-board). Amenities include Wi-Fi, a pool, and a private pier leading to the Aegean's translucent waters. The better rooms boast stunning sea views, as well as antique-chic decor. Serving Turkish fare and grilled fish, the onsite seaside restaurant is a bonus. Set in a chili garden after which the hotel takes its current name, **(Biber Evi** (0286/721-7410, www.biberevi.com, 230-270TL, half-board), Chili House, is one of the priciest hotels in town. The property is 150 years old and was formerly owned by a rich acorn trader. The current proprietor is British expat Jacqui, who together with award-winning chef Lütfi Oğuzcan, dazzle with a rustic and spare environment and, as you might expect, a menu replete with chili recipes. The rooftop terrace is *the* spot in town to view the sunset over one of Oğuzcan's collection of aged whiskeys.

Barely five years old, the **Nazlıhan Boutique Hotel** (Assos Iskele Mevki, 0286/721-7385, www.assosedengroup.com, 180–230TL) spells rustic all the way down to brick walls and the antique tiles in the baths. But only 8 of the property's 37 rooms offer sea views. The Nazlıhan includes half-board, with traditional Turkish meals served buffet-style in one of three restaurants. Its laid-back Eden Port café, by the harbor, welcomes with fluffy pillows, crackling fire, delectable array of coffees, and narghile. Hotel guests enjoy a complimentary stretch of beach at the Assos Group's superior Fenerlihan restaurant, located by the harbor.

On a vertiginous cliff above the seemingly yet-to-be-discovered Sivrice Bay is the secluded **Berceste Hotel** (Sivrice Feneri Mevki, Bektaş Köyü 1, 0286/723-4616, www.bercestehotel.com, 150TL). This castle-like property, owned by a retired army general and his wife, features Turkish chalet-style decorated rooms with a to-die-for panorama of the Sivrice cove, the island of Lesbos, and the sea beyond. Ditto for the ample terrace, which doubles as a restaurant and a locale from which to behold ridiculously beautiful sunsets serenaded by the resident cicadas.

On the low-budget end, but packing tons of charm, right in Behramkale, the **(Eris Pansiyon** (Behramkale Köyü 6, 0286/721-7080, erispansiyon.com, d. up to 120TL) is owned by a retired American couple from New York. No pretense here, just five simple rooms, an old brick house, Mediterranean gardens, stunning mountain views, irresistible organic food, and owner Emily Vickers' melt-in-your-mouth cookies.

Food

You'll find the finer food at restaurants along the coastal highway. Come evening, tables and chairs are laid out beachside, making this an ideal spot to view the sunset and the ruins above. Fish is king along the Aegean and **Fenerlihan** (Harbor, 0286/721-7017, 12TL) is a great place to try the daily catch or their dressed-up Turkish fare. But a trip to Assos is not complete without trying the award-winning dishes of thespian-turned-chef extraordinaire Lütfi Oğuzcan at **Biber Evi Restaurant** (0286/721-7410, www.biberevi.com, 17TL). Foodies are drawn to Biber Evi (Chili House) for its connoisseur's wine list, its bread sticks baked fresh from the village bakery, and produce plucked from the kitchen garden.

One of the few diners open year-round, **Lembas Café & Winehouse** (0286/721-7391, www.assos.de/lembashouses/cafe.htm, 12TL) is an eye-catching residence that boasts Assos' best cup of Joe. With a cellar boasting regional wines and strong homemade cherry liqueur, the menu's cosmopolitan entrées are enhanced when drizzled with the house's pressed olive oil.

Getting There and Around

Coach service linking Ayvaçık or Küçükkuyu from Çanakkale, Istanbul, Ankara, Izmir, or Bursa is available through Çanakkale Truva or Kamil Koç. Hop on the **Assos Birlik** minibus from the Ayvaçık stop or hail a cab from **Ida Taxi** in Küçükkuyu. In the summer months, May–mid-September, a *dolmuş* service (1.5TL) linking Behramkale and Assos runs frequently; these function as taxis (3.5TL) during the winter.

AYVAÇIK

Serving as a transit point through southwest Biga Peninsula, Ayvaçık also thrives as a market town come Fridays when *Yörük Turcoman* women (nomadic herders) peddle produce gathered from Mount Ida's high plateaus at stands pitched near the *otogar* (bus station). Natural, authentic *Yörük kilims* (rugs) are for sale at ridiculously inexpensive prices at the **Yörük Hale** (9 A.M.–5 P.M. daily) cooperative, adjacent to the bus station.

Just south of town, the gallery at **Doğal Boya Araştırma ve Geliştirme Projesi** (DOBAG, Natural Dye Research and Development Project, 0286/712-1274, www.dobag.com, 9 A.M.–6 P.M.) displays some of the world's most stunning carpets made of naturally-dyed lamb's wool by regional weavers. Although the cooperative has focused on exporting its products to an international clientele since 1982, the pricey exhibits are rarely for sale, but are certainly worth a look.

Getting There

From the E87 Highway that links Çanakkale to Izmir, Route 17-51 leads straight into Ayvacık. Coach service to Çanakkale is available hourly from Ayvacık's *otogar* (bus station). With Assos just 20 minutes away by *dolmuş* (4TL), it's easy to stay in Assos and hop on one of the half-dozen vehicles that make the trip daily.

BAY OF EDREMIT

Just beyond the shores of the long Bay of Edremit, scrub lands reveal unexpected ruins that denote its protracted Hellenic history, towering Mediterranean oak trees, and miles of protected olive groves that produce the region's prized product. Processing plants pepper the coastal road that winds along the bay to the last resort town of Ayvalık. Midway through, Kaz Dağı Milli Parkı—Homer's famed lush Mount Ida—soars over the azure Aegean, making it an ideal alpine roadside stop. From start to finish, the 100-kilometer excursion snakes through some of the country's most fertile land along the Aegean's resplendent waters, punctuated only by charming villages dedicated to farming and a budding tourism industry.

Adatepe

Starting in Küçükkuyu, the **Adatepe Zeytinyağlı Müzesi** (Adatepe Olive Oil Museum, 0286/752-1303, www.adatepe.com, 9 A.M.–5 P.M., free admission) is Turkey's first and only exhibit space devoted to the succulent fruit and the millennia-old practice of extracting its golden liquid. Rows of ancient amphorae and an original stone wheel are exhibited in this refurbished old soap factory. Stop for infused herb tea at the adjoining café, prior to continuing on to Adatepe, just four kilometers to the north.

One of the last traditional, picture-perfect villages in the North Aegean, **Adatepe Village** rests on the furthest western slope of Mount Ida. The mere dozen abodes that make up the town sit on the periphery of its square, which is centered on a single towering plane tree. Its canopy provides the preferred resting spot for the parish's summer residents—mainly intellectual *Istanbullus,* relaxing over a book and strong tea.

One of Adatepe's traditional brick houses is the rustic **Adatepe Pansiyonları** (Adatepe Village, 0286/752-6803, www.adatepe.net, 120TL). Set in two village buildings, nine simple, more-than-adequate rooms come with pristine en suite bathrooms and two decadent meals. Decide what's for dinner from Mount Ida's ripest produce and the Aegean's tantalizing fish.

Altınoluk

This small resort town boasts a five-kilometer sandy beach overshadowed by the bay's eco-tourist attraction of **Mount Ida.** Extending from Assos to Ören, the mountain offers a variety of trails that can be explored from almost any point. But Altınoluk—the summer haunt of Ankara's bourgeoisie—is the preferred launch for a full-day **guided tour** provided by **Mare & Monte**'s travel agency (Fatih Cad. 13, 0266/396-1730. www.hotelmaremonte.com, 50TL). The excursion snakes through mountain villages, canyons, and waterfalls. It

DOBAG CARPETS

Carpet weaving was a thankless job in the 20th century. Cheaper synthetic dyes and fabrics replaced the time-honored values and crafting techniques of nomadic carpet weavers, forcing them literally out of business due to the high price sought in return for the months spent on their heirloom rugs. New carpets were soaked in lightly-chlorinated baths and caustic soda to create an antique "patina"; designs followed fashion, not custom; and, worst of all, the tradition of dyeing and design creation almost went the way of the dodo.

While there are still quite a few original-fakes on the market, the *Doğal Boya Araştırma ve Geliştirme Projesi* (Natural Dye Research and Development Project) – or DOBAG – virtually restored the traditional art of carpet weaving in 1981. The DOBAG project is the end result of an 11-year, painstaking research program on the original weaving and dyeing techniques of antique carpets performed by German teacher and chemist Harald Boehmer. Once assembled, dyeing recipes and techniques were taken to the mountain villages of Ayvacık in northwestern Turkey, where ancestral patterns and weaving expertise still lived on. Through the union of Boehmer's coloring techniques and the village women's knotting expertise, original quality rugs could be once again be woven. Today, DOBAG rugs are famed for their dramatic designs and deep, naturally-produced colors.

DOBAG is in essence a self-financing co-op.

The venture directly exports rugs, while the lady weavers raise their own socioeconomic status and that of their village peers. In 2003, the venture involved some 350 families in 35 villages. At the project's launch, three decades ago, families resettled en masse from their mountainside hamlets. Today, the exodus to the city has ceased, proving that traditional carpet weaving can be a sweet business indeed. Weaving is home-based and no child is involved.

Like most rugs, DOBAG rugs are priced according to the knot count; the more knots, the higher the price. For instance, a 6 by 9 foot carpet can have upwards of 600,000 knots, and takes about four months of weaving labor. Shearing the rough fleece off the village goats (washing, sorting, carding, spinning, and dyeing it), set-up time, fringe weaving, and the final washing and drying of the rug are not included. FYI, it takes the wool of 10 sheep to knot one square meter of rug.

Each original carpet carries a leather tag with DOBAG's internationally registered trademark, the weaver's name and village, the actual knot count and certification number. The same data is kept on file at Marmara University, the DOBAG's administrator.

Unique in the world, the project's limited size ensures that there are only a few true *kilims* (Turkish carpets). True DOBAG rugs are hard to come by, only available through authorized dealers outside of Turkey, and are valued collectibles.

includes lunch and a chance to view the innumerable varieties of indigenous flora and fauna. Going without a group is feasible from the next village of Akçay, but securing a permit and a compulsory guide may prove thornier and pricier. The folks at Mare Monte are big on promoting the area's eco-tourism trove, and offer a slew of outdoorsy activities, like trekking, creek fishing, camping, and jeep safaris. Experienced hikers can opt for a longer stint by contacting **Kaz Dağı Milli Parkı Ekoturizm Organizasyonları** (Goose Mountain National Park Ecotourism Organizations,

0266/377-2523, www.kazdagiekoturizm.com). Specializing in all-inclusive, one- to three-day packages (50–260TL), KDMPEO's certified and English-speaking staff secures all the necessary permits and provides safari-type transportation, local *Yörük* (nomadic herder) meals, and camping equipment.

Edremit

Pushing east past the resort of Altınoluk and the village of Akçay, the transportation hub of Edremit looms. Today, it's just a pit stop along the road for tourists and a shopping axis for summer residents of outlying areas. But as history's **Adramyttium,** the ancient colony was featured in Homer's *Iliad* and the New Testament. The harbor is where Paul the Apostle sailed almost 2000 years ago en route to Rome to appeal for Caesar's leniency for having illegally brought a Gentile into a Jewish temple. Unsuccessful, Paul languished in prison until Nero condemned him to death by beheading in A.D. 67.

With coach service linking the entire country, Edremit's *otogar* (bus station, 0266/373-1070) is located on Yilmaz Akpınar Bulvarı, half a mile from the town center. Along Edremit's main street, Menderes Bulvarı, has a **PTT** (post office, 9 A.M.–11 P.M., to 7 P.M. in winter), banks, and ATMs. The closest **tourism office** (Barbaros Meydanı, 0266/384-1113) is located in Akçay, 3.5 kilometers west of Edremit.

Ören and Burhaniye

Busy from mid-June to mid-September with vacationing nationals flocking to its long stretch of sandy beach, the small resort town of Ören is staunchly protected from hungry developers who've had to look south to stake their claim. The Greek village has remained undisturbed since most Hellenes were exchanged in the early 1920s. The main pedestrian drag, Central Çarşı Caddesi, is flanked by shops selling summer trappings, sidewalk cafés, and ice cream shops. Ören is reputed for its wine and olive oil, which is hailed August 16–18 with the annual **Olive Festival** (0266/412-6450, www.burhaniye.bel.tr).

Ören is Turkish for ruins—check them out in the plot along the esplanade. The town's posh Wednesday street market is known for dirt-cheap beachwear in the summer.

The town's large camping ground, along with pensions, is packed come summer, but finer lodgings are just a few steps away. The four-star **Artemis Ören Holiday Village** (0256/416-3776, www.artemis.gen.tr, from US$70) overlooks the picturesque esplanade. Bright comfy rooms with sea views, plus tons of relaxing amenities—like sauna and private beach—and a sumptuous complimentary

breakfast served daily on the esplanade await Artemis guests. For food on the go, head for Çarşı Caddesi's stalls; they specialize in *kumpir* (stuffed taters) and *Ayvalık Tostu* (sandwich filled with almost everything but the kitchen sink). Or, converge at the tiny stools of the tented bar/café **Ida Yörük Cadırı** for narghile, Turkish coffee, or a quick sandwich.

About two kilometers east of Ören is Burhaniye. It's stormed on Mondays by shoppers who come to the town's weekly market, from as far away as Lesbos, to stock their refrigerators and wardrobes. Burhaniye is growing annually, as more *Yörüks* (nomadic herders) leave their mountain stead for the ease of city life. If onsite on January 27, don't miss the annual **camel wrestling** matches that take place on the outskirts of Burhaniye. There's no blood involved during the bouts, which is rather interesting as these mammoth bulls vie for supremacy by butting heads as they would in a herd.

Dolmuş service is available between Ören and Burhaniye, which itself is connected by municipal minibuses to Edremit, 15 kilometers to the north. From June through the end of August, public boats cross the Bay of Edremit frequently from Ören marina to Akçay. Burhaniye's *otogar* (bus station, 0266/422-1165) offers bus service connections to Turkey's west, Ankara, and Istanbul.

AYVALIK

The arrival into Ayvalık proper is misleading, with its slew of prosaic, two-story compounds, not exactly the resort guidebooks praise. Adding insult to injury, smog fills the air, along with the reeking odors that emanate from its olive presses. Ayvalık is a busy town that capitalizes on fishing, tourism, and the olive, in all of its incarnations, for its sustenance. The city of 30,000 year-round residents is sprinkled with decaying Ottoman Greek houses along cobblestone back alleys. On the main island of Alibey—a.k.a. Cunda—some of these stone townhouses have found new life as B&Bs and lively cafés. Although not spectacular, its coast leads to a stunning archipelago set against

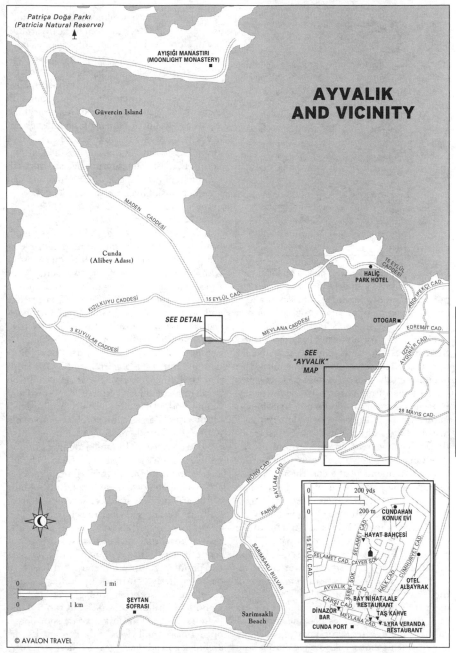

Patriça Doğa Parkı
(Patricia Natural Reserve)

AYIŞIĞI MANASTIRI
(MOONLIGHT MONASTERY)

Güvercin Island

AYVALIK
AND VICINITY

MADEN CADDESİ

Cunda
(Alibey Adası)

15 EYLÜL CADDESİ

HALİÇ
PARK HOTEL

KIZILKUYU CADDESİ

15 EYLÜL CAD.

ABDI İPEKÇİ CAD.

3 KUYULAR CADDESİ

SEE DETAIL

MEVLANA CADDESİ

OTOGAR ■

EDREMİT CAD.

İZZET AYGÜNER CAD.

SEE
"AYVALIK"
MAP

29 MAYIS CAD.

NORTHERN AEGEAN COAST

İNÖNÜ CAD.

SAYLAM CAD.

FARUK

SARIMSAKLI BULVAR

0   1 mi
0   1 km

ŞEYTAN
SOFRASI
■

Sarimsakli
Beach

© AVALON TRAVEL

0   200 yds
0   200 m

CUNDAHAN
KONUK EVİ

HAYAT BAHÇESİ

15 EYLÜL CAD.

SELAMET CAD.

ÇAYER SOK.

SELAMET CAD.

ŞEREF SOK.

HALK CAD.

CUMHURİYET CAD.

AYVALIK CAD.

ÇARŞI CAD.

BAY NİHAT-LALE
RESTAURANT

OTEL
ALBAYRAK

DİNAZÖR
BAR

MEVLANA CAD.

TAŞ KAHVE

CUNDA PORT ■

LYRA VERANDA
RESTAURANT

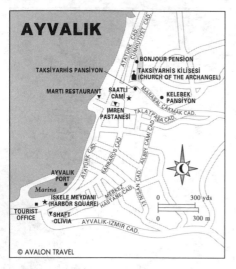

AYVALIK

TAKSİYARHİS PANSİYON

BONJOUR PENSION
TAKSİYARHİS KİLİSESİ
(CHURCH OF THE ARCHANGEL)

MARTI RESTAURANT SAATLİ
CAMİ

KELEBEK
PANSİYON

İMREN
PASTANESİ

AYVALIK
PORT

Marina

İSKELE MEYDANI
(HARBOR SQUARE)

TOURIST
OFFICE SHAFT
OLİVİA AYVALIK-İZMİR CAD.

0   300 yds

0   300 m

© AVALON TRAVEL

turquoise seas and heady pines. The local government is unfortunately bending under the pressure of greedy developers and slowly allowing construction of unsightly rows of summer villas on some of the once idyllic isles.

Historically, Ayvalık dates back to the early Bronze Age. But it was only in the 16th century that Greeks, fearing the constant wrath of pirates on the isles of Lesbos and Crete, pled the Ottoman Empire for permission to stay. In time, the town then known as Kydonies—quince trees in Greek—grew to encompass a distinct local culture, based on Greek traditions, language, religion, and customs. It become one of Asia Minor's most prosperous Greek settlements of the era, thanks mainly to luck. The Kydonieans plucked Ottoman grand vizier and fleet Captain Cezayirli Hasan Paşa from the sea, after he was defeated by the Russian navy in 1792. Ever so grateful to the locals, Hasan lavished the town with special privileges, like tax exemption, self-rule, and even banned Muslims from settling in the region. But it wasn't until after the massacres of the Greek Revolution of 1821 that the settlement truly hit its stride as a chief olive oil and soap producer. Kydonies became second in cultural import after Izmir, boasting an academy, printing house, renowned hotels and

cafés, and over two dozen churches and monasteries. While Greek can still be heard around town, more than 90 percent of Ayvalık's population is Turkish. Minarets may have been added to Orthodox basilicas, but the chimneys of dilapidated 19th-century Greek olive factories remain. Interestingly, the population exchange of 1923 swapped the Greek-speaking Turks of Lesbos for Ayvalık's Hellenes, an ironic twist of fate that has kept the language alive. The island was renamed Alibey after a hero of the Turkish resistance. Most Turks call it Cunda, but true locals of Cretan origin call it Moschonisi, Greek for scented island.

Sights

Starting at İskele Meydanı (harbor square), head up one of the cobblestone lanes linking the shore to the hill to **Saatli Cami** (Mosque with a Clock). Today's mosque was actually the Agios Ioannis Church, which converted to a mosque in the early 19th century. The belfry and clock attest to its original Greek Orthodox status. No longer inside, Agios Ioannis' frescoes were whitewashed in the conversion.

Steps away, Ayvalık's **Agios Georgios** is its most remarkable church today. It blends neoclassicism with rich Byzantine tradition through meticulously restored iconostasis and ceiling, both rich in gilded details. Amid a small plot behind a street-side porch, **Taksiyarhis Kilisesi** (Church of the Archangel) also avoided conversion. Its famed architecture and marble artisanry survived since the church's inauguration in 1873, but the building's frescoes and iconography are in poor condition. Many of the artwork was stolen or severely defaced, leading city elders to close the church.

South of Ayvalık's downtown, along the coastal road that snakes past historical waterfront mansions, verdant Çamlık crosses the popular, seven-kilometer sand beach of Sarımsaklı. It continues up a steep climb through the scented pine groves of Orta Çamlık to a hilltop known as **Şeytan Sofrası** (Satan's Table). This lofty, scenic spot boasts open-air cafés and views of the verdant 15-islet archipelago and the Aegean's bluest waters.

Across a long jetty, about a mile north of Ayvalık's main square, lies **Cunda**—a.k.a. Alibey Adası. Aside from its busy Thursday farmer's market, which regularly draws in boatfuls of Greek islanders, abandoned churches, souvenir shops, and villas crowd its southern shores. The undulating road that leads to the northern **Patriça Doğa Parkı** (Patrica Natural Reserve) features curbside fountains and an ever-changing scenery of olive groves and thyme bushes, with the coast never too far from view. The prize at the end of the road is **Ayışığı Manastırı** (Moonlight Monastery), which was built in 1751 for an Orthodox brotherhood. Of the eight friararies founded on Cunda, Agios Dimitrios Ta Selina—Moonlight Monastery's Greek name—was by far its most famous.

Scuba-Diving and Cruises

The shores off of Ayvalık are rumored to hold the lost city of Atlantis. Try your luck at discovering its remains or just enjoy the water with one of the few certified dive operators in the region: **Körfez Diving Center** (Atatürk bulvarı Özaral pasajı 617a–30, 0266/312-4996, www.korfezdiving.com, 50–500TL). Packages vary from a one-day dip and dive to a full-fledged, three-day course for budding divers in the spectral underwater world of the roughly 15 isles around the bay.

For a tour of Lesbos, a Greek island stuck in the past, just off Ayvalık's coast, contact **Meander Travel** (0266/312-2456, 104 min., 6 P.M. daily mid-May–Oct., 50€ one-way). Throughout the high season, the return from Lesbos is scheduled for 8:30 P.M. Mondays, Thursdays, and Saturdays only. In the off-peak season, November–mid-may, the crossings wind down to a couple per week.

Particularly beautiful on a clear night are the **moonlight cruises,** which snake through the islands on most evenings form Cunda's harbor. Just head to the pier and hop on one of the ongoing vessels.

Accommodations

Lodging in Ayvalık runs the gamut: from antique B&Bs to unpretentious guesthouses. Most of these request that shoes are removed upon entering the house, so bring slippers. Not particularly pricey but oozing with charm, the architectural ♦ **Bonjour Pension** (Fevzi Çakmak Cad., Çeşme Sok. 5, 0266/312-8085, www.bonjourpansiyon.com, 70TL) exemplifies Ayvalık's past. The entrance is filled with ornate antiques and century-old ceilings, while the quiet rear gardens welcome with a breakfast feast (an additional 8TL). Only some of the rooms have en suite baths and air-conditioning.

Another good choice is the **Taksiyarhis Pansiyon** (Marasal Cakmak cad. 71, 0266/312-1494, taksiyarhispension.com, 70TL), located next to the Taksiyarhis church. The decor is chockfull of regional antiques, *kilims* (Turkish carpets), and cushions in a communal, homey space. You'll also have to share the baths. Also in old town Ayvalık, the **Kelebek Pansiyon** (Mareşal Çakmak Cad. 108, 0266/312-3908, www.kelebek-pension.com, 70TL) is owned and meticulously run by the German-born Kiray family. The seven large rooms come with a copious complimentary breakfast and private baths; only a few rooms have air-conditioning and sea views.

On Cunda, ♦ **Otel Albayrak** (Şafak Sok. 15, 0266/327-2633, www.otelalbayrak.com, from 90TL) boasts impeccable rooms in a classic Greek brownstone, steps from the isle's sandy shores. Organic brick walls grace the rooms, which feature modern coveniences like LCD televisions, air-conditioning, and Wi-Fi, as well as sea views. Also, **Cundahan Konuk Evi** (Selamet Cad.,Tepebasi Sok 13, 0266/327-1681, www.cundahan.com, 180TL) is a bit pricey, but luxuriously appointed. The pool is a welcome bonus in an island B&B. One of the few five-stars in the area, the **Haliç Park Hotel** (15 Eylül Cad 1, 0266/331-5221, www.halicpark.com, 290TL) offers an all-inclusive, pre-packaged vacation option with private beaches and loads of activities for the youngest guests.

Food

Warmer waters bring *papalina* (baby sardines),

NORTHERN AEGEAN COAST

which Turks drive across the country to to Ayvalık to feast on. Nowadays, most restaurats run out of the fish quickly because it is so cheap: 10TL for an overflowing plate. As is the case throughout the Aegean, tons of seafood and fresh herbs, like *istifno* (a kind of greens) and *radika* (chicory), show up in a myriad of appetizers which are best enjoyed along Cunda's pier or Ayvalık's seaside promenade.

In Ayvalık, the trendy **Martı Restaurant** (Gazinolar Aralığı 19, 0266/312-6899, 15TL) serves up amazing olive oil–based and regional dishes, as well as seasonal fish varieties. For dessert head to local fave, **Imren Pastanesi** (Talatpaşa Cad. 47, 0266/312-1213, 3–10TL) for mastic ice cream or *lor tatlısı* (dessert made of crumbly mascarpone-like cheese). For an after-dinner drink, **Shaft Olivia Bar** (Atatürk Cad. 1, Sok. 7, 0266/312-2231, until 4 A.M.) serves up live rock and blues from the converted main space of an olive factory.

The place to eat on the island is ⟨ **Bay Nihat-Lale Restaurant** (Alibey Adası Iskelesi, 0266/327-1063, 13TL). A darling of restaurant critics, the diner is often packed, which more often than not translates into a long wait before the entrée arrives. If the waitlist is too long, then head toward the other end of the pier to Ali Gülören's ⟨ **Lyra Veranda Restaurant** (Alibey Adası Iskelesi, 0266/327-2412, www.lyraveranda.com.tr, 12TL). Lyra's service is great; its assortment of mezes are succulent, chiefly garlicky fresh mountain greens dressed with olive oil or yogurt. Locals in the know head for **Hayat Bahçesi** (Garden of Life, Selamet Cad. 7, Alibey Adası, 0266/327-2926, hayatbahcesi.com, 8TL) for their farm-fresh breakfast and anytime sandwiches and light meals. Cafés also abound along the pier. And there's no better stop for tea, Turkish coffee, or even ice cream than at the 150-year-old **Taş Kahve** (Stone Coffee, along the esplanade).

It's a regional landmark with tall stained-glass windows and lofty ceilings. Take a seat along the terrace and hear locals chat in Cretan dialect. Cunda's after-hours spot remains **Dinazor Bar** (Sahil Boyu 49, 0266/327-2194). It's a super trendy bar in a converted olive plant, with live Turkish music until 2 A.M. during the summer.

Information and Services

Ayvalık's **tourism office** kiosk (0366/312-2122, 9 A.M.–7 P.M. daily May–Sept.) is located along Iskele Meydanı's esplanade. The **PTT** (Atatürk Blv. 49, 0266/312-1003, 8 A.M.–11 P.M. Mon–Sat.), banks, and ATMs are on Atatürk Bulvarı, the town center's main thoroughfare.

Getting There and Around

Coach connection to Ayvalık can be arranged with any of the national companies, such as **Varan** (Otogar No. 54, 0266/331-5777 or 0212/444-8999, www.varan.com.tr), one of the safest and most reliable firms. Their office in Ayvalık is located in the bus station, which is about 1.5 kilometers north of Iskele Meydanı. From there, connecting to Çanakkale with Çanakkale Truva is possible. Also inquire with the larger coach companies about their shuttle service to and from the *otogar* (bus station). There's an **Avis car rental** (Talatpaşa Cad., 0266/312-2456) for those wishing to explore the greater area by car.

The municipality's public transportation is dependable. Most buses run the length of Atatürk Bulvarı to the beaches of Sarımsaklı to the south and to the *otogar* and Cunda/Alibey Island (1.5TL). White with red stripes, Ayvalık's *dolmuşes* (communal taxi, 2TL) run the same route from their main stop in Armutçuk in the north to Sefa, near the marina. A **boat shuttle** connects Ayvalık's harbor to Cunda in just 15 minutes (1.5TL).

Bergama (Pergamum)

Ideal as a full day-trip from Ayvalık, Pergamum's succinct historical layers make it a living testament to Asia Minor's tumultuous past. Two of the Mediterranean's best archaeological sites are located here—the Acropolis and the Asclepion of ancient Pergamum. The city, called Bergama in Turkish, is also home to the Red Basilica—today's Kızıl Avlu (Red Court)—which appeared in the Bible's *Book of Revelation*. But aside from its tourist trappings, Bergama's cobblestone lanes, home to rickety Ottoman abodes, and its industrious downtown are well worth an overnight stay in one of its B&Bs.

Ancient Pergamum is noted for its stunning ruins, most of which date back to Eumenes II's illustrious reign (197–156 B.C.). Found in the elevated Acropolis—the old city's cultural, religious, and legislative hub—the ruins include a bluff-hugging amphitheater, the ornately chiseled gate of the Temple of Athena, and remnants of colossal palaces. Pergamum's ordinary citizenry thrived in the city below. Just about the only vestige bearing their passage are the remains of the Asclepion, one of the earliest and most prominent medical centers of antiquity.

the remaining arches of the largest library at Pergamum – today's Bergama

© FUAT TAMTÜRK

HISTORY

While Pergamum traces its beginnings to the 10th century B.C., Lydian king Croesus brought it to the forefront in 560 B.C. A little more than a decade later, the Persians conquered Pergamum as part of the Lydian realm and ruled the city until Alexander the Great's powerful army reclaimed the whole of Asia Minor in 334 B.C. Upon Alexander's untimely death 11 years later, his top general and administrator of Asia Minor, Lysimachus turned the city into a military base and treasury for a reported 9,000 talents (as much as 540,000 pounds!) of gold. But while Lysimachus was away campaigning he entrusted his favored lieutenant, Philetaerus, with the guard of the city and its wealth. When Lysimachus died in 281 B.C., Philetaerus the Eunuch adeptly

managed to stay in control and used this trove to found the dynasty of the Attalid Kings. In the following 15 decades, Pergamum flourished into the capital of what in time would become Anatolia's most important kingdom, and one of the most revered cultural centers of Ancient Greek civilization. Additions like the Altar of Zeus and the grand library under the reign of Pergamum's most illustrious king, Eumenes II, propelled Pergamum's grandeur to rival those of Alexandria's and Antioch's during the first half of the 2nd century B.C. But Attalus III, lacking a direct heir, bequeathed the city in 133 B.C. to Rome. Four years later, the kingdom of Pergamum became the Roman province of Asia, losing some of its economical and political prowess, but continuing its growth as a cultural and intellectual epicenter. During Byzantine rule, Pergamum was a considerable Christian center. Its church was mentioned as one of the Seven Churches of the Revelation.

NORTHERN AEGEAN COAST

In A.D. 262, the marauding Goths arrived, signaling the beginning of a lengthy demise.

It wasn't until 1871 that Karl Humann, a young German engineer managing the construction of a road through Pergamum, "discovered" the ruins of Pergamon, while scavenging the area for building material. Switching professions on a dime, the budding archaeologist uncovered an impressive cache, including the Altar of Zeus and the Temple of Athena's ornate propylaeum. Both were sent to the Pergamum Museum in Berlin.

SIGHTS

Navigating the sites around Pergamum starts at the town center, where an archaeology museum puts the ancient city's achievements and timeline into perspective. A couple of miles west lies Pergamum's famed medical center of Ascelpion, which can be followed by a visit to the Acropolis, 4.5 kilometers to the north. The town synchronized the opening hours of all sites, which are 8:30 A.M.–6:30 P.M. during the summer and until 5 P.M. the rest of the year. Alongside the parking lots of the acropolis and asclepion are merchants peddling handsome souvenirs—like onyx statues and vases—at 50 percent of Istanbul prices. A word to the wise: Stock up on a couple of water bottles sold here, particularly during the heat of summer, which can top 40°C (104°F).

Arkeoloji Müzesi (Archaeology Museum)

Pergamum's small, but highly informative, Arkeoloji Müzesi (Cumhurriyet Cad. 10, 0232/631-2883, 5TL) displays discarded objects the Germans didn't think worthy of carting off to Berlin, mainly statues and gravestones found among Pergamum's extensive ruins. Aside from a mock Altar of Zeus painstakingly reproduced by museum staff, look out for the remains of the famed Roman thermal baths at Allanoi and ornate examples of Pergamum's famed sculpting style. Also of note, the museum's nod to the Ottomans

NORTHERN AEGEAN COAST

© JESSICA TAMTÜRK

The Red Basilica was built by Roman Emperor Hadrian in the 2nd century in honor of the Egyptian god Serapis.

the Asclepion – the world's first psychiatric hospital

© JESSICA TAMTÜRK

Asclepion (Temple of Healing Arts)

One of the foremost medical centers of its time, the Asclepion (10TL) was both a sanctuary and a healing center built to honor the god of healing, Asclepius. It was founded in the 4th century B.C. by Greek poet Archias, an Antiochian who had been cured at a similar center in Epidauros in Greece. Pergamum's Asclepion was the world's first psychiatric hospital. Its residents, such as Marcus Aurelius and Hadrian, were treated with massage, dietary, and bathing therapies derived from dream-based analysis.

But it wasn't until Galen, the foremost Roman physician after Hippocrates, that the center truly hit its stride. Born in Pergamum, Galen utilized anatomical studies he conducted on animals and observations of human bodily functions he gathered from his formal medical studies performed in Smyrna, Alexandria and Corinth to cure severely traumatized patients at Pergamum's gladiator school. His insights into the circulatory and neural system remained in use until the late 1500s.

A stroll through the Asclepion begins along the cobblestone Via Tecta—Pergamum's Sacred Way, once flanked with bustling shops—to the remains of a column carved with snakes, the symbol of Asclepius. Heed the signs leading to the Pergamum's famed library to the right and the Roman theater, both utilized to entertain patients. Nearby is the **Sacred Well,** where modern visitors still benefit from its alleged curative attributes. Finally, listen to the trickle of the water below the **Temple of Telesphorus,** the long vaulted tunnel honoring a mythic god who symbolized recovery from illness.

To reach the Asclepion, head west by following signage along Galinos Caddesi. Walking is feasible, but a taxi is advisable in the heat of summer. Also, bear in mind that this route edges a large military installation; all nearby streets are closed to through-traffic at sunset. Refrain from taking photos outside of the ruins.

includes ethnographic displays of indigenous *kilims* (Turkish carpets) and crafts, as well as clothing and manuscripts.

Kızıl Avlu (Red Basilica)

Known as Red Basilica after the color of its building stones, the 2nd-century A.D. Kızıl Avlu (Kinik Cad., 5TL) was built under the reign of Hadrian, as a temple to honor Egyptian gods Isis, Serapis, and Harpocrates. This humongous pile of red bricks straddles the Bergama River, which flows into two tunnels below the structure. Just before entering the site, the **Kurtuluş Camii** (Liberation Mosque) is tucked inside one of this great church's towers.

Mentioned as one of the Seven Churches of Revelation in the Bible, Saint John the Apostle sent one of his ominous letters to this church, noting that the city held the throne of Satan, perhaps in reference to the Altar of Zeus. The Byzantines converted this huge edifice into a basilica in the 5th century A.D.

◖ Acropolis

Some 1200 feet in elevation along steep terraces that reveal stunning views of the modern

NORTHERN AEGEAN COAST

ALLIANOI

During the construction of the Yortanlı dam in the forlorn valleys near the village of Ivrindi, 18 kilometers northeast of Bergama, the ancient site of Allianoi was accidentally discovered in 2003, right beneath the modern baths that had been onsite since the early 20th century.

Allianoi is the only Roman baths complex discovered so far that includes a recreation site right on top of a thermal spring; one that was left as is, and not morphed to reflect the whims of subsequent empires. The site sprawls over 10,000 square meters, but so far only 20 percent has been excavated.

If the Turkish State Water Works has its way, the dam project will go as proposed and Allianoi, which lies amidst the proposed reservoir, will be flooded, halting the prospect of future excavations altogether. Repeated protests from ICOMOS, UNESCO, and the European Union have done little to delay the project.

Historically, the baths at Allianoi were mentioned once by the 2nd century orator Aelius Aristides, a man of weak health whose diary, *Hieroi Logoi* (Sacred Tales), recorded his illness and subsequent recovery. Aristides writes that his recuperation was greatly facilitated by the frequent visits to thermal baths in Izmir, Pergamum, and Allianoi. The baths here are part of the 2nd century A.D. expansion of public works that Roman imperials commissioned in and near large cities throughout Asia Minor. Bridges, streets, middle-class tenements, a Connection Building, *propylon* (temple entrance), and *nymphaeum* (shrine dedicated to a nymph) onsite all date from this period.

Allianoi is close enough to Pergamum for a detour. It's not an official site, so there are no entrance booths, nor admission charges.

city below, the Acropolis (10TL) was the center of the Attalid Kingdom. Disregard the suggested tour and head straight to the location where the Acropolis' most tantalizing site, the **Altar of Zeus,** once stood. Just the foundations of the altar beneath two large evergreen trees can be seen, but this is enough to imagine the grandeur of this shrine until the Turkish government succeeds in its legal battles to have it return to its original location. The shrine was commissioned by Eumenes II to honor his father's victory against the Gauls in the late 2nd century B.C.

The partly reconstructed **Temple of Athena** is missing its propylaeum (porch of this sacred enclosure), which was carted off to Berlin's Pergamum Museum in 1871. The Temple is adjacent to Pergamum's noted **library.** Some 200,000 texts were housed in this structure, which was greatly expanded by cultural esthete Eumenes II. He's said to have borrowed tomes from some of Antiquity's largest libraries without returning them, and even exchanged gold for the works of Aristotle. Eumenes's unrelenting aim to build the library so concerned Egyptian kings—the sole producers of papyrus during the era—that they stopped exporting the printing medium to Pergamum, fearing that its book repository would exceed theirs in volume. Eumenes, ever the problem solver, launched a race to find an alternative printing medium, sweetening the pot with a large reward. And that is how *pergamenum* (parchment), the ancient Egyptian method of specially treating and extending animal skin, was revived. In the end, Mark Anthony ransacked the library and lavishing his beloved Cleopatra with the repository's greatest titles.

Just over the edge, Ancient Rome's steepest **amphitheater** once seated 10,000 comfortably. Some 80 rows extend in three tiers over 108 feet on the flank of a vertiginous cliff side. Its innovatively portable stage was carted off between performances to allow free access to the **Temple of Dionysis,** located stage left.

Doubling back up the hill leads to the **Temple of Trajan,** which was built in A.D. 125 by Roman emperor Trajan's successor,

Hadrian, in his and Zeus's honor. This shrine's also been partly reconstructed by German archaeologists; its splendid Corinthian columns are a mixture of original material and aptly etched modern marble blocks. For dizzying scenery of the valley and aquifer beyond, cross the ruins of the ancient city's walls and the remains of barracks behind Trajan's temple to the pillared cistern.

On the return back to the entrance, the road leads through the remains of six royal residences, including the **Palaces of Attalid I** and **Eumenes II.** If not wishing to miss a thing, walk past the Altar of Zeus to the **Roman baths,** the **Middle City** with its **gymnasium,** the **Temple of Demetre,** and Pergamum's **Lower Agora.**

ACCOMMODATIONS AND FOOD

If you must stay overnight in Pergamum, make a beeline past the rundown pensions to ℂ **Akropolis Guesthouse** (Kayalik Cad. 5, 0232/631-2621, www.akropolisguesthouse. com, from 95TL). Eight neat and ample rooms come with modern amenities like satellite television, Internet access, and air-conditioning. A relaxing backyard pool and an onsite restaurant set in a refurbished barn, and a small tower in a rear garden that affords views of the acropolis add to the location's allure.

Small and homey, the **Odyssey Guest House** (Abacihan Sok. 13, 0232/631-3501, www.odysseyguesthouse.com, from 60TL) exemplifies Turkish hospitality, thanks to its youthful owner Ersin Kirmaz. Mostly patronized by foreigners, this B&B is set in a 150-year-old Greek townhouse, boasting seven comfy rooms with Internet access and a rooftop terrace. Complimentary generous breakfasts are served on the terrace.

Between visiting the sites, the hungry can refuel at ℂ **Meydan Restaurant** (Istiklal Meydanı 4, 0232/633-1793, from 6TL). It's the town's oldest diner. It boasts fine local cuisine that's based primarily on bready concoctions, like *pide* (flat bread topped with cheese or tiny lamb cubes) and their succulent moussaka. Another good choice is **Paşam Restaurant**

(Izmir Yolu, on the left before entering town, from 8TL). This place's patio boasts a trout-filled pool, whose denizens are served as a main meal. Don't miss the mezes, like the seaweed drizzled with lemon and olive oil and fresh regional veggie salads.

INFORMATION AND SERVICES

With just so-so maps of the city and the typical brochures produced by the Turkish Ministry of Tourism, Pergamum's **tourist office** (Izmir Cad. 54, 0232/631-2851, 8:30 A.M.–7 P.M. Mon.–Sat. in summer, until 5 P.M. in winter) is located next to the archaeological museum. All bank and mail services are located along this stretch of Izmir Caddessi as well.

GETTING THERE AND AROUND

If driving, the 50-kilometer back road (35-04) to Pergamum, just north of Ayvalık, is infinitely more enjoyable than the drab highway that leads directly to town. It winds through the Madra Mountain's evergreen forests, giant rocks, and myriad of natural springs. A string of 13 regional villages, known collectively as Kozak—the world's premier pine nut–harvesting center—lie just off the main road. Alternatively, follow the Izmir-Çanakkale Yolu (E87) three miles past Ovacık, and turn onto the D240, where roadside signs lead motorists the remainder of the way.

Pergamum's new *otogar* (bus station) lies at the junction of D240 and Izmir Caddesi. There are hourly buses to and from Ayvalık and Izmir, while connections to Istanbul and Ankara are offered at least once daily. Hop on a taxi (14TL) or the regular *dolmuş* (2TL) service for the seven-kilometer commute into town from the *otogar.*

Navigating around Pergamum's somewhat remote sites by foot is feasible during the winter season. Otherwise, and particularly for the sake of time, negotiate a tour of the four main sites—the archaeology museum, Red Basilica, Asclepion, and Acropolis—with a taxi (if you don't have a car). Keep in mind that taxis only allow for a short hop through the various sites and should cost no more than 50TL from town. Add another 15TL if touring from the *otogar*.

FOÇA

If the north Aegean is the oyster of Turkey's western coast, then Foça must be its pearl. Its Greek townhouses and Ottoman mansions lie side-by-side and fill to the brim with cultivated *Istanbullus* come June. The harbor town's population then soars well beyond its 15,000 locals. Its cool coastal waters are also reputed as a resting ground for the Mediterranean monk seal, one of the world's most endangered mammals, estimated to be just 400-strong. Thanks to strong winds and heady currents, Foça is a haven for sailboards.

Essentially divided into two parts, Yeni and Eski Foça—for New and Old, respectively—the old part of town sprawls along two bays and a small harbor. This is where the action is. Twelve miles away from its sister city, much smaller Yenifoça seems forlorn in its remoteness, and hopefully will remain so as long as local governance continues its adamant efforts to keep development at bay in order to protect the local flora and fauna, as well as what's left of its historical remains. Eski Foça has two bays: Büyük Deniz (Large Sea) to the north is home to a commercial port; Küçük Deniz (Small Sea) to the south is where the touristy enclave lies. While half a day should suffice to tour what's left of its historical sites and the picturesque area, most first-timers find Foça's charm intoxicating and inevitably stay longer.

Historically, Foça was known as Phocaea, the original Ionian city which dates back to the 9th century B.C. Phoecaeans were able long-distance seamen and went on to found Massalia—the French city of Marseille—in 600 B.C., and a host of other colonies ringing the Med. They traded as far south as Egypt and most likely assisted in settling Amisos—present-day Samsun—on the Black Sea, and Lampsacus on the European flank of the Dardanelles. But when Cyrus the Great of Persia conquered Lydia in 547 B.C., and all of its previously annexed Ionian territories, Phocaeans abandoned the city, rather than succumb to Persian rule. As for Yeni Foça, it may

Two fishermen return for the day to the rustic resort of Foça, just north of Izmir.

be called new, but it was actually settled by the Genoese in 1275. It remained the more prosperous of the two cities during the Middle Ages, thanks in part to its alum-rich mines. By the 13th century, it fell to the Turks. And in 1455 it was annexed to the fledgling Ottoman Empire. Both Foças were controlled by Greece during the Greco-Turkish war of 1919–1922, which explains the richness of their Greek architecture.

Sights

While the remains of **Ancient Phocaea** are minimal, there are a few destinations around town worth checking out. On the way in from the Izmir-Çanakkale Highway, the **Taş Ev,** an odd-looking monumental tomb dating back to the 4th century B.C., is believed to have been the burial chamber of a Persian king. Also, the recently discovered **Temple of Athena** near Foça's high-school unveiled an equine head thought to date back to the 5th century B.C.

The town's oldest remnant is the Genoese fortress of **Beşkapılar** (Five Gates). The Ottomans repaired its fortifications in 1455 and added the watchtowers in the process. The castle's boathouse now serves as an open-air theater. The fortress houses the 15th-century **Kayalar Cami** (Mosque of the Rocks), which beckons with its 200-year-old lighthouse-like solitary minaret. Its rectangular base and the wooden flat roof are interesting in that they predate the Ottoman architecture's domed roofs and square bases. Its recently renovated *şadırvan* (ablution fountain) stands due west.

Also of note is **Şeytan Hamamı** (Devil's Baths), which is a tomb carved from the hillside of Candede Mount, just over 1.5 kilometers east of the city center. The 4th-century B.C. tomb opens to two burial chambers beyond its arched entrance.

The dilapidated **Dış Kale** (External Castle) was built in the 17th century to guard from seaborne invasion along the tip of the peninsula that delineates the town's southwestern-most point. Stone cannon balls found during underwater archaeological research may have been hurled from catapults at this location to deter approaching enemy armadas.

Cruises

Not to be missed, boat trips **Delphin Boat Tours** (0232/812-5011, May–Sept., 20TL) depart from either Küçük Deniz or Büyük Deniz harbors for a seven-hour day cruise that winds through the various isles. These include Siren Rocks, north of Foça, and environmentally-protected areas. Departing around 11 A.M., the boat anchors several times for a swim and lunch on board.

Accommodations

Much like Assos to the north, Foça brims with B&Bs in renovated Greek and Ottoman mansions along the esplanade of Küçük Deniz. It also boasts economical pensions much further north and a newly opened all-inclusive resort. For complete information on hotels and restaurants in Foça, as well as the newest merchants, log onto the exhaustive website, www.focarehber.com.

The best B&B in town is **❰ Foçantique Hotel** (Küçükdeniz Sahil Cad. 154, 0232/812-4313, www.focantiquehotel.com, 160–250TL), just a step away from the bay's alluring sandy shores and clean coastal waters. Refurbished in 2004 from an old stone mansion, 11 lofty rooms are packed with colorful antiques, individual baths—a suite even comes with its own hammam—and a rooftop café that specializes in pleasing night owls.

For mid-range lodgings, the **Hotel Grand Amphora** (Ismetpaşa Mah. 206 Sok. 7, 0232/812-3930, www.hotelgrandamphora.com, 80–110TL) has 18 sparsely appointed rooms with pristine individual baths. This is the only small hotel in town with a pool. It is loaded with amenities at a very decent prices and remains open year-round.

Also, the large **Hanedan Resort & Beach Club** (4. Mersinaki Koyu, 0232/812-3650, www.hanedanresort.net, €76–104) boasts a plethora of relaxing and fun activities indoors and outdoors, from a hammam and spa to sports galore. Large, airy, well-appointed rooms with private baths, and all the modern fixings await distinguished guests.

On the low-budget end, the youthful meeting spot of **Iyon Pansiyon** (Ismetpaşa Mah. 198/8, 0232/812-1415, www.iyonpansiyon.com, 35–45TL) offers small, sparsely furnished rooms with showers and televisions in a renovated Greek mansion a block from the shore. The outdoorsy types can revel in activities like sailing lessons and bike tours with amiable owner Umut Tutar.

Food

Foça's best eateries are located around the bay of Küçük Deniz's esplanade, with prices traditionally listed at the entrances of restaurants. Fish is the only exception, as the catch, and its price, vary—sometimes greatly—from day to day, or even per customer! Once again, expect some of the best Foçan dishes to revolve around finned creatures, but determine its price per serving prior to placing the order to avoid any misunderstanding. In summer, ask the concierge of your hotel to secure restaurant reservations instead of trying your luck at the door.

Among the city's eight fish eateries, **❰ Celep**

Restoran (Sahil Cad. 48, 0232/812-1495, 15TL) is a tradition. It offers a romantic ambience in which to enjoy its fish grills and limitless array of mezes. Not as trendy, but just as busy, **Kordon** (0232/812-6191) is another hands-down favorite for fish and grilled lamb with weekending *Izmirlis*. Both eateries are located along the small square at the southernmost end of the esplanade, where lobsters from sunken baskets are plucked per order.

The boardwalk cafés are an ideal location to people-watch and recharge during the long stroll around the esplanade. Whatever the reason, an atmospheric place to enjoy either is **Anfi Tiyatro Café** (Sahil Cad. 33, 0232/812-3334), where owner Recep Aydın can often be found taking orders, from simple *köftes* (meatballs) to cappuccino. Pick up a game of backgammon or a drink among the friendly young locals at **Café Neco** (Sahil Cad. 10, 0232/812-5020). On a particularly torrid day, cool down with a scoop of *mastic* (diet ice cream) or any of the other 35 ice cream flavors at **Nazmi Usta** (0232/812-5471).

Information and Services

The **tourism information** office (Cumhuriyet Meydanı, 0232/812-1222, 8:30 A.M.–6 P.M. Mon.–Fri., 10 A.M.–8 P.M. Sat. and Sun.

May–Sept.; 8:30 A.M.–5 P.M. Mon.–Fri. Oct.–Apr.), banks, PTT (post office), and ATMs crowd the main square, just north of the bay of Büyük Deniz. All hotels listed offer Internet access; if need be, these services can also be found at **Kaptan Net** (Fevzi Paşa Mah. Sok. 26/A, 0232/812-3411, 2TL), a street behind the PTT office.

Getting There and Around

Foça is located at the end of the 35-79 Yolu, which connects in about 20 kilometers to the Izmir-Çanakkale Yolu (E87). The distance from Pergamum to Foça is about 70 kilometers or a 45-minute drive. The **Foça Rent-A-Car** (Fevzi Paşa Mah. 191/7, 0232/812-2496) provides vehicle rental options. For those wishing to bike their way through, **Motor Rent** (0232/812-1969, across form the coach station) offers bike rental services, as well as motorbikes, starting at 20TL per day.

The *otogar* (bus station), on the northern edge of Büyük Deniz, has coach service operating to Izmir every 90 minutes (6:30 A.M.–9 P.M., until 11 P.M. May–Sept., 7TL). **Municipal buses** shuttle the 25 kilometers between Eski and Yeni Foça regularly from the *otogar* (4TL).

Izmir

Turkey's third largest city, Izmir, extends along the belt of a 56-kilometer-long gulf, ringed entirely by beautiful mountains—a natural inheritance that's lured a list of conquerors since its recently discovered Neolithic beginnings (6000 B.C.). Aristotle claimed that Izmir (old Smyrna) was the birthplace of Homer (900 B.C.).

But Izmir is much more than the sum of its early parts. It enjoys mild weather year-round, with the exception of hot and dry summers; a healthy tourism sector; and an agricultural trove based on tobacco, figs, and raisins. It's also the country's second largest port and home to a bustling economy, comprised of trade and industry. With a population of at least three

million, Izmir's import is further emphasized as the seat of NATO Southwest and by a hefty annual calendar of international trade expositions.

The city's boom, however, has had its downside. Three decades of unchecked housing and industrial development has led to a pitiful urban wasteland, where smoggy ghettos on its outskirts teem with the screech of auto repair shops and sweatshops that incessantly crank out replicas of the latest Gucci jeans. But thanks to municipal beautification and restoration efforts, the wealthy coastal areas like the Kordon—a lushly landscaped esplanade on the banks of the Aegean—and the historical

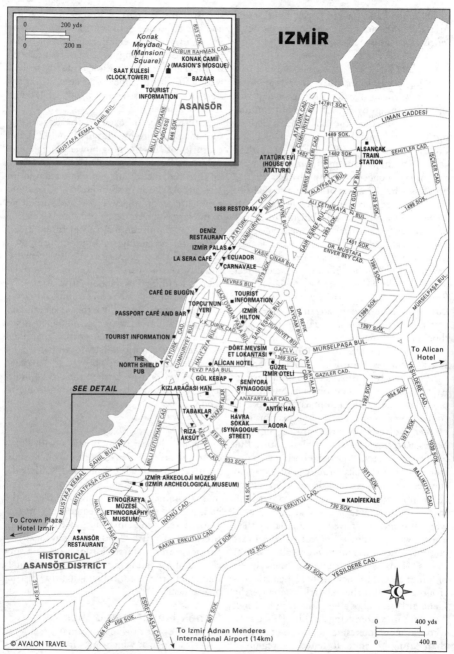

NORTHERN AEGEAN COAST

neighborhood and age-old Greek mansions of Aslancak to the north, are what draws the city's tourists.

HISTORY

Ungoing excavations at Yeşilova Höyük in Izmir's Bornova district have rewinded the city's beginnings by at least three millennium back to 6500 B.C. to the Chalcolithic Period. But until we know the full extent of what the site unveils, theories of Izmir's first settlers vary. Some historians maintain that a warring Amazon queen—most probably a Hittite priestess—by the name of Myrina settled the city, and used a corruption of her name to come up with Smyrna. Local historians, however, place Izmir's first settlement at about 3000 B.C., according to ongoing archaeological research being conducted at a site in modern-day Bayraklı. By the 1500s B.C., the city feel under the rule of the Central Anatolian Hittite Empire. By then Smyrna's population—the Luwians—practiced an advanced cuneiform system and polytheistic rituals, in tune with those of their rulers.

Two centuries after the fall of the mighty Hittite Empire (1200 B.C.), Ionians flooded their previously controlled colonies in western Asia Minor. Under their tutelage, Smyrna exploded as a cultural metropolis, much like its contemporary Troy. It is around this time that Homer was born, along the banks of Smyrna's Meles River, according to Herodotus. But high times attracted the neighboring Lydians, who battered the city around 600 B.C., and the Persians who arrived decades later. Even these mighty eastern warriors proved no match for Alexander the Great in 334 B.C., who subsequently arrived in Smyrna, by then a mere village. Shortly thereafter, Alexander commissioned a brand new city atop Mount Pagus—today's Kadifekale—at the request of Smyrnians. This new truly Hellenistic metropolis was absorbed shortly thereafter by General Lysimachos's Pergamum in 323 B.C. Two centuries later, King Attallus III's, a man who was more interested in growing tomatoes than ruling his state, forfeited the region to

the Romans. As part of Rome's Asian realm and the subsequent Byzantines, old Smyrna was resurrected, receiving magnificent buildings while remaining largely independent in political affairs. Its maritime trade was revitalized, and with it came a vast cultural expansion, until the massive earthquake of 178 B.C. flattened the city.

Smyrna was annexed to the developing Ottoman Empire by Murad II in 1425 after centuries of flip-flopping power struggles between the Byzantines and Selçuks. The city—by then renamed Izmir—became a haven for Jews fleeing the Spanish Inquisition. Thanks to a measure according sweeping trade privileges to foreigners, Izmir developed into the ebbing Ottoman Empire's most successful commercial center, attracting wealthy European merchants. By the beginning of the 19th century, the city was home to a large Greek population and a myriad of religious structures, serving Christians, Jews, and Muslims. After the Ottomans' defeat in WWI, the Greek military occupied Izmir for three years, hoping to annex the city and much of the Aegean to mainland Greece. But a nationalist movement led by Mustafa Kemal Atatürk proved too massive for the Greeks, who burned the city's minority neighborhoods before retreating to mainland Greece.

SIGHTS

Izmir sprawls over many districts, with sights centered in the southeast. Its most notable tourist attractions, like the Agora and Kadifekale, lie to the east of Konak Meydanı, the city's most prominent square, which doubles as the banking and government center along the seafront. Extending northbound from Konak Meydanı, Atatürk Caddes, known locally as Birinci Kordon (First Cordon), offers a succession of appealing terrace eateries and hotels that end in the historical and nightlife district of Alsancak.

Konak Meydanı and Vicinity

Konak Meydanı (Mansion Square) is a large pedestrian plaza, which owes its name to the yellow Ottoman gubernatorial mansion on its periphery. It was built in 1865 when the seat of the province of Aydın moved to Izmir. From Konak's center soars **Saat Kulesi** (Clock Tower). It was commissioned in 1901 to the French architect Raymond Charles Père to commemorate the 25th anniversary of artsy Sultan Abdülhamid II's ascension to the throne. The 25-meter-tall marble structure was inspired by North African themes and features four fountains on its cardinal points, as well as mechanical movements gifted by German emperor Kaiser Wilhelm II. The other historical structure amid this aggressively modern square is the nearby mid-18th-century **Konak Camii** (Mansion's Mosque), whose facade is stunningly tiled in Kütahya faience.

A ten-minute stroll southwest of Konak, just off Mithatpaşa Caddesi, the **Asansör** neighborhood lies in the city's old Jewish quarters. Look for a hill-hugging brick tower. It was built in 1907 to taxi wealthy Levantines to their plush mansions on the hill from the business hub below. The tower features a recently refurbished elevator, which zooms up to an onsite café with unending views of the bay. The café is best enjoyed at sunset over a hot glass of tea or a meal.

Bazaar

As the closest commercial center for Izmir's bustling textile and leather industry, the bazaar (9 A.M.–9 P.M. Mon.–Sat. May–Sept., until 5 P.M. Oct.–Apr.) is well worth a few hours' foray for that perfect bargain. Getting lost in this antique mall is half the fun of shopping here. Stalls of pungent leather garments, clucking fowls, baskets piled high with olives, and bathroom fixings crowd the dozen lanes that constitute this historical mall. Ambling up its main artery of Anafartalar Caddesi, jewelers and shoe and clothing sellers loudly bid for space and the next sale. Adjacent Fevzi Paşa Bulvarı and its perpendicular passages are the place to bargain for leather. Tucked just west of Aanafartalar Caddesi is the covered 18th-century **Kızlarağası Han**—the place to haggle for colorful carpets.

Agora

One of Izmir's last pre-Ottoman remains, the Agora (just south of Anafartalar Caddesi, 0232/425-5354, 8:30 A.M.–noon and 1–5 P.M. daily, 5TL) lies in ruins at the bottom of Izmir's highest hill. This was old Smyrna's marketplace, commissioned in the 4th century B.C. by Alexander the Great. Thanks to reconstruction efforts conducted by Faustina, wife of Roman emperor Marcus Aurelius, the Agora was entirely rebuilt after the massive earthquake of A.D. 178. Of the several Corinthian columns that once delineated the Agora's northern and western flanks, only one colonnade bearing the likeness of Faustina in one of its arches still stands. The Altar of Zeus that once stood in the marketplace's center was somewhat "lost," but the statues of Poseidon and Demeter believed to have been part of said altar are exhibited in the local archaeological museum. While exploring the Agora's ruins, look out for blocks from the four original gates, identifiable trading stalls, coats of arms, and gravestones dating from the site's stint as a Byzantine and later Ottoman cemetery.

To reach the Agora, it's best to hire a taxi to avoid the questionable shanty town that lies beyond Anafartalar Caddesi and the numbered streets to the east. The perimeter to the Agora's main gate is a short walk away after turning right from 940 Sokak.

Kadifekale

Southeast of the Agora, the perpetually floodlit Kadifekale crowns ancient Mount Pagus. This lofty location, which was chosen by Alexander the Great to reconstruct Smyrna in 334 B.C. after driving the Persians from the city, now serves mostly as a playground for young soccer players and a busy selling point for women hailing from Anatolia's remotest corners.

Today's Kadifekale (Velvet Fortress) is a product of Byzantine and subsequent Ottoman reconstructions of the Roman structure that was devastated by a late 2nd-century tremor. The fortress's remnants are disappointing after the long stroll to reach the site, but the sunset viewed from this location is stunning, particularly during the summer when a café provides libations and seating for the daily affair.

To reach Kadifekale hop on bus 33 from Konak to the terminus, which is located less than 350 meters from the fortress. Hiking up the hill from the Agora is possible, but the last stretch threads through a poor gypsy neighborhood and you may feel uncomfortable. If you opt to walk, walking with a companion and a good city map to navigate the web of back streets that lead uphill are highly recommended.

Museums

Izmir Arkeoloji Müzesi (Izmir Archaeological Museum, Halil Rifat, near Konak Meydanı, 0232/489-0796, 8:30 A.M.–5:30 P.M. Tues.– Sun., 5TL) regroups Greco-Roman artifacts from the town's ancient Agora and Tepekule (Old Smyrna), as well as from Pergamum, Iasos, and Ephesus. The grounds include an array of Hellenistic amphorae. In the lobby, maps detailing the country's lengthy history are probably the museum's most informative offerings. The floor above contains an ornately etched sarcophagus dating to 3000 B.C., the head of the statue of Roman emperor Domitian from Ephesus, and a collection of ceramics, glass, gold, statues, and mosaics arranged chronologically in an effort to retrace Izmir's history. The lower floor boasts the statues of Demeter, Poseidon, and Artemis found during a Turco-German archaeological excavation in the Agora during the 1930s.

Izmir's **Etnografya Müzesi** (Ethnography Museum, next to the Archaeology Museum, 0232/489-0796, 8:30 A.M.–5:30 P.M. Tues.– Sun., 3TL) picks up where the Archaeology Museum left off. It opened in the late 1980s in the converted late-19th-century Sainte Roche Hospital with four floors of accumulated folk exhibits that shed light into local traditions and craftsmanship. There's a reconstructed kiln used to cast *boncuks* (blue and white beads that cast off the evil eye); dioramas detailing the manufacture of pottery and felt; and a camel-wrestling exhibit. Before leaving, head to the lower floor to check out traditional *Izmirli*

housing, from the wooden Ottoman house to the posh Levantine townhouse of Christian and Jewish traders.

Both museums are a short walk southeast of Konak Meydanı along Milliküphane.

Synagogues

Izmir's rich Jewish heritage still thrives in its Asansör quarter. Three of its nine historical synagogues along 927 Sokak (originally Havra Sokak—Synagogue Street) were recently renovated and are open to the public during services on Saturday mornings. The most active, the two-centuries-old **Seniyora Synagogue** (927 Sok. 77) on is open every morning. A guided tour through Izmir's Jewish heritage is offered through its tourism office (1344 Sok. 2, 0232/483-5117, 8:30 A.M.–7 P.M. daily June–Oct.; 8:30 A.M.–5:30 P.M. Mon.–Fri. Nov.–May).

Kordon

Extending from Cumhuriyet Meydanı to the tip of the posh enclave of Alsancak, the busy Kordon is lined with luxury high-rise buildings, hotels, and consulates. This strip is also noted for its string of terraces where deep-pocketed *Izmirlis* hustle for tables, from which to nosh while gazing at the sunset. Strolling the three-kilometer-long Kordon is a popular evening pastime for local families. The best method to experience the length and vivacity of this esplanade is by horse-drawn phaetons (30TL for a full tour).

On the way, pay tribute to the father of the Turkish republic at **Atatürk Evi** (House of Ataturk, Atatürk Cad. 248, 8:30 A.M.–noon and 1–5 P.M., free), where the premier stayed while visiting his mother, Zübeyde Hanım, who resided in Izmir. The wooden townhouse, converted into a museum, offers an inner look at the sumptuous digs of the one-time local aristocracy. This gives a preview of the few remaining 18th- and 19th-century mansions— once home to wealthy Europeans who escaped the 1922 blaze. These are located on 1453 and 1482 Sokaks, which run perpendicular to the main drag.

NIGHTLIFE

The Kordon has hands down the best bars in Izmir, but the Alsancak neighborhood has begun to divert the younger-set with a collection of watering holes and buzzing nightclubs along Sokak 1482. Keep in mind that the lifespan of clubs and bars average about two years, and what's in today may soon be outdated. But before cutting that rug, join the locals along the Kordon in the traditional evening stroll—the *passegiata*—Izmir inherited from its Italian ancestors.

Pick up a game of backgammon with the locals at **Passport Café and Bar** (Atatürk Cad. 140, Konak, 0232/425-3901). A puff of narghile over *çay* (tea), a piping hot demi-tasse of Turkish coffee, or a heady stein-full of Turkey's most popular beer, Efes, can all be had at this local hangout. Also, **La Sera Café** (Atatürk Cad. 190A, 0232/464-2595, www.lasera.com.tr) is just across from Deniz Restaurant. Its atmosphere is livelier than at any other location, particularly during the summer. Just let the sounds of live Turkish contemporary music guide you to this spacious boardwalk location, which features flaming red ottomans—as in seating—and clear plastic bar stools. For something a little more chic, try **The North Shield Pub** (Atatürk Cad., 0232/483-0720). It opened to rave reviews in 2007 as an exact replica of their successful bar in Istanbul. The Hünal family launched this latest branch in a modern mall reconstructed from Izmir's old French Customs building, just over the water. The seating is configured to best enjoy the lapping sea of the Gulf of Izmir and the sun that stunningly sets over it. All young *Izmirlis* into trance, house, and Turkish pop music head to **Carnavale** (Atatürk Cad. 158, 0232/484-7650) or the adjacent **Ecuador** (Atatürk Cad. 176, 0232/464-2517) for surprisingly good Latin music and late-night nosh.

FESTIVALS

In the first half of March, Izmir hosts a two-week-long **Izmir Avrupa Caz Festival** (Izmir European Jazz Festival, Mithatpaşa Sok. 138, 0232/482-0090, www.iksev.org, concert tickets from 30TL). Unlike the similar event

in Istanbul that highlights mostly North America's greatest performers, Izmir focuses solely on European Jazz.

ACCOMMODATIONS

Izmir thrives as an international convention center. The lack of available hotel rooms in its finer hotels attests to its success in bringing businesspeople to town throughout the year. It pays to reserve well in advance, preferably online to secure the best deals. Otherwise, you're bound to pay at least ten percent more onsite. The city's best hotels are located along the Kordon, while the newly refurbished mansions of Alsancak now serve as somewhat plain—and even gritty—B&Bs.

Under 75TL

Regrettably, only one hotel is worth mentioning in the budget category. The 55-year-old **Güzel Izmir Oteli** (1368 Sok. 8, 0232/483-5069, www.guzelizmirhotel.com, from 64TL) provides spotless, no-frills accommodations, with individual showers. At thes e prices though, it's recommended to check out the many available rooms—a common practice in Turkey—before settling into one.

75-150TL

Full of character, the **Antik Han** (Anafartalar Cad. 600, 0232/489-2750, www.otelantikhan.com, from 140TL) is, as its name suggests, an old building. Two entrepreneurs saved this structure from demolition to build in its stead a friendly and comfy inn with 30 charming, but basic, rooms. At last check, the facility was just being remodeled to include individually air-conditioned rooms and even a playroom with the prerequisite PlayStation for its junior guests. The Antik's draw remains its landscaped courtyard, which provides ample quiet space, inside a hotel that's located amid the lively and noisy bazaar on Anafartalar Caddesi.

Another good choice is **Alican Hotel** (Fevzipaşa Bulv. 15, 0232/484-2768, www.alicanotel.com, €65), a modern gem right in the heart of Izmir. It's also been entirely renovated. Its 30, once drab, floral rooms were revamped

NATURAL HOT SPRINGS

Turkey's West Coast is a hot spring hub, with most of its 17 natural spas centered around the fertile and volcanic soil of the Marmara and Aegean regions. Their mineral-rich waters are purported to cure a slew of skin and nerve ailments, but luxuriating for an hour or two in their warmth remains, for most, their prime benefit. No matter where the destination along Turkey's western littoral, there's bound to be a celebrated hot spring nearby. Plan an outing that will simultaneously enhance your health, put a spring in your step, and feed your appetite for culture and history.

The ancient Anatolians were onto the rejuvenating powers of mineral springs. In fact, Hierapolis – today's Pamukkale – was built atop a mineral-rich fountain of youth in the 2nd century B.C. Ditto for the ancient Lycians, who headed to the city of Caunos for restorative mud baths in the nearby Köyceğiz Lake. Ottoman sultans followed the emperors who came before them and continued building health-promoting temples in cities like Termal and Bursa.

Pamukkale: The stunningly beautiful travertines (rocks deposited from mineral springs) of Pamukkale are one of the country's biggest draws. Here, calcium-laden waters springing from the earth to the tune of 400 liters per second cascade over a cliff, forming dramatically white basins as they cool. The water has a temperature range of 33-38°C (91.4-100°F). Its calcareous content is believed to alleviate a range of disorders, ranging from dermatological to digestive maladies and physical exhaustion.

Termal: The Romans bathed in the many pools of Termal, which lies 11 kilometers southwest of Yalova. To get here, it's an hour's ride by fast ferry across the Sea of Marmara from Istanbul's central port of Yenikapı. Restored and greatly embellished by Ottoman sultans, the indoor and outdoor pools, as well as the verdant gardens and woods that surround them, were a favorite of Kemal Atatürk. The springs gush at 15 liters per second, with a temperature of 57-60°C (134-140°F). They're rich in sodium chloride, calcium sulfate, and fluoride: a therapeutic mix thought to help fight neurological and urological disorders, as well as metabolic problems. The complex also boasts dry and underwater massages, as well as drinking cures.

Çekirge: A suburb of the green city of Bursa, Çekirge's spa hotels are all built around the town's collection of slow-gushing mineral springs (39-58°C/102-136°F). In Atatürk's Hotel Çelik (the aptly-named Mineral Hotel), Lybian king Idris was lounging with Turkey's premier when he learned that he had been overthrown during a coup schemed by a certain colonel Khadafi. The

with a super modern decor, all the way down to regally-red bedspreads. Its seafood restaurant, whose menu was also revamped into contemporary cuisine–style fare, welcomes guests in the morning with a generous complimentary breakfast. With the recent additions of a sauna, pool, and hammam, the Alican Is the best deal in town.

Over 150TL

Crowning the list of hotels are two international chains that feature their namesake brand luxuries and, it goes without saying, a great attention to detail. Izmir's only five-star hotel, the ◖ **Crowne Plaza Hotel Izmir** (Inciraltı

Sok. 67, 0232/292-1300, www.ichotelsgroup.com, from €90) is a sleek modern tower overlooking the azure waters of the Gulf of Izmir. It excels at providing a relaxing ambience with top-notch facilities like spa, health club, and sporting arenas. Every ample, luxurious room boasts impressive views of the bay. The hotel's two restaurants are noted for culinary excellence, while the Lomboz Bar on the 20th floor boasts a dizzying panorama, as well as live music.

The **Izmir Hilton** (Gazi Osmanpaşa Bulv. 7, 0232/441-6060, www.hilton.com, from €135) opened its doors in 1992. The rooms, service, and facilities are immaculate. A lot of care goes

area's calcium, magnesium sulfate, and bicarbonate-rich thermals reputedly alleviate rheumatic, hepatic, gall bladder, and gynecological ailments.

Sültaniye Baths: Just a few kilometers north of the Mediterranean resort of Dalyan in the pastoral town of Köyceğiz are the Sültaniye Baths. These mineral-laden hot springs and mud baths border the tranquil Köyceğiz Lake. The springs (30-38°C/86-100°F) contain sodium chloride, hydrogen, sulfur bromide, and fluoride, and are naturally radioactive; the mix is hailed for easing rheumatism and dermatological and gynecological illness. These health benefits far outweigh the risk of reeking of sulfur bromide, which is akin to the smell of rotten eggs. Downriver is the resort of Dalyan, with its 2,400-year-old rock tombs of Caunos kings, and the loggerhead turtle nesting ground at İztuzu Beach.

Balçova: Located in the Aegean port city of Izmir, Balçova thermal springs are built atop the Baths of Agamemnon. This sulfur-rich tap with a relatively high pH balance takes its name from mythological Macedonian king Agamemnon who, according to Homer, was advised by an oracle to bring his injured troops here during the campaign against Troy in the 13th century B.C. Norway's health ministry took notice, and in 1997 signed an agreement with the Balçova Thermal Hotel to send more than 1000 rheumatism sufferers annually for therapeutic treatments. At 90-95 percent, the success rate is almost miraculous and attests to the restorative powers of the springs. A fully-certified staff works at the adjoining state-of-the art spa.

Çeşme: This scenic peninsula 70 kilometers south of Izmir boasts various resort hotels built atop natural hot springs. Some feature natural hot springs, while others offer thalassotherapy services provided by the sodium-rich seawater. Çeşme is one of Turkey's hottest resorts, and as such the thermal hotels here compete with some of Europe's finest, with accommodations and spa services at a fraction of the price.

Kangal Hot Spring: Unique in the world for the fish (10-12 cm in length) that nibble on the diseased skin of bathers, the Kangal spring runs at a 36°C (96°F) with a pH of 7.3. The bicarbonate, calcium, magnesium sulfate, chlorine, sodium, and magnesium heal a slew of ailments, including rheumatism and neurological disorders. But it's the simultaneous presence of carbon dioxide gas, crucial in curing psoriasis and eczema, and the "toothless" fish, which vacuum off affected areas of the epidermis, that are hailed by Turkish scientists to cure the peskiest of skin ailments in under 21 days.

into its management and it shows through its highly knowledgeable and dignified multi-lingual staff. Every need is addressed, with three restaurants, two bars, indoor swimming pool, two tennis courts, health club, and spa, as well as a slew of professional services, from a tour desk to a shopping arcade.

The locally-owned **Izmir Palas** (Atatürk Bulvarı, 0232/465-0030, www.izmirpalas. com.tr, from €90) is the oldest hotel in town. Built in 1927, the three-star, cozy Palas was entirely renovated in 2005. It's located on the prestigious Kordon, so expect panoramic sea views. It sidewalk Deniz Restaurant is reputed for its tasty regional fish dishes.

FOOD
Izmir's renowned for its coastal seafood. Mussels are offered ubiquitously at finer restaurants—the safest place to try them—and from tray-balancing street peddlers. Choose from *midiye dolma* (mussel stuffed with spiced rice) or fried incantations at the finer establishments. Remember that buying from a street vendor during the hot summer months increases the risk of seafood poisoning. Typically Aegean, the *çipura* (gilthead bream) is a delicacy that's outrageously tasty when grilled. Another regional specialty is fried or grilled *barbunya* (red mullet). The really adventurous can try *tuzda balık* (fish cooked in salt) or even fish that's

NORTHERN AEGEAN COAST

been simmered in milk. Meat lovers will delight in the local *çöp şiş* (trash kebab, literally). But don't let its name scare you: they're simply grilled skewers of giblet-less "leftover" lamb. For a regal meal among Izmir's *société*, head to Kordon's brimming terraces. Or better yet, further north to the restored mansions of Alsancak, where you'll find cafés, bars, and restaurants along Kıbris Şehitler Caddesi and its perpendicular streets. For a quick snack during the day, early birds should aim their fork to the bazaar's typical street fare of *pide* (flat bread) and kebabs. While these close at 7:30 P.M., the majority of Izmir's eateries remain open until well past 11 P.M.

Cafés and Desserts

Riza Aksüt (863 Sok. 66, Kemeraltı, 0232/484-9864, 4–10TL) has satisfied the sweet tooth of *Izmirlis* since 1957. Try their homemade ice cream or the scandalously tasty *bal kaymak* (clotted cream drizzled with honey). This popular family hangout serves puddings and cakes to perfection, and rivals any of Istanbul's finer pastry shops. Also, **Café de Bugün** (Atatürk Cad. 162, Kordon, 0232/425-8118) hails back to Izmir's European heyday as evidenced by its opulent cosmopolitan decor. With specialties originating from Western Europe's capitals, this café serves authentic tiramisu, as well as an array of very American cheesecakes.

Fusion

For the best views, head to **Asansör Restaurant** (Dario Moreno Sokağı, 0232/261-2626, 50TL). Listen to live music from 8 P.M. on, as you savor a succulent variety of international fare, listed in the language of the country the dish originated.

Meat

Near Cumhuriyet Meydanı, **Topçu'nun Yeri** (Kazim Dirik Cad. 3, 0232/425-9047, from 8TL) is another meeting place for upmarket *Izmirlis*. The attraction is not its posh atmosphere, but Topçu's noted *çöp şiş* (wooden skewers stacked with tiny beef shish kebabs)

which are the best in town. The award-winning **Dört Mevsim Et Lokantası** (1369 Sok. 51/A, 0232/489-8991, from 10TL) has for years been synonymous with Izmir. Turks from as far as Ankara file in to its packed quarters for a chance to reaquaint their taste buds with the house specialty of *köfte* (meatball) served with chili sauce. It also features an *ocakbaşı* (open grill), which continually offers baked delicacies, like stuffed-eggplant kebab. While in the bazaar, visit **Gül Kebap** (Anafartalar Cad. 415, 0232/425-0126, open until 5 P.M., 6TL) for ridiculously inexpensive but consistently good meaty fare. This *kebapcı* (kebab/grilled meat restaurant) has served the bazaar merchants for more than 50 years.

Seafood

Deniz Restaurant (Atatürk Cad. 188/B, 0232/464-4499, 15TL, reservations necessary) is not only considered the best eatery along the Kordon, it's also the place where Turkey's glitterati refuel. Try the specialty of *balik kavurma* (morsels of a roasted flaky Med catch served in a traditional earthenware pan). And sweeten the pot with fried ice cream for dessert.

For inexpensive fish, **Tabaklar** (872 Sok. 132, 0232/482-2708, 12TL, until 7 P.M., closed Mon.) serves both local small catch like red mullet and their specialty of *dil şiş* (sole kebab). It's extremely popular with the locals who can't afford the more expensive fish diners along the Kordon.

For exquisite grilled seafood, head to **1888 Restoran** (Cumhuriyet Bulv. 248, 0232/421-6690, 15TL). In the lovely Alsancak quarter, this restaurant graces the lobby of a refurbished 18th-century mansion and its name states the year in which it opened its doors. It serves the once popular Sephardic and Spanish dishes, as well as great mezes of regional wild greens, dressed simply with olive oil and lemon juice.

INFORMATION AND SERVICES
Tourist and Travel Information

Izmir's main **tourism information office** (1344 Sok. 2, 0232/483-5117, 8:30 A.M.–7 P.M. June–Oct.; 8:30 A.M.–5:30 P.M. Mon.–Fri.)

Nov.–May) is located inside the fancy-fronted government building, marked *Il Kültür ve Turizm Müdürlüğü*. A larger tourism office branch is on the ground floor of the Büyük Efes Otel (Gazı Osman Paşa Bulv., 0232/445-7390); it adheres to the same operating hours as the one in town. Both locations, which are run by the municipality, distribute city guides and assist with hotel and area information. Their helpful, multi-lingual staff may even book concert tickets and specialty tours. There's a **tourism information kiosk** (0232/274-2214, 8:30 A.M.–8:30 P.M. daily May–Oct., until 5 P.M. Nov.–Apr.) in the airport arrival hall. Additional maps and local tourism brochures are usually stocked at the Konak Meydanı branch of the municipal **turism polis** (0232/489-0500, 8:30 A.M.–8:30 P.M. daily May–Oct., until 5 P.M. Nov.–Apr.), near the central Saat Kulesi.

For guided excursions in and around Izmir, one of the most reputable tour operators in Izmir is **Vespera Travel** (1721 Sok. Melek Ishanı, 4/312, 0232/364-2705, www.vespera-travel.com). Vespera's multi-lingual staff specializes in tours of Sardis, Ephesus, Chios, Pergamum, and Ayvalık. Their exhaustive daily tour of Izmir, which departs in the morning, averages €120 per couple, with guide, lunch, and all entrance fees.

Banks and Currency Exchange
Banks and 24-hour ATMs are located on Cumhuriyet and Konak Squares, as well as along Fevzi Paşa Bulvarı. For added safety, withdraw money from automated tellers located inside banks, if available. For the lowest exchange rate, trade currency at **Izmir Döviz** (Fevzi Paşa Bulv. 75, 0232/441-8882, 7 A.M.–7 P.M. Mon.–Sat.).

Communications
For postal services, money transfers, and currency exchange, Izmir's main **PTT** office is also located on Cumhuriyet Square. It remains open 24 hours a day. For Internet services, **Internet Café** (1369 Sok. 9, 9–1 A.M., 1.50TL/hr) has modern equipment and a friendly staff.

Head for **Artı Kitabevi** (Cumhuriyet Bulv. 142/B, 0232/421-2632) to purchase English books and magazines. This bookstore has the best selection of foreign books available in Izmir.

Emergency Services
The staff of the municipal **turizm polis kiosk** (0232/489-0500, 8:30 A.M.–8:30 P.M. daily May–Oct., until 5 P.M. Nov.–Apr.) in Konak Meydanı answers any and all emergency needs in English. Additional branches are available in Basmane (1207 Sok., 0232/446-1456), and in Alsancak (0232/464-9360), located next to the hospital.

The **American Consulate** (Kazim Dirik Sok. 13, Floor 8, Pasaport District, 0232/441-2203) can assist with urgent requests and emergencies. Its staff regularly refers U.S. citizens needing medical assistance to the local **American Hospital** (1375 Sok., 0232/484-5360). It's staffed by NATO physicians and treats NATO personnel.

GETTING THERE
By Air
One of the country's busiest airports, Izmir's **Adnan Menderes Airport** is serviced by all Turkish charters and THY (Turkey's national airline), KLM, British Airways, and other international carriers. **Turkish Airlines**'s local offices are located just below the Büyük Efes Hotel (Gazı Osman Paşa Bulv. 1/F, 0232/484-1220) and at Izmir's airport (0232/274-2424). Also in the airport departure hall, **Pegasus Airlines** (0232/274-6231) flies throughout Turkey, as well as some Western European destinations. Other carriers include **Lufthansa** (0232/4223622); **British Airways** (Cumhuriyet Bulv. 109, 2nd Floor, Alsancak, 0232/441-3829).

By Bus
Most vacationing tourists arrive and depart from Izmir by bus. Roughly five kilometers northeast of Konak Meydanı, the city's *otogar* (bus station) is one of the largest vehicular hubs in the nation. There are virtually dozens of agents,

crowded shoulder-to-shoulder vying for their next customer. Don't be tempted to purchase the cheapest ticket to your next destination or the earliest departure. Opt instead to travel with one of the more reputable companies, like **Ulusoy** (0232/444-1888, www.ulusoy.com.tr) and **Varan** (0232/472-0389, www.varan.com). During the hectic summer months, reserve at least 24 hours in advance of departure and at least two days ahead for weekend travel. Sales offices for regional carriers, serving Pergamum, Efes, Sart, Çeşme, Selçuk, and other regional destinations, are on the upper floor. These buses depart several times during the day, either on an hourly basis or, at the very least, every two hours. Sales offices for national or international bus travel are on the 1st Floor. The terminus for public buses that crisscross Izmir leave from a small plaza just outside the entrance.

By Train

Most intercity trains arrive at the **Basmane Garı** (0232/484-8638), while the historic **Alsancak Garı** (0232/464-7795) is reserved for cross country lines. There are three express trains serving Ankara (5:45 P.M., 6:25 P.M., and 7:30 P.M. daily, sleeper 70TL) via Eskişehir (18TL), departing from the latter. Get off at Eskişehir to join the connection for Istanbul. Departing at 8:30 A.M., the **Marmara Ekspressi** reaches the port town of Bandırma in about six hours, from there a boat headed for Istanbul's Yenikapı port can be boarded. If traveling by train to Istanbul, the latter option is by far the best choice since it shaves off several hours of travel time.

GETTING AROUND

Izmir's severe congestion almost makes walking a necessity. Taxis do run the gamut and start the meter at about 2TL, with evening fares costing 50 percent more. There's an underground **metro** (6 A.M.–midnight daily, www.izmirmetro.com.tr, 2TL/token) that zips from Basmane (near the *otogar*) to Konak Meydanı in about ten minutes.

Izmir's Basmane Garı (Basmane Train Station) is one of the city's lovingly renovated 19th-century Levantine public buildings.

© JESSICA TAMTÜRK

Izmir's dependable **municipal buses** depart from **Konak Otobus Istasyonu** (bus terminal) at Konak Meydanı. Tickets (1.50TL) can be purchased either from the bus driver or at white kiosks along the larger thoroughfares.

Ferries (1.50TL/token) crossing the Gulf of Izmir and linking the jetties of Alsancak, Konak, and Pasaport are an enjoyable way to travel, and to beat the bumper-to-bumper traffic along Cumhuriyet Square.

Driving in Izmir, just like commuting by private vehicle in Istanbul, can be nightmarish due to the city's heavy congestion. Patience is king when negotiating bumper-to-bumper traffic, particularly when the headache gets compounded with Izmir's confusing roundabouts. Keep in mind that Fevzi Paşa and Gazı Bulvarıs are one-way thoroughfares. Parking along city streets is supervised by city employees, who charge a flat fee, starting at 2.5TL per hour. For those wishing to explore further afield, rent a car from **Avis** (Airport, 0232/274-2172, www.avis.com.tr, 24 hours), **Hertz** (Airport, 0232/274-3610, 24 hours), or, **Europcar** (Airport, 0232/274-2163, 24 hours).

MANISA

Manisa occupies the southern edge of the abundant Gediz Valley, which sprawls beneath the lofty Spil Dağı (ancient Mount Sipylus). Through a twist of fate, *Manisalıs* have always enjoyed noteworthy status, no matter which occupiers—rich Lydians, the mighty Ottomans, or today's industrial Turks—controlled the city. Today's Manisa is reminiscent of bustling Bursa: green, industrious, and affluent. It's a pleasant 45-minute road trip from Izmir, and traditionally serves as a pit stop on the way to the legendary Lydian capital of Sardis.

Historically, Manisa was once Magnesia ad Sipylus—the site where the mighty Roman army of consul Lucius Cornelius defeated the army of Persian king Antiochus III in 190 B.C. But for more than 16 centuries, the town remained a mere road stop for the invaders du jour. That is until the Turkish Saruhan Emirate captured the city in 1313 and appointed it their capital. It continued to prosper as a provincial center after

the Ottomans absorbed the Saruhan chieftain in 1410, but Manisa's status catapulted to the forefront after it became the training ground for *şahzades* (crown princes). Impressive early Ottoman mosques and *konaks* (mansions) were commissioned by the soon-to-be sultans and their mothers, who'd tagged along to ensure the well-being of their sons. But the majority of these were destroyed when the Greeks left Asia Minor in 1922.

Up until the late 20th century, Manisa thrived on agriculture, mostly from olives and grapes, whose production was supported by the water flowing from nearby Mount Sipylus. The runoff was reduced to a trickle when the mount's flow was diverted to Izmir and further southwest to support the region's booming development.

Aside from the few remaining Ottoman monuments and a small museum worth seeing, there isn't much to detain visitors for more than a half-day. For more information, the **tourism information office** (Mustafa Kemal Cad. 606, 6th Floor, 0236/231-2541, 8 A.M.–noon and 1–5 P.M. Mon.–Fri.) stocks city guides.

Sights

Of the six mosques still standing, Manisa's **Muradiye Camii** (Mosque of Murad) was commissioned by Sultan Murad in 1585. Murad, an incurable womanizer whose harem ballooned to 1,200 beauties and progeny included some 103 children, was born in Manisa. He requested that a grand structure be built to commemorate his hometown and passage, and tasked Ottoman master architect Mimar Sinan with the job. Manisa's Mosque of Murad turned out to be his last architectural masterpiece before his death just three years later. Its impressive interior boasts dazzling tile artisanship and stained glass windows that filter daylight into the prayer hall in a variety of colors. The Muradiye's adjoining soup kitchen today serves as **Manisa Müzesi** (Manisa Museum, 9 A.M.–5 P.M. Tues.–Sun., 3TL). Its displays include impressive mosaics, marble Byzantine statues, and tombstones discovered in nearby Sart.

The dilapidated **Ulu Camii** (Great Mosque

of Manisa) is the oldest structure in town. Built in 1366, the forlorn mosque sits atop a terrace in a park that towers over the city. The teahouse next to it provides a perfect spot from which to inspect the Selçuk structure. This nearly-seven-centuries-old structure was commissioned by Saruhan emir Ishak Çelebi (1357–1388). Manisa's Great Mosque constitutes the first step towards the development of the intricate spatial composition of classical Ottoman mosques. The complex, a great big brick block, consists of a mosque, *medrese* (Islamic seminary), *türbe* (tomb), and ablutions fountains. Its hammam is located about 80 meters northeast of the mosque.

The third mosque of interest is **Sultan Camii** (Sultan's Mosque); it faces Murad's Mosque. Built in 1522 for Ayşe Hafize, Süleyman the Magnificent's mom, the mosque is part of a large *külliye* (religious complex). Its *darüşşifa* (hospital) was in use as a mental facility until about a century ago.

Festivals

Every year on the third Sunday in March, the **Mesir Şenlikleri** gets into full swing. It's a wild festival that honors *mesir macunu,* a spicy paste mixed with some 41 ingredients served in the form of a chewy candy. It's supposed to restore health, youth, and potency, and is often referred to as the tongue-in-cheek Turkish Viagra.

The story goes that Merkez Efendi concocted this mixture in 1522 in the hope of curing the sick at the Muradiye's hospital. When Ayşe Hafize, the mom of Sultan Süleyman the Magnificent, suffered from a mysterious ailment, her perplexed doctors prescribed this potent mixture after trying all known cures. Following a speedy recovery, she distributed the aphrodisiac to Manisa's populace.

Today, thousands take part in the festivities that include historical reenactments and a free-for-all *mesir macunu* distribution, in which the muezzin throws packets of the chew from high atop the minaret to awaiting crowds below. Locals believe that the *macun* (paste) will keep them disease- and pain-free until the next festival. The concoction is also believed to immunize against scorpion and snake bites.

Accommodations and Food

If deciding to stay a while, however, there's really only one accommodation worth recommending: **Anemon Otel Manisa** (Manisa Girişi Kuva-i-Milliye Anıt Mevkii, 0236/233-4141, www.anemonhotels.com, 180TL). This four-star hotel boasts satellite television and Internet access. Large modern rooms feature the latest technology to please its considerable business clientele.

Manisa is lacking in remarkable eateries, other than those featured in its larger hotels. The popular, **Teras 2** (Ibrahim Gökçen Bulvarı, Belediye Kultur Sitesi, 0226/231-3393, 18TL), however, stands out for its superior Turkish fare.

Getting There and Around

If you're not visiting the area with a tour company, the best way to reach Manisa is by bus through Izmir. The 45-minute ride costs about 8TL. From the *otogar* (bus station), walk about ten minutes south, in the direction of the mountain, to reach the central thoroughfare of Doğu Caddesi, or hop on an awaiting *dolmuş* (1TL) to reach the center of town.

(SART (SARDIS)

The ancient site of Sart lies on the outskirts of its namesake farming village, at the foot of the Tmolus Mountains overlooking the fertile Hermus River Plain. Its roots dig so deep into history that it's hard to define its early beginnings. A joint archaeological research team from Harvard and Cornell Universities, however, claims that the site's been a major metropolis for at least four millennia. Suffice it to say that most first-timers who gaze at its restored, early 3rd-century Lydian gymnasium are awed by its grandeur. The discovery of its adjoining 3rd-century synagogue even stunned historians by validating that Judaism was not only alive, but thriving during the Roman era. Sardis's ruins are an eye-popping experience for armchair archaeologists,

© JESSICA TAMTÜRK

The ancient city of Sardis is home to the 1,500-year-old marble remains of a synagogue.

history buffs, or anyone wondering about humankind's lengthy past.

Sardis is a must-do day trip from Izmir and can be undertaken with **Vespera Travel** (1721 Sok. Melek Ishanı, 4/312, 0232/364-2705, www.vesperatravel.com). Vespera personnel take guests by air-conditioned vehicle from Izmir on an eight-hour tour to Sardis's ruins for €57 per person, inclusive of all entrance fees and lunch.

History

To understand the ruins, at least some of Sardis's protracted history must be retraced. Whether it goes by its modern monikers of Sardis, Sardes, or Sardeis; Sparda in Persian; or Sart in Turkish, the one thing that academics can agree on is that it was the capital of the Lydian Empire (8th–6th century B.C.). At its height the realm extended from the Aegean Sea well into central Anatolia. Noted for its fertile soil and rich deposits of gold and silver form the nearby Patolus Çayı (river), Sardis quickly

gained affluence. Lydian kings were the first to mint the electrum (coins of silver and gold). The renowned King Croesus (563–546 B.C.) made a fortune from trade, facilitated by the newly minted coins that had replaced a barter system. This wealth lingers to this day in the dictum "rich as Croesus." But this prosperity raised the attention of the Persian King Cyrus the Great, who in 546 B.C. conquered Sardis after a 14-day siege in which poor Croesus was burned alive. Under the Persians, Sardis marked the last stop on an administrative route that began in Persepolis—today's Susa in Iran. Industry and commercial trade made Lydia one of the richest kingdoms of its time, with a lifestyle reputed for its extravagance. But during the Ionian Revolt (499 B.C.), the Ionian Greeks to the west launched a systematic rebellion against the tyrannical rule of the Persians, burning Sardis to the ground in the process. Any subsequent attempt to repel the Persians from Asia Minor proved unsuccessful until Alexander the Great's great army successfully accomplished the feat in 334 B.C. Sardis surrendered to Alexander. The great warrior tasked his architect with returning the former Lydian capital to its former architectural magnificence, but a massive earthquake in A.D. 17 devastated much of these marble structures. One of Sardis's crucial sculptures, a stone shrine to the mother goddess Cybele, survived the earthquake untouched. It's one of the earliest Ionic temples and earliest examples of Ionic architecture (6th century B.C.). During the ensuing Greek era, after the death of Alexander, Pergamum kings coveted Sardis's exotic wealth. And in 282 B.C., the city became the Seleucid capital and an independent Greek city-state. The colossal Artemis Temple on site dates from this era. Under the Romans, the shrine was greatly enlarged with a bath-gymnasium complex.

Sardis continued to play a major role in religion. The seat of a Christian bishopric, Sardis's church was the third of the Seven Churches of the Revelation to receive an ominous letter from Saint John the Apostle in the 1st century A.D. It also had a thriving Jewish community, who sponsored the creation of one of the largest ancient synagogues outside of Palestine.

Sardis remained one of Asia Minor's major metropolises until the late Byzantine era. Flip-flopping raids and conquests of the lush surrounding Hermus Valley between the Turks and the Christians had by the 11th century cut most vital routes to and from the city. Sardis's citadel fell to the advancing Turks in 1306. And less than a century later, Mongol warlord Timerlane destroyed the once grand capital. It never recovered.

Sights

The **ruins of Sardis** (8 A.M.–7 P.M. May–Oct., until 5 P.M. Nov.–Apr., 5TL) are clustered into two main groups, which are easily approachable from the main road. Informative signposts lead visitors through the entire site. The first includes the stunningly restored gymnasium and adjacent synagogue, which are reached by following the **Roman Road** that leads past **Byzantine shops** and **Byzantine latrines.** The tunnels that drained these ancient communal toilets can still be seen along the shops' rear walls. These vertical partitions backed into the adjoining synagogue. Among the clearly marked businesses along this ancient commercial lane, the names of their owners, Sabbatio and Jacob, keep recurring. The former was a benefactor of the synagogue, while the latter may have been one of its elders.

A left turn at the end of the road leads to Sardis's **synagogue.** The floors of this 3rd-century A.D. structure feature original mosaics; the ones on the walls, however, are replicas. The originals are housed in Manisa's municipal museum. At over 100 meters in length, the Sardis synagogue is the largest of its kind. Tiled columns and walls offer historical information. Look for a plaque listing the mostly North American benefactors who've enabled the renovation process of this *havra* (synagogue).

Right next door to the synagogue is the site of a once impressive **gymnasium and bath complex,** which was destroyed by the Sassanian-Persians in A.D. 616. Beyond it stands an astonishingly tall and meticulously restored **Marble Court.** It may have been completed in A.D. 211 or 212, according to the dedicatory inscription that honors Roman emperor Geta, who only ruled for those two years. Beyond the structure's finely striated columns is an entrance that leads to the court's marble **swimming pool** and resting area. Judging from the magnificence of its forecourt, the bath was used to honor the imperial cult.

Current archaeological research has unveiled parts of **city walls** dating back to the Lydian era, and a **Roman residence,** which, naturally, sits atop an earlier Lydian abode.

TEMPLE OF ARTEMIS

Heading west from the synagogue, past the tea houses of the village of Sart—short for Sartmahmut—the Temple of Artemis (8 A.M.–5 P.M., 3TL) boasts the remnants of six 18-meter-tall columns. The construction of this impressive Roman temple began in 300 B.C., but was never finished. Researchers believe that a wall may have been planned as a division to allow each deity a separate chamber. The West-facing hall was meant to be shared by the god Artemis and Roman empress Faustina; while the East-facing chamber was allocated to Zeus and the exalted Antonine emperor. By the mid-4th century A.D., the temple was "cleansed" of its pagan past and a **Byzantine church** was built among its ruins.

Before leaving the site, there are two ruins worth a detour. The first, the Altar of Cybele, lies in the center of the Sardis archaeological site, next to the Lydian gold refinery. It's facing east, and flanked on either side by crouching lions—felines considered sacred to the Anatolian Mother Goddess Cybele. The mid-6th century shrine was erected during the rule of Lydian King Alyattes. The second set of ruins, more than 100 burial grounds, is located on the right side—or North —of the highway leading away from Sardis. The series of tumuli are saucer-like burial mounds that entomb Lydian royalty.

Getting There and Around

The best way to visit the Sardis ruins is with a regional agent (Vespera Travel, 1721 Sok.

Melek Ishanı, 4/312, 0232/364-2705, www.
vesperatravel.com). If touring solo, however,
getting to Sardis is easy through the *dolmuş*
(communal taxi, 1.5TL) that connects the town
of Sartmahmut to the district center of Salihli.
Salihli can be reached by bus from Izmir (less
than 10TL); it's a pleasant 90-minute (96-km)
ride along the E96 from Izmir's *otogar* (bus station). Departure from Manisa's *otogar* to Sahili
(50 km) is also available.

ÇEŞME PENINSULA

Two decades ago, a trio of diehard sailboards
"found" what they called paradise on earth: the
beaches of Çeşme's windswept, scrubby coastal
shores. A few years later Bodrum's summer residents "rediscovered" the location's cooler and
drier climate and made the peninsula what
it is today—a weekend escape for Istanbul's
youthful elite. Some 74 kilometers southwest of
Izmir, Çeşme is blessed with more than a dozen
sandy shores and pristine aquamarine waters.
The Greek island of Chios looms at an eight-
kilometer distance across the Aegean. The peninsula is a contradiction in spades: Its ringed
coast is a bastion for unchecked hedonism,
while its sluggish interior is purely prosaic. Its
agricultural landscape lays claim to the noted
mastic gum trees, fields of aniseed, sesame, and
artichokes, scattered with fig and olive trees. Its
un-spoilt bays provide sunbathers and swimmers absolute peace.

The peninsula is named after the fort town
of *Çeşme* (drinking fountain) at its tip. The
name of Çeşme itself is labeled after the myriad
of Ottoman fountains that were built atop natural springs. Discovered in the late 18th century, these gushers were long forgotten until
recently. Turkey's tourism magnates are finally
exploiting that natural richness with the opening of several uber-luxurious spa resorts.

You could spend a week exploring Çeşme's
fine beaches and secluded coves, lounge in
its exclusive haunts, and investigate its back
country. But 48 hours should suffice to visit
the uniquely Greek village of Alaçatı and its
nearby surfing paradise, the golden shores
of Altınkum, the village of Ildiri (ancient

the charming town of Çeşme

COURTESY OF TURKISH MINISTRY OF TOURISM

Erythrae), and enjoy some R&R in transit.
Çeşme's international harbor is a great spot
from which to take one of the daily ferries
to the nearby island of Chios, or as a departure point for a jaunt to Italy or other Greek
islands.

Çeşme

A 14th-century **Genoese castle** looms over
the handful of cobblestone lanes that comprise the picturesque enclave of Çeşme. Shortly
after conquering this Aegean outpost, Sultan
Beyazit I strengthened the fortress. It later
served as a watchtower from which guards
surveyed the horizons for marauding pirates.
Unlike Bodrum's fortress, the citadel here is
disappointedly barren, but does offer a stunning panorama of the Aegean Sea and Chios.
Its museum, **Çeşme Müzesi** (Çeşme Museum,
8 A.M.–5 P.M., 4TL), however, boasts wonderful artifacts discovered from the nearby ancient
village of Erythrea. Just outside the castle lies
the statue of Cezayirli Gazi Hasan Paşa, a naval
commander of the Battle of Chesma (1770)

NORTHERN AEGEAN COAST

who later became grand vizier. The lion he's caressing represents his infamous pet. Also nearby is **Öküz Mehmet Paşa Kervansaray**—a *han* commissioned in 1528 by Süleyman the Magnificent. For centuries, this trading post marked the end of the transcontinental Silk Road for the hordes of caravans that made their way from the Middle East into the arid steppe of Central Anatolia and beyond. From this point, Asian goods were unloaded from camels and exported to Europe. While today it's been converted into a luxury hotel, its solid stone architecture is intact and its courtyard provides a nice location to escape the blazing heat of summer.

Amid Çeşme's back streets, you'll find the 19th-century Greek Orthodox **Church of Agios Haralambos.** It serves today as an art gallery. Along Bağlar Çarşı Caddesi is the restored 18th-century **Belediye Hamamı** (Municipal Hammam, 0232/712-5386, 10 A.M.–10 P.M., mid-June–mid-Sept., 40TL); its staff is renowned for providing rough rubs that'll remove pounds of dead skin.

ACCOMMODATIONS AND FOOD

The pearl of Çeşme, the �`C` **Piril Hotel Thermal and Beauty Spa** (Inönü Mahallesi, 0232/444-0232, www.pirilhotel.com, 160–225TL) proves that a full-service resort doesn't necessarily have to be an eyesore. A compilation of pleasing glass and concrete, this structure boasts 140 sunlit rooms that tend to be on the small side. As its name suggests, a veritable smorgasbord of luxurious treatments are available in its 4,000-square-foot mind and body retreat.

Also worth noting, the centrally located **Ridvan Otel** (Cumhuriyet Meydanı 11, 0232/712-6336, www.ridvanotel.com, 80–125TL) offers large basic rooms with balconies that overlook the square. This five-story hotel boasts all modern amenities, in addition to a pool, private beach, and large breakfast buffet.

The overall best deal, however, is the **Yalçin Hotel** (Kale Sok. 38, 0232/712-6981, www.yalcinotel.com, 72TL with breakfast), which features 15 immaculately clean, basic rooms with stunning views of the fortress from its lofty location. Throughout July, the Yalçin typically offers a daily rate of 50TL per person, including breakfast and dinner.

For the best dining in town, Turks return to year after year to 🌑 **Imren Lokantasi** (Inkilap Cad. 6, 0232/712-7620, 10TL). The Kadağan sibling quartet has been serving simple, yet spectacularly good, traditional Turkish entrées and veggie appetizers since 1960. Try their specialty of *çiçek dolması* (stuffed marrow flowers), followed by *Karnıyarık* (meat stuffed eggplant) for a truly traditional meal.

Altınkum

Translating into golden sands, Altınkum gets its name from a series of pristine, undeveloped beaches and coves. This delightful coastal strip, six miles southwest of Çeşme, remains free of monster hotels thanks to the protected status it enjoys. But don't worry, there are still rudimentary restaurants and plenty of idyllic camping sites. By far the winner among these is **Cennet Camping** (0532/394-0131, tent rental 25TL), which is set right off the beach. It also boasts a restaurant, where both sea and land yields are combined to perfection. Those into windsurfing, parasailing, and the like will find equipment rental at the **Fun Beach** (from 75TL/day). To get to Altınkum, hop on the *dolmuş* (communal taxi, 2TL) that departs from the rear of Çeşme's *turizm danışma* (tourism office). The last car returns to Çeşme at sunset. Keep in mind that most of Altınkum's tourism facilities are open June–mid-September.

🌑 Alaçatı

The place to be seen, Alaçatı has been transformed into a platform for country living. It's become a year-round weekend escape for Istanbul's and Izmir's elite and wannabes. It remained a pleasant Greek village, replete with gorgeous 19th-century stone abodes, until one was turned into the posh Taş Otel (hotel) in the mid-1990s. This B&B proved so popular that a number of copycats followed suit. Then came the trendy restaurants and cafés, whose cosmopolitan or Turkish menus alone command a trip to the peninsula. Due to strict building regulations, the town's antique architecture remains intact, at least in the town center, where cobblestone streets are rimmed with tiny souvenir and antique shops, as well as art galleries. Although each year sees the tourist season lengthening, most hotels and restaurants are open mid-May–mid-October and on school and end-of-the-year holidays. Hotels reservations are strongly recommended.

Alaçatı's beach is located about three miles south of the city's main drag of Kemalpaşa Caddesi. The waters here are superb for sailboards, though strong winds can be a nuisance for sunbathers. A *dolmuş* (communal taxi) service connects Çeşme to Alaçatı.

Ildiri

Located about 16 kilometers north of Çeşme, the fishing village of Ildiri makes for an ideal lunch destination. Its coast unfurls along a small bay that's protected from the batter of the wind by a couple of small islets just offshore. *Ildirlis,* numbering just under 400, thrive on fishing and the harvest of artichokes, gum, and olives. A couple of pleasant fish diners line the docks, but nowhere can one enjoy the serene scenery of the area's rolling fields with a backdrop of the blue sea than at the tented cafés, located on the road into town. They're the perfect spot to enjoy a *gözleme*—a pancake-like flat bread filled with cheese, herbs, or meat—with a piping cup of hot *çay* (tea).

Once sated, head to the town limits to visit the nearby remains of the ancient city of **Erythrea** (8 A.M.–5 P.M., free). While most ruins languish unexcavated under acres of cultivated fields, random archaeological digs have unearthed a 3rd-century B.C. amphitheater; some ultra luxurious 2nd-century B.C. villas, replete with their mosaic forecourts; and, a 6th-century B.C. Temple of Heracles. Climb the hillock where the amphitheater is located for some incredible coastal views and to inspect the remains of an antique basilica.

Sports and Recreation

Çeşme's renowned as one of the world's top four windsurfing destinations. The planet's best pros crash its shores en masse during the annual Windsurf Turkey Cup and its Çeşme Sea Festival (early July); the rest of the summer, eager layfolks by the hundreds try their hand—and balance—at this demanding sport, rendered even more challenging by this area's forceful gusts and shallows.

B&G Surf (0232/716-6170, www.alacati. com, closed Nov.–Mar.) employs knowledgeable instructors that won't make you feel like a total tenderfoot. They also rent gear: board and wetsuit (80–120TL/day). A two-hour private lesson runs about 100TL. Another good choice is **ASPC** (Alaçatı Surf Paradise and Club, Liman Yolu, 0232/716-6611, www.alacati.de, mid-March–Oct.). As the largest surfing center in Turkey, it enjoys a long-standing reputation with professional surfers. Top-quality equipment rental includes all sorts of boards as well as paragliding gear (75TL/day, 300TL/week). ASPC has a variety of board- and kite-surfing classes for both beginners and advanced surfers (6–10-hour lessons, from 175TL).

For those seeking more relaxing water activities, **day cruises** depart every morning from the Çeşme marina and provide roughly seven hours of snorkeling, swimming, or just sunbathing fun. Along the route, island hop on a trio of isles—**Eşek Adası** (Donkey Island), named for its wild equestrians; **Blue Lagoon;** and Black Island. These cruises run the gamut, from the typically crowded, music-blasting boat to private day cruises with lunch included (20–90TL/person with lunch). Secure space the day before for lower rates and don't be afraid to negotiate if paying in cash. Boats—typically wooden *gullets*—leave the marina at 10 A.M. to return around 5 P.M.

Deep-sea diving around the several shipwrecks that line Çeşme's seabed is another possibility with **Dolphin Land** (0232/337-0161, www.divecesme.com). This outfit offers fully certified diving instructors and provides full-day diving trips, as well as refresher courses and PADI certification for those itching to earn their fins in this underwater sport.

Some of Turkey's finest beaches are in Çeşme. **Pırlanta Plajı** scores high on the country's top ten. It earns its name of "diamond" from the mile-long strip of sand that glitters in the sun's rays. Located southwest of Çeşme, this public beach faces north toward the peninsula's craggy shores and features slightly warmer waters.

Information and Services

Most banks, ATMs, transportation offices, **tourism information office** (Iskele Meydanı 6, 0232/712-6653), hotels, and restaurants all radiate a couple of blocks from Cumhuriyet Meydanı, Çeşme's main square. For Internet service, **Triatek** (3048 Sokak, 10 A.M.–1 A.M.) remains open the longest and has the most modern technology available. The **PTT** (8 A.M.–midnight) is located along the esplanade, just north of the ferry port.

Getting There

One of Turkey's most modern *otoyols* (expressways) links Izmir to the Çeşme peninsula in less than an hour. Unless you're coming by car or with a tour, all bus connections in and out of Çeşme transit through Izmir. Buses heading for Izmir depart from Çeşme's *otogar* (every 15 minutes, 6 A.M.–6 P.M., 10TL). Çeşme's otogar is inland, at about a 15-minute walk from the marina. It's served through the minibus service that links Çeşme, Ilica, and Alaçatı from the parking lot just south of Çeşme's tourism information office.

Car-and-passenger ferryboats link Çeşme to Chios and various other European destinations from the harbor. The service to Chios runs five times weekly in high season and twice weekly in the winter; it generally departs Çeşme at 9 A.M. and returns from Chios at 5 P.M. Tickets to this Greek island can be purchased from **Ertürk Travel Agency** (Beyazıt Cad. 6, 0232/712-6768, www.erturk.com. tr, round-trip 100TL, vehicles from 150TL). Ferries heading to the Italian ports of Brindisi, Ancona, and Bari leave at least once weekly during the summer and less frequently the rest of the year. To learn about scheduling, fares, and purchasing tickets, visit the ticket sales office of **Marmara Lines** (Turgut Özal Bulv., 0232/712-2223, www.marmaralines.com), one of the largest and most dependable Turkish ferryboat companies. The embarcadero is less than a 15-minute walk following the bay from Çeşme's square.

NORTHERN AEGEAN COAST

THE SOUTHERN AEGEAN COAST

The southern Aegean coast is one of the most fertile regions in Turkey, and one which comprises the world's densest concentration of antiquities per square kilometer. It sprawls over the lush deltas formed by the life-giving Küçük and Büyük Menderes Rivers. From their banks spread fields of tobacco, grains, and cotton, while woods of fir and olive groves unfurl as far as the eye can see. So valued were these streams during antiquity that the twists and turns along their course inspired early Greek lexicographers to coin the word *meander*.

It's this natural abundance, combined with an ideal topography and a close proximity to the Aegean, that produced some of the world's earliest tribes. As centuries passed, Greek islanders colonized the coast, creating the mighty Ionian realm and some of the first advancements in the fields of science, history, and art.

The Aegean's star metropolises once included Sardis, Pergamum, and Ephesus. The latter may be the crown jewel of Turkey's ancient cities, but its lesser-visited sister cities nearby—Miletus, Didyma, and gorgeous Priene—are packed with ruins and certainly worth a trip. Rebuilt stele-by-stele, Priene stands hundreds of feet up on a hill overlooking the lush delta. Its Acropolis is second in importance after the Delphi in Greece. But aside from history, its lofty location affords breathtaking views of cultivated fields as far as the eye can see. The Ephesus region also features Meryemana (House of the Virgin Mary); the few remains of the Temple of Artemis, one of the Ancient World's Seven Wonders; and other

© JESSICA TAMTÜRK

HIGHLIGHTS

◖ Efes (Ephesus): In this ancient Ionian metropolis, stroll by such spellbinding monuments as the Library of Celsus (page 217).

◖ Şirince: Bask in the preserved Greek beauty of this elevated little village, renowned for its orchards and heady wines (page 223).

◖ Priene: Climb up to this astonishing ancient city's restored Acropolis to take in spectacular views of the Büyük Menderes valley below (page 229).

◖ Bafa Gölu (Bafa Lake): On the shores of Bafa Lake, visit the rural village of Herakleia – lunch at one of its many water-lapped cafés and wander through ruins of 1,300-year-old Byzantine monasteries (page 235).

◖ Hierapolis: Take a dip in the lily-white travertine pools of this surreal mineral-laden spot in the Roman ruins in Pamukkale (page 242).

LOOK FOR ◖ TO FIND RECOMMENDED SIGHTS, ACTIVITIES, DINING, AND LODGING.

dazzling sites that have borne witness to the founding of Christianity.

Today, the coastal highway follows the Menderes, a.k.a. the Cayster River, in its meanderings through the southern Aegean coast. Tented stands occupied by farmers, who tirelessly signal travelers to stop for a taste of the juiciest tomatoes and figs, pepper the artery's grassy shoulders. Further south, the two-lane road hugs the southern bank of Bafa Gölu (Bafa Lake). On its sandy shores lies the rarely visited Herakleia under Latmos—a bucolic village seemingly untouched by the wave of local modernization that's gripped western Turkey in the last 20 years. This marks the starting point of Carian country, an area that was home to an indigenous people more than 12 centuries ago.

Other destinations include the small village of Şirince—renowned for its wines, picturesque architecture, and panoramas. It's smack in the middle of all of the major sites and provides an idyllic, peaceful base from which to relax after hours of ambling through so much history. The nearby coastal resort of Kuşadası, with its abundance of mammoth vacation resorts and nighttime activities, will satisfy those seeking a fuller serving of entertainment with their sightseeing.

Regarding leisurely pursuits under the sun, the playground of Bodrum is one of the most happening spots in the Med. This summer colony offers sandy strips covered with *uber*luxurious hotels and evening haunts that await those who can afford to play with the international

SOUTHERN AEGEAN COAST

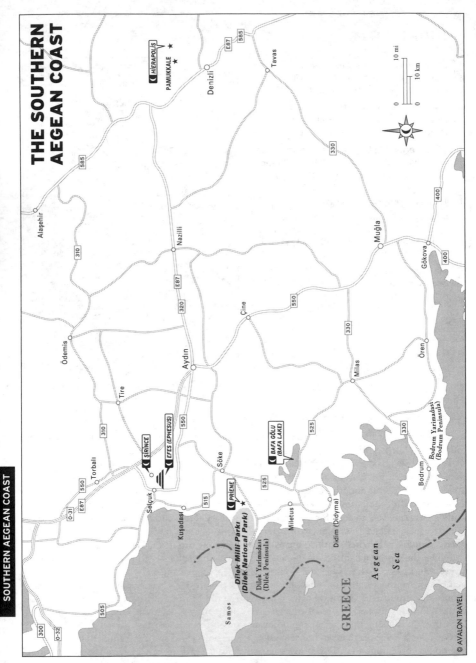

THE SOUTHERN AEGEAN COAST

jet-set crowd. From downtown Bodrum rises an impressive Venetian castle built on the ruins of the Mausoleum of Halikarnassus, another of the Seven Wonders of the antiquity. Its lobby houses the globally renowned museum of underwater archaeology, boasting 8,000-year-old barnacle-encrusted amphorae.

The area is more than just the coast and its many distractions, a two-hour drive inland from Kuşadası leads to Pamukkale, where surreal, snow-white outcrops of calcium jut from the earth, creating majestic ledges pocked with shallow thermal pools. These mineral-rich springs are hailed to be therapeutically beneficial in curing most maladies. This must-do day trip, and countless others—at last count there were more than 40—provides an ideal getaway in an area brimming with sights.

PLANNING YOUR TIME

If you have just three days to explore this region, plan on doing two things: schedule a longer return trip and plan carefully to include choice destinations. Basing your efforts in the pretty, blue-collar town of Selçuk for a 72-hour whirl through this region is a possibility. This allows for a variety of half- or full-day side trips to archaic Ephesus, the charming mountain village of Şirince, the Temple of Artemis, the House of the Virgin Mary, and the PMD (Priene, Miletus, and Didyma) excursion. A visit to further-off Pamukkale is also an option. But that barely scratches the surface of what's to see, so set aside at least six days to do this region justice.

Plan to land at Izmir's Adnan Menderes Airport, where a pre-booked airport transfer with the hotel of choice or a rental vehicle await departure for the Selçuk region. Alternatively, travel by bus from either Istanbul, Ankara, or pretty much any other point to Selçuk's *otogar* (bus station). Booking with a larger hotel has its rewards, which include the added option of an in-house travel service to reserve those must-do excursions, and free rides within Selçuk, to the resort of Kuşadası, and other locations of interest. While tours and coach transportation are readily available, renting a vehicle allows for

the stunning Library of Celsus in Ephesus

COURTESY OF REPUBLIC OF TURKEY CULTURE AND TOURISM MINISTRY

SOUTHERN AEGEAN COAST

more independence and a more relaxing option than the impossibly rushed schedules of tour companies.

This suggested itinerary takes off from Selçuk. Plan a solid two days to visit the ancient Ionian cities of Ephesus, Priene, Miletus, and Didyma, followed by a tour of the bucolic wine bastion Şirince, and a pilgrimage to the venerated Meryemana (House of the Virgin Mary), 4th-century Basilica of Saint John, and the intricate 14th-century Isabey Mosque. Mix-and-match another 48 hours for a day cruise along the gorgeous coast of Kuşadası, a picnic on the shale beaches of Dilek Peninsula National Park, or a visit to Pamukkale's ethereal travertine pools. The last two days can be spent traveling southbound toward Bodrum. A stop at Bafa Gölü (Bafa Lake) is in order; it's just a 45-minute drive south from Kuşadası. This large body of water, aside from being a natural and historical reserve, heralds the most bucolic stretch of Turkey's west coast. Donkeys and horse carriages appear at every turn, and so do ruins after ruins. A great example of this is Herakleia under Latmos, a lakeside outpost in the shadow of the 4,100-foot Beşparmak Dağı (Five-Fingered Mountain), which boasts Byzantine monasteries and thousands of birds nesting atop olive trees. Here, join the two-hour cruise that covers the lake's five islets, before claiming your table at one of the lakeside eateries known for their grilled trout.

Climate

The region's mild temperature makes any season ideal for touring. Perhaps the worst time is at its busiest, during the hot summer season, when this stretch is assaulted with busloads of tourists and highs of above 38°C (100°F). Beach space is at a premium, ditto for restaurants and hotels, and bars are a-hopping. Obviously, some revel in this brouhaha, while others find it dreadful. The southern Aegean is best enjoyed during the months of May and September, when temperatures are milder and tourism is reduced to a trickle. Coastal waters remain warm and cafés still enjoy outdoor seating. While the region enjoys the sought-after Mediterranean climate, winter can dip to 2°C (35.6°F), and summer temperatures can sink to 16°C (62°F). The rest of the year (mid-Nov.–mid-Mar.) exhibits a quieter atmosphere along the coast. This is a great time to engage with the local culture and enjoy a solitary stroll through the ruins that pock this region. Keeping in mind that both hoteliers and restaurateurs synchronize their clocks with the official summer season, more than 60 percent of establishments close shop during the rest of the year.

Tours

Consider contacting Ingrid Peetermans of **Anker Travel** (İnönü Bulvarı, 14; Kuşadası, 0256/612-4598, ingrid@ankertravel.net, www.ankertravel.net) to arrange tours, transportation, lodging, and entertainment in the area. With more than two decades of specializing in Turkey's travel sector from her adopted home base of Kuşadası, Peetermans is a master planner with arguably the deepest knowledge of the area; she's a Belgo-Turk who speaks at least four languages fluently. Just ask and she delivers: book a cruise to the Greek Islands or Italy; rent a car (€42–88/day); request airport transfers from Izmir (one way/round-trip, €84–173 for 1–4 people); or book a side-trip. The popular regional excursions like Pamukkale (Mon., Thurs., and Sat., €50/person, incl. museum entrances); Ephesus (daily in July and Aug., €50–55); and Priene/Miletus/Didyma (every Wed., €40) are available June 15–September 15. Call her for arrangements during the off-season.

The Ephesus Region

What constitutes the ancient Ionian territory sits atop verdant land once covered by the Aegean Sea. The sea gradually retreated due to silting, but left watery remnants of its erstwhile reach, creating the broad natural reserve of Bafa Lake. It is in this ever-changing landscape that history's main hubs were formed by eastern Hellenic migrants from mainland Greece and its isles. Later, metropolises like Ephesus, Priene, and Miletus gave rise to the arts and sciences, thanks to early philosophers like Thales and Miletus, a.k.a. "the Father of Science," as well as the famed architect Isidore. It was also in this region that Christianity's early beliefs coalesced. Saint John brought the Virgin Mary here from Jerusalem in A.D. 41. Just a decade later, Saint Paul riled local officials by preaching the gospel to local pagans.

While ancient Ionia owes its advancement to the amount of Greek settlers who colonized its shores, it wasn't until the 1980s that the area was "discovered" by tourists. Tour buses started trickling in, and the nearby fishing village of Kuşadası slowly transformed into the hedonistic, pub-infested mecca for Northern Europeans that it is today. Its renewed boardwalk and splendid beaches please those with a few hours to spend among the throngs. Selçuk also capitalized on the onslaught of vacationers with attractions of its own: Steam Train, Ephesus Museums, famed camel wrestling festival, bird paradise at nearby Pamucak beach, and bustling Saturday street bazaar. Add to it the mountain village of Şirince—known for its splendid fruity wines and pastoral abodes—just a short *dolmuş* (communal taxi) ride away from Selçuk, and there is just as much to explore inland as on the coast. Then, there's the marvelous Dilek Peninsula National Park on Dilek Peninsula, with its wide woody expanses that plunge dramatically into the crystal clear coastal waters. A hike to the park's isolated shale beaches provides a possible glimpse of the rare Anatolian cheetah or a pack of wild horses.

(EFES (EPHESUS)

One of the highlights of the ancient world, Ephesus (0232/892-6010, 8 A.M.–4:30 P.M. Oct.–Apr., 8 A.M.–6:30 P.M. May–Sept., admission 20TL, parking 4TL) is the best preserved ancient city in the Eastern Mediterranean. It played a key role in the birth and advent of both Western thought and Christianity. About 40 points of historical, archaeological, and religious interest are located within this large open-air museum. As such, a brisk tour of the ancient city can be accomplished in as little as a couple of hours; a full tour can take up to a day. Summers are particularly scorching and crowded, so stock up on water and wear comfortable shoes.

To learn more about this ancient city's critical role throughout antiquity, read *Ephesos: Metropolis of Asia* by Helmut Koester. Or, browse www.ephesus.us for interactive maps and extensive background details on each of the Ephesian ruins. Also, consider hiring the services of one of the guides at the entrance (75TL for a two-hour tour) or tour the site with the assistance of an **audio guide** (student 4TL, adult 8TL, available just past the shops). Don't want to DIY, the specialized **Ephesus Excursions** (Meander Travel, Kibris Cad. 1/A, Kuşadası, 0256/614-3859, www.ephesusexcursions.com, US$57–155, entrance fees and English guide included) adeptly walks groups through the entire site, offering tons of comical anecdotes and little-known historical facts.

History

Myths surrounding the founding of Ephesus abound. Some say the Amazons were there first. Others claim that in the 10th century B.C. Androclus, the son of Athenian King Crodus, followed an Appollo prophecy pinpointing the exact location of his next great Ionian colony: a place where the boar meets the fish.

Fables aside, Ephesus was already a prosperous trading center under the Mycenaeans (11th century B.C.). Word of this wealth reached

EPHESUS AND THE BIRTH OF RELIGION

Ephesus, just outside of Selçuk proper, is the world's best preserved archaeological and historic site. Unlike its contemporaries – such as Rome and Athens – Ephesus' treasures have remained in splendid condition. This antique site was abandoned centuries ago for the coast, remaining virtually untouched by development.

Ephesus' remains reveal the existence of one of the largest ancient trade centers and regional capitals of the ancient Greek colonial period. Its strategic location along the Aegean Coast made it a crucial geographical foothold for virtually every eastern Mediterranean empire that has roamed its soils. From the Hittites and Persians to the Byzantines and Ottomans, this was not only a ground zero port but also the ultimate conquest.

So it comes to no surprise that religion also arose here. The Temple of Artemis, one of the Wonders of the Ancient World, lies in ruin in Ephesus. This temple to the Anatolian goddess of fertility and the hunt drew hundreds of thousands from the empire's four corners in its time. Artemis predates the 6th century B.C., and is thought to be a corruption of the even older Hittite goddess Kybele. As the Greeks colonized what is today Turkey's western coast, they adopted the cult. And so did the Romans (3rd century B.C.).

But as minority religious cults arose throughout the empire, such as the cults of Isis and Mithraism, the Romans' stability became wobbly. One of these was Jewish Christianity. And, thanks to the apostles, Paul and Peter, who allegedly ministered here in the A.D. 30s and 40s, this once-pagan city became one of the foremost Christian pilgrimage sites. Peter is even said to have brought the Virgin Mary here and built a house on the slope of Ephesus.

The Nicene Creed, the yardstick of correct Christian belief, was even ratified as the universal creed of Christendom by the First Council of Ephesus in 431. The city remained one of Christianity's capitals, and remains so even today. Original church elders considered it the epicenter from which the Gospel was spread to the Roman Empire. And from this spot, bishops were installed throughout Asia Minor, extending east to the great city of Antioch.

Unfortunately, a natural build-up of silt flowing from a nearby river, the rise of Constantinople under Christian Emperor Constantine the Great, and the Muslim westward push ended Ephesus' run as one of the prime centers of the ancient world. Today, archaeologists onsite report that only about 15 percent of this once massive city has been unearthed.

rich Lydian King Croesus. He invaded and annexed Ephesus in 560 B.C., and essentially drove out the Ephesians to an area known as Artemision. But the Persians, seeking access to the Mediterranean, toppled Croesus' reign less than two decades later, thus incorporating all of Asia Minor's cities into their growing empire. The proud Ephesians rebelled against the Persian rule by joining in the Ionian Revolt in the Battle of Ephesus in 498 B.C. Ionians gained their independence, but greater Anatolia was only liberated from Persian control about 150 years later when Alexander the Great defeated the Persians in the Battle of Granicus in 334 B.C. After Alexander's untimely passing, Lysimachus, one of his generals, ruled

over much of Asia Minor. During Lysimachus's reign, Ephesus was moved 2 kilometers inland, between Bülbüldagı (Mt. Koressos) and Panayır Dağı (Mt. Pion), beginning its geographical ties with modern Selçuk.

The daily life of Ephesians didn't change much with the power upheavals. Immigrants easily assimilated, education was at the forefront, and so was trade. The cult of the female goddess Artemis, which drew pilgrims from throughout the Ancient world during the Classical Period, was a symbol for women's rights. Female artists thrived, according to the writer Pliny, who later wrote of having seen a depiction of the goddess Diana by the Ephesian painter Timarata.

By the end of the 3rd century B.C., the Syrian King Seleucus I Nicator bloodily removed Lysimachus and absorbed Ephesus into the expanding Seleucid Empire. An ensuing tug of war between the Egyptian Ptolemies and the Seleucids lasted for over a century before the city finally was absorbed by the Romans in 133 B.C. By this time, Ephesus became the capital of Asia Minor, with a reported population of over 250,000; as the largest metropolis in the empire after Rome, it enjoyed a bustling intercontinental trade with the Middle East.

During the 1st century A.D., as the cult of the goddess Diana (Artemis) slowly lost steam, a budding Christian movement, centered around Ephesus, began to take root. Saint Paul, who preached the teachings of Jesus and converted many Ephesians during his three-year stay in the city (A.D. 53–56), was largely responsible for the change. Even the Virgin Mary, led by Saint John the Apostle in A.D. 41, allegedly settled and lived the rest of her days in Ephesus.

In the end, the constant deposit of dirt and sand pushed the city even further inland, near modern-day Selçuk. Despite attempts during the imperial reigns of Nero and Hadrian to divert the flow of the Menderes, the harbor—now five kilometers inland—silted up. Landlocked, Ephesus began its long decline. But it still ranked high as a Christian center; Emperor Theodosius even chose the city's Church of Mary as the setting for the Third Ecumenical Council in A.D. 431.

Sights
GYMNASIUM OF VEDIUS
The first ruins just south of the main entrance are those of the ancient gym and stadium. Built in the 2nd century A.D. by the order of wealthy Ephesians, Publius Vedius Antoninus and his wife Flavia Papiana, the Gymnasium of Vedius is dedicated to the goddess Artemis and to Emperor Antoninus Pius. Its eastern entrance leads to a *palaestra* (courtyard) encircled by tall marble pillars. Along the walls of the Imperial Hall, notice the statues of the gym's benefactors above floors intricately inlaid with mosaics.

Traditionally, gymnasiums were the breeding grounds for the youth, where the arts, sports, literature, drama, and speech were taught daily. At its height, this gym housed cold (frigidarium) and warm (tepidarium) baths; the frigidarium's pool was filled by a large amphora held by a statue of the god of the Cayster/Menderes River. The statue is currently on exhibit at the Izmir Museum.

DOUBLE CHURCH
This 2nd-century A.D. Roman cultural and educational center was known as the Hall of the Muses. When Christianity was adopted as the official religion of Rome, the 260-meter-tall structure became the Church of the Virgin Mary. It owes it name to one of the two aisles in its interior, which was dedicated to the Virgin Mary; the other was dedicated to St. John. The church's baptistery is the best preserved in Asia Minor.

Emperor Theodosius II called the Third Ecumenical Council in this church in A.D. 431. Some 200 bishops attended the multi-day debate that culminated in defining the double nature of Christ as god and man, and Mary as the mother of god. It also denounced as heresy the teachings of the Archbishop of Constantinople, Nestorius, who rejected the divine nature of Christ and claimed Mary not as the mother of god, but as the mother of a human being.

ARCADIAN WAY
This 11-meter-wide pedestrian lane is situated between the Harbor Baths and the great theater. Traders and sailors entering the city from the harbor first set foot along this once magnificently marbled street. Lofty colonnades were added along the 530-meter-long stretch during the reign of Emperor Arcadius (A.D. 395–408). Shops and galleries filled both of its flanks. At its height, it was one of only three lit avenues throughout the Roman Empire, along with avenues in Rome and Antioch. Some 50 lights lit up its colonnades; sewers ran along its length beneath the marble flagstones.

Just east of Arcadian street sits Ephesus'

© TOM DEMPSEY

A graveyard for gladiators was discovered in 2007 beneath the 2,000-year-old remains of Ephesus's Grand Theater – the ancient world's largest amphitheater.

Grand Theater, on the slope of Panayır Dağı (Mt. Pion). Built under the reign of Lysimachus (3rd century B.C.), the theater was greatly enlarged by the Romans three centuries later. It's the largest of its kind in Anatolia, with a seating capacity of 25,000. It took excavators about six decades to carve this arena from the side of the hill. Sixty-six rows of seats are divided by two *diazomas* (aisles), forming three horizontal sections. The lower section's marble seating with sweeping backs was reserved for dignitaries; the Emperor's Box is nearest to center stage. The rest of the populace entered from the top. Reliefs, statues, and niches once ornamented the facade of the three-story-high stage building. During its heyday, this gigantic arena held the big events of the day, whether it'd be a play, sermon, philosophical discourse, or gladiator bout. St. Paul delivered a sermon condemning paganism on its stage in the 1st century A.D., riling shopkeepers who made a bundle on the Artemisian cult. Make sure to climb to the upper *cavea* (tier) to check out the striking view of the archaeological park.

Exiting the theater, the first building on Arcadian Way is the impressive ruins of the two-story **Theatre Gymnasium.** This structure was mainly used as a sports arena. The four-story **Harbor Baths,** located on the opposite end of the street, were built in A.D. 2. Nicknamed the Baths of Constantine on account of the restoration that was undertaken by the Roman emperor in the mid-3rd century, this was the lane's largest building with a width of 160 meters and a length of 170 meters. A peristyle forecourt led to a central bath-gymnasium complex, with rooms of various sizes that served for cultural and spiritual instruction.

SACRED WAY
So named because it once led to the Temple of Artemis beyond Panayır Dağı (Mt. Pion), the Sacred Way today spans the distance between the Grand Theater and the Library of Celsus. The Marble Road, its other moniker, was originally laid in the 1st century A.D., but was rebuilt 400 years later. Its western flank delineates the State Agora's wall, upon which a higher platform was constructed during Nero's reign to accommodate pedestrians. Look for the footprint next to the ridge; it leads to the brothel, and may constitute history's very first advertisement campaign!

The **State Agora** was *the* original mall, and arguably one of the largest in Asia Minor. Built in the 3rd century B.C., today's ruins date from the wicked Caracalla's reign (A.D. 211–217). The 110-square-meter marketplace was surrounded by columns and had three gates: one leading to the theater on the northeast; one facing the harbor to the west; and a third opening to the Library of Celsus. Its northern wall was wide open, while a portico with rows of bustling shops ringed its remaining perimeter. A sundial and water clock were featured in its center.

LIBRARY OF CELSUS
The Library of Celsus is Ephesus' most memorable building. Astonishingly well preserved,

COURTESY OF REPUBLIC OF TURKEY CULTURE AND TOURISM MINISTRY

The Temple of Hadrian at Ephesus was commissioned in the 2nd century by its namesake Roman emperor.

the library was constructed in A.D. 117 by the Consul Julius Aquila as a mausoleum for his father, Roman Governor of the Asian Provinces Julius Celsus Polemaeanus. Celsus' grave remains beneath the ground floor, across from the entrance. A statue of Athena, the goddess of wisdom, once stood guard over his remains; the statue's current whereabouts are unknown. The library's collection of volumes, an estimated 12,000 scrolls, constituted the world's third-largest collection after Alexandria and Pergamum. The rolled tomes were kept in cupboards in wall niches, with double walls behind them to temper the effects of atmospheric conditions, particularly humidity.

The two-level facade, which actually hides a three-story book repository, consists of three entrances interspersed by statues. But these are only copies of the originals, which somehow found their way to the Ephesus Museum in Vienna in 1910. The goddesses of wisdom (Sophia), knowledge (Episteme), intelligence (Ennoia), and valor (Arete) symbolized Celsus' virtues. A fire ravaged most of the library's

interior; its exterior was redeemed centuries later with the addition of a monumental pool.

CURETES WAY

One of Ephesus' three main thoroughfares, the Curetes Way slices the city diagonally from the State Agora to the Library of Celsus. Early 20th-century archaeologists named the road according to an inscription found in one of the stones that referred to the Curetes (a.k.a the priests of Artemis). In its heyday, statues and shops lined both its flanks, along with fountains and monuments. During one of the many earthquakes that beleaguered the city, many structures, particularly the colonnades, were damaged. Blocks and other columns salvaged from Ephesus' other buildings were used in their reconstruction.

The most stunning structure along this stretch is the **Temple of Hadrian.** Built around A.D. 120 by Publius Quintilius, a relatively unknown bourgeois person of the time, the temple was dedicated to the Emperor Hadrian, Artemis, and the Ephesians. The facade's four

SOUTHERN AEGEAN COAST

Corinthian columns bolster a curved arch, which features a relief of the goddess of victory, Tyche, in its center. Interestingly, the side colonnades are square. The monument's interior bears four friezes that depict the various myths related to the creation of Ephesus. The inscribed pedestals fronting the temple facade bear the names of Galerius, Maximianus, Diocletianus, and Constantius I, suggesting that the statues of these imperial gents may have stood above them. They too disappeared into the ether.

Along the way, you'll notice the **Slope Houses** (15TL) near the Library of Celsus on the rise of Bülbül Dağı. This is the proverbial jewel in Ephesus' crown, a definite must-see for visitors! The city's upper class lived among these residences during the 1st–7th centuries A.D. Their impressively colonnaded and tiled interiors were impeccably preserved, thanks to the alluvial silting that buried them over time. Reached by a steep flight of stairs behind the shops on Curetes Way, Slope House 1 and 2 are currently on display. More than any others in this region, these buildings put all historical rhetoric aside to show, in stunning details, the lifestyle of the period.

The **Fountain of Trajan** once stood on Curetes Way. Unfortunately, not much remains of the towering statue of the early-2nd-century emperor, aside from a single marble foot. The awesome statues of Dionysus that beautified this monument are now at the Ephesus Museum in Selçuk.

At the intersection of Curetes Way and the Marble Road stands Ephesus' **brothel.** Funny how the mere mention of this structure evokes comments from tourists; during its heyday, swinging by was just as common as going out for a jug of olive oil! Its lobby to the west of the entrance has a colorful mosaic floor, which captures the four seasons. The main bath next to it has an elliptical pool, which boasts a pretty mosaic featuring a trio of women eating and drinking, a server, and a couple of house pets nibbling on crumbs. The chambers on the 2nd floor were used to entertain clients. A statue of the Hellenic fertility god

Priapus, an overly endowed midget, was discovered near this structure. It also resides at the nearby Ephesus Museum.

Ephesus' **latrine** was built in the 1st century A.D. The use of these men-only communal toilets wasn't free. Taking a closer look beneath the carved marble, one realizes that the system was rather advanced for its time. The gutter below was constantly awash with running water. The "bench" was covered by a roof, while the public room's center remained open to the elements. A sunken pool in its center was used for catching rainwater; the rest of the floor was tiled in mosaics.

The **Hercules Gate** marks the end of Curetes Way. Named after the large Herculean reliefs on its posts, the gate is believed to have arrived at its current location in the 4th century A.D. This new entrance narrowed access to the street, preventing vehicular access.

ON THE HEIGHTS

Directly to the right of the Hercules Gate is a side street that leads up to the **Domitian Square.** It's so named for its central **Domitian Temple,** built to honor Roman Emperor Domitian (1st century A.D.). To its left, you'll find the **Polio Fountain,** which distributed water that flowed straight to the city from aqueducts through a clever system of terra cotta pipes. Opposite, the **Memmius Monument** commemorates the noted Roman orator Memmius.

Ambling further up the hill, the scattered ruins of the **Prytaneion** come into view. The building was dedicated to Hestia, the goddess of the hearth, and contained Ephesus' perpetually burning sacred flame. The pit, once the center of the Prytaneion, marks the spot of the flame. All of Ephesus' religious and official ceremonies were held here since Lysimachus ordered its construction (3rd century B.C.). Today's ruins, however, date from a renovation undertaken during the reign of Augustus (1st century A.D.). Two crucial statues of Ephesian Artemis were discovered in the Prytaneion; they're housed in the Ephesus Museum. The last set of ruins on the climb are those of the

Beuleterion/Odeon. This small theater, with a capacity of 1,500, held meetings of the *boulea* (senate) and also functioned as a concert hall. Dating form the 2nd century A.D., the building's benefactors were the wealthy Ephesians Publius Vedius Antoninus and his wife Flavia Papiana.

The alleged **Tomb of St. Luke** is located on the other side of Meryem Ana Yolu, marked along the highway just beyond this last set of ruins. The remains of Luke the Evangelist, the author of the Gospel of Luke and the Acts of the Apostles, were allegedly buried in the circular building onsite before they were transported to Istanbul's Church of the Holy Apostles—today's Fatih Mosque.

GROTTO OF THE SEVEN SLEEPERS

A paved road heads east about 0.8 kilometers from the Gymnasium of Vedius to the Grotto of the Seven Sleepers. As legend has it, seven young Christian boys, fearing the Decian Persecution (A.D. 250), fled to the cave in an attempt to sidestep Roman guards. Being Christian at the time was a serious crime. Once the guards reached the grotto they callously barricaded the boys inside. The septet fell asleep for what seemed a night, and woke up to the tremors of an earthquake that miraculously reopened the cave. Famished, the boys then walked to town only to realize they were strolling through 5th-century Ephesus. In the two centuries that had elapsed, their religion, once condemned, was now the common faith. The Seven Sleepers, who later died of natural causes, were buried in the grotto. The Sleepers also appear in the Koran. But in this version, the boys, accompanied by a dog, slept 309 years. A church, made of crypts, was built above this grotto. Christians fleeing Roman persecution built similar structures throughout Anatolia. A rural concession stand serving *gözleme* (Turkish pastry) and *ayran* (yogurt beverage) faces the grotto.

Festivals

The first week of May heralds Ephesus' International Festival of Culture and Tourism, a time that highlights the antique park's rich past through historical reenactments and colorful folkloric performances.

During June and July each year, the antique Grand Theater comes alive with the **International Izmir Festival** (www.iksev. org). Attending one of the concerts and ballet performances by world-renowned talents, like Elton John and the Vienna Chamber Philharmonic, is highly recommended.

Getting There and Around

If you haven't opted for a tour or a rental vehicle, a *dolmuş* (communal taxi) service from Selçuk (2TL) runs the three-kilometer stretch between Ephesus and Selçuk. Taxis (10TL) are also widely available.

The main entrance to Ephesus is located just south of Dr. Sabri Yayla Bulvarı. The southern entrance, Güney Kapısı, is off of Meryem Ana Yolu (D550 Hwy.), near the tomb of Saint Luke. Walking is the best way to get around.

◖ ŞIRINCE

One of the most attractive villages on the Aegean coast, Şirince—meaning pretty—is set amidst sprawling peach orchards and olive groves in a bowl set at 1000 feet above sea level. It's surrounded by pine-blanketed hills and boasts 100 or so historic residences, all commanding spectacular views of the lush valley below. Whitewashed stucco abodes with red-tiled roofs are a throwback to the 19th century, when the town was predominantly Greek.

Historically, Ephesian Christians retreated to Şirince when the Islamic Selçuks conquered the Aegean in the 13th century. The local *Şircelis* were later displaced to the Greek Macedonian town of Kavala during the population exchange of 1924. In turn, Muslim Kavalans trickled into Şirince, bringing along their Baltic winemaking skills. Thanks to this rich heritage, the town has earned historic preservation status.

Today, Şirince, with its rustic charm, is enjoying tremendous popularity. Its narrow streets and town center teem with village women peddling tatted lace, homemade

SOUTHERN AEGEAN COAST

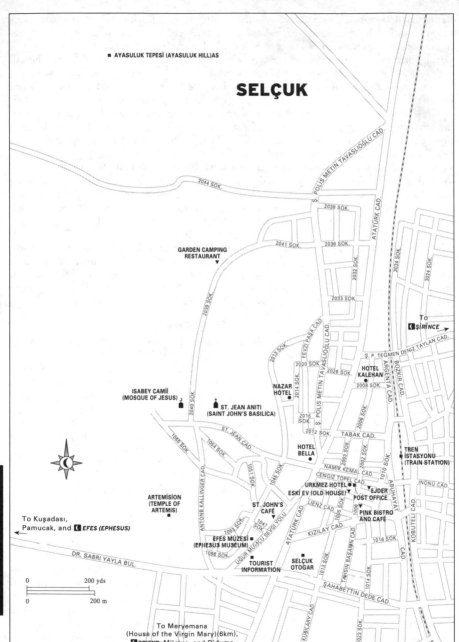

SELÇUK

AYASULUK TEPESİ (AYASULUK HILL)AS

POLİS METİN TAVASLIOĞLU CAD.

2044 SOK.

ATATÜRK CAD.

2038 SOK.

2041 SOK.   2036 SOK.

GARDEN CAMPING
RESTAURANT

2039 SOK.

2032 SOK.

3024 SOK.

3074 SOK.

2033 SOK.

2013 SOK.

To
ŞİRİNCE

FEVZİ PAŞA CAD.

Ş. P. TEĞMEN DENİZ TAYLAN CAD.

2020 SOK.   2028 SOK.

HOTEL
KALEHAN

BOZKIR CAD.

ARGENTA CAD.

2008 SOK.

ISABEY CAMİİ
(MOSQUE OF JESUS)

2040 SOK.

NAZAR
HOTEL

2014 SOK.

POLİS METİN TAVASLIOĞLU CAD.

2026 SOK.

ST. JEAN ANITI
(SAINT JOHN'S BASILICA)

2016
SDK.

2012 SOK.

TABAK CAD.

2006 SOK.

2003 SOK.

1065 SOK.   1064 SOK.

ST. JEAN CAD.

HOTEL
BELLA

2002 SOK.

1010 SOK.

TREN
İSTASYONU
(TRAIN STATION)

İNÖNÜ CAD.

NAMIK KEMAL CAD.

CENGİZ TOPEL CAD.

1063 SOK.

ARTEMİSİON
(TEMPLE OF
ARTEMIS)

ANTONB KALLINGER CAD.

1061 SOK.

1045 SOK.

URKMEZ HOTEL

ESKİ EV (OLD HOUSE)

LIENZ CAD.

1095 SOK.

EJDER
POST OFFICE

ABUHAYA

1066

PINK BISTRO
AND CAFÉ

KOBUTELİ CAD.

CAD.

ST. JOHN'S
CAFÉ

1062 SOK.

1047
SOK.

UĞUR MUMCU SEVGİ YOLU

ATATÜRK CAD.

KIZILAY CAD.

1016 SOK.

To Kuşadası,
Pamucak, and EFES (EPHESUS)

DR. SABRİ YAYLA BUL.

EFES MÜZESİ
(EPHESUS MUSEUM)

1066 SOK.

TOURIST
INFORMATION

SELÇUK
OTOGAR

TAHSİN BAŞARAN CAD.

1013 SOK.

1014 SOK.

ŞAHABETTİN DEDE CAD.

KUBİLAY CAD.

1023 SOK.

0   200 yds

0   200 m

To Meryemana
(House of the Virgin Mary) (6km),
PRIENE, Miletus, and Didyma

© AVALON TRAVEL

jam, and succulent olive oil to the busloads of visitors. Local fruity wines draw hordes to Artemis, a restaurant housed in the village's most eminent building—an adeptly restored 19th-century schoolhouse. Adding to Şirince's fame are the feisty Nişanyans, a couple of celebrated travel writers who fled Istanbul's rat race in the mid 1990s to open a B&B in the village. Also worth a look are the fading frescoes of the **Church of Saint John the Baptist,** which is currently being restored thanks to donations from the American Society of Ephesus George B. Quatman Foundation. Built on the ruins of an early church, this stone building dates back to 1805.

Şirince is located seven kilometers east of Selçuk. A *dolmuş* service connects the village from the Selçuk train station, every 15–25 minutes.

Accommodations and Food

If you fall to temptation and decide to overnight in Şirince, there's no better spot than **◖ Nişanyan Eveleri** (follow signs from the town entrance, 0232/898-3208, www.nisanyan.com, 100–260TL). Müjde and Sevan Nişanyan converted several properties into a series of inns that appeal to all budgets, from the barest of rooms to suites with complementary breakfast of black caviar and French champagne. There are three private residences, five charming Ilyastepe cottages, the quirky five-room Nişanyan Inn, and the inexpensive seven-room Kilisealtı Guesthouse. The makeshift restaurant, recently expanded to six tables, is reminiscent of Tuscany. Try their version of the homey dish of *Kuzu Inçik,* a roasted lamb shank so tender it falls off the bone.

The **◖ Şirince Terrace Houses** (see website for directions, 0232/898-3133, www.ephesushousessirince.com, €130, additional adult €15) offers three large cottages that are beautifully appointed in a traditional Turkish decor. Each of owner Ömer Samlı's chalets comes equipped with a large kitchen, bathroom, and several guestrooms. This is a great choice for families on a budget.

Drawing on its Baltic, Hellenic, and Ottoman roots, the cuisine of Şirince is farm-fresh and luscious. The village's schoolhouse remains one of its biggest tourist attractions, made even sweeter when a sly restaurateur revamped it as **Artemis** (0232/898-3240, www.artemisrestaurant.com, 15TL). This wine boutique/restaurant features 20 locally produced wine varieties, and arguably the best bites in town.

Try the local dish of *keşkek* (barley lamb stew) with a sprinkling of the sneeze-inducing local red pepper at **Arşipel Greek Café and Restaurant** (0232/898-3216, 12TL). This place is notoriously busy with tour groups, who not only come for the food but also for the stunning views from its broad terrace.

SELÇUK

Selçuk seems a castoff transportation hub in the shadow of Ephesus' spectacular ruins, just three kilometers to the west. But there's way more to it than meets the eye. It boasts a busy, colorful street market each Saturday (check out the ridiculously cheap genuine-fake designer clothing). It's also the much-lauded nesting haunt for hundreds of storks. The town of Selçuk is probably best known for its centuries-old camel and oil wrestling festivals. Ruin-wise, the pint-sized Ephesus Museum is nothing short of stunning; it houses the remains found at Ephesus. That is, whatever wasn't ruthlessly carted off to European museums. The House of the Virgin Mary, the 6th-century Basilica of St. John, and the eons-old Temple of Artemis—one of the Seven Wonders of the ancient world—are also popular sights. With so much to see, you may find this charming, blue-collar town's less expensive inns well suited as a base. For exhaustive information about Ephesus and Selçuk, visit the municipality of Selçuk's informative website (www.selcuk.bel.tr/eng).

Sights

Thankfully, the opening hours of Selçuk's attractions are synchronized. Museums and monuments open daily, with the exception of Mondays, 8 A.M.–7 P.M. May–September and 8 A.M.–5 P.M. October–April.

EFES MÜZESI
(EPHESUS MUSEUM)

The five sections of the Efes Müzesi (a block west of Atatürk Cad., across from the Tourist Information office, 0232/892-6010, 5TL) are chock-full of Ephesian relics dating from the Archaic period all the way to the Turkish era. What holds the attention of most tourists, however, are the artifacts that date from Artemisian, Roman, and Byzantine eras. Allow 90 minutes, at the very least, to stroll through its five sections.

The displays open with the **Terrace Houses Section,** whose Roman relics have been gradually unearthed in the last 50 years. These include plans of the hillside houses of Ephesus' privileged class, and photos of the excavations. Several showcases contain medical and cosmetic artifacts, as well as religious and cultic items. In an adjacent niche are a 3rd-century fresco of Socrates and a statue of Artemis the Huntress; both were retrieved from one of these plush abodes, attesting to the importance of philosophy and spirituality in everyday Roman life. To the left is a 2nd-century A.D. bust of Roman emperor Marcus Aurelius, along with statuettes of the virile Greek god Priapus and Egyptian deity Bes. Despite their enormous phalluses, neither gods were esteemed for their manhood. Rather, Priapus was a guardian deity who thwarted the evil eye. His peer, the ugly, stumpy Bes, protected households, but particularly kept an eye on mothers and children. The pièces de résistance, however, is the large bronze statue of **Eros with Dolphin,** once a centerpiece of a 2nd-century fountain, and a copy of a Roman statue of Eros by Greek sculptor Lysippos (4th century B.C.).

The room of the **Fountain Artifacts** reveals relics from the Pollio, Trajan, and Laecanus fountains at Ephesus. To the left of the entrance are a bust of **Zeus** and a headless statue of **Aphrodite,** both dated to the 1st century A.D. Just beyond is a display of statues of Greek mythological deities Odysseus and Polyphemus, which adorned the Pollio fountain near Ephesus' Dolmitian Square. Two impressive stunningly carved statues of

Dionysius, the Greek god of wine, are also on display. The first is with a satyr, a male companion versed in poetry; the other is his dazzling marble likeness flanked by the imperial family. There's also the enchantress Aphrodite with her trusty oyster shell, among a variety of other statues. The series of busts on the right once belonged to the statues gracing the Laecanus Bassus Fountain.

The **Recent Findings Room** features Ephesian discoveries unearthed in the last three years. The display case to the right of the entrance holds Byzantine relics. Amid the collections of coins and jewelry on the left, there are a few pre-Roman Ephesian coins depicting the city symbol and a bee on one side and Artemis' deer on the other. There are also theater masks fashioned of leather, which were recovered inside Ephesus' Grand Theater. This room also features the stunning **Ivory frieze** excavated from an upper terrace of one of Ephesus' hillside houses; it details a war scene involving Roman emperor Trajan and his soldiers fighting eastern barbarians.

The **Garden** section contains gravesite-related artifacts, including a sarcophagus dating back to the 2nd century A.D. It's stunningly adorned with figures of Moses, and was recycled, according to the inscription on the lid, during the Byzantine era.

The **Grave Artifacts Room** boasts exhibits discovered inside regional tombs. To the left are depictions of Anatolian burial customs. But the small relics, found in a grave in front of the Basilica of St. John, are perhaps the most telling exhibit in this museum. They date back to the Mycenaean age (13th century B.C.) and single-handedly attest to Ephesus' long history.

Of the last two sections, the **Artemis Room** is perhaps the most striking, and undoubtedly the exclamation point to an essential visit to the Ephesus Museum. This section, commemorating the Mother Goddess Artemis, contains impressive statues and related artifacts. These statues (1st century A.D.) were found by accident in Ephesus' Prytaneion, the town's religious and ceremonial center. Both, the Great Artemis and the Beautiful Artemis, are covered with rounded protrusions. These were once believed to be accessory breasts. But scholars now believe these mounds may have been sacrificed bull testicles, further emphasizing this most venerated goddess's role in fertility.

ARTEMISION
(TEMPLE OF ARTEMIS)

One of the Seven Wonders of the Ancient World, the remains of Artemision (on the road to Kuşadası, between Ephesus and Selçuk, free) are frighteningly dismal. Just the scrappy foundations of this once surreal monument attest to what was once one of the largest constructions of antiquity. Financed by the wealthy Lydian King Croesus, it took 120 years to erect the marble monument; Cretan architect Chersiphron and his son Metagenes did the initial design and construction. The original temple was built in 550 B.C., with just 36 columns, each about four meters in height. And, according to Roman author Pliny the Elder (A.D. 23–59), this marshy site was specifically selected for the monumental build due to its softer ground. The idea behind this theory was that the soil's softness would absorb the shocks of eventual seismic activity. Others believe that the Temple of Artemis was erected on this site, already sacred to Kybele, the ancient Anatolian Mother Goddess, to carry on a cultic tradition.

The temple was constructed and destroyed several times. It first fell prey to a mad arsonist and later toppled during a massive earthquake in the beginning of the 4th century B.C. Within a century, a new and improved Artemision was erected right atop its previous location. This newer structure contained 127 columns, each measuring a whopping 18 meters, delineating a space that spanned 115 meters in length and 55 meters in width. That's four times the size of Athens' Parthenon! It stood for the better part of six centuries before being razed by the Goths in their furious assault of the region in A.D. 262. Two centuries later, as the majority of Ephesians were converting to Christianity, the Temple of Artemis lost its cultic allure and became a ready-made quarry for the construction of local churches.

ST. JEAN ANITI
(SAINT JOHN'S BASILICA)

After bringing the Virgin Mary to Ephesus in A.D. 41, St. John the Apostle spent the last years of his life in the region, preaching the gospel and writing some of his momentous texts. He was buried in the southern slope of Ayosoluk Hill. During the 4th century, a small chapel was constructed over the grave to commemorate the 300th anniversary of his death. The building was enlarged to a magnificent basilica (to the right of St. Jean Cad., located just 500 m. west of Atatürk Cad., 5TL) during the reign of Emperor Justinian (A.D. 527–565). The monumental church was constructed of stone and brick in the shape of a cross, topped by six domes. Rather than the typical square base crowned with cupolas, this layout was a rarity for its time. St. John's marble tomb was exalted as one of the Middle Ages' most sacred sites; it's in the center of the sanctuary, right beneath the lofty central dome. During the 7th and 8th centuries, ramparts were erected around the structure to fend against constant Arabian attacks. But by 1330, the Selçuk Aydınoğlu Emirate had conquered Selçuk. The basilica was converted into a mosque. Tamerlane's fearsome Mongols razed the building in 1402. And whatever was left of the basilica's original stones were pillaged in the subsequent centuries for use as construction material.

There are some exhibits onsite worth checking out. These include the columns in the courtyard, which bear the monograms of Emperor Justinian and his wife Theodora. There's also a 5th-century baptistery located north of the nave, while the interior houses 10th-century frescoes that depict St. John and Jesus. The excavations around the basilica's periphery continue under the supervision of Ekrem Akurgal and the financial support of the American Society of Ephesus George B. Quatman Foundation.

SOUTHERN AEGEAN COAST

© JESSICA TAMTÜRK

one of the few building blocks remaining amid the shell of the 6th-century Saint John's Basilica

ISABEY CAMII
(MOSQUE OF JESUS)

The Mosque of Jesus (at the intersection of St. Jean Cad. and 2040th Sok., dawn–dusk, free) is the most ornate example of Selçukian architecture still standing today. It was conceived by the master Syrian architect Ali son of Mushimish al-Damishki between 1374 and 1375. The Mosque of Jesus features stones and columns culled from Ephesus' great monuments. Its asymmetric interior design was highly unorthodox for its time; none of its windows, doors, and domes were designed to match. But a mosque it is, all the way down to the geometric carving and Koranic calligraphy etched in stone that adorn its lofty marble entrance. Inside, the dome, tiled in turquoise and blue tiles, seemingly floats above a *mihrab* (niche in wall pointing to Mecca) and pulpit, both sculpted of marble.

MERYEMANA
(HOUSE OF THE VIRGIN MARY)

It's believed that Saint John brought the Virgin Mary to Ephesus in the mid-1st century A.D., and later built her this small house (dawn–dusk, parking 5TL) atop present-day Selçuk's lofty Bülbül Dağı. Missionaries from Izmir discovered the four dilapidated walls that upheld the small stone abode in 1891, following German nun Anne Catherine Emmerich's visions (more than 50 years earlier) of Mary's final whereabouts. The Izmir missionaries further learned that the Christians of Ephesus visited the site annually on August 15. This yearly service continues since the days when the Christians of Ephesus made the pilgrimage to this site from distant mountain villages. Although the Vatican has yet to officially recognize its authenticity due to the lack of scientific evidence, four popes, including the current Pope Benedict XVI, visited the holy site.

The House of the Virgin Mary is considered holy for Muslims as well. Christ was referred to as a great prophet in the Koran, and his mother is the sole woman referred to by name in the Islamic scriptures. Muslims also make pilgrimages to this house, marking their

SOUTHERN AEGEAN COAST

visit with scraps of cloth or paper pinned to a wooden casing inside the entrance. A wish is made during the process, with the strong belief that the sanctity of the site will assist in its materialization.

Mass at the House of the Virgin Mary is held Monday–Saturday at 7:15 A.M. and 6:30 P.M. An additional service takes place on Sundays at 10:30 A.M. The woodsy grounds include resting areas ideal for picnicking. The pleasant **Café Turco** (0232/894-1010, from 7TL) serves a variety of special coffees, as well as salads and sandwiches.

The House of the Virgin Mary is located 7 kilometers from the center of Selçuk. Since there's no *dolmuş* (communal taxi) servicing the site, hiring a cab (15TL) or visiting by tour is just about the only way to get there.

Priene, Miletus, and Didyma

Cheekily referred to as PMD by the local tourism sector, Priene, Miletus, and Didyma are among the best-preserved ancient cities of the Ionian realm in Anatolia. While these history-packed locations are mere diminutives next to the magnificence of nearby Ephesus, an outing will prove its worth in gold. The views of the lush Büyük Menderes Valley from Priene's heights is worth the trip alone. Note that all three parks keep the same hours of operation and entrance fees: 8 A.M.–7:30 P.M. daily in summer, until 5:30 P.M. in winter; 3TL. Detailed maps and historical guides are sold at each park's entrance.

Consider slating a day to trample around these ruins—and a dip in the Aegean Sea at Altınkum Beach as an added bonus—by either joining one of the myriad tours offered by local travel companies and cooperatives or by renting a vehicle. Most regional hotels provide similar tour arrangements through contracted agencies; ask them to schedule the PMD tour when you make the hotel reservation, keeping in mind that the availability and frequency of tours are greatly reduced in the off-season. If driving the PMD route from Kuşadası, head southwest on the D-525, following the haphazard signposts for Söke. Continue just one kilometer past Güllübahçe's outlet malls and restaurants to Priene (about 36 km. from Kuşadası). Miletus is another 22 kilometers due south through the vast cotton fields on either side of the Menderes River delta. The ancient site of Didyma—a.k.a. Didim or Yenihisar—lies 19 kilometers south of Miletus. Altınkum Beach is a five-minute drive south from Miletus, along Didim's Atatürk Bulvarı.

PRIENE

Propped on a small mesa, the antique settlement of Priene (0256/547-1165) stands in the shadow of the looming Mount Mykale, overlooking the vast and incredibly green Büyük Menderes flood plain. From its lofty location, it's hard to believe Priene was once a port city with its lowest level lying at the mouth of the river and offering sweeping views of the Aegean from its acropolis atop the city. Priene was built on a military-inspired grid plan, essentially duplicating the innovative city design of Miletus. It rose to fame in the 4th century B.C. as the entertainment center and member of the mighty Ionian League of Cities. Much of what can be seen today are remains of the sweeping monuments constructed to bolster its political status during the rise of Asia Minor. These include the **theater,** the once wooden-roofed **bouleuterion** (senate house), parts of its seven-meter thick city walls, sprawling private houses, gymnasium, and stadium. Interesting for its grandeur—and apparent lack of deterioration—is the roomy claw-footed imperial seating located in the center of the first row of the theater. But the most prominent monument, however, is the **Temple of Athena,** which was built by Pythius of Halicarnassus, the architect of the famed mausoleum in Bodrum.

MILETUS

After Priene's sublime views, the marshlands surrounding the ruins of Miletus (Balat Köyüm, Didim, 0256/875-5206) provide a stark geographical difference between the two erstwhile Ionian cities. It's interesting to realize that today's landlocked Miletus once also sat on the edge of the Aegean. Much like

Ephesus, it finally succumbed to constant silting during the Selçuk era (12th century A.D.). The area today holds some remains of Miletus' prominence, which lasted for 14 centuries (700 B.C.–A.D. 700). Some of its lofty natives gave rise to new schools of thought, at a time when mainland Greece was entrenched in its bleak, cultural Dark Ages. Chief among Miletus' luminaries was the pre-Socratic philosopher Thales of Miletus, who was one of the Seven Sages of Greece and also considered the "father of science" for his breakthroughs in the fields of astronomy and geometry. But there was also Hecataeus of Miletus (550–446 B.C.), the first historian of ancient Greece; he actually coined the word "history." Even Miletus' alphabet was adopted by ancient Greece as its official alphabet. The ruins that remain today mostly date back to a Roman beautification project (2nd century B.C.). Among them is the striking 15,000-spectator **Roman amphitheater,** best seen from its top tier, and the **Baths of Faustina,** a complex of water fountains dedicated to the god Meander and named after the wife of Marcus Aurelius (A.D. 164). For majestic views of the valley and the entire site, climb to the Turkish fortress above the theater.

DIDYMA

Rounding out the archaeological outing is Didyma (0256/811-0035). The impressive **Temple of Apollo** (a.k.a. *Didymaion*) was fronted by 120 20-meter-high columns. It was chief among the oracles of Ancient Greece, rivaling the size of the Delphi in Greece. The largest monument of its time (6th century B.C.), the Temple of Apollo was constructed entirely of alabaster marble. Priests waited just beyond the colonnaded entrance to communicate queries to and answers from the oracle. A walk through the stone rubble will reveal a colossal **Head of Medusa.** The road that connects Didyma to Miletus today stands directly atop the Sacred Way, which served essentially the same purpose. But Trajan made sure that it did so on a grand scale when he commissioned it in the 1st century A.D. Spectacular sarcophagi, sphinx, and lion statues graced the shoulders of the antique road.

Entertainment and Events
FESTIVALS

Every year in late January (usually the third weekend), **Camel Wrestling Festivals** are in full swing along the Aegean littoral. Selçuk is considered one of the centers of this centuries-old tradition, in which hundreds of spectators watch these colorfully-garbed, 900-kilo stags "wrestle" each other. Since 2000, the matches have been organized in a desolate field close to Pamucak Beach (5–7TL). Since there's no seating, bring along a garbage bag to sit on, as well as adequate clothing to protect from the seasonal cold and rain. Make sure to arrive early; the competition for space lining the field is fierce.

For a different kind of contact sport, Selçuk's **Oil Wrestling festival** (first Sunday in May) rates second in popularity after Edirne's. It features dozens of *pehlivans* (wrestlers), slicked in olive oil from head to toe, who take on each other to the point of surrender or exhaustion, whichever comes first. Event organizers make sure that there's plenty of plastic seating available for spectators.

The **Selçuk/Efes Festival** (first week in September) features traditional Turkish—and worldwide-folk song and dance at the Roman theater at the ancient site of Ephesus. The town also comes alive with a variety of music concerts. It's also an arts expo, filled with artisans displaying their mastery in carving, weaving, pottery and ceramics. The event translates into a great opportunity to purchase a truly indigenous piece of art.

NIGHTLIFE

A night on the town in Selçuk always involves heading to **Pink Bistro and café** (Siegburg Cad. 24, 0232/892-9801, 10 P.M.–4 A.M. daily high season, until 2 A.M. in low season, mixed drinks 10TL). It's Selçuk's oldest pub, where Efes beer (3TL) seems to grace every table on the crowded street terrace near Cengiz Topel Caddesi.

Accommodations

For those wishing to avoid Kuşadası's raucous resorts or if Şirince's charming B&Bs aren't your thing, the hotels in Selçuk are a more centrally located choice—one that's inexpensive to boot. The best by far is (**Hotel Bella** (St. John Cad. 7, 0232/892-3944, www.hotelbella. com, from 70TL). Just across from St. John's Basilica, the Bella excels with its friendly staff and its generous made-to-order breakfasts. Traditional in decor, each of the 11 guestrooms boasts a hand-woven *kilim* (Turkish carpet). The spacious, yet cozy, rooftop terrace/café is fabulously Ottoman and very unpretentious. The free Wi-Fi and transportation to local sites, as well as Bella's succulent Turkish fare, are all definite bonuses.

The **Nazar Hotel** (2019 Sok. 14, 0232/892-2222, www.nazarhotel.com, €35 with a/c) is one of the few inns with a pool in Selçuk. This is certainly a plus when visiting in the heat of summer. While the rooms at the family-run Nazar are larger than expected, with modern en suite baths, not all come with air-conditioning—a must July–September. A generous four-course dinner of homemade Turkish delicacies costs (15TL) is one of the best spreads in town.

Aside from its affordability, the **Urkmez Hotel** (Namik Kemal Cad. 20, 0232/892-6312, www.urkmezhotel.com, s. €14–20) truly stands out with simple, yet immaculately clean, accommodations. The Ozkan duo of brothers who run this charming set of 15 rooms are delightfully funny and ready to please. The rooftop terrace, which overlooks Castle Hill and the stork nests over the nearby aqueduct, is a nice setting for an evening drink. Expect all the regular conveniences in this centrally-located hotel, without a high price tag.

The **Hotel Kalehan** (Atatürk Cad. 49, 0232/892-6154, www.kalehan.com, US$65–120) is Selçuk's largest hotel. The Kalehan promotes a boutique feel, thanks to collections of Ottoman antiques strewn throughout its public spaces. The inn is comprised of a pair of historical townhouses with a total of 52 rooms. Owner Hakan Ergir succeeded in creating an easy-going atmosphere throughout every room in the hotel. The pool, surrounded by a manicured garden, is the prerequisite oasis for traveling families or those seeking quietude after a long day of traipsing through ruins. Turkish Mediterranean fare is served in the Kalehan's rustic dining room, which, hallelujah, remains open all day.

Food

Selçuk is a bastion for simple traditional meals, comprised of farm-fresh meat and cold veggie dishes. *The* restaurant to people-watch and taste the local bounty is (**Ejder** (Cengiz Topel Cad. 9, 0232/892-3296, 8:30 A.M.–11 P.M. daily, 7–15TL) in the center of town. While travelers swoon over *köfte* (meatball) platters, the real delicacy in this region is meat on a skewer. The Ejders excel at this, with delectable grilled lamb and chicken kebabs. Vegans will be pleased with this mom-and-pop's large variety of locally produced veggie sides drizzled in olive oil.

Eski Ev (Old House, 1005 Sok. 1/A, 0232/892-9357, 8:30 A.M.–midnight, 6–14TL) provides an unbeatable atmosphere. This family-run restaurant is set in an old house with an attached terrace, filled with the cackle of birds and rich with fruit trees and blooming perennials. Grab one of the rattan chairs outback and order the house's much-lauded meat stew, which comes piping hot atop a copper plate.

Located behind the hill of the Selçuk castle, **Garden Camping Restaurant** (Kale Altı 4, 0232/892-6165, 8 A.M.–11 P.M. high season only, 7–14TL) is a welcome culinary reward after the trek to Castle Hill. While the camping site and lack of diners do little to encourage patronage, the onsite restaurant is inviting with a breezy garden and shady pavilion. The trout pond ensures that the fish featured on the menu are as fresh as can be. But the tour de force here are the veggies, grown in an adjoining patch, that make up the most succulent dolma dishes.

After so many cups of instant coffee, the espresso at (**St. John's Café** (Uğur Mumcu Sevgi Yolu 4/C, 0232/892-4005, 9 A.M.–11 P.M.

daily, 6TL) is a welcome relief. St. John's menu extends past fresh juices and custom java to include tasty salads and sandwiches. Try the house toast with turkey, cheese, and apples. The locale is a popular non-smoking meeting point for locals; it doubles as a teensy gift store filled with traditional local crafts.

A night on the town in Selçuk always involves heading to **Pink Bistro and Café** (Siegburg Cad. 24, 0232/892-9801, 10 P.M.–4 A.M. daily high season, until 2 A.M. in low season, mixed drinks 10TL). It's Selçuk's oldest pub, where Efes beer (3TL) seems to grace every table on the crowded street terrace near Cengiz Topel Caddesi.

Information and Services

Selçuk's **tourism office** (Agora Cad. 35, 0232/892-6945, www.selcuk.gov.tr, 8 A.M.–noon and 1–5 P.M. daily Apr.–Nov., Mon–Fri. Dec.–Mar.) is located directly across from the Ephesus Museum. The area is also staffed with a **Tourist Police Office** (0232/892-8989, 24 hours a day), located in a booth across from the bus station. The local state **hospital** (Dr. Sabri Yayla Bulv., 0232/892-7036) employs a multilingual staff and houses all modern diagnostic equipment. Banks and ATMs are located on Namık Kemal Caddesi. The **post office** (Cengiz Topel Cad. 13, 0232/892-6480, 8:30 A.M.–12:30 P.M. and 1:30–4:30 P.M. Mon.–Fri.) provides services such as currency exchange, money transfers, and faxing.

Getting There

BY AIR

Located 60 kilometers from Selçuk, **Izmir's Adnan Menderes Airport** (Airport Headquarters, 0232/274-2424, www.adnan-menderesairport.com) is the point of arrival for daily flights from Istanbul and Ankara, as well as some western European cities, Iran, and Israel. A bus (every 30 minutes, 7TL) leaves for Selçuk from the Tansaş, Gaziemir bus stop, about a 10-minute taxi ride away from the airport terminal. Transfers from Izmir's airport can also be arranged through hotels (approx. €40).

BY BUS

Both long-distance and regional buses arrive at Selçuk's *otogar* (bus station), located along Atatürk Caddesi across from the park. If traveling on a long-distance bus, ask company staff if the route includes a stop at Selçuk's *otogar*. Often, buses that continue through to southwestern Turkey, drop passengers by a *durak* (stop) along the E87 Highway, about eight kilometers northeast of Selçuk. If this is the case, contact your hotel ahead of time to arrange transportation from that point.

BY TRAIN

Trains are unfortunately not as frequent and dependable as coach service, and by far more crowded on weekends and holidays. Having said that, opting to travel by train is considerably cheaper (about 2TL) and practically transports guests door-to-door. Train service links Izmir's airport to Selçuk's *tren istasyonu* (train station). There are four daily scheduled departures from the airport to Selçuk (8 A.M., 9:30 A.M., 3:45 P.M., and 7:35 P.M.) and six scheduled departures from Selçuk to the airport (6:25 A.M., 7:15 A.M., 8:30 A.M., 12:10 P.M., 5:40 P.M., and 7:05 P.M.).

Getting Around

Commuting within Selçuk is a snap. Walking seems to be the locals' favorite mode of transportation. That's good news because the majority of the sites are contained within a small area. Taxiing around is possible, particularly for destinations that are outside the city center like Ephesus, the House of the Virgin Mary, and the Grotto of the Seven Sleepers. *Dolmuş* (communal taxi, 2TL) service crisscrosses the city from Selçuk's *otogar* (bus station) all the way to Ephesus' Lower Gate. Kuşadası is just 18 kilometers west of town; frequent *dolmuş* service to Kuşadası departs from the city square (5TL).

KUŞADASI

Local farmers regale in telling stories of an undefiled Kuşadası, one with no high-rises in sight, no mammoth vacation resorts . . . heck, without even a paved road. But that was in

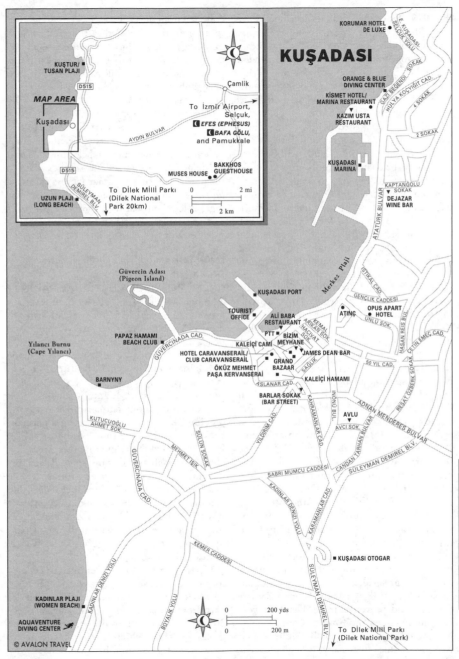

KORUMAR HOTEL
DE LUXE

E. KUŞADASI
SELÇUK YOLU

KUŞTUR/
TUSAN PLAJI

D515

MAP AREA

Kuşadası

Çamlik

KUŞADASI

ORANGE & BLUE
DIVING CENTER

GAZI BEĞENDI SOKAK

HULYA KOÇYIĞIT CAD.

KISMET HOTEL/
MARINA RESTAURANT

KAZIM USTA
RESTAURANT

4 SOKAK

2 SOKAK

To İzmir Airport,
Selçuk,
EFES (EPHESUS)
BAFA GÖLU,
and Pamukkale

AYDIN BULVAR

SÜLEYMAN
DEMIREL BLV.

D515

KUŞADASI
MARINA

KAPTANOĞLU
SOKAK

DEJAZAR
WINE BAR

ATATÜRK BULVAR

UZUN PLAJI
(LONG BEACH)

BAKKHOS
GUESTHOUSE

MUSES HOUSE

To Dilek Millí Parkı
(Dilek National
Park 20km)

0   2 mi

0   2 km

Güvercin Adası
(Pigeon Island)

KUŞADASI PORT

Merkez Plaji

ISTIKLAL CAD.

GENÇLIK CADDESI

HASAN REIS BUL.

ÇETIN EMEÇ CAD.

TOURIST
OFFICE

ATINÇ

OPUS APART
HOTEL

UNLÜ SOK.

KEMAL
ARSLAN SOK.

ALİ BABA
RESTAURANT

Yılancı Burnu
(Cape Yılancı)

PAPAZ HAMAMI
BEACH CLUB

GÜVERCINADA CAD.

PTT

KALEİÇİ CAMI

HACIVAT
SOK.

BIZIM
MEYHANE

JAMES DEAN BAR

50 YIL CAD.

RESAT ÖZBERK SOKAK

HOTEL CARAVANSERAIL/
CLUB CARAVANSERAIL

GRAND
BAZAAR

SAĞLIK

ÖKÜZ MEHMET
PAŞA KERVANSERAI

KALEİÇİ HAMAMI

BARNYNY

ISLANAR CAD.

BARLAR SOKAK
(BAR STREET)

KAHRAMANLAR CAD.

AVLU

AVCI SOK.

ADNAN MENDERES BULVAR

KUTUCUOĞLU
AHMET SOK.

YILDIRIM CAD.

İNÖNÜ BUL.

SABRI MUMCU CADDESI

CANDAN TARHAN BULVAR

SÜLEYMAN DEMIREL BLV.

GÜVERCINADA CAD.

MEHMET IŞIK

SÜLON SOKAK

KADINLAR DENIZLI YOLU

KARAMANLAR CAD.

KEMER CADDESI

KUŞADASI OTOGAR

KADINLAR DENIZLI YOLU

BOYALIK YOLU

SÜLEYMAN DEMIREL BLV.

KADINLAR PLAJI
(WOMEN BEACH)

AQUAVENTURE
DIVING CENTER

0   200 yds

0   200 m

To Dilek Millí Parkı
(Dilek National Park)

© AVALON TRAVEL

the 1970s. Since then, zealous developers have chomped at the bit, constructing ever more massive holiday resorts and blocks of summer housing for Western Europeans who heeded the call of Ephesus' ever-growing popularity. Some even purchased vacation homes, and others loved it so much they chose to expatriate to Kuşadası's warm, golden coast.

Despite its packaged-holiday atmosphere and its undaunted growth and slightly British cachet, Kuşadası (Bird Island) still beckons tourists by the boat- or bus-full. Its year-round population of 50,000 soars to nearly half a million come summer. This popularity stems, in part, from the busy port, where mammoth cruise ships dock on their Mediterranean foray. The town's subdued Turkish feel, great beachy resorts, rambunctious nightlife, splendid coastal region, and the availability of countless excursions—from the archaeological to the cultural—all add to the ultimate summer trip for both families and partygoers. If you're willing to overlook its consumer-centric aspects, Kuşadası is a great all-inclusive base for exploring this incomparable slice of Turkey.

Sights

Kuşadası sprawls inland on either side of its central causeway, which leads to Güvercin Adası (Pigeon Island). Aside from inspiring the town's name, the popular isle is home to a diminutive **fortress,** a few beach clubs, and plenty of kid-friendly animals. The stone structure is usually closed, but that's okay because its appeal lies more in its history than whatever relics it contains. During the 16th century the pirate Khair ad-Din—a.k.a. the feared Barbarossa—based his operations, that swept throughout the Mediterranean, from this point. Later he was "asked" to lead Sultan Süleyman the Magnificent's Ottoman navy.

The town centers around the **Öküz Mehmet Paşa Kervanserai,** a 40-foot-high Ottoman castle built in 1618 by Sultan Osman II's vizier to accommodate overseas trade. That same year he commissioned the **Kaleiçi Cami,** nearby **hammam** (bathhouse), and **city walls,** which were all sustained financially through proceeds

collected from the caravansary. A thorough restoration in the 1960s led to the caravansary's grand opening as Club Karavanserai—a hotel and nightclub. Slightly southwest of this ancient *han* (caravansary) lie a handful 19th-century timber townhouses, boasting the regional architecture of the period.

The **Grand Bazaar** is home to roughly a thousand stalls, where virtually any Turkish ware—be it ornate carpets to "genuine-fake" designer purses, watches, and clothing—is sold for pennies on the dollar. Shopaholics will also delight in the weekly bazaar (across from the *dolmuş* station, Fri.), when villagers from the region flock to town with their carts of fruits and vegetables, towels and lace, and locally-made clothing.

Day Trips
DILEK MILLI PARKI
(DILEK PENINSULA NATIONAL PARK)

The Dilek Milli Parkı (8 A.M.–6:30 P.M., admission 2TL, vehicle 5TL) is one of Turkey's most pristine natural reserves, whose natural peace and splendor are juxtaposed against a heavily militarized buffer zone between the Greek island of Samos and the Turkish mainland. This 28,000-acre park is a hilly extension of the Samsun Mountain, cloaked with pine and indigenous fauna until it naturally juts into the Aegean Sea, creating a peaceful backdrop for sun and nature worshippers alike. Here, protected fauna like the rare Anatolian cheetah, as well as even rarer majestic sea turtles and monk seals, can be glimpsed. The beaches and picnic areas of Dilek Peninsula National Park beckon sun-seeking eco-tourists April–October. Tracking and climbing opportunities abound deeper within the woods and up to the park's highest point, Dilek Tepesi (Dilek Hill, 1237 m.).

Getting to the Dilek Peninsula (20 km. south of Kuşadası) is easiest by car. There's a *dolmuş* (communal taxi) service (3TL) that departs from Kuşadası's *otogar* (bus station) every 30 minutes, but it drops off passengers by the park's entrance, which is still 10 kilometers away from the coveted beaches. That's why

İçmeler Köyü, a shady, sandy strip less than a kilometer away from Dilek's entrance, is usually blanketed with sunbathers. Keep in mind that İçmeler offers no public facilities. But those at the less crowded beaches of **Aydınlık** and **Kavaklı,** located at five and seven kilometers from the park entrance, respectively, do. Both stretches are covered with pebbles. A large dirt track, signposted as *Kanyon* and a pedestrian symbol, snakes up the summit of Dilek Hill. Dilek's furthest beach, **Karasu Burun,** is well worth the schlep. It's a pebbly strip straight across from the Greek isle of Samos. There are plenty of facilities here, including showers and changing rooms. Each beach has a snack bar that's open during the high season. The dirt track further ahead, signaling *Yasak Bölge* (Forbidden Area) signals the start of the militarized zone.

◖ BAFA GÖLU (BAFA LAKE)

Located 69 kilometers south of Kuşadası, Bafa Lake is a large body of water that's both a stunning natural and historical preserve. It sits snugly in a valley shadowed by the mystical **Beşparmak Dağı** (Five-Fingered Mountains). Up until the 5th century B.C. the lake was a long serpentine bay of the Aegean Sea known as the Gulf of Lade. But gradual alluvial deposits from the Büyük Menderes River formed the marshes to the west, thereby land-locking the lake for posterity. Its southeastern and northern shores are home to a couple of untouched rural villages, one of which is **Kapıkırı**—antiquity's **Herakleia under Latmos.**

Herakleia is filled with the unrestored ruins of a dozen Byzantine monasteries. These friaries were built at the beginning of the 8th century by monks who fled to Latmos from the coast in an effort to avoid the wrath of Arab invaders. The mountain face just above Kapıkırı is pocked with caves, some of which were once home to hermits. More than 170 prehistoric rock paintings dating back to 6000 B.C. have been discovered in these cliffside grottos by a German research team led by archaeologist Anneliese Peschlow.

LOVER'S TRYST AT LATMOS

Kapıkırı unfurls amidst boulders and rocks fallen from the slope of the 1,400-meter-high Beşparmak Dağı. This sacred mount, known throughout classical history as Latmos, is squarely rooted in Greek mythology. The story goes that the beautiful moon goddess Selene fell for a handsome young local shepherd called Endymion. Fearing the lad's mortality, the goddess pleaded with his father, Zeus, to keep her lover in perpetual sleep so that he would live eternally. He is rumored to still be asleep in a local cage, thousands of years since his lover, Selene, paid him nightly conjugal visits. The stunning Selene allegedly bore him some 50 daughters. Endymion was so revered for his skills of selflessness that he inspired a pagan cult of asceticism centered around Latmos. Carian hermits, followed centuries later by Christian monks, made pilgrimages en masse to this location. The legend continues to this day, as locals believe that the lovers still have a tryst every full moon.

The area is also a boon for bird and nature lovers. More than 255 different bird species are said to be native to Bafa Lake. Herakleia is particularly renowned internationally as the nesting ground for the showy Collared Pratincole. More than 9,000 waterfowl migrate to the lake annually, including the sack-billed Dalmatian pelican. Sure they come for the milder weather around the Aegean Coast, but they also come to feed on Bafa Lake's large populations of eels, trout, and other finned creatures—a bounty sure to appeal to fish fans.

It's easy for time-strapped visitors to despair when surveying the wide breadth of area to cover. With just that in mind, a couple of entrepreneurs, who also happen to be local inn and restaurant owners, came up with lake cruises. These stop at the must-see sites: the lake's three largest islands and the lake's largest sandy beach. Lunch is provided on the return. One of these is **Selene Pansiyon and Restaurant** (Bafa Lake, 0252/543-5221, www.latmosherakleia.com, lake tour €50). They specialize in a variety of tours from the shortest—a three-hour, 12-kilometer trek (€50) that showcases caves and monasteries—to the largest-an eight-day, all-inclusive packages (€400, includes airport transfers, full board, six guided tours) of bird-watching, shopping in nearby Milas, trekking through ruins, and island-hopping. Aside from being a fully renovated rustic inn (B&B €30, half-board €60, chalet €100), boasting a large pool and air-conditioned lakeside rooms with en suite bathrooms, Selene has a restaurant right on the lake. Time and again this restaurant remains the top-seeded stop among nationals wishing to savor delicious local samplings of veggie dishes followed by a perfectly grilled lake trout.

The town of Bafa is located 89 kilometers south of Kuşadası, at the end of the lake. The main freeway (D525), which connects Söke to Milas, skirts the lake. Once there, look out for the sign that indicates a sharp left turn to Bafa.

The ruins of Herakleia in Kapıkırı are 10 kilometers further, along the back road that circles the lake from Bafa.

Beaches and Water Sports

The reward for a day of traipsing through ancient rubble and visiting museums is a soak in the Aegean's crystalline waters. Unfortunately, the advent of massive amounts of summer escapists, combined with unchecked development, has rendered the area around Kuşadası and a good part of the coast a sorry sight for those seeking rest and relaxation on a public beach. While the tiny, municipal stretches of **Merkez Plajı** (Downtown Beach) and **Kadınlar Plajı** (Women's Beach)—so called for its once topless vacationing sirens—are two highly-praised options best avoided, there are some sun-kissed spots worth venturing to.

A great sandy strips near Kuşadası is **Uzun Plajı** (Long Beach), which is situated six kilometers south of town. Here, you'll find cafés and restaurants, chaises lounges and parasols, and water-sports facilities. Ditto for **Kustur/**

Kuşadası's famed Kadinlar Plajı (Women's Beach)

Tusan Plajı, just five kilometers to the north of town. This locale offers a kilometer-long sandy shoreline with the expected facilities, warm limpid waters, and thick crowds come summer weekends.

Also, you won't go wrong by opting to lay your towel at one of the **beach clubs,** where space is restricted to allow for maximum hedonism. Kuşadası's coast is dotted with them; a good choice for its location is **Papaz Hamamı Beach Club** (just left of the Pigeon Island's causeway). Even better, **Bar NY** (www.barnewyork.net), at the entrance of Yılancı Burnu (Cape Yılancı), located just 1.5 kilometers south of town, allows for superb views of the bay and fortress.

If you're into water sports, head to the **Orange & Blue Diving Center** (Carisma Delux Hotel, Akyar Mevki 5, Kuşadası Setur Marina, 9256/618-1524, www.kusadasidivecenter.com). Orange & Blue's fully-certified instructors specialize in scuba and open-water diving instruction (€250). The agency provides undersea outings, like cave and night diving (1 dive €30, 10 dives €300), and can even organize underwater wedding ceremonies! **Aquaventure Diving Center** (Kadinlar Denizi, Miracle Beach Club, 0256/612-7845, www.aquaventure.com.tr) offers similar services and prices, and its location at Women Beach is more centrally located.

Nightlife

If rowdy, inebriated crowds, raucous Irish pubs, and cheesy karaoke dives are your bag, then head to Barlar Sokak. But for a tad more class walk down to Kuşadası's old town, to the mesh of narrow streets between Barbaros Hayrettin Bulvari and Sağlik Sokak. The night scene here never gets going before midnight, that is, in mid-March–mid-November; it's practically non-existent the rest of the year.

A trip to Turkey wouldn't be complete without checking out an evening Turkish folklore show. And **Club Caravanserail** (Atatürk Bulv. 2, 0256/614-4115, Thurs.–Sun., starts 7:30 p.m., €50), is one of the best places to experience the cabaret-type festivities. Attendees line up at a gigantic banquet table filled with innumerable appetizers, just as the show starts. Then, a basic Turkish main course arrives as a variety of traditional Turkish dances are performed. There are also the requisite belly dancers and spoon-clicking musicians, as well as a nod to more international ditties like "La Vie En Rose."

Kuşadası's best bar by far is **James Dean Bar** (Sakarya Sok. 14, 0256/614-3827, until 5 a.m.). It's set in an attractive two-centuries old townhouse with outdoor merriment amid fruit trees, just steps away from the marina. The clientele is comprised of moneyed nationals, slugging from pricey bottles of Miller beer (15TL) while bebopping to Turkish pop music.

When in Turkey do as the Turks do: revel at a *meyhane* (Turkish tavern). **Bizim Meyhane** (Sakarya Sok. 10, 0256/612-2208) is just the place to enjoy the anise-flavored *rakı* with a few tasty *mezes* to delay inebriation. A darling of the Turkish media, Bizim is owned by a brother-sister duo who have collected an impressive array of stringed instruments. These hang from the property's brick walls, waiting to be picked up by one of the siblings in their nightly song and dance. This place is best described as an *alaturca* country bar, and perhaps the best antidote to Kuşadası's cookie-cutter entertainment choices.

Accommodations

Finding lodging in Kuşadası depends entirely on budget. Accommodations run the gamut, from the economical pension to the pricey five-star; at last count, there were more than 400 properties! But buyer beware, most all-inclusive (AI) resorts in town often deliver vacation packages à la Club Med, but on the whole fall pitifully short of providing the latter's consistency and the personal touches expected at those prices.

Guidebooks rarely reveal the minutiae of booking a room in resort towns; here's what I've learned about Kuşadası. The region's mammoth resorts typically have two booking arrangements: a B&B quote or an AI rate. The latter is by far more expensive—by as much as 25 percent—but includes free use of all facilities on site. The B&B rate is just that—bed and breakfast. A room with seaside views and use of the facilities—say, the sauna—will be add-ons to the published quotes. Lodging in the center of town may seem the smart way to go to save time commuting, but the incessant din may keep you from getting those replenishing Z's. Only about a quarter of Kuşadası's hotels are open year-round; the rest operate only April–November. To find additional properties and useful discounts of up to 20 percent, log on to www.kusadasihotels.com.

UNDER €50

Who said comfy, clean accommodations, charm, and good eats have to mean big bucks? Obviously not the folks at ℂ **Opus Apart Hotel** (Kitaş Özazman Sitesi, in the rear of the garage, 0256/622-3010, www.opusapart. com, from €15). Rated high by DYI travelers, each of the 48 apartments can sleep up to four adults comfortably; some even boast balconies. The accommodations are basic, clean, and have en suite baths and equipped kitchens. Public spaces include a large pool, entertainment center, indoor and outdoor restaurants featuring Turco/European cuisine, and a disco bar to get your groove on. The Opus is within walking distance of the city center (700 meters).

€50-150

While the buzzword around town is boutique, most fall short of the charm. But, ℂ **Muses House** (Kirazli Köyu 158, 0256/667-1125, www.museshouse.com, children over 14, €115–140) gives any B&B in Tuscany a run for its money. Since its inception in 2006, there have been nothing but raves from guests who've stayed at this property. Welsh owner Steven has transformed two country houses in the farming village of Kirazli into a set of five regally decorated rooms, plus a rear villa with pool (330TL). Each room, inspired by one of the five muses of mythology, boasts luxurious fabrics and high ceilings, as well as attached large marble baths, equipped with toiletries. The grounds feature a

pool and sprawling marble terraces. The cuisine served outside or around a family-style dinner table inside is divinely Turkish.

Nearby, the **Bakkhos Guesthouse** (just above Kirazli Köy Yolu, 0256/622-0337, www. bakkhos.com, Apr.–Nov., €50–70) is another B&B option. It's a typical Turkish country house that's been transformed into a 12-room rustic inn. It may be 6 kilometers from Kuşadası, but booking with the Özbaş's—the Turco/Dutch couple who own the property—has its merits. All rooms boast Mediterranean porches, surrounded by blooming gardens and lofty palms; interiors ooze country charm and simplicity. Public quarters promote amity with an oversized pool and wraparound sofas that are perfect for a late afternoon cup of tea with friends. The Kuşadası *dolmuş* (communal taxi) passes conveniently on the road just below the village of Kirazli.

For a truly unique experience, bask in Ottoman history at the **Hotel Caravanserail** (Atatürk Bulv. 2, 0256/614-4115, www.kusadasihotels.com/caravanserail/, from US$110). This four-centuries-old *han* (caravansary), commissioned by an Ottoman vizier in 1618, features 26 immaculately clean rooms, bearing centuries-old detailing, including inset stone fireplaces. The inner courtyard, where breakfasts and dinners are served in summer, is magically transformed with a live Turkish dinner show Thursdays–Sundays.

Another good, centrally-located option is the **Atinç** (Ataturk Bulv. 42, 0256/614-7608, www.hotelatinc.com, from €50). Economical lodgings, smack dab on the coastal road, are hard to find. That's what Atinç provides, with an impressively attentive staff. Each room bears a different flowery motif and comes with a balcony, television, air-conditioning, and mini bar. The accommodations are a bit bland, but the unending sea and town views from the oversized rooftop pool sure makes up for it in spades.

OVER €150

The ℂ **Korumar Hotel de Luxe** (Gazi Beğendi Mevkii P.K.18, 0256/618-1530, www.

korumar.com.tr, open year-round, €81–265) is the most luxurious resort close (2 km.) to the city center. The Korumar is one of these double-rate hotels, so beware when booking. Consider spending a little more on an airy seaside room with balcony; the sunsets seen from the protected pebbly cove where the property lies are incomparable. Safes, satellite TVs, mini-bar, and bathtubs all await; but no free Wi-Fi.

Close by is the choice of royalty, the **Kismet Hotel** (Atatürk Bulv. 1, 0232/618-1290, www.kismet.com.tr, from €150), owned by Hümeyra Sultan—the granddaughter of the last sultan of the Ottoman Empire. Set on a rocky promontory overlooking the Kuşadası port, *Kismet* (fate) has welcomed most of Europe's royalty, including Queen Elizabeth. Kismet's decor is unexpectedly modern and airy. The seaside rooms benefit from phenomenal views and large baths. What seals the deal, however, is the view from the Marina Bar and Terrace, seated amid immaculately-landscaped grounds. Once there, feast on, yes, succulent Ottoman cuisine, as well as Mediterranean fare.

Food
EUROPEAN
A mix of fine Med/British cuisine awaits at the recently opened (**Dejazar Wine Bar** (Ataturk Bul. 84, 0256/618-2821, www.dejazarwinebar.com, 11 A.M.–midnight, 18TL). Functioning more as a brasserie than what its name entails, Dejazar's Scottish owners hit the bull's eye by placing British faves on the menu; the grilled pork chop with baked apple and bread pudding are luscious. But for those not sated on red meat, the rib-eye with peppercorn sauce is also highly recommended! Make sure to visit the bathrooms: they're whimsically charming, with purse-shaped mirrors.

FISH
No self-respecting Turk vacations in Kuşadası without dining over a fish entrée at (**Kazım Usta Restaurant** (Liman Cad. 4, 0256/614-1226, 11 A.M.–midnight daily Apr.–Nov., 20TL) at least once during their stay.

Open since 1956, Kazım is not only the oldest restaurant in town, but it's also considered Kuşadası's finest locale for grilled fish. Try the house specialty of eggplant salad, followed by a locally caught *çıpura* (gilthead bream), which is cooked superbly over a charcoal grill. This fine meal, combined with the marina atmosphere, is a memorable outing.

The dishes and the service at **Ali Baba Restaurant** (Belediye Turistik Çarsisi 5, 0256/614-1551, 11 A.M.–midnight, 20TL) has yet to disappoint, even during the evening rush.

TURKISH
(The family-owned **Avlu** (Cephane Sok. 15, 0256/614-7995, 9 A.M.–midnight, 5TL) has remained *the* diner of choice among locals for decades. And, thanks to happily-sated guidebook writers, getting a table at lunchtime seems harder these days. Simplicity and consistency are key here. The meals of the day stand at attention in a counter waiting for the next in line to pick them. Veggies rule, but the house's chili pepper sauce and crowd-favorite *semizotu* (purslane with garlicky yogurt) are some of the best I've ever had.

(**Marina Restaurant** (inside Kismet Hotel, Atatürk Bulv. 1, 0256/618-1290, www.kismet.com.tr, noon–3 P.M. and 7–11:30 P.M. daily, 14TL) is over the top in satisfaction. It features lots of tasty *hamurlu tatlar* (flour-based dishes), like an innovative *börek* (lightly fried Turkish roll) served with crispy vegetables and a red pepper sauce. The Kayseri *mantı*—a dish of tiny dumplings served in garlicky yogurt sauce—truly deserves a nod. While the nightly dinner banquet (30TL) amazes, there's an à la carte menu featuring poultry, red meat, and lots of salads. Ditch the center and aim your fork toward this romantic getaway overlooking the bay of Kuşadası.

Information and Services
Kuşadası's **Tourist Information Office** (Iskele Meydanı, 0256/614-1103, 8 A.M.–noon and 1–5 P.M. daily May–Oct., closed weekends Nov.–Apr.) offers town maps and hotel listings. For more information on activities and a

full hotel and restaurant listing online, log on to the Kuşadası guide at www.kusadasi.net. The **PTT** office (Barbaros Hayrettin Paşa Bulv. 23–25, 0256/612-3311, 8 A.M.–midnight daily in high season, 8:30 A.M.–5:30 P.M. Mon.–Sat. Nov.–Apr.) provides all postal services, currency exchange, and money transfers, as well as a faxing and calling center. **Banks** (8:30 A.M.–5:30 P.M. Mon.–Fri.) and 24-hour ATMs are located along the Barbaros Hayrettin Paşa Bulvari. To connect to the Internet, head to **Kismet Internet café** (Liman Cad. 1, 0256/612-3580, noon–at least 11 P.M., 3TL/15 min.) provides not only English-speaking staff, but English keyboards to boot! It's located right across from the entrance to the marina.

Kuşadası's private **hospital** (Özel Kuşadası Hastanesi, Anıt Sok. 17, 0256/613-1616) is located just three kilometers north of the town center.

Getting There

BY CAR
From Izmir, travel along the region's main highway (E87) about 60 kilometers south to the Selçuk/Izmir connector (D550), which will take you past Selçuk toward the turn-off leading onto westbound Aydın Bulvarı (Rte. 35–42). This road and adequate signposts lead right into the town center (about 120 km.). From the south, the Selçuk/Izmir connector (D550) leads northbound toward Aydın Bulvarı.

BY BUS
Kuşadası's central *otogar* (Kahramanlar Cad., 0256/614-9571) is located less than one kilometer out of the town center on the main road. Although *dolmuşes* (communal taxis) are aplenty, hailing a taxi (6TL) to travel to your

hotel is about the best way to ensure door-to-door service. The offices of major bus companies are all located along İsmet İnönü Bulvarı; these provide convenient shuttle service to the *otogar* (bus station). There you'll find buses heading to Bodrum (15–20TL, 2.5 hours) three times a day during the summer. To travel to Söke, go by *dolmuş* (4TL, every 20 min.) during the off-season.

BY BOAT
Ferries connect at the port of Kuşadası and the Greek island of Samos daily. Regular departure to Samos is at 8:30 A.M.; the return to Kuşadası is at 5 P.M. There are two additional services in May–mid-October. The first departs from Samos at 8:30 A.M.; the other leaves Kuşadası at 5 P.M. (€30 one-way, €35 same-day return, €50 open return, 75 min.). Tickets can be purchased online through **Anker Travel's** (Adnan Menderes Bulv. 38, 0256/213-2044, www.ankertravel.net/www.feribot.net). Keep in mind that passports are checked at each port prior to embarking, so arrive at least 45 minutes ahead of departure.

Getting Around
Commuting in Kuşadası on the cheap is easy by hopping on a *dolmuş* (communal taxi, 2TL). These take off from the *garaj* (station) on Adnan Menderes Bulvarı, but can also be boarded from any spot in town. Route details are posted on the left side of the windshield. The *dolmuş* for Selçuk (3TL) departs approximately every 15 minutes and includes Ephesus among its stops. The coastal minibus travels along Atatürk Bulvarı and Güvercin Ada Caddesi, making stops at Kadınlar Denizi. The service heading north to Kuştur Beach takes off from the intersection of İstiklal Caddesi and Atatürk Bulvarı.

Pamukkale

The travertine pools at Pamukkale command attention even from miles away. These sparkling white cascading terraces are one of a kind; the outcrop is known among Turks as the world's eighth wonder. The terraces sprawl over 200 meters up the Çaldağ Mountain chain from the Curuksu Plain. A full exploration of this winter white wonderland reveals pools reminiscent of lily pads and others of gigantic seashells. This dramatic geological anomaly is the result of eons of calcium-laden accumulation brought forth by hot springs spurting from rifts in the earth, created over time by seismic activity. All scientific data aside, this once magnificent outpost has been Anatolia's ultimate spa resort since antiquity. Roman imperials bathed in the colonnaded Sacred Pool corralled in a plateau halfway up a cliffside. From its pine-blanketed flanks unfurl the ruins of the ancient city of Hierapolis and its 2,000-year-old ruins.

It's hard to believe that these ruins, and the integrity of the entire locale in fact, almost didn't survive the wrath of greedy developers. By the late 1980s, the pools at Pamukkale (Turkish for "cotton castle") had turned brown from sewage water runoff, and local tourism had all but stopped. Baffled as to exactly how to reinvigorate the site's international popularity, local authorities called in the United Nations. A UNESCO designation followed in 1988, leading the way for the displacement of all hotels to the local town of Karahayit and a major clean-up of the area's springs. While the site today is just a fraction of its original, Pamukkale deserves a visit nonetheless.

A trip to the ruins at Hierapolis inevitably involves a soak in its pools. Keep in mind that the typical day-trip option, offered through travel agencies from Kuşadası, allows for rarely more than a three-hour swim and tour. As

COURTESY OF REPUBLIC OF TURKEY CULTURE AND TOURISM MINISTRY

Pamukkale's white travertine pools are an ethereal geological anomaly.

SOUTHERN AEGEAN COAST

highly enjoyable as these tours are, even better is to set aside a couple of days to experience all that the region has to offer. Overnighters need to book lodging in the plush, yet dirt-cheap, resorts in the town of Karahayit, just five kilometers north of Pamukkale. There, you'll also find thermal baths, but these are unimpressive in comparison. These springs are considerably warmer (42–56°C) and slightly tinged red, due to the iron content of the village's springs. If time allows, plan a day to travel to the ancient city of Aphrodisias.

The best time to plan a stopover is any time outside the mad tourist rush and searing heat of summer, preferably during the months of May and October. Though, to catch Pamukkale's annual nod to the arts—its International Music and Culture Festival—come in June, when national talents vie for first place and distinction.

◖ HIERAPOLIS

Adjacent to the parking lot near the northern entrance is the **Pamukkale Arkeoloji Müzesi** (Pamukkale Archaeology Museum, 0258/272-2034, 9 A.M.–12:30 P.M. and 1:30–5:30 P.M. Tues.–Sun., 2TL). This small but outstanding museum, housed in the southern roman baths (2nd century A.D.) of Hierapolis, helps to shed light on Hierapolis' movers and shakers, as well as its prolonged history. There's an outstanding collection of statues and reliefs, along with other artifacts like coins, sarcophagi, medical objects, and jewelry, most dating back to the Romans.

Scattered all about, the ruins of Hierapolis (0258/272-2077, always open, 5TL plus parking fee), Greek for "Sacred City," attest to the importance the ancients gave to the site and its potent springs. From its founding in 190 B.C. by Eumenes II, the king of Pergamum, Hierapolis was centered around the temple of Hiera. This monument had, in fact, predated the city by at least 200 years, and may have been the inspiration for its name. Incidentally, Hiera was the gorgeous wife of Telephus—the son of Hercules, grandson of Zeus, and mythical founder of the kingdom of Pergamum.

Ancients firmly believed that the Greek god Apollo was responsible for Hierapolis' wild outcrops, while the odorous fumes emanating from the pools were linked to the God of the netherworld, Pluto.

But it wasn't until the 2nd century A.D. that Hierapolis experienced its heyday. Sure its spa was the main reason for its fame, but its textiles, particularly wool and dyes, also put the city squarely on the commercial map. By the time Roman Emperor Hadrian arrived in town, Hierapolis' infrastructure badly needed an overhaul after a series of earthquakes. Roman Emperor Hadrian abided, and buildings like the theater were added. After the advent of monotheism, the metropolis was home to a large Jewish community, as well as an important Christian center. In the 5th century, the Byzantines added a handful of churches and the large Martyrium of St. Philip the Apostle.

To fully experience the 10 or so ruins of Hierapolis, devote at least half a day. Most tours whisk you through in under two hours; but fans of religion and history require as much as an entire day. No matter how time is allotted, start first with a dip in the Sacred Pool; it'll add the oomph needed to carry you through.

Sacred Pool

It's not hard to see why tourists barely wait for the buses to stop to join other bathers in the crystalline thermal pools of this snowy-white natural wonder, reminiscent of a waterfall. The place to jump in, however, is directly in the Sacred Pool (Pamukkale Thermal, 0258/272-2024, www.pamukkalethermal.com, 8 A.M.–8 P.M. May–Oct., until 5 P.M. Nov.–Apr., adult 18TL, children ages 6–12 12TL, children under 6 free, locker 2TL, towels 7 15TL), preferably early in the morning when everyone is gorging on the all-you-can-eat breakfast. The waters are slightly radioactive, rich in calcium, magnesium sulfate, bicarbonate, and carbon dioxide, and possess a pH of 6.

Note that the entrance fee allows for a two-hour access, but this regulation is rarely observed by park attendants. The water filling the pools throughout the natural reserve spills from this ancient bathing spot, which is inside the only modern structure that's escaped relocation to Karahayit more than 15 years ago. The Pamukkale Thermal, which now functions as a rather large reception area, houses the pool, verdant grounds, and a tea house. The pool is littered with fluted Roman columns and marble drums—a reminder of Hierapolis' historical significance.

A walk down the length of the shimmering cascade takes about 15 minutes, and leads to the town of Pamukkale. Keep in mind that shoes are not allowed, so barefooting it is about the only way to go.

Ruins

Just northeast of the Sacred Pool, the ruins of Hierapolis are a startling collection of not only the ancient city's historical pedigree, but also an amalgam of religious sites that single-handedly relate the advent of faith through Anatolia, from its early pagan roots to the dominance of Christian and Jewish creeds. Most of the site's archaeological treasures were discovered over six decades by an Italian team of researchers, led by archaeologist Paolo Verzone, who worked on site for more than 30 years. The closest structure to the Sacred Pool is the Roman amphitheater, the third largest of its kind in Asia Minor and arguably the best preserved.

Originally built by Titus Flavius Vespasianus in A.D. 60 on the slope of Hierapolis' hill, the grand amphitheater's size was increased by Hadrian in the mid-2nd century. But Septimius Severus upped his two Roman predecessors a century later by extending the seating by another tier of 25 rows and capacity to 15,000. Intricate busts, statues, and reliefs depicting the myths of Dyonisios, Apollo, and Artemis, were discovered in the two-story proscenium (raised stage). These are on display at the Hierapolis Museum. Musical and theatrical performances are presented annually on this stage during the **Festival of Pamukkale** (late May–early June).

A pretty good hike up the hill leads to the **Martyrium of St. Philip the Apostle,** where St. Philip's remains are thought to be buried. One of the original 12 apostles, Philip, according to the Bible, was killed by upside-down crucifixion in Hierapolis. Although not a thing has been discovered to attest to the whereabouts of his tomb, researchers have at least determined that this octagonal basilica dates from the 5th century. A blaze ravaged through the structure just a few decades later and its columns still bear the marks.

A few meters down the hill are the strewn remains of the **Temple of Apollo,** the sun god and main deity who ruled over the city during Hellenic times. Only the altar's foundation remains, but if you descend the remains of the monumental staircase on the other side of the temple, you'll reach the **Plutonion.** Essentially a small cave of about 10 meters in length, surrounded by a fence, the Plutonion is a death chamber filled with lethal carbon dioxide emanating from an open fault line below. In those days, only eunuchs, serving the Temple Cybele, were able to withstand the noxious fumes during the animal sacrifices which were conducted in this rock chamber. And that's with the help of up to four layers of cloth wrapped around their head! The emissions are still potent, which explains why the Plutonion's gate is sealed off.

Next to the temple is the **nymphaeum,** a monumental fountain that distributed water throughout the city. It was built in the 4th century A.D. with three walls surrounding a bowl of water to which steps led on the open side.

Heading west and just south of the martyrium is a **necropolis.** This is one of the largest ancient cemeteries in Asia minor and the best preserved. Among the 1,200 tombs, mostly constructed of local limestone, are ornately-etched sarcophagi, circular tumuli, and mausoleums. Both locals and those who visited for medical reasons were laid to rest here, explaining the variety of burial structures designed according to tradition and rank. This whopping 1.5-kilometer-long cemetery begs to question the validity of the curative powers ascribed to the springs!

SOUTHERN AEGEAN COAST

Further down the hill is the 5th-century **Byzantine Gate,** which was built as an outpost from which to guard the city from Arab invaders. This gate led to the colonnaded street called the **Plateia.** This was Hierapolis' main drag; it spanned 0.8 kilometers from the **North Gate** to the monumental **Domitian Gate.** The latter was built around A.D. 83 by Julius Frontinus, the Roman proconsul of Asia Minor (A.D. 84–86). Originally two stories high, the two once massive towers, connected by three arches, was the entrance of Frontinus Street. This was downtown Hierapolis, with covered walkways on either side housing shops and ateliers.

APHRODISIAS

No tourist visiting Pamukkale should miss a trip to Aphrodisias (it makes an excellent day trip). One of the finest archaeological sites in the Mediterranean region, Aphrodisias—adjacent to the city of Geyre—is an often missed treasure trove of some of the best preserved ruins, detailing a whopping 7,000-year wedge of history. And thanks to the archaeological team from New York University, currently excavating onsite, the landscaping is sensational and the entire site is virtually free of rocks. If you've got a car, then by all means, don't miss it. If not, book this excursion right from your hotel.

History

Aphrodisias was associated with a fertility cult and may date as far back as the 5th millennium B.C. From the accumulated ruins rose its central acropolis (8th century B.C.) and, in time, its nearby temple to the goddess of love. The outpost grew into a significant town around the 2nd century B.C., known in particular for its Aphrodisian sculptures, an artistic form which was facilitated by the marble quarries of the nearby mount of Babadağ. Pilgrims arrived from the coastal regions in increasing numbers to pay their respect to the Temple of Aphrodite. And when Julius Caesar overnighted in Aphrodisias with his troops on his way to northern Turkey to crush the armies of the Pontic King Pharnaces II (47 B.C.), he lavished the temple with a golden statue of Eros. Soon after Caesar's visit, the temple earned a reputation for its unruly fertility rites and orgies. When Christianity took hold, the temple was converted into a church and its marble blocks were used to build a delineating wall. To ensure that the town was rid of its sinful past, Aphrodisias was renamed Stavropolis (the City of the Cross) in A.D. 350. The town prospered under the Byzantines, but finally succumbed to repeated attacks from the west-marching Selçuks. Ancient Aphrodisias became the muse of Turkish/American archaeologist Dr. Kenan Erim, who excavated most of the ruins visible today from 1961 up until his death in 1990. Erim's book, *Aphrodisias: the City of Venus Aphrodite,* recounts his life's work.

Ruins

The entire site of Aphrodisias (0256/448-8003, 9 A.M.–7 P.M. May–Oct., until 5:30 P.M. Nov.–Apr., 10TL) covers some 520 hectares and comprises 14 main sites, the majority of which dates from the 2nd century A.D. Naturally, the first stop has to be the **Temple of Aphrodite.** It was built in the 1st century B.C. and converted into Christian Basilica around the 5th century A.D. Just a baker's dozen, its lofty columns linger interspersed between the remaining rubble of this once amazing shrine to the goddess of love.

Near the park entrance, the stunning **tetrapylon**—Aphrodisias' monumental gate—greeted lovelorn pilgrims to the city in true Ionic architecture. To the left, you'll find the gravestone of Dr. Erim amid a beautifully landscaped plot. Following a cobblestone path, the impressive **stadium of Aphrodisias** was one of Asia Minor's largest in its heyday. Measuring at 262 meters in length and 59 meters in width, this arena accommodated 30,000 spectators. Seating was arranged according to guilds, as some of the inscription in the marble tiers reveal. After a particularly damaging earthquake during the 7th century A.D., part of the stadium underwent a renovation to accommodate the public events that previously had been staged in the theater. The 7,000-seat **theater** was entirely crafted of alabaster marble. Take time to walk between the tiered seating, you'll notice chiseled renderings of a menorah, gladiators, even the name of Nikoforos—a seemingly important thespian who commissioned a small dressing room next to the stage.

Getting There

For a carefree visit to Aphrodisias, book a tour through a hotel in Pamukkale, or shop around various travel agencies in your port of entry. Most day trips heading to Pamukkale include a guided mini-tour through Aphrodisias. If driving from Pamukkale, head south to Denizli, then to Tavas. There, take the D585 turnoff indicating Karacasu, and follow the signs leading to Aphrodisias (110 km).

ACCOMMODATIONS AND FOOD

With close to 30 properties to choose from in and around Pamukkale, picking the right one is like looking for a needle in a haystack. Considering all the larger hotels are five kilometers out of town, the family-run B&Bs within a short walking distance from the ruins and pools are the smarter choice.

A highly recommended B&B is the charming (**Melrose Allgau Hotel** (Tahsin Cad. 19, 0258/272-2767, www.allgauhotel.com, d. €30, suite €50). The rates are so super economical that expectations are not sky-high. But the en suite doubles, decorated with lip-smacking bursts of colors, are spacious and super clean. The Allgau's owners, Ummu and Mehmet Güleç, add to the wow factor with their boundless Turkish hospitality. Ummu is the attendant chef and whips up the most amazing yogurt soup and *sarma* (stuffed grape leaves). Top all that with in-room air-conditioning, free Internet access, and two pools to choose from, and you'll have to wonder why everyone else is choosing a five-star hotel when you have it all right here. Next door is another inn of choice, the (**Venus Hotel** (Tahsin Cad. 16, 0258/272-2152, from €30). The Venus is a facsimile of the Allgau when

it comes to conveniences. The decor, however, is purely traditional Turkish, all the way down to the bright red wraparound sofas in the lobby. The color scheme even rears its head in the fabrics used in the large rooms upstairs, which boast a quaint continental flair. There's a pool and plenty of relaxing spaces, including a wraparound patio restaurant where traditional Turkish fare is on the menu. Note that the springs and ruins are just a 10-minute walk from these inns. The owners of both inns can arrange a variety of side trips in the region.

Need more than a room and a meal? Then the **Colossae Hotel Thermal** (Karahayit, 0258/271-4156, www.colossae.com.tr, 143–190TL) may be just what the doctor ordered. Among a slew of contenders, the Colossae excels with consistent service, although its institutional accommodations are a bit dated. Guests come for the top-notch spa treatments, like reflexology, aromatherapy, reiki, and even an onsite Clarins Beauty Center. The beautifully landscaped gardens feature an Olympic-size pool, thermal springs, mud baths, and tennis courts. And with six restaurants on the premises, you'll be stumped as to where to go for dinner.

Finding good eats outside of hotels in Karahayit and the pensions closer to the ruins is not an easy feat. Few restaurateurs in town are able to compete with the convenience and offerings of onsite hotel dining. Those who are successful, however, invariably add a few inn-type rooms and become B&Bs. So head to one of these for sustenance. Or, better yet, do a 360 back to the hotel and order room service.

If hunger hits in the center of town, check out **Ünal Restaurant** (Belediye Altı, 0258/272-2451, 11 A.M.–10 P.M., under 15TL). One of the few local diners open year-round, this *lokanta* (diner) offers a daily set menu option, which includes soup, seasonal salad, a Turkish entrée, topped with tea or coffee. Owner Mustafa Ünal is also known for his grilled *köfte* (meatball) and creamy *sutlaç* (rice pudding).

INFORMATION AND SERVICES

Pamukkale's **Tourism Information Office** (0258/272-2077, 8:30 A.M.–12:30 P.M. and

1:30–5:30 P.M. Mon.–Sat.) is at the top of the travertines, right behind the archaeological museum. Here, you'll also find the local offices of the PTT and ATMs, as well as a small infirmary and police station. You'll have to travel to Denizli for banking services.

GETTING THERE

Day trips to Pamukkale can be arranged from most travel agencies headquartered in coastal cities, such as Kuşadası, Bodrum, Izmir, and Antalya. But keep in mind that traveling by bus from any of these points to the travertines entails a six- to eight-hour round-trip commute, leaving at most three hours onsite, including a one-hour stop for lunch. If Pamukkale is in the cards during your trip to Turkey, do yourself a favor and overnight locally.

By Bus

The only company serving Pamukkale is **Pamukkale Seyahat** (toll free 0212/444-3535, Istanbul Esenler 0212/658-2222, www.pamukkaleturizm.com.tr Turkish only). But it only does so in the high season. The rest of the year buses arrive directly into Denizli, and from there connect to a regional service to Pamukkale. Pamukkale Seyahat services the Aegean and a good portion of the Black Sea coasts through its larger stations in Istanbul (8 hrs.) and Ankara (5 hrs.); ticket prices vary 20–50TL, depending on the distance of travel. Warning: ensure that the final destination on the ticket is Pamukkale, otherwise you'll be stranded 25 kilometers away in Denizli. A municipal bus connects Denizli and Pamukkale (3TL) every 15–30 minutes until 10 P.M., depending on the time of year. You can also hire a cab for about 30TL, but you'll have to negotiate that rate.

Pamukkale is not privvy to its own *otogar* (bus station). Instead travelers arriving into

town are dropped off at the bottom the resort's hill at the minibus stop. From there, catch the *dolmuş* (communal taxi) headed for Karahayit; it conveniently stops at the parking lot at Hierapolis.

By Train

The **Pamukkale Ekspressi** (Istanbul Haydarpaşa station 0216/336-0475, Denizli 0258/268-2831, sleeping car 65TL/person) departs Istanbul's Haydarpaşa train station daily at 5:35 P.M. en route to Denizli, with the return departing at 5 P.M. and arriving in Istanbul at 8:34 A.M. The 15-hour trip winds through mostly agricultural country, including the gorgeous Menderes Valley, with a total of six stops before its terminus. A diner is available onboard, with porters announcing meal services to passengers three times daily.

GETTING AROUND

The quickest way of ascending the park is through the **northern entrance,** which is situated 2.5 kilometers up the windy road that leads to Karahayit from the town of Pamukkale. Pass the entrance booth at the top of the climb, and travel another one kilometer alongside Hierapolis' necropolis to reach the main ruins and the Sacred Pool. The second option is to enter through the town of Pamukkale, but this involves a 15-minute hike barefoot up the travertines. The last resort is the **south entrance,** which also requires a 15-minute walk past ongoing archaeological excavations from the park's southern parking lot. There's a fee of 5TL at each entrance.

Most visitors walk the kilometer distance from the arched gate of Karahayit to the park's northern entrance. Figure at least three kilometers, or up to 20 minutes, to get to the Sacred Pool from most hotels. Alternatively, most hoteliers provide rides to the park entrance.

THE TURQUOISE COAST

Aptly named for the deep blue of its Mediterranean waters, the Turquoise Coast is a sea lover's paradise of hidden coves, bays, and isles, all set against jagged cliffs of the westernmost crags of the Taurus Mountains. The landscape is dramatic, to say the very least. Conifer-filled canyons drop steeply right into the sea in some places or form the tiniest sandy beaches in others. This slice of Turkey is stunning, second only to majestic Istanbul.

This lush craggy coastline lures millions of visitors. One major draw is Bodrum, a less pompous version of the French Riviera. This peninsula covers 649 square kilometers and comprises 13 beachside villages. Each has its own culture, from the laid back Bay of Akyarlar to the exclusive Türkbükü. The richness of this area extends all along the coast, as it juts out and tucks itself in, for more than 650 kilometers, all the way to Antalya. The second of two sinewy peninsulas just past Bodrum signals the Eastern Med and a premier sailing paradise. If you can detach yourself from the beauty of the coast, you'll find a rural Turkey with postcard-perfect villages like Kaş and Üçağız at the tip of southwestern Turkey's Gulf of Finike.

Outdoorsy types will find the Turquoise Coast particularly appealing. Enjoy the venerated Blue Cruise aboard a *gület,* the traditional Turkish wooden yacht. Dive the underwater canyons in Kaş; paraglide above Ölüdeniz's stunning Blue Lagoon. For those not so keen on water, canyon-seekers will revel in Saklıkent Gorge near Fethiye and hikers will dig the serpentine 500-kilometer-long

COURTESY OF REPUBLIC OF TURKEY CULTURE AND TOURISM MINISTRY

THE TURQUOISE COAST

HIGHLIGHTS

◖ **Marmaris Day Trips:** Discover picturesque seaside villages and Hellenic ruins where the Aegean meets the Med on the Hısarönü andthis Reşadiye pair of historic peninsulas (page 267).

◖ **Ölüdeniz:** Glide above, or laze on, the white sands of Turkey's very own Blue Lagoon (page 283).

◖ **Xanthos:** Investigate the Lycian League's 3,000-year-old ruins at Xanthos (page 296).

◖ **Patara:** Walk amidst seaside ruins abutting one of the Med's longest beaches (page 297).

◖ **Kekova Bay:** Dive offshore to the sunken

Roman ruins of Üçağız or climb above the picturesque village of Kaş to Kaleköy's small fortress for spectacular sea views (page 303).

◖ **Aspendos:** The best way to enjoy this 2000-year-old Roman theater – the best preserved in Asia Minor – is during the classical concert and ballet season which takes place every summer (page 318).

◖ **Chimaera, Olympos, and Çıralı:** Check out this the must-see ancient village of Olympos for its untouched Çıralı Beach, decrepit marble temples amid pine-cloaked mountains, treehouse lodges, and especially for the eternal flame of Chimaera (page 320).

LOOK FOR ◖ TO FIND RECOMMENDED SIGHTS, ACTIVITIES, DINING, AND LODGING.

Lycian Way. Along the way, there's also the nesting ground of the majestic loggerhead turtles near Dalyan.

While this coast may be reflected in tourist brochures as the end-all of sandy destinations, much of it is now dotted with new developments. Mega resorts and summer residential tracts still mushroom interspersed with old Turkey and the innumerable remains of civilizations past. This dichotomy exists throughout,

as designer-bag toting city slickers share space with head-scarfed farmers.

PLANNING YOUR TIME

Plan to travel through this area for at least a week to really enjoy both its panoply of sights and its relaxation idylls. A two-week itinerary is recommended, however, to allow for at least a couple of days in both Bodrum and Antalya as bookends to this scenic journey. To

TWO WEEKS ON THE TURQUOISE COAST

The following two-week itinerary incorporates all major sights, a marine jaunt, and the necessary couple of days of beachside tranquility in Bodrum and Antalya.

DAY 1

Earmark the morning of the first day in Bodrum to sightseeing its castle and the ruins of ancient Halicarnassus, before savoring bluefish carpaccio for lunch at the harborside restaurant, **Yağhane** (Neyzen Tevfik Cad. 170, 0252/313-4747, www.yaghanebodrum.com). From there, rent a vehicle and tour the perimeter of Bodrum's scenic peninsula. Stop along the way in Yalıkavak for a seaside stroll before another remarkable dinner at Bodrum's premier fish haunt, **Hasan'in Yeri** (Gerişaltı Mevkii, Yalıkavak, 0252/385-4242, www.hasaninyeri.com).

DAY 2

Board a *gület* (motorized sailboat) to explore the cape's best offshore destinations. Snorkel, waddle in a mud bath, and take a relaxing snooze.

DAY 3

Head out in a pre-booked rental car to catch the 9 A.M. hydrofoil ferry to the port of **Datça** on the Reşadiye Peninsula. Spend the rest of the morning surveying the **ancient Dorian ruins** strewn around the terraced headland at Knidos, before traveling back to the mainland by way of the memorable hamlet of Reşadiye – home to traditional Aegean/Turkish architecture – and the fishing village of Datça. In Datça, have a late lunch at **Zekeriya Sofrası** (Zekeriya's Table, Yalı Cad. 60-62, 0252/712-4303), which serves ridiculously good and cheap Turkish down-home cooking. Gloriously sated, head out to explore the second cape – the **Hisarönü Peninsula.** The string of sandy beaches, rustic fishing villages, stunningly aquamarine coves, and a waterfall all await along the 40-kilometer coastal road that leads to the tip of the historic promontory. Head to Marmaris by nightfall.

DAYS 4-8

Explore the Marmaris castle in the morning before boarding a *gület* en route to Fethiye on a pre-booked, four-day **Blue Cruise** (Turkey Travel Tours, Sat. only 3:30 P.M., US$230-600 pp depending on the time of travel). Sail to the 2,500-year-old **Lycian ruins** and **rock tombs at Dalyan** and snorkel or sunbathe in some of the prettiest bays in the eastern Med along the way to Fethiye.

DAYS 9-10

In Fethiye, explore the loggerhead turtle nesting ground at **Kaplumbağ Plajı** (Turtle Beach); parasail over the natural splendor of Ölüdeniz; white-water raft in the Dalaman River, discovering the hidden caves and canyons at Saklıkent Gorge; or better yet, just relax on Fethiye's splendid four-kilometer-long sandy stretch.

DAY 11

Rent a car to survey the 84 kilometers of destination-packed coastline between Fethiye and Kekova. Stops along the way include **Butterfly Valley's** deep canyon that descends straight into the sea; Kalkan, the location of ancient **Xanthos** now replete with whitewashed shoe-box houses trailed in showy bougainvillea; Gelemiş, ancient **Patara** and its Temple of Apollo; and, the rustic village of Kaş – home to sponge divers and more Lycian relics. Then, head to the nearby village of Üçağız for a romantic dinner and an overnight at the rustic **Kale Pansiyon** (0242/874-2111, www.kalepansiyon.com, €70-80).

DAY 12

Continue onto **Antalya** (102 km.). The drive along miles of beaches and headlands include some enticing activities: wade among the sunken eons-old ruins at Kekova; visit Demre, the home of Saint Nicholas's splendid 2nd-century church; and, trek through Olympus's national park, where the eternal flame of Chimeara blazes.

DAYS 13-14

The last 48 hours of this itinerary are spent based at **Mediterra Hotel** (Barbaros M Zafer S 5, Kaleiçi, 0242/244-8624, www.mediterraart.com, US$97-115) in Antalya. The provincial seat of one of Turkey's most beautiful regions, the city possesses a prize-winning archaeological museum, phenomenal beaches, loads of Selçuk architecture, trendy shops, and numerous Greco-Roman antiques.

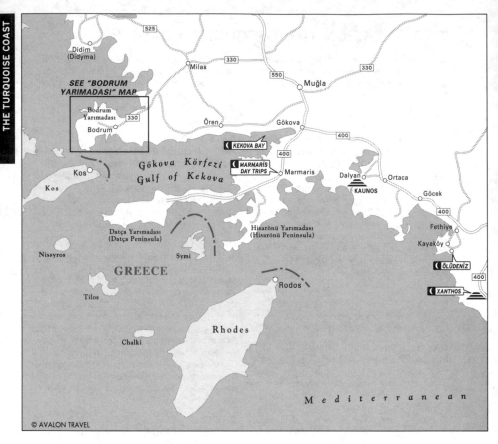

experience local culture, a one-day drive is included from Fethiye to Antalya—hands-down the best coastal scenery along the coast; and, four days are set aside for the Blue Cruise. Just one consideration, however, book your itinerary around the cruise departure day, which is a Saturday.

The absolute best time to travel through this region is during the shoulder season, during the spring months of April and May and autumn months of October and early November. Avoid the summer season altogether, if you can. Starting in mid-June–mid-September the Turquoise Coast's population swells, sometimes by 300 percent in the summer playgrounds of Bodrum, Marmaris, and Antalya. Hotel rates

also follow the upward arc and so will the cost of everything you'll drink, eat, rent, or ride.

Climate-wise, the region's mild temperatures make any season ideal for touring. Perhaps the worst time is at its busiest, during the torrid summer season when this stretch is assaulted with busloads of tourists and highs of above 40°C (100°F). Beach space is at a premium; ditto for restaurants, hotels, and bars. Obviously, some revel in this brouhaha, while others find it dreadful. That's why this slice of Turkey is best enjoyed during the spring and fall months when temperatures are much milder and tourism diminishes to a trickle. Coastal waters remain warm and cafés still have outdoor-seating. While the region enjoys

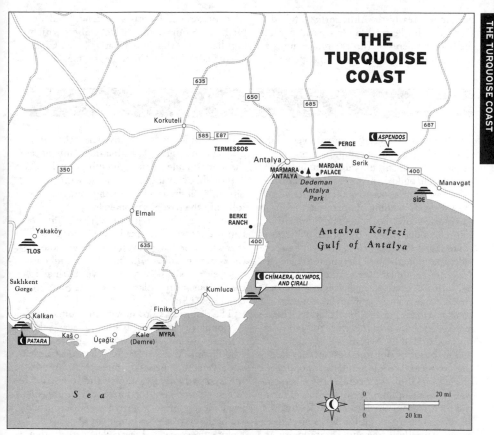

the sought-after Mediterranean climate, winter temperatures can dip to 9°C (48.2°F) during the day, and to 3°C (37.4°F) in the evening. And—yes—there is even the rare frost. Average summer low temperatures hover around 19°C (66°F). The winter months create a different atmosphere on the coast. This is a great time to engage with the local culture. Keeping in mind that both hoteliers and restaurateurs synchronize their clocks with the official summer season, more than 60 percent of hotels close shop during the rest of the year. Spring in places like Butterfly Valley offer nature lovers a unique chance to check out wild flower displays and herbs that paint and scent its deep gorge.

The annual festival season gets into gear all along the coast in May, and doesn't stop until December. One of the most awaited celebrations nationwide is Antalya's Aspendos Opera and Ballet Festival, which occur for two weeks starting in mid-June in ancient Aspendos's colossal Greco-Roman amphitheater. Eight to ten classical performances of such classics as Adolphe Adam's ballet *Giselle* and Georges Bizet's opera *Carmen* are performed to packed crowds in the arena. The month of May marks the start of the yachting season with the Marmaris International Yachting Festival. And two internationally reputed yacht races officially end the season: Bodrum's Sailing Cup in October and Marmaris's Yacht Regatta in

November. Yearly, the Altın Portakal (Golden Orange) Film Festival in October recognizes the biggest talents of Turkey's movie industry with Cannes-like celebrations and showings.

Also of note is Demre's International St. Nicholas Symposium in December, which highlights its 4th-century native Santa Claus to coincide with the Christmas season.

Bodrum

The Bodrum Yarımadası (Bodrum Peninsula) seems to be the end-all summer destination in Turkey, with, thankfully tons of unblemished real estate to build on its appeal. The peninsula's secret, aside from some 65,000 hectares of rolling hills with nothing but decrepit windmills and grazing cows, lies in its long littoral. About a dozen unique villages, comprised of blocks of whitewashed low-rises draped in showy bougainvillea, promote the Med's celebrated dolce vita. And, unlike similar über resorts like Kuşadası or Marmaris, development here is mostly kept in check. Aside from a highway that connects the peninsula to the provincial seal of Muğla, there's just a single back road that rings this large, scenic headland in the Aegean Sea.

The proof of Bodrum's popularity lies in the numbers. With a permanent population of about 33,000, the peninsula swells to upwards of one million in the summer. During the high season, the locale double-duties as an ultimate party point for billionaires in exclusive bays like Torba and Türkbükü, or as a laid-back refuge in idyllic bays like Akyarlar and around the cafés overlooking the sunken ruins off the port of Gümüşlük. The rest of the year, however, the peninsula reverts back to a sleepy resort of anglers, farmers, and boat builders.

What truly grabs first-time visitors is the unrivaled excitement of the harbor town Bodrum. The medieval Castle of St. Peter commands the cape from downtown Bodrum's yacht-filled harbor. Near this looming fortress are the foregone remains of the Halicarnassus Mausoleum—one of the Seven Wonders of the Ancient World. Both offer plenty to keep sightseers busy during daytime. Come nighttime, the port roars to life with a laser light

display letting everyone know where the party is. And that's usually at Halikarnas Club, once the loudest and largest nightclub in the Med. Although, today it has to contend with a slew of similar clubs and the blaring lounges that roll onto the harbor's promenade.

So whatever the inkling, the Bodrum Peninsula seems ever ready to please. But, if that's still not enough, you can always take to the water aboard a gület (motorized sailboat) from either one of Bodrum's two marinas to the various nearby islands or on the romanticized Blue Cruise.

The peninsula's downtown, Bodrum, owes its popularity to Turkish scribe Cevat Şakir Kabaağaçlı. Exactly a century ago, Sultan Abdülhamid II exiled Kabaağaçlı to the Castle of St. Peter for a period of three years for writing sympathetically about army deserters. When he arrived at the fortress, the dungeon was closed, so the local governor—an admiring fan of the essayist—set him up in a house overlooking the gorgeous Aegean. There, the author waxed poetic about the scenery and the sweet life of what was then a small fishing community. He amassed tons of essays and later books aimed directly at Istanbul's intelligentsia. By the 1950s, Turkey's educated class had moved in for the summer. And less than two decades later, Bodrum couldn't keep up with the demand from tourists and real estate developers.

Sure today's overly commercial center looks nothing like the sea-lapped outpost Kabaağaçlı memorialized in prose, but the blue of the water that so tantalized him remains, and so does the friendliness of anglers by the port. During summer, Bodrum's centrum is the eye of the tourism storm with an unrelenting whirlwind of cruise boats, yachts, and tour buses. If you thrive in

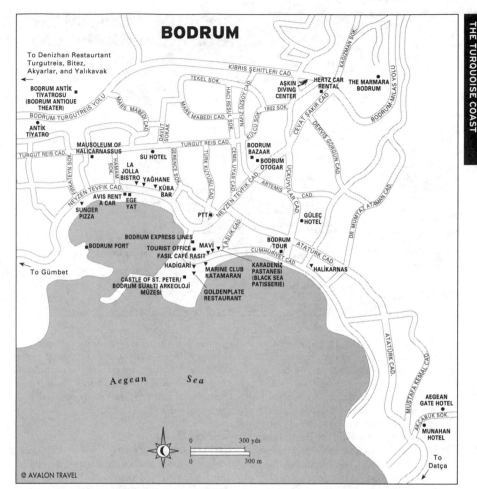

BODRUM

To Denizhan Restaurant
Turgutreis, Bitez,
Akyarlar, and Yalıkavak

KIBRIS ŞEHITLERI CAD.

TEKEL SOK.

AŞKIN DIVING CENTER

HERTZ CAR RENTAL

THE MARMARA BODRUM

BODRUM-MILAS YOLU

BODRUM ANTİK TIYATROSU (BODRUM ANTIQUE THEATER)

MARS MABEDI CAD.

HACI RESUL SOK.

ZAFER SOK.

KÜLCÜ SOK.

1802 SOK.

BODRUM-TURGUTREIS YOLU

DAVUT DERE SOK.

MARS MABEDI CAD.

CEVAT ŞAKIR CAD.

DERVIŞ GÖRGÜN CAD.

ANTİK TİYATRO

AYKICI SOK.

TURGUT REIS CAD.

BODRUM BAZAAR

ÜÇKUYULAR CAD.

BODRUM OTOGAR

MAUSOLEUM OF HALICARNASSUS

GERENCE SOK.

TÜRK KUYUSU CAD.

CEMIL UYAR CAD.

ARTEMIS CAD.

TURGUT REIS CAD.

SU HOTEL

DR. MÜMTAZ ATAMAN CAD.

LA JOLLA BISTRO

HAMAM SOK.

YAĞHANE

KÜBA BAR

NEYZEN TEVFİK CAD.

NEBRATEN SOK.

AVIS RENT A CAR

EGE YAT

NEYZEN TEVFİK CAD.

GÜLEÇ HOTEL

SUNGER PIZZA

PTT

TAŞLIK CAD.

ATATÜRK CAD.

BODRUM EXPRESS LINES

BODRUM PORT

TOURIST OFFICE

MAVİ

BODRUM TOUR

CUMHURIYET CAD.

FASIL CAFÉ RASIT

HADİGARİ

HALIKARNAS

To Gümbet

MARINE CLUB KATAMARAN

KARADENIZ PASTANESİ (BLACK SEA PATISSERIE)

CASTLE OF ST. PETER/ BODRUM SUALTI ARKEOLOJİ MÜZESİ

GOLDENPLATE RESTAURANT

KAZIZMAN SOK.

Aegean   Sea

ATATÜRK CAD.

MUSTAFA KEMAL CAD.

AEGEAN GATE HOTEL

AKÇABÜK SOK.

MUNAHAN HOTEL

To Datça

0   300 yds
0   300 m

© AVALON TRAVEL

TURGUT REIS CAD.

the middle of the action, then this place is for you. Or you might also enjoy the lively enclave of Gümbet, a beachside village popular for its British bar scene and international restaurants. Otherwise, base your efforts elsewhere around the peninsula and *dolmuş* (communal taxi) back to the center for sightseeing.

HISTORY

The history of Bodrum—or ancient Halicarnassus—is deeply entwined with its port. The first Hellenic colony to capitalize on the seaside outpost were the Dorians in the 11th century B.C. This strategic location didn't elude the Persians either when they stormed Asia Minor in the mid-6th century B.C. They selected the locale as the capital of the Carian satrapy (province), a title which relinquished a significant amount of autonomy to the locals, particularly when it came to spending the proceeds that arose from prominent local boat-building and trading guilds. And as booming economies typically went hand in hand with the advent of culture during Antiquity, it

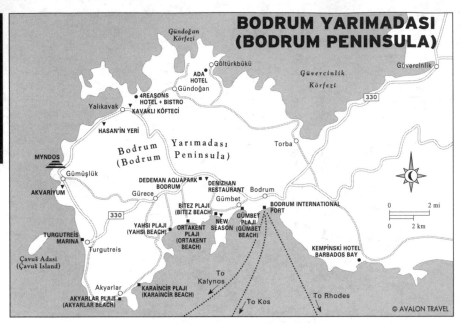

wasn't long before the area spawned great minds. One of them was the great Herodotus of Halicarnassus (484–425 B.C.)—the father of history.

The single testament that speaks of the port city's Ancient history is the Mausoleum of Halicarnassus. Built in the 4th century B.C., the structure became a tribute to Carian Princess Artemis II and Mausolus and their unfathomable wealth and love. The remains of this impressive tomb—one of the Seven Wonders of the Ancient World—lie just a couple of blocks inland from the fortress.

By the 12th century, the Selçuk Turks ruled the Aegean city, only to relinquish it to the Knights of Saint John in 1404. These chevaliers waltzed in and built the Castle of St. Peter atop a diminutive Selçukian fort with stones culled from the mausoleum. The town was renamed Mesy, and served until the onset of the 16th century as a refuge for Christians fleeing from the Islamization of Anatolia.

It was from a nearby ivy-covered farmhouse that Cevat Şakir Kabaağaçlı, the popular 20th-century Turkish essayist, romanticized the fishing village. In his seafaring tales all along the Aegean littoral, he coined the term *Mavi Yolçuluk* (Blue Cruise) and this became the commercial name for the trendy nautical voyage along the Lycian Coast.

SIGHTS
Castle of St. Peter

Bodrum's main attraction is one of the largest and best preserved castles of the Knights of Rhodes, and the world's hands-down best underwater archaeology museum. If that doesn't grab your attention, come for the fantastic sea views best seen from the five-centuries-old refectory high atop the French Tower.

The garrison lies atop an earlier Selçukian fort on what was once the island of Zephyria, named after Zephyros, the Hellenic God of the Western Wind. This spot was hand-picked by the knights, and bankrolled by their various European duchies and the Vatican, for a new garrison (after losing their foothold in Izmir to Tamerlane and his rapacious Mongol troops in 1402). According to Turkish historians, the knights were handed free reign of the littoral by Ottoman Sultan Mehmet Celebi, who also feared the wrath of the Mongols. The then Pope Callixtus III, who was intent on renewing a crusade against the westward marching Turkish infidels, personally appointed German knight and architect Heinrich Schlegelholt to launch the build. The pontiff even went as far as to guarantee laborers eternal life in heaven for their holy "participation." It took decades for the fortress, originally a set of moats and fortifications, to gain its current size. And in 1522, just months before the mighty Ottoman army of Süleyman II the Magnificent captured most of the Eastern Med, the knights uncovered Mausolus' burial chamber and its booty, while searching nearby for additional stones to strengthen the garrison. The fortress became a prison under the Ottomans, and storage space for the numerous undersea finds after Mustafa Kemal Atatürk's rise to power in 1923. The 600-year-old castle has withstood the test of time and repeated earthquakes remarkably. With more than 240 coat of arms, varied inscriptions, and armor along the garrison's five towers, the interior and exterior spaces make the fortress a foremost example of European medieval history.

The looming structure has been formally opened to the public as the **Bodrum Sualtı Arkeoloji Müzesi** (0252/316-2516, www.bodrum-museum.com, 8:30 A.M.–noon and 1–5:30 P.M. Tues.–Sun. in winter, until 7 P.M. in summer, 10TL) since 1963. It's an impressive repository for the countless booty collected from nine offshore shipwrecks, some dating as far back as the 14th century B.C. These undersea treasures are strewn throughout, aptly mixing the site's comprehensive history. Aside from vast collections of barnacle-encrusted amphorae, stunningly ornate gold and silver jewelry, oil lamps, and copper tools, shipwrecks have been perfectly reconstructed just as they appeared undersea when errant sponge divers discovered them. One of these exhibits is the 3,400-year-old **Uluburun Shipwreck.** Its cargo include a gold chalice and a remarkable gold scarab inscribed with the name of ancient Egyptian queen Nefertiti.

the resort town of Bodrum's medieval gem, the 15th-century Castle of St. Peter

Aside from historical artifacts, the fortress' grounds feature samples of almost every flora found in the Mediterranean. Take note of the myrtle tree in the main court. Dedicated to Aphrodite throughout history, the plane tree was sought by royalty for its health-promoting benefits.

Slate at least a couple of hours to tour this gem while on the peninsula. It's arguably Turkey's best museum, thanks to the conserted efforts of Turkey's Ministry of Tourism and the Institute of Nautical Archaeology at Texas A&M University.

Mausoleum of Halicarnassus

When the Carian satrap (governor) Mausolus grew tired of having to answer to his higher-ups in the Persian capital of Persepolis, he revolted (362 B.C.). Mausolus then moved the ancient seat of the Carian satrapy (province) from Mylasa (Milas) to Halicarnassus—today's Bodrum. From this new coastal seat he went on to invade Lycia and Ionia, accompanied by his wife/sister, Artemis II. The duo spared no expense to beautify their new capital, and in the process devised a burial ground that would attest to their accumulated riches for eons to come. Unfortunately, Mausolus died at the tender age of 24 (353 B.C.), leaving his sister and widow with the task of completing the grave. Artemis obliged by seeking out the best architects and sculptors to complete the impressive shrine. The final product was a massive marble square measuring 45 meters in height, which was divided into three equal parts: the base featured bas-reliefs of lions and demigods; a colonnaded terrace encircled a marble tomb; and, a pyramidal roof supported a colossal horse-drawn chariot containing the grander-than-life statues of Artemis and Mausolus. The term mausoleum—or monumental grave—derives from Mausolus. Despite various pirate raids in the mid-1st century A.D., the tomb stood pretty much intact until a series of devastating earthquakes destroyed most of its roof around the first millennium. The 36 columns that surrounded the grave and the structure's base were used as fodder for the construction

of a Selçukian fortress in the 12th century. The Knights of St. John further picked whatever remained to build the Castle of St. Peter.

The site of the Mausoleum (Turgutreis Cad., 8:30 A.M.–5:30 P.M. Tues.–Sun., 5TL) is a pleasant landscaped courtyard. The remains of the monumental grave are strewn haphazardly and are still under excavation. These include some fluted columns, marble drums, one of the grave's grand stairways, and rubble culled from its chambers. Of note, however, are fragments of friezes that appeared on the base of the Mausoleum and a collection of models and representations of what the burial shrine itself and the town of Halicarnassus may have looked like more than 2,300 years ago.

Bodrum Antik Tiyatrosu (Bodrum Antique Theater)

Bodrum is privy to its own Antique amphitheater. The Bodrum Antik Tiyatrosu (on the main highway of Kıbrıs Şehitler Cad., 0252/316-8061, 8:30 A.M.–5:30 P.M. Tues.–Sun. in winter, until 7 P.M. in summer, 5TL) has a capacity of 13,000. It's a compact venue that doubles as an outdoor music hall during the concert season. From its location high atop Bodrum's hillside, the views of the marina and the Greek isle of Kos are reason enough to visit. Historically, the theater is another 4th-century B.C. brainchild of architectural aesthete Mausolus. The Romans renovated, enlarged, and enriched it in the 2nd century A.D. Check out the rows of seating for clues etched in stone pertaining to the wealthy benefactors who contributed in the makeover. Climb above the theater to peek at recently excavated rock tombs that actually predate the surrounding structure.

ENTERTAINMENT AND EVENTS

Bodrum is reputed throughout Europe and beyond for its nightlife. And the race is on, as Bodrum proper's gaudy haunts vie for prominence against the jet-set magnets of Göltürkbükü (municipality of Gölköy and Türkbükü) on the opposite side of the peninsula, keeping the foreign press giddy with praise and the paparazzi on their toes for the latest star to hit town. But generally, Bodrum's nightlife starts along the terraced diners, bars, and booths selling trinkets on the narrow, but packed, Dr. Alimbey Caddesi. It then flows along the broader Cumhuriyet Caddesi *(Barlar Sokağı)*, where British pubs share acreage with sophisticated dens catering to virtually all lifestyles. But no matter what the location, entertainment is not restricted to nighttime. Seaside bars and beach clubs guarantee a generous flow of beer, big screen TVs, and boisterous games of backgammon all day long. Dance clubs and bars get going around 11 P.M. until last call, which is usually until at least 2 A.M. around the peninsula. But the *rakı*-fueled fun continues well into the wee hours of the morn in Bodrum proper.

Nightclubs

A trip to Bodrum warrants an evening at **Halikarnas** (Cumhuriyet Cad. 178, 0252/316-8000, www.halikarnas.com.tr, 10 P.M.–5 A.M. Apr.–Oct., weekday 30TL, weekend 35TL). So incomparable is the ambience here that even Mick Jagger was left speechless during a visit in the 1980s. This stylish theater-discotheque is Las Vegas' larger-than-life showmanship, Amsterdam's nocturnal permissiveness, and London's club scene all rolled into one. There's so much here that this outdoor party mecca's 5,500 guests (capacity) come back night after night. Hint: call or log online to reserve a table on the upper levels away from the throbbing mass of humanity on the dance floor.

The uniquely decadent **Marine Club Katamaran** (Dr. Alimbey Cad. 1025, 0252/313-3600, www.clubbodrum.com, 10 P.M.–4 A.M. daily Apr.–Oct., weekday 30TL, weekend 35TL) takes 1,500 revelers nightly to the high seas, with shuttles ferrying guests to and from the marina every 15 minutes. Boasting five bars, this giant floating dance floor sails off by 1 A.M. to the tunes of top international DJs, interspersed with fashion shows and Turkish pop stars.

Head north to Göltürkbükü's posh **Bianca** (Akdeniz Cad. 35, Gölköy, 0252/357-7474, www.biancabeach.com, daily June–Oct.,

50TL), which remains one of the Med's most exclusive nightclubs. Bee-bop with designer-clad socialites to Latin music, R&B, or to the sounds of whichever Turkish top-40 artists happen to be on the scene.

Bars

Küba Bar (Neyzen Tekvik Cad. 62, 0252/313-4450, www.kubabar.com, 9 A.M.–4 A.M. daily May–Nov.; until 2 A.M. Wed.–Sun. Dec.–Apr., drinks 20TL, entrées 40TL) is the only bar/restaurant able to lure the national elite from their hillside hideaways to the marina. A sleek whitewashed stone terrace welcomes bar-hoppers with black marble bars and aluminum fittings, while the pricey, reservations-only restaurant is set in the rear.

The bar responsible for launching Bodrum's night scene more than 30 years ago is **Hadigari** (Dr. Alimbey Cad. 37, 0252/316-0048, www.hadigari.com.tr, daily June–Oct., admission 20TL after midnight). Located just left of the castle in a converted power plant, Hadigari—meaning, let's go folks!—lures foot traffic with gigantic torches flanking its harborside entrance. This all-in-one space does dining best from 7 P.M. onward, although it doubles as a busy bar and upscale nightclub after hours.

For a nice alternative to the techno-pumping dens of Bar Street, head to **Fasıl Café Rasıt** (Cumhuriyet Caddesi, 0252/316-1895). Here, traditional belly dancers and Turkish musicians perform 11 P.M.–3 A.M.

Festivals and Events

Every year, the third week of October commemorates the official end of the sailing season with Bodrum's much-awaited **International Bodrum Cup** (ERA Bodrum Sailing Club, www.bodrumcup.com), which attracts hundreds of national and international sailors. The race not only features competing dozens of crews, all vying for the winning pennant and cup, but also promotes the sport worldwide. The last two weeks of August herald the **International Ballet Festival** (0252/313-7649, www.bodrumballetfestival.org). Held at the Castle of St. Peter, the event

THE BLUE VOYAGE

Imagine spending a week or two with nothing but scented pine-clad mountains to break the interminable blue of the sky melding into that of the water. That's what's on offer on the **Mavi Yolculuk** (Blue Voyage). This unique sea-born journey was made famous in the late 1920s when the intelligentsia got wind of an article penned by the erudite poet and travel writer Cevat Şakir Kabaağaçlı. Known as the "Fisherman of Halicarcanass," Kabaağaçlı spent the first year (1927) of a 36-month exile in Bodrum's Genoese fortress for riling politicos in print. Imagine being "jailed" in Bodrum! But instead of serving his time shackled and repenting, the author flew the coop and toured Turkey's southwestern coast with village fishermen and sponge divers. He was the first to chart and wax lyrical about what he coined the Blue Voyage.

In the eight decades since, the nautical jaunt has become the highlight of a trip to Turkey – one that allows first-time travelers to visit coastal villages, like Kekova, that are only accessible by boat. This tremendously popular sea trip comes in all sizes and shapes, so it pays to be informed about what's on offer.

The *gület* is the traditional boat of this region; it's a wooden, two-masted motorized sailboat that offers a variety of main features. Being larger and wider than most crafts, *gülets* offer spacious decks and larger public areas, in addition to private cabins with showers and modern amenities. A typical *gület* with a crew accommodates 8-12 people. Day-trip boats can carry up to 25.

Experienced sailors can also choose the bareboat charter option – or a boat without a crew – that allows passengers way more independence and the possibility of a do-it-yourself adventure. Captained boats, on the other hand, keep the crew but do away with all other passengers, leaving you and your party alone to chart the course.

Then, there's the most popular option: chartering a cabin on scheduled cruises. The typical sailboats used for cabin charters are the least attractive – and oldest – models of an operator's fleet. These ships usually don't receive the TLC lavished on newer, larger crafts, like annual maintenance, for instance. They can show wear and tear, faded decks, malfunctioning plumbing, and antiquated cabins. As in everything else, you get what you pay for, and dishing out a bit more cash will go a long way.

The favored Blue Voyage route departs from Bodrum to the Gulf of Gökova, for a classical seven-day outing that combines plenty of opportunities for swimming and traipsing through the ancient site of Knidos. Other trips setting sail from Bodrum sail straight through either the North (Kos, Kalymnos, and Patmos) or South (Rhodes and Simi) Dodecanese Islands, adding an escape to the irresistible Greek islands. But most first timers to Turkey's turquoise coast opt for the popular Marmaris option, which heads to Fethiye and back, pausing at Cleopatra's Baths, Göcek, İztuzu Beach, Dalyan, Kaunos, and Ölüdeniz. Seven-day sails are also available from Antalya and Fethiye; these feature the idyllic spots of Ölüdeniz, Kaş, Kekova, and Gemiler Island.

Blue voyages are organized during mid-April through at least the end of October. Booking with a local or international travel agent can pay off big time in the long run. Most cruises are seven days long and typically depart on Sunday morning. But operators will match any request, anywhere from the two-day stop-and-go to the three-week leisurely cruise. Seven-day cruise packages run €285-465 per person; luxury versions start at €525 per person and include gourmet meals and larger, more posh cabins. Mini cruises, which run four days around the stunning Marmaris-Fethiye, run €205-275.

highlights Turkey's top ballet stars in modern and classical ballet performances.

SPORTS AND RECREATION

With a landscape so stunningly varied, at least a day should be set aside to fully experience Bodrum by trekking through its outback. Aside from the must-do, ridiculously hip day-long boat tours, you'll also find jeep safaris and horseback riding. And, while you're at it, why not rent a scooter for a DIY trip of the peninsula? All one really needs to do is walk through Bodrum's center, and along its harbor, to realize the myriad touring possibilities.

Boat Tours

To join the requisite day cruise, head for Bodrum's harbor the evening before you plan on setting out. There you'll find handfuls of deckhands and even captains peddling the standard seven-hour cruise (from 25TL). Typically departing around 10 A.M. and returning by 5:30 P.M., wooden *gülets* (motorized sailboats) run a cookie-cutter itinerary. Stops include five favorite swimming locales, among them offshore caves, scenic bays, and a therapeutic mud bath at **Karaada** (Black Island).

No one else does maritime travel better than Bodrum outfitters, thanks to the variety of providers in and around the marina. Whatever the desire, whether a two-week trip through the Greek islands, the venerated seven- or eight-day Blue Cruise, or even custom itineraries, there's a company to oblige. One notable cruise and charter company is **Ege Yat** (Aegean Yacht, İçmeler 54, Bodrum Center, 0252/313-2655, www.aegeanyacht.com). A darling of the national and foreign press, Aegean Yacht leads the pack of yacht service providers in Turkey, thanks to a highly varied fleet of boats and an impeccable safety record. Aegean provides six-hour boat tours (daily, €15) and the largest selection of eight-day cruises, including eight casual Blue Cruise itineraries (€260–440 full board) and the Royal Cruise (€1050–1900 full board). The latter takes passengers in high style from Bodrum along the Hisarönü Peninsula and the Greek isle of Kos.

Horseback Riding

If you'd like to hoof it equestrian-style, then check out the **Turgutreis Country Ranch** (Yukarı Mah., Turgutreis, 0252/382-5654, www.irismaritime.com, €25). Turgutreis Country Ranch offers a five-hour horseback-riding trip through the hills, valleys, and beaches surrounding Turgutreis, after which refreshments can be enjoyed in the utmost serenity of this ranch's cafeteria.

Jeep and Trekking Tours

Four-wheel drive and trekking safaris are really hitting their stride in Bodrum. Touring by jeep is a fun way to take in the peninsula, enjoy a swim or two, and make friends with local farmers and visiting city-slickers alike. A contender for the all-around best tours is **Bodrum Tour** (Üçkuyular Cad. 5, next to Hotel Alize, 0252/313-3009, www.bodrumtour.com). Guided by Bodrum natives, the 130-kilometer jeep safari (9 A.M.–5 P.M. daily, €30) hits all the essential spectacular spots, as well as the peninsula's secret idylls and loftiest peaks. The lunch stop in Mazı, a sleepy beachside hamlet, includes a swim in one of Bodrum's least visited and most stunning bays. The eight-hour trekking tour (daily, €35) is just as exciting, with stops on Bodrum's highest stepped terraces and crags, all boasting majestic scenery.

Bodrum's central location makes it an ideal base for one-day excursions. Bodrum Tour, along with most agents in town, offer these side trips (about €30) to coincide with local market days in specific destinations: Pamukkale (Tues. and Fri.); Ephesus (Wed. and Sat.); and Dalyan and Kaunos (Thurs. and Sun.).

Water Sports

Bodrum is the epitome of hedonism, particularly when it comes to activities that involve water. The translucent coastal sea beckons scuba divers to explore the superb fauna and flora, as well as the expected relics of its underwater reefs, islands, and caves. The shore is dotted with more than 30 public beaches and beach clubs.

For underwater exploration, **Aşkın Diving Center** (Kibris Şehitleri Cad., Ataman Iş Merkezi E/3, 0252/316-4247, www.askindiving.com) is *the* diving provider of choice. The dives are led by owner Aşkın Canbazoğlu, an archaeologist who was affiliated with Bodrum's Underwater Archaeology Museum for eight years before going commercial. Aşkın leads divers to Bodrum's offshore archaeological sites, while snorkelers are free to explore the surface. Full day dives (€50) include the use of equipment, boat trip, two dives, and lunch. Night dives (€40), non-diving trips (€15), equipment rental (€15/per day), and one- to four-day PADI-certified instruction (includes theory and international license, €50–320) are also on offer.

Kitesurfers and windsurfers head to **Bitez Plajı** (Bitez Beach). The surfing season runs late May–early November. Winds are mild in the morning, and pick up dramatically by mid-afternoon. Owner Rush of **Rush Windsurfing** (Bitez Beach, board rental 85TL/day, 425TL/week) is a jovial European and a patient instructor. Equipment rental is available for intermediate to advanced surfers. Windsurfing lessons (130TL/2hr, 320TL/10hr) are typically organized in the mornings.

Beaches and Beach Clubs

Bodrum's best beaches are located on the southern side of the peninsula. **Akyarlar** tops my list. It even appeared on *Forbes Magazine*'s "15 Best Sandy Strips in the World." It owes its reputation to the powdery sand and the string of traditional Greek stone houses that line its tiny, concave bay. Coming in second for its traditional Turkish restaurants is **Karaincir**'s long sandy stretch, just next door to Akyarlar. Coming in third is **Bitez**, a beach that mixes shallow depths, that are ideal for children, and offshore wind conditions, that lend to some of the best surfing and waterskiing on the peninsula. **Ortakent, Bardakcı,** and **Bağla,** nearby, are also recommended.

Alternatively, the posh beach clubs in the northern enclave of **Göltürkbükü** and **Yalıkavak** are just that, expensive havens

for the highly privileged. The top destination remains **Bianca Beach Club** (Akdeniz Cad. 35, Gölköy, 0252/357-7474, www.biancabeach.com, 50TL). A card purchased at the entrance entitles guests to purchase chintzy snacks and libations for up to the card's monetary value. Bianca's pillared beachfront and snazzy pool come replete with a business center for guests who must keep tabs on their financial portfolio. For low-key luxury, head to **Xuma Beach Club** (south side of Yalıkavak, 0252/385-4775, 10TL). Here, mostly money-eyed nationals seesaw between the beautifully landscaped grounds around the beach and one of the many international restaurants onsite. Note that whichever shoreline you decide to slather your sunscreen on comes with an availability of chaise lounges and parasols; this luxury is offered on the understanding that you will order meals during your stay at the establishment's shorefront.

Water theme parks around the promontory ensure the overall satisfaction of kids in the family. But, when it comes down to safety, not all parks are created equal. Scoring high for the quality of its staff and equipment is the recently opened **Dedeman Aquapark Bodrum** (Scala Beach, Ortakent, 0252/358-5888, www.aquaparkdedeman.com, adult 33TL, children ages 7–12 23TL, under 6 and over 60 free). The four-hectare space is filled with exciting and teen-friendly water slides and surf pools. The lazy pond, splashing spots for tots, and three fast food stands are geared to satisfy the rest of the clan.

ACCOMMODATIONS

While there is an exception or two, finding all-around pleasant accommodations in the center of town is difficult, unless you venture further up Bodrum's hill. The nightly hubbub around both marinas can keep early-to-bed visitors counting sheep until 4 A.M. Pension owners swear by the efficacy of double-glazed windows, but even this proves no match to the din—and light—emitted by the gargantuan clubs nearby. But if action is what you're after, and you'll be cutting a rug until the wee hours anyway, then by all means, do base your efforts around the port.

Otherwise, the best plan of action is to opt for an idyllic B&B or one of the many sleek resorts along the peninsula. Most hotels are closed November–April, opening for the two-week New Year's holiday. For an exhaustive list of Bodrum's more than 400 properties, check out www.bodrumhotels.net.

Under €100

Ask a tourism professional to recommend a mid-priced boutique hotel in Bodrum and 【 **Aegean Gate Hotel** (Guvercin Sok. 2, Bodrum, 0252/316-7853, www.aegeangate-hotel.com, May–Oct., €65–100) is the sure-fire answer. And here's why: It's within walking distance of all the sites, relatively inexpensive, and an ultimate retreat among gorgeously land-scaped grounds high on a rocky mound above Bodrum. Taking time to meet with each guest, Irish owners Rory and Gary are another plus to staying at the Aegean Gate; they're a virtual gold mine of information when it comes to the peninsula. The Aegean has only six rooms, and they go fast.

Su Hotel (Turgutreis Cad. 120, Bodrum, 0252/316-6906, www.suhotel.net, €75–95) is the rare property smack in the center whose location guarantees quietude. The building, tucked in along a pedestrian side street, opens into a large white relaxing courtyard, which boasts a refreshing pool and colorful bougain-villea. Each of the large 26 rooms bursts with a palette of lip-smacking color and homey touches like handmade quilts. Modern en suite baths and an onsite restaurant and bar add to this pleasant stay.

The most affordable escape in Bodrum is **Güleç Hotel** (Uçkuyular Cad. 18, Bodrum, 0252/316-5222, www.hotelgulec.com, €55–65). The 18 spare units provide bare, yet immaculately clean, amenities. This family-run pension also boasts a breakfast bar, which is included in the price of the room and served under an overgrown pergola, as well as a large tangerine orchard filled with blooms and birds of every color.

€100-200

The **Munahan Hotel** (Akcabuk Sok. 14, Bodrum, 0252/313-6482, www.munahan.com.tr, €95–125) is another B&B that excels at creating a serene environment amid down-town Bodrum's clatter. Each inspired by a different herb, the charming nine doubles and suites are sparingly filled with antiques and feature immaculately kept baths. The rooms and suites surround the striking courtyard that greets guests just past the entrance. The court-yard has a pool that curves around a lovingly tended garden.

Another reputable B&B in Bodrum, just minutes from the town center, is 【 **Antik Tiyatro** (Antique Theater Hotel, Kibris Sehitleri Cad. 169, 0252/316-6053, www.antiquetheaterhotel.com, €100–225). It boasts designer touches in a tiny property steps away from Bodrum's 2,000-year-old amphitheater. The staff is highly professional and amiable. The guest rooms are somewhat narrow, yet sumptuously decorated with wood furnish-ings, miles of marble, original etchings, hand-made quilts, and antique mirrors. Seemingly floating over Bodrum's twin harbors, the pool beckons both waders and loungers for incom-parable summer sunsets over the bay. Antik is renowned globally for serving a French-inspired Turkish cuisine at pool-side tables; the *New York Times* hails it as one of the best hotels in Turkey.

A darling of the national media, the **4reasons Hotel+Bistro** (Bakan Cad. 2, Yalıkavak, 0252/385-3212, www.4reasonshotel.com, €115–200) is set high above the long—and as yet untouched—bay of Yalıkavak. The four reasons why guests swoon over this prop-erty, according to its owners, Esra and Ali Akin, are serenity, design, quality, and atti-tude. You'll find all of those things and gor-geous island views, lush fruit orchards, and white-on-white spacious rooms that exude easy-going yet refined Med charm. Add the eclectic Middle East–meets-French cuisine offered at the posh onsite bistro and you won't want to leave, much less sup elsewhere.

Over €200

For unbridled luxury head to the secluded **Kempinski Hotel Barbaros Bay** (Kızılağaç Köyü, Yalıçiftlik, 0252/311-0303, www.kempinski-bodrum.com, €145–470). One of Bodrum's top three decadent resorts, the Kempinski's guest rooms are modern in design, each with balconies and an endless array of amenities. But what truly surprises here are the grounds: The pool features sunken replicas of minarets and domes, and the decadent 5,500 square-meter spa facility offers detox and Asian services. Four top-notch, five-star restaurants, lounges, and even a 24-hour library are some of the extra touches.

The Marmara Bodrum (Yokusbaşı Mah., Suluhasan Cad. 18, 0252/313-8130, www.themarmarahotels.com, €150–360) is a luscious hotel clinging over Bodrum's hillside with unadulterated views of the castle and bay. The relaxed atmosphere in the lobby, which unfurls in a sea of modern pearly white furnishings, extends to the 61 immaculately designed guest rooms. Large inviting king-size designer beds are propped on posh parquet and surrounded by airy wicker furniture and bulky custom-design ebony consoles. The Marmara's attention to detail extends to its exterior design, more white, combined with stone that echoes the surrounding boulders; its thermal spa; and the eclectic Med menu served at its gourmet restaurant, the Marmara Tutti.

Thanks to the able efforts of hotelier Vedat Semis the **Ada Hotel** (Tepecik Cad. 128, Türkbükü, 0252/377-5915, www.adahotel. com, US$250–600) is the ultimate in boutique sophistication. Ada epitomizes modern Mediterranean decor on the outside, while its interior blends fascinating Turkish touches and antiques—like four-poster beds and handmade carpets—in wood-accentuated block stone spaces. Just a rubdown at the gorgeous Turkish hammam makes the steep room rates worthwhile. High above the expensive playground of the gulf of Türkbükü, the property's terraces include a pool, exclusive lounges, a library, a serene courtyard centered around a 150-year-old olive tree, and a crypt, which doubles as a

Bodrum's Akyarlar beach and bay

© JESSICA TAMTÜRK

wine cellar for an eclectic collection of wines. Uncork a bottle at the open-air or indoor fine-dining settings.

FOOD

Making recommendations for Bodrum's ever-changing restaurant scene is just as difficult as choosing the area's best hotels. But aside from seeking that proverbial needle in the haystack, the choices listed here are reputable main-stays among savvy travelers and plugged-in lo-cals. There are culinary treasures throughout the peninsula, so it pays to schedule a dinner trip out of Bodrum proper. Make sure to re-serve a table in advance, particularly on the weekends.

As in any other resort town, prices listed on menus are geared towards the wealthier clientele and more than double during the high season. Snacks purchased on-the-go throughout town rarely disappoint in taste or price. If you're in the mood for fish, find out whether the cost is quoted by weight or per order before ordering to avoid any misunderstanding. Bodrum's cuisine revolves around the plentiful Aegean seafood, the fruit and oil reaped from olive groves dotting the peninsula, and zucchini flowers stuffed with herbed rice filling.

Cafés

A hybrid café/bar, **Mavi** (Cumhuriyet Cad. 175, 0252/316-3932, 9 A.M.–4 A.M. June–Oct.) welcomes a sophisticated clientel for breakfast with a mean espresso and a rack stocked with the day's newspapers. Since 1983 live Turkish or Latin music shows take place nightly (tickets required) during the high season.

International

New Season Restaurant (Bitez Bay, 0252/363-8477, www.newseasonrestaurant. com, 8 A.M.–midnight, 18TL) brings Asian and Mexican influences to local produce, fish, and meat. This eclectic mix delivers sumptuous dishes, like sesame-encrusted lamb chops on a bed of greens. Locals know that the best time to head to Seasons is for its weekend brunches,

which feature an array of fruit, salad, meat, and eggs. And if you need transportation, they'll provide that too!

La Jolla Bistro (Neyzen Tevfik Cad. 174, 0252/313-7660, www.lajollabodrum.com, 9 A.M.–midnight, 18TL) opened in 2001 by star restaurateur Serdar Toprak. He learned the fine art of pasta-making in Naples, prior to sweating in some of the most illustrious kitchens of San Diego, California. La Jolla evokes the Golden State's eclectic cuisine and serves it up marvelously to the waiting throngs of well-heeled *Istanbullus*. Aside from nine luscious pasta dishes, the grill menu includes a rare filet mignon cooked to perfection and served with a red wine sauce. There's also a popular sushi bar, Bodrum's largest wine and coffee bars, and cheesecakes to die for.

Pizza lovers delight in the affordable and always busy **Sunger Pizza** (Neyzen Tevfik Cad. 218, 0252/316-0854, 12TL). A hailed lunch haunt for yachters and hip businesspeople alike, Sunger's pizzas are good. And its garlic bread is even better. But the actual specialty here is the *çökertme kebab,* which is a sandwich filled with fries and thinly sliced sirloin, topped with a garlic yogurt sauce. Try this local flavor at the rooftop terrace; it boasts incredible views of Kos and the castle.

Seafood

When it comes to seafood, **Hasan'in Yeri** (Hasan's Place, Gerişaltı Mevkii, Yalıkavak, 0252/385-4242, www.hasaninyeri.com, 11 A.M.–11 P.M., dinner with wine 60TL) remains the restaurant to beat on the peninsula. *Istanbullus* fly in just to savor Hasan's reputed specialties, like cold octopus and calamari appetizer followed with grilled *lagos* (Aegean grouper), drizzled with garlic- and thyme-infused olive oil. But the real culinary gem is the assortment of bite-sized Turkish sweets, which come on a tray with heavenly, sinful double-clotted cream. Set along Yalıkavak's dreamy waterfront, Hasan is a reputed romantic getaway, particularly during the month of August's breathtaking sunsets.

Akvariyum (Aquarium, Yalı Mevkii, Gümüşlük, 0252/385-4151, www.aquariumgumusluk, 11 A.M.–midnight, dinner with wine 50TL) is another favorite fish haunt in nearby Gümüşlük. I've yet to try the more than 40 recommended dishes here because I'm stuck on the *tuzda balık* (seabass cooked in salt), which is showily flambéed tableside. With a handful of small fishing boats bopping in the waters nearby, the terrace's candlelit tables only add to the poetic charm of this romantic setting.

Located in a restored olive oil processing plant, **Yağhane** (Neyzen Tevfik Cad. 170, Bodrum, 0252/313-4747, www.yaghanebodrum.com, 11 A.M.–midnight, dinner with wine 70TL) proposes Aegean fish fare like no one else in and around Bodrum proper. The high notes here remain the *balık pastırması* (cured bluefish carpaccio served with marinated calamari and caviar), heightened only by Yağhane's seabass drizzled with a *rakı*-infused sauce—a dish Ottoman sultans served visiting dignitaries. With a seafront location, this busy, rustic locale also doubles as an art gallery featuring the works of local painters.

Sweets and Quick Bites

Karadeniz Pastanesi (Karadeniz Patisserie, Dr. Alim Bey Caddesi/Meyhane Sokak, Bodrum, 8 A.M.–8 P.M.) not only sells the fruit and cream cakes displayed at the window, but also some of the most filling sandwiches to eat on the go.

No one leaves Bodrum without trying one or two scoops of the organic ice cream served at **Bitez Dondurmacısı** (Geris Altı Mevkii, Yalıkavak, 0252/363-9345, scoop 2.50TL). Owned by Ahmet and Ramaza İhtiyar, the ice cream shop offers more than 14 flavors to perpetual queues hugging the refrigerated showcase. The cognac-flavored chocolate and the Marachino cherry are exquisite.

Turkish

Goldenplate Restaurant (145 Sok., Bodrum, 0252/316-9613, www.goldenplatebodrum.com, 25TL) is one of the town center's most popular restaurants. Its broad menu is centered around Turkish dishes, like its signature dish Amphora Kebab (stewed lamb baked and served in a tall clay pot). Chef-owner Zekeriye Altuntabak doesn't shy away from dabbling in a host of international cuisines to satisfy the demands of foreign palates. Goldenplate is one of the very few seafront diners open year-round; staff even take guests free of charge on a short sunset cruise in the Bodrum Bay on Tuesdays, Thursdays, and Saturdays in summer.

For the meaty tastes of Eastern Anatolia, carnivores should aim their fork at **Denizhan Restaurant** (Turgutreis Yolu, 0252/363-7674, www.denizhan.com, 25TL). Situated about 2.5 kilometers from the town center, the decade-old Denizhan is such a fixture among Bodrum's glitzy residents that it now remains open year-round. All produce is grown organically onsite: The proof is just out the window in the hill-clinging vegetable plot. Denizhan prides itself by trucking in daily the tenderest lamb and beef for their specialty *şiş kebab* from Bandırma; a no-salt cheese for their memorable *künefe* dessert from Istanbul; and the health-inducing turnip juice known as *salğam suyu* from southeast Turkey. The abundant list of domestic vintages only heightens the feast.

Kavaklı Köfteci (Main Square, Yalıkavak, 0252/385-4748, www.kavaklikofteci.com, 11 A.M.–11 P.M., 8TL) is a great introduction to the famous Turkish *köftes* (beef meat balls). In fact, that's all it serves, with the prerequisite side dish of *piyaz* (white bean salad) and a healthy complimentary serving of grilled fresh bread. Reserve ahead of time to bypass the long queues waiting for a table.

INFORMATION AND SERVICES

Bodrum's main **tourist office** (Merkez, 0252/316-2760, 9 A.M.–6 P.M. daily) obliges with very simple maps. Locate an issue of **Bodrum Life** (www.bodrumlife.com, monthly May–Sept.) for more in-depth information, maps, and a listing of destinations and accommodations. The **PTT office** (Cevat Şakıir Cad., 0252/316-2760, 9 A.M.–5 P.M. Mon.–Fri.) has 24-hour telephone services year-round. **ATMs** and **currency exchange** bureaus are located near the harbor along Dr. Alim Bey Caddesi and Cevat Şakir Caddesi, while **bank** offices line the main highway, Kıbrıs Şehitleri Caddesi.

GETTING THERE
By Air

The airport servicing Bodrum is about 36 kilometers (30min) from the town center, and actually closer to the provincial seat in Milas. The two terminals at **Bodrum-Milas Havalimanı** (Bodrum-Milas International Airport, 0252/523-0101, www.milasbodrumairport.com) welcome charter flights daily in the high season from most European capitals, in addition to national airlines, such as Pegasus, Turkish Airlines, and Onur Air. Thanks to a fierce competition between these carriers, tickets can usually be purchased well ahead of time for less than 75TL, and are even cheaper during the shoulder seasons. **THY** (Kıbrıs Şehitler Cad., Oasis Shopping Center, 0252/317-1203) currently runs five flights daily and **Pegasus** (at the airport, 0252/523-0293) has one daily service from Istanbul.

Havas (0252/523-0040, www.havas.com, 15TL) shuttles are the pain-free transport to and from Bodrum. These take off from Bodrum's *otogar* (bus station), stopping on the main highway at Güvercinlik and Torba, two hours prior the departure time of each international flight. Note that seating availability on shuttles is on a first-come first-serve basis. Alternatively, the convenient **Taxi Coop** (at the airport, 0252/523-0024, www.bodrumairporttaxi.com, 24 hours) shuttles passengers directly into town (80TL) or to any villages around the peninsula (80–100TL) anytime of the day or night.

By Car

Most international car rental agencies have branches at the Bodrum airport and in town. **Avis Rent a Car** (at the airport, 0252/523-0201; Neyzen Tevfik Cad. 92, Bodrum, 0252/316-2333, 8 A.M.–8 P.M. daily) rents compact vehicles for about 120TL per day. Rental rates are easily negotiated down, sometimes as much as the tax rate, once onsite.

Take time to shop around, particularly during the off-season.

The Bodrum Peninsula is connected to Milas (48km) by Highway D330. From there Highway D-525 connects through Aydın to the Trans-European Highway E-87 toward Izmir (250km) and further north to Istanbul (710km).

By Bus

Although nationals have just discovered the convenience and affordability of air travel, most tourists are still arriving into Bodrum by bus. This mode of travel is the cheapest way to get to the peninsula from virtually anywhere in the country. **Varan** (0252/316-7849) is the most dependable but also the costliest, while **Kamil Koç** (0252/313-0468) typically provides the best rates. All coach service departs from the **Bodrum Otogar** (bus station), which is centrally located on Cevat Şakir Caddesi, less than a kilometer northeast of St. Peter Castle.

By Boat

Boat service connects the Greek islands of Kos and Rhodes, as well as the Reşadiye Peninsula and other Aegean ports, to Bodrum. Additional runs to the Greek isle of Kalymnos and Turkish ports of Marmaris and Dalyan are provided during the high season, mid-April–end of October. For more information and timetables, contact either **Bodrum Express Lines** (Kale Cad. 18, 0252/316-1087, www.bodrumexpresslines.com) or the **Bodrum Ferryboat Association** (Kale Cad. 22, 0252/316-0882, www.bodrumferryboat.com). Tickets can be purchased right at the dock or through any of the many travel agents in town.

Bodrum Express Lines provides ferryboat service daily to Kos from Bodrum at 9:30 A.M. (May–Sept., 55min, one-way €28), with the return leg departing Kos at 4:30 P.M. (3:30 P.M. in winter). These stop at the Turgutreis marina on both legs (10 A.M.–4:30 P.M.) during the high season. A hydrofoil service is organized daily during the high season, departing Bodrum at 9:30 A.M. and leaving Kos at 5 P.M. (20min, one-way €32). Only ferries operate to

Kos during the winter season, departing on Mondays, Wednesdays, and Fridays. The service to Rhodes runs on Monday and Friday April–September; these depart at 8:30 A.M. from Bodrum and at 4:30 P.M. from Rhodes (2.25hr, one-way €60). Allow at least 30 minutes prior to boarding time for passport formalities, more if a ticket needs to be purchased. Americans are required to purchase a visa when entering Turkey for the first time, but not if traveling to ports in the EU. Tickets purchased in Turkey include port fees, while port costs are paid up front when arriving in Greece.

Ferryboats (2hr, one-way 25TL, round-trip 40TL, car 65TL) to the Datça Peninsula depart twice daily (9 A.M. and 5 P.M.) from Bodrum during the high season. Bus transfers from the port in Körmen to the town of Datça (15min) are included in the fare.

GETTING AROUND

Bodrum's center, with its web of narrow cobblestone streets, is small enough to cover by foot. Another option is the popular scooter, which can be rented for next to nothing; it allows for quicker transits and easy parking. For those staying outside of Bodrum's center, frequent *dolmuş* (communal taxi, 1–2TL) service connecting the peninsula's bays and villages is available from the *otogar* (bus station). Renting a car for a day or two will give you more freedom to explore the peninsula.

Marmaris

Marmaris has grown into one of the most popular resorts on Turkey's west coast. Much like its sister-cities, Kuşadası and Antalya, it's fallen prey to a huge population explosion and overbuilding to accommodate the summer influx of European escapees. The word Marmaris originates from the Greek for glittering, a name that was certainly inspired by the effervescence of its waters. Turkish locals, however, often claim that its name was coined from a condemnation Süleyman the Magnificent angrily uttered after seeing the repulsive construction of a castle he had commissioned in 1522. *"Mimar as"* ("hang the architect"), were the sultan's words. While history doesn't divulge whether his wishes were abided, locals tell the tale tongue-in-cheek, politely emphasizing that Marmaris's boundless natural appeal is cursed by well-meaning builders.

Tourism is Marmaris's bread and butter. Its year-round population of 20,000 explodes to 350,000 come summer. Whether by the busload or the boatful, tourists come on cheap package tours in June–September, turning the town into more of a noisy blight than a peaceful summer escape. Interestingly enough, Marmaris is one of only a handful of towns in Turkey where improprieties aren't scoffed at, rather they are expected. This is evident along the town's stark beach to the west, where topless maidens and inebriated males congregate.

While it's true that the town is just a shadow of the fishing backwater it once was, with barely a road to its name, it's always been blessed with striking topography. Surrounded by the steep pine-covered Taurus Mountains, Marmaris sits at the end of a long azure inlet. Its spectacular harbor is home to Turkey's largest and most modern yacht marina, as well as a castle that owes its presence to long-gone crusaders. The recently revamped tree-lined promenade, along with the new "traditional" Aegean two-story buildings, goes a long way to recapture the village feel. But traffic-clogged commercial side streets and the buzzing bazaar relay the fact that Marmaris is primarily geared to satisfy the needs of its main industry: tourism. Expensive designer fakes and an array of Turkish knick-knacks are for sale everywhere. Town eateries capitalize on British staples like fish and chips and baked potatoes, rather than try to win over fickle palates with Turkish fare.

To imagine what the former Marmaris

looked like, you need only to explore the coastline jutting from the overgrown harbor town. A day-trip to the Hisarönü and Reşadiye Peninsulas provides the antidote to mass commercialization. Interlaced bays, backed by lushly forested mountains, reveal sandy beaches touched only by the bluest waters. Further out, the peninsulas unfurl like gnarly fingers, divulging sleepy hamlets and the architectural footprints of the ancient Greek islanders who colonized the coast.

Marmaris's port makes a one-day foray to the Greek island of Rhodes doable. Alternatively, follow the itinerary the Turks prefer: Travel north of Marmaris, either by land or sea, to discover the Bay of Gökova's untouched farming bastions and picturesque bays. The same can be accomplished in the southbound direction, towards Dalyan and Fethiye.

SIGHTS

The **Castle of Marmaris** now functions as the **Marmaris Müzesi** (0252/412-1459, 8:30 A.M.-noon and 1–5:30 P.M. Tues.–Sun., 3TL). Set aside an hour to visit the bastion's five separate displays, some of which focus on the region's ethnography. Nautical knick-knacks comprise the Castle Commander room, and there's also an archaeological trove of amphorae, earthenware, glassware, and coins excavated from the ancient Dorian cities of Knidos, Burgaz, and Hisarönü nearby. While the exhibit is far from jaw-dropping, the view of Marmaris, the sea, and islands beyond is well worth the price of admission.

According to the ancient Greek historian Herodotus, a castle has been present on Marmaris's hillock since 3000 B.C. Around the time Alexander the Great swept through Asia Minor to repel its Persian occupiers (334 B.C.), the town's 600 inhabitants realized they were no match to Alexander's 40,000 troops and retreated to the hills, but not before burning their valuables inside the castle and destroying the structure. An entire overhaul of the fortress was commissioned in 1522 by Süleyman the Magnificent in order to proceed with his scheme to invade the Greek island of Rhodes.

◖ DAY TRIPS

Short jaunts out of the touristy hustle of the bay to the verdant suburbs reaffirms why nationals dub this part of the coast *Yeşil* (Green) Marmaris. There is the option of venturing northward toward the splendidly authentic Gökova Bay or visiting the two peninsulas that jut out to sea just north of Marmaris. Renting a car makes getting around easy.

The Datça-Marmaris region is served by two dedicated travel specialists, or rather connoisseurs, who offer a variety of tours and experiences. You can participate in a village baking project; hike, mountain-bike, rappel, or raft in the surrounding lushness of the Taurus Mountains; or swim and explore on the 10-hour sea excursion to Knidos. Whatever the desire, Gerard Oude Hergelink and his wife Shenda Tüfekcioglu of **Titco Tours** (0216/418-2949, www.marmaris-datca/travel, €22–35) are sure to have a corresponding day trip.

Hisarönü Yarımadası (Hisarönü Peninsula)

On a day trip south toward the fiercely protected Hisarönü Peninsula, the first stop is usually the sheltered bay of **İçmeler.** This revered mooring spot on the Blue Cruise is also a base for avid trekkers bound for the 20-kilometer trail which winds westward, and uphill, to the charming forest village of Değirmanyanı.

Two kilometers south of İçmeler lies the village of **Turunç.** Thanks in part to its isolation, Turunç is hanging on to its rustic roots, despite its increasing appeal with vacationers. Long transplanted from Marmaris, locals clad in traditional colorful shalwars are here, hawking irresistible handmade goods like tatted lace, scented olive oil soaps, and some of the most fragrant honeys.

The road that goes to the cape's heights takes motorists even further southwest (20km) to the fishing outpost of **Selimiye.** Perhaps the loveliest outpost on the peninsula, this *Yörük* (local nomadic herders) settlement earns its keep from boat-building, fishing, and almond production. Enjoy the odd yet mouth-watering octopus omelet and locally-caught lobster at **Mavi Deniz Selimiye** (Selimiye Beldesi, 0252/446-4220, 15TL) along the bay. Or, just gawk at the beauty of Kameriye, the small islet that bears the remains of a Greek monastery just across the bay.

From Selimiye, either continue to the tip of the peninsula to the centuries-old, traditional boat-building settlement of Bozburun (6km) or make your way back—ever so slowly—towards **Orhaniye**. En route, refresh at the waterfall at Turgutköy, before wading at the kilometer-long shallows at Orhaniye's Kızkumu beach. Break for succulent jumbo shrimps at the seaside terrace at family-run **Dogan Restaurant** (next to the marina in Orhaniye, 0252/487-1074, 18TL).

Gökova

The traditional Ottoman town of Gökova is 35 kilometers north of Marmaris on the road to Muğla. Gökova, which translates to heaven's plain, seems like a major tourist spot, but is actually far from it. This Blue Cruise way station is not much more than a diminutive town boasting a shale beach and a river, backed by towering forested cliffs. It's home to traditional Muğlan architecture—the wooden two-story arcaded townhomes made famous by the prize-winning Turkish architect Nail Cakirhan. Don't leave before enjoying Halil Usta's tempting mackerel grill at **Halil'in Yeri** (0252/243-5173, 15TL), by the river. Blue Cruise veterans alighting in Gökova head straight for this 40-year-old diner that's also renowned for its farm breakfast.

Reşadiye Yarımadasi (Reşadiye Peninsula)

Those looking for yet another reason to bolt from the rowdiness of Marmaris need look no further than the sinewy Reşadiye Peninsula. Seemingly untouched by time—and development—the peaceful cape, also dubbed the Datça Peninsula, is the actual boundary between the Mediterranean and Aegean Seas. Aside from its geography, the cape is venerated throughout the country for its three Bs: *Balık* (fish), *Badem* (almond), and *Bal* (honey). And it's hailed internationally for the historical

vestiges at the ancient site of Knidos on the headland's very tip. It's best to reach Datça, the cape's main town, from the sea from either Marmaris or Bodrum.

The cape's natural wealth and its central location are the reasons why the Dorians colonized this spot. What little remains of **Knidos** (0252/226-1011, 8 A.M.–6 P.M., 5TL) was, in fact, part of the Dorian Hexapolis—a federation of six ancient cities. The ancient Greek historian Strabo (64 B.C.–A.D. 24) described Knidos as "a city that was built for the most beautiful of goddesses, Aphrodite, on the most beautiful of peninsulas." Knidos gained prominence in the 4th century B.C. as a center for Doric art and culture. The stepped headland gives way to the site's double harbor: one harbor in the Med and the other in the Aegean. An agora, amphitheater, and odeum, as well as temples honoring Dionysus, the Muses, and the revered Knidian Aphrodite were unearthed here. Most of the architectural wealth, mainly statues, has made its way to the London and Vatican Museums. The 38-kilometer (45min) drive from Datça to Knidos is rough, to say the least. Boats (25TL) depart from the harbor in Datça at 9 A.M. en route to Knidos.

The splendid coves of Palamut Bükü, Musediye, Domuzçukuru, and Akvaryum line the peninsula's southern flank. Remote enough to deter mass tourism, these bays maintain some of the purest and bluest waters in the Med. Adding to this coastal beauty is the main port town of Datça and a couple nostalgic hamlets nearby. On the road south to Körmen from Datça (7km), **Eski Datça** (Old Datça) is postcard-perfect. Its narrow cobblestone paths flanked by stone dwellings, decked in stunning bougainvillea, hark back to decades past when this tiny hamlet was entirely populated by Greeks. Aside from the superb Greek architecture, not much has changed: Gender divisions are still omnipresent with the men congregating at the central piazza's sole café, while the women ply the most opulent silk crafts. Homemade silk needlework, perhaps one of the cape's best kept secrets, can be purchased at souvenir shops in the Saturday street market. Nearby, the town of Reşadiye boasts some fine examples of coastal Turkish architecture.

NIGHTLIFE

Marmaris's vibrant nightlife is legendary, and gives Bodrum and Antalya a run for their money. The local *barlar sokağı* (bar street), located along narrow Hacı Mustafa Sokak (a.k.a. 39th Sokak), officially gets going by 7 P.M., truly hits its stride at midnight, and rages on until about 4 A.M. Atypical for a party town is Marmaris's lack of entrance fees. Prices for beer (from 9TL) and spirits (12–20TL) are quite affordable as well. Dress codes are scoffed at; shorts and tube dresses are the norm. The motto is come and party just as you are.

In recent summers, the top club venues included **Bar X** (Ataturk Cad., 0252/413-3213) and **Salt 'N Pepa.** They're located side-by-side on a street locals call Uzunyalı; just head toward the lightshow synchronized to the blaring techno beat. Another in-vogue venue is **Crazy Daisy** (39 Sok. 121, 0252/412-5846). Packing about 1,300 dancers nightly in the heat of summer, the water and foam shows are popular with the bikini-clad clientele.

If all the twenty-something ruckus is not appealing, head for the infinitely calmer nighttime entertainment options at the **Netsel Marina** (0252/412-2708). Just east of the Old Quarter, Netsel has ten smart restaurants and cafés, like the upmarket **Divan Pub,** a shopping arcade, as well as an open air cinema that features the latest movie releases in English nightly.

SPORTS AND RECREATION
Boat Tours

The cookie-cutter boat excursion through the region's wealth of flora and geological splendor is highly recommended. Marmaris's coastline functions as the largest maritime expo of boat-charter contenders, each one trying to outbid the other for business. The itinerary traditionally sets off aboard a *gület* (motorized sailboat) at around 9:30 A.M. and returns by 5:30 P.M., and includes lunch. Inquire whether the cruise includes stops at the popular locales of Turunç, Umlu, Cadirgan, Çiftlik Bays, and Cleopatra's (Sedir) Island—the beach covered in fine white sand the sultry princess imported from an Egyptian desert. If not, keep on shopping. Chartering a boat for the day costs 350–400TL (for up to six people), or about 35TL for single bookings. Bear in mind that getting the best quote involves some haggling. Also, mariners officially start the season in May and end towards the last week of October. Off-season cruises are also possible, but require a little coaxing. Cruises that explore the Mediterranean, the resort of Dalyan, the impresssive Lycian ruins, and the mud baths at Kaunos are also available (two-day trips or longer, 600–1,000TL).

Diving

Diving takes on a whole different meaning in Marmaris's splendid underwater landscape. For a day of snorkeling or undersea exploration, **Paradise Diving Center** (Namik Kemal Cad. 25, 0252/417-6366, www.paradisediving.net) offers day and evening dives, as well as diving courses for newbies to the sport. Booths all along the harbor also tout catamaran outings, waterskiing, and surfing.

Beaches

Downtown Marmaris is awfully short of palatable beaches. The closest sandy idylls are **İçmeler,** some eight kilometers south of the town center, and **Turunç,** two kilometers further. The highly pleasant Sea Taxis that depart from Kordon Caddesi and the frequent *dolmuş* (communal taxi) that takes off from the intersection of Ulusal Egemenlik Bulvarı and General Mustafa Muğlalı Caddessi shuttle people to the beaches and back from Marmaris. Fares for both start at 2.50TL.

ACCOMMODATIONS

Should you choose to stay on the cape for dinner or the night, there's a handful of little-known oases that provide dining and lodging facilities. One of the most beautiful residences on Reşadiye, and as such an unofficial museum, is

Mehmet Ali Aga Konağı inn (Kavak Meydanı, 0252/712-9257, www.kocaev.com, €190–700). Known locally as *Koca Ev* (Big House), this rustic, yet entirely renovated mansion is on land awarded to Ali Ağa for his successful stint in the Ottoman navy in the late 17th century. His progeny, the Tuhfezade family, founded the old Elaki quarter—or today's Reşadiye. Albeit pricey, 12 regal rooms comprise this elegantly appointed inn. The inn stands as a virtual warehouse for Ottoman and Turkish antiques, as well as the family's collection of Western European antique furniture.

Another charming lodging option is **Eski Datca Evleri** (Old Datça Houses, Eski Datça Mah. D1 Sokak 26, 0252/712-2129, www.eskidatcaevleri.com, 110–125TL). Tucked behind a historical stone facade, this inn opens to a trio of arcaded Greek houses. Sparse traditional decor prevails in the Almond and Olive Houses' comfy studios, ditto for the Fig House's roomy doubles. There's a wireless Internet connection throughout the property. The outdoor Ede Café serves a traditional farm-fresh breakfast.

Forming their own Grecian "hamlet," the 12 two-story villas at **Marphe** (Onuncu Cad. 34, Datça, 0252/712-9030, www.hotelmarphe.com, 160–550TL can accommodate entire families. The ambience is muted luxury, based on the ever popular white palette, pocked by hardwood antiques and *kilim* (Turkish carpet). Peace rules in this pine-clad collection of Greek whitewashed stone houses that offer a variety of accommodations: roomy suites, apartments, and spacious villas. It may not be seaside, but the large inviting pool in the center of the meticulously tended grounds does the trick.

Alternatively, opt for the **Olive Garden Hotel** (Musedıye Bay, Ovabükü, 0252/728-0056, www.olivegardenhotel.com, US$40–45). Located on one of the peninsula's remotest bays, this 14-room inn appears out of nowhere on the rise of a scrubby hillock, with nothing but blue ahead and rolling hills on either side. The basic doubles and family suites are air-conditioned and comfy. The olive tree-filled grounds en-

courage laziness with pristine white hammocks and a cleverly-camouflaged sunken pool.

FOOD

One of the finest fish and seafood restaurants in and around Marmaris is **Yalı Restoran** (around Datça's port, 0252/712-9366, 15TL). Ali Ozcaylan serves his dedicated clientele year-round with his memorable yet inexpensive versions of grilled local catch. Come for the stunning sunset over the marina in early September.

For sumptuous Turkish home food **Zekeriya Sofrası** (Zekeriya's Table, Yalı Cad. 60–62, 0252/712-4303) is the place. It's dirt cheap and ridiculously good; so good in fact that Zekeriya keeps enlarging the place to accommodate larger crowds. House specials change daily.

ACCOMMODATIONS

Marmaris proper has some decent hotels, but if it's peace and a pristine coastline you're seeking then head to the nearby resort of İçmeler. Or, better yet, opt for the charming country B&Bs on the Hisarönü Peninsula, just 20 kilometers south of town. From İçmeler and Hisarönü Peninsula, nightlife and shopping are still just a short car- or boat-ride away.

Under €100

The **Royal Maris Hotel** (Atatürk Cad. 34, 0252/412-8383, www.royalmarishotel.com, €50–85) is one of a handful of properties open year-round. A roof-top pool and terrace are some of the highlights of this anti-resort hotel. With 71 typical yet very affordable rooms (44 with sea views), Maris meets the stringent requirements of its no-nonsense business clientele with its refurbished modern decor. And it does so with friendly service and leisure amenities that include a hammam, private beach, and gym at no extra cost.

Just seven kilometers south of Marmaris, the **Pupa Yat Otel** (Adaağız Mevkii Yalancı Boğaz, 0252/413-3566, www.pupa.com.tr, €55–75) is one of these undiscovered gems where repeat guests—mostly yachters—have known each other for years. Lushly landscaped, with adult palms and eucalyptuses, the property delineates the region's famed frankincense forest. It boasts its own beach, as well as mooring space, overlooking the harbor of Marmaris from a distance. The taxi booth outside ensures easy transport into town. Recently remodeled, the 19 units are modest but brightly lit and each boast a balcony with a sea view.

In Turunç, the **Lavanta House** (Turunç, 0252/476-7822, www.lavantaturunc.com, 90–125TL) is a 13-room B&B set on a steep cliffside that boasts 180-degree views of the scintillating blue Med. Lavanta is owned by Hale, a transplanted Istanbulite, who brought her cosmopolitan flair to this remote bay. The rooms are whitewashed with grown-up touches of gingham. Farm-fresh fare reflects a rich Aegean culinary heritage with generous breakfasts, tempting seafood grills, and mezes.

Villa Florya (Kumlubuk, 0252/476-7553, www.villaflorya.com, US$65–95) is situated high atop a limestone headland that bisects the three-kilometer sandy strip of Kumlubuk. To its rear, a cluster of farmhouses and pensions dot a secluded and undeveloped bay. The three-story building boasts 13 roomy units that are colorfully stylish, each possessing splendid sea views. The beach welcomes with bright, overstuffed cushions, and a traditional Turkish restaurant.

Over €100

The five-star resort 🄲 **Maritim Hotel Grand Azur** (Kenan Evren Bulv. 17, 0252/417-4050, www.hotelgrandazur.com, from €130) offers a vacation without ever leaving the hotel. The property boasts a large private beach, fully stocked with banana boats, water skies, speedboats, and even a diving school. Lush tropical plants, redwoods, and palm trees line the grounds. A gargantuan central pool offers twists and turns through the landscape until it finally meets the indoor pool and exclusive fitness center. Large rooms are neat and sparsely decorated in modern decor; But who needs super fancy accommodations with so much to do onsite?

Way off the beaten track, but well worth every inch of its remoteness, is the 🄲 **Golden Key**

Bördübet (Bördübet Mevkii, 0252/436-9230, www.goldenkeyhotels.com, from €260). This property, split by a rivulet that trickles through the surrounding pine forest, lies 12 kilometers away from Marmaris, in nearly tropical grounds. Aside from a cantankerous family of geese and meandering tortoises, this chalet-like hotel is sublimely peaceful. The balconied rooms evoke a semi-zen atmosphere with decadently appointed custom-made country furnishings. The Golden Key's super private cove can be accessed by boat, bicycle, or via a pleasant 20-minute walk through the woods. The restaurant serves authentic, superior Turkish cuisine, bolstered by a long wine list.

The best lodging in İçmeler is the seafront **Marti Resort Deluxe** (İçmeler Köyü, 0252/455-3440, www.marti.com.tr, €130–308), a collection of wooden and stone buildings melding into the surrounding pine woods. The property's landscaping features burbling fountains and verdant gardens that extend down to a long private beach. Totally renovated in 2008, the now five-star property's 178 standard rooms each boasts a balcony and bathtub. The 78 deluxe rooms have parquet flooring and hands down the best sea views. Families will dig the added space of the 12 villas (51–160 sq meters), each with a balcony, terrace, kitchenette, one or two bedrooms, and a whirlpool tub. It's also a one-stop vacation spot, with a popular nightclub, four restaurants, and five bars.

FOOD

None of Turkey's top culinary prizes have ever been awarded to chefs toiling in Marmaris. The town's lack of memorable eateries—that is, if you're not into fish and chips and entrées doled out by the ladle—proves it. As in any city along the coast, fish reigns supreme. And for that, one must head for the marina, not the pier, where the fish joints serve run-of-the-mill grills to an unenlightened international clientele with prices to match. When in Marmaris, do as the locals do and head for an authentic Turkish meal around the hole-in-the-wall eateries near the castle and bazaar. One of them is the well-reputed **Ney Restaurant** (26 Sok. 24, 0252/412-8792, 18TL), a historic Greek abode in the castle area. Expect delightful Turkish treats at affordable prices and great views of the marina.

For those who've been smitten by delectable miniatures, also known as Turkish mezes, **Meza** (Kemal Seyfettin Eligin Blv. No. 71, 0532/247-5866, appetizers 10TL) offers a large quantity of mostly cold starters, including lots of veggie options. House specialties include grilled steak served in a spiced red wine and the ever-popular fried calamari appetizer.

《 Uno Restaurant (two locations: near the harbor and by the Tansaş supermarket on Ulusal Egemenlik Cad.; 0252/413-8211, 18TL) is in essence an Italian restaurant, with tasty pizzas to prove it. But the plank steak is a rarity, and, when a specimen comes cooked to perfection, even rarer. Also highly recommended, the piped mashed potatoes are indeed amazing, so was the Mexican chicken baguette sandwich for lunch and the friendly service.

INFORMATION AND SERVICES

Marmaris's **tourist office** (Iskele Meydanı 2, 0252/412-1035, 8 A.M.–noon and 1–5 P.M.) faces the Atatürk statue, which is in the center of the city's main square. A second location, serving the Hisarönü Peninsula, is located at the Datça harbor (0252/412-7277, 8 A.M.–noon and 1–5 P.M.). The **PTT** (60 Sok 2/4, 0252/412-8381, 8:30 A.M.–midnight) offers 24-hour phone service. **ATMs** and **Banks** line Ulusal Egemenlik Caddesi and Yeni Kordon Caddesi. To connect to the Web, head to **Bell@ Internet Café** (62 Sok. 24, 0252/412-6921, 4TL/hr), just north of Atatürk Caddessi.

GETTING THERE
By Air
Marmaris is served by the modern **Dalaman Airport** (ATM Dalaman Havalimanı, 0252/792-5555, www.atmairport.aero), which is 105 kilometers east of Marmaris. **Turkish Airlines** (Atatürk Cad. 26B, 0252/412-3751, www.thy.com) operates at least two daily flights to Marmaris from Istanbul year-round. Low cost carriers **Onur Air** (toll free 444-6687, www.onurair.com.tr), **Pegasus** (toll free 444-0737, www.flypgs.com), and **Atlas Jet** (toll free 444-3387, www.atlasjet.com) also serve the region from various points in Turkey. The international charters airlines **Easyjet** (www.easyjet.com) and **Thomas Cook** (www.flythomascook.com) fly into Dalaman as well.

Havas Shuttles (toll free 444-0487) transport passengers arriving into Dalaman to Marmaris's main bus terminal. The trip lasts 90 minutes and costs 23TL. Alternatively, a 24-hour **taxi** co-op provides rides into Marmaris, with a fare of about 140TL for the one-hour ride. Three rental car companies have branches at Dalaman: **Avis** (0252/792-5118, www.avis.com.tr); **Budget** (0252/792-5150, www.budget.com.tr); and **Eropcar** (0252/792-5414, www.europcar.com.tr).

By Bus
Close to the main highway, Marmaris's *otogar* (bus station, 0252/412-3037) is situated three kilometers north of the town center. Bus ticketing offices are located in the Tansaş Shopping Center on Ulusal Egemenlik Bulvarı. Some bus companies provide complimentary transportation into town. If not, a *dolmuş* (communal taxi) service bound for the city center takes off from the bus station at least every 15 minutes in the high season. Hiring a cab (5TL) may be the smarter choice for those not traveling light.

Long distance bus service from Istanbul (14 hrs, 850km, 70TL) departs at least once a day, while connections to Ankara (11 hrs, 590km, 65TL) are more frequent; both depart around 11 P.M. Buses to Antalya (6.5 hrs, 590km, 30TL) depart twice daily. Regional buses run to Bodrum (3.5 hrs, 165km, 15TL), north to Izmir (4 hrs, 320km, 25TL), and to Fehtiye (3 hrs, 170lm, 12TL) at least hourly during the high season. Long-distance *dolmuşes* serve Datça (1.5 hrs, 8TL) and Ortaca/Dalyan (1.5 hrs, 7TL), departing at least every 90 minutes year-round.

THE TURQUOISE COAST

By Boat

A direct ferry connects Bodrum to Marmaris thrice weekly on Mondays, Thursdays, and Sundays during the high season, April–October. The cruise is organized by **Bodrum Express Lines** (0252/316-1087, www.bodrumexpresslines.com), and departs from Bodrum at 8 A.M. and 6 P.M., arriving in the quaint seaside hamlet Gelibolu. From there, passengers are transferred by bus to Marmaris, a 75-minute ride. The transfer is included in the ticket price (one-way €25, round-trip €30). Alternatively, a car ferry, run by **Bodrum Ferryboat Association** (0252/712-2143 in Datça, 0252/316-0882 in Bodrum, www.bodrumferryboat.com, 2 hrs, one-way 25TL, round-trip 40TL, car 65TL), connects Bodrum to Datça, leaving at the same time from both ports, at 9 A.M. and 5 P.M. Passengers disembark in the desolate port in Körmen, then board a bus bound for the town of Datça (6.5km, 15min). The bus transfer is included in the ticket, which can be purchased at the company's offices in either destination.

Catamarans ply the sea route between the Greek isle of Rhodes and Marmaris twice daily, from either port April 15–November 1. The service, which is run by **Yeşil Marmaris Tourism & Yacht Management** (Barbaros Cad. 13, 0252/412-1033, www.yesilmarmarislines.com, one-way €50, same-day return €50, open return €75, includes port taxes), departs from Marmaris at 9 A.M. and the return from Rhodes takes off at 4:30 P.M. Charges for vehicles range €120–200; children up to 13 years of age are €32.50.

The maritime operators listed here accept online reservations. Tickets can also be purchased from any travel agent around the Marmaris harbor. Passengers leaving Turkey are required to show their passports; those planning to return to Turkey, even on the same day, are required to purchase another visa. Arrive at least 60 minutes prior to departure for passport control.

GETTING AROUND

Commuting around Marmaris by public transportation is a snap. There are *dolmuş* (communal taxi) services, which vary in color to signify their route (what a spectacular idea!). Of the five separate routes taking off from the town center at Iskele Meydanı, the orange line heads north to İçmeler; the pink minibuses head south to Yalancı Bay; and the popular green service hits all the intercity spots. Destinations and fares (1.50–3TL) are posted on the windshield.

To explore destinations further afield like, Datça and the various coves in and around Marmaris, consider renting a vehicle. Hotel concierges can negotiate a cheaper rate for a rental—whether a jeep or scooter—than those proposed at vehicle rental companies. To avoid any misunderstandings, secure the model of the vehicle and its rate prior to delivery.

A taxi between İçmeler and Marmaris can cost upwards of 30TL when it really shouldn't set you back more than 15TL. To avoid unwanted charges, make sure the rate is settled prior to boarding. An alternate taxi boat (5TL) runs the same route from the central harbor during the high season.

Dalyan

Another gem of the Aegean that's managing to maintain its rural charm, the old river town of Dalyan is a bastion of serenity in the sea of packaged-tourism resorts along the coast. Its appeal lies mostly around the spectacular wetlands of the Dalyan Çayı (Dalyan River), a natural water canal which connects Köyceğiz Lake to the north to the Mediterranean Sea to the south. The riverside cafés and hotels are the heart of Dalyan come summer, when boatloads of tourists arrive from Marmaris and Fethiye. They come to gawk at the stunning temple tombs hewn from the steep rocks that rise from the marshes, and the ruins of the antique Lycian port at Kaunos. There's also the reputed open-air mud baths to the north and the thermal baths of Köyceğiz Lake further upstream. İztuzu Beach, the natural sandbar that lies at the mouth of the Dalyan River, protecting it from the Med, is one of the few remaining nesting grounds for the graceful loggerhead turtle.

Dalyan actually owes its popularity with tourists to this tame yet endangered reptile, whose dwindling numbers earned the beach a high-protection status after a very publicized dispute between developers and environmentalists in 1986. And thanks to international vigilance, the village of Dalyan has also managed to retain its quaint hamlet feel, making this often-overlooked spot a great base from which to explore the region's ecotourism opportunities by foot, bike, kayak, snorkel, jeep, or boat.

Just to the south, the bay of Göcek—a favored mooring destination for wealthy Turkish yachters—makes for a perfect day trip. The pine-clad hills that surround this deep inlet are valued by luxury hotel developers wishing to capitalize on the annual arrival of the sailing season. You might also consider the sleepy lake town of Köyceğiz as an alternate base when visiting this region and its spectacular natural wealth.

SIGHTS

Most sites can be explored within a day by hopping on one of the boats awaiting passengers at

Dalyan's harbor. Forgo tourist traps and opt for the ride offered by **Dalyan Tekne Kooperatif** (0252/284-3254 or 0537/359-1918, 25TL with lunch). The excursion typically departs at 10:30 A.M. daily. Jovial owner Kamuran Özgen sets a playful mood as he encourages friendship among passengers, even allowing them to take the helm.

Kaunos

Facing Dalyan halfway along the river, ancient Kaunos (0252/614-1150, 8:30 A.M.–8:30 P.M., 5TL) was, according to the 5th-century historian Herodotus, the capital of the region between Lycia and Caria. Its steep slopes were first settled by native Anatolians around 3000 B.C., but Kaunos didn't gain prominence as a major trading port until the 5th century B.C.

© TOM DEMPSEY

Built high up on a hillside, 2,400-year-old Lycian tombs line the harbor of ancient Kaunos.

More than 40 years of archaeological excavations have revealed a dual harbor, which included a pier designated strictly for commerce (mainly salt and slaves) and another for military purposes. Other principal Kaunian remains include an acropolis standing amidst city walls, a theater, four temples, an agora, stoa, nymphaeum, baths, palestra, churches, a cistern, and, of course, the majestic funerary monuments carved in the steep riverbanks.

According to the 1st-century Roman poet Ovid, Kaunos's namesake founder was the son of Miletos and the water nymph Kyane who fell in love with his twin sister Byblis. This illicit affair was the chief reason why Kaunos fled home to found a city in a place far enough away that she would never find him. All the major players in Asia Major, from the early Persians (600 B.C.) and Carians to the Egyptians and finally to the Romans (A.D. 200), had a hand in Kaunian culture and architecture. But no building reflects the Lycians' strong Eastern influence more than the rock-cut tombs, which, as opposed to their Carian neighbors who buried their dead communally outside of town, were not only integrated within the city, but also beautified it. Kaunos's fate, like a good portion of its neighbors along the coast, was sealed when its port finally silted up by sediment from the Dalyan River. The bubonic plague of the mid-5th century A.D. just added insult to injury by wiping more than half of its inhabitants off the map and essentially quashed an already ailing trade.

Tour boats moor at the edge of the 15-meter-wide Dalyan River, at a wooden *dalyan* (fish weir) located about 100 meters from Kaunos's entrance. The path to the right leads to the Roman theater. There, you'll find two statues inscribed with the names of 4th-century B.C. Carian governor Mausolus and his sin Hecatomnos. Farther up the Acropolis hill are the ruins of a defensive sea wall; the sea retreated more than five kilometers south since the time Lycian sentries stood guard here. The Roman baths and a Byzantine basilica are located northwest, and just above these are the remains of a 2nd-century A.D. Roman temple

to Apollo. Some of the rock tombs below can be seen from here; those with ornate colonnades belonged to kings, while others are just simple chambers intended for governors. Whatever the Romans did not quarry was ravaged by treasure seekers.

İztuzu Beach

With the tall reeds rustling in the background and pristine waters backed by some of the lushest hills, İztuzu Beach stands as one the prettiest of its kind in the region. The endangered loggerhead turtles are of the same opinion as they return annually to this seven-kilometer-long sandy strip where they were born. It's one of only three remaining nesting grounds for the air-breathing sea reptilian (Caretta Caretta) in Turkey, and one of a handful of sites across the Med. İztuzu Beach became headline news in 1986 when a pair of convservationists successfully fought an attempt to develop a luxury resort onsite. As these reptilians lay their eggs after sunset May–September, beach access is restricted before 8 A.M. and after 6 P.M. in order to not interfere with the egg-laying turtles. Chaise lounges and parasols are rented at the beach; concession stands remain open throughout the day.

A *dolmuş* (communal taxi, 5TL) from Dalyan reaches the beach, and so do boats after winding their way down the canal through the marshes to the open tip of the beach. İztuzu comprises two beaches: a private stretch used for disembarking the multitudes of visitors and a much quieter option near the road.

Sultaniye Kaplıcaları (Sultaniye Hot Springs)

Just south of Köyceğiz Gölü, the open-air mud baths and hot springs of Sultaniye Hot Springs (0252/266-0077, 4TL) are said to rid the bather of wrinkles. At least Cleopatra thought so, but it's doubtful she waited the recommended half hour for the muck to do its thing. Located upstream near the lake, the hot thermals (40°C) gush the most radioactive waters in Turkey. The baths' high calcium, sulphur, iron, potassium, and salt contents are

The Sultaniye Hot Springs, just north of Dalyan, boast sulfur-rich silt that's credited with healing rheumatism and skin ailments.

said to allay afflictions from acne to rheumatism. These baths hark back to the Kaunian era and have seen the likes of thespians Dustin Hoffman and Jack Nicholson since.

A *dolmuş* boat (6TL) departs for Sultaniye Hot Springs from Dalyan at least hourly; chartering a private excursion boat can also be negotiated.

Göçek

The splendid Bay of Göçek, at the northern tip of the pine-clad Gulf of Fethiye, has long been the exclusive mooring station of the Med's moneyed mariners. The arrival of a couple of high class holiday resorts has transformed this superbly scenic fishing hamlet—and its celebrated marina—into the secluded playground known among yachters as one of the pearls of the Mediterranean. And, thanks to strict laws regarding development, it seems that Göçek's allure won't be blemished any time soon by cookie-cutter resorts like its sister cities along the coast.

It all started in 2003, when two trendy hotel chains each opened their highly awaited resorts along the coast. The **Swissôtel at Göçek Marina** (Cumhuriyet Mahallesi, 0252/645-2760, www.swissotel.com, May 1–October 31, €140–378) was the first to capitalize on the fashionable yachting crowd with a beautifully landscaped property that not only provided the brand's upscale accommodations, but beach real estate (rare in Göçek) and a full array of leisure amenities to boot. The other resort, **Göcek Lykia Resort Hotel** (Cumhuriyet Mahallesi, 0252/645-2828, www.goceklykiaresort.com, €100–140) is a throwback to Hellenistic architecture all the way to its colonnaded entrance and oversized pool. Some 95 colorful rooms won't break the style meter, but who needs fancy digs when virtually every conceivable tour of the area is offered on a silver platter.

And while you're in Göcek don't miss a meal at **Barbaros Café Restaurant** (Iskele Meydanı 4, 0252/645-3056, 18TL). With patio tables lining a refreshing outdoor fountain, Barbaros is one of the superior fish restaurants around

LOOKING FOR LOGGERHEADS

Mediterranean loggerhead sea turtles, known in Turkey by their scientific name *Caretta caretta*, are solitary creatures that ply great distances to spawn. The variety that nests along Turkey's Mediterranean Coast returns annually to lay its clutch, which can vary from 70–150 eggs, in the same place where the adult turtle was born. The species is endangered. Only about 60,000 egg-laying females have survived the species' greatest threats: poachers and the frequent, unintentional capture in the nets and long-lines of the world's fisheries.

The most common turtle in the Mediterranean, the reddish-brown loggerhead prefers pristine, empty, and quiet sandy beaches to lay its eggs. But tourists do, too. And the rise in development to accommodate the needs of vacationers during the 1980s and 1990s encroached on a large part of the turtle's spawning sands. To make matters worse, just a few soft-shelled hatchlings ever make it to the sea. The baby turtles that make it past the lizards, crabs, and seabirds are often eaten by fish. Only one or two of the hatchlings from one nest is expected to survive.

The species and its breeding grounds along the Mediterranean seaboard now enjoy a protected status in Turkey, thanks to the tireless efforts of the World Wildlife Federation. Stringent schedules restrict sunbathers and swimmers from beaches frequented by the loggerhead, usually from dusk to sunrise May–October. Because these turtles bury their eggs deep in the sand, local scientists place string cages over the buried nests, helping to protect the nests from accidental human destruction.

Mature loggerheads live an average of 30 years, but their life span can extend to 50 years. Tipping the scales at about 120 kilos, an adult turtle measures about 92 centimeters. They feed on bottom-dwelling invertebrates, and sea mollusks, easily crushing their shells with their powerful jaws.

Although the laying grounds for the loggerheads extend into most of the Turquoise coast, Dalyan remains the best place to view the turtles. İztuzu Beach, down river from Dalyan and about 80 kilometers south of Marmaris, is a favorite location of loggerheads. The blue crabs teeming in the Dalyan delta are a favorite snack of these marine reptiles. A couple of adult females have even ditched their migratory lifestyle to gorge on the colorful mollusks and amuse thousands of tourists year-round. The beach at Patara is another great location to watch these fascinating creatures.

---

the harbor. There are more than 30 different appetizers to savor—try the sea bass in mayo—and, if you haven't tried it yet, Barbaros does a great version of the west coast specialty of *tuzda balık* (fish baked in salt).

NIGHTLIFE

Dalyan's nightlife revolves around Maraş Mahallesi, where quiet pubs and rowdy beer joints share real estate in an effort to reel in the UK crowd. There are also charming and outdoor cafés like the riverside **Sun Ray Lounge/ Grand Café** (Maraş Cad., www.sunraylounge. com, 1 P.M.–1 A.M.). Sprawling over two floors, it's simultaneously classy and unpretentious and the only café with live acoustic music and views of the riverside tombs.

For serious drinkers of fruity concoctions, **Jazz Bar** (Gülpınar Cad. 30, 0542/371-6585, 9 A.M.–1 A.M.) serves both smoothies and mixed drinks. It's Dalyan's oldest quayside watering hole and it recently added live music (jazz, blues, and rock 'n' roll) on Mondays, Wednesdays, Fridays, and Saturdays. Specialty coffees and luscious homemade desserts are also rated high on Jazz's menu.

ACCOMMODATIONS

Dalyan has yet to be invaded by mass tourism resorts. And by the look of things, and increasingly stringent protectionist regulations, it'll be awhile before any large developer in his right mind comes in with a luxury hotel scheme. That's good because family-run

278 THE TURQUOISE COAST

pensions still thrive here, despite the arrival of the more grown-up options along the riverbank. All in all, there are accommodations for every budget. Keep in mind that summer signals Dalyan's dreaded mosquito season. To ensure a sting-free stay in a swanky river-view room, ask hotel staff to provide an electric mosquito repellent.

Perhaps the oldest hotel in Dalyan, the **Kano Otel** (Maras Cad. 70, 0252/284-3000, www.otelkano.com, 85–105TL) is a riverside property smack across one of the most splendid cliffside Lycian tombs. The two-story building boasts 10 immaculately clean units that reflect the quirkiness of the property's owner, renowned Turkish psychiatrist Can Bulucu, with unexpected splashes of color throughout. All rooms overlook the welcoming wooden deck along the river. The onsite restaurant features modern Italian cuisine with an incredible pasta entrée in a mushroom and blue crab sauce and a sumptuous *tarte flambée* on its dessert menu.

Another great budget option is the **Sultan Apart Hotel** (338 Sok. 51/A, 0252/284-4704, www.sultanhanaparthotel.com, 100–140TL). Despite having to pay extra for breakfast (8TL), the Sultan offers a large pool surrounded by seven roomy apartment units less than one kilometer from the center of town. Each apartment features a large veranda, open kitchen with appliances, plenty of seating, and air-conditioning, making this property ideal for groups of up to four adults in its larger rooms (165–250TL).

The **Happy Caretta Hotel** (Kaunos Sok., 0252/284-2109, www.happycaretta.com, 155–180TL) is one of the top choices of the two dozen properties that line the river. This family-run hotel boasts a garden shaded by century-old cypresses, by the river across from some of the best specimens of the cliffside tombs left by the Lycians. Here you'll find the Turkish version of a Tikki hut that doubles as a well-equipped bar. There are a lot of landscaped grounds for little ones to run around. Borrow one of the hotel's bikes for a five-minute ride into town or join Dalyan's turtle population in a refreshing plunge in the river.

By far one of Dalyan's most luxurious options, **Sultan Palas Hotel** (Horozlar Mevkii, 0252/284-2103, www.sultanpalasdalyan.co.uk, d. B&B €65, half-board €75) can only be reached by boat from Dalyan. This utterly serene idyll on the river's rarely trodden west bank boasts, aside from a turreted castle-like appearance, 26 suites heavy on British detailing. And that's what constitutes the majority of the Palas's devout clientele, who, like the turtles of İztuzu, vacation here annually from the UK. Welcomed improvements to the en suite baths and the outdated infrastructure, as well as the necessary service of a river ferry, were undertaken in 2007. All suites feature air-conditioning and a balcony. The balconies overlook lush gardens, an oversized pool, and the splendid, untouched countryside.

Dalyan Dostları Evi Boutique Hotel (Savkar Sok. 1, 0252/284-5521, www.dalyandostlarievi.com, €80–120) is a stylishly modern hotel. It boasts seven spacious rooms with refined yet understated decor, as well as two suites and a large pool onsite, from its location further inland. If traveling with Fido, you'll find that four-legged guests are equally encouraged to stay.

FOOD

Riverside dining has never been so good, particularly after sunset when the antique cliffside tombs are awashed in spotlights. The only problem here is the relentless mosquitoes who are also looking to score a meal. Just bring along bug repellent and you'll be golden. Also note that most restaurants in Dalyan close shop from mid-November through at least the beginning of March, opening only during the busy holiday season, 9 A.M. until midnight or so.

Caretta Caretta Restaurant (Maraş Cad. 124, 0252/284-3039, www.carettacaretta.net, 15TL) boasts succulent Ottoman fare sprinkled with traditional European dishes, as well as a children's menu. Their beef roulades stuffed with shrimp, mushrooms, onions, and cheese is surprisingly sumptuous. Call ahead to secure one of the outdoor tables filling the riverside deck on busier summer weekends.

Riverside Restaurant (Maraş Mah. Sağlık Ocağı Sok., 0252/284-3166, 18TL) is Dalyan's finest fish restaurant in a long line of copy cats along the riverbank. The long tree-shaded terrace looks straight across the canal to the tombs just above the reedy marshes. Inside, owner Sami Şengül recently opened a wing just for kids, where they can pretend to dine like grown-ups and then frolic in the adjacent playground while the parents get a well-deserved dinner break. If sightseeing got the best of you, consider ordering in a tasty dish from Riverside's special delivery menu.

Bistro Clou (Pazar Yeri Sok., 0252/284-3452, 7TL) is a small family-run diner with traditional Turkish country cuisine. Try their *güveç*, an oven-baked one-pot meal that hits the spot, or their great rendition of the Muğla specialty of *çöp şiş* (grilled lamb skewers). Live Jazz provides welcome entertainment during hot summer evenings.

INFORMATION AND SERVICES

The **Tourist Information Bureau** (Maraş Cad. 2C, 0252/284-4235, 8 A.M.–noon and 1–5 P.M. Mon.–Fri. Nov.–Apr., until 7 P.M. May–Oct.) is opened longer hours during the high season. There's one solitary **bank** (Tükiye İş Bankası, Cumhuriyet Meydanı 11, 0252/284-2024) and a couple of ATMs, including one adjacent to the central **Postal Office** (Maraş Mah. Sarısu Sok. 2/A, 0252/284-2212, 8:30 A.M.–5:30 P.M. Mon.–Sat.). For Internet services, **Easy Internet** (11 Sok. Blok 10/6, 0252/284-3888, www.easydalyan.com, 10 A.M.–midnight, 5TL/hr) is foreigner-friendly, with loads of services like Web surfing and gaming, faxing, translation, and even free Dalyan tips just for the asking.

GETTING THERE

There is no direct public transportation to Dalyan from the regional airport at Dalaman (35km away). The shuttle service run by **Havas** (0252/792-5077, www.havas.com.tr, 25TL) takes passengers from the airport to Ortaca, about 12 kilometers away. From there, the *dolmuş* (communal taxi, runs every 30min,

4TL) service to Dalyan is about the only way to go. To avoid this complicated itinerary, just opt for the more convenient and faster, door-to-door taxi service through Dalaman Airport's taxi cooperative (65TL). The most reasonable return transfer to Dalaman is through **Kaunos Tour** (Maraş Mahallesi, in the town center, 0252/284-2816, www.kaunostours.com, 1–3 passengers 28–67TL).

Bus companies do not have direct service to Dalyan. The only option is to request to be dropped off at the Ortaca *durak* (stop) on the Muğla/Fethiye Highway, and then board a cab (30TL) to travel the eight kilometers into Dalyan. There's also an irregular regional *dolmuş* service to Dalyan from either Marmaris (80km, 1.5hr) or Fethiye (75km, 1.25hr) for less than 10TL.

Alighting in Dalyan by boat is not only recommended to take in the sheer beauty of its coast, but also one of the easiest ways to get into town. Arrange for a one-way trip with one of the tour operators located at either the Fethiye or Marmaris harbors.

GETTING AROUND

The preferred mode of transportation in Dalyan is the river boat. Boat *dolmuşes* (communal taxis), run by the local taxi cooperative, organize excursions south to İztuzu Beach (departing Dalyan: 9 A.M.–1 P.M.; returning to Dalyan: until 6 P.M., round-trip 5TL). Unlike the comparable road service that takes off when full, riverboats depart once a certain number of passengers have boarded. It's a good idea to take off for İztuzu early in the morning to ensure space on an earlier return service. The cooperative has a similar service running north to Köyceğiz Lake, stopping en route at Sultaniye Hot Springs; it departs daily in summer at 9 A.M. and returns around 3 P.M. Also, when booking accommodations, look for a hotel that provides their guests complimentary boat commutes—or special day-trip options; this saves time on the local commute. Of the many tour providers located in Dalyan's main square, **Kaunos Tours** (0252/284-2816, www.kaunostours.com) provides an almost unlimited range of tourist excursions, like horse and jeep safaris, as well as bike and trekking tours. Jeep, scooter, and mountain-bike rentals can also be arranged through them.

Alternatively, *dolmuş* routes out of Dalyan's center go to the town of Köyçeğiz (30min), İztuzu Beach (15min), and Ortaca (15min) for a flat fare of 4TL.

Fethiye

Fethiye is picture-perfect: an idyllic topography of piney mountains outlined by the most beautiful bays of white sands and gleaming waters. It's in this backdrop that seashores like Ölüdeniz—Turkey's spectacular Blue Lagoon—elicit inertia. While the rocky cliffs beyond, mixed in with the offshore isles, beg to be experienced and their ancient history explored.

Fethiye is tucked into the southeastern coast of its namesake bay, in the center of a region that boasts forsaken villages, remnants of Lycian eras past, and unsurpassed vegetation that covers some of the Eastern Med's sheerest cliffs. The town itself is rooted in history, but a massive earthquake in 1856 shook its forbearer—the ancient Lycian port Telmessos—to its core, and another powerful tremor finished the job in 1957. So today's Fethiye is modern and, aside from its pretty harbor, which is sheltered by the offshore Şövalyie Adası (Knight Island) and a long seaboard, offers a handful of ancient relics amidst plenty of the expected tourist fare.

The pot of gold is outside Fethiye, where the stomping grounds of ancient Anatolians, known as the Lycians, left rock tombs and other monuments. There's also the ghost town of Kayaköy, an open-air museum set in a lush valley just eight kilometers to the south. And, hidden 50 kilometers east among the cliffs that encircle the coast are the rushing torrents of icy cold water that cut the narrow Saklıkent Gorge. Lest we forget, Turkey's poster-child for tourism, Ölüdeniz, is a sun-drenched cape that majestically halves the splendidly turquoise still waters of the Med's very own blue lagoon.

This natural abundance, laced with tons of history, makes the Fethiye region *the* destination of choice for thrill-seekers or those looking for their own square footage of inanely splendid sun-kissed sands. An innumerable amount of bays—most accessed only by sea—and the cliffs just behind them are fodder for a slew of active pursuits like paragliding, diving, trekking, and mountain-biking. Spend a week or two, or a lifetime, in this idyllic spot, one of the Blue Cruise's top destinations.

SIGHTS

Among the buildings saved from two-centuries-worth of seismic calamities are a handful of monuments that attest to each of Fethiye's most illustrious eras as the ancient town of Telmessos. Those alighting from the sea get an eyeful of the **Roman Amphitheater,** which was built in the early 2nd century B.C. to accommodate 5,000 spectators.

But what makes Fethiye unlike any other cosmopolitan resort along the southern coast is that it was rebuilt entirely around impressive 2,500-year-old Lycian **sarcophagi.** The best example lies just northeast of the Belediye Dairesi (Town Hall) on Atatürk Caddesi. The two sides of its Gothic-style lid bear war scene carvings, while its two-story facade's etchings resemble wooden, square joists. Long stripped of their contents, burial chambers like this one are all over town, both in public and private spaces.

The hills that surround Fethiye bear most of its historical pedigree. Behind town, there's a **Crusader Fortress,** which was built by the Knights of St. John in the late 15th century, atop what is thought to be the remains of a Hellenistic acropolis. The fort stands where the city was first founded some 2,400 years ago; the walls surrounding it date from the 11th century.

Fethiye's heights are dotted with rock-cut tombs. The most impressive is the

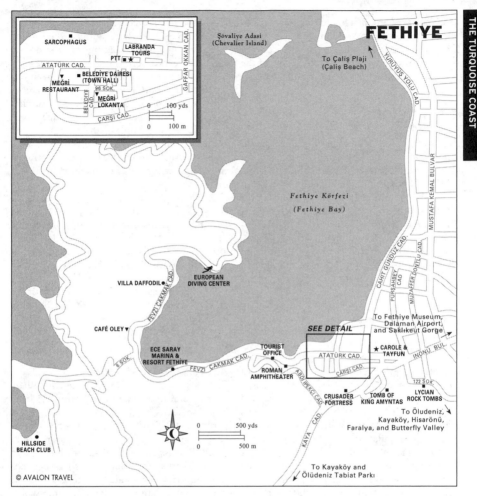

FETHIYE

(Map labels:)
SARCOPHAGUS
LABRANDA TOURS
PTT
ATATÜRK CAD.
GAFFAR OKKAN CAD.
MEĞRİ RESTAURANT
BELEDIYE DAIRESİ (TOWN HALL)
96 SOK.
BELEDIYE CAD.
MEĞRİ LOKANTA
ÇARŞI CAD.
0   100 yds
0   100 m

Şövaliye Adasi (Chevalier Island)

To Çaliş Plaji (Çaliş Beach)

YÜRÜYÜŞ YOLU CAD.

Fethiye Körfezi (Fethiye Bay)

MUSTAFA KEMAL BULVAR

VILLA DAFFODIL
EUROPEAN DIVING CENTER
FEVZİ ÇAKMAK CAD.
CAHİT GÜNDÜZ CAD.
PÜRSAHBEY CAD.
MUZAFFER DOĞUŞLU CAD.

CAFÉ OLEY

SEE DETAIL

To Fethiye Museum, Dalaman Airport, and Saklıkent Gorge

ECE SARAY MARINA & RESORT FETHIYE
6 SOK.
FEVZİ ÇAKMAK CAD.
TOURIST OFFICE
ATATÜRK CAD.
CAROLE & TAYFUN
İNÖNÜ BUL.
ÇARŞI CAD.
ROMAN AMPHITHEATER
ABDİ İPEKÇİ CAD.
122 SOK.
CRUSADER FORTRESS
TOMB OF KING AMYNTAS
LYCIAN ROCK TOMBS
KAYA CAD.

To Öludeniz, Kayaköy, Hisarönü, Faralya, and Butterfly Valley

HILLSIDE BEACH CLUB

0   500 yds
0   500 m

To Kayaköy and Ölüdeniz Tabiat Parkı

© AVALON TRAVEL

Tomb of King Amyntas (0252/614-1150, 8:30 A.M.–8:30 P.M., 5TL). This Ionic temple, adorned by an arcaded portico, was built in 450 B.C. for Amyntas, the son of Hermapias, who ruled Hellenic Telmessos. A steep hike is required to reach the tomb, which, incidentally, can be seen just as well from afar. If you still decide to scale the cliff, head off before noon to avoid both higher temperatures and early evening crowds who tend to congregate for the impressive sunsets from this venue. Far better

to head 500 meters east to the lesser-visited temple-type tomb that stands with one of its columns broken. An afternoon of exploration will reveal other traditional Lycian rock-tombs and various pigeonhole-like graves carved in a rectangular pattern in the rock face.

The **Fethiye Museum** (Fethiye Müzesi, Okul Sok., 0252/614-1150, 8:30 A.M.–5:30 P.M., 2TL), focusing on archaeology and ethnography, is tiny, but don't let its size fool you. Among the exhibits, which are mostly columns culled from Telmessos's acropolis, is the stele discovered at Letoon. The etchings on this single piece of stonework are in three languages (Aramaic, Lycian, and Greek); its discovery in 1973 proved crucial to decoding one of the two Lycian dialects spoken until the 1st century B.C.

EXCURSIONS
Kayaköy

Romanticized in a mesmerizing novel based on an inter-ethnic love affair during the decline of the Ottoman Empire and the ensuing WWI battle at Çanakkale, the village of Kayaköy was author Louis de Bernières's pick of the Anatolian litter when it came to selecting a locale from which to base his sweeping 570-page bestseller *Birds Without Wings*. The historical epic's vivid descriptions of Eskibahçe—Kayaköy's fictitious moniker in the book—barely prepare the reader for the village's haunting scenery.

While the town was originally founded by the Lycians as Carmylessus, it wasn't until the 17th century that Greeks resettled it as Levissi. Kayaköy (0252/614-1150, 8:30 A.M.–8:30 P.M., 5TL) is the name of the ghost town today. It stands as a grim reminder of the impact of the population exchange between Greece and Turkey in 1923. After the latter succeeded in gaining its independence, both nations agreed to swap Turkey's Ottoman Orthodox Christian population for Greece's Muslims. Hordes were uprooted and respectively "sent home" to a country most had never visited before. And in the case of Levissi, its former Christian population of over 6,000 went on to found the town of Nea Levissi in the Athenian suburbs. Most of their Muslim counterparts from Greece shunned the inland village—by then renamed Kayaköy—to "repatriate" along the coast.

To add insult to injury, Kayaköy's collection of 300 buildings were severely damaged during a series of earthquakes, most notably in 1957. The "ghosts" of monasteries, schools, workshops, and homes, all built in the 19th century, were left roofless and crumbling. A long-haul rebuilding effort launched in 1988 by Turkey's Association of Travel Agencies and its Council of Architects is slowly revamping the hillside village's single-story buildings back to a state worthy of exposition. Built in a manner as to benefit from spectacular views of the green valley below, the buildings adopt a golden ember glow as the sun sets. The town's two churches have long been denuded of their gilded icons, but still retain enough of their original wall friezes and mosaic flooring to warrant a trip. The largest, Panaghia Pyrgiotissa, sits amidst the village, while the church of Taksiyarhis is up on the slope.

A *dolmuş* (communal taxi) travels to Kayaköy from Fethiye (8km, 3TL) on the half hour during the summer, and almost on an hourly basis November–April. There's also a minibus that connects to the anglicized town of Hisarönü (3TL, 5km), where a frequent *dolmuş* bound for the beach of Ölüdeniz (4km, 2.5TL) can be boarded. Alternatively, you can hit the trail signposted Kayaköy behind Fethiye's fortress. Count on about a two-hours' walk, preferably before 10 A.M. to avoid the blazing afternoon sun.

ACCOMMODATIONS AND FOOD

For those wanting to experience the village over several days, one of the nine feel-like-home spacious rooms at **Misafir Evi** (Kaya Caddesi, 0252/618-0162, www.kayamisafirevi.com, 30–120TL) does just the trick. They come replete with air-conditioning and en suite baths. The rooms are sparsely decorated to maximize modern comforts without any chintz. Misafir's popular restaurant, which remains open during the off-season, deserves a nod for its garden- and farm-fresh dishes, particularly its superb *künefe* (cheese dessert) and hearty vegetables stews.

Top off your excursion to Kayaköy with a visit to **Kaya Winehouse** (Gökçeburun Mah. 70, 0252/618-0454, www.kayawinehouse.com, meals 25TL) for traditional Turkish eats. Set on the grounds of a beautifully restored Greek house, Kaya owner Ilkay Bey serves white, red, and fruit wines, created by small independents vintners in the region.

C Ölüdeniz

If heaven could resemble an earthly place, then one contender for a prime location would be Ölüdeniz (Dead Sea). This large, splendid sandbar, which bisects the tiniest of the country's innumerable bays, and its sheltered Blue Lagoon within, is reason enough to visit Turkey. The approach is half the fun: The road that crosses pine-covered country opens up to reveal the bluest of waters, pocked only by a long sandy arm below. Remember, however, that you won't be the only one taking a gander at this location. So opt instead for the off-season visit to bypass the crowds.

The protracted beach on its white-sand piney cape and the turquoise still waters of the reputed Blue Lagoon make up **Ölüdeniz Tabiat Parkı** (Ölüdeniz National Park, Ölüdeniz Cad., 8 A.M.–8 P.M., admission 4TL, parking 5TL). Incidentally, Ölüdeniz is also the name of a village situated some six kilometers northeast of this protected coastal wonder. Although it's thankfully protected from development, you'll find lounge chairs and parasols, as well as concession stands, toilets, and showers to ensure a pleasant day at the beach. To stake a piece of sun-kissed acreage, arrive before 10 A.M.

A lauded landing site for the daring paragliders who fearlessly jump off from the nearby towering summit of Babadağ, **Belcekiz Plajı** (Belcekiz Beach) is attracting more and more hotel resorts and a nascent entertainment scene that will in time rival anything found 15 kilometers northwest in Fethiye. Here, you'll find a propensity of tours and spectacular white sands lining the iridescent blue-green waters. Families love the entire region for its warmer waters, but Ölüdeniz's shallower sea makes it particularly irresistible for those with smaller children.

A *dolmuş* (communal taxi, 15km, 4TL) departs from a stop across from Fethiye's hospital en route to Ölüdeniz at least every 15 minutes in the high season, and at least twice hourly November–April. Its itinerary includes stops in the resort towns of Ovacık and Hisarönü.

Popular with sunbathers and yachters, the protected paradise of Ölüdeniz is a blue lagoon framed by an extended strip of white sand.

ACCOMMODATIONS AND FOOD

If you're planning to extend your stay, ditch the resorts for Ölüdeniz's handful of charming boutique hotels. Leading the pack is **Jade Residence** (Belcekiz Mevkii 30, Sok. No.1, 0252/617-0690, www.jade-residence.com, €130). Undoubtedly named for the color of the sea just beyond this beachfront property, the Jade can't be beat for its friendly staff and its clientele (no boisterous teenage boppers here). The rooms, just eight to choose from, are spacious and add to the serenity of the place with spare, tasteful furnishings and French windows overlooking a tropical garden, refreshing pool, and topaz coast beyond. Gaze at breathtaking sunsets while savoring regional mezes and grilled fish at the onsite restaurant's terrace.

Don't miss **La Mare Italian Restaurant** (Ölüeniz Cad., next to the Tokgöz Shopping Center, 0252/617-0666, 17TL) for arguably the tastiest spaghetti bolognese and thin-crusted pizza east of Bologna. Open since 2007, La Mare has become the restaurant of choice with locals for its alfresco dining, which also includes the rare T-bone steak (22TL).

Tlos

One of Lycia's major cities, Tlos (Saklıkent Yolu, 0252/614-1150, 8:30 A.M.–8:30 P.M. daily, 5TL) was also its oldest and most commanding, thanks in part to its highly defendable location high atop the Xanthos Valley. The Romans were awed by its might and citizenry, referring to city as "the very brilliant metropolis of the Lycian nation." Historically, however, inscriptions on Hittite records recently unearthed reveal that Tlos was founded well before 2,000 B.C. When the Hittite Empire was absorbed by the Lydians in the 12th century B.C., Tlos folded into Lycia, only to be absorbed by the Romans about a millenium later. According to archaelogical excavations conducted jointly by Antalya's Akdeniz University and the Lycia Research Center, Tlosians were divided into three *demes* (districts) named for Greek mythological heroes Bellerophon, Iobates, and Sarpedon. A Jewish populace comprised yet another subdivision with its own political representatives.

The city was an important bishopric under the Byzantines and, interestingly enough, one of the very few to thrive well into the 19th century under the Ottomans.

From its towering seat at the eastern end of the Xanthos Valley, Tlos flows down the cliffside from the ancient city's acropolis. Tlos offers remarkable examples of temple-like rock caves, carved right into the sheer northern cliff. The several freestanding sarcophagi nearby leave an indelible first impression. All other ruins stem from monuments dating back to a mid-2nd-century A.D. reconstruction of the city, commissioned—and bankrolled—by two Roman philanthropists, following the massive earthquake of A.D. 141. If you can bypass the flocks of curious goats grazing around the entrance of the theater, you'll be able to read the ancient carvings on its stage walls. Much like other Hellenic arenas, this one was built on a slope with 34 rows of seats, supported by an intricate structure of underground vaults. Climbing further up the hill first leads to the city's walls, which were added by the Byzantines and later fortified by the Ottomans. These last occupiers added a large garrison in the late 14th century atop the summit to keep an eye on the wide Xanthos Valley below; come here February–May to gawk at acres of blooming flora, including wild orchids and showy poppies.

To reach Tlos and Yayaköy from Fethiye follow the highway leading southbound to Antalya/Korkuteli, passing the bridge over Eşen Çayı (20km), or until the roundabout. Once there, follow signage toward Korkuteli for about 500 meters and hang a right (south) at the road bearing a Saklıkent/Tlos marker. Continue down the country road until the left-hand turnoff to Tlos (about 10km). Alternatively, a *dolmuş* (communal taxi) connects Fethiye to Saklıkent, stopping at the hamlet of Güncşli. Unfortunately, the only way to reach Tlos and Yakaköy from the turnoff is to hike the three kilometers due east; or hitch a ride with one of the friendly locals.

YAKAKÖY

Right below the ancient city of Tlos lies the

traditional farming village of Yakaköy. By its entrance is a trout farm whose owners have ingenuously opened as an entertainment park and popular restaurant. Yaka Park Trout Farm or **Yaka Parkı** (Yakaköyü, 0252/634-0391, 9 A.M.–10 P.M., meals 25TL), with its old water windmill and trout pond, offers their guests an opportunity to play with a fish before ordering it for lunch. Also interesting is the bar, which has been filled with tiny trout, and the cackling ducks all around. The staff dares guests to try the onsite pool, but do so at your own risk since it's been filled with freezing runoff from Ak Dağı (White Mountain). Lounge the day away on an oversized cushion on Yaka's soft rolling hill or pick one of the terrace tables shaded by adult pines. By the way, the unlimited mezes are good, but the trout grilled to a crisp is even better.

If you decide that you just can't part with the prevailing serenity of Yakaköy, the quaint B&B **The Mountain Lodge** (Yaka Yolu 2, 0252/638-2515, www.themountainlodge. co.uk, €72–106) will be happy to oblige visiting guests. The property includes a Turkish/Continental restaurant and an anglicized pub, which lures in a sizeable British expat clientele from Fethiye. So, like many guests have done in the past, stop in for a beer and you may end up staying the week in a decently-sized guest room or in the homey studio with attached kitchenette.

SAKLIKENT KANYON (SAKLIKENT GORGE)

Great tacked onto a trip to the ruins of Tlos, or even better as an active day excursion of its own, Saklıkent Gorge (8:30 A.M.–8:30 P.M., 5TL, free Nov.–Apr.)—a.k.a. the Canyon of the Hidden Valley—is a natural phenomenon. Eons of torrential runoff from Ak Dağı (White Mountain) have formed a 500-meter deep crevasse. Getting there from the top of the gorge is not for the faint-hearted; it requires wading through waist-high waters so cold you'll go numb after just five minutes. The canyon is so steep and narrow that the sun barely hits the stream and the 18-kilometer-long gorge

renders even mid-August temperatures chilly. Alternatively, opt for the more sedate entry at the foot of the canyon, where the official entrance to this natural preserve lies next to the parking lot, concession stands, and lines of tour buses.

A narrow 150-meter-long catwalk attached to the cliff-face leads up to the gorge, where the flow of the Gökçesu and Ulupnar Rivers meet on their way down from Babadağı. In transit, wooden platforms, that seemingly hang in mid-air, allow for breathtaking scenery of precipices that have been sanded to a shiny luster. Some of these wooden decks were creatively transformed into the **Saklikent Gorge River Restaurant** (0252/659-0074, www. saklikentgorge.net), a nice open-air joint to savor traditional "wintery" oven-baked dishes, seated on mats around low tables with waters rushing at an arm's length away. The restaurant's owners, the Ulutaş brothers, also own the nearby River Bar and Tree Houses, where twenty-somethings hang out for days of endless fun in kayaks by daylight and narghile parties by night. You can enjoy splashing and sliding through the water and mud, or wading through rapids while holding on to a rope; just bring water shoes with a good grip and you'll be golden. Otherwise, a pair can be rented onsite for about 3TL.

Tours by air-conditioned minibus or jeep safari head daily for Saklıkent Gorge during the summer, with stops at the ruins of Tlos and lunch at Yaka Parkı. Book a tour easily by contacting one of Fethiye's premier travel agencies, **Carol & Tayfun** (Atatürk Cad., above Ataman Market, Fethiye, 0252/612-3228, www.caroletayfun.com, 18–41TL). Departing at 9 A.M. and returning by 6 P.M. every day, except Mondays and Saturdays, the price of the excursion includes lunch and transfers, as well as guide and park entry fees.

A *dolmuş* (communal taxi, 45min, 6TL) leaves Fethiye's minibus station when full (every 15min) for the 42-kilometer drive southeast to Saklıkent. Or, if you're driving, follow the Antalya/Korkuteli highway and turn left at the road marked for Saklıkent/Tlos. Pass the left-hand turn to Tlos and continue another 10 kilometers to another left turn toward Saklikent.

Faralya and Butterfly Valley

For an excursion that will satisfy fans of ecotourism, outdoorsy types, and archaeology buffs, head to the ancient Lycian city of Faralya high above the fiercely-protected natural reserve of Kelebek Vadisi (Butterfly Valley). This stunningly beautiful dale, lined by pristine beach acreage, owes its name to the 30 species of butterflies that paint its skies and deep gorge in technicolor June–September. In addition to the year-round presence of some 40 nocturnal moths, it's also a hatching spot for the rare, cherry-red Jersey tiger butterfly in April and May. The heady scents emanating from the 350-meter-deep valley's abundant Mediterranean flora—mainly mint, jasmine and thyme—is what draws these winged fauna.

Taking off from the beach, an easy hour-long hike into the valley along densely vegetated trails leads to a refreshing, 60-meter-high waterfall (3TL). Take the rocky path to the right (south) that leads uphill through the canyon to the headland on which the village of Faralya sits. Make sure to follow the trail, part of the Lycian Way, by heeding the red-dotted signs. A sturdy rope was added to facilitate passage through the steeper, narrower inclines. This method of reaching Faralya takes about an hour. Wear a pair of sturdy hiking shoes and bring water.

Faralya, with a population of 500, barely had a road to its name until a few years ago. Today, it's the summer home of the earth-friendly Turco-British couple who run the **Yuva Eco-Holiday Center** (Faralya, 4417/675-5888). *Yuva* in Turkish translates into *den,* and that's just what founders Atilla Sevilmiş and Caroline Clipson have created by offering soul-nurturing programs such as yoga, reflexology, and detox in a spectacularly unblemished wilderness. With the turquoise sea just a hike away and traditional Turkish country cuisine, the seven-day program (all

meals, activities, lodging, and group airport transfers included, 415TL pp) helps reconnect its guests to nature—both their inner nature and the great outdoors.

The most enjoyable way of reaching Butterfly Valley is by using the taxi minibus service (May–Sept., 30min ride, round-trip 12TL) that leaves from Belcekiz Beach three times a day (11 A.M., 2 P.M., and 6 P.M.), with three returns (9 A.M., 1 P.M., and 5 P.M.) from the valley to Belcekiz Beach. Alternatively, a *dolmuş* (communal taxi, 25min ride, 5TL) departs for Faralya from Fethiye (8km), by way of Ölüdeniz, five times per day in summer, twice a day in winter.

ACCOMMODATIONS

For those who are left stranded in Faralya, the rustic, authentic accommodations at the water-lapped **Oyster Residences** (Faralya, 0252/642-1063, www.oysterresidences.com, €230–250) await with surroundings that defy even superlatives. Defining the property's dramatic rocky seafront lined by heady, crooked pines as splendid drastically falls short of what it is. One thing's for certain: The sparsity of the interior decor in each of the chalets, including the finest white linen and prime organic fabrics, only heightens the enchanting surroundings. A stay here is life enhancing, if you have the loose purse strings to afford it. The pampering by the onsite valet, İsmail, just furthers the enchantment with epicurean feasts fit for a gourmet.

More affordable digs are available at **George's House** (Faralya, 0252/642-1102, www.georgehouse.net.tc, 60TL). This all-inclusive, half-board inn has 11 bare-bone bungalows or larger en suite rooms. George's also offers tents (10TL) or just meals (breakfast and dinner, 18TL), as well as tree houses for those ready to snooze under the stars. Either way, at these prices you can't go wrong. The hotel's reputedly good and inexpensive farm-fresh fare and modest lodgings remain grounded in Turkish simplicity, an island in a sea of recently-launched pricey B&Bs boasting trendy nouvelle cuisine.

NIGHTLIFE

It's hard to beat the all-inclusive resorts for their nightly entertainment schedule, variety of bars, and nightclubs. A good example of this is **LykiaWorld** (Kıdrak Mevkii, Ölüdeniz, 0252/617-0200, www.lykiaworld.com) whose nighttime party begins with family-friendly dance lessons and staged shows and ends with blasting top-40 tunes on their sweeping dance floors until the wee hours of the morning. Most hotels and resorts accept non-guests; nightly programs are typically listed near the reception desk.

Fethiye and a few of its hamlets have a lively bar/nightclub scene worth checking out. Fethiye's Old Bazaar quarters has a good variety of restaurants and British-style bars, which all liven up after 7 P.M. Tucked in its narrow lanes, merchants take advantage of the heavy foot traffic to sell kitschy baubles until at least midnight. In Ölüdeniz, the promenade along Belcekiz Beach replicates the fun with its few nightclub/bar hybrids that lure the young and rowdy with ear-splitting music. The best option along the promenade is **Buzz Bar & Restaurant** (Belcekiz Beach promenade, 0252/617-0526, www.buzzbeachbar.com). One of the top-rated—and sexiest—beach bars in the world; the young and beautiful congregate there for delectable frozen strawberry Smirnoffs (15TL) or sumptuous chocolate cheesecakes. There's also live beach percussion sessions on Fridays and Saturdays. For a quieter and definitely more sophisticated evening, head up the cliff toward **White Dolphin Restaurant (Beyaz Yunus)** (Oyster Residences, Faralya, 0252/642-1063, www.oysterresidences.com). There, candle-lit tables and soft music lures a clientele of millionaires, who moor their megayachts in the crashing waves below.

The almost entirely British hamlet of Hisarönü, on the road to Kayaköy, gets wild and crazy during the summer. An innumerable amount of beer bars, restaurants, and trinket shops line this expat enclave's overcrowded pedestrian streets. Hisarönü's "in" night spot is **Time Out Bar** (Hisarönü, 0534/618-5226); it's a karaoke bar where a ripped bar staff (also the owners) dance to the tune of ear-splitting music and howls from the crowds.

SPORTS AND RECREATION
Beaches

Ironic as it may seem, the nearest beach to Fethiye proper is named **Çalış** (work). It's located five kilometers north of downtown, along Fethiye bay, and perhaps received the moniker because its three-kilometer length requires a long walk to reach its end. It's actually two strips in one: The touristy strip at Çalış gives way to the surf-haven of **Koca Çalış**, at its northern tip. The former provides the expected array of identical hotel resorts and concession shops, touting sunscreen and humongous beach balls. While its crowded shores are best avoided during the day, a visit to view the sun setting over offshore islands in mid-summer may turn out to be one of the highlights of your trip. Wind-battered Koca Çalış, to the north, thankfully remains too wild for mass tourism and just perfect to enjoy its unblemished natural setting.

Çalış Beach can be reached by water *dolmuş* (communal taxi, 5TL), which takes off right from Fethiye's marina every 30 minutes. Or, there's the frequent street *dolmuş* (2TL) that connects Çalış from the minibus station, stopping in between to pick up passengers.

If you were planning to rent a vehicle—a jeep preferably—during your stay, why not visit the pristine cove of **Gemiler Beach** after an outing to the museum-village of Kayaköy? Untouched by development, this beach boasts picturesque mountains in the distance and the possibility of swimming or boating to **Gemiler Adası** (Boat Island). This diminutive landmass is home to the ruins of the 1,300-year-old Byzantine **Saint Nicholas Monastery** (5TL), named after the benevolent saint who once lived here. Back on the beach, you'll find a boat rental booth and a makeshift café, known for its toothsome fish fare.

For immaculate sands worth the attention of sunbathing pundits, plus an impromptu walk through Byzantine ruins, board the water *taksi* from Fethiye's marina to the offshore **Şevalye**

Adası (Chevalier Island). And, of course, don't forget the beach resort of **Belcekız Beach** and the Blue Lagoon of nearby **Ölüdeniz** for, irrefutably, the best costal scenery in the Eastern Mediterranean.

Cruises

Join the hyped **12-Island Tour** by **Labranda Tours** (Atatürk Cad. 78, 0252/612-0323, www. labrandatour.com, 25TL pp, includes lunch)—actually 12 stops comprising the six main islands—right from Fethiye's marina. Departing at 9 A.M. and returning at 6 P.M., boats circle the Bay of Fethiye as their load of semi-inebriated passengers bop to the tunes of Turkish pop music. Don't let that deter you from signing up; the scenery is indescribably stunning. This mini Blue Cruise stops for dips in the turquoise waters just off Yassicalar Adası (Flats Island) and Tersane Adası (Shipyard Island). But the wow-effect of the entire day is a snorkel session above the sunken Byzantine baths at Hamam Bay, a.k.a. Cleopatra's Bath, and at Gemiler Adası (Boat Island). A stop at Turunç Bükü's rocky outpost allows for a truly wild experience of jumping off from a dangling rope straight into the iridescent waters below. A stop at the beach and therapeutic mud baths at Kızıl Ada (Red Islands) marks the last stop on the itinerary. Expect to pay a little more November–April.

If you'd like to extend the sea-borne adventure beyond the nine hours of a day cruise, consider booking a short (3 nights, 4 days) version of what most consider the "best of" the Blue Cruise, along the Turkish Coast. There's a panoply of travel agencies and even boat captains who offer this shortened option from Fethiye through ancient Lycian country, with an itinerary that typically includes the ports of Ölüdeniz, Gemiler Island, and the formidable Patara Beach, before switching for the land portion of the tour at Demre/Myra to the last stop at Olympos by bus. Among dozens of travel agencies purveying similar tours, the Turco-Belgian owners of **V-GO** (Iskele Meydani, below Dedeoğlu Hotel, Fethiye, 0252/612-2113, www. bluecruisesturkey.com) are not only multilingual, but highly recommended by the national

tourist association and some of the largest European tour operators. Cruises are priced at €175 July 1–September 30 and at €155 April 1–June 30 and October 1–December 1. A 30 percent deposit is required at the time of booking. The fare includes hotel transfers to the boat, all meals, harbor fees, and the use of snorkeling equipment, but does not cover drinks onboard or the tip for the crew.

Horseback Riding and Jeep Safaris

What better way to enjoy the scenery of shrubby countryside, mixed in with its jaw-dropping coastal splendor, than to wander through Fethiye's back mountain roads on a safari. There are two horseback-riding options, each about 3.5 hours long: one tours the Xanthos Valley to the archaeology at Kayaköy Village, while the other treks through fragrant pine forests to the astonishing Blue Lagoon of Ölüdeniz. Horses or ponies are available to suit riders of all experiences and ages; reliable hard-hats and tacking are provided. **Carol & Tayfun** (Atatürk Cad., above Ataman Market, Fethiye, 0252/612-3228, www.caroltayfun.com, 15TL) provide these horseback-riding tours daily, with hotel transfers included. The morning ride runs 8:30 A.M.–noon; the afternoon jaunt runs 3:30 P.M.–6 P.M.

Carol & Tayfun, along with a panoply of others around the region, also offers exhilarating **Jeep safaris** through dirt roads in Fethiye's back country. Either drive or be driven through most major sites around Fethiye in an open-topped four-wheeler, as part of a daily convoy that begins with a stop at the rock temples at Tlos. After an open buffet feast at Yaka Park Trout Farm, the ride continues to Saklıkent Gorge, where the convoy will follow the river to Xanthos to discover the ruins. The excursion finishes with some R&R at Patara, one of Turkey's longest sandy beaches. The safaris (15TL) take off daily at around 8 A.M. and return by 6 P.M., May–October, and include hotel transfers, lunch, and a guide. It gets grimy, dusty, wet, and muddy; appropriate clothes are highly recommended.

HIKING THE LYCIAN WAY

Brainchild of hiker extraordinaire Kate Clow, a 60-something Brit expat who's called Antalya home for more than a decade, the Lycian Way winds its way along ancient Lycia. Clow cleared and waymarked this path that swoops through the Tekke Peninsula, a headland that juts dramatically into the Med, and she continues to maintain it. The mountains soar from the pined coast, forming pygmy coves, astounding vistas, and excellent trails along this southwestern part of Turkey. Along the way, the Lycians' impressive burial chambers in their ancient architectural style can be explored, as well as a myriad of other ancient sites.

Winding along a 509-kilometer waymarked footpath, the Lycian Way loops from Fethiye to Antalya. The hike is graded medium to hard since it's not level. The road ascends and descends as it approaches and swerves away from the sea. The trail consists of footpaths and mule trails, and tends to be limestone, hard, and often shingly. The going is easy near Fethiye and gets more difficult as it winds its way southward. Spring (Feb.-May) or autumn or (Sept.-Nov.) are the recommended times to hike this path. Stay away from the summer season; 2009 saw temperatures in late July and early August around the mid-40s°C with high humidity. Hotels and pensions pepper the start of the route, around Patara, Kalkan, Kaş, Myra, Finike, Adrasan, Olympos, Çıralı, and Tekirova. Village houses and camps dot the rest of the way. Camping does not require any special permission.

Along the trail you'll encounter: Myra's stunning theater masks and the church of the Angel Gabriel in the hills above; dazzling walks along the slopes of Baba Dağı, with paragliders soaring above; the spectacular slope into Faralya from the cliffs of the protected Butterfly Valley; Patara's 12-kilometer-long beach; the pebbly coasts of the resorts of Kaş and Kalkan; the Genoese Castle, harbor and sunken Hellene city at Üçağız; the feel-on-top-of-the-world walk on the mountain ridge leading to Finike; the overnight stay at Cape Gelidonia; the rough climb up Mount Olympos (2,388m); wading through the canyon at Göynük; and, the ruins of out-of-the-way Lycian cities. That's all, aside from meeting gregarious villagers and encountering old country abodes and lush green forests, juxtaposed against the snow-white rocks and the startling blue of the Mediterranean.

Clow and avid hiker and photographer Terry Richardson provide a list of accommodations on the 33 burgs and cities along the route. There's tons of information online at www.lycianway.com, or in the highly recommended book *The Lycian Way*, authored by the duo. Clow guides groups through the various trails she's marked; she also recommends contacting **Middle Earth Travel** (Gaferli Mah. Cevizler Sok. 20, Göreme, Nevşehir, 0384/271-2559, www.middleearthtravel.com) to join one of the three Lycian Way tours. The seven-day Pirates Coast Trek costs €550, a price that includes transfers (to and from Antalya), accommodations, guide, hotel transfers, meals, and mule support. One evening meal, all soft drinks, beer, and tips are not included as well as entrance fees to historical sites and museums. The eight-day Seven Capes Trek runs €480, which includes all meals and transfers to Dalaman, and guide; and, the 15-Day Trek costs €1,050 with amenities and services included.

Paragliding

Ölüdeniz is one of the premier paragliding locations for professionals in the world. The sheer drop-off from Mount Babadağ (1,969m.) over the natural spectacle of the Blue Lagoon of Ölüdeniz, combined with the area's mild offshore winds and gnarly thermals rising from the sun-beaten earth, makes an ideal setting for this adrenaline-packed sport. Among Ölüdeniz's dozen paragliding outfitters, **Sky Sports** (Deniz Kamp, Ölüdeniz, 0252/617-0511, www.skysports-turkey.com, mid-April–Oct., tandem flight 180TL) rates highest when it comes to quality of equipment, experience, and insurance. Groups take off four times a day (9 A.M., 11 A.M., 2 P.M., and 4 P.M.)

for the two-hour flight/tour that includes an hour-long mini Jeep safari to reach Babadağ's summit from Ölüdeniz. Rated first in Fethiye's long list of must-do activities, jumps are highly popular and sell out fast. Book online if at all possible, or at least 24 hours in advance.

Water Sports
DIVING
There are more than 20 dive sites around the Gulf of Fethiye to please scuba divers at any level. In fact, the area's underwater caves are world-famous for their unparalleled scenery. Thanks to shallow depths—less than 30 meters below the surface—and large entrances, daylight filters through easily. Colorful mollusks, large fish, and colonies of seahorses and shrimp by the million reside alongside 3,000-year-old amphorae littering the seabed.

Day tours from Fethiye include two 30-minute dives to visit the area's noteworthy caves, like the caves at Şahin Bükü to the east of Fethiye: the Afkule, Turkish Bath, and Mexican Hat caves. Established in 1989, **European Diving Center** (Fevzi Çakmak Cad. 133, Fethiye, 0252/614-9771, www.europeandivingcenter.com) is the most reputable diving center in Turkey, with branches in vacation destinations throughout the littoral. Daily excursions (53TL) for qualified scuba divers include three dives, lunch, equipment rental, and certified guides. Great for families, the "beginner's day" (49TL) involves a quick lesson about the basics of diving concepts, followed by two sea dives in small groups with an instructor. Other instructional packages include a two- to three-day scuba diving (160TL) program and a three-day PADI open water diving (270TL) program, as well as weeks-long master diver holiday programs (399–1450TL). Fethiye's larger hotel resorts, like LikyaWorld, also run their own programs.

SURFING
Of the handful of surfing schools that opened shop, **Fethiye Surf Center** (Pk.170 Çalış Plajı, 0252/622-0753, www.fethiyesurfcenter.com), in Çalış Beach, is run by a trio of siblings, headed by national kitesurfing champion Taner Aykurt. Eight instructors specialize in windsurfing and kitesurfing, offering options like an hour-long kitesurfing taster (€30); their popular three-lesson basic windsurfing course (€50); advanced windsurfing lessons (€90–130); and board rental by the hour (€10–12), day (€25–70), or week (€210–235). Fethiye Surf Center's onsite café makes an outing great for the entire family, with comfy oversized cushions for lounging and great Turkish fare, cooked by none other than Taner's mom.

WHITE-WATER RAFTING
The Dalaman River offers white-water rafting enthusiasts an opportunity to ride the rapids on the swift currents that flow between heady canyons. While this popular activity can be achieved from any point along Southwestern Turkey, Fethiye's proximity to Dalaman (57km) allows for quick transfers, enabling guests to save on travel time. Virtually all tour companies offer the packaged tour (40TL) that includes transportation to Dalaman, lunch, instruction, and equipment. A good choice is **Alpine Rafting company** (Köprülü Kanyon, Beşkonak Köyü, Antalya; 0534/301-9536; www.turkeyrafting.com), who offers an all-day outing that begins at 8 A.M. and finishes at 5 P.M. The tour (€20) includes a 15 km rafting ride down the Dalaman River, transfer from hotel, and professional guide. Daily rafting excursions typically take off at 8 A.M. and return around 6 P.M., May–October.

ACCOMMODATIONS
Packed with activities and day trips, and as the departure point for the shortened version of the must-do Blue Cruise, Fethiye offers the ideal base for a pleasingly varied vacation. The problem is that the town is not long on superior hotels, nor boutiques for that matter. Instead, it's got scores of identical resorts, aimed at mass tourism and lots of basic pensions. As the center of the region, however, Fethiye is hard to beat when it comes to satisfying the modern traveler with a centralized network of entertainment, dining, and shopping establishments,

conveniences you just won't find out in the boondocks.

For a beach hotel, stay close to Fethiye's Çalış Beach. Just two kilometers north of the town center, inexpensive pensions are lined up side-by-side, just off the sand, touting super basic rooms to a backpacker clientele. The larger properties at Ölüdeniz's Belcekız Beach tend to be crowded and packed with families—particularly British—with inflated room prices that reflect their European clientele's greater purchasing power. Excellent family-run B&Bs and self-catering accommodations are on the rise, providing alternatives to the ubiquitous all-inclusive holiday resorts.

Veering off-center you'll find pleasing lodging around Fethiye's satellite villages. In historical Kayaköy, for example, life continues unaffected by year-round tourism amid the lush Xanthos Valley. Here, you'll find a trio of boutique inns that capitalize on their peaceful surroundings to offer their guests unparalleled charm and location, as well as unbeatable serenity. Midway between Fethiye and Kayaköy, Hisarönü and Ovacık are expanding to include ever more holiday villages—and rather garish entertainment facilities—to titillate the British proletariat. The only property worth a mention, that is, if you're looking for self-catering accommodations, is Hisarönü's **Orka Private Villas** (Ovacık village, 0252/616-6794, www.orkaclub.com/eng, 2-bedroom 108TL, 3-bedroom 120TL, 4-bedroom 132TL).

Also worth considering are the blissfully remote properties peppering the hills, seacoast, and valleys just outside of downtown Fethiye. Serenely secluded beachfront chalets, spa and holistic retreats, and luxuriously refurbished villas are all possibilities for those who thrive in supreme quietness reminiscent of a *Lost* episode. Consider checking out the independently-run Su Değirmeni in Faralya and other small hotels like it.

Lastly, booking with one of the better properties in Fethiye can prove problematic, particularly during the summer time. Holiday packagers tend to monopolize hotels for the entire season, sometimes even year-round,

thereby leaving individual travelers high and dry. Unnerving as this may be, join them rather than try to beat them at their own game. You might just be pleasantly surprised by the type of deals available through holiday hyper-marketers like **Thomson Holiday** (U.K., 0871/231-4691, www.thomson.co.uk) or **Thomas Cook Holidays** (U.K., 0871/895-0055, www.thomascook.com). Also, keep in mind that most services are quoted in British pounds, and that the majority of hotels in and around Fethiye are closed mid-November–March.

Under €50

Kaya Cottages Kayaköy (Kayaköy, 0537/579-2050, www.kaya-cottages.co.uk, 185–300TL/week) appeal to self-caterers with two cottages which individually accommodate up to four adults. In the able hands of Clare Bunkley, these two once-crumbling historical farms were transformed into alluring vacation dens. A pool was even added to titillate guests looking to flee from hectic Fethiye. The larger unit, the Smokehouse, boasts high-beamed ceilings, a modern bath, fully-appointed kitchen, balcony, and patio.

Oykun Otel (1000 Sok., Caliş Beach Fethiye, 0252/613-3111, www.oykunhotel.com, €40–52) is currently the centrally-located budget hotel to beat in Fethiye. Awarded three years in a row as the best three-star hotel in Fethiye by Thomson Holidays, the family-run Oykun oozes with friendly services and activities geared for the entire family. Some 90 doubles and 10 suites are cozily spacious, albeit a bit frayed around the edges. But who cares at these prices and with a location near the beach at Çaliş (500m)? All the money saved can be used to splurge on a windsurfing course or on the hotel's daily fishing or boat trips. Nightly BBQs, indoor games that include billiards and table tennis, and a lively pool setting all encourage Oykun's predominantly British clients to mingle.

Villa Daffodil (Favzi Çakmak Cad. 115, Fethiye, 0252/614-9595, www.villadaffodil.com, 35–45TL) is one of those rare residences that stays open year-round. Its proximity to the beach, unbelievable Ottoman charm, and popularity with tour groups make it a sell-out virtually year-round. The property, which is run by a retired Turkish colonel, features 27 basic rooms that are immaculately kept. Eight boast diminutive balconies with sea views, while others share a courtyard. A small pool is located in the rear verdant garden. Villa Daffodil guests have the option of chartering Colonel Hussein's seven-cabin *güllet* (motorized sailboat), which is moored in the bay just 100 feet away from the hotel.

€50-150

Club Belcekiz Beach (Ölüdeniz, 0252/617-0077, www.belcekiz.com, 75–115TL) is the answer to a no-fuss vacation, particularly with kids in tow. With a location at the very tip of Ölüdeniz Beach, with Babadağ looming in the background, the gorgeous setting promises an active vacation. And, as a vacation village, Club Belcekiz Beach obliges with a slew of guided outdoor trips organized daily and onsite facilities that include immense pools, a full-range spa, and traditional hammam, as well as a no-charge Kids' Club, all in a property boasting beautifully manicured gardens. Rooms, each with modern tiled baths and patio or balcony, are identical in either section of the hotel. This hotel is in demand, and securing a room is not an easy feat, but well worth it at these prices.

Su Değirmeni (Hisar Mah. 4, Uzunyurt, Faralya, 0252/642-1245, www.natur-reisen.de, €55–70/day, €375–485/week). Taking its name from an onsite watermill, Değirmeni sprawls over terraces tucked in a mountain crevice overlooking Butterfly Valley. The two-story stone houses, which include nine suites, two doubles and a single, are totally secluded and surrounded in lush Mediterranean fauna. The large rooms boast traditional *kilims* (Turkish carpets), custom pine furniture, and spectacular views of the valley. With more than two decades in hotel management and tour planning experience in the Fethiye area, owners Ferruh and Brigitte Özbali are experts when it comes to satisfying their predominantly German clientele's penchant for the outdoors.

Jade Residence (Belcekiz Mevki, Ölüdeniz, 0252/617-0690, www.jade-residence.com, from €110) was recently built out of an historic merchant abode to accommodate the extra clientele its sister property, Oyster Residences (next door) couldn't. All modicums of luxury can be found in the eight rooms of this residence, as well as a refreshing pool. It's the perfect B&B, conceived by restaurateur Mehmet Günel and his charming wife Günsenin, the folks behind White Dolphin Restaurant, one of Turkey's best fish eateries. The reason why Jade wins over Oyster is its onsite diner. The property is just steps away from an inviting, relaxing beachfront and miles from noisy tour groups.

Over €150

One of Fethiye's most exclusive resort hotels, the remotely-located, all-inclusive **Hillside Beach Club** (Kalemya Koyu, 4km due west of Fethiye, 0252/614-8360, www.hillsidebeachclub.com, minimum three-day stay, from €900) is built and run by Alarko Group, Turkey's premier developer. Their upscale touch is pervasive here: way superior spa facilities; five types of larger rooms boast a spare, but selective decor, and either a seaside terrace or balcony to make the most of this massive property's private cove; and, 15 sport activities free-of-charge, including all off-shore activities like pricey sailing instruction. Custom touches include an innovative Pillow Menu, where guests can choose from buckwheat pillows to an anti-reflux contender; and a "festival" of food offered on miles of buffet tables at the six onsite restaurants (there's even a sushi bar!). Hillside Beach Club offers a stylish, no-brainer vacation that may be pricier than most, but it's well worth it!

Reminiscent of the imperial palaces lining the Bosphorus, the coastal **Ece Saray Marina & Resort Fethiye** (Yat Limanı 1, 0252/612-5005, www.ecesaray.net, €185–310) is centrally-located at the end of Fethiye's marina. Since 2003 the Ece has filled the niche between Fethiye's down-and-low inns and pricey accommodations. The decor is pure Levantine, both outside and in, with a proper British gentleman's lounge at Cigar Bar, Parisian-inspired wrought-iron balconies running the height of the facade, and even a modern spa that offers a host of Asian and Scandinavian treatments with an innovatively colorful hammam. The exquisite pool is magnificently landscaped, with greens and colorful blooms that pop against its stark white granite surrounds; the setting is even more striking against the lapis lazuli seas in the background. It's the meeting place of choice for affluent yachters. The location also boasts the chic Levante Restaurant, Fethiye's best grown-up restaurant.

LykiaWorld Ölüdeniz (Ölüdeniz, 0252/617-0400, www.lykiaworld.com, US$236–650 full board) is one of the largest all-inclusive holiday villages in Turkey. Conceived by the German developer Robinson's, Lykia boasts a 5.5-acre Children's Paradise that include a water-theme park, eight swimming pools, 20 water slides, and playgrounds including Treasure Island, Pirate's Forest, Hidden Caves, and even a beach for babies. Meanwhile, parents will be free to renew body and spirit with thalassotherapy treatments or one of the 10 massages at the hands of Balinese and Turkish specialists at the Manolya Spa. Lykia's beach is Ölüdeniz's best, and so are its host of outdoor activities. There are more than 17 pools on the premises and nine restaurants covering virtually every cuisine under the sun.

FOOD

Fethiye has its fair share of street food, from *dürüm* (rolls) and *pide* (pita) sandwiches to the highly popular corn doused in salted butter-substitute. These might come in handy when enjoying a day at the beach or on a stroll, but it won't make foodies green with envy. Actually, there are not many restaurants in Fethiye that will, unless a kebab or a British-inspired meal will do the trick. But a slight venture out of Fethiye proper toward, say, Kayaköy or Ölüdeniz, will reap its weight in gold. Most restaurants open their doors by 9 A.M. and close by midnight in the summer.

Cafés

A great find for breakfast or afternoon tea, **Café Oley** (Eski Meğri Sok. 3, Fethiye, 0252/612-9532) features homemade cakes and an extensive coffee bar. Its fresh ice-cold fruit juices and ice creams are refreshing on sultry summer afternoons. Oley's Mediterranean menu also features a variety of sandwiches, tantalizing snacks, and full-fledged meals all day long. There is also Wi-Fi and an English book exchange to while away the hours over espresso served by friendly staffers.

Fish

For seafood-lovers across Turkey, the Fethiye region is synonymous with ◖ **Beyaz Yunus** (Kidrak Yolu Uzeri 1, Ölüdeniz, 0252/617-0068, 6 P.M.–1 A.M., 20TL). If you can afford to dine à la Prince Charles then try this romantic seafront restaurant, which overlooks the stunning turquoise Med from its very own secluded cliff at the end of Belcekiz Beach. Actually, the affordable mezes here are fabulous, including the *sarma* (grape leaves, 8TL) and the octopus salad (12TL)—served whole with a good drizzle of the house's own olive oil.

Meğri Restaurant (Lika Sok. 8 and 9, Fethiye, 0252/614-4040, 9 A.M.–midnight, 30TL) is a Fethiye staple. Right in the center of Fethiye, hidden in a back street lining the bazaar, Meğri is actually a compilation of three venues: a corner café, an unassuming traditional *lokanta* (diner), and the original location which has consistently wowed crowds of locals forever. During the summer, the tables of this elegant restaurant spill out into the town square, creating a jolly atmosphere from which to enjoy a succulent and crafty mix of French, Mediterranean, and Turkish cuisine. The fish is the house specialty, however, with the popular calamari headlining the menu. For affordable Turkish meat grills without the pomp, try the adjacent **Meğri Lokanta** (Çarsi Cad. 26, 0252/614-4047); you'll still get to enjoy a dinner under the stars in the lively courtyard come summer evenings.

Greek

◖ **Levissi Garden Winehouse & Restaurant** (Kayaköy, 0252/618-0108, www.levissigarden. com, 19TL) is another one of Kayaköy's historic stone farm cottages that was lovingly restored to a restaurant/winehouse with indoor and outdoor dining. Its original stables now house a large cellar where more than 2,000 bottles of domestic wines are stored. Topping the Greek-inspired menu are tantalizing falafel and the strained yogurt dip tzatziki. Main course specialties include oven-baked prawn and feta casseroles and the Levissi steak in a creamy yogurt sauce with green peppers.

Meat
Cin Bal (Kayaköy, 0252/618-0066, www.cinbal.com, 11 A.M.–1 A.M.) is a 20-year-old restaurant that's made its fame selling meat by the kilo (22TL). Once the cut—boar, chicken, lamb, or beef—has been picked and served, guests can then cook it themselves on sidetable grills. For those not keen on red meat, there's chicken and fish. Appetizers, sides, and drinks are complimentary with the cut of meat, but these always seem superfluous after such a carnivorous feast. The place oozes atmosphere nightly as locals cheer and sing along with wandering gypsy dancers and musicians.

INFORMATION AND SERVICES
In Fethiye proper, the **Tourist Information Office** (Iskele Karşısı 1, 0252/614-1527, www.oludeniztourism.org) is located across the marina next to the antique theater. In Ölüdeniz, there's a privately-run **Tourism Development Cooperative** (Belcekiz promenade, 0252/617-0438). Banks, ATMs, and currency exchange booths are all located on Atatürk Caddesi.

GETTING THERE
By Air
Fethiye is served by the **Dalaman Airport** (ATM Dalaman Havalimanı, 0252/792-5555, www.atmairport.aero), which is about 70 kilometers northeast of town. A large number of national and international airlines and charters arrive at Fethiye including Turkish carriers like **Onur Air** (www.onurair.com.tr) and **Atlasjet** (www.atlasjet.com.tr). **Easyjet** (www.easyjet.com) and **British Midland** (www.flybmi.

com) are the most popular among the handful of European charter airlines that fly into Dalaman.

While flying into the busier Antalya Airport might seem feasible on the map, the drive is more than four hours long and takes a rather big bite out of your travel schedule. If time is not an issue, then by all means, drive up to enjoy the highly scenic seaside route northwest to Fethiye.

Transferring into Fethiye from Dalaman is easy to do with **Havas Shuttles** (toll free 444-0487, www.havas.com) that await passengers just outside Dalaman Airport's terminal, before taking off to their destinations on the Southern Aegean and Mediterranean coasts. The white buses are marked with their respective terminus; those headed for Fethiye (1hr, 20TL) drop-off passengers by the marina. A **taxi** from Dalaman Airport will set you back 120TL. A vehicle can be rented from one of three counters right in front of the airport's main gates.

By Bus
Varan (Çarşı Cad. 9, Fethiye, 0252/614-6524 or toll free 444-8999, www.varan.com.tr) or **Ulusoy** (toll free 444-1888, www.ulusoy.com.tr) drive the route from Fethiye to Istanbul once-daily, passing through Denizli (12.5hr, 90TL). Pamukkale (toll free 444-3535) runs the Fethiye-Izmir route daily, passing through Ortaca (6hr, 30TL), and also travels to Antalya (4.5hr, 25TL). All buses depart from the *otogar* (bus station), which is about 1.5 kilometers east of the town center. A frequent *dolmuş* (communal taxi) runs to the marina (2TL); a taxi will cost you about 12TL to cover the same route.

GETTING AROUND
By Car
The best way to get around Fethiye and its suburbs is by car. To rent one, head to the local car-rental offices located around the marina, or simply request the concierge at your hotel to do the negotiating for you. Like most hotels, rates for car rentals are quoted in British

pounds and tend to be steeper than those found in Bodrum or Antalya. For this reason, it might also be easier—and less costly—to book your vehicle online with either **Avis** (www.avis.com) or **Hertz** (www.hertz.com). International carriers are represented in Fethiye through travel agents; Avis vehicles are rented through **Panama Tourism** (Yat Limani Körfez Apt. 9/A2, 0252/612-3719), where a compact vehicle rental is available for as little as 25TL per day. Check out the local Fethiye **Rent-a-Car** (Atatürk Cad. 106, 0252/612-2281, www.fethiyerentacar.com) for compact cars and jeep rentals, from 22TL per day.

You might also want to consider renting a scooter from **Kaan Rent-a-Car** (Fevzi Çakmak Cad. 31/A, 0252/612-9563, www.

kaanrentacar.com, 30TL/day). These come in handy in town for small jaunts to Çalış Beach or even to Kayaköy, although the gravelly back roads can sometimes be hard to negotiate.

By *Dolmuş* (Communal Taxi)

Fethiye's main *dolmuş* (flat charge 2.50TL) stop is located at the intersection of Atatürk Caddesi and Sedir Sokak. Leaving approximately every 15 minutes during the summer, the minibuses follow Atatürk and Çarşısı Caddesi to the *otogar* (bus station), and east and west of center. The Ölüdeniz Minibus runs hourly shuttles between Fethiye and Kayaköy (4TL); those driving the Fethiye-Faralya/Kabak route depart at least once every two hours.

Kalkan

Reminiscent of the Italian Riviera, minus the attitude, Kalkan has gone through more transformation than any other resort along the littoral. Its classical Greek Ottoman charm was all the rage with glitzy Turks looking for a remote hideaway in the 1960s. Word got around the Med, and by the mid-1980s, wealthy Europeans were arriving in hordes to this quiet hideaway. The construction of a tiny yacht marina followed, and unfortunately, so did development. But thanks to lack of space in Kalkan proper, these sprawling holiday complexes were—and still are—being built on the outskirts. Today, German and British expats, particularly retirees, claim the majority of the high season's population, which swells more than twice its winter numbers to 8500. British travelers rule in summer; in fact, English may be the only language heard for hours on end. But locals, who earn their keep mainly from tourism, don't seem to mind. Independent travelers do, however, after learning that rooms are hard to come by since most hotels are booked months in advance. This continuously increasing demand has pushed prices sky-high, and ensures that most entrées reflect the British palate.

The seaside village sprawls steeply downward from the main road on terraces that culminate in a diminutive, postcard-worthy harbor. Along the streets are the traditional Kalkan houses: two-storied, whitewashed stone townhouses that boast contrasting woodwork in the way of shuttered windows and timber balconies. During the high season, the narrow lanes are abuzz with vendors touting custom silver trinkets and the colorful *kilims* (Turkish carpets) of the region.

Kalkan became important as a trading port in the mid-19th century, accommodating a maritime trade surpassing that of even Fethiye or Antalya. Then known as Kalamaki, the town was both Greek and Turkish and so thrived from the trade of regionally-produced charcoal, silk, olive oil, cotton, and wine, as well as lumber culled from the cedar and pine forests, that a customs house was built at the turn of the 20th century. And, as the population exchange of 1923 rolled around, Kalkan's Greek population was repatriated to its ancestral origin on the nearby Greek island of Meis (Castellorizo).

While Kalkan's mixed Bohemian-upmarket

feel offers loads of romanticism, its proximity to a host of historical sites and stunning shore and offshore beauty also makes it a convenient base from which to discover Turkey's Western Mediterranean coast. For more information on hotels and activities, visit Kalkans's exhaustive website at www.kalkan.org.tr.

EXCURSIONS
Xanthos Valley

The jagged coastline, offshore islands, and underwater caves around Kalkan provide outdoor thrill-seekers ample opportunity for myriad land and sea excursions. Discovering the Xanthos Valley and its ancient Lycian cities, as well as the island of Kekova and its sunken city are worthy outings. The only single-day excursions offered in Kalkan are through **Club Lycia Travel & Tours** (Mustafa Kocakaya Cad. 23, Kalkan, 0242/844-3794); Lycian sites and Kekova tours are available at 18TL and 25TL, respectively.

Kalkan's close proximity to the Xanthos Valley enables day tourists quick and easy access to its ancient Lycian sites, which include Xanthos, Patara, and Letoön. Ideally, the tour is best performed by rental car, with each site situated close the main road (D-400). But there are also *dolmuş* (communal taxi) and bus services that navigate this popular route in season.

Free maps of ancient Lycian sites are widely available throughout Kalkan and its surrounding resort towns. Outside the site, a concession stand sells water, as well as books covering the ancient kingdom, of which George E. Bean's *Lycian Turkey: An Archaeological Guide* is by far the most comprehensive. Before departure, however, log onto to the Lycian Turkey website at www.lycianturkey.com for information about the Lycians.

(Xanthos

The nearest ancient Lycian settlement to Kalkan is Xanthos (Kinik Beldesi, 0242/845-4799, 9 A.M.–7:30 P.M. daily, 3TL).

© JESSICA TAMTÜRK

Of the two 5th-century B.C. funeral monuments gracing the theater in Xanthos, the Harpies' Tomb (right) is by far the most famous.

As Lycia's oldest city (8th century B.C.) and its capital, Xanthos played a major role as a center of culture and commerce for the Lycians, as well as the Persians, Macedonians, Greeks, and Romans who later governed it and its sister cities in the Lycian League. The most striking events attesting to the fierce independence of the Lycians are two suicide missions undertaken by the men after killing their wives, children, and slaves, and destroying their own acropolis in 540 B.C. and in 42 B.C. to escape submission to the Persians and Brutus's Roman troops, respectively. Only the 80 families who were out of town during the onslaught survived when the Persians marched in. The site, along with 17 others throughout the valley, was discovered in 1838 by Sir Charles Fellows. Fellows dismantled the city and carted its most stunning monuments to the British Museum in London a few years later.

Two of the site's most impressive monuments actually lie on the road to Xanthos from the village of Kinik. The **Xanthos Gate,** which was built during the Hellenistic era, is on the right, while to the left rises an arch dedicated to the Roman emperor Vespasian—a gift from the locals, largely in thanks for his philanthropic interests in Xanthos. Further to the right are the sporadic remains of the magnificent **Nereids Monument;** the prized pieces are now on display in the 7th hall of the British Museum. Heading left towards the town's **original Acropolis** you'll see the 2nd-century A.D. ruins of a **Roman theater.** Next to it are Xanthos's most memorable monuments: the 5th-century B.C. **Harpies' Tomb** (named after the sirens who were thought to carry off the souls of the dead which were carved on the original marble frieze that stood atop the column tomb); the **Lycian Tomb;** and, the distinctively unique **Roman Pillar Tomb.** Farther back, the tall Obelisk, with its Greek and lengthy Lycian inscription (250 lines), was critical in deciphering the enigmatic Lycian tongue. Across the road is the **newer Acropolis,** home to a **Byzantine Basilica,** whose only remains are its original magnificent mosaic flooring. Nearby, an untended path follows an ancient wall to

the **Necropolis.** Take the time to visit this often-overlooked site, where through a scattering of **sarcophagi,** you'll find three intricately-carved tombs: the Belly Dancer Sarcophagus, the Lion's Tomb, and a 2,400-year-old tower tomb.

◖ Patara

Patara (Kinik Beldesi, 0242/843-5018, 9 A.M.–7:30 P.M. daily, 10TL) was Lycia's main port city. That is, until its location at the mouth of the Xanthos River silted up and its marshes became a breeding ground for malaria-carrying mosquitoes. Its stunning 12-kilometer-long Patara Beach, one of the world's top beaches, lies just a 10-minute stroll away from Patara's major ruins. Today, Patara is a national park noted for its rich bird-life.

Much of Patara remains undiscovered, buried in the shifting sand brought along by the fierce winds that batter the ancient city. According to legend, Patara was founded by Patarus, son of Apollo, some time in the mid-1st millenium B.C. It was noted throughout antiquity for its temple and oracle of Apollo, which was second only to that of Delphi. Patara's high priestess interpreted omens only during the six summer months, since Appolo is thought to have spent that period here and the remainder at Delphi.

Patara's present claim to fame, however, is as the birthplace of St. Nicholas, bishop of Myra—a.k.a. Santa Claus. St. Paul stopped here during his second missionary journey (A.D. 49–51). He helped to propel Patara as an important Christian center. But by A.D. 600, continuous pirate attacks, the silting up of its harbor, and malaria virtually wiped out its population.

Through ongoing excavations of layers of sand, parts of the ancient city beyond Patara's imposing main gate—the triple-arched **Triumphal Gate of Modestus** (1st century A.D.)—are being discovered. One of these discoveries is the Lycian League's bouleuterions (senate), whose rows of seats form a semi-circle much like the arrangement found in the American Congress. Another recent find is believed to be the world's oldest **lighthouse.**

Patara Beach is located at a the end of the road, about one kilometer south of the ruins. The village of Gelemiş—a haven of family-run pensions, ideal for low budget travelers—is 3.5 kilometers south of the highway. A *dolmuş* (communal taxi, 1.50TL) service departs frequently for the beach from Gelemiş's main square.

Letoön

Just 10 kilometers south of Xanthos, the ancient city of Letoön (9 A.M.–7:30 P.M. daily, 5TL) is a UNESCO Heritage Site. It's situated in a fertile plain by a quiet farming village, whose ravenous flocks of sheep are often grazing onsite. Rising from waterlogged terrain, the ruins are a refreshing escape during the hot summer months.

Xanthos and Letoön are considered a double-site, since the two were closely linked, with the former governing the latter. Together they are one of Turkey's' most remarkable archaeological sites. Letoön was Lycia's center for the sacred cult, the realm's primary sanctuary. It was founded to honor the three main Lycian deities: Leto, and the twin children Apollo and Artemis, which she bore during an insipid love affair with Zeus. The **temples** (4th–5th centuries B.C.) honoring each deity stand in the center of the site. A frog-filled **nymphaeum,** used for baptismal services, and a recently discovered mosaic floor delineate a 6th-century **Byzantine Basilica.**

NIGHTLIFE

Kalkan twinkles come nighttime with lights around its harbor and up its web of streets, where atop Greek houses reside atmospheric rooftop cafés and bars wooing both affluent travelers and locals. Below them you'll find the odd Arabic-themed clubs with belly dancers, gypsy bands, and folkloric music, as well as a narghile café and even sports bars—like **NoName Bar,** where live soccer matches always draw a crowd. The excitement extends to the breezy harborfront, where roaming vendors vie for space with souvenir shops, modern pubs, and upscale restaurants.

Among Kalkan's bars along the marina, a trio deserve special notice. To the west, **Sandal Bar** (0242/844-2453) offers a romantic location with plenty of seating surrounding a small dance floor. **Yacht Point** (0242/844-2084), fronting the mosque, offers the same fare. Further east along the marina, **Kleo Bar** (0242/844-3330) is much smaller, but no less atmospheric with seating that extends almost to the beach and nightly live music shows. But if it's an all out party you're in the mood for, then head to **Ice Blue Bar,** located smack in the center of Old Town.

BEACHES

Kalkan's central beach is more of a beach club, which, interestingly enough, is known as the **Yacht Club.** Located on the other side of the marina's breakwater, the "Club" provides a variety of stands that cater to sunbathers, which include umbrellas and lounge chairs (both for less than 10TL) and affordable refreshments. The onsite water sports outfitter, **Blue Marlin** (0242/844-2783, www.bmwatersports-kalkan. com, Apr.–Oct.), provides a slew of extreme sports alternatives and relaxing water activities (fishing tours), as well as boat rental. A artificially-made shale beach, just east of the marina, provides an alternative from the Club's water-lapped deck.

Definitely more enjoyable than Yacht Club is **Kaputaş Beach,** which is nothing more than a thimble-size sandy cove and beach backed by a massive gorge. About a 500-meter swim to the left of the strip is **Mavi Mağara** (Blue Cave), which is named for the color of its luminescent interior. Bear in mind that no lifeguards patrol this beach, so proceed carefully among the jagged rock face. Located about seven kilometers east of Kalkan (15min), Kaputaş Beach can be reached by *dolmuş* (communal taxi, 2.5TL). It drops off passengers by the highway railing, which leads to the steep stairway that connects to the beach.

The other sandy strip that doubles as a poster child for Turkey's Tourism Board is **Patara Beach.** At 50 meters wide and 12 kilometers long, this sandy strip is by far the country's

Midway between Kaş and Kalkan, Kaputaş Beach is where steep, pine-covered cliffs dramatically join the Med.

longest and arguably its most beautiful. The only drawback is that it can get scorching hot in the summer. The absence of trees translates into little or no shade. But you'll find beach umbrellas (5TL) and a concession stand offering the necessary refreshments. Also note that Patara Beach is a nesting ground for sea turtles; it closes at dusk when the reptiles begin their approach. Reaching the beach by *dolmuş* (communal taxi) has its rewards in the form of free entrance; if driving, parking near the ruins means having to pay the 3TL entrance fee to get to the beach.

Just 1.5 kilometers from Kalkan, Kalamar Bay is privy to the romantic **Kalamar Beach Club** (0242/844-3061). Sprawling over a series of roomy, well-outfitted cement decks just above the Med's clear sparkling waters, the Club boasts a great restaurant/bar and concession stand. The prices here are the steepest in Kalkan, but don't worry, a cab fare to the Club will be reimbursed and the return will be assured through the Club's complimentary hotel drop-off service. Lounge chair and umbrella

rental costs about 10TL a day. Aside from the immaculate shower rooms onsite, other facilities include the **Kalkan Dive Center,** and its sister company **Aquasports** (0242/844-2361). Both provide countless opportunities for undersea exploration (1–3 boat dives €45–120) and water sports (rentals of water skis start at 50TL/10min).

ACCOMMODATIONS

Kalkan offers a wide array of inexpensive, romantic B&Bs and self-catering villas up on its heights or just outside of town. Those included here are far enough away from the marina's decibel-pounding cafés and bars to ensure a restful stay. And with less than 15 units to let, most still offer facilities, including a pool and, at the very least, an onsite café for a fraction of the price of hotels found elsewhere along the coast. If you prefer the grand all-inclusive resort hotels, look in Kalamar Bay, accessible through a convenient water taxi service.

Keep in mind that you'll be competing for accommodations with **Tapestry Holidays**

(0208/995-7787,www.tapestryholidays.com), which books an entire range of local hotels months in advance. So you might consider joining one of their tours, which requires a minimum seven-day package that includes accommodations and flights from London's Gatwick Airport (535–1500TL). The majority of hotels are open April–end of October.

Under €100

Centrally located with stunning views overlooking Kalkan's diminutive gulf, **Ⓒ Rhapsody Hotel** (Nilufer Sok. 48, 0242/844-2575, 36–70TL) is the location to beat price-wise. The sparkling blue waters of the pool contrast with the sprays of pink bougainvillea cloaking the whitewashed walls of this large property. Among the 30 modish units, the stellar Terrace Suite—a bargain at 70TL—boasts its own spacious terrace with a whirlpool tub. Rhapsody's overall decor is an elegant mix of modern quirkiness, from its glassed-in, sparkling white reception area to the padded red velvet wall that backs a plush, crimson sitting area. The overflowing breakfast and dinner buffets, as well as an onsite Turkish hammam, top off a long list of this hotel's delectable surprises.

Hotel Fidanka Houses (Kisla Mevkii, 0242/844-1245, €60–100) distinguishes itself with accommodations that belie their affordability. So what if it sits in a newly developed area east of town that is arguably Kalkan's least alluring? The hotel makes up for this disadvantage in spades, with quirky accommodations and loads of valuable Anatolian antiques throughout. Of the 13 charming units, wrapped around an infinity pool overlooking the resplendent Med, there are 11 spacious suites, each boasting classic furnishings, seaside terraces, seating areas, and baths. Alternatively, opt for one of three rustic Timber Houses or the posh private villa (₺170), which sleeps up to four. A platform beach lies just 150 meters down the hill from the property's enchanting garden.

At the very top of one of Kalkan's winding lanes is **Türk Evi** (Yalıboyu Mahallesi, 0242/844-3129, www.kalkanturkevi.com, €30–40). The Turco-Norwegian owners have imbued this family-friendly B&B with loads of the charm and warmth typical of Turkish hospitality. Share truly memorable complimentary breakfasts around their farm-style kitchen or mingle with other guests over a barbecue dinner on an outdoor patio trailing with vines. Türk Evi features nine simple, but pleasantly decorated, non-air-conditioned rooms.

The **Allegra Hotel** (Zeytinkayasi Mevki, 0242/844-2436, €55–85) is about one kilometer from Kalkan proper. This sunny, yet boldly modern, boutique hotel, run by a charming Turco-French couple, features spectacular sea views from each of its nine rooms' balconies. No beach here, however, but an exclusive beach club lies at a five-minutes' steep walk down the hill. Complimentary breakfasts are served around the pool, while dinners of Turkish and French specialties are provided on demand only. And at these prices, opting for a larger rooftop retreat (€85) won't break the bank.

Over €100

Lauded by the international press for its irresistible charm, the cliff-topping **Ⓒ Villa Mahal** (PK 4, Kalkan, 0242/844-3268, €160–340) offers breathtaking views of a slanted hill, cloaked with a sweeping olive grove, that culminates in the deep indigo waters of Kalkan's bay. Its distinctly brilliant whitewashed facade, with its blue accents, evokes the true Med atmosphere of the region. The Mahal provides the ultimate romantic escape in understated luxury. Choose from 13 elegant units, each varying in size, from the Moonlight to Deluxe rooms, as well as secluded duplexes (one with a private pool). All units boast private terraces with sea views that defy superlatives. Descend the 180 steps through the Mahal's large gardens of morning glories to the rocky beach—a platform with lounge chairs—after feasting on a delectable breakfast at the Rooftop Restaurant. Then, just loll the day away or nosh seaside at the Beach Restaurant. A frequent shuttle service provides transportation to Kalkan's central marina from the hotel's platform.

Stunningly exclusive to say the least, the **Ⓒ Patara Prince** (0242/844-3920, www.

clubpatara.com, rooms €180–320, villas €390–1650), along with its sister property, Club Patara, offer 250 villas and a 60-room hotel gracing a steep hillside opposite Kalkan's marina. The dream of renowned Turkish architect/designer Turhan Kaso, the property's slightly-rounded natural stone buildings combined with lush greenery entirely blend into the environment—a clever site plan that sets this magical hotel apart from the massive resorts along the littoral. The traditional hotel complex boasts chic suites, some featuring whirlpool tubs or fireplaces. The Mediterranean Room (from €210) is a treat with 180-degree sea views, wraparound terrace, and a marble bath with inset ceiling. There are three swimming pools and a myriad of sunning spots along cascading terraces. An array of water sports activities are organized at the onsite beach platform. Four fine-dining restaurants (one open year-round), four bars and one nightclub, a full-service spa, and a free shuttle service to Kalkan top the Patara Prince's list of amenities.

FOOD

Kalkan boasts more upmarket restaurants—68 at last count—and bars per capita than any other resort on Turkey's Med coast. And local restaurateurs have been quick to gauge meal prices according to what their predominantly European guests can afford. This means that you'll also be rolling out a lot more dough to nosh in the village than almost anywhere else along the coast. But quality doesn't have to mean nouvelle cuisine dished out in funky plates. Head to a quaint Turkish-style *lokanta* (diner) for a simple, delectable meal that won't ruin your holiday budget. Good ones to try are **Bezirgan's Kitchen** (0242/844-2106, at the town's entrance) and **Deli Deli Tomato** (0542/337-7790, down the street from Bezirgan, next to the PTT), for traditionally Turkish fare.

For an innovative outing, aim your fork for the **trout restaurants** of **İslamlar,** eight kilometers from Kalkan. In this tiny village nestled high on a mountainside with splendid views of vineyards and the turquoise waters of the

Med in the distance, the first of these terraced diners is **Mahmut'un Yeri** (Mahmut's Place, Islamlar Köyü, 0242/838-6344, set menu 14TL). Owner Mahmut Arga is rumored to have started the trend that's placed İsmalar on the map for delectable locally-grown produce and fish. Nosh on the region's super peppery arugula, pan-fried halloumi cheese, and soft eggplant salad over a glass of the local vintage (priced at 50 percent less than in town) prior to an entrée of perfectly-grilled trout.

Also, most of the mid-size to larger B&Bs in this area offer sumptuous local/Mediterranean cuisine at their restaurants, which are open to the public. But, since chefs only stock by the day for the day's head count, you'll need to make a reservation at least a day in advance. And finally, keep in mind, that most restaurants close their doors end of October–early April.

Fish

◖ **Korsan Fish Terrace** (at the Marina, 0242/844-3076, www.korsankalkan.com, 9:30 A.M.–midnight daily, 25TL) atop the hotel Patara Stone House is Kalkan's most celebrated fine-dining establishment for fish. Since opening his original restaurant (Meze) in 1979, owner Uluc Bilgutay has added two other locations to please both fish fans and consummate carnivores: **Korsan Meze** (0242/844-3622) serves tantalizingly-modern versions of its namesake dishes by the tray-full; and, **Korsan Kebab** (located behind Meze, 0242/844-2116, open year-round), a meat-only diner featuring a more casual style. All have stunning views and exquisite food, with prices to match. Each location has its specialty: the Terrace dishes out a meticulously sauteed crayfish in garlic butter, while the Meze on the seafront is known for its contemporary East-meets-West fares and its free appetizers of freshly-baked garlic bread, dried apricots, and a spicy salsa relish. The minted lamb chunks inside boule bread is Meze's other specialty.

Turkish Fusion

◖ **Aubergine Restaurant** (at the Marina, 0242/844-3332, www.kalkanaubergine.com,

9:30 A.M.–1 A.M., open year-round, 30TL) is fine-dining par excellence. Chef-owner Mehmet Bilgiç adapted more than a decade of experience in some of Europe's finest kitchens to the cuisine minted at Istanbul's Ottoman palaces. *Müthiş* ("outstanding" in Turkish) are the resulting dishes, which vary from a list of slowly-roasted game—wild boar and ostrich—to beef cuts grilled to perfection. Grilled fresh concoctions, like the Mediterranean *lagos şiş* (skewered chunks grouper), are time and again my favorites. Bilgiç recently launched **Daphne Terrace & Cocktail Bar** (0242/844-3547), a few steps away from Aubergine, behind the mosque. From high above its rooftop terrace, this new location offers a racier menu of East-meets-West cuisine, heavy with Mediterranean influences. The chic bar, on the first floor, comes in handy for after-dinner drinks, or for a casual dining menu at any time, 6 P.M.–2:30 A.M.

Another great choice is ❤ **Ilyada** (entrance behind Iskele Sok., near the mosque, 0242/844-3157, www.ilyadarestaurant.com, 9 A.M.–midnight daily, 18TL), one of Kalkan's newer restaurants that's gaining popularity for its inexpensive daily set menu. You'll have to look hard to find a great meze platter, followed by a perfectly-grilled sea bass or sea-bream, salad, and desert with Turkish coffee at the bargain of 25TL. The friendly staff—with their hard-to-miss white attire—are master performers when it comes to presenting *testi*

kebabi (flaming terra cotta pots filled with lamb chunks and veggies). Ilyada's bar is also proving to be a watering hole of choice among well-heeled Brits.

INFORMATION AND SERVICES

Unfortunately, Kalkan is not privy to a tourist office. Instead, the municipality runs a website (www.kalkan.org.tr) that features exhaustive information pertaining to the village. The PTT, banks, and ATMs are located on Süleyman Yilmaz Caddesi.

GETTING THERE AND AROUND

Like Fethiye and Dalyan, Kalkan is served by the **Dalaman Airport** (ATM Dalaman Havalimanı, 0252/792-5555, www.atmairport. aero). The airport is situated 155 kilometers southwest of Kalkan center and not many options are available for transfer into Kalkan. A cab ride, provided by the **Dalaman Taxi Coop,** costs 190TL. A less costly option is to ride the **Havaş Shuttles** (toll free 444-0487, www. havas.com) to Fethiye, and from there take a minibus (1.5hr, 83km, 10TL). This alternative should cost no more than 35TL.

If traveling regionally, *dolmuş* (communal taxi) service runs about every 30 minutes from Kaş (4TL); from Antalya (3.5hr, 20TL) the road is long and curvy, but the picture-perfect landscape is well worth the extra commuting time.

Kaş

Backed by lofty pine-clad mountains, Kaş sits amid a small bay within arm's reach of the small Greek island of Meis (Kaştellorizo). Like Kalkan to the north, Kaş was a small fishing enclave with whitewashed stone houses lining the cobblestone lanes that jut from a small harbor. But unlike its neighbor, the latter maintained most of its original charm and relaxed atmosphere, thanks partly to high domestic tourism and the absence of major European tour package operators. Rare are the mammoth holiday resorts here. In their stead are charming B&Bs and excellent restaurants, praised among the Turks for their simplicity of services and unpretentiousness. By day, the action revolves around the marina, where fishers tout their catch, and around the square's shaded *çaybahçes* (tea gardens), where tea and political conversations abound. Come nightfall, Kaş's cobblestone lanes are thronged with upper-class Turks and foreign tourists all vying for prime space at the terrace tables of lively restaurants and bars.

Amateur archaeologists wade past the partly-sunken Lycian ruins in the Kekova Bay.

Kaş grew placidly among the ruins of the ancient Roman port city of Antiphellos, and during the Ottoman era it was a place of exile for political dissidents. With more than 300 days of sunshine and clear tepid waters, it's not a bad location to serve time. Today, its drawback, some say, is also its savior: Kaş's lack of long sandy beaches makes it less appealing than other resorts along the littoral. But it redeems itself with a coast that's peppered with alcoves. And reminiscent of Ölüdeniz's Mount Babadağ to the north, Kaş has its own mountain—albeit much smaller at 500 meters high—in the form of Yatan Adam (Sleeping Man). Here, the extreme sport of paragliding is taking off. And so are a slew of other outdoor activities, like hiking and scuba diving. It's also an ideal and restful base from which to tour the coast, starting with an excursion to Kekova and its sunken city, the Xanthos Valley with its Lycian ruins, and south towards Antalya.

SIGHTS
Antiphellos Ruins
The sparse remains of Kaş's ancient Roman forerunner, Antiphellos, endure, attesting to the village's lengthy history as a Hellenistic center. The **amphitheater,** 500 meters west of the main square, is the most impressive monument still standing. There's a **monumental tomb** located east of the town square, up the hilly Uzun Çarşı Caddesi. Mounted on a tall base, inscribed with yet-to-be deciphered Lycian text, this handsome sarcophagus bears a Gothic lid and is embossed with lions. While the city was once filled with a variety of burial chambers, the other remaining examples are those carved into the hillside above Yeni Yol Caddesi.

◖ Kekova Bay
Before hitting the high seas, take time to explore the sleepy fishing and farming village **Üçağız** and its vicinity. Üçağız boasts a collection of stunning **Lycian tombs,** which are located at the rear of the village. Easily accessible by boat, the submerged tombs of **Aperlai** and the spectacular acropolis of **Apollonia,** due west of Üçağız, are two well-preserved ancient sites that are worth an hour's side trip.

THE GREEK ISLAND OF KASTELLORIZO

The Turks call it *Maïs,* the Arabs *Mayas,* and the ancient Crusaders *Kastellorizo,* combining the Italian words *castello* (castle) and *rosso* (red). The Greeks simply refer to it as *Megísti,* meaning "largest." But, at almost 12 square kilometers, the isle is ironically the smallest of the Dodecanese Islands. It earned its name for being the largest of a small archipelago of a perfect baker's dozen of islets, all of which are Greek with the exception of Kekova.

No matter which name is used, Kastellorizo is incredibly charming and perhaps the most peaceful isle in the Mediterranean. No roads crisscross this natural and biological haven, just paths large enough to accommodate Kastellorizo's one small shuttle bus and a taxi. The utter quiet and lack of pollution enables flora and fauna to thrive unlike any other place around. Loggerhead turtles, dolphins, and monk seals are frequent marine guests.

Kastellorizo is located just 1,300 meters from the rocky coast of Kaş — one of western Turkey's most beautiful resorts. Kastellorizo is tiny and oh-so charming. Fishing and tourism are the isle's mainstays; almost all of its needs, including drinking water, must be shipped in from the isle of Rhodes, about 110 kilometers east. The town of Megísti sprawls from a tiny harbor; there are a handful of taverns and a castle that harks back to the Crusaders. The wear and tear seen today along the traditionally white and blue-roofed Greek abodes provides a rich patina, one that prompts its first-time visitors to ponder its lengthy history.

Kastellorizo is Greece's easternmost island, and a victim of 80 years of political unrest between two geographically and historically close-knit neighbors. The isle's population topped 13,000 in 1920, at a time when it thrived as a trade port between the Anatolian city of Makri — today's Fethiye — and the Lebanese capital of Beirut. Products like coal, grain, timber, and pine bark arrived from Anatolia, while rice, sugar, coffee, tissues, and yarns arrived via Lebanon from Egypt. Kazzies, the Aussie moniker for the locals, also reaped the benefits of a developing charcoal production, which the Egyptians used for narghile, as well as from sponge fishing. At the turn of the 20th century, Kastellorizo's economy free-fell along with the reigning Ottoman Empire. The population exchange of 1923 that hit mainland Ana-

Frozen in time, the remote village of **Kaleköy**—Antiquity's Simena—is a popular tour destination for day-trippers arriving from Kaş. Its harbor is overshadowed by the **Byzantine Fortress of the Knights of St. John** (admission 5TL). Interestingly enough, the knights built the castle's perimeter walls around a tiny Hellenic **amphitheater,** rather than taking it apart during the construction. No roads cross this village, just dusty lanes lined with decrepit stone houses that lead to rock-hewn **Lycian tombs** and 10-foot-tall **sarcophagi.** Kaleköy's jetty is lined with great fish restaurants, offering grilled fish fare that begs to be enjoyed while relaxing at a terrace table overlooking the crashing waves. Spend an afternoon swimming off a couple of the sandy spots around the village. Or, if that's not enough time to take in this picturesque spot,

stay the night at one of the four basic rooms at the waterfront **Sahil Pansiyon** (Kaleköy 145/A, 0242/874-2263, www.sahilpension.com, from €35).

ENTERTAINMENT AND EVENTS
Festivals
Every year during the last week of June the **Kaş Lycia Festival** (Kaş Municipality, Süleyman Sandikçi Sokak, 0242/836-1020, www.kas.bel.tr in Turkish)is in full swing. It's not only an opportunity for both international and regional folk dancing troupes to display their culture, but also a time for the city of Kaş to shine and present its regional artistry.

Nightlife
Much like Kalkan, Kaş's nightlife begins at 7 P.M. and goes well into the night. The

tolia added insult to injury, when the island's predominantly Greek population was sent packing. And just 20 years later, British troops disembarked on Kastellorizo and systematically evacuated the thousands who had remained to Egypt in an effort to protect them from German air attacks during WWII. The displaced took advantage of an offer from the British government to immigrate to Australia; today, about 50,000 Kazzies call Perth and Sydney home. The island rejoined Greece in 1948.

Kastellorizo's ancient history mirrors that of Asia Minor. The Mycenians were the isle's earliest settlers who, according to archaeological finds excavated onsite, arrived some time in the mid-3rd millennium B.C. The Dorians and Lycians settled here from their home in Asia Minor. A grand Lycian tomb, dating from the 300s B.C., is the island's most famed relic. The Crusaders arrived in the 14th century and deemed the isle so strategically well-placed that they built a castle on the ruins of a 2,500-year-old Dorian fortress.

Kastellorizo has some sites that are worth checking out on a day trip from Kaş: There's a 700-year-old castle of the knights, a few yards away from the harbor's quay; an impressive Lycian temple tomb; and many religious monuments. The churches of St. Constantine and Eleni were built in 1835 with marble quarried from the Great Temple of Apollo on the mainland's antique Lycian prefecture. There's also the monastery of St. George of the Mountain and a petite Archaeological Museum. But locals will tell you that the most beautiful thing to see in Kastellorizo is its blue cave. Known as one of the most beautiful grottos in the Med, it is 75 meters long, by 40 meters wide, and 35 meters high, replete with stalactites and stalagmites. Its name comes from the deep sapphire blue reflected from its depths by the morning sun. It can only be visited by boat, and so are a handful of similar caves where monk seals and loggerhead turtles gather.

Altuğ Tours (Merkez Süleyman Çavuş Camii Necip Bey Cad. 34, Kaş, 0242/836-2158, www.altugtours.com) in Antalya runs a passenger boat that departs for Kastellorizo from Kaş every morning at 9 A.M. It takes about 30 minutes to cross; the fare costs 45TL and the Turkish boat crew takes care of the visa formalities.

---

atmosphere is relaxed, so shorts and t-shirts are acceptable.

The **Hideaway Café & Bar** (Cumhuriyet Cad. 16/A, 0242/836-3369) truly deserves its name because it's removed from the street in the rear garden of a restored Greek house. If you blink, you'll miss it. Nicknamed "The Blues Man," owner Erdem, and his girlfriend Nur, love American music. Be it Blues or Rock, count on sipping Erdem's lime-infused sugarcane special, the caipirinha—Brazil's national alcoholic drink—tucked away in one of the corner lounges. Along with a wide private collection of wine, Hideaway offers succulent dessert options and a Sunday farm-fresh breakfast buffet.

The **Meis Bar & Disco** (Liman Sok. 20, 0536/475-4021) opens into a posh bar that was once, believe it or not, the main seaside entrance to Kaş's forerunner, Antiphellos. Below, a 2,300-year-old Lycian water cistern was discovered by chance when the owner looked into building a disco within its massive walls. Since the Meis is the favorite hangout for the fickle Turkish upper-crust, dress to impress.

Mavi Bar (Mütfü Efendi Sok., 0242/836-1834) is the nightly hangout of choice. Located a step behind the marina, Mavi is the oldest bar in town. For years its nightly summer party extended onto the sidewalk because, starting as early as 9 P.M., there's not even standing room inside. Just follow the crowds and the sounds of rock music, as you head east along the harbor.

At the small, plain yet incredibly-cozy **Hi-Jazz Bar** (Deniz Sok., 0242/836-1315), it's all about jazz. Owner Yilmaz, a 50-something retired New York cabbie who discovered his passion for music in New Orleans, chose to return home to build this relaxing spot, tucked in a back alley. The live music goes on nightly, starting with smooth jazz at 7 P.M.

SHOPPING

Gracing the first floors of many a historic abode in Kaş are tiny shops touting uniquely crafted items. *Kaşlıs* and their immediate neighbors are famed for their artisanship. Custom-made jewelry of semiprecious and precious metals is popular with foreigners, while Turks swoon over hand-woven *kilims* (Turkish carpets) and *tülbent* (decorative edging on natural fabrics) scarves, as well as trinkets—spoons and tiny boxes—hand-carved out of walnut. These is not the mass-produced–sold-as-unique items you've been seeing since your arrival. If a particular item catches your eye along the mercantile street of Uzunçarşı, be prepared to bargain its price down by *at least* 25 percent from the original quote. Also, the weekly farmer's market takes place every Friday just across from the marina.

Mencilis Art Silver (Uzunçarşı Cad. 13, 0242/836-2897, www.mencilis.com) actually designs its own products and ships them out for production. The resulting baubles are sometimes massive, gem-encrusted pieces that are sure to become family heirlooms. Incidentally, the top floors above this cavernous jewelry shop have recently been renovated as the neat Mencilis Apart Hotel—worth a look if you're strapped for lodgings.

Modern ceramics and porcelains are the specialty at **Atölie Anatolia** (Hükümet Cad. 2/1, 0242/836-1954, www.atelieanatolia.com). Personalized one-of-a-kind collections, like the "forget-me-not" tea or coffee service for six, make an ideal souvenir or, better yet, a great gift for the consummate host.

The Old Curiosity Shop (Çukurbağlı Sok. 1, 0541/879-7054) certainly fits the name that it borrowed from an old Charles Dickens novel. This antique shop's cavernous interiors burst with Ottomania: antique lanterns, silver samovars, and even some meticulously-embroidered caftans vie for precious space. International shipping is available.

SPORTS AND RECREATION

Beaches

Just 1.5 kilometers south of the town center—or a pleasant 10-minute stroll—Kaş's solitary beach is the picturesque **Büyük Çakıl Plajı**. This cove is aptly named for its cover of large pebbles. And, unlike its neighbor to the north **Küçük Çakıl Plajı** (Small Pebble Beach), it's large enough to accommodate a couple of rows of lounge chairs and a few restaurants, whose staffs vie to snatch drink orders.

Straight across the bay, you'll find **Liman Ağızı**. This pebble-covered stretch boasts transparent waters and a few outdoor diners.

Boat Trips

Kaş may lack sandy acreage, but its on- and offshore beauty beg to be discovered. Jagged mountain cliffs, pygmy islands, protected bays, and a smidgen of coral cliffs provide the perfect backdrop for outings galore. While there are a dozen ways to explore the region around Kaş, the most popular is a three-hour boat trip (€15) to Kekova and Üçağız, which includes numerous stops to explore ruins and to swim. Book a spot with any of the travel agents along the marina, or contact **Bougainville Travel** (Çukurbağlı Cad. 10, 0242/836-3737, www.bougainville-turkey.com). Owned by a Turco-British trio of adventure travel and outdoor activities specialists, Bougainville touts a kayaking excursion to the sunken city of Kekova Bay (€35), a canyon trip (€50) through the gorges of Saklıkent or Kaputaş, and paragliding (€90) off the 1000-meter-high Asas mountain, among a host of other outdoor thrills. All day-trips include lunch, guide, and transfers to Kaş.

Kekova Adası (Kekova Island) and its surroundings offer beautiful scenery with an unmatched rusticity along its fishing and farming villages. The whole area is littered with massive ruins that have succumbed to the sea. Topping the list of archaeological sites is **Batık Şehir** (Sunken City), which lies buried six meters beneath the crystal clear waters of Kekova Bay, on the northern tip of the island. The most stunning relics are those of city walls and private homes that once comprised the residential area of ancient Simena; these relented to the sea during the massive earthquake in the 2nd century A.D. To preserve the integrity of the site, boats are forbidden from entering the site. Unfortunately, swimmers and snorkelers are also restricted from exploring the stairways, terraces, and amphorae lying beneath the water. The boat trip (from €25 pp, including lunch and guide) departs typically around 10 A.M. from the Kaş marina. The excursion stops along the way at Kekova and **Tersane Adası** (Boatyard Island), followed by lunch on board and an hour-long excursion to the untouched village of Kaleköy. The excursion includes a climb to Kaleköy's Byzantine fortress and stops to swim or snorkel and to explore area caves.

To get a better glimpse of the bay of Kekova and its spectral undersea landscape, board one of the glass-bottom boats (€30) that depart at 10 A.M. daily from Üçağız and return by 5 P.M. If touring solo sounds more appealing, then try to arrive in Üçağız no later than 9 A.M., while space is still available. Alternatively, you can negotiate a chartered trip (from €200) on a private boat. Be prepared to haggle with the local boat owners, who are charging increasingly higher—sometimes exorbitant—rates for a day out at sea.

Jeep Safari

With the Biga Peninsula along the northern Aegean and much of south eastern Turkey, the region between Kalkan and Antalya is filled with the remains of more than 25 Lycian sites, some of which remain buried along with their legacy. Teimiussa (Üçagiz) and Simena (Kaleköy) are the most popular in this region. But other sites, like Apollonia, Myra, Andiake, the ancient entertainment center of Arykanda, and the water-lapped ruins of Aperlai, contain enough ruins to warrant a visit. The hinterland ruins of ancient Lycia can be discovered on a Jeep safari (€30), offered by **Bougainville**

Travel (Çukurbağlı Cad. 10, 0242/836-3737, www.bougainville-turkey.com). Alternatively, consider proceeding solo by car, armed with a good map, plenty of water, and good walking shoes. Just let the brown road signs that indicate historical sites be your guide.

ACCOMMODATIONS

Kaş teems with lodging options in its center. Also, at a five-kilometer-distance due west, the tranquil Çukurbağ Peninsula, a four-kilometer-long spit of rock with steep cliffs that descend to pristine waters, offers a handful of boutique hotels. The sea is all around and it has a stunningly deep, rich color. The Greek island of Castellorizo is a mere 1.5 miles from the Turkish coast at this point. Rather remote, unless you have your own wheels, Çukurbağ's cape is reached by turning right from Kas's central roundabout, right before the marina.

Under €100

Hotel Per Se (Koza Sok. 23, Kaş center, 0242/836-4256, www.hotelperse.com, from €75) boasts crisp, modern Italian design inside and out, with spectacular 180-degree views of the azure Med and the tiny Greek isle of Meis. The spare, yet elegant neo-chic, design extends to nine roomy units, each boasting its own balcony. Every hint of color has been expertly placed to break the hotel's palette of white-on-white furniture and walls, enhanced only by strong wooden accents. The pool is tiny and only takes a handful of waders at a time, but, just steps down a long sweeping staircase, the shale beach of Küçükçakil accommodates more waders. Owner Cengiz Unsal has carried on the Italian theme all the way to the table, with succulent pasta dishes, an excellent tiramisu, and the best espresso in town. At a three-minute's walk from Kaş's harbor, the Per Se is close enough to town and far enough to provide a supremely serene environment.

A few doors closer to the marina, the **Begonvil Hotel** (Koza Sok. 13, Kaş center, 0242/836-3079, www.hotelbegonvil.com, €35–45) takes its name from the deep magenta

THE TURQUOISE COAST

bougainvillea that creeps up its facade. Owners Serap and Onur Cöl lived in Switzerland for many years, and, since 1996, have imbued this family-run hotel with the quality of service the European country is known for with their own brand of Turkish hospitality. The 15 units are standard, but each feature their own air-conditioning unit and balconies, either overlooking the sea or the unspoiled mountain scenery. The hosts meet with each guest in the breezy, rustic breakfast nook each morning to ensure their stay is nothing short of perfect. The lobby features a small library; a wireless Internet network is provided free of charge.

Over €100

Diva Residence Hotel (Ibrahim Cingay Sok. 4, Çukurbağ Peninsula, 0242/836-4255, www. divakas.com, €85–135) is a spacious residence featuring 11 sea view units. Choose from 42-square-meter or 82-square-meter apartments, each with a living room and private balcony; the larger suites can sleep up to six. The property is lined with splendid gardens and a large pool, overlooking the island of Meis. Big fireplaces add to the charm of this sparsely-decorated, modern boutique hotel. Below, a wooden deck built on rock doubles as Diva's private beach, which is reached down a long flight of stairs. While there's a café by the sea, heading back up to the tented Deck Bar with its overstuffed floor cushions is hard to resist. The cuisine is progressive but also caters to vegetarians, with a menu of fresh home-cooked meals offered buffet-style or à la carte.

◀ Hadrian Hotel (Doğan Kaşaroğlu Sok. 10, Çukurbağ Peninsula, 0242/836-2856, www.hotel-hadrian.de, half-board €115–130) is a bright B&B that hugs the end of the rocky Çukurbağ Peninsula. The sunny courtyard, which centers around a large, sophisticated saltwater pool, and the pavilion below, are covered in magenta bougainvillea and open to superb views of the entire bay. A flight of stairs leads to the hotel's rocky beach platform below, which is located above waters so deep they're ideal for diving and snorkeling. The Hadrian offers 14 roomy units, among which

upscale resort town of Kaş
© JESSICA TAMTÜRK

10 rooms are doubles and 4 are two- or three-room suites (€160–300). At capacity, the hotel accommodates 40, but its open decor was expertly designed to make guests feel anything but cramped in a small property.

Club Çapa Hotel (Cukurbağ Peninsula 8, 0242/836-3190, www.clubcapa.com, $150) is nothing short of mystical. Crowning a cliff that overlooks Kaş, the Çapa unrolls over a series of terraces, where you might find the property's saltwater pools, a jasmine garden, or a tented café, all the way down to a sea deck filled with inviting cushions. Each of the 21 units are a bit small, but each expands through French doors unto a balcony overlooking the stunning bay of Kaş, keeping the rooms breezy, light, and airy. The hotel provides a shuttle service to Kaş, day trips around the region, and a host of outdoor activities.

FOOD

Much like Kalkan, Kaş is also overrun with fine-dining establishments. It's a fierce environment, with a quick turnaround rate; what's "in" this season might not be around the next. For this reason, I try to lean to the established B&Bs and boutique hotels, whose celebrity-chef in-the-making truly exert themselves to provide the freshest and most appealing fare. And, in so doing, try to get the attention of newspaper pundits. While Kaş does offer fine-dining establishments, scams are not unheard of, even at the better restaurants. Closely review the bill before paying to ensure that there isn't an extra charge.

Turkish

(Mercan Restaurant (Kaş marina, 0242/836-1209, http://mercankas.net, 20TL) has a lot to do with propelling Kaş to one of *the* culinary destinations on the western coast. For more than five decades—it's actually the oldest restaurant in town—Mercan has served a simple, winning combination of meat and fish specialties. Among the stand outs are the Turkish-style moussaka and the succulent swordfish shish kebab.

Sultan Garden Restaurant's (by the marina, 0242/836-3762, www.sultangarden.co.uk, 9 A.M.–1 A.M., 22TL) quality, price, and location are truly hard to beat. The lengthy Turkish menu features a variety of beef cuts grilled to order. Try the generous T-bone; it's excellent. The Sultan's Delight—succulent lamb morsels stewed in tomatoes served over eggplant purée—repeatedly thrills this die-hard Turkish cuisine lover. The seafront Sultan has houses in one of Kaş's oldest harbor buildings and has two Lycian tombs and a Lycian water cistern gracing the landscape of its surrounding gardens.

The range of strictly Turkish fare at **Sampati Restaurant** (Uzuncarşi Cad., Gürsoy Sok. 11, 0242/836-2418, www.sempatirestaurant.com, 18TL) vies for "best-of" status among Kaş's gourmet establishments. What owner Sevim Özenen excels at here, though, is hospitality. Sampati exudes homey charm from its shelves of planted pots lining its interior wall to the miniature boutique where locally-made jewelry is for sale. The welcoming streetside terrace is an ideal setting to enjoy favorite dishes,

like the tandoori-baked lamb, cooked so slow it requires a six-hour advance order. Or, nosh on equally sumptuous appetizers like *çerkez tavuğu* (cold meze of chicken and walnuts in a garlic sauce).

International

(Chez Evy (Terzi Sok. 2, 0242/836-1253, 30TL) offers the only French haute cuisine fit for a gourmet on Turkey's entire western seaboard. Located in one of Kaş's quieter side alleys, Evy decorates and cooks herself; she even visits her customers tableside when the kitchen is quiet. The prices are higher than anywhere else in town, but the portions are twice as big. The hidden garden is a lovely setting for one of Evy's specialties, for instance, the house fillet steak with eight different char-grilled vegetables; though I prefer the Béarnaise sauce version. There's also a three-course meal for two (€80), which includes wine. If the temperature is just too hot to bare, escape to the air-conditioned, collectibles-filled inner room. Reserve a table at least a day in advance during the summer. You'd be remiss not to dine here in the off-season, just call to see if they can accommodate.

INFORMATION AND SERVICES

The **Tourist Information Office** (Cumhuriyet Meydani 5, 0242/836-1238) is located on the main square. Banks and ATMs line the main drag of Atatürk Caddesi.

The *otogar* (bus station, 0242/836-1020) is located at the intersection of Uğur Mumcu and Süleyman Çavus Caddesi, less than two kilometers from the harbor. The best way to transfer safely to a hotel or to the town center is to take one of the taxis waiting at the bus station.

GETTING THERE

Kaş is served through the Dalaman Airport, about 190 kilometers due south. There aren't many options available for transfer into Kaş, except a costly cab ride, provided by the **Dalaman Taxi Coop** (210TL). Alternatively, the **Havaş Shuttles** (toll free 444-0487, www.

havas.com, 25TL) will get you into to Fethiye, and from there you can take the hourly minibus service (112km, 1.5hr, 14TL) to Kaş. This alternative should cost no more than 40TL. Arriving from Antalya (180km) is feasible but will cost you more by taxi, and the highway makes bus travel (15TL) tedious; count on at least 3.5 hours to arrive in Kaş.

Traveling by long-distance coach through Turkey is highly enjoyable and affordable. Since Kaş and Kalkan are almost synonymous when it comes to distances and destinations, most buses arriving in either serve the other. Of the companies that have routes through

Southwestern Turkey, **Pamukkale** (toll free 444-3535, www.pamukkaleturizm.com.tr) leaves nightly at 10 P.M. from Istanbul (906km, 14hr, 65TL) or at 12:30 and 10 P.M. from Izmir (453km, 8.5hr, 40TL).

Regional **minibuses** drive the Kaş-Fethiye route via Kalkan (1.5hr, 14TL) and travel to Olympos (110km, 2.5hr, 12TL) about every half hour. A connection to Antalya leaves hourly (180km, 3.5hr, 15TL). It takes as long as 4.5 hours, if traveling during rush hour. To avoid bumper-to-bumper traffic, travel early in the morning. Note that minibuses also leave frequently for the beach of Patara.

Kale (Demre)

Not a major geographical destination per se but remote enough from major cities to warrant its own sub-section, Kale has become somewhat of a cult-hit for those still believing in Santa Claus. It's also an important stopover on the increasingly-popular biblical tour of Turkey.

Arriving from Kaş, the main road descends through the rocky slopes of Mt. Alaca to the fertile alluvial Kale plain, which surrounds the city of Kale. For now Kale still earns its keep from agriculture, as the propensity of fields and green houses that surround its perimeter suggest. But soon, thanks to the preservation and investment schemes of its mayor, it may be on its way to becoming a tourist destination. And that's due in part to a 4th-century bishop by the name of Nicholas of Myra.

Before it became Kale—for the record, Demre is its other name—the city was known as the Roman town of Myra and was situated 1.5 kilometers north of the city's current boundaries. Apostle St. Paul stopped on his way to Rome from Caesaria in A.D. 60. Of the many bishops who served in Myra, Saint Nicholas—of Santa Claus fame—became celebrated worldwide for his extreme generosity.

Myra attests to its lengthy Lycian past with a magnificently-preserved set of rock-

hewn Lycian tombs, set high on the steep cliff flanking its ancient amphitheater. The restored Basilica of St. Nicholas is definitely worth the trip: this elevated necropolis, which still bears some of its original cream color, is Kale's major tourist treasure.

Due to effluvial silting, Myra, like much of its neighbors on the western littoral, gradually became landlocked during the Byzantine era; it now sits five kilometers east of the Mediterranean. It's far from the playful coastal resorts, and, outside of the church and Lycian ruins, the busloads of tourists just swing through for a couple of hours. Outside of its rustic charm and the beauty of its rolling fields, there's not much here to entertain a curious traveler.

SIGHTS
Aya Nicola Kilisesi
(Church of St. Nicholas)
The Church of St. Nicholas (Müze Cad., 0242/871-6820, 8:30 A.M.–7:30 P.M. daily, until 5:30 P.M. in winter, 5TL) was built right after the death of Saint Nicholas in the mid-3rd century. The building was badly damaged during the earthquake of 529, and was later reconstructed as a grand basilica by Emperor Justinian, with the addition of two domed

THE LEGENDARY SANTA CLAUS

Sainted just decades after his death in A.D. 343 for his exceptional benevolence, Nicholas the Bishop of Myra was born with a silver spoon in his mouth. He was a Hellene from the Lycian city of Patara – Demre in modern-day Turkey – when Asia Minor was under Roman rule. Nick was so devout as a young boy that he was said to have rigorously observed the Coptic fasts every Wednesday and Friday. After his parents succumbed to one of Lycia's famed epidemics, he went on to live with his uncle. The elder tonsured – shaved the top of his head in preparation for entering a religious order – young Nicholas was to become a reader, subsequently a priest, and finally a bishop.

Legend has it that Nick used a large inheritance to bestow secret gifts on villagers by dropping coins in the shoes of those who left them out for him. Another legend says he saved three poor village girls from prostitution by dropping satchels of gold to be used as dowries. Another account even claims he resuscitated three boys whose bodies had been left to "cure" in brine by a malevolent butcher wishing to sell them off as pickled pig meat on a nearby island during a famine. However, no text attests to his being rotund nor bearded, but his crimson outfit is indicative of his ordained position in the church.

Nick's ornate tomb, gaping hole and all, can still be seen inside his namesake cathedral in Demre. His remains were taken furtively by sailors from the Italian town of Bari in 1087, despite critical outrage from local Orthodox monks. But no one listened. Myra was then ruled by Muslim Selçuks. Saint Nick's bones arrived in Italy on May 9, 1087. Some called the sailors thieves and pirates, while others claimed the act was justified by a vision of Saint Nicholas personally pleading to have his remains carried away from impending doom and saved for posterity.

Whatever the reason, their removal prior to the Muslim domination of Asia Minor resulted in making the legends even bigger. On December 28, 2009, the Turkish government declared that it would make a formal request to its Italian counterpart for the return of Nicholas's remains to Turkey, citing two reasons for their return: that he himself had expressed his wish to be buried in the church he commissioned in the city of his birth; and the fact that they were taken without permission. Whether or not his bones will lie again in their original tomb, Saint Nicholas – the American Santa Claus, the Dutch Sinterklaas, and the Italian San Nicola – continues to be a fixture for children eagerly awaiting their presents during the month of December throughout the world.

chambers. The church was reconstructed twice more, following the rampaging of its inner sanctum at the hands of marauding Arabs in the mid-9th century and again in 1034. Emperor Constantine ordered its restoration in 1043, requesting that a monastery be built alongside the sanctuary. As to the remains of the saint, the Vatican attests that they were taken by Italian merchants to Bari, Italy, where they were enshrined in a cathedral. The basilica was renovated most recently in the mid-19th century under the order of Tsar Nicholas I; this time adding the belfry. Also worthy of note, this church is one of the few that has escaped religious conversion.

Despite the wrath of nature and humans,

some of the original mosaic floor has faired very well. Albeit faded, the wall and dome frescoes are still visible. St. Nicholas's empty tomb is located on the south aisle between two pillars and behind a broken marble screen. The sarcophagus dates from the Greek era, and was obviously reused (Saint Nicholas died penniless!).

Myra Ruins

Just two kilometers due north of Müze Caddesi lie the ruins of Myra (8:30 A.M.–7:30 P.M. daily, until 5 P.M. in winter, 5TL). Of the structures that have withstood the test of time are a mid-1st century A.D. **Hellenic amphitheater** and a well-preserved pseudo-tenement of **Lycian**

© JESSICA TAMTÜRK

A stone block that once graced the theater at Myra shows carvings of ancient actors.

tombs. Intricately carved stage masks litter the theater area. Befitting the status of a Greek temple, the nearby cliffside tombs were carved right out of the rock face, with supporting columns and pediments, in the 4th century B.C. Charles Fellows wrote that when he discovered the ancient city of Myra in 1840 these funeral chambers were "a riot of color, colorfully painted red, yellow, and blue." As a side note, Saint Nicholas may have ordered the demolition of Myra's Acropolis and its once grand Temple of Artemis to prevent reversion to idolatry among the locals.

Çayağzı (Andriake)

Just a four-kilometer *dolmuş*-ride west of town, today's Çayağzı (Stream Mouth) is a mere collection of ruins. It was once Andriake, a natural harbor town annexed to the city of Myra, which stood at the exact location where the Demre Creek flows into the sea. Andriake's most important ruin is an eight-room triangular granary, which was built in the 1st century A.D. during the reign of Roman emperor Hadrian. The site also contains the remains of two Byzantine basilicas, a harbor street, a necropolis, a bath, and aqueducts, all straddling the stream/marsh (stream in the summer; marsh in the winter).

The ruins extend widely on either side of the river, whose mouth forms Çayağzı Plajı (Çayağzı Beach). A handful of boatyards and fish mongers, as well as a decent restaurant, make up this fishing port. The sea's particularly shallow waters are ideal for families with smaller children; the restaurant makes an even better location to experience the onshore minutiae of rural life.

ACCOMMODATIONS AND FOOD

After seeing the ruins and prattling around the beach, there isn't much to keep an avid traveler in Kale. At least that's what I thought until I had the pleasure of staying the night at Süleyman Hacımusaoğlu's luxurious boutique hotel. **Hoyran Wedre** (Hoyran Köyü PK 2, Demre, 0242/875-1125, www.hoyran.com,

€80–150), rated high on my Turkey best-of boutiques list, is located in a rural village that feels as if it's seen little change since the Lycians populated the Kale basin. The smell of thyme pervades ubiquitous olive orchards, which are interspersed by oak trees so large they must be at least five centuries old. Built lovingly of adobe, wood, and travertine so as not to clash with the sanctity of eons past, The Hoyran Cottages boast 15 rooms that are sparsely furnished with cherished antiques and *kilims* (Turkish carpets); some even boast fireplaces. Outside, and just a mere 0.5-kilometer descent away from the property, the cobalt sea stretches out to the horizon.

If the munchies strike while in Demre, there are a couple of choices. Either stave off your hunger until you reach the seafront restaurant in Çayağzı Plajı, or head to the traditional diners along the pedestrian drag in front of the Church of St. Nicholas. The very unassuming **Ipek Restaurant** (100m to the left of Church of St. Nicholas, 0242/871-5150, 12TL) is the locals' choice for meat in all of its incarnations.

GETTING THERE
Demre lies 48 kilometers east of Kaş and 225 kilometers southwest of Antalya. Both minibus and *dolmuş* (communal taxi) service connect Demre to Kaş (45min, 5TL), Fethiye (3hr, 18TL), and Finike (25min, 4TL) several times a day. Alternatively, you can tack on Demre to an outing to Kekova Island. Just head to the town center of Üçagiz, where you'll find frequent connections to Demre throughout the summer.

Antalya

Nudged inside a long gulf (Antalya Körfezi), Antalya sits on an enormous travertine plateau formed over eons by the innumerable springs flowing toward the Med from the Taurus Mountains. The beauty of this once Roman-Ottoman port, with its lengthy history and miles of sun-kissed beaches, is only eclipsed by towering snow-capped Beydağları (Gentleman's Mountains) just beyond its periphery.

The city of Antalya is the center of Antalya province, which stretches all the way northwest to Kalkan and east to Alanya. This strip, known as the Turkish Riviera, boasts more sandy acreage and resort hotels than the coasts of Italy and Spain combined. The surge of wealthy Russians choosing the city as their summer escape, and their compatriot mega-developers who've heeded the call for superior accommodations, have redefined Antalya as one of the sexiest, most luxurious resorts along the Turkish littoral. In fact, the recently-opened, 1.5-billion-dollar Mardan resort has put some of Las Vegas's priciest destinations to shame.

But if you've thought that Antalya is just about the sea, sex, and sun, you're sorely mistaken. Its peripheral mountains burst with geological wonders, from gushing waterfalls and deep gorges, to trickling streams and lush plains. Canyon-seekers, white-water rafters, long distance hikers and bikers, golfers, and divers revel in the region's off- and onshore outdoors potential. There's also a good day's stroll through the well-preserved Kaleiçi quarter, a web of cobblestone alleys that has delineated Antalya's center and harbor since the Roman era. And, while on the subject of history, the award-winning Antalya Archaeological Museum lays claim to the innumerable pre-Classical and Hellenic artifacts found in the region's ancient settlements of Perge and Aspendos. But aside from sports and museums, the number of fine dining— and wining—establishments are enough to make a gourmet burst with excitement.

At a short walk due west of historic Kaleiçi, the decidedly modern enclave of Konyaaltı awaits with a wide shale beach, fringed by a palm tree–lined promenade. There, you'll find an outdoor mall perfect for the entire family to spend the day: parents can dine while the

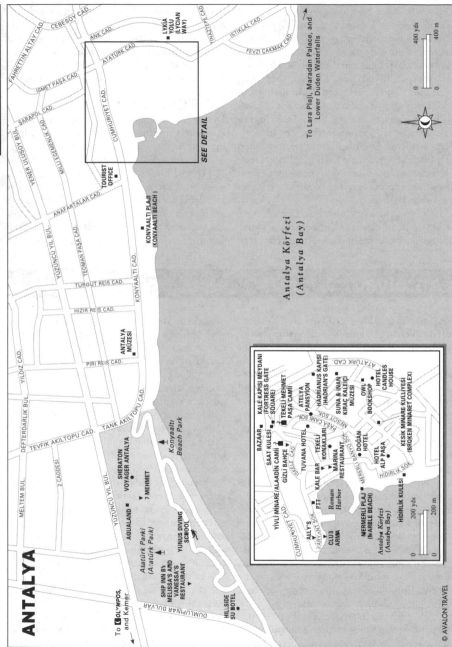

ANTALYA

To **OLYMPOS,**
and Kemer

Antalya Körfezi
(Antalya Bay)

To Lara Plaji, Maradan Palace, and
Lower Duden Waterfalls

400 yds
400 m

SEE DETAIL

LYKIA
YOLU
(LYCIAN
WAY)

CEBESOY CAD.
ANK CAD.
ATATÜRK CAD.
İSTİKLAL CAD.
FEVZİ ÇAKMAK CAD.
YİNAZTEPE CAD.
FAHRETTİN ALTAY CAD.
İSMET PAŞA CAD.
CUMHURİYET CAD.
SARAPOL CAD.
MİLLET ESEMENLİK CAD.
YENER ULUSOY BUL.
TOURIST
OFFICE
ANAFARTALAR CAD.
YÜZÜNCÜ YIL BUL.
TEOMAN PAŞA CAD.
KONYAALTI PLAJI
(KONYAALTI BEACH)
KONYAALTI CAD.
TURGUT REİS CAD.
HIZIR REİS CAD.
YILDIZ CAD.
ANTALYA
MÜZESİ
PIRI REİS CAD.
DEFTERDARLIK BUL.
TEVFİK AKILTOPU CAD.
TANK AKILTOPU CAD.
2 CADDESİ
MELTEM BUL.
YÜZÜNCÜ YIL BUL.
Konyaalti
Beach Park
SHERATON
VOYAGER ANTALYA
AQUALAND
7 MEHMET
Atatürk Parki
(Atatürk Park)
YUNUS DIVING
SCHOOL
SHIP INN B's
MELISSA'S AND
VANESSA'S
RESTAURANT
HILLSIDE
SU HOTEL
DUMLUPINAR BULVAR

Detail inset

BAZAAR
SAAT KULESİ
GİZLİ BAHÇE
KALE KAPISI MEYDANI
(FORTRESS GATE
SQUARE)
TEKELİ MEHMET
PAŞA CAMİİ
ATELYA
PANSİYON
HADRIANUS KAPISI
(HADRIAN'S GATE)
ATATÜRK CAD.
SUNA & İNAN
KIRAÇ KALEİÇİ
MÜZESİ
OWL
BOOKSHOP
HOTEL
CANDLES
HOUSE
KESİK MİNARE KÜLLİYESİ
(BROKEN MINARET COMPLEX)
YİVLİ MİNARE/ALAADİN CAMİİ
TUVANA HOTEL
KALE BAR
TEKELİ
KONAKLARI
DOĞAN
HOTEL
HOTEL
ALP PAŞA
HIDIRLIK SOK.
PTT
MARINA
RESTAURANT
Roman
Harbor
CUMHURİYET CAD.
ALLY'S
VARYANT SOK.
CLUB
ARMA
MERMERLİ PLAJI
(MARBLE BEACH)
Antalya Körfezi
(Antalya Bay)
HIDIRLIK KULESİ
200 yds
200 m
PAŞA CAMİ SOK.
MESCİT SOK.
İSKELE CAD.
MERMERLİ BANYO SOK.

© AVALON TRAVEL

young ones shoot paint balls or climb the monkey bars at the kiddie park. With so much to offer to history, culinary, and outdoor buffs, it's easy to see why Antalya is the destination of choice.

HISTORY

The Hellenes couldn't have chosen a better name when they called the 115-kilometer-coastal area between ancient Lycia and Cilicia—today's Antalya province—*Pamphylia* (Greek for "all tribes"). And throughout history, starting from the pre-historic nomads who roamed Antalya's mountainous periphery some 52,000 years ago to today's modern Turks, a long list of civilizations either settled or trod through this province's realm.

While it's known that the Hittites and various Greek colonies settled the region, Antalya doesn't officially enter historical annals until the 3rd century B.C. That's according to the accidental discovery in 2008 of a necropolis and its 361 graves during an excavation of a business center in Doğu Garajı. This find is particularly interesting because Antalya's foundation can no longer be attributed to Pergamum King Attallus II. His father—same name minus a Roman numeral—was then responsible for naming the settlement Attaleia in his honor. But it's safe to say that the city, until further findings, remains younger than its sister metropolises of Perge, Termessos, and Aspendos by at least seven centuries. And why Antalya still thrives, while the others are relegated to history may be due to its location at the end of an easy-to-defend gulf. At least Attalus I thought so, and his harbor town continued to flourish well after his son bequeathed it, along with the entire Pergamene Empire, to the Romans in A.D. 133. And just three years later, a spectacular triumphal gate was built to honor the momentous visit of Roman Emperor Hadrian.

The Romans and subsequent Byzantines ruled the region until the arrival of the Selçuk Turks in A.D. 1207. A new rule required another name change and a new logo to symbolize Attaleia's conversion to Islam; it was renamed Antalya and the *Yivli Minare* (Fluted Minaret) became its trademark. During the next 200 years sovereignty vacillated between the Mongols and the Hamidoğulları, another Turkic emirate, until Antalya's absorption into the Ottoman Empire in 1391.

After WWI, the Ottoman Empire dissolved and Antalya was entreated to the Italians. Mustafa Kemal Atatürk's armies put an end to foreign rule in 1921 after winning the War of Independence and reclaiming the former Ottoman port as a major city that now constitutes Turkey's seventh largest city.

SIGHTS
Kaleiçi
(Old Town)

Get to the nitty gritty of a visit to Old Town Antalya by first checking out its most impressive monument, **Hadrianus Kapısı** (Hadrian's Gate). Built in A.D. 130 to honor the visit of Roman Emperor Hadrian, this triumphal

Antalya's tiny marina is flanked by fortifications that date to the 2nd century B.C.

gate—also called *Üç Kapısı* (Three Gates)—gets its name from its trio of arches that connect to the ancient city walls on either side. It's located on Cumhuriyet Caddesi and leads straight into the Kaleiçi.

About 500 meters north along Imaret Sokağı is **Kale Kapısı Meydanı** (Fortress Gate Square). On its western flank lies **Saat Kulesi** (Clock Tower)—a timepiece that was probably added during the 19th century. It graces one of two watch towers (only one remains) built by the Selçuks to protect the gate.

Just across the square, the **Yivli Minare** (Fluted Minaret) was built in true Selçukian architecture alongside—not atop—the adjoining mosque by Sultan Alaaddin Keykubad in 1225–27. The fluted thick brick structure has come to symbolize the city of Antalya. At 38 meters tall, the minaret's 90 steps were climbed five times a day by the muezzin to broadcast the *adhan* (call to prayer). The adjoining **Alaadin Camii** is a converted Byzantine church; it gained its multi-domed appearance during a mid-14th-century reconstruction. Also in the mosque complex is a **Mevlevi Tekke** (Whirling Dervish Monastery), which was built in 1255. This sufi seminary now houses the interesting **Antalya Devlet Güzel Sanatlar Galerisi** (Antalya Public Fine Arts Gallery, Cumhuriyet Cad. 55, 0242/248-7076, free) in one of its four halls; art collections from local artists are displayed in its small, plain chamber September–May. In the complex's lush gardens are a pair of tombs: one belonging to Sufi Sheik Zincirkıran Mehmet Bey (1377) and the other to Nigar Hatun, the wife of Ottoman sultan Beyazid II.

Directly south of the square, just off Uzun Çarşı Sokak, is the **Tekeli Mehmet Paşa Camii.** This petite mosque boasts particularly intricate Koranic inscriptions on colorfully-tiled panels. Its commissioner, Mehmet Paşa, was one of Sultan Mehmet III's illustrious public servants who began his 60-year career as a sergeant major in the Ottoman army and ended up serving as the governor of Van in 1616.

Wandering southwest towards the harbor, the busy old quarter of Kaleiçi—now fiercely protected from development by the municipality—is lined with restored **Ottoman houses.** Most of these were reborn as inns, B&Bs, and, touristy shops during an award-winning restoration project launched in the late 1970s.

Kaleiçi's southern section is not only more peaceful, but also features a handful of interesting sights. One of them is the ruined **Kesik Minare Kulliyesi** (Broken Minaret Complex, Hesapcı Sok.). Built in the 13th century, this single-galleried Selçukian minaret Islamized the Byzantine basilica of Panagelia (5th century A.D.) already onsite. The minaret earned its name after losing its crown in a fire in 1896. While the structure was finally transformed into a "proper" mosque in 1467 by the Turkish Sultan Korkut, its remarkable interior prayer hall still bears the church's original twin sections in the shape of a double cross, as well as an arched gate and marble columns that belie this building's original faith.

Crowning a rocky ledge just below Hesapcı Sokak is the 14-meter-tall **Hidirlik Kulesi.** Also known as the Red Tower, this 2nd-century fortress was originally part of the city walls and functioned as a lighthouse.

Kaleiçi Müzesi (Kaleiçi Museum)

Located in the center of Kaleiçi, the **Sunan & İnan Kıraç Kaleiçi Müzesi** (Kocatepe Sok. 25, 0242/243-4274, www.kaleicimuzesi.com, 9 A.M.–noon and 1–6 P.M. Thurs.–Tues.) comprises two buildings which were meticulously restored in the mid-1990s. The first, a traditional Turkish mansion, features typical ethnographic recreations of daily rituals and the rites of passage of the Ottomans. The other structure, the former Greek Orthodox church of Aya Yorgo (1863), is definitely more interesting both for its interior and exterior design. It contains an extensive collection of Turkish ceramics collected by the Kıraçes.

Antalya Müzesi (Antalya Museum)

The Antalya Müzesi (Cumhurriyet Cad., 0242/241-4528, 9 A.M.–6 P.M. Tues.–Sun.,

10TL) is Turkey's second most important archaeological museum, after Istanbul's, and definitely deserves a visit even if you're in town for just a day. Located 1.5 kilometers west of Kaleiçi, this museum is a repository for the bulk of the relics excavated in the Antalya province-one of the world's richest cultural centers. Some 5,000 archaeological artifacts are displayed in 14 exhibitions halls and more than 25,000 are currently in storage. It opens with a prehistory hall that includes a mind-blowing collection of artifacts excavated from the Karain Cave at Burdur. The longest continuously inhabited cave in Turkey, Karain contained tools and figurines that were over 50,000 years old when it was discovered. These are displayed chronologically from the Paleolithic Era to the late Bronze Age, giving visitors a grasp of the timeline.

Even for those not interested in statues, the Hall of the Gods truly amazes with the usual suspects from Greek mythology. Grander-than-life effigies of 16 gods include incredibly well-preserved statues of Zeus, Apollo, Aphrodite, and Athena. The Hall of the Emperors, next, is dedicated to mortals of "grandeur," such as Roman Emperors Hadrian and Traian. These were uncovered in the 1970s during excavations of Perge and Aspendos.

Then, there's the Hall of Burial Culture, which retraces funeral rites from the 2nd century A.D. The tomb of Hercules is the most prominent of all the finely carved wall burial chambers on display. The remaining halls are considerably smaller, but no less stunning with exhibitions of Byzantine religious icons; pre-Hellenic coin collections; and Selçuk and Ottoman ceramics, carpets, and Koranic texts, among a plethora of household articles.

DAY TRIPS

The Province of Antalya spans 115 kilometers in length along its coast and extends 45 kilometers inland. With so much geography to cover, picking the ideal day trip can be daunting, especially considering that more than two dozen outings—outdoorsy, archaeological, cultural, or just plain fun—are available from the town

center. The ones to seriously consider are excursions east to the ancient cities of Aspendos and Perge; or west to the burning flame of Chimaera or the mountaintop fortress at Termessos. Renting a car is always my preferred means of transport, but day tours in air-conditioned minibuses or Jeep safaris are also possible. Antalya's well-organized *dolmuş* (communal taxi) cooperative also makes it simple and economical to tour the sites, without having to spend hours in transit. A safe and trouble-free alternative is to pre-book a tour prior to travel: check out **Natta Travel Services** (100 Yil Bulvarı, Sheraton Voyager Resort & Spa Hotel 4, 0242/238-6134, www.nattatravel.com). They specialize in stylish half- and full-day tours of the region with a focus on outdoor activities. Among the 15 excursions to choose from are Jeep safaris through the Taurus Mountains (€50), rafting in Köprülü Canyon (€45), ballooning over Aspendos (€200), and a boat tour of Phaselis (€50). Trips depart 7:30 A.M. or 8:30 A.M. and return by 5:30 P.M., and include English-speaking guides, lunch, round-trip hotel transfers, and equipment use where applicable.

Perge, Aspendos, and Side

Adding the ancient cities of Perge and Side to the requisite outing to Aspendos extends a three-hour jaunt by five hours (for a total of 8). Rather smart, I'd say, because in the process you explore Aspendos' magnificent theater and also get a decent bird's eye view of the whole of ancient Pamphylia and its ruins-packed trove of ancient cities. Trotting a little further east along the Med also allows for a couple of truly magnificent pit stops to refresh at the gushing waterfalls of Manavgat and to bask in Side's irresistible sunsets. Although this itinerary seems packed, it truly isn't, since the furthest point is only about 80 kilometers east of Antalya. Getting an early start and spending an hour or so at each stop will still get you back to Antalya by mid-evening.

PERGE

The ancient Pamphylian capital of Perge (18km east of Antalya on the Antalya-Alanya Hwy.,

COURTESY OF REPUBLIC OF TURKEY CULTURE AND TOURISM MINISTRY

The Aspendos Theatre is one of the few amphitheaters of the ancient world that has its own opera and ballet season.

0242/426-2748, 9 A.M.–7:30 P.M. daily, until 5 P.M. in winter, 15TL) lies 20 kilometers east of modern Antalya. Entirely relegated to history, the ancient city was settled as "Parha" by the Hittites in the 15th century B.C. Saints Paul and Barnabas evangelized among the gentiles here while on their missionary journeys to Antioch (A.D. 42). The ruins today are widely scattered, but are still impressive enough to warrant a visit. While not much remains of its Bronze Age acropolis, one of Antiquity's oldest, Perge does boast a stunning stadium. It's one of Asia Minor's best-preserved sporting arenas, after Affrodisias's; it accommodated 12,000 spectators in its 2nd-century A.D. heyday. Below the rows of seating were a total of 30 chambers, every third chamber was used as an entrance or shop; the arcades still bear the engravings of the shopkeepers' names. The 15,000-seat amphitheater is purely Greco-Roman, as evidenced by its position on the hillside. The stage area dates back to the 2nd-century and features ornate reliefs of mythological scenes.

ASPENDOS

Time has not been kind to Aspendos (48km east of Antalya on the Antalya-Alanya Hwy., 0242/735-7337, 9 A.M.–7:30 P.M. daily, until 5 P.M. in winter, 10TL). Not much remains of this city, which was originally settled in 1000 B.C. by Argives—colonists from the Peloponnese city of Argos. But its one remaining monument, the **Aspendos Theatre,** is worth the trip to and from Antalya. It's by far the best-preserved theater complex of Asia Minor, thanks to periodic maintenance and reinforcements provided by the Selçuks of Rum, who converted its stage into a palace at the turn of the 1st millennium and a caravansary by the mid-1300s. The best way to experience this monument is to try to coordinate a visit with one of the nighttime performances during the national opera and ballet festival mid-June–early July.

SIDE

Lying on a one-kilometer-long peninsula, the ancient metropolis of Side (75km east of Antalya on the Antalya-Alanya Hwy., 9 A.M.–7:30 P.M. daily, until 5 P.M. in winter, admission 10TL) overlooks a contemporary, yet picturesque, summer resort. In 30 years, this once idyllic Turkish fishing hamlet with its unspoiled white sandy beaches and spectacular Roman ruins has transformed itself into an upcoming tourism powerhouse. But while most of the incoming tourists are Turks, who are more interested in sunny pursuits than history, Side's main claim to fame are its ruins. The most spectacular is the Temple of Apollo (southwestern tip of the harbor), which has crested a hillock overlooking the Med since the 2nd century A.D. It's magnificently well preserved, and, along with the adjacent Temple of Athena, is arguably Turkey's most enchanting site of ruins. Exploring it at dusk, with the sounds of the crashing waves and spotlighting added for effect, makes for a truly memorable experience. Side's Roman **theater** was Pamphylia's largest, with a capacity of 20,000 spectators. Since Side lacks a hillside, this massive 2nd-century A.D. structure was constructed in the Roman style, using an arch-plan to support the sharp verticals, rather the typical Greek style of hollowing out a foothill. Other buildings include an agora, a library, and a 6th-century Byzantine basilica. The building blocks of most of these are so unstable that the park has had to install chain-linked fencing to restrict access. Before leaving the site, stroll through the Roman baths that now house the **Side Museum** (0242/753-1006, 9 A.M.–noon and 1–7:30 P.M. Tues.–Sun., until 5:30 P.M. in winter, 10TL). It's a small, yet impressive, repository of the statues and sarcophagi found intact on the site.

Side is a perfect point to tarry a while. The town gushes with excellent restaurants, all boasting sea views from which to enjoy the phenomenal sunsets. As of summer 2009, the restaurant to beat, for quality and overall atmosphere, is **Soundwaves Restaurant** (Barbaros Cad., 0242/753-1059). Owner Ali Bey and his Australian wife, Penny, burst with joviality and an unmatched attentiveness that pervades their yacht-themed diner. The overall

tantalizing menu's best picks are the creamed, garlicky mushroom appetizer, the pricey, but superbly grilled *kuzu balığı* (leer fish), and their succulent avocado dessert.

Just eight kilometers northeast of Side, the **Manavgat Waterfalls** (Manavgat Şelalesi, 2TL) provides another highly popular-and refreshing-escape to the scorching temperatures along the coast. This touristy spot, at the point where the Taurus Mountains' waters cascade down, forming the Manavgat River, is renowned for its trout. Plenty of riverside diners offer grilled or baked fish. To reach the falls head west from Side to Manavgat (4km), then another four kilometers north straight to the park.

Termessos

The citadel city of Termessos crests a lofty mountaintop in the center of the rugged **Güllük Dağı Milli Parki** (Güllük Mountain National Park, 0242/423-7416, 8:30 A.M.–7:30 P.M. daily, until 5:30 P.M. in winter, admission 10TL, parking 8TL). With an elevation slightly above 1,050 meters, even the mighty Alexander the Great couldn't conquer the walled-city he later referred to as an "an eagle's nest." Sure the terrain proved tough to climb for this uber-conqueror, but the Termessians—a rebellious and hot-under-the collar indigenous people of this former Pisidian metropolis—bravely defied his valiant efforts. Perhaps this is why the Seleucids, and the Romans after them, complied—albeit reluctantly—with Termessos's wishes to remain an independent ally.

Termessos is an impressively-preserved ancient site, ideally situated high amid sheer cliffs and dense pine forests. Its most stunning remains—both for its historical value and its mind-bending views of Antalya through dense cloud cover—is its **Roman theater.** Like most of what remains of this magnificent, expansive city, the theater dates to the 2nd century B.C. and was crafted from boulders cut from the surrounding peaks. Also of note are a collection of magnificent **rock-cut tombs** and the pair of **sarcophagi**—those of Alex's general Alcates and ancient Greek geographer Agatemeros.

Water from the Düden Waterfalls flows dramatically into lakes filled with trout.

Exploring Termessos can be tricky; the site is steep, vast, and exposed to the elements. Plan on arriving early with plenty of water (none provided on location), comfortable hiking shoes, sunscreen, and a hat. City plans, provided free-of-charge at the ticket booth, will assist you in navigating through Termessos's 14 points of interests. Once onsite, follow the sign-posts toward the tombs, along the long, sometimes steep, narrow footpath that snakes past rock-hewn tombs, part of the upper city walls, and the odd sarcophagus. After accomplishing the site's most intense climb, turn back and go down to Termessos's center, where the theater and 90 percent of the ruins are located. A quick, early morning foray shouldn't last longer than two hours. Double that if the excursion is during the busy, grueling hot afternoon, or if you plan at pausing at every historic boulder.

Termessos is located 35 kilometers north of Antalya, about 10 kilometers southeast of the Antalya-Denizli Highway (E87). Doing it solo in a rental vehicle is possible, but an excursion with a knowledgeable guide is highly recommended. Contact tour packager **Turkey Golden Tours** (Peykhane Sk. 34, Sultanahmet, 0554/797-2646, www.turkeygoldentours.com) to book this half-day trip (€40), which also includes a visit to the sublimely picturesque and refreshing **Düden Şelalesi** (Duden Waterfalls). All entrance fees, English-speaking guide, and air-conditioned transportation are included in the cost of the trip.

◖ Chimaera, Olympos, and Çıralı

Perhaps one of Antalya's top day trips, and one of the Med's yet to be discovered idylls, the area comprising the **Olimpos Beydağları Sahil Millî Parkı** (Olympos Bey Mountains Coastal National Park) boasts three of Antalya's best kept secrets. The first, nestled in a valley in the foothill of Tahtalı Dağı (Timber Mountain; or, *Olympos,* Greek for "Great Mountain"), is the ancient city of Olympos. The two others are the long sandy beach of Çıralı, one of the Med's few remaining nesting grounds for the endangered loggerhead turtle, and the eternal flame of Chimaera, set deep in the lush pine forest.

CHIMAERA

The Chimaera, or *Yanartaş* (Burning Rock) in Turkish, is a series of flames once thought to have been a mythical fire-breathing monster that roamed the Olympos mountain spitting flames from its three heads. Part goat, part lion, and part serpent, Homer's legendary behemoth was so feared among ancient Anatolians that the rocky slopes of Olympos were to be avoided at all costs until Greek geographer Strabo debunked the toponym as just a natural combustion phenomenon. Actually, this earthly marvel is attributed to methane gases rising from deep beneath the earth through a fissure and igniting at a precise point where the serpentine hills rise from the limestone shelf. But thankfully, the Greeks also believed that the Chimaera was slain by Bellerophon while riding his winged horse, Pegasus. Chimaera lies seven kilometers, or a one-hour hike, uphill from the village

© TOM DEMPSEY

The eternal flame of Chimaera, near modern Olympos, spontaneously ignites after being extinguished.

turn of the 15th century, Olympos was abandoned. The vast site is overgrown and scattered throughout with fragmented ruins, so make sure to grab the map available at the ticket booth. If you're not keen on seeing the ruins, come to peek at rare Mediterranean flora—splendid wild orchids, oleanders, and lavenders—or to pick wild figs from the hundreds of fruit trees that line the burbling rivulet.

ÇIRALI

A few steps north from the point where the Ulupınar stream meets the sea is **Çıralı Plajı** (Çıralı Beach), one of Turkey's few beaches that has remained entirely undeveloped. It extends about 3.5 kilometers, and the roads that line its sands include a slew of fine family-run pensions. If you're considering a remote setting to base your eastern Turkish Med adventure, feasible only with a rental car, or an extension of a day trip, then Çıralı may just be the perfect answer. Crowning the list of sublimely rural B&Bs is **Olympos Lodge** (Çıralı, Kemer, P.O. Box 38, 0242/825-7171, www.olymposlodge. net, €140–200 with half-board). Passing the pricey sedan-filled parking lot, the entrance's kaleidoscope of blooms breaks the green of perfectly clipped grass and fragrant thickets. A hammock here, a pond there, and the calls of the odd chicken, goose, or peacock add surprising touches to this remote escape, which is backed by the snow-capped giant of Mount Olympus. Some 12 elegantly-spare bungalows are zen-inspired in swatches of linen and white, and all feature cedar flooring and large modern baths.

For a more economic option, check out the **Myland Nature** (Çıralı, Kemer, P.O. Box 71, 0242/825-7044, www.mylandnature.com, 140–190TL). Engin and Pınar, pals from university, scrimped their pennies for a decade to purchase 15 acres of mostly clearings and fruit orchards on which to build their dream inn. And in 1999, their hope became reality with Myland. Slightly set back from the beach (70m), due to a law introduced to protect the adjacent nesting ground of loggerhead turtles, the property features 13 timber cabins, each

of Çıralı. And, as you approach, don't be surprised by the barbecue odors emanating from the site; a couple of sly entrepreneurs are roasting kebabs and boiling water for tea right atop the flames.

OLYMPOS

The ancient settlement of Olympos (0242/892-1325, open daily, 3TL), set in a verdant coastal valley straddling the Ulupınar Çayı (Great Spring Stream), enters recorded history in the 2nd century B.C. One of the main six cities of the Lycian federation, Olympos, according to Roman philosopher Cicero (1st century B.C.), was a city filled with great culture and extensive riches. With the Chimaera flame just steps away, it's no wonder that Olympos grew as a pilgrimage center honoring Hephaestus—a.k.a. Vulcan, the god of fire—until the advent of Christianity in the 2nd century A.D. Throughout the Middle Ages, Genoese and Rhodian Crusaders erected a pair of fortresses along its coast, but by the

boasting a veranda with hammock and deck chairs. Many activities are provided for guests, including a free yoga class daily at 8 A.M. led by owner Pınar herself.

GETTING THERE

Situated about 110 kilometers south of Antalya's center, the Çıralı/Yanartaş exit is located along the Antalya Highway (D400). The turnoff leads to a bumpy road that follows a lush riverbed for about six kilometers. Either cross the bridge leading into Çıralı to reach the "official" entrance to the mountain footpath leading to the Chimaera (1.5km); or, take the road right before the bridge to go straight to the beach. The Antalya-Fethiye minibus stops hourly at the restaurant located on the highway, one kilometer north of the junction into Olympos. From May to November, the Olympos *dolmuş* (communal taxi, 3TL) leaves every half hour until 7 P.M. for the site and the service to Çıralı leaves every two hours. Check with your hotel for the availability of transfers either to the main road, the Antalya bus station, or the airport.

ENTERTAINMENT AND EVENTS
Nightlife

There are several options for nighttime outings in Antalya. You can to take to the streets of Kaleiçi, where a stroll might see you winding through the souvenir and carpet shops, stopping at an ice cream parlor, and ending the evening at an exclusive bar in the antique harbor. Another choice is to head to Konyaaltı's Antalya Beach Park, where clubs and restaurants spill out onto the sand on the beachside of the promenade, and convivial *meyhanes* (Turkish taverns) line the other. To find the local flavor of Antalya, check out the pricier bars and clubs/restaurants lining Atatürk Kültür Parkı or hang with the proletariat at Karaalioğlu Parkı. Also, check out what's on tap at the major resorts and hotels; some bars and clubs—like the Monkey Club and Jazz Bar of Mardan Palace and Marmara's onsite bars over in Lara—are welcome to the public. And don't forget the odd Turkish or 1001 Arabian Nights evening shows touted by most travel agencies in the area. There's no strict dress code, but since Antalya is slightly more eastern European than the resorts in the west, a smarter dress may be called for than, say, that of Fethiye's and Marmaris's accepted beachwear.

Club Arma (Iskele Cad. 75, 0252/241-6260, 11 P.M.-4 A.M., 15TL) is Antalya's snazziest club, at least in the Kaleiçi district. Enjoy a peaceful seafood dinner by Kaleiçi's docks at the indoor restaurant before tripping the light fantastic under the stars.

Kale Bar (Memerli Sok. 2, Kaleiçi, 0242/248-6591, 11 A.M.–2 A.M.) is an upper-class bar that boasts the best sea views in Kaleiçi from its location above the Old Harbor's battlements. Drinks are pricey (over 15TL for mixed drinks), but the elegance is bar none. You'll find Kale Bar inside Tutav Türk Evi Hotel, alongside its Pink House and Green House restaurants.

Ally's (Sur Sok. 4/8, Kaleiçi, 0242/244-7704, www.ally.com.tr, cover charge 25TL) is a 4,000-square-meter facility atop the antique city walls, boasting nine elegant bars and restaurants. Ally's is one of Antalya's entertainment trademarks for its laser shows and line-up of Turkey's top singing acts and Europe's reigning DJs. With waist-high white tables and its fuchsia accents, Ally's welcomes more than 3,500 guests decked out in their finest duds nightly during the summer.

Out in Kemer is one of the coast's largest—and trendiest—clubs after Bodrum's Halicarnassus, **Club Inferno** (Deniz Cad. 1, Kemer, 0242/814-5335, www.infernoclub.net, 10 P.M.–5 A.M., daily during summer, 15–25TL) is known for its themed parties and racy cabaret acts. But be warned that the atmosphere here is more, say, of a new-age gentleman's club, rather than just a dance club. At capacity, dance the night away with 3,000—mostly Russian—guests.

Festivals

Every year during the last week of September, Turkey's movie stars and media pundits head to

Antalya for the **Altın Portakal Film Festivalı** (altinportakal.tursak.org.tr). Showings and an award ceremony, held in Aspendos's ancient amphitheater, feature the best national talent. Also of note is the festival of **Lara Sandland** (www.larasandland.com, May–Nov.), which exposes the talents of dozens of the world's top sand sculptors as they create inane-and unfortunately temporary-architectural masterpieces along the beaches of Antalya's Lara quarter. In 2009, the theme was mythology: In 25 days five artists molded 1,000 tons of sand into a Chinese dragon , a creation which entered the Guiness Book of World Records for largest sand sculpture.

SPORTS AND RECREATION
Beaches
The entire province of Antalya is lined by a long sandy strip hugging the Med, so snatching a good spot to catch some rays won't be difficult. But why bother traveling that far when the Konyaaltı quarter, smack in the center of town, boasts a 1.5-kilometer pebbly beach with world-class amenities aimed to entertain entire families? Its **Beach Park** (0242/249-0900, www.beachpark.com.tr) includes the kid-tailored **AquaLand,** Turkey's fourth largest water park, and **DolphinLand** (15TL). Otters, white whales, and bottle-nose dolphins thrill spectators during one-hour performances scheduled twice daily in the summer; for an extra 75TL, you can even swim with dolphins. Of the seven beach clubs currently in operation, **Eleven** (Beach Park 11, 0242/249-0922, www.eleven-beach.com) commands the largest clientele for its luxurious, parasol-covered couches in the sand and for its tasty menu of grills and fresh salads. No matter which beach club you choose, each contender features its own restaurant and water-centric or fashion- and music-filled activities—some even organize boat tours—along with the expected beachfront outfitted with comfy lounges, umbrellas, and changing and bathing facilities. Entry varies 5–12TL per day. As day turns into night, these beach clubs turn into posh outdoor night clubs. The Antalya Beach Park is located just three kilometers west

of Kaleiçi, and can be accessed by riding the tram until the *Müze* stop. A 200-meter stroll westward leads to the main entrance.

The second option is the long sandy strip of **Lara Beach,** situated 12 kilometers east of Kaleiçi. But the prospect of spending the day here after visiting Konyaaltı's beachy amusement mall is less than inspiring. A trip to the newly-opened Mardan Palace, nearby, might provide enough jollification to make trekking all the way to Lara worthwhile. *Dolmuşes* (communal taxis, 30min, 3TL) driving the route between Kaleiçi and Lara stop along the beachfront.

Unique to Antalya are the icy springs that find their way from high above the Taurus Mountains to the sea, creating some stunning scenery in the process and plenty of soaking opportunities for the brave. The best one is **Aşağı Düden Şelalesi** (Lower Duden Falls), where the torrential waters cascade into the Mediterranean. It's located 10 kilometers east of Antalya, right before Lara, and best reached by boat. Or, head north 10 kilometers to **Yukarı Düden Şelalesi** (Upper Duden Falls), where you'll find teahouses and cafés. Another glacial spring spurts from right below Mermerli Park, just east of Kaleiçi, at a point called **Memerli Plajı** (Marble Beach). Accessed through Memerli Restaurant, this small public beach is cordoned by Antalya's ancient city walls.

Not satisfied? Then head out from the town center by car. But before you do so, you'll have to choose between sand or pebble; your selection will determine the direction. Pebbly beaches are west of Antalya. The best one is the resort of Kemer, 45 kilometers away. A rare wonder of successful municipal planning in Turkey, Kemer is an idyllic setting, benefitting from absolutely calm waters, the splendid scenery of Mount Olympos, and an open-air shopping drag. Now, for sand, set the compass east for the exclusive resort of Belek's **İleribaşı** public beach. Crystal clear waters earned Belek's coast the coveted blue flag award. The beach itself is pristine, with lifeguard facilities and lounge chair and parasol rentals. The municipality strictly maintains the strip's opening hours (9 A.M.–6 P.M.) to make way for the loggerhead turtles who return annually to spawn (May–Sept.).

Cruises

The **Phaselis and Three Islands** day cruise provides a pleasant sea-born option for visiting Antalya's fantastic coast. Either join one of the many tours that depart from the docks at Antalya's ancient marina or pre-book with local agent **Natta Travel Services** (100 Yil Bulvarı, Sheraton Voyager Resort & Spa Hotel 4, 0242/238-6134, www.nattatravel. com). Opting for the latter is smart since it departs—aboard a well-stocked *gület* (motorized sailboat)—50 kilometers north from the new marina, near Kemer; this allows for a much broader tour of the region both on and off land. This particular trip stops first at Phaselis, the ancient port founded by Greek pirates in 674 B.C., and moves on to picturesque Ayışığı Bay and Pirates Cave. But others, particularly those setting off from the old harbor, are varied. These tours include one- and two-hour-long excursions of the Gulf of Antalya (€25-35), its offshore islands, and the Lower Duden Waterfalls. Other cruises take off for much longer itineraries that might include stops as far north as Kale/Demre, Olympos, and even Kaş. Also keep in mind that the type of lunch served onboard affects the price of a cruise; this ranges between a sandwich and soda to a three-course grilled fish meal.

Diving

The Gulf of Antalya's sea floor is littered with the remains of two French World War II ships and fighter planes. The wrecks provide another dimension to diving among the area's kaleidoscopic display of flora and fauna, which include giant sea sponges, rare Mediterranean Monk seals, and glittering schools of blue fin tuna. Mild winds and shallow caves also make this bay ideal for discovery divers.

Diving schools and services are provided at major resort hotels from Kemer to Belek. Courses and individual dives are popular, so it may be smart to book in advance. Antalya's

outfitter and instruction facility of choice is **Yunus Diving School** (Konyaaltı Beachpark 5-6, 0242/238-4486). Led by Cumhur Tuğ, the founder of the Antalya Underwater Sports Association, Yunus offers two-hour dives and week-long certification programs, starting at 50TL (not including equipment rental).

Golf

Antalya, Turkey's premier destination for golfers, now boasts six championship golf courses. And the race to build PGA-endorsed greens continues, as evidenced by the recent addition of an 18-hole championship course designed by world-class golfer Jack Nicklaus. Ensconced between the surrounding mountain peaks of the Taurus Mountains, the bulk of golf schools, resorts, and clubs are situated in Belek, 47 kilometers east of Antalya. **Millennium Golf** (Güzelbağ Mah. Zeybek Sok. 117, 0252/349-3131, www.millenniumgolf.gen. tr) offers golf enthusiasts a range of information and hotel and club packages. Their very own Millennium Golf School runs half-day programs for beginners and intermediate putters seven days a week, year-round.

The property to beat for the moment is **LykiaWorld & Link** (Denizyaka Köyü, Köprüçay Mevkii, 0252/617-0200, www.lykiagroup.com). Designed by acclaimed course architect Pete Dye, this demanding 18-hole course is the only links course in Turkey and also the only one hugging the Med. It features loads of pot bunkers, rye grass, elevated tees on curvaceous sand dunes, and shifting Mediterranean winds to challenge the seasoned golfer along its par-72 course. Greens fees start at €105 per round and go up to €475 for a five-round package.

Hiking

Turkey's first long-distance, waymarked trekking route, the **Lykia Yolu** (Lycian Way), and the more recent **St. Paul Yolu** (St. Paul Trail) were realized by British expat and avid hiker Kate Clow. She, along with her partner in crime, Terry Richardson, spent years signposting these spectacularly scenic courses. The

509-kilometer Lycian Way winds through ancient Lycia, from Fethiye to Antalya, along rocky footpaths and mountainous mule trails that never stray too far from sea. This medium-to-hard course involves several steep climbs and descents, difficulties that are only accentuated by the summer's blistering heat. The second path leads northeast from Perge (10km east of Antalya) over the Taurus Mountains to ancient Antioch in Pisidia, in the stunning Eğirdir lake region. This more rigorous 500-kilometer route partly covers Saint Paul's first missionary journey through Asia Minor. It involves 2,200-meter climbs, with two optional 2,800-meter ascents for more seasoned trekkers.

Clow created an extensive website (www.lycianway.com) and penned two companion books with detailed maps. The best time to hike either trail is during the months of February–May and September–November. And while the Lycian Way is generously signposted, the Saint Paul Trail only has officially approved white and red waymarkers.

ACCOMMODATIONS

Since the early 1990s a latent race to build grander hotels along Antalya's miles of sun-kissed coast and emerald green foothills has been brewing. The 2009 opening of the surreal Mardan Palace earned its owner, Russian industrialist Telman Ismailov, the lead, at least for the time being. The Las Vegas-style Mardan and its dozens of worthy competitors all along Antalya's Turkish Riviera are prized destinations that feature regular or all-inclusive accommodations available by the night or by the week. There are a handful of tried-and-true, four- and five-star resorts steps east of Antalya's Kaleiçi quarter. But the recently opened Antalya Beach Park in central Konyaaltı, and its baker's dozen of deluxe hotels, has filled the need to entertain entire families wishing for an ideal Med escape. Just a decade ago, this type of lodging was only available on the periphery.

B&B lovers, such as I am, are certainly not to be left out. The center, particularly Kaleiçi, has a wealth of historical Ottoman mansions lovingly restored into family-run inns. Most of these boast their own pint-size luxuries, with rarely more than a dozen cozy rooms lining a landscaped courtyard or a pool. These inner havens transform in the evening into romantic dining terraces from which to savor succulent Turkish fare. And, with the ancient harbor just steps away, you'll be situated within a short walking distance to Antalya's famed bar and restaurant scene.

There are hundreds of hotels competing for guests on Antalya's hotel strip. Discounts of up to 10 percent are available to early-bookers, online shoppers, and those paying in cash. Large hotels offer extremely competitive rates to local travel agents, who in turn pass the savings along to their customers; so it may be wise to got that route. If you happen to be in Turkey before traveling to Antalya, pick up a Turkish newspaper and look through the pages of hotel ads for some of the lowest rates around.

Under €100

Boasting a budget traveler's dream accommodations, **(Hotel Alp Paşa** (Hesapçı Sok. 30, Kaleiçi, 0242/247-5676, www.alppasa.com, €60–250) oozes with yesteryear charm and luxury. This 150-year-old collection of *konaks* (residences) that once belonged to wealthy Ottoman merchants were entirely restored; two of the original structures—the *selamlık* and haremlik (men and women's quarters)—were painstakingly scoured clean of layers of paint and cement. Carved doors, intricate ceilings, and building stones dating from Roman and Byzantine times were discovered underneath. Inside, the rooms are ample, sparsely decorated with Ottoman touches, and boast individual air-conditioning units and tiled baths. Some feature canopied beds, others whirlpool tubs. Outside, a timeworn water pond, surrounded by an original mosaic-tiled courtyard, became the perfect spot to add a small pool. An overflowing breakfast buffet welcomes guests every morning, while an á la carte restaurant also offers a dinner buffet option for €10 per guest.

Atelya Pansyion (Civelek Sok. 21, Kaleici,

0242/241-6416, www.atelyahotel.com, €50) is a collection of three ravishing Ottoman houses owned and operated by Hakan Kacaroğlu. The refined Antalya native has infused the property with loads of character, evidenced by the landscaping of the center courtyard, which bursts with the scent of jasmine, and the burbling sounds of an antique fountain. The accommodations in the original building are basic, but quite roomy with wooden floors and appealing *kilims* (Turkish carpets) gracing the walls. The Sultan abode (refurbished in 2003) is adorned with traditional accouterments fit for an 18th-century imperial, but the samovars and animal pelts gracing the floor may be a little over the top for today's traveler. Meals are provided on request.

Hotel Candles House (Kandiller Sok. 6, Kaleici, 0242/243-2790, www.hotelcandleshouse.com, €50) is a petite guesthouse tucked inside the sinewy, narrow alleys of Kaleiçi. You won't have to go far to explore the sights; Hadrian's Gate and the Fluted Minaret are just around the corner. Okay, so this is more like staying in a friend's house, but that's exactly why Candles is so charming. While the four small rooms offer the bare minimum-a bed, an air-conditioning unit, TV, and bath-the restaurant downstairs welcomes 40 guests, to indoor seating or to a landscaped terrace, with a tantalizing Turkish menu crafted by the brother-sister team who run the show.

Tekeli Konakları (Dizdar Hasan Sok., Kaleici, 0242/244-5465, www.tekeli.com.tr, US$80–115) comprises six historic Turkish mansions in the heart of Old Town Kaleiçi, centered around two split-level courtyards that features a small, welcoming pool. The nine sparsely-adorned rooms are all purely Anatolian in style, with flooring crafted of fragrant cedar and naturally-dyed linens. Each boasts its own personality, in the form of a hand-woven Turkish carpet over here, an antique Ottoman stained-glass panel over there, and doorknobs fashioned of Kütahya faience. During the summer, the upper courtyard transforms into a terrace restaurant crowded with local gourmets. The noise of tinkling glasses and particularly the hubbub from the disco next door may undermine a good night's sleep.

Doğan Hotel (Mermerli Banyo Sok. 5, Kaleiçi, 0242/241-8842, www.doganhotel.com, €80) is another collection of restored historic houses near Antalya's ancient harbor. The location is simply superb, just 100 meters from Kaleiçi's small beach. The Doğan is the oldest family-run inn in town, and its 41 guestrooms were recently upgraded; wooden floors were re-planked and so were some of the ceilings. Expect plush fabrics, individual air-conditioning units, ceiling fans, and satellite TV throughout. Set your sights for the *Çatı Odası,* a mansard room that boasts its own balcony overlooking the harbor. The highlight here is the garden oasis, impregnated throughout with the delicious fragrance of orange blossoms and the sounds of cascading water.

€100-200

The **Marmara Antalya** (Şirinyalı Mah., Lara, 0242/249-3600, www.themarmarahotels.com, €95–155) is the quirky addition to the Marmara Group's list of exclusive hotels. Located in Antalya's Lara quarter, just five kilometers from central Kaleiçi, it commands spectacular views of the bay. The 208 superior rooms are bright and contemporary, and well worth every penny. But, plan to splurge a little more to snatch one of the 24 doubles (€154) on the tri-level "Revolving Loft." Its floating apparatus is unique in the world in that it slowly revolves in its own "pool." The result is a constantly changing scenery of mountains, the sparkling Mediterranean Sea, and the Marmara's vast grounds. Aside from an award-winning spa facility, the deluxe amenities feature a lily-white beach deck, an immense outdoor pool, and a 297-meter-long kayaking canal that crisscrosses the property. Rounding out the list of amenities are a stunning Turkish bath and sauna, tennis courts, four café/bars, and one of the Marmara Group's celebrated Tuti restaurants.

The **Sheraton Voyager Antalya** (100. Yıl Bulvarı, Konyaaltı, 0242/249-4949, www.sheratonantalya.com, €95-185) is perched on a cliff above the shaded public park of Konyaaltı.

The property boasts a stunning botanical garden, crisscrossed by burbling streams. Impressive in size and design, its main building seems ready to take flight with two long wings, surely designed to avail the majority of its 395 large rooms with splendid views of the entire Gulf of Antalya. Large marble baths, filled with custom-made toiletries, redeem the guestrooms' ordinary decor. Other plusses include slippers and fluffy bathrobes, LCD TVs, and large balconies. An outdoor swimming pool boasts a two-level water cascade-great for kids of any age-and a circle of graceful adult palm trees. Other facilities include a splendid spa oasis, nearby golf courses, complete array of water- and land-sports, travel agency, three restaurants, and six café/bars.

The **Dedeman Antalya Park** (Lara Yolu, Lara, 0242/321-3930, www.dedemanhotels. com, €75–115) manages to retain the Dedeman chain's luxury cachet in a fun-filled environment geared towards families. Its adjacent Aquapark, free for hotel guests, promises water-filled enjoyment with river rides, a colossal wave pool, and more than a dozen water slides. Inside, the 483 rooms, including 35 suites, are standard-size and come in pastel hues. One of the largest hotels serving Antalya's convention center, the Park functions at capacity almost year-round. Its small beach earned the coveted blue-flag award for the cleanliness of its waters. A full-service spa, gym, water- and land-sports activities are also available.

Over in Kemer, the **Berke Ranch** (Akcasaz Mvk. PK:76, Kemer, 0242/818-0333, www.hotel-berkeranch.com, €120–170) may just be the woodsy antidote to allay a Mediterranean overdose. Trust me, it does get to you after a while! Unlike the majority of hospitality giants that capitalize on their proximity to the sea, Berke makes no bones about its intent to provide a riding and holiday club away from the sandy coast. It's located in one of the scenic foothills of Lycia's famed Mount Olympus, amid fragrant orange orchards. The vast property includes its stubby main building, numerous two-story villas, and a superlative honeymoon suite. City slickers dig the four- to seven-day

riding adventures through the mountainous Lycian outback, while the idlers among them bask by the large elliptical pool. The 29 standard-size rooms (and three suites) boast a country chic decor, highlighted by white linens and dark wood accents. Boasting either an á la carte menu or buffet-style dining, depending on occupancy, the restaurant features a wooden deck that overlooks Twin Peaks—a cooky land formation of two gigantic granite spires that jut from the verdant plain.

Over €200

Mardan Palace (Kundü Köyü, Oteller Mevkii, Lara, 0242/310-4100, www.mardanpalace.com, €320–600) successfully blends Istanbul's historical landmarks with the pomp of Las Vegas's Caesar's Palace. With a total of 560 rooms, including two Royal Suites with private pool and butler (€14,000 per night!), the 1.4-billion-dollar Mardan encompasses three buildings and a series of garden villas that surround a five-acre sparkling pool, or this insane property's version of the Bosphorus. In its center, the bridge, inspired by Da Vinci's original plan for the Galata Bridge, also spans a gondola track devised to transport guests on a 30-minute ride across the pool. Within the pool is a sunken aquarium that houses some 3,000 fish and doubles as the decor for the underground Aquamarine, the exclusive fish restaurant that shares acreage with 23 other upper-class wining and dining facilities. The list of amenities goes on: Jack Nicklaus signature golf course; a 7,500-square-meter full service spa; toddler and teenager clubs and spas; and a dramatic, Greek-style amphitheater. While the Mardan is touted as the most expensive resort on the Mediterranean, the Anatolian Wing's stunning superior rooms, which command a €320 per night rate, are not that far-fetched, considering their palatial decor, velvety Hermés linens, marble baths with rain showers, and sumptuous views.

Hillside Su (Konyaaltı Cad., 0242/249-0700, www.hillsidesu.com.tr, from €240) brings Miami Beach to Antalya's posh

Konyaaltı neighborhood. A vision in white, from white floors and walls to the inch-thick linens gracing the stainless steel bathroom racks, Hillside is far from stark. Its Saturday Night Fever-inspired lounge, featuring four gigantic disco balls, large welcoming atrium, and whimsical red accents throughout, makes up for the lack of color in spades. The bonus of the sizable rooms (255 doubles, 39 suites) are the relaxing lounge beds provided on balconies that either open to splendid views of the Med or the Taurus Mountains; and, the Hillside Su has personalized pillow menu. From its single (yep, white!) tower, the property sprawls along perfectly clipped lawns. A blue-flagged beach, a sparkling teak-decked pool, and Sushi, one of Antalya's best Asian-themed restaurants, round out its outdoor facilities. Other amenities include a full-service spa and gym, six international restaurants, three bars, and an indoor pool.

Tuvana Hotel (Karanlık Sok. 18, Kaleici, 0242/244-4054, www.tuvanahotel.com, €150-220) is a 46-room B&B that surpasses, by leaps and bounds, its competition in the old town of Kaleiçi. Located on a quiet side street, sheltered from the fray of touristy boutiques, Tuvana comprises the four mansions of Abdi Effendi, a high Ottoman officer who threw lavish parties for visiting dignitaries during the first half of the 18th century. Today, his great-grandson Aziz Tankut and his wife Nermin Sumer continue that hospitality hands-on. The reputed B&B's main house features simple guestrooms with opulent drapery and bed linens, as well as the owner's prized antiques. The deluxe rooms are located in the other properties, and feature LCD TVs; Ottoman-style, gold-leafed ceilings; and crystal lighting. Outside, the walled courtyard welcomes with a full-size swimming pool. Orange, tangerine, banana, plum, and pomegranate trees offer mounds of fruit for the picking, but if real hunger strikes, head to one of the three onsite Turkish restaurants. Bikes are available to tour Old Town should you wish to detach yourself from this truly magnificent property.

FOOD

Antalya can be considered Turkey's second culinary capital, after Istanbul, not for any particular food tradition, but for its sheer number of restaurants. Included in the calculations are the industrial buffets and the eateries featured in the hospitality behemoths along the coastal corridor. Only Antalya's sought-after diners and time-revered establishments are included here. It's a good idea to ditch the shorts and don the slacks to visit these; reserving a table ahead of time will guarantee space and seating arrangements. If it's the local flavor you're after, then head to *lokantas* (diners) around Kaleiçi or the inexpensive dining haunts further north along Atatürk Caddesi.

International

Stella's Manzara (Lara Cad. 40/1, Lara, next to Dedeman Aquapark, 0242/243-3931, noon-midnight daily, 20TL) has changed locations four times in 17 years, requiring a name change every time it fine tuned its location. Confusing? I would say so, particularly for the food critics who try to keep up. Now in its fourth rendition, Stella's added "Manzara" to its name (for the awesome sea views of the Med the location offers) and Mexican and French inspiration to its already established Italian and Mediterranean menu. Awesome choices here include pizzas and pastas, but for a walk on the wild side order fish, chicken, or beef. The meat comes raw with hefty side dishes, seasonings, and a portable barbecue-like contraption filled with volcanic rocks that allows guests to grill tableside. After 10 P.M., Stella's morphs into the Garden Bar—a night club meeting spot for Antalya's finely dressed summer denizens.

Marina Restaurant (Mermerli Sok. 15, Kalçiçi, 0242/247 5490, www.marinaresidence.net, noon–midnight daily, 25TL) offers award-winning fine dining in the heart of Old Town. Sublime French dishes pop up among a menu boasting Mediterranean-inspired Turkish fare with unexpected twists. The recommended T-bone steak, highlighted by a zesty chili sauce, is superb. A live piano serenade adds to the romantic poolside location.

Ship Inn by Melissa's and Vanessa's Restaurant (Atatürk Culture Park 329, 0242/238-5235, 11:30 A.M.–1 A.M., 25TL) adeptly blends Swiss, Turkish, and Med cuisines with a menu heavy on meat and fish. Pastas and meat fondues round out the family-friendly meals. Grilled marinated beef ribs, extremely rare as a main dish in Turkey, please the Yankee in all of us. In summer, Ship Inn's interior turns into a giant covered terrace deck from which to enjoy the marshy artificially-made lake in Atatürk Culture Park. Just bring the mosquito repellent and you'll be golden.

Seafood
Club Arma (Iskele Cad. 75, 0252/244-9710, 11 A.M.–midnight, 25TL) is located in a refurbished 19th-century gashouse located on a diminutive bluff at the north end of Antalya's ancient harbor. Long gone are the signs of the sacks that were kept here when the building was later used as a silo; in their stead, tables dressed in white linen occupy a setting that evokes European dining at its best. The fish and meat dishes appearing on the menu are grilled to perfection, but Arma's seafood—from grilled lobster to the jumbo prawns and avocado appetizer—is succulently addictive. By 10 P.M., Arma earns its "Club" prefix by welcoming hundreds of partygoers on the outdoor platform adjacent to the restaurant.

Yedi Mehmet (Atatürk Culture Park 333, 0242/238-5200, www.7mehmet.com, 11 A.M.–midnight, 25TL) opened a quarter of a century ago, and its popularity has never waned. It features all the Turkish standbys, but the fish steals the show. The wine list is short and a bit overpriced, offering diners a great opportunity to try aniseed-flavored *rakı* (Turkish aperitif). Wondering where the name comes from? It's a moniker owner Mehmet earned from his elementary school friends for the scar in the shape of a seven on his forehead.

Turkish
Gizli Bahçe (Dizdar Hasan Bey Sok. 1, Kaleiçi, 0242/244-8010, www.gizlibahce.net, 18TL) doesn't stray from its Anatolian roots by going Continental. Regional appetizers like yummy *şakşuka* (yogurt-slathered, garlicky appetizer of sauteed eggplant, zucchini, and tomato) and *tahinli piyaz* (white bean salad in tahina sauce) are reasons enough to try their menu. Also, the fish *köftes* (balls) served on arugula and the Ottoman Special—stewed lamb served on caramelized eggplant and drizzled with unexpected orange juice—are delectable entrées. Gizli wins the race for best setting for its romantic location up on the ramparts overlooking the sea.

INFORMATION AND SERVICES
Antalya's **Tourism Office** (Çumhurriyet Cad., 0242/241-1747, 8 A.M.–7 P.M.) is located less than 300 meters west of Kaleiçi, right before Anafartalar Caddesi, on the sea side of the street. Fliers, maps, and brochures are available at this location; the same information can also be found at larger travel agencies and hotels around the harbor. For an exhaustive Internet resource about Antalya and its districts, log onto **Antalya Guide** (www.antalyaguide.org); the website has up-to-the-minute information about weather and happenings around town.

For more details about the area and some light reading, head to **Owl Bookshop** (Akarçeşme Sok. 21, Kaleici, 0242/243-5718, 10 A.M.–10 P.M.). Run by an English-speaking Turk, the shop has new and used English books, which can be bartered for the ones you read on the flight to Turkey.

Banks, ATMs and currency exchange booths are located on Kazım Özalp Caddesi and Ismet Paşa Caddesi, on either side of Antalya's Bazaar, just north of Cumhuriyet Caddesi. The main **PTT office** (Anafartlar Cad. 9, 0242/243-4575) is located 200 meters west of the tourism office.

GETTING THERE
By Air
Antalya Havalimanı (Antalya International Airport, 0242/330-3030, www.aytport.com) continues to expand to accommodate the increasing international traffic pouring in year-round. To put it into perspective, in 2007, the year the second international terminal opened,

the arrivals totaled 15 million. In the first quarter of 2009, arrivals had already surpassed the nine-million mark, promising a record-breaking year despite the gripping global recession. With more than 200 flights arriving daily during the summer, finding a connection from anywhere on the continent is a breeze. National carriers **Turkish Airlines** (toll free 444-0849, www.thy.com), **Pegasus** (toll free 444-0737, www.flypgs.com), and **Sun Express** (toll free 444-0797, www.sunexpress.com.tr) provide international flights to and from Antalya daily. While international carrier British Airways and British charter Thomas Cook fly directly from Gatwick, and Swiss Air does so from Zurich.

The competition is just as tight for the domestic routes, with five of the main Turkish carriers providing about three dozens flights daily: **THY** (toll free 444-0849, www.thy.com), **Pegasus** (444-0737, www.flypgs.com), **AtlasJet** (toll free 444-3387, www.atlasjet.com), **Onurair** (toll free 444-6687, www.onurair.com), and **SunExpress** (toll free 444-0797, www.sunexpress.com) all compete for fares, with the latter typically offering the best deal.

Antalya's airport is located 12 kilometers from the city center. Turkish Airlines' **Havaş Shuttles** (toll free 444-0487, www.havas.com, 10TL) runs a half-hourly service from the airport's three terminals 24 hours a day. Destined for its terminal at the *otogar* (bus station), four kilometers northwest of Kaleiçi, the shuttle winds along Konyaaltı Caddesi to the town center. The only hotel it stops at is the Sheraton; if you didn't book there, then a taxi from *Merkez* (center) is just about the only way to get to your final destination. For the return to the airport, the only way to board one of these shuttles is to head to THY's ticketing office (Cumhuriyet Cad. 91, 0242/243-4383); the service departs hourly for the airport. Alternatively, taxi fares run about 2.5TL per kilometer, so expect to pay somewhere around 30TL for the same ride.

CAR RENTAL

The airport has a dozen rental concessions, most of which are located in the domestic terminal. If you're coming from abroad, it's a good idea to pass the international terminal's agencies and head straight for Terminal 2 (Domestic). There you'll find a broader selection of agencies and greater availability of vehicles at such locations as **Avis** (0242/330-3073), **Hertz** (0242/330-3465), and **National** (0242/330-3316).

By Bus

With flight prices starting as low as 65TL, traveling cross-country by bus for about the same rate doesn't make much sense. Figure in travel time of, say, 12 hours from Istanbul to Antalya, as opposed to less than an hour by plane, and you'll end up wasting a lot of time. Nonetheless, Antalya is still a huge hub for bus companies; at last count there were more than 150 companies serving regional, cross-country, and international routes.

The largest providers serving Antlaya are **Varan, Ulusöy,** and **Kamil Koç,** just to name a few. Ticket prices vary slightly between companies, here are the rough estimates: Istanbul (710km, 11hr, 66TL); Izmir (550km, 7hr, 47TL), Ankara (555km, 7hr, 43TL), and Göreme (Cappadocia, 490km, 12hr, 40TL).

Bus travel is just about the only means of getting around the region inexpensively. Minibuses depart west for Fethiye (222km, 4hr, 23TL) and Kaş (185km, 4hr, 15TL) or, east towards Mavagat (75km, 1hr, 19TL) and Alanya (135km, 2.5hr, 24TL).

Antalya's *Yeni Garaj* (bus station) is a massive dual terminal situated just four kilometers northwest on the Antalya-Burdur Highway. A *dolmuş* (communal taxi, every 30min, 1.75TL) drives a sinuous route from the *Yeni Garaj* to the center of town, a four-kilometer-trip that takes about 45 minutes. A taxi makes a lot more sense, particularly if you're toting bags. It may cost upwards of 20TL during rush hour. An additional 50 percent is added to regular fares between the hours of midnight and 6 A.M.

GETTING AROUND

You're in luck if your base is Kaleiçi; you'll be able to walk to most of its historical sites within 15 minutes. For destinations just outside this historic district, a very convenient **tramway** service (1TL) stops at 14 locations along its coastal and inland itinerary. Starting west at the Antalya Museum, just a few hundred meters from the entrance to Konyaaltı's Beach Park, it winds its way inland along Cumhuriyet Caddesi, stopping at Kale Kapısı, and continuing southeast along Atatürk Caddesi.

Antalya's center is grid-locked from morning to night. Commuting by car or taxi is not a good idea. Clogged one-way streets make it horrendous for those not used to the center. Even transiting the two kilometers west from Kaleiçi to Konyaaltı may prove faster—and much cheaper—by foot (20min) than by car or taxi. But if you're planning to fully experience the entire district, then renting a vehicle becomes a must. Major companies run offices at Antalya's airport, with most branches available at the domestic terminal. **Avis** (Fevzi Çakmak Cad. 30, 0242/248-1772, www.avis.com.tr) and **Budget** (Fevzi Çakmak Cad. 27, 0242/243-3006, www.budget.com.tr) have offices in town.

CAPPADOCIA AND CENTRAL ANATOLIA

Much of Central Anatolia remains a secret to foreigners, perhaps with the exception of the Turkish capital of Ankara and Cappadocia's fairy chimneys—the phallic-looking monuments of soft-volcanic ash carved by nature's whimsical gales. This region lies on a steppe, by definition a large area of flat unforested grassland in the world's eastern hemisphere. But shake any notion of windswept wastelands. In fact, this humongous, elevated plain, roughly 1,000 feet above ground, ensconced between Turkey's two lofty mountain ranges, the Pontic Alps to the north and the Taurus Mountains to the south, is anything but bland.

There's history that still remains buried deep in the earth's layers. Suffice it to say that this strategic corridor, stuck between the East and the West, was the center of trade routes for eons. First, the Assyrians were lured by the wealth of ancient Anatolians some 20 centuries before the birth of Jesus. Then marched in the proud Persians, the stoic Greeks, the rowdy Romans, and the Selçuk emirates; each group left behind its cultural stamp. Places like neolithic Hattusa, patrician Cappadocia, and Selçukian Konya are imprinted with the trails of the ancients. While Atatürk's famed capital, Ankara, is a perfect mix of the old, found in its pre-Hittite Citadel district, and the new, seen in its spectacular mid-20th century edifices, hailing the not-so-old Turkish Republic and its founder. So while Cappadocia's spectacular lunar landscape still remains central Anatolia's pearl, the rest of the region sure gives it a run for its money.

COURTESY OF REPUBLIC OF TURKEY CULTURE AND TOURISM MINISTRY

HIGHLIGHTS

(Göreme Acık Hava Müzesi (Göreme Open-Air Museum): Explore this immense outdoor park's collection of no less than 10 rock-hewn churches and their remarkably well-preserved frescoes (page 340).

(Ürgüp: Experience Cappadocia's rich wine history and five-star cave accommodations (page 352).

(Ihlara Vadısı (Ihlara Valley): More than 100 rock-carved churches await discovery in this valley along the banks of the magnificently lush Ihlara Valle Melendez River (page 357).

(Underground Cities: Probe underground at **Derinkuyu** and **Kaymaklı,** two subterranean cities that date back to the Hittites (page 359).

((Mevlâna Müzesi (Mevlâna Museum): Pay your respect to the legendary Sufi mystic and poet Rumî by visiting the visually stunning 13th-century mausoleum built in his honor (page 361).

(Anıtkabir (Atatürk Mausoleum): Join the legions of Turks who visit the massive mausoleum in the heart of Ankara, built to commemmorate Mustafa Kemal Atatürk (page 373).

(Anadolu Medeniyetleri Müzesi (Museum of Anatolian Civilizations): Take a walk through Anatolia's past, where a parade of civilizations unfurls, from cave-dwell-

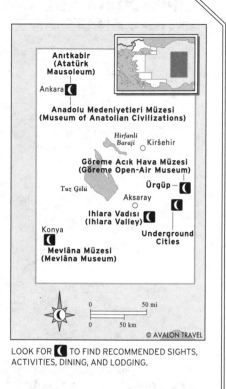

LOOK FOR **(** TO FIND RECOMMENDED SIGHTS, ACTIVITIES, DINING, AND LODGING.

ing relics, through Paleolithic cult statues, all the way to the Greeks, Romans, Selçuks, and Ottomans (page 374).

PLANNING YOUR TIME

A decent exploration of Cappadocia requires three days. If you're tacking on Konya and Ankara to the mix, double it to six. The best time to visit arid Central Anatolia is in the off-season, during spring and autumn. The summer months are torrid—upwards of 40°C—in the unshaded valley of fairy chimneys, making the going tough and, quite frankly, too exhausting. Cappadocia's cave hotels are the recommended

accommodations in the area, since these remain cool throughout the day. There's also a significant difference between day and night temperatures, sometimes as much as 20°C. The winters in the Anatolian heartland are freezing, with an average temp of -2°C December–February. The plus side, however, is that the already magical scenery gets even better with a thick cover (20–30cm) of snow. This climate in no way hinders sightseeing. As a matter

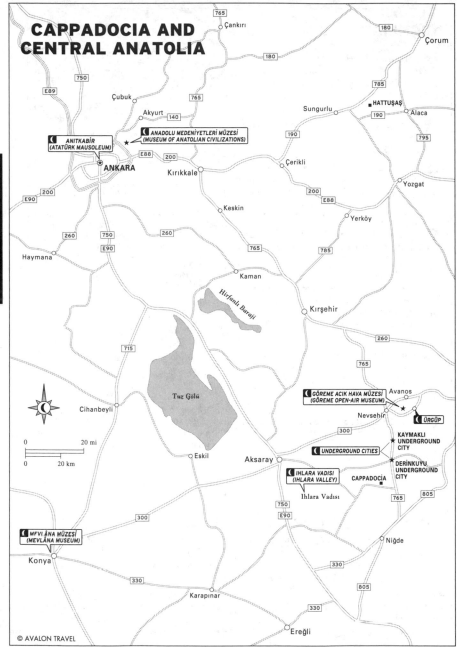

© AVALON TRAVEL

COURTESY OF REPUBLIC OF TURKEY CULTURE AND TOURISM MINISTRY

CAPPADOCIA

A light snowfall highlights the stunning geography of Cappadocia.

of fact, it gets even better when nearby Mt. Erciyes (Argeus) opens up to skiers and plenty of heart-pounding ATV touring opportunities. Cappadocia is best seen in spring, March–May, when the temperature hovers at 15°C. Spring also hails the eventual, light downpour, which rarely lasts for more than two hours and seldom impedes popular hot-air balloon rides. The months of September–November, which see the highest tourist traffic, are generally warm (around 20°C).

The Konya Rumî celebrations in mid-December are a great time to plan a journey here, but you'll have to brave the cooler temperatures of winter and perhaps even the occasional snowfall if you plan to visit Cappadocia and Ankara. Ankara is best visited on Independence Day, August 30, when the capital throws a big celebration. But no matter how and when you tour Central Anatolia, even for a couple of days in the broiling heat of summer, one thing's for sure: The lunar landscape of Cappadocia, the sheer amount of history and culture, and the region's exclusive haunts will absolutely stun you.

SIX DAYS IN CENTRAL ANATOLIA

This suggested itinerary covers a packed two days in Ankara, 24 hours in Konya, and three days in Cappadocia. This can be done in less time by covering only the crucial landmarks, but you'll have to bypass the side trips that flavor the region. And since there are no direct flights to these destinations, a car rental is necessary from the second day in Ankara through the end of the trip. This itinerary can also be achieved by bus, but you'll lose precious time on the road.

DAY 1

Arrive early at Ankara's Esenboğa Airport head directly to your hotel. A good budget option is the Dedeman Ankara, but if you want to splurge, book the Swissôtel. After checking in and dropping off your luggage, walk up to the historic **Hisar** – Ankara's oldest, pastoral citadel – to explore its 1,400-year-old fortifications and gate, Roman ruins, and cobblestone streets lined with Ottoman mansions (now swanky restaurants).

From the main gate, go to neighboring **Çengelhan.** This 16th-century caravansary was renovated into a museum dedicated to the history of transportation, communications, and industry. Take a couple of hours to walk through the interesting and interactive exhibits (perfect for little ones). Have lunch at Divan Çengelhan Brasserie, built inside an impressive *han* (inn); this will add the final exclamation point to a history-filled morning.

In the afternoon visit the spectacular **Museum of Anatolian Civilizations,** one of the world's finest repositories of archaeological artifacts, chronicling Anatolia's peoples, from cavemen to the modern Turks. Plan an early dinner in the hip brasseries of Kavaklıdere.

DAY 2

Begin bright and early with an hour-long visit to **Anıtkabir** to pay your respect to Atatürk, as is expected of visiting dignitaries. Then pick up your pre-booked rental car and make a beeline to **Hattuşaş** with the hope of completing the 2.5-hour drive by lunchtime.

Drive straight to Hattuşaş Restaurant, where a meal of grilled meats will fill you up for a 3-4-hour exploration of one of western Asia's oldest settlements. After walking through Hittite territory – hopefully without forgetting to check out the stunning nearby shrine of Yazılıkaya, return to the capital city's Citadel district to dine among diplomats and politicians at Kale Washington.

DAY 3

Drive the 2.5-3 hours south along the modern D715 highway to Konya. Once there, head straight for the **Mevlâna Museum and Shrine** in central Konya to pay homage to the ancient Sufi poet Rumî.

Just beyond the museum's immaculately landscaped grounds, have lunch at Mevlevi Sofrası, where regional lamb dishes reign. Sated, head to the lofty Alladdin Tepesi for some killer views and to tour the Selçuk **Alaeddin Camii.**

Next, make the two-hour road trip to Cappadocia, or you can always return to town to check out a whirling dervish show.

DAY 4

Drive to the area's famed rock-hewn caves by heading to the monastery complex and open air museum of the **Zelve Valley.** The fairy chimneys here are actually more striking than those of Göreme, so make sure not to bypass this stop in favor of a direct jaunt to the hotel. After climbing through Zelve's tufa sanctuaries, head to the **Göreme Open-Air Museum,** where sublime frescoes in early Christian churches and Byzantine basilicas await.

Afterwards, the hungry can feast over delectable Ottoman and regional fare at A'laturca Restaurant. Check out the modern village of Göreme, with its antique pottery and rug shops across from the central *otogar.*

Load up on water bottles, before heading to **Üçhisar**'s fortress for a climb to the top to experience the best view, bar-none, of the valley.

DAY 5

The second day in Cappadocia entails either the insanely popular hot-air balloon ride, which needs to be booked way in advance, or a horseback ride through the valley. The balloon ride returns by noon, leaving the rest of the day to trek by car, foot, bike, or horseback through the valley. No matter how you plan to get around, make sure to visit **Avanos,** one of the ceramic capitals of Turkey. Lying just above the Kızılırmak (Red River), the red silt that gave the river its name has been shaped by regional potters since the time of the Hittites.

Stop for dinner at Bizim Ev and dig into an unreal version of the sumptuous regional dish of *mantı* (tiny raviolis stuffed with lamb and doused in a garlicky yogurt sauce and spiced butter), before going the five kilometers east to the 12th-century **Sarıhan** caravansary for the nightly whirling dervish show at 9 P.M.

DAY 6

The last day takes you 100 kilometers southwest of Nevşehir to the Ihlara Valley's honeycombed Byzantine churches and underground

the St. Barbara Chapel in Cappadocia's Göreme Open-Air Museum

villages. You'll enter **Ihlara Vadısı,** a 14-kilometer-long gorge, through the village of Ihlara and exit through Belirsima, where a lunch of kiln-baked kebabs can be enjoyed.

Sated, drive northeast to the **underground cities of Derinkuyu, and Kaymaklı.** You'll climb up and down steep and narrow stairways to visit entire towns built by the ancients to hide from the invaders of the day. Return to Üçhisar for dinner under the stars at the impossibly appealing Ziggy's Shoppe and Café, a cave restaurant. Either drop off the car locally and fly straight to Istanbul, or drive the 276 kilometers (3-3.5 hours) to Ankara to return the vehicle.

© TOM DEMPSEY

Cappadocia

Ask any regional government official as to the actual geographical boundaries of Cappadocia and they'll be hard-pressed for an answer. The fact is that no one knows with certainty its eastern and western confines. We just know that it's bordered to the south by the Taurus Mountains and to the north by the Pontic Alps.

Its history is not as nebulous, however, and it's generally agreed that the Hittites were the first to settle the land of fairy chimneys some time in the 18th century B.C. Following their downfall, the Persians entered the scene and named the region *Katpatuka,* which translates into the *Land of Beautiful Horses.* And these fine, wild equines were indeed famed throughout Classical Antiquity, and often gifted to Assyrian and Persian imperials. Smack in the middle of Anatolia, this are was an important stop on the Silk Road. Power struggles oscillated between history's eastern and western empires, and, finally, between Arab warlords before the advent of the Selçuks and Ottomans. These incessant power shifts often involved the annihilation of locals, so it's no wonder that the natives found a way to carve the soft tufa landscape to create underground hideaways to escape hostile invaders. Persecution continued, but this time in the name of religion. Deemed heretics before Christianity became a bona fide religion, early Christians enlarged these boltholes into complex monastic cities that continued to be used during the somewhat peaceful Byzantine Era. These once again reverted to hideaways during the Arab invasions of the 7th century. Conversely, Cappadocian Christians were free to worship under Muslim rulers.

The region's importance waned over time; its rock-hewn treasures long forgotten. That is, until the arrival of French explorer Paul Lucas at the turn of the 18th century. Lucas thrust this geological marvel back into scientific annals. Cappadocia's natural boundaries may still perplex cartographers, much like its unique architecture baffles the millions of tourists who arrive on this steppe annually.

The effects of wind and erosion on Cappadocia's volcanic tuff make for a visually baffling backdrop.

GÖREME

Göreme is the original heart of Cappadocia, ground-zero of an expansive slice of volcanic geography whose massive popularity has yet to falter on its sky-high path. It's a small village with a high density of tall fairy chimneys and rock-carved houses, some of which are still inhabited by locals. Small churches pop up unexpectedly on the 1.5-kilometer stroll from Göreme to its main attraction: the Göreme Open-Air Museum. But what makes Göreme truly unique is its hiking potential along sometimes steep trails that boast some of Cappadocia's most stunning landscape.

To be entirely truthful, the town has earned a bad rap for its cheap back-packer crowds and their infringement on its countryfied atmosphere. But this is only a myth based on comparisons with the nearby luxury hotel-packed hamlets of Ürgüp and Üçhisar. As a matter of

GÖREME

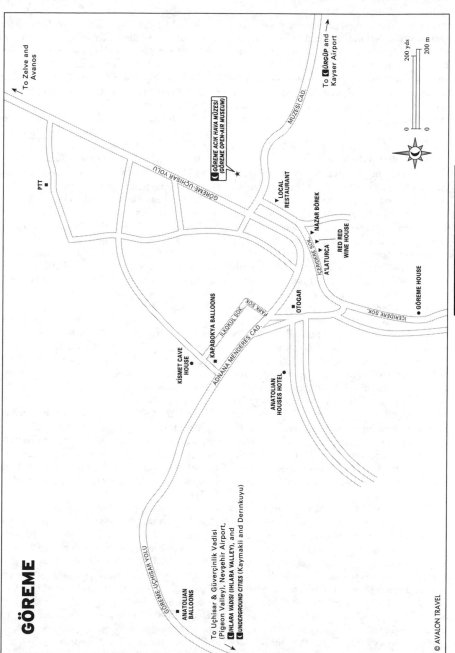

To Zelve and Avanos

PTT

GÖREME UÇHISAR YOLU

GÖREME AÇIK HAVA MÜZESI
(GÖREME OPEN-AIR MUSEUM)

MÜZESI CAD.

To ÜRGÜP and Kayser Airport

LOCAL RESTAURANT

NAZAR BÖREK

RED RED WINE HOUSE

CERIDERE SOK.

ALATURCA

GÖREME HOUSE

CERIDERE SOK.

KAPADOKYA BALLOONS

ILKOKUL SOK.

PARK SOK.

OTOGAR

KISMET CAVE HOUSE

ADNANA MENDERES CAD.

ANATOLIAN HOUSES HOTEL

GÖREME UÇHISAR YOLU

ANATOLIAN BALLOONS

To Uçhisar & Güverçinlik Vadisi (Pigeon Valley), Nevşehir Airport, IHLARA VADISI (IHLARA VALLEY), and UNDERGROUND CITIES (Kaymaklı and Derinkuyu)

200 yds
200 m

fact, a new breed of restaurateurs and hoteliers is slowly refurbishing its dated cafés into chic diners and lackluster pensions into appealing B&Bs. This renewed vitality not only provides an ideal—and much less expensive—base from which to poke around the geological labyrinth, but also provides that elusive authentic village atmosphere.

◖ Göreme Acık Hava Müzesi (Göreme Open-Air Museum)

Cappadocia's most noted site is the Göreme Acık Hava Müzesi (1.5km from the town center, 0347/271-2167, 8 A.M.–7 P.M. daily, until 5 P.M. in winter, admission 12TL, parking 2TL). While you'll find plenty of troglodyte habitations, much more striking are the collections of frescoed cave-churches. These were carved out of soft volcanic rock and embellished with light-reflecting frescoes by orthodox Christian monks during the Middle Ages.

Eastern Monasticism, the practice of eastern religious education, was partly founded and diffused to the West by St. Basil the Great, the Byzantine bishop of Caesarea (modern Kayseri), as a result of his unwillingness to adhere to the Church's growing matrerialism. St. Basil, a recognized theological philosopher of his time, prescribed a communal life for men that emphasized poverty, piety, liturgical prayer, and manual labor as a means to fully devote one's life to spirituality. His message so reverberated with early Christians that they opted for the pious life in the honeycombed rock houses of Cappadocia over the hedonistic life in the coastal cities.

The Open-Air Museum is a testament to the piety of these early Christians, with a collection of 30 churches and chapels, as well as rectories, abodes, and religious schools; the build ings form a roughly circular monastic complex carved entirely in the tufa. From the diamond-shaped roundabout just past the entry, look for the clearly signposted path that'll take you through the park and the sights in a counter-clockwise direction.

The frescoes throughout are stunning, despite minor damage caused by the elements. A few were badly marred during the Byzantine Iconoclastic decade during the 8th century A.D., while most of the eyes were gouged by Muslim locals out of fear of the evil eye.

The first church on the itinerary is **St. Basil's Church.** Its rectangular nave boasts niches and a trio of arches. The narthex, or lobby, features tombs in the floor, which have been interestingly left open. This church's north wall bears frescoes depicting Saints George, Basil, and Theodore. Check out the three Maltese crosses on the nave's vault; these are thought to represent the Trinity.

Dating from the mid-11th century, **Elmali Kilise** (Apple Church) owes its fruity name to the red orb clenched by St. Michael the Archangel in a fresco near the entrance. In reality, the saint is known for holding a red shield, not an apple. The frescoes inside depict saints, bishops, and martyrs. Another boasts a Last Supper scene with a large fish—the codified symbol of Jesus.

Just behind the rock that houses the Apple Church lies the **Azize Barbara Kilisesi** (St. Barbara Chapel). It has a cruciform layout, with three apses embellished with simple red figures on white plaster. On one wall a giant locust representing evil faces two crosses on another wall.

The **Yılan Kilisesi** (Snake Church) is named for the dragon St. George is seen slaying on one of its murals. Beyond the barrel-vaulted narthex, renditions of the hermit St. Onophrius, fronted by a sapling, can be seen, along with one depicting the church's founder, St. Basil, holding a book in one hand.

The most impressive of all rock-carved churches is **Karanlik Kilise** (Dark Church). An extra fee of 10TL is required to view its frescoes, which are the best-preserved specimens in Cappadocia. Thanks to its hidden location, this church escaped the wrath of Iconoclasts, leaving intact most of its murals. Also, the lack of direct sunlight in the inner halls kept the vivid frescoes from discoloration. Visitors rarely go through the trouble of paying the extra fee, so the Dark Church is not crowded.

Azize Katarina Kilisesi (St. Catherine

Chapel) rises from a Greek-cross floor plan, with a domed central crossing and barrel-vaulted transepts. Interesting for its number of graves onsite, the chapel has four beneath the floor and two situated in niches. The St. Catherine Chapel, built by a donor named Anna, dates back to the 11th century.

Çarıklı Kilise (Church with Sandals) earns its moniker for the pair of footprints situated in the narthex, right under the Ascension scene. Inaugurated in the early 13th century, this space is relatively new compared to the others and its frescoes are much more elaborate. Look for the inner fresco of Jesus the Pantocrator with the busts of angels, right below the central dome.

Tokalı Kilisesi (Church with Clasp) is just outside the museum; a ticket to the museum grants visitors access. Of all the rock churches in Cappadocia, Tokalı boasts the greatest amount and most detailed paintings narrating the life of Christ. The complex sprawls over four chambers, with a barrel-vaulted, single-nave Old Church (10th century) leading the way to the rectangular New Church. There are three vertical sections painted in bands of vivid green, reds, and indigo depicting St. Basil and other saints.

The paintings and decorations represent a flowering of a uniquely Cappadocian artistic style, while the Byzantine architectural features of the churches, like arches, columns, and capitals, are interesting in that not one of them is necessary structurally.

Excursions from Göreme
AVANOS

The ubiquitous pottery displayed throughout Cappadocia comes from Avanos, a town located eight kilometers northeast of Göreme's center. Like its peers throughout the region, the city of Avanos (pop. 15,900) is entirely hewn from indigenous volcanic rock; but unlike the others, it is the only one to lie along the banks of the Kızılırmak (Red River), Turkey's longest river. This waterway, which incidentally separates Avanos from the rest of Cappadocia, gets its name from the red sediment that tints

its waters. It is from this abundant silt that ceramic clay is formed to produce the pottery so unique to Cappadocia.

The practice dates back to well before the Hittites, according to their 3,500-year-old records. Once so predominant, the craft was practiced by each *Avanoslu:* children collected silt and dads manned pottery wheels in a workshop attached to every household. Today, Avanos thrives on clay products for commercial sale, like roof tiles and building blocks. But there's also a variety of household pottery, such as the traditional Avanos handled urn, for sale in some three dozen shops around town. Some shopkeepers invite onlookers to try molding at the kick wheel, a tactic that always guarantees a sale. Be prepared to haggle for that perfect piece; once acquired, have it shipped rather than risk damaging it on the long way home. Aside from terra cotta pottery, alabaster trinkets and hand-woven rugs are also produced locally.

To get a piece of the "terra cotta pie," or just

Avanos has had a bustling ceramics trade for over 3,500 years.

COURTESY OF REPUBLIC OF TURKEY CULTURE AND TOURISM MINISTRY

CAPPADOCIA

learn the tricks of Avanos's master potter, head to **Chez Galip** (www.chezgalip.com). Galip Bey's seven-room, bric-a-brac of an atelier confirms the fact that he's nuts for the art of pottery. And nuts for hair; he's collected thousands of strands of hair from customers over his five-decade-long career. His extensive collection of unique and popular-themed fine ceramics leaves clients hard-pressed to choose.

While plenty of inns and boutiques thrive in this burg heavily patronized by French tourists, I don't recommend spending the night in Avanos. It's just too far off center and a bit chintzy for my taste; three hours of prodding around the tiny streets should suffice. If you've come this far, there's no reason not to continue another five kilometers southeast to reach the spectacular **Sarıhan** (Yellow Caravansary). This 13th-century caravansary is the last—and perhaps the finest in Turkey—built by the Selçuks. Its finely-ornamented architecture adheres to tradition, except that its mosque appears over the gateway and not in the courtyard. *Semas* (whirling dervish ceremonies) are organized here nightly, at 9 P.M. in winter and 9:30 P.M. in summer. Tickets for the hour-long rite and transportation are €25 and can be secured through most travel agencies in the region.

Sticking out like a sore thumb in Avanos's bleak culinary front is **Bizim Ev** (Baklacı Sok. 1, Avanos, 0384/511-5525, www.bizim-ev.com, 9 A.M.–midnight daily, 9TL), which sprawls out over four dining rooms, two of which are caves. There is a surprisingly elegant atmosphere, with smart white linens and shining glassware, juxtaposed over the ever-present Cappadocian stone architecture and barrel-vaulted ceilings. Try the delectable house special of *bostan kebabı*, which incorporates tender chunks of chicken, turkey, or beef stewed with mushrooms, eggplant, onions, and peppers, crowned with cheese, and presented in a clay pot. The rest of the menu highlights Turkish veggies cooked in olive oil, grilled meats and fish, as well as a good variety of Anatolian desserts.

To reach Avanos, situated at the northeastern tip of Cappadocia, some 12 kilometers north of Ürgüp, hop on the regional minibuses that drive the road between Nevşehir and Avanos hourly, 8 A.M.–5 P.M. (winter) and until 7 P.M. (summer). A taxi costs about 15TL from Göreme and 20TL from Ürgüp, and as much as double that amount from Nevşehir.

ZELVE

The community of Zelve, like hundreds of others in Western Anatolia, was once inhabited by Greeks. In fact, it's one of the earliest—and longest—monastic settlements in Anatolia. The rock-hewn monasteries and their adobes remain; the Anatolian Greeks, who inhabited this once-devout settlement, were removed during the population exchange—more like compulsory repatriation—to mainland Greece and its isles to be replaced by Ionian and Thracian Turks during 1922.

Zelve Open-Air Museum (0384/411-2525, 8 A.M.–5 P.M. daily, until 7 P.M. in summer, 5TL) is located on the outskirts of the village of Aktepe. Zelve was emptied of its inhabitants in 1952, when the dwellings of this UNESCO-protected national park were deemed unsafe. The population was moved to Aktepe. Today, Zelve's eerily-empty monasteries, some built as early as the 9th century A.D., were built by Christians who fled in droves from the Persian and Arab invasions of the Middle Ages.

While it's true that the chapels and monasteries may not be as striking as those in the Göreme Open-Air Museum, the land is dramatic, to say the least. These hills are peppered with housing of all types. Walking though the cliffs to explore this historic park's nooks and crannies is a feat for the fit. To guard from invaders, the settlement was built like a veritable maze: foothold-only entrances, long concealed tunnels, and underground footpaths. A full exploration of Zelve takes about four hours and requires an adept climbing and hiking ability. Since navigating the settlement and terrain can be tricky, with some of the structures crumbling, it's best to join one of the outstanding tours organized by **Argeus Travel** (Istiklal Cad., 7 Ürgüp, 0384/341-4688, www.argeus. com.tr) or **Turkish Heritage Travel** (Yavuz

Sok. 1, Göreme, 0384/271-2687, www.goreme. com). Travel agencies throughout Cappadocia provide similar group or personal guided tours of the area that typically include the village of Avanos.

The Zelve Open-Air Museum is located on the way to Avanos, some five kilometers northeast of Göreme. There's no regular public transportation to the Zelve Valley, so you either have to rent a vehicle, hire a taxi, or join a tour.

PAŞA BAĞLARI

Formerly known as Monk Valley, **Paşa Bağları** (Pasha's Vineyard, 2km northeast of Göreme, adjacent to Zelve; admission included with the purchase of a Zelve ticket) proudly owns the most striking earth pillars, smack in the middle of a vineyard. Some of these tufa formations—there are hundreds of them—dramatically split into smaller cones midway through. Incidentally, these chimneys are dubbed mushrooms. Some of history's most self-effacing Christian stylites (hermits) built their monastic communities in these sometimes double- or triple-headed chimneys.

Such was the Hermitage of Simeon monks, who, during the 5th and 6th centuries A.D., mirrored the ascetic existence of their patron, Saint Simeon. A tri-level chapel, which was dug out of a 15-meter-tall cone, was dedicated to Simeon. Inside, the rooms boast five-meter-high ceilings and walls adorned with frescoes depicting his life, and the self-imposed hardships he withstood while in Aleppo.

Tours

Unless you want to poke around the entire valley hit-and-miss style, you'll need to join a tour. I highly recommend this, not only because it's the most fool-proof way to hit all the sites within a relatively short period of time, but also, and this is especially true in Cappadocia, because there's just such a wide variety of activities and destinations. Picking the right tour, depending on your preferences, is easy enough; selecting a tour company, however, seems to be a major bone of contention.

Horror stories abound from the fly-by-nights who overcharge (sometimes as much as four times regular rates); are just unknowledgeable of the area; or, don't provide the necessary insurance on active outings like those that involve ATVs, horses, and even hot-air balloons. The regular full-day guided tour of the valley, with lunch and wine-tasting, is about €30; mountain bike tours €30; Jeep tours €75; and ATV tours €90; and the wildly sought-after hot-air balloon tour €160–250.

Specializing in Cappadocia, **Argeus Travel** (Istiklal Cad., 7 Ürgüp, 0384/341-4688, www. argeus.com.tr) is rated high among its mostly North American clientele as one of the best comprehensive travel agents in the region and for its recommended traditional or adventure tours of Konya, Istanbul, Antalya, the Ionian Country, and the Lycian Triangle. Be it a day tour or a two-week jaunt throughout the Turkish mainland, owner Aydın Ayhan Güney's staff of local, English-speaking travel veterans not only show you the sites, but proudly unearth the valley's—or whichever destination's—little-known secrets. Their day-long itineraries through Cappadocia (there are four to choose from) start at 9:30 A.M. with a hotel pick up and aim to tour only the sites included in the schedule. No shopping excursions here, just a pause for the delicious à la carte lunch, included in the tour (from US$110 per person; US$80 for groups of six or more, with all entrance fees included). Their attention to detail, much smaller group sizes—up to eight people per local tour—unwavering customer service, and overall professionalism has earned them recommendations by Turkish Airlines and TURSAB (the national association of travel agents).

Turkish Heritage Travel (Yavuz Sok. 1, Göreme, 0384/271-2687, www.goreme. com) is Göreme's tour leader and a specialist in adventure tours. Based at the Kelebek Hotel, and run by Cappadocian native Ali Yavuz, Heritage runs a dozen custom or outdoors tours, all led by highly experienced, friendly guides. They're multilingual and are locals with an endless knowledge of the area's lesser-known attractions. Heritage is great for budget travelers since their full-day outings (9:30 A.M.–5:30 P.M.) start at around €30 per person; professional guidance, entrance fees, lunch (some tours include wine-tasting), and transportation are included in the cost. Hiking (from €20), horseback riding (from €40), ATV (€35–90), Jeep (€90), professional photo safari (€100), and the must-do hot-air balloon (€150–260) tours are all offered.

Turkish Cuisine Tours (www.turkishcuisinetours.com), a spin-off of Turkish Heritage Travel, offers guests instruction in three of Turkey's most favorite dishes: hand-rolled *manti* (meat-stuffed mini raviolis) and *sarma* (grape leaves) and Turkish coffee. Guides pick up guests at their hotel at 9:30 A.M. en route for a cave house whose kitchen is staffed by local women eager to share their secrets to perfectly-rolled, herby, rice-filled vine leaves. The eight-hour lesson includes lunch and hotel drop-off ($50 per person).

Another highly-respected touring outfit for international travelers, **Cappadocia Tours** (Istiklal Cad. 19/9, Ürgüp, 0384/341-7485, www.cappadociatours.com) is owned by Cappadocia, Turkey, and Middle-East travel specialist Süleyman Çakır. Off-the-beaten-track day trips are this outfit's specialty, like Cappadocia's Underground City and Traditional Villages tour, which allows momentary immersion in a rural life that hasn't changed in centuries in traditional Greek or early Turkish settlements. Their full-day Ihlara Walking tour is also highly recommended. All tours depart at 9:30 A.M. and return at 5 P.M.; the cost of €50 (cash only) includes all entrance fees to museums, English-speaking guide, lunch, transportation, and taxes.

Sports and Recreation

If there ever was a region that's best explored through non-traditional methods, Cappadocia has to be it. Gliding over the tufas in a balloon at sunrise, hiking the myriad of easy-to-medium trails above and through caves, and safariing through the entire valley, camera in hand, guarantees a highly memorable trip.

HOT-AIR BALLOONS

The first must-do that comes to mind is the hour-long hot-air balloon ride, in which on average 20 passengers take off in a gigantic wicker basket. This air-bound enclosure, dangling from cables attached to colorful balloons shoots up above a majestic fantasyland of fairy chimneys and the stark moonscape to reach a maximum height of 1,500 feet, all the while heading east towards the rising sun. In season, a veritable aerial ballet can be seen over the region as balloons by the dozens bop along the prevailing winds in their colorful splendor.

Heading out at 4:30 A.M. isn't fun, but that is easily forgotten once off the ground, gliding high above the tree tops. Early morning take-offs are best since the prevailing winds during this time are typically calm and cool, ensuring gentle and stable flights, mild landings, and maximum lifting capacity. This time of the day is also ideal for photography, as the sunrise enhances the valley's earthy colors. Here is what to expect from a traditional flight: hotel pick-up and drop-off, snacks before flight, ceremonial champagne, and certificate after landing. Reservations are required prior to flights; in season, book at least a week in advance either by phone or online.

Since Lars and Kaili Kidner pioneered the hot-air balloon flight in Cappadocia in 1980, and the resulting success of their company, **Kapadokya Balloons** (Nevşehir, 0384/271-2442, www.kapadokyaballoons.com, €250/person), a slew of contenders have hit the scene. Needless to say, Kapadokya is the most experienced, with a staff of a half-dozen highly-trained pilots. Flights are year-round, providing the weather is clement.

Anatolian Balloons (Adnan Menderes Cad. 34, Göreme, 0384/271-2300, www.anatolianballoons.com, 60- to 75-min flight, €160–230) claims to be the largest hot-air balloon company in the world and one of Göreme's oldest. To reach and maintain this title, Anatolian Balloons has extended its operations to Antalya and meticulously maintains and upgrades its equipment and insurance. Through commercial agreements with automotive and beverage companies, among others, to place company logos on its balloons, Anatolian undercuts most of its competitors' prices. Ditto for **Göreme Balloons** (Koyunyolu mevkii 1, Ürgüp, 0384/341-5662, www.goremeballoons.com; 60min/90min flight, €160/€230), who not only enjoys wide acclaim from passengers but also from balloonists who use their commercial balloon indoor and outdoor storage, maintenance, and refueling facility. To gauge just how popular this outing is, Göreme Balloons experienced more than a 300 percent increase in passengers from 2004 to 2008. They also fly year-round.

HIKING

Even for those not fond of sneakers, Cappadocia's pastel-colored dunes are a dream of a stroll. And with scenery like that, I've yet to find a hike that wasn't up to par. By day or night, particularly guided by a full moon, through summer's floral splendor or wintery snows, meditative types revel at the sites around the region's near dozen diminutive valleys, which bear names like **Vine Valley** (Bağlıdere), **Honey Valley** (Ballıdere), **Rose Valley** (Güllüdere), **Pigeon Valley** (Güvercinlik), and **Sword Valley.** They're relatively easy trails that take anywhere from one to three hours to complete. If you're lucky enough to have the entire day earmarked for outdoor exploration, you can easily piggyback a couple hikes since most trails are interconnected.

To guarantee a safe and comfortable outing, wear sports shoes and a light coat to stay warm when the sun goes down and the temperature suddenly dips. Carting water and a picnic in a backpack is also a good idea for those who wish to break bread under the ever-present Cappadocian apricot tree. A word to the wise: Directional markings lead to trails, but there's no waymarkers while en route. One of the most striking outings is the Red Valley (Kizilçukur Vadisi), which extends for about four kilometers, from Çavuşin to the entrance of Ortahisar, along varied rock formations and rock-cut chapels. Pigeon Valley is another easy four-kilometer stroll through magnificent dovecotes;

it starts on the south side of the fortress of Uçhisar and ends at Göreme village. Avid hikers love the challenge of the White Valley hike, which extends about six kilometers from Uçhisar to Çavuşin village, and winds through local gardens and Love Valley—named for its more phallic-looking fairy chimneys.

For a no-hassle hiking experience through Cappadocia's popular trails and secret caves and churches, Göreme native Mehmet Güngör, of **Walking Mehmet** (0384/271-2064 or 0532/382-2069, www.walkingmehmet.com, year-round, €40), is both an exhaustive resource of local knowledge and a die-hard walker; he's clocked in some 1,350 kilometers guiding 8,000 guests on foot-tours of the area. For a fee of €50, he'll take out a group for 3–5 hours from Roma Café in Göreme, his very own café.

HORSEBACK RIDING

Cappadocia inherits its name from the Persian *Katpatuka,* meaning "land of fine horses." Equines were bred in the valley from as early as the mid-second millenium B.C. Cappadocia was renowned throughout the Classical period for its stables and honoring area landlords with horses became a tradition. So why not carry on the custom of the ancients and pay tribute to the valley's horses by riding one of them through their indigenous backyard of verdant dales and wide dust bowls?

The **Akhal-Teke Horse Riding Center** (Camikebir Mah. Kadi Sok. 1, Avanos, 0384/511-5171, www.akhal-tekehorsecenter.com) has 30 horses available for riders of all types, from beginner to experienced, as well as an onsite restaurant. Week-long, all-inclusive, horse-riding holidays cost US$875–1300 depending on group size; nights are spent in local homes or in tents. Hour-long rides wind along the banks of the red-hued Kızılımak River (€20); the two-hour excursion takes to the mountains and the natural spring (€35); the four-hour tour takes riders through the Cappadocian outback, the Zelve Open-Air Museum, Paşabağı, and the village of Çavusin (€70); the all-day ride starts in Üçhisar, looping through Göreme and Çavusin (€95).

GOLF

Cross-golfing, and since June 2009 cross-country golfing, aims to be hotter in the region than hot-air ballooning. And with tourists spending fortunes on activities, golf is on its way to being a worthy rival. In this variation of the widely popular sport, there are no putters. Bright orange and red golf balls are aimed at nets, not holes; fairy chimneys and cones are the obstacles, replacing traditional sandbanks or water features. Caddies, always at the ready to offer a refreshing drink, ride atop donkeys with the traditional Anatolian, colorful woolen harnesses, not four-wheel carts. Ömer Tosun, the creator of the venture and owner of the Museum Hotel and Matiana Travel, also added a unique clubhouse nested on a rocky peak with wow-inducing views of the valleys. Needless to say, **Cross Golf Cappadocia** (Orta Mah. Uzundere Sok. 7, Göreme, 0384/271-2351, www.crossgolfcappadocia.com.tr) is the only golfing "green" that is UNESCO-protected. Nine "net" games cost €150 per person, €120 for groups of 6–10, or as low as €80 for larger groups, and include taxes, soft drinks, and hotel transfers. Club rentals and caddie service are €20.

Accommodations

More than 80 percent of Göreme's hotels offer inexpensive accommodations; the remaining 20 percent boast some of the most exclusive hideouts of the entire valley. But however romantic the idea of staying in a cave might be, their lack of light and ventilation can be problematic. The remedy is to book accommodations outfitted with a window.

The town's top-end B&B is **(Anatolian Houses Hotel** (Gaferli Mahallesi, 0384/271-2463, www.anatolianhouses.com.tr, €250–550). Tucked at the end of a winding lane, the inconspicuous gate of this surreal property opens to a stunning outdoor/indoor pool. Upper-level rooms, "carved" into the soft bedrock, are lit either by skylights or clever floodlit recesses. Also deserving a nod are the collections of antiques displayed in niches throughout the property. Luxury amenities include a sauna and hammam, as well as a gastronome's restaurant.

Göreme's best bargain accommodations, hands-down, are those offered at the **Kelebek Hotel** (Yavuz Sok. 1, 0384/271-2531, www.kelebekhotel.com, €45–120). This family-owned B&B offers one of the largest assortments of accommodations, from cave and traditional arched rooms to a duo of private fairy chimneys. The spacious suites are bright—a rarity in the region—and appointed with locally handmade furniture and fabrics; the en suite baths boast marble walls and unique hammam basins, power showers, and hot tubs. Kelebek's forte lies in providing a full service experience, with a variety of tours, a restaurant that specializes in Cappadocian cuisine, and the recently-added pool and fully-staffed Turkish bath.

Kismet Cave House (Kagnı Yolu 9, 0384/271-2416, www.kismetcavehouse.com, breakfast included, €56–135) is owned by Faruk Keleş. If awards were given to best hotel host, then this charming eight-room B&B's owner would snatch the prize. He personally arranges airport transfers from Nevşehir (free for stays of three nights or more), shows guests "his" Cappadocia, and goes out of his way to ensure guest satisfaction. Inside, good-size accommodations ooze with the warmth of richly colored, hand-woven bedcovers from Afghanistan and antique furniture. Down comforters, hot tubs in the en suite baths, and fireplaces are additional luxuries.

Göreme House (Eselli Mah. 47, 0384/271-2060, www.goremehouse.com, from €65) is charming beyond description. Its postcard-worthy courtyard is in the center of a two-storied, historic mansion, once owned by a regional elder. Inside, 13 arched rooms exude Anatolian allure, with dark wood and colorful linens, and feature particularly roomy en suite baths. Satellite TVs, mini bars, and a tea and coffee service station round out the amenities. Another plus is the top-floor balcony that offers stunning views of the Cappadocian moonscape. This property lies on the supremely quiet outskirts of Göreme—a bonus that turns out to be a bane when the muezzin at the mosque seemingly next door calls the faithful at 5 A.M. But ear plugs should remedy that situation.

Food

Göreme has less restaurants than hotels. Rather odd, considering that nourishment—at least for me—rates higher than sleep. Its diners, however, tend to offer excellent menus based on a delectable Cappadocian cuisine that's rich in meat and veggies bred and grown from the extremely fertile land. Two local dishes that must be experienced are *Kayseri Mantısı* (tiny lamb- or beef-filled raviolis drenched in a garlicky yogurt sauce) and platters of beer-battered Anatolian cheeses fried to a crisp. You'll also find smidgens of continental food—pastas, grilled steaks, and chicken dishes—throughout to please those who have overdosed on Anatolian fare. And let's not forget the succulent local vintages and grapes, as well as the fruits of the fêted local potato and caper crops. Reservations are a must at the

COURTESY OF REPUBLIC OF TURKEY CULTURE AND TOURISM MINISTRY

The dish to try while in Central Anatolia is *mantı* – tiny ground beef-filled ravioli, served with garlic yogurt and a pepper-butter sauce.

better eateries during the summer and major Turkish holidays.

The ◖ **Orient Restaurant** (located at the entrance of Göreme, 0384/271-2346, www. orientrestaurant.net, 8 A.M.–midnight daily, 15–30TL) is the oldest and finest dining establishment in Göreme. It's earned its lofty reputation by consistently serving sumptuous fare, the best of which has to be the rack of lamb—bar none the best I've had in my two decades in Turkey. The pleasant meal starts with warm homemade rolls, served with olives and roasted tomatoes. Not a devout carnivore? Then pass on the delectable minute steak and dive into the less meaty *karnıyarık* (Chinese eggplants stuffed with a herby ground lamb filling and baked to absolute tenderness). The fine wine list features local Melen vintages—rated among the best in Turkey—along with French and other Turkish selections. Orient is cozy yet elegant, offering an ideal spot for a quick breakfast or lunch, or the perfect destination for a candlelit tête-à-tête on their outdoor patio.

◖ **A'laturca** (0384/271-2882, www.ala-turca.com.tr, 10 A.M.–11 P.M. daily, 20TL) opened in 2003 to provide a more refined dining environment than what was already onsite. Since then, it's not only been attracting tourists, but locals as well. Why? The answer is just simple yet delicious meals, served in a dressed-up country atmosphere that's purely Anatolian, with loads of hand-woven fabrics and rich furnishings. A lawn outside, outfitted with beanbag seating, doubles as a groovy night hangout, made even more alluring with a fully-stocked bar. New and super convenient are their catering facilities, which make takeout and hotel deliveries as easy as going online or picking up the phone.

Nazar Börek (Müze Yolu, 0384/271-2183) is renowned for being inexpensive and truly deserves its reputation for the freshest, homemade savory and sweet pastries. Try the Turkish herby-cheesy pancake of *gözleme* (Turkish pastry), also served with meat or spinach, or choose from a collection of fila dough–baked savories known as *böreks*. A couple of meaty dishes were added to the menu, including a yummy daily soup special. It's small, but you can't miss it; look for the busiest patio on the main street.

Local Restaurant (Müze Yolu 38, 0384/271-2629, 30TL) is incorrigibly charming and inexpensive to boot. Pink-tableclothed tables imbue an air of fine-dining, and what you get is just that—great fare straight from the farm. Enjoy meze followed by a meat entrée with wine right on the outside patio, watching the foot traffic along the intersection of Göreme's main street and the road to Göreme Valley.

Once sated, head out for a nightcap at **Red Red Wine House** (Müze Yolu). This tiny bar, renovated from a stable with a low-arched ceiling, I'm told, welcomed Carlos Santana. At least that's according to Red's loquacious owner, Muharrem Serinsu, who never tires of informing his clientele of his bar's lengthy history. It's a locals' favorite that remains open year-round, even during the coldest winter evenings. And, as the name of the place suggests, there's an extensive collection of local wines, beer, and rakı (Turkish aperitif) flowing here.

Information and Services

Göreme is a bustling burg, centered around its otogar (bus station) and a bazaar right behind it. Most of its shops, hotels, and restaurants are located in the streets flowing from this center; its main site, Göreme Open-Air Museum, is one kilometer to the east.

Most businesses honor credit cards; a trio of ATMs are located in town around the otogar and one at **Deniz Bank** around Müze Caddesi, the only financial institution in town. The **PTT office** (Bilal Eroğlu Cad. 1/A, Göreme, 0384/271-2900) provides telecommunications services as well as money exchange.

Göreme's Tourism Society, **Göreme Turizm Derneği** (located in the otogar, 0384/271-1111, www.goreme.org, 8:30 A.M.–7 P.M. Mon.–Fri.), was created by area merchants and hoteliers. The service aims to point traffic to the Society's benefactors and not to offer the traditional services and information expected from a traditional tourist office. Infinitely more useful will be the information, maps, and tips provided by

locally-bred hotel concierges or B&B owners, or the helpful staff at the many travel agencies located inside the otogar.

Getting There

The most inexpensive flights to Cappadocia—6–12 a day depending on the season—arrive through **Kayseri Erkilet International Airport** (0352/337-5494), about 75 kilometers, or an hour's travel time, from Göreme. Local travel agencies, or shuttles waiting for passengers heading to all the major destinations within Cappadocia, provide airport transfers for a fee of around €10; some hotels run a similar shuttle service that may even be complimentary, depending on the length of stay. The decade-old **Nevşehir Airport** is closer, but the 35-minute transfer compounded with the hard-to-find tickets (there's only one Turkish Airlines flight per day) is too much of a hassle to make it worthwhile. **Turkish Airlines** runs at least five flights a day from Istanbul's Atatürk Airport to Kayseri for as low as 69TL; total travel time from Istanbul is about 70 minutes.

Larger bus companies serving Göreme drop passengers a couple of blocks from the otogar (bus station on Uzundere Cad.), and provide minibus service the rest of the way. Once there, a taxi ride is the quickest way to the hotel. The regional dolmuş (communal taxi) winds its way every hour from the Ürgüp otogar to Zelve, Avanos, Göreme, Üçhisar, and then back to its point of origin. **Metro Tourism** (toll free 444-3455, www.metroturizm.com.tr) runs the most domestic lines in Turkey. From Istanbul, the fare costs 50TL and the trip lasts about 10.5 hours.

Getting Around

Primarily flat and rather small in size, Göreme lends is an ideal walking town. ATVs, scooters, and bicycles are available through the travel agencies around the otogar (bus station). **Heritage Travel** (Aydinli Mah. Yavuz Sok. 1, Göreme, 0384/271-2687, www.goreme.com) rents scooters and bicycles for a two-hour period for about $15; car rentals are $65 per day.

ÜÇHISAR

Traveling eastward from Cappadocia's capital town of Nevşehir, an eerie landscape unfolds in a series of dust bowls pocked by soft yellow and pink dunes, cones, and fairy chimneys. The mighty **Erciyes Dağı**—the once-active volcano responsible for this mad lunar landscape—stands guard with a 3,920-meter height that extends well into the cloud cover. This fantastic scenery alerts the traveler that arrival in Üçhisar is imminent.

It's a slumbering troglodyte village that

CAPPADOCIAN WINE HERITAGE

Wine was the favored drink of Anatolian royalty 4,000 years ago. The Hittites may even have launched the practice of drinking this holy firewater during early pagan rites performed in Asia Minor. In fact, a rock-relief of 8th-century B.C. Tabalian King Warpalawas and Storm God Tarhunzasin holding grapes and toasting each other with goblets, found in the village of Ivriz, attests to rampant inebriation during the Bronze Age. This sacred fermented grape-extraction in time led to the ancient Greek myth of Dionysus, the god of wine, mystic ecstasy, and orgiastic excess.

Cappadocia's famed vineyards, which were first tilled and tended by the Hittites, are extremely productive. That is due to the region's fertile volcanic soil and its pliable rock, where ideal underground cellars were easily carved out. Outside of the Kavaklidere, Turasan, and Kocabağ wineries, viniculture is more of a household undertaking than an industrial one. The rather small size of vineyards (40-70 acres) and arable terrain wedged between Cappadocia's profusion of hills may have a lot to do with this.

Wine production is a family affair. The peasants here still apply the skills handed down through the generations. The traditional Öküzgözü (Ox-Eye) grapes intended to be used at home are either eaten whole (55 percent of production); boiled down to produce the grape syrup, pekmez (35 percent); or are earmarked for wine production (about 4 percent). The tilling, replanting, and reaping of the vines are left to the older folks, who can often be seen in a horse carriage on the way to their crop early in the morning. Collection starts early in the A.M., early September–beginning of October. The first fruits are black and intended to be consumed whole or used for their juice. The end of the season signals the white grape harvest, with the finest specimen, "Emir," being picked from mid-September on.

The Vitis Vinifera grape genus is used to produce wine. While more than 1,500 grape varieties are cultivated in Turkey, only 1,100 kinds are domestic, with 12 of foreign origin. In Cappadocia, both well-known grapes, like Cabernet Sauvignon, Merlot, and Chardonnay, are being cultivated alongside unbelievably subtle and unique domestic genera, like Narince, Emir, and Öküzgözü by all three major wine makers, who produce a collective 18 million liters of wine annually. But **Kocabağ** (www.kocabag.com), an internationally-heralded boutique winery located in Üçhisar, is the preferred producer according to oenological pundits. Their Öküzgözü vintage – a genus originating from the eastern Turkish city of Elaziğ – is applauded for being simple, crisp, and fresh, with tart overtones.

Other grapes worth sampling are Boğazkere. Also from Elaziğ, this red grape genus imbues its rich hue into its juice, which when fermented produces a well-structured wine with strong dried fruit and fig overtones. Kalecik Karası is another dark indigenous grape, known for its deep ruby hue. Its rich, well-balanced structure provides a strong aroma of red fruit, vanillin, and cocoa, with a finish that's light, fresh, and elegant. Among the white grape varieties, the Narince genus is a soft, gently spicy peer of other fair varietals cultivated solely in Turkey, like Sültaniye and Emir.

Eons before wine was considered a luxurious European import, indigenous Anatolians were imbibing the stuff. And a trip to Cappadocia wouldn't be complete without a foray into the viticulture heritage fermented down from the ancients.

stretches out from the base of a fortress. Here, you'll discover an old-time Cappadocian village with plenty of lore. It's by far more peaceful than the bustle of Göreme and more down-to-earth than posh Ürgüp, and a preferred destination for southwestern European tourists.

Üçhisar's stone fort is the highest volcanic outcrop in Cappadocia; its apex is a favorite panoramic destination for tourists, particularly at sunset. **Üçhisar Kale** (Üçhisar Castle, 0384/219-2618, 8 A.M.–7 P.M. daily, 3TL) is bisected below ground by artificially-made tunnels and its faces are pocked by hand-crafted lookout windows. Ottomans in the 15th and 16th centuries, as well as the Selçuks before them, utilized these natural formations, in conjunction with similar chimneys in Ortahısar, Ürgüp, Tıgraz, and Çavuşin, both as observation and defense points. Guards used a system of mirrors to warn against invaders, sending messages in relay all the way to the empire's capital of Istanbul.

The valley that encircles Üçhisar reveals the geological tale of the entire Cappadocian valley, with rock formations in various states of disintegration. Upon closer inspection, rocky channels can be explored along the valley's ridge; and, below, the Güvercinlik Vadisi (Pigeon Valley) reveals myriad pigeon houses, all painted white to lure the winged animals and their precious droppings.

Accommodations

Plenty of hotels can be found in Üçhisar, but what used to be the mainstay—pensions—have trickled down to just three. Accommodations run the gamut from just bed-and-breakfasts to superb cave hotels that would make Istanbul's five star establishments blush from embarrassment. Now what you pay is not necessarily what you get. And, let's face it, a trip to Cappadocia is not meant to be spent in a room fit for a sultan, but rather meant to be spent outside visiting the entire valley. Go for a clean

COURTESY CF MUSEUM HOTEL

Luxurious cave hotels, like the Museum Hotel, offer their guests amenities that exceed even five-star standards.

bed and shower and the prospect of an organic farm morning meal included in the price of the room.

UNDER €50

Les Terraces d'Üçhisar (Eski Göreme Yolu, Üçhisar, 0384/219-2792, www.terrassespension.com, s. €33, d. €39, suite €80) is not only economical, but the rooms and service onsite don't reflect the price. There are a total of 14 rooms, 7 of which are caves, with some featuring barrel-vaulted ceilings. At the price of €80, the suite, with its series of adjoining rooms that can accommodate up to five, is a steal, particularly for families. Expect traditional pension accommodations with ample tile or stone flooring. Les Terraces' owner Marcos Venon is an avid cook, whose ability shines in the four-course meal (€10) he concocts nightly; he's also a consummate hiker, who leads hotel guests (for free!) on morning hikes to Göreme. The breakfasts are generous, with make-your-own-omelet options and an opportunity to practice your French. The drawbacks here are no central heating, just additional blankets and electrical heaters, and no daily maid service.

La Maison du Rêve (Tekeli Mahalle 17, Üçhisar, 0384/219-2199, www.lamaisondureve.com, s. €20, d. €35, tr. €45) crowns Üçhisar's hill. As such, it is privy to some of the most beautiful views in Cappadocia; an ideal place to watch the sun set or rise, as it colors the valley below in shades of orange and purple. Locally born and bred owner Metin Gökgöz runs the 30-room pension; son Fatih, a professionally-trained cook, runs the kitchen and the terraced diner. The property spreads out over three floors of no-frill rooms with en suite baths. The Gökgözes also rent out scooters and bicycles, as well as personally lead walking tours of the valley.

€50-100

Villa Cappadocia (Kaya Başı Sok. 18, Üçhisar, 0384/219-3133, www.villacappadocia.com, s. €60, d. €70–80) boasts 12 roomy units in a property that graces the panoramic flank of the fortress hill and boasts spectacular views of Pigeon Valley. Each room comes with ample, fully-equipped modern baths that affirm the hotel's recent arrival on the Üçhisar hospitality scene. Outside, a collection of terraces— rooftop, along the walkways, and adjoining the property—are ideal spots to chat of the day's conquests over a glass of steaming hot tea. Utterly romantic, the onsite cellar restaurant (10–25TL) features a haute-cuisine take on local dishes.

Taşkonaklar (Gedik Sok. 8, Uçhisar, 0384/219-3001, www.taskonaklar.com, d. from €60, suites from €130) sits amidst a meticulously-renovated property that used to house a baptistery, praying rooms, and grape-crushing rooms. The liturgical silence of yesteryear still reigns supreme along the walkways and grassy terraces that lead to the hotel's 14 spacious rooms. Of the inexpensive doubles—there's three to choose from—the Upper Console Room (104) boasts 25 square meters of barrel-vaulted living space, a fireplace, and an ample slate bath with shower enclosure. But spring for the diminutive Middle Grapevine Suite, which is 10 square meters larger and boasts its own terrace overlooking wide grass-topped dunes. Amenities include restaurant, bar, free Wi-Fi, and private parking.

OVER €100

The ❰ Museum Hotel (Tekeli mah. 1, 0384/219-2220, www.museum-hotel.com, d. €120–225, suites €235–2,200) defies classification. If the sultans of yesteryear had built palaces in this ethereal valley, this property and its lavish interiors would definitely have fit their artistic requirements. Immediately striking is the collection of textiles and antiques from Museum owner Ömer Tosun's private collection, amassed during his previous life as a fine carpet and fabric dealer. True to its name, the property's wow-inducing pieces can be found in the 12 double rooms, in the way of 6th-century Roman jars, antique brass beds, and antique Selçuk and Ottoman rugs throughout. The Khayyam's Suite, named for the 11th-century mathematician, poet, and astrologer, boasts his quatrain poems and books, all rarities, and an awe-inspiring bath, replete with a fine marble whirlpool tub and shower combo overlooking a scenic window that overlooks a gigantic Cappadocian boulder. Amenities fit for royalty include: award-winning Lil'a restaurant onsite; adjoining cross-golf driving range; a state-of-the-art wellness center and mosaic-tiled infinity pool; and a rooftop panoramic terrace.

Les Maisons de Cappadoce (Belediye Meydani 6, Üçhisar, 0384/219-2813, www.cappadoce.com; studio €140–190, houses €240–980) is the brainchild of French architect Jacques Avizou, who labored lovingly for 15 years to renovate some 17 self-catering houses and studios among the crumbling rock formations of the lofty Üçhisar community. Ideal for the independent traveler wanting nothing but utter relaxation or a romantic getaway, each house (sleeps up to seven) and studio (sleeps up to four) boasts colorful Anatolian *kilims* (Turkish carpets), furniture hand-crafted by local artisans, and fine earthenware made in Avanos. But the true feat here is in the way the sculpted portals, stone fireplace, vaulted ceiling, and panoramic terrace of each residence blends magically with the surreal beauty of the surrounding landscape.

Food

A dressy alternative, touting a European/Turkish menu among the string of small and inexpensive cafés lining the city center, (**Elai** (Eski Göreme Cad., Üçhisar, 0384/219-3181, www.elairestaurant.com, 18–25TL) replaced a nicotine-tarnished *çayhane* (Anatolian teahouse). Today, it's a swanky restaurant boasting high wood-beamed ceilings and a cavernous interior. A terrace, shaped of the local stone, offers an ideal place to watch the setting sun over a glass of Emir-Sultaniye, Kavaklidere's finest vintage. The food leans heavily towards classical Anatolian cuisine and the imperial cuisine of Istanbul. But the style is kept unabashedly simple, such as in the melt-in-your mouth carpaccio of sea bass marinated in *rakı* (Turkish aperitif) and spicy *mercimek köftesi* (red lentil meatball). European classics featured on the menu include rack of lamb and duck à l'orange.

Incidentally, the restaurant's name is short for Kubilay, the owner of one of Cappadoccia's best fine-dining establishments.

WINERY

A little secret, even to the most devout Turkish oenophiles: There exists a wine house in Üçhisar by the name of **Kocabağ** (0384/219-2979, www.kocabag.com), where wine lovers throughout Cappadocia come for the finest of local wines. Internationally recognized for a superior Turkish wine and ranking in the top five in the country, Kocabağ only produces 300,000 liters per year, making their annual vintages highly sought-after. The house bottles three floral and fruity whites, and four intensely fruity reds. But the most distinctive wine is the Kalecik Karası, an elegant, lightly spicy claret with rich pomegranate, plum, and cherry undertones.

Getting There and Around

A **minibus** service organized by the Nevşehir municipality drives the road between the Nevşehir and Üçhisar. A regional *dolmuş* (communal taxi) originating from the Ürgüp *otogar* (bus station) winds its way to Zelve, Avanos, Göreme, and Üçhisar. The route requires at least 90 minutes; it's a great way to crisscross the whole valley, except during the summer when high temperatures make riding in a vehicle sans air-conditioning less than palatable.

(ÜRGÜP

Just six kilometers east of Göreme, Ürgüp is the center of Cappadocia; though, not its capital. The distinction is akin to 17-million-strong Istanbul and Ankara, with the former strangely playing second fiddle to the latter's status of capital. Nevertheless, Ürgüp is an ideal base for a Cappadocian holiday, with its superior hotels, fine-dining restaurants, lively nightlife, and high-class shopping—albeit more costly than anywhere in the valley. Tourist arrivals are soaring and revenues are sky-rockcting from all the luxury tourism. Ürgüp has become a bastion of hospitality, with every crumbling shack reborn as a five-star cave hotel or fancy restaurant. This area is now defined by Turkey's finest hoteliers and restaurateurs as one of the country's major resorts. This growth, for the time being, has yet to whitewash the town of its indigenous Anatolian culture.

Sights
TEMENNI HILL
To discover the lay of the land, one must scale to its loftiest point for a view. In Ürgüp, nothing could be more satisfying. The town's highest point, Temenni Hill (a.k.a. Wishing Hill), is a 1,100-meter-high column that towers over the town's piazza. This natural rock formation, which was reinforced by a layer of concrete after a massive rockfall in 2006, is home to two interesting monuments. The first is the *türbe* (tomb) of Selçuk Sultan Kiliç Arslan IV, who dodged an assassination attempt through lethal poisoning in Aksaray only to be caught and killed by his executioners in Ürgüp in 1266. His remains were later relocated to the Selçuk Empire's capital of Konya, and a shrine was built onsite in 1863 to commemorate his passing. Close by, an Ottoman-era library features a neat teahouse, but also an interesting photo collection detailing Ürgüp and offering one of the few snapshots taken of the now-demolished 19th-century Church of Saint John.

Temenni Hill lies just outside the town center on the way to Göreme. It can be accessed by hiking up the street fronting İnkilip Primary School.

SARICA KILISESI (SARICA CHURCH)
The restoration of the Sarıca Kilisesi (in Kepez Valley), one of the oldest Byzantine Churches in Cappadocia (mid-6th century A.D.), was undertaken by the private company Vasco Travel in 1997, at a time when the Turkish government supplied little or no funds to revamp historical sites throughout the region. For centuries this basilica was not only damaged by erosion, but also by the accumulation of pigeon poop, during its spell as an aviary coop and bird dropping–storage facility. So when work began in

2001, crews had to scour layers of aviary dung to reach the artistic bounty that lay beneath, on the walls and floors of this magnificent rock-carved basilica. What they found were elaborate mosaic floorings and frescoes upon vast ochre walls. The architectural details are even more striking, such as intricately carved niches, arched vaults, and lofty columns. What originally seemed like another far-fetched undertaking paid off a decade later when project manager Cengiz Kabaoğlu received the 2007 European Union Architectural Heritage.

The Sarıca Church is located on the way to Mustafapaşa, three kilometers south of Ürgüp.

AYVALI
An example of Anatolia at its purest is the village of Ayvalı, which remains untouched by modernism; in fact, it hasn't changed in centuries. The village (pop. 1,200) is bisected by the Içeridere River. This brook crosses the valley to Golgoli Tepe (Golgoli Mountain), a seven-kilometer-hike through ghostly caves and rock-hewn chapels. Moseying along town, you will find a multi-domed Selçuk mosque (always open outside of prayer times) and a myriad of caves and houses hewn out of Cappadocian stone.

The **Aravan Evi** (0384/354-5838, www.aravanevi.com, s. €45, d. €60) is a charming boutique hotel that boasts five highly affordable standard/double rooms, irresistible local dishes on its veranda restaurant, and a big helping of Turkish hospitality that's made this hotel one of the most popular in the region. The Yazgans' donkeys, three of them, are available for trips about pastoral Ayvalı. Be prepared to drink *çay* (tea) in the home of every villager you cross on your way; that's just how friendly the folks in this tiny valley are.

Ayvalı is located 10 kilometers south of Ürgüp.

Winery
Turasan Şarapevi (Turasan Winery, Çimenli Mevkii, Ürgüp, 0384/341-4961, www.turasan.com, 9 A.M.–sunset daily, winery tour 10TL, tour and wine-tasting 18TL) is the region's

and one of the country's largest wine producers. Founded in 1943, Turasan is based in Cappadocia and features a collection of the area's finest vintages and oenological heritage tours. Cappadocia's history has been bound to winemaking for millennia; Turasan offers a good overview of this accumulated culture in an affordable trio of table wines: Turasan Red, White, and Rose. Come for a wine tasting at sunset to enjoy a vintage and spectacular view.

Nightlife

Aptly filling in Cappadocia's lack of upscale nighttime haunts, **Sirios Bar & Wine House Prokopi** (Istiklal Cad. 20, Ürgüp, 0384/341-8878, www.siriosbarprokopi.com, 11:30 A.M.–5 A.M. daily in summer, from 5:30 P.M.–3 A.M. in winter) is an after-hour destination for a little of everything: It's a wine bar, attached to a 16th-century winemaking "cave"; an art gallery, featuring work from a different artist each month; and, a live jazz space on weekends. The venue spreads over two floors in a classical Greek abode. The upper story's monastic-like, candlelit "wine" chamber feels either romantic or spooky; I've yet to decide! But downstairs, the front room is dominated by a central bar, lined with dark wood stools leading into a barrel-vaulted cave filled with tables for two. It's just perfect for couples!

Accommodations
UNDER €150

4ODA Cave House (Esbelli Sok. 46, Ürgüp, 0384/341-6080, www.4oda.com, s. €95–110, d. $130–145) launched the restoration in the Esbelli quarter. This troglodyte adobe boasts five delightful rooms—one more than the name of the property suggests—that highlight the Greek heritage of the region, like stone carving and grape presses. The sitting room, whose ceiling is arguably the loftiest in Cappadocia, is both homey, with a personal collection of classic books and musical instruments ready to be strummed, and artsy, with reproductions of paintings by European master painters. But 4ODA is known for its big complimentary breakfast—more like a brunch—that includes a huge variety of cheeses, homemade jams, and pastries. Elvan Ozbay, who manages the property with husband Sermet, was the host for "The Cities of the Underworld," shown on the History Channel.

The decade-old **Gamirasu Cave Hotel** (Ayvali Köyü, Ürgüp, 0384/354-5815, www.gamirasu.com, d. €80–100, deluxe and suites from €100) is located a bit off-center in the quiet and-yet-untouched village of Ayvalı. Run by a local family, the Gamirasu is situated on the edge of a creek in one of Cappadocia's more verdant valleys. Boasting its very own rose garden, the grounds and interiors of the hotel remain as quiet and sequestered as the monastic cells built in the caves adjoining the property more than 1,000 years ago—an ambience that's definitely a bonus come tourist season. Some 18 rooms in seven exquisitely restored houses offer a true Anatolian experience with handmade cotton mattresses and colorful *kilims* (Turkish carpets)—also available in the barrel-vaulted monk cells—and a veritable farm-fresh feast for the complimentary breakfast. Horseback riding around the village is also complimentary, and so is a host of other agricultural or culinary activities, like winemaking and bread-making in stone ovens, or drying and harvesting fruits, in and around the village.

€150 AND UP

Elkep Evi (Eski Turban Oteli Arkasi 26 Ürgüp, 0384/341-6000. www.elkepevi.com, s. €65–110, d. €90–140) boasts larger rooms than its competitors in Ürgüp's Cavern Hill. Other bonuses include private terraces carved right into the cliff, each boasting dramatic views of Cappadocia's moonscape. Historically, this hotel was built right atop a network of Agarthan caves, so named for a monastic culture which withdrew into a labyrinth of subterranean cities to maintain their secrets and were ruled by the mysterious Inner World government. All legends aside, Elkep boasts three types of singles and doubles, ranging from the simple to those featuring either whirlpool tubs or Turkish baths. A complimentary, full breakfast spread, which includes herb- and cheese-filled pancakes known as *gözlemes* and freshly-squeezed orange juice, can be enjoyed from the Hilltop Garden, which boasts unparalleled views of Ürgüp.

◖ Serinn House (Esbelli Sok. 6, Ürgüp, 0384/341-6076, www.serinnhouse.com, closed Nov.–Mar., d. €150) is a study in opposites. Some five cool, monochromatic caves are sparsely furnished in luxurious, colorful modern pieces, creating spaces that are utterly relaxing yet grown up enough for today's discerning traveler. Colorful shag rugs highlight black lacquer four-poster beds and metal chairs that come in lip-smacking colors. This is the Flinstones meets the Guggenheim. The property is really "cool"—that's also what the hotel's name translates into—among a backdrop of properties that highlight the area's Anatolian heritage. Owner Eren Serpen, a hospitality maven who engaged the fine talents of renowned Istanbul architect Rifat Ergör and chef Defne Koryürek to craft this gem of a hotel deep in Cappadocia's hotel row.

One of the priciest hotels in the area, **Yunak Evelri** (Yunak Mahallesi, Ürgüp, 0384/341-6920, www.yunak.com, s. €150, d. €170) was the brainchild of exclusive restaurateur Yusuf Gürürgöz. After rocking the Istanbul dining scene to its core, Görürgöz reaped the profits and purchased six crumbling caves along one of Ürgüp's bluffs that date back to the 5th century A.D. The long rebirthing process gave rise to Yunak, an environmentally-friendly, fairy-tale hotel that boasts 30 rooms. Accommodations include exotic, upscale caves and multi-chamber suites. The hotel emanates a romantic Mediterranean vibe, with hardwood parquets flooring, creamy whitewashed walls, antique *kilims* (Turkish carpets), and locally-handcrafted furniture and ceramics. Personal touches, added in by Gürürgöz himself, include decadent fabrics throughout (from bed linens to thick white cotton bathrobes) and white marble baths that boast Swedish jet and stream showers and whirlpool tubs, as well as

electronic gadgets like the latest in audio systems. Each room comes with its own balcony or shared patios.

Sacred House (B. Hayrettin Sok. 25, Ürgüp, 0384/341-7102, www.sacred-house. com, d. €140–190) is a diminutive cave tucked in the quieter back streets of Ürgüp. A dozen thematically-inspired rooms, among which are three ridiculously-luxurious suites, are jammed-packed with antiques and one-of-a-kind pieces that evoke medieval nobility. The Sultan's Armory, for instance, boasts religious icons and a free-standing, stone-crafted fireplace in niches. And, oh, its bathroom, outfitted with the finest of white marble, is nothing short of a genius in design and über-sumptuousness. Sacred House's creator, Turan Gülcüolğü, combines his training in top-hotel management and previous experience at Kapadokya Lodge Country Club, with his Armenian wife Talin Sarıoğlu's more down-to-earth touches. Turan is totally hands-on in the kitchen, whose delectable menu reflects Ottoman, Cappadocian, Armenian, and Greek influences, as well as the eons-old Byzantine fare of Kapama—bite-size lamb chunks simmerred with vegetables served with vermicelli-peppered pilaf. While there are more sensible places to stay in town, Sacred House is one-in-a-thousand and by far one of the best all-around hotels featured in this tome.

Food

The place to beat in Ürgüp, **◖ Şömine Café & Restaurant** (Cumhuriyet Meydanı 9, Ürgüp, 0384/341-8442, www.sominerestau-rant.co, 9 A.M.–midnight daily, 12TL) offers alfresco and indoor dining to discriminating diners. As its name suggests (*şömine* is "fireplace" in Turkish), you'll find a large hearth here. This provides the needed warmth during Cappadocia wintry nights. Marble floors and linen-covered tables belie a menu that's actually quite affordable. While the house special of *testi kebab* is highly recommended, my choice remains Şömine's delectable *beğendi kebab*—tender morsels of stewed lamb or beef served over a cheesy eggplant purée. Call ahead for reservations on weekends or during the summer season.

Ziggy's Shoppe & Café (Tevfik Fikret Cad. 24 Ürgüp, 0384/341-7107, 11 A.M.–1:30 A.M. daily, 7–15TL) sprawls over four rock-hewn terraces, strewn with table-and-chair or couch-and–coffee table seating arrangements. The menu is light, with pasta and salad fare and a long, albeit pricey, drink menu (great for sunset aperitifs or an after-hours hangout for grown-ups). Two suggestions to try are the "Endless Joy" Turkish Meze platter (35TL pp) and the innovative fresh fettuccine with Kayseri pastırma. Inside, a collection of fireplaces warms up chilly winter nights.

Another must-do dining destination while in Cappadocia is **Dimrit Café & Restaurant** (Tevfik Fikret Cad. 40, Ürgüp, 0384/341-8585, www.dimrit.com, 9 A.M.–midnight daily, 11TL). Expect an all-out Turkish feast in this renovated stone adobe, set high among one of Ürgüp's loftiest hills. A 2nd-floor terrace boasts chic white tabletops and a 270-degree view of dusty rolling hills, while interior, barrel-vaulted alcoves offer an ideal setting for couples. Although you'll find a similar atmosphere at Şömine, the views here are unbeatable.

Old Greek House (Mustafapaşa, Ürgüp, 0384/353-5141, www.oldgreekhouse.com, 10TL) is a bit of Hollywood in the Cappadocian burbs, with a menu offering an excellent mix of Anatolian and Ottoman dishes. A favorite filming location, this old Greek mansion—featured in the runaway Turkish hit TV series *Asmalı Konak*—was purchased in 1938 for the whopping sum of 10TL by the Öztürk family. A couple of generations later, Süleyman and Fuat Öztürk converted the property into a hotel/restaurant that is widely known for its decadent five-course meal. Recommended dishes include *karnıyarık* (eggplants stuffed with stewed ground lamb), an excellent *mantı* (Turkish ravioli), and *köfte* (meatballs), served with potatoes. While the entirety of the wood-paneled interiors of this two-story classic adobe have been refurbished, the duo of dining rooms located on the 2nd floor still bear the remains of striking frescoes.

Panorama Café & Restaurant (Camii Kebir Sok. 16 Ürgüp, 0534/511-5194, www.panoramacafe.net, 9 A.M.–11 P.M. daily, 8TL) is the destination for an economical yet scrumptious Anatolian meal. Ideal for breakfast, lunch, or dinner, Panorama has earned kudos not only for the "panoramic" views to be had from its lofty position, but also for its homey ambience, delectable *mantı* (Turkish ravioli, slathered in a garlicky yogurt sauce), and the true Turkish hospitality of its owner Ismael Bey.

Information and Services

Ürgüp's **Tourism and Travel Information Office** (Kayseri Cad. 37, 0384/341-4059; 8 A.M.–6 P.M. daily, closed Sun. in winter) is redundant at best since all hotel concierges and owners in the area, as well as travel agents, are better at answering queries, providing maps, or talking about Cappadocia's history from an infinitely more personal point of view.

A couple of small bank offices, area hospital, and a police station can be found along the multitudes of small souvenir shops lining the town's main thoroughfare, Kayseri Caddesi.

Getting Around

Walking around Ürgüp by foot is highly recommended, but be advised that the town's Esbelli neighborhood is situated up a rather steep hill. Scaling it up and down during the heat of summer can be unbearable, so hiring a cab may be the way to go.

You can tour Cappadocia from this location without a tour guide since most of the region's car rental agencies are located in this busy tourist center. Among them, **Europcar** (Istiklal Cad. 10, 0384/341-8855) and **Avis** (Istiklal Cad. 19, 0384/341-2177) offer compact vehicles starting at 90TL per day. Local companies, like **Kapadokya Car Rental** (İstiklal Cad. 2, 0384/341-8838, www.kapadokyarentacar.com), offer lower rates (from 70TL/day for up to 7 days) for vehicles that are typically a year older. **Bicycles, scooters,** and **ATVs** are available to rent from smaller outfitters around town.

◖ IHLARA VADISI (IHLARA VALLEY)

Located about 120 kilometers southwest of Göreme, Ihlara Vadısı (0382/453-7005, 8 A.M.–7 P.M. daily, 5TL) is a dramatic gorge, carved out of the volcanic Cappadocian rock base by the Melendez Stream. The landscape is unparalleled, with greenery that is unique in the region. It is this rare affluence of both water and highly fertile soil that has drawn communities here since the beginning of time.

Ihlara is a testament to piety, with about 105 rock-hewn churches, as well as eerie monasteries, tiny chapels, austere hermit caves, and thousands of troglodyte dwellings, some dating as far back as the 6th century. Today, village life continues along the banks of the Melendez: Goats scurry up its flanks as boys play "street soccer" among the dusty lanes that lead from the stream. Once known as Peristrema, the Ihlara Valley is a 16-kilometer-long canyon whose flanks jut in some spots as high as 100 meters, and that snakes along the contours of the sometimes-rushing stream below. The banks of the Melendez are lush with poplars, neat rows of pistachio trees and vineyards, and populated by a rich wildlife of croaking amphibians, colorful butterflies, and birds.

Hiking through Ihlara Canyon can take as little as two hours or as much as a day. For the shortest tour, enter through **Ihlara Vadisi Turistik Tesisleri** (Ihlara Valley Touristic Facility, Güzelyurt İlçesi Center, AKSARAY, 0382/453-7482, 8 A.M.–6:30 P.M. daily) along the valley's western perimeter, two kilometers north of Ihlara Village. Here you'll find what I call "satan's stairway"—a grueling 360-step descent into Ihlara Valley National Park. It's a rather difficult entry point, but since it's located closest to the sights, it allows for the quickest tour (about three hours if you're in good shape). To avoid scaling back up the stairs, start from the valley below and hike southward towards Ihlara Village, the southernmost point of this national park. This approach should take no more than four hours. For the longest route, but one that's sure to capture all vantage points, troglodyte dwellings, and sanctuaries, take the

3.5-kilometer hike north to Belisirma—the canyon's midpoint—from the village of Ihlara (can take up to six hours).

Sights

For the most part, the churches of the Ihlara Valley are a testament to time and constant erosion. Some date back to the mid-8th century; the frescoes gracing their inner walls, however, were added sometime later, during the 10th and 12th centuries. Interestingly, the churches vary in architecture: Those clustered around Ihlara Village reflect the coptic style utilized throughout Egypt and later Syria, while the churches located in the village of Belisirma are strictly Byzantine.

The **Ağaçaltı Kilisesi** (Church Under the Tree) is the first religious building on the route; it's the cross-vaulted structure hidden behind a mount of rocks on the left side of the stream. Also nicknamed the Church of Daniel for the fresco of the Saint Daniel flanked by two lions on the wall facing the main entrance, this church was actually consecrated to Pantenossa, a religious icon typically depicted in the hands of the Virgin Mary. Modern Orthodox Christians believe that it has the power to cure cancer. The crude, muted-colored frescoes and the geometrical shapes—checks and rosettes—reflect the Eastern coptic style of architecture.

Continuing to the right of the stairway, Ihlara's two other noteworthy churches, **Pürenli Seki Kilisesi** (Church with the Heather Terrace) and the **Kokar Kilisesi,** house additional religious frescoes.

The **Eğritaş Kilisesi** (Church with the Crooked Stone) is located about 500 meters past the old wooden footbridge on the stream's other bank. Considered to be a funerary chapel and the valley's oldest and most ornate church, Eğritaş consists of a vaulted chapel with an apse, and burial chapels below it. The ceiling is covered by a gigantic, gilded Greek cross, with three rows of chiseled frescoes on either side. The Crooked Stone moniker refers to the church's eroded state, not for any faulty construction! Again, this structure reflects

CAPPADOCIA AND CENTRAL ANATOLIA

an Arab influence in its composition and is a prime example of early Eastern Christianity's pre-Iconoclastic art.

Returning to the other bank of the river on the way to Belisirma, the 10th-century **Yilanlı Kilisesi** (Church of the Serpents) receives its name from the fresco showing adders in the act of admonishing four female sinners. The punishment of women who were thought to be the root of temptation and sin was a popular theme in early Christian belief.

Aptly named for the hyacinth in the fields that surround it, the **Sümbüllü Kilisesi** (Hyacinth Church) can be found on the stream's left bank. This two-level structure's facade of pillars and arched niches hewn from the surrounding rock is unique and recalls the ornate tombs made popular by the Lycians. Adjoining the many cells are chapels bearing some relatively unmarred frescoes, including a Byzantine reproduction of the Annunciation.

Three kilometers north of Ihlara and 50 meters away from the river's west bank, the **Kırk Damaltı Kilisesi** (Forty Checkered Church) is also known as the Church of St. George, and is the valley's newest church. The wall paintings are a reflection of the religious and cultural mix present during the structure's construction in the late 13th century. Of particular interest is the dilapidated fresco of Georgian princess Thamar and her husband Basil Giagupes, a Greek minister who ruled the region during the reign of Selçuk Turkish Sultan Mesud II, presenting a model of the Church of Saint Georges. Thamar funded the vineyard attached to the monastery and the frescoes within—gifts, which at the time entitled her the status of sole benefactor and creator. Basil is shown cloaked in a Selçuk kaftan and headdress, and the title of *Amirarzes* (Emir) suggests that he was granted a fief, with the caveat that he would supply troops to assist the Selçuks whenever necessary. This panel is regarded as an expression of Christian gratitude for the tolerance of the Selçuks.

Bahattin'in Samanlığı Kilisesi (Bahattin's Granary Church) is 300 meters further past Kırk Damaltı Kilisesi. It's named for the local grain gatherer who stored straw in this small, barrel-vaulted church, which dates back to the 11th century. Its apse is adorned with niches and some 20 portraits depicting the life of Christ.

At the end of the shortened tour is Belisirma. Before the arrival of Selçuk Sultan Kılıçarslan II in 1156, this village was an ancient center of medicine. The medical school, which focused primarily on a process of mummification that was widely practiced in the valley, was transferred later to the Selçuk Sultanate capital of Aksaray.

Food

Belisirma offers dining options to satisfy the trail-weary. The riverside **Belisirma Restaurant** (0382/457-3057, 9 A.M.–10 P.M. daily, 12TL) juts over the Melendez Stream. Settle in at a table on the 2nd-story terrace, overlooking the family of dabbling ducks, or lounge on the tiny wooden piers outfitted with cushioned sofas. House specialties are baked in earthenware; the lemony trout is succulent.

Getting There

Visiting Ihlara Valley is best done with a guided tour. You'll save time this way and garner a greater appreciation of the valley's history when you hear it told by a person who has made it his or her business. It's difficult to accurately grasp the region's background and the historical and architectural nuances between churches while hopping on either side of the stream for kilometers trying to find your bearings from a map. Arriving with a group by bus has the additional benefit of a drop-off by the main entrance. Driving to Ihlara means parking at either end of the 16-kilometer canyon, in Belisirma or Selime, which means an additional hike up or down the gorge to retrieve the vehicle. Parking at the main entrance at Ihlara Valley Touristic Facility is also feasible, but includes a hike back along the 3.5-kilometer trail and the dreaded 360-stair climb.

If you're game to hiking the Ihlara Valley solo, do plan for an entire day out. The drive alone is about 90 minutes from Ürgüp or

Göreme. To get there from central Cappadocia, follow the Nevşehir-Aksaray Road to Aksaray, which leads to Ihlara. The main entrance is located two kilometers north of the village. There isn't much in the way of public transportation outside of a *dolmuş* (communal taxi) service that drives the route between central Cappadocia and Nevşehir, requiring passengers to hop on a transfer to Aksaray, and yet another transfer for Ihlara. Once there, a taxi is about the only way to get to the main entrance.

◖ UNDERGROUND CITIES

More than 200 underground cities have been discovered in Cappadocia, the volcanic rock–rich region between Kayseri and its capital of Nevşehir. Only about a fifth of these cities span three or more underground levels. Derinkuyu overshadows all the cities with its 11 stories of churches, dwellings, storage rooms, kitchens, and even olive presses.

The history of Cappadocia's famed subterranean communities is as nebulous as their deepest levels, which remain closed to the public. Based on Hittite artifacts found in the vicinity of the caves, the general assumption is that these ancient central Anatolians may have carved the top levels to hide from Phrygian invaders around 1200 B.C. These caverns were subsequently inhabited by early Christians fleeing Roman persecution during the 1st and 2nd centuries, and were later expanded into complex troglodytic cities by later generations fleeing the Arab invasions of the 7th and 8th centuries.

Inconspicuous entrances belie complex underground metropolises, which, in the case of Derinkuyu, extend 85 meters below the ground and may have been populated by as many as 50,000 people. Miles of secret passageways leading from these discreet portals allowed for a quick retreat underground when invading armies marched through. While the actual number of cities remains a mystery, their interconnectedness was revealed from these tunnels. From above, millstones were used ingeniously to both conceal and seal off each key entrance. A tiny hole in the center of this hefty circular stone, which can measure up to 1.5 meters and weigh as much as half a ton, provided a lookout to the outside world. Beneath, a similar closing aperture further sealed every floor's main access points. An ideal system of defense, these underground caves provide a chilling look at the ingenuousness and tenacity of early Cappadocians.

Derinkuyu

Derinkuyu means deep well and **Derinkuyu Yeraltı Şehir** (Derinkuyu Underground City, 0384/381-3194, 8 A.M.–5 P.M. daily in winter, until 7 P.M. in summer, 10TL) bears its name well, since it's the deepest and most expansive subterranean settlement discovered to date in Cappadocia. Though only 8 of the 11 levels are open to the public. Derinkuyu exhibits the typical amenities found in other underground complexes: cellars; wine and oil presses; stables and storage rooms on the upper floors; kitchens; chapels; and hundreds of private dwellings. Derinkuyu bears a couple of unique features, including a vast gallery that was utilized as a seminary. This large barrel-vaulted room is located on the 2nd floor and is flanked on the left by small cells which are thought to have been used as studies. Lying on the lowest level, the cruciform church is also a one-of-a-kind; it's entered through a vertical stairway located between the complex's 3rd and 4th levels. A massive ventilation shaft extending some 55 meters not only aired all levels beneath, but also appears to have been used as a well. This reservoir provided water to villagers above ground, and to the subterranean levels, when the world outside was sealed off.

A network of wells, storage rooms, and air shafts—the majority of which extend to 30 meters deep—gave locals the possibility to hide from the outside world for months at a time. Varying in size (2,000–7,000 square feet), each floor had an entrance that could be sealed with a donut-like millstone.

Derinkuyu is located 26 kilometers south of Nevşehir. A guided visit by bus from central Cappadocia is the quickest and most advantageous way to fully experience the area.

Kaymaklı

While Derinkuyu's sheer size is impressive, **Kaymaklı Yeraltı Sehir** (Kaymaklı Underground City, 0384/218-2500, 8 A.M.–5 P.M. daily in winter, until 7 P.M. in summer, 10TL) offers a much better understanding of how a troglodyte community actually functioned. Still in use today as storage facilities and cellars, the nearly 100 tunnels—all smaller in height and width and steeper in incline than those found in Derinkuyu—that crisscross this complex connect to at least one of the dwellings beneath. The city's layout is also unique in that each space is situated near a ventilation shaft, making both dwellings and public spaces dependent on the location of air vents. The 1st floor holds a stable that is so small it's led archaeologists to believe that Kaymaklı may have had other similar rooms in sections that have yet to be excavated. To the left of the stable, a millstone entrance gives way to a minute chapel and confessional; while, to the right, are some rooms believed to be living quarters. The 2nd level comprises a church with nave and two apses, as well as a baptismal font. And along the walls are seats carved right out of the soft rock. Interestingly enough, names of individuals appear both on graves inside the church and are engraved in an area just outside, pointing to the possibility that the people entered here may have been the church's benefactors or possibly religious leaders. The entire structure's depth has been estimated at 20 meters, with the capacity to hold upwards of 15,000 people for months at a time.

Clues pointing to Kaymaklı's possible role as a regional commercial center include its high number of storerooms, wine and oil presses, as well a higher number of kitchens. These are located on the 3rd floor, and even extend to the 4th floor, where yet another large number of rooms were consecrated to the storage of clay jars used to stockpile highly valuable oil an wine. Also of interest is an immense hollow block of textured andesite, a dark volcanic rock prevalent throughout the troglodyte complex, that was utilized as a vat in which copper was melted. The sides of this cauldron-like fixture is pierced with 57 holes of about 10cm in circumference each; the semi-molten metal would be place in each of these holes to facilitate molding.

Elaborate systems of communication and engineering throughout are also apparent. Small holes carved right into the floor allowed the transmission of messages with the occupants above. This came in particularly handy, when each floor was sealed off with the hefty millstone. The air shafts, which extend well beyond the last level of the complex, not only ventilated the entire compound but also allowed for the dissipation of kitchen fumes.

Getting There

The best way to visit both Kaymaklı and Derinkuyu is to join avday tour that includes the magical valley of Ihlara and nostalgic Güzelyurt. **Urgup Travel** (Duayeri Mahallesi, Ahmet Asim Yalvac Cad.12/A, Urgup, 0384/341-5015, www.urgiptravel.com, € 60per person, 9 A.M.–5:30 P.M.) provides a highly informative day-long outing to Kaymaklı and its pastoral and archeological surroundings. Or,you can rent a car and do it solo. A haphazard Nevşehir-Nidğde *dolmuş* (communal taxi) stops at both underground complexes; but this necessitates another transfer from central Cappadocia.

Kaymaklı and Derinkuyu are located 19 kilometers and 28 kilometers south of Nevşehir, respectively, on the Nevşehir-Nigde Road (D765). Tack on another six kilometers to the trip if coming from Ürgüp.

Konya

The administrative center of its namesake province—Turkey's largest in terms of area—Konya is a dichotomy in spades: It's at once a bed of fervent conservatism and one of the country's economic powerhouses. After its Turkicization by the mighty and devout Selçuk Empire (circa 12th century), Konya became the capital but only for about 150 years. Despite its fluctuating political status, the city continued under various occupations—even to this day—to welcome Islam's most venerated leaders. One of these is the great Sufi mystic Mevlâna Jelaleddin Rumî, who settled here and went on to found the Mevlâna Order.

Konya, a Turkish derivative of *Iconium* in Latin, relates its colorful past through its extensive architectural legacy, with an array of Selçukian and Ottoman mosques, ornate hammams, caravansaries, and *medreses* (Islamic seminaries). Today, the old is giving way to the new and the contrast is interesting: Konya's hip University district diverges from its conservative roots, particularly during *Cuma* (Friday) prayers when the jeans-clad youth rubs elbows with the bearded patriarchy outside the city's centuries-old mosques.

While Konya's not high on the traditional traveler's map and gets somewhat of a bad rap as the country's religious hotbed, the tomb of Mevlâna remains a pilgrimage site for millions of Muslims and spiritual aesthetes. A visit goes hand-in-hand with experiencing a famed *sema*—the meditative Sufi whirling ritual symbolizing man's spiritual ascent from the confining ego to the eternal. Konya also offers a culinary detour through the richness of its centuries-old roasting and baking legacy, with dishes like *fırın kebap*—tender slices of fatty mutton piled on pillowy bread. Just bear in mind that its rare to find a restaurant that offers alcoholic beverages.

HISTORY

Recent findings at the Çatalhöyük, an archaeological dig just southeast of Konya, proved that the area may have been inhabited as early as the 8th millennium B.C. But it wasn't until the Hittites' arrival, sometime in mid-2000 B.C., that modern Konya received its first moniker of Kuwanna. Then the continuous line of usual suspects renamed the city at will: Kowannia under the Phrygians (8th century B.C.), Iconium under the Romans, and finally the Turks presented it with its current name. Incidentally, Konya is a Turkicized cognate of *eikon* (Greek), from which stems the Hellenic legend that accredited the iconic Medusa head that assisted Perseus during his legendary victory over the natives and founding of the city. By the mid-1st century A.D., the city had grown into such a regional commercial hub that Saints Paul and Barnabus deemed a layover on their missionary journeys throughout Anatolia necessary. Their repeated visits placed Iconium on the liturgical map as one of the early Christian communities, leading to its selection as the site for one of early Christianity's church councils.

Once the Selçuks crushed the Byzantines at Manzikert in 1071, they moved west from Isfahan in Iran and established their seat on Alaeddin Hill in Konya and re-minted themselves as Sultanate of Rhum. Under Sultan Alp Arslan, the Selçuks encompassed most of Anatolia for the next century. Early on, the accumulated spoils of war were used to fund dozens of fine buildings, boasting an erudite Selçukian architectural style strongly rooted in Persia, while reflecting more ornate Byzantine influences. Some structures have stood the test of almost nine centuries; unfortunate others, like Konya's official symbol—the crumbling stone wall of Sultan Kılıç Arslan's Palace (mid-12th century A.D.) braced by a concrete arch—have not.

SIGHTS
Mevlâna Müzesi (Mevlâna Museum)
The Mevlâna Müzesi (Mevlana Mah.,

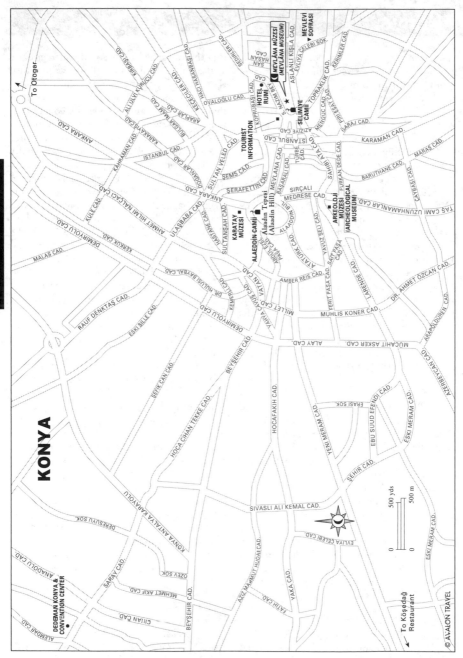

KONYA

the Mevlâna Mosque and Museum

0332/351-1140, www.mevlana.net, 9 A.M.–6:30 P.M. daily, opens at 10 A.M. on Mon., 5TL) no longer houses a traditional Mevlevi order, but is the original *tekke* (lodge of the Mevlevi Dervishes). The entire complex, measuring at 18,000 square meters (194,000 square feet), consists of a *semahane* (open room for the whirling ritual), a *şadırvan* (fountain for ritual ablutions), a *masjid* (small mosque), living and teaching quarters, a library, and the mausoleum housing the tomb of Mevlâna Jelaleddin Rumî, the founder of the mystical sect who posthumously received the title of Mevlâna ("guide" in Arabic). This sprawling complex grew over several centuries; it began as the shrine of one of Mevlâna's successors, Hüsamettin Çelebi, built over Jelaleddin's grave in 1274. In true Selçukian architectural form, the cylindrical drum of the dome once rested on four columns. The conical dome is tiled with turquoise faience that was added in 1854, while the interior decorations and the intricately-carved wooden catafalque were the work of Ottoman sultan Selim I.

The **Mevlâna Shrine** bursts with enameled reliefs and Islamic scriptures, and contains Jelaleddin's tomb, as well as that of his son, Sultan Veled, and his father, Bahaeddin Veled. Those shrouded in velvet bearing Islamic scriptures belong to eminent dervishes. A silver gate crafted in 1597 heralds Mevlâna's tomb, the largest in the complex. Notice the patriarchal hierarchy in which Veled's tomb stands upright next to Mevlâna's, a sign denoting respect.

Adjacent to the shrine lie the **mosque** and *semahane* (open room for the whirling ritual), which were added in the late 15th–mid-16th centuries by Mehmet the Conqueror and Süleyman the Magnificent, respectively. Beneath the crystal lamps donated by Selim I in the late 16th century, lie a collection of Mevlâna's robes, musical instruments utilized during ceremonies, and an array of Selçuk and Ottoman memorabilia, including some gilded Korans dating back to the 13th century. The mosque also contains a priceless collection of ancient silk and wool prayer rugs, as well as a chest containing tufts from Mohammed's beard.

In September 1925, Atatürk banned all religious sects throughout the country. But the

THE LEGACY OF MEVLÂNA JELALEDDIN RUMÎ IN THE MEVLEVI SUFI ORDER

So few texts suggest acceptance and tolerance like the verses etched on the tomb of Mevlâna Jelaleddin Rumî:

Come, come, whoever you are.
Wonderer, worshipper, lover of leaving.
It doesn't matter.
Ours is not a caravan of despair.
Come, even if you have broken your vow
a thousand times
Come, yet again, come, come.

Born in 1207 in Balkh, in modern-day Afghanistan, Mevlâna Jelaleddin Rumî became one of liberal Islam's most celebrated poets and philosophers. Mevlâna, which actually means our guide in Persian, came from a noted family of poets and jurists. Like his teacher/father, Baha'uddin, Mevlâna wrote and ministered in Persian, the literary language of the Selçuks in his day. He accompanied his father to Aleppo, Damascus, and throughout much of today's southeastern Turkey, before finally settling in Konya in 1228, at the behest of Sultan Alaeddin. At the time, Konya was the capital of the Selçuk Turkish Sultanate of Rum. Mevlâna even earned the moniker Rumî, denoting that he was of Rome, or of former Roman lands.

Perhaps most critical in Rumî's prose and inspiration overall was his friendship with renowned Sufi mystic Shams-i Tabrizi. Considerably older than his cadet, Shams introduced Rumî to spiritual dance, music, and poetry. But within three years of his appearance, Shams simply vanished. Some say he may have been killed by Rumî's jealous acolytes. No matter, Rumî was so bereft, he withdrew for years. The mystic penned 50,000 verses during this hiatus; some expound on his deep loss and even refer to Shams as his soul mate. His collected works are known as the Mesnevi, a set of five tomes, each written in Persian.

Rumî lived another quarter century, in which time he was often seen whirling through Konya in sheer ecstasy. And on December 17, 1273, a night known as Seb-i Aruz (wedding night with god), Rumî finally met his maker.

THE MEVLEVI ORDER

The Mevlevi Order, a Sufi (Islamic mystic) sect, was founded by Rumî's son, Sultan Veled, to carry on the master's teachings and practices. For 700 years, the sect has been led by Mevlâna's direct progeny. The current Çelebi, Faruk Hemdem, is the 20th great-grandson of Mevlâna; and he's also the 33rd Celebi to lead the order. Mevlevis, as noted on the tomb's epitaph, extend an invitation to people of all faiths. Their main task in pursuing their 13th-century master's teachings are to bring love and compassion to the lives of all.

Throughout the history of the Ottomans, the Mevlevi sect (known as the Çelebis) and the Osmans (the empire's founding family) were irrevocably united. And when the descendant of Sultan Veled, Devlet Hatun, married Sultan Beyazid I in 1450, both families were forever tied by blood. Their son, sultan Mehmed I Çelebi, elevated the order to become the most respected in the empire and bestowed the sect with many gifts. Some dervishes even rose to fame with their poetry and music; such was the case of Sheikh Ghalib, whose literature and songs greatly influenced the empire during the 17th century through his friend Sultan Selim III. Known among Mevlevi ranks as Galip Dede, the Sufi poet was indoctrinated at the Galata Mevlevihanesi, which was the first Mevlevi monastery to be built in Istanbul in 1491. As the Ottoman Empire spread, so did the order, reaching as far west as the now-defunct Yugoslavia and extending east and south into Syria and Egypt. Mevlevis are still active in these two countries, where their sect retains the Arabic name of Mawlawi. A Mevlevi regiment even served in Syria and Palestine during World

War I. The 800-strong battalion was formed in December 1914 in Konya, and was sent to Damascus to fight the British.

As the new secular Republic of Turkey was being formed, Mustafa Kemal Atatürk issued an order to close all sects on December 13, 1925. That included all Mevlevi *tekkes* (dervish lodges). Mevlevi assets were confiscated and all ceremonies thenceforth banned. Two years later, the Mevlâna Mausoleum in Konya was allowed to reopen, but only as a museum. But by the 1950s, the Turkish government had again permitted the order to hold its annual whirling performance in Konya to commemorate the death of its master. Today, the Mevlâna Museum is open year-round and the city of Konya holds a Mevlâna festival during two weeks in mid-December.

THE *SEMA*
The Mevlevis are also known as *semazens* (whirling dervishes), or those who practice the *sema* (whirling dervish ceremony). Their whirling *dhikr* (Muslim supplication) is accompanied by music. A *sema* consists of seven distinct parts. Each represents a step in a mystical journey which reflects a person's spiritual ascent through ego to arrive at the "perfect" and return as a person who has reached a greater depth of enlightenment and perfection. These two qualities are necessary to pursue the principles of Mevlâna, which consist of coming closer to god, as well as loving and being of service to the whole of creation, regardless of genus, creed, or religious inclination.

Mevlevi historians believe *sema* was created by Rumî. The story goes that one day, as the master was ambling through Konya's marketplace, he heard the rhythmic hammering of goldbeaters. Their chants in praise to Allah: "la elaha ella'llah" (no god, but god) so enthralled him that he stretched his arms out to his sides and began spinning in a circle.

The performance follows a strict prescribed ritual. The dervishes spin in circles around their sheikh (the order's elder), who is the only one to revolve in place. Dervishes wear a white gown, symbolizing the ego; a black cloak, signifying the world; and, a conical headdress stands for the ego's tombstone. The arms are crossed across the torso, a movement representing their testament to their bind with god. The dervish crosses his arms, at first, to testify his unity with god. Arms are slowly stretched out as whirling begins on the right foot. The right palm is turned to the skies to receive god's blessings, while the dervish looks at his left palm, which faces the earth and passes the benediction to those on Earth. Revolving occurs counter-clockwise, from right to left, around the heart, embracing all of humankind and creation with affection and love.

The first part is the eulogy of *Nat-I Serif*, in which the Prophet Muhammed, who represents love, and all the prophets before him, are praised. Then, *Naat* follows with a chant in praise to Muhammed, accompanied by the beating of the drum. Third is *Taksim*, or the playing of the reed *ney* (flute), which signifies the divine breath, or the first breath that gives life to everything. *Devr-i Veled* ensues, with each dervish bowing his head to his peers to acknowledge the divine breath that each of us has received, as the sounds of the *peshrev* symbolize their souls greeting each other from beneath their earthly bodies. The *Four Selam* are the centerpiece of the *sema*. The *semazen* represent the moon, spinning just outside of the sheikh, who personifies the sun. The four *selams* (salutations) represent the entire spiritual journey that every Mevlevi goes through: the first recognizes the existence of god; the second acknowledges the existence of his unity with all, the third one represents the ecstasy experienced in a state of total surrender; and the fourth involves the sheikh joining the dance as a symbol of peace of heart achieved after uniting with the divine. After another *Taksim* is performed, the ceremony concludes with recitations from the Qu'ran and a prayer by the sheikh.

mystical sect survived as a religious order: Special permission was granted by the Turkish government in 1957 to the Mawlawi order of Konya to perform their ritual whirling dances for tourists for two weeks each year during the commemoration of Mevlâna's birth in December. Konya has welcomed a steadily increasing stream of pilgrims daily since the mid-1990s.

The **Selimiye Camii,** located in the park across from the museum's entrance, is a traditional Ottoman mosque. Construction was completed in 1587 and funded by sultan-in-training Selim II during his training as the governor of Konya.

Access to the museum, as in all Muslim sites, requires the removal of shoes. Visitors bearing a little too much skin may be asked to cover up with shawls provided at the museum or mosque entrance. Also, plan the two-hour visit for well after lunch to coincide with the departure of dozens of tourist buses, usually after 2 P.M.

Alaeddin Camii (Alaaddin Mosque)

Konya's second most important building is the Alaeddin Camii, (Alaaddin Tepesi, at the end of Mevlâna Cad., 9:30 A.M.–5 P.M. daily). Built by a Damascene architect in 1221 to commemorate the reign of Alaeddin Keykubat, this plain looking Selçukian edifice sprawls over Alaaddin Tepesi, Konya's original acropolis. Past its restrained stone entrance, the mosque's interior is a surprising collection of marble pillars, crowned by Roman and Ionic capitals, most probably quarried from the collection of churches that the Selçuks razed upon arrival. Of special note are: the intricately-carved wooden *minbar* (pulpit); an antiquated marble *mihrab* (niche indicating the direction of Mecca), adorned with typical black and blue Selçuk Islamic calligraphy; and one of the two *türbes* (tomb) said to contain the remnants of eight Selçuk sultans.

Alaeddin Hill's *çaybahçes* (tea gardens) are the preferred hangouts of students attending the local university. A highlight of a tour through Konya is watching the sun set from one of the verdant tea gardens.

Karatay Müzesi (Karatay Museum)

The Karatay Müzesi (0332/351-1914, 8:30 A.M.–5:30 P.M. daily, 3TL) is a ceramic museum housed in a *medrese* (Islamic seminary) built in 1252 by Selçuk Emir Calaleddin Karatay. The collection of rare Selçuk tiles housed within is a must-do detour, even if you're just in town to visit the shrine. The faience on display, albeit small in number, offers examples of the restrained decorative style of early Selçuk masters, but also finely highlights the uniqueness of each of the noted production centers throughout Anatolia. The most striking representation is the octagonal tiles recovered from the 13th-century summer palace of Selçuk Sultan Kubadabad. Outside, the **Ince Minare** (Thin Minaret) highlights Selçukian restraint for overbearing decorations; it appears quite plain from afar, but notice the intricately carved Islamic scriptures on its circular stone face.

The exquisitely carved stone portal of the Ince Minare in Konya is a perfect example of Selçuk architecture.

Arkeoloji Müzesi (Archaeological Museum)

Konya's Arkeoloji Müzesi (Gültepe Mah. Larende Cad., 0332/351-3207, 8:30 A.M.–5:30 P.M. daily, 3TL) used to be a veritable hangar for the artifacts excavated from Kültepe—an ancient Assyrian colony (2000 B.C.), located 14 kilometers north of Kayseri. While much of it has been moved to its new location at the Kayseri Archaeological Museum, what remains are ancient Assyrian bills of sale in the way of carved tablets, and some odd-looking lighting implements. If you don't have time to visit the Neolithic settlement of Çatalhöyük, 50 kilometers southeast of town, Konya's Archaeological Museum has a good array of artifacts, like jewelry and fragments of wall paintings, some as old as 8,000 years.

FESTIVALS

One of Islam's most awaited commemorations is the **Mevlâna Festival** (mid-Dec.), which takes place annually in Konya. Seb-i Aruz, or the "wedding night," is held on December 17, and culminates in a 10-day-long observance to celebrate Mevlâna's final breath on that day in 1273, ascension to heaven, and his wedding to the Divine. Mevlâna taught complete tolerance, awareness of God through love, and union with God through dance. For schedules, exhaustive information, and tickets for the December celebrations, contact **Konya Il Kültür & Turizm Müdürlüğü** (Konya Provincial Cultural and Tourism Directorate, Mevlâna Cad. 73, 0332/351-1074, www.konyakultur.gov.tr, €15). Tickets for the one-hour ceremonies that occur thrice weekly throughout the year are available through the **Mevlana Kültür Merkezi** (Mevlana Cultural Center, Aslanlı Kışla Cad., Karatay, 0332/352-8111, www.mkm.gov.tr, about €15), local travel agencies, and hotels.

ACCOMMODATIONS

Konya's hospitality scene runs the gamut from the barest of accommodations to high-class five star hotels. Expect overpriced accommodations; even the national chains charge the same or more than the sea-view rooms found in the coastal tourist belt. And while you may not be able to find booze in town, you may be pleased to find a well-stocked minibar in some hotels. Also, the sound of the first call to prayer emanating from the sheer number of mosques in the center makes sleeping in almost impossible.

Hotel Ulusan (Şukran Mah., Kurşunçular Sok. 22, Meram, 0332/351-2420, s. 30TL, d. 45TL) is located in the Meram quarter, just 200 meters south of Alaadin Tepesi. With a 10-minute walking distance to reach most sites, the Ulusan is the ideal choice for those on a budget; not only are the rooms inexpensive, but you'll also save on transportation. Some rooms have shared baths, but these are so large and clean that you may not mind sharing them, especially when you're saving so much dough on accommodations. Owner Ali Bey is a super friendly and hospitable guy, who never tires of enlightening his guests on the ins-and-outs of the city. Internet access and a full, succulent breakfast are complimentary.

Can't beat the **Hotel Rumi** (Durakfahki Sok. 5, 0332/353-1121, www.rumihotel.com, s. US$90, d. US$115) for its location; it's right across from the Mevlâna Museum. Opened in 2005, this business hotel boasts 33 immaculately-clean rooms (including three suites), each with modest yet modern furnishings and black-and-white tiled baths. As a plus, booking half-board or full-board for $10 or $20 respectively, makes looking for your next meal easy. A café and restaurant with a terrace, sauna and hammam, as well as indoor gym and billiard room round out the facilities.

Considering that the Dedeman chain of hotels is one of the most reputed in Turkey, particularly when it comes to business travel, it came as no surprise when the ◖ **Dedeman Konya and Convention Center** (Ozalan Mah., Sille Kavşağı, 0332/221-6600, www.dedeman.com, €99–139) not only lives up to its expectations, but well exceeds them. The tallest building in Konya, the Dedeman features 206 rooms (140 standards) decked in the latest electronics, including LCD TVs, individual

Internet connections, and even built-in screens that allow guests to leave a "do not disturb" video sign. A fully-stocked roof-top bar affords the best views of the city, while the Safran restaurant introduces a modern twist to Turkish cuisine and tasty continental favorites. Guests will dig the oversized hammam, the full service spa, and the indoor and outdoor pools.

FOOD

Mevlevi Sofrası (Aziziye Mah. Çelebi Sok. 1, 0332/353-3341, www.konyamevlevisofrasi.com, 10 A.M.–11 P.M. daily, 11TL) is located next to the Mevlâna Museum and offers several interior dining rooms oozing with Anatoliana: colorful halls juxtaposed against even more vibrant chintz, carpets, and bric-a-brac. Outside, several terraces lure diners with views of the museum's Selçukian domes and Ottoman minarets just beyond splendidly tended flower beds. As expected for this region, meat-and-bread concoctions highlight the menu. Try the traditional *tirit*—chunks of tandoor-roasted lamb and bread served with homemade yogurt and drizzled with melted butter. The beverages menu consists of strong teas, Arabic sherbets, and *ayran* (slightly salted, watered-down yogurt drink). There's a complimentary *sema* (Whirling Dervish ceremony) at 9 P.M. nightly.

Konak Konya Mutfağı (Akçeşme Mah., Piriesat Cad. 5, 0332/352-8547, www.konak-konyamutfagi.com, 11 A.M.–10 P.M. daily, 11TL) has been a hands-down favorite since it opened in 1994. A darling of international food critics, Konak moved to a larger location to accommodate its increasing clientele and changed its name from *köşk* (chalet) to *konak* (mansion). The house also expanded its excellent meaty offerings, but drink choices have remained limited (*sans* alcohol). Sample the homemade yogurt set served in a clay bowl before diving into the house specialties of Konak Kebap—stewed lamb on the bone, topped with fresh tomatoes and tangy creamy feta and the veggie juice, laced with tamarind, cinnamon, and other spices that are secret (I've been told repeatedly).

Köşedağ (Meram Tarihi Köprü Karşısı, 0332/325-2757, www.kosedagrestaurant.com, 9TL) has thrived for more than two decades by offering the typical Konyan feast: tons of roasted mutton. This place does stand apart, however, for its freshly-picked veggies that end up in a mouthwatering array of salads and mezes. The *Köşedağ tava* is a weird twist on Mexican fajitas, minus the cumin, the heat, and the condiments; and they've ditched the side of tortilla for lavash. The recently added Köşedağ Café, just across the restaurant's rear lawn, offers nightly live music, narghile, and strong tea (sorry no alcohol!) year-round; roasted chestnuts and the warmth of a roaring hearth in winter.

INFORMATION AND SERVICES

Konya's streets extend from the circular road that wraps around Alaaddin Tepesi. Mevlâna Caddesi runs east for about one kilometer to the Mevlâna Museum; along this road are the municipal and provincial government hubs. ATMs, Banks, police station, and the **tourist office** (Mevlâna Cad. 21, 0332/351-1074, 8 A.M.–7 P.M. Mon.–Sat., until 5 P.M. in winter) also line Mevlâna Caddesi.

GETTING THERE
By Air

Domestic air travel has truly become the best alternative since the additions of hundreds of inexpensive daily flights to and from Turkey's major cities. **Turkish Airlines** (THY, toll free 444-0849, www.thy.com) runs four daily flights from Istanbul for about 160TL (incl. taxes); **Pegasus** (toll free 444-0737, www.fly-pgs.com) runs one service per day for about 80TL. Konya's **airport** (332/239-1343) is situated 16 kilometers northeast of the city center. **Havaş Shuttles** (www.havas.net, 0332/239-0105, 25min, 8TL) runs a shuttle for every departure and arrival, to and from the Konya's **THY office** (Mevlâna Cad. 9, 0332/351-2000) and the airport.

By Bus

National and regional bus companies connect

to all domestic destinations. The most reputable companies are **Ulusoy** (toll free 444-1888, www.ulusoy.com) and **Kontur** (toll free 444-4042, www.kontur.com). These and other companies offer service to Istanbul (10hr, 48TL); Ankara (3hr, 22TL); Antalya (6hr, 25TL); and Nevşehir (3.5hr, 20TL), among other destinations.

Konya's *yeni otogar* (new bus station) is located about seven kilometers from the town center; a taxi ride (20min, 15TL) will get you into town. If you're traveling light, opt for the municipal tramway (just left of the terminal, 45min, 1.5TL) or a *dolmuş* (communal taxi, 25min, 2TL) to Alaaddin Tepesi.

By Car

If you happen to be based in Antalya or Nevşehir, Konya makes for an excellent day trip. Arriving east from Cappadocia, the trip takes you through 225 kilometers (3hrs) of open country; from the southern hub of Antalya, the three hours spent on the scenic road are actually a travel highlight on their own, as the brand new, three-lane highway climbs over the western end of the majestic Taurus Mountains. Reaching the city center from any of Konya's three outlying highways can take up to 45 minutes; navigating through and parking along the web of antiquated roads running perpendicular to Mevlâna Caddesi can be problematic.

By Train

Konya's **train station** (0332/322-3670, 7 A.M.–11 P.M. daily) lies three kilometers southwest, in the suburb of Meram. The **Meram Ekspressi** (12.5hrs, 70TL) line departs from Istanbul's Haydarpaşa train station; the trip is long, but it allows first-timers a great and safe way to experience western Anatolia, all in the comfort of a sleeper and dining wagons with full Wi-Fi connections. An Ankara-Konya High Speed train—expected to shave off 9.25hrs hours of travel time—and a similar project between Istanbul and Konya are in the works.

GETTING AROUND

Since the lion's share of tourist sites is located in close proximity to Mevlâna Caddesi, walking to and fro is a highly viable alternative to dishing extra dough for cab fare. A stream of *dolmuşes* (communal taxis) run the length of Mevlâna Caddesi; this is a great way to go from the museum to Alaadin Tepesi. Getting to the airport, train, or bus station, all located in the periphery, do necessitate transportation. A half-hourly *dolmuş* (1TL) drives the road between the *otogar* (bus station) and town. Taxis will get you just about anywhere else for a much higher fare, and don't expect cabbies to be knowledgeable about hotels or restaurants.

CAPPADOCIA

Ankara

Even after 86 years of being Turkey's capital, Ankara still sadly remains in the shadow of Istanbul. In fact, some Westerners still erroneously call the latter Turkey's capital. But in all fairness this metropolis has blazed trails in the last decade, an evolution that has gone hand-in-hand with the popular rule of the Justice and Development Party. Ankara is enveloped in a dynamic spirit, most evident by its growing number of suburbs, its thriving café culture, and even a nascent culinary scene. It's a modern city that primarily caters to a large population of foreign diplomats and embassies, national politicians and the businesses that serve them, and some of the country's superior universities and research facilities. On the cultural front, the presence of the State Opera and Ballet, State Theater, and the Presidential Symphony Orchestra ensure that the city continues to beckon Turkey's artistic youth. Theoretically, Ankara has all the ingredients to bear the status of capital, but its lack of individuality, its youth, and its second-fiddle ranking to Istanbul deter it from being as memorable as its European peers.

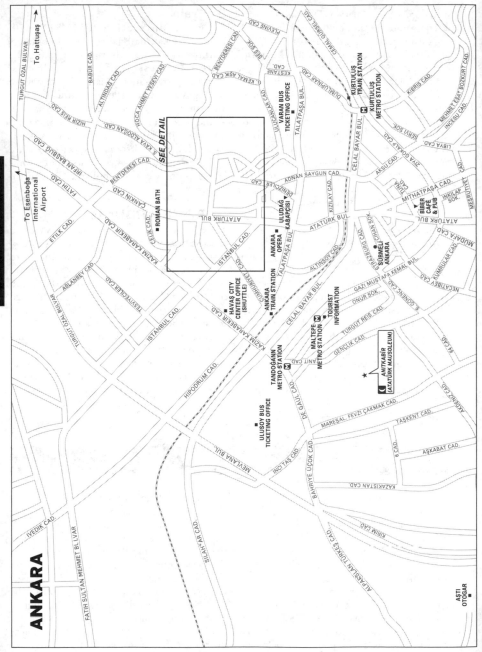

CAPPADOCIA

ANKARA

CAPPADOCIA

500 yds
500 m

TEKMAR CAD.

BAĞLAR CAD.

BAĞLAR CAD.

BELLGON SOK

BÜLBÜLDERESİ CAD.

ANKARA HILTON/ MURPHY'S DANCE BAR
SHERATON HOTEL & CONVENTION CENTER
ANKARA

FILISTIN SOK.
TRILYE

NENE HATUN CAD.

RESIT GALIP CAD.

KULELI SOK

8 CAD.

2 CAD.

ZIYAUR RAHMAN CAD.

EMBASSY OF THE UNITED STATES

PAPER MOON
NOKTAL SOK.
ATLANTIN CAD.

T. EMEKSIZ CAD.
IRAN CAD.

S. EHSAN CAD.

ÇANKAYA CAD.

THE LORD KINROSS

R. TAGORE CAD.

1 MARTI CAD.

SIMON BOLIVAR BUL.

SWISSÔTEL

ESAT CAD.
ÖZEL ÇANKAYA HOSPITAL

KIRÂNKAYA CAD.

TANRAM CAD.

GÜNIZI SOK.

TUNALI HILMI CAD.

HERTZ RENT-A-CAR
AVIS RENT-A-CAR
ÖZEL BAYINDIR HOSPITAL
BEST HOTEL

J.F. KENNEDY CAD.

ATATÜRK BUL.

KUĞULU KVS.

PARIS CAD.

EMBASSY OF CANADA

CINNAH CAD.

A. AZIVEL SOK

CAFÉ DE PARIS

DEDEMAN ANKARA

HERTZ RENT-A-CAR

TUNUS CAD.

AKAY CAD.

HACI YOLU SOK

YAPRAK SOK

BANKACI SOK

PARIS CAD.

EMBASSY OF GERMANY

EMBASSY OF ITALY

ÖMUR SOK.

ALI DEDE SOK.

EMBASSY OF FRANCE

KUVEYT CAD.

THE NORTH SHIELD PUB
FARABI CAD.

GÜVENLIK CAD.

MESNEVI CAD.

EMBASSY OF GREAT BRITAIN

PIYADE SOK.

HÖSERE CAD.

KUZGUN SOK.

GÜVENLIK CAD.

DIKMEN CAD.

PORTAKAL ÇIÇEĞI SOK.

HÖSERE CAD.

SEDAT SIMAVI SOK
A. MITHAT EFENDI SOK.

MİLLİ

İSMET İNÖNÜ BULVAR

İSMET İNÖNÜ BULVAR

ZIYA BEY CAD.

BOSNA HERSEK CAD.

TURKOCAĞI CAD.

OSMANLI CAD.

T CAD.

BANS MANÇO CAD.

MEVLANA BUL.

ESKIŞEHIR YOLU

48 CAD.

48 CAD.

48 CAD.

KALE
WASHINGTON
DIVAN
CENGELHAN BRASSERIE

CENGEL HAN RAHMI M. KOÇ MÜZESİ

HISAR (ANKARA CITADEL)

İPEK CAD.

ALIFSA SOK.

KARAMAN SOK.

AKKAN SOK

ANADOLU MEDENİYETLERİ MÜZESİ (MUSEUM OF ANATOLIAN CIVILIZATIONS)

BENTDERESİ CAD.

REVGIRLI

TEMPLE OF AUGUSTUS AND ROME
HACI BAYRAM CAMİİ (HACI BAYRAM MOSQUE)

BOYACILAR SOK.
GÜVERCIN SOK.

HISAR PARKI CAD.

KONYA SOK.

IŞIKLAR CAD.

NAFARTALAR CAD.

SUŞAM SOK

HÜKUMET CAD.

COLUMN OF JULIAN

TELGRAK SOK.

ANAFARTALAR CAD.

NAFARTALAR CAD.

BOĞAZIÇI LOKANTASI

DENIZCILER CAD.

RUZGARLI CAD.

ULUS SQUARE/ EQUESTRIAN ATAURK STATUE

SANAYI CAD.

ATATÜRK BULVAR

ADNAN SAYGUN CAD.

ÇANKIRI CAD.

KURTULUŞ SAVAŞI MÜZESİ (MUSEUM OF THE WAR OF INDEPENDENCE)

CUMHÜRIYET MÜZESİ (MUSEUM OF THE REPUBLIC)

CUMHÜRIYET CAD.

İSTANBUL CAD.

ULUS METRO STATION

250 yds
250 m

© AVALON TRAVEL

Paris or London, it's not. And that's exactly the reason why most travelers snub it all together for the sun-kissed coasts to the west and south or the fairy chimneys of Cappadocia. But there's still plenty here to keep tourists entertained for 48 hours. Two sights in particular, Atatürk's evocative mausoleum and the exceptional Museum of Anatolian Civilizations, head a long list of to-dos in town. Ankara's streets throb with a palpable nationalist pride. Reminding Turks of their past are busts and statues of Atatürk bedecking most public spaces: the Victory Monument, in Ulus Square, stands as a reminder of the three million lives lost during the country's war of independence; and, the Monument to a Secure and Confident Future reminds the Turkish youth "to be proud, work hard, and have self-confidence." But if that's way too deep, venues like the ancient citadel bring tales of the late Bronze Age back to life. The cafés, restaurant terraces, museums, and souvenir stalls around the cobblestone streets of Ankara's original acropolis can keep families entertained for an entire day.

HISTORY

Ankara lies at a trade crossroads smack in the center of Anatolia, an area first trodden some 5,000 years ago by the late Bronze Age Hatti civilization. In fact, ancient Mesopotamians referred to the entire Anatolian plateau plate as the "Land of the Hatti." But it wasn't until the Hittites, who invaded the region in the 2nd millennium before the birth of Jesus, that the city received its first name, Akuwash. Later, the Phrygians in the 10th century B.C., then the Lydians, and subsequently the Persians all successfully ruled this important trading center. That is until the Persians were ousted by Alexander the Great's troops in 333 B.C., paving the way for the arrival of the Pontus Greeks from the Black Sea coast. It was at the turn of 3rd century B.C. that the city truly saw its first expansion as a commercial center, a nexus from which goods were traded between the Black Sea ports and Crimea to the north; Assyria, Cyprus, and Lebanon to the south; and Georgia, Armenia, and Persia to the east.

The Pontus Greeks aptly named this important commercial post Ànkyra ("anchor" in Greek). The city's first stint as a capital came under the Galatians, a Celtic race who migrated west from Thrace in the mid-3rd century B.C. But they only ruled about two centuries until Augustus Caesar vanquished them, immediately annexing Ankyra, along with its estimated 200,000 inhabitants, to the Roman Empire and even making it one of three administrative centers in central Asia Minor.

The Byzantines held on to the city despite the push and pull of the Persians and the Arabs, that is, until 1071 A.D. when the Selçuk Turks literally bulldozed the city, which subsequently was renamed Enguriye. The westward expansion of the Ottoman Empire left most of central Anatolia unsupervised. Ankara's population declined to 5,000; the grand trading post was left a mere grazing land for its prized Angora goats. But the tide turned a decade after the Ottomans lost WWI, when Atatürk selected the city as the provisional seat of government in 1920. After the successful War of Independence, Ankara became the capital of the fledgling Republic of Turkey on October 29, 1923. With the help of Europe civic engineers and urban architects, the city was split in two: the old section, Ulus, still comprises ancient buildings, lining narrow winding streets dating back to its aggregate Roman, Byzantine, and Ottoman past; the new section, Yenihisar, sprawls from Kızılay, with modern features like wide streets, swanky hotels, theaters, and shopping malls, as well as high-rises, government buildings, and a slew of foreign embassies. In the 9th decade since its founding, Ankara's population has swelled from 35,000 in 1924 to almost 5 million today; its two original suburbs became eight suburbs.

ORIENTATION

Ankara Bulvarı is Ankara's main artery. It connects the newer section of town in Çankaya—home of the presidential palace—in the south to Ulus Square, the capital's oldest quarter in the north, passing through Kızılay and trendy Kavadlıdere. Ulus Meydanı (Ulus Square) is ornamented with a massive statue of Atatürk on horseback. Museums are located around this plaza. The city's Roman remnants are located slightly north of this square. The AŞTI bus station and the central office of Havaş airport shuttles are situated three kilometers south of Ulus.

The Hisar (Citadel) quarter is less than two kilometers east of Ulus Square. Get there directly by following the uphill slant of Hisarparkı Caddesi, and turning right onto Ipek Caddesi; the end of this street marks the entrance of the Museum of Anatolian Civilizations. Right behind the museum lies the Cengel Han Rahmi M. Koç Museum, and you'll also find the gate to the historically pastoral Kale quarter—one of Ankara's landmarks.

You can easily foot your way through Ankara, a car rental is not necessary unless you're considering visiting Hattuşaş or the outskirts of the capital.

SIGHTS
◖ Anıtkabir
(Atatürk Mausoleum)
Foreign dignitaries visiting Ankara are expected to pay respect to Atatürk at Anıtkabir (Anıtteppe Cad., 0312/231-7975, 8:30 A.M.–5:30 P.M. Tues.–Sun., free). In doing so, they join the millions of Turks who travel to the capital annually to honor the man who founded the country. Completed in 1945, the colonnade strictly abides by the Turkish architectural movement of the period, which utilized strong symmetrical designs and unadorned cut-stone in the design of monument-like public buildings. The memorial stands atop overlooking the capital. Inside, the Hall of Honor houses a 40-ton sarcophagus, under which a tomb room encloses Atatürk's remains. Based on an octagonal floor plan, duplicating Selçuk and Ottoman building styles, this central structure's pyramidal ceiling is inlaid with gold tiles and the mosaic walls recall Anatolia's various empires. Outside, a gallery wraps around the main building and leads to various exhibit areas, including: a small museum housing Atatürk's clothing, books, and official automobiles; a gift shop; and the recently opened the War of Independence Museum, which honors the republic's founding father through dioramas and photos of war campaigns. At each

Anıtkabir is the monumental mausoleum dedicated to Mustafa Kemal Atatürk.

corner of the building stands a guard; stick around to experience the impressive Changing of the Guard ceremony, which takes place every half hour.

◖ Anadolu Medeniyetleri Müzesi (Museum of Anatolian Civilizations)

Ankara's Museum of Anatolian Civilizations (Hisarlar Cad. Gözcü Sok. 2, 0312/324-3160, www.anadolumedeniyetlerimuzesi.gov.tr, 8:30 A.M.–5 P.M. Tues.–Sun., 10TL) alone warrants a trip to the city. This archaeological museum, one of the finest of its kind in the world, takes up most of one of the oldest and largest Ottoman caravansaries. This 15th-century *han* (caravansary) and covered bazaar—or fireproof *bedesten* (marketplace) where valuable metals and jewelry were traded—were completed during the reign of Mehmet the Conqueror. Since its inauguration in 1968, the museum inside this double-domed structure continues to detail not only the history of the region, but also the evolution of humankind in Anatolia, with the best artifacts collected throughout the country.

The museum is arranged like most museums of its kind in Turkey, with displays starting at the right of the entrance and continuing chronologically in a counterclockwise fashion. Right off the bat, the remains (2.5 million years ago–8000 B.C.) discovered inside Antalya's Karain Cave—one of the oldest subterranean cities ever found—detail a caveman's hunter-gatherer existence, with tools carved of stone and bone.

The Bronze Age collections relate to the Hatti tribes, which populated Anatolia during the 3rd–2nd millennium B.C. On display is a recreation of a burial ceremony that includes solar discs, deer-shaped statuettes, and loads of gold jewelry that emphasize the importance of religious practices during the Bronze Age.

The Southern Hall gives way to the Assyrian Trade Colonies (1950–1750 B.C.). This era saw the rise of trade and writing in Anatolia. More than 20,000 Assyrian clay tablets, inscribed in cuneiform, relate to business deals and law.

According to deciphered tablets, goods were exchanged for silver and gold.

The Great Hittite Empire collection (1750–1200 B.C.) centers around the impressive relief of the God of War, which was taken from the King's Gate Boğazköy (Hattusa). Near the reconstructions of Hittite religious rites and the King's Gate at Boğazköy, you'll discover a tablet inscribed in Akkadian scripts (1275–1220 B.C.), which constitutes what is perhaps the most important artifact relating to the period. It's a correspondence from Egyptian Queen Nefertari (wife of Ramses II) to Hittite Queen Puduhepa (wife of Hattusili III), written after the peace treaty of Kadesh. This is history's first peace treaty.

Exhibits in the central *bedesten* (marketplace) section vary, but mostly accommodate the latest archaeological finds discovered in Anatolia. Displays located in the lower level relate to the Classical Period (Hellenistic, Roman, and Byzantine Eras) and provide a rundown of Ankara's historical highlights.

Haci Bayram Camii (Haci Bayram Mosque)

Completed in 1428 by Haci Bayram, founder of the Sufi Bayrami sect, who was also a poet and hymnodist, the Haci Bayram Camii (Ulus, dawn–dusk, free) depicts a traditional Selçuk floor plan. The modest lines and decor of Selçukian style were revamped with the ornate touches of the illustrious Mimar Sinan in the 16th century.

This is by far Ankara's prettiest and most significant mosque, both for its combination of design styles and its benefactor. A hexagonal rosette, framed by six rows of flowered borders, dominates a large ceiling constructed entirely of wood. Kütahya tiles were added in the 18th century above the windows; a border of hand-carved palm fronds borders the faience.

Much like Rumi's tomb, sufi pilgrims visit the **Haci Bayram Türbesi** (Haci Bayram Mausoleum) that is adjacent to the mosque's *mihrab* (a niche indicating the direction of Mecca). Bayram died in 1429 and his remains lie beyond the marble facade of a diminutive square building, topped by a stone octagonal drum, crowned by a lead dome. The structure's original wooden exterior and interior entrance doors are now on display at the Ankara Ethnography Museum.

The Haci Bayram Mosque and Mausoleum are located just to the right of Hükümet Caddesi, which is reached easily from Hisar Parkı Caddesi, one of the main streets jutting out from Ulus Square.

Hisar
(Ankara Citadel)

Ankara's original acropolis, Hisar is located in the old town of Ulus. This fortress, which dominates Ankara's tallest hill, was either built by the Galatians or the Hittites. The *kaleiçi* (inner walls) date back to the 6th century A.D., while the outer walls were commissioned 200 years later by Byzantine Emperor Michael II to provide an extra layer of fortification.

Inside, the tiny citadel district sprawls along narrow winding lanes, flanked by traditional two-storied wooden and adobe houses, whose large wooden gates open to pebbled courtyards and fragrant gardens. Like a pearl within its oyster, the citadel is a traditional Turkish village in the heart of one of the eastern hemisphere's most important capitals. The majority of the abodes are now functioning as craft or antique stores, and restaurants that serve some of Ankara's finest treats. A walk straight up from the gate along Kalekapısı Sokak leads to a cluster of ancient marble sarcophagi, fountains, and column drums (across from the Kınacı Restaurant). Also along this stretch is the And Café. Located on the 2nd floor, past a stone archway, this café is a great place to linger over tea or lemonade and its location in the tower affords superb views of northern Ankara.

Çengel Han Rahmi M. Koç Müzesi

Ankara's north/south and east/west trade routes stopped at the Çengel Han Rahmi M. Koç Müzesi (across from Hisar's entrance, Sutepe Mah.,Depo Sok. 1, Altındağ, 0312/309-6800,

CAPPADOCIA

Home of the Galatians during the 3rd century B.C. and the Hittites well before that, Hisar is situated 978 meters high atop Ankara's tallest hill.

THE HISTORY OF ANATOLIA

Making sense of Anatolian history is enough to make one's head spin. With a whopping 30,000-year-long past, this steppe served as an impressive crossroads for the most important civilizations of its time. It's crucial to think of Anatolia, or what the Greeks called *mikrá asía* (Asia Minor), as not only the buffer between the East and the West, but also as a land of such wealth that ambitious leaders from as far east as Mongolia to the western Crusaders were green with envy for eons.

So with that in mind, here's a quick-reference guide to keep the facts, civilizations, and, most importantly, the timeline in check as you hop between ancient sites.

AGE/CULTURE	TIME
Neolithic Age	9000-5000 B.C.
Chalcolithic Age	5000-3000 B.C.
Bronze Age	3300-1200 B.C.
Hattians	2500-2000 B.C.
Akkadian Empire	2400-2150 B.C.
Assyrian Traders	1950-1750 B.C.

AGE/CULTURE	TIME
Hittites	1700-1220 B.C.
Ionian Collusion	1300-700 B.C.
Neo-Hittite Kingdoms	1200-800 B.C.
Phrygian Kingdom	1200-700 B.C.
Troy I-VIII	3000-700 B.C.
Aegean and Balkan Migration	1200 B.C.
Urartu Civilization	900-600 B.C.
Classical Antiquity	700-330 B.C.
Phrygians	750-300 B.C.
Lydia, Caria, and Lycia	700-300 B.C.
Ionians	1,050-300 B.C.
Persian Empire	559-331 B.C.
Kingdom of Alexander the Great	334-301 B.C.
Seleucid Empire	305-64 B.C.
Kingdom of Pontus	302-64 B.C.

www.rmk-museum.org, 10 A.M.–5 P.M. Tues.–Fri., 10 A.M.–7 P.M. Sat.–Sun., adult 6TL, children 3TL) during the 16th and 17th centuries. Completed during the reign of Süleyman the Magnificent in 1522, this caravansary was a gift to the sultan's daughter from her husband, Damat Rüstem Paşa. It was meticulously restored by Turkish business magnate Rahmi Koç, as a gesture towards his father, Vehbi Koç, who had began his illustrious career in 1917 at a small grocery store located inside. The 26-room inn opened as a museum dedicated to Rahmi Koç's passions in 1995. Displays include engineering, road and maritime transport, and scientific instruments; there are lots of interactive exhibits to thrill the little ones.

Temple of Augustus and Rome

Attached to the Haci Bayram Mosque, the Temple of Augustus (open to the public, free) was built by the Galatians in A.D. 10 as a tribute to their commitment to Roman Emperor Augustus, and reconstructed during the 2nd century by the Romans. Like most ancient monuments dating from the Classical Period, this one was built from the remains of a temple honoring the Phrygian Goddesses Men and Kybele. Just before his death, Augustus penned

AGE/CULTURE	TIME
Attalids of Pergamon	282-129 B.C.
Kingdom of Armenia	190 B.C.-A.D. 428
Roman Republic	133-27 B.C.
Roman Empire	27 B.C.-A.D. 330
Middle Ages to Today	A.D. 330-present
Byzantines	A.D. 330-1453
Selçuk Sultanate of Rûm	1077-1307
Ottomans	1299-1922
Republic of Turkey	1923-present

The Hittites, believed to have been a people of Balkan origin, are generally considered to be the first settlers to take advantage of Anatolia's fertility and more temperate climate. They were a super power of the Bronze Age, rivaling the Egyptians and Babylonians. This massive empire imploded sometime in the 12th century B.C. due to civil war, nasty internal feuds for the throne, and relentless pressure from the Sea Peoples to the west. Assyrian trading colonies capitalized on the more strategic location of central Anatolia, and engulfed the Hittites' inland realm. The coastal region saw the growth of indigenous states – like Phrygians, Lydians – until about the 8th century B.C., when the Greek islanders colonized Anatolia's western seaboard.

The Achaemenid Empire marched in from Persia – today's modern Iran – in 560 B.C. And the reign of Croesus, the Lydian king known for his fortunes, was abruptly put to an end. The Greek colonies to the west fell to the Persians like dominoes. Some 200 years later, Alexander the Great repelled the Persians in one long sweep back to the borders of modern Iran, once again returning the whole of Asia Minor to the Greeks. After the Romans conquered the seaboard in the 2nd century B.C., the region enjoyed centuries of peace. Under the subsequent Byzantine Empire, Asia Minor was one of antiquity's cultural and religious centers and was sliced by a crucial trade route. As the Byzantines declined, Arabs and Mongols began nibbling at its far eastern reaches. By the 14th century, a feudal system of Turkish *beyliks* (emirates) was in place over the whole of Anatolia. By the mid-15th century, the Ottoman Turks conquered most of northwestern Anatolia, Thrace, and finally the Byzantine capital of Constantinople. The Ottoman Empire ruled over Anatolia until 1922. In a year, and with a War of Independence, Kemal Atatürk's Turkish Republic engulfed the whole of what the Greeks call Asia Minor.

CAPPADOCIA

the document *Res Gestae Divi Augusti* (*Deeds of the Divine Augustus,* written in both Greek and Latin). This will of sorts contains four sections, each detailing a different aspect of his regal career: political deeds, public benefactions, military accomplishments, and political stance. He instructed his senate to dispatch the document throughout the empire to be displayed carved in stone on monuments or temples. Many of these have survived, but Ankara's copy is the only copy appearing almost in full form. In 2002, the temple made its way onto the World's Monument Fund's list of endangered sites, entitling it to a full restoration. The monument is currently closed to public viewing and totally hidden from sight by scaffolding. The slabs are meticulously—and slowly—being restored through the collaborated efforts of the University of Trieste in Italy and the Middle Eastern Technical University in Ankara.

The Column of Julian

Known by locals as the *Belkis Minaresi,* the Column of Julian (Ulus Square, free) was built to honor Emperor Julian in A.D. 362. The 15-meter-tall column is topped by a Corinthian capital, thought to have been added two centuries later.

Roman Bath

The Roman Bath (Çankiri Cad., Ulus, 8:30 A.M.–noon and 1–5:30 P.M. daily, 2TL) was built during the reign of Roman Emperor Caracalla (A.D. 211–217) in honor of the god of medicine Asklepios. What remains of this once considerably large building are the three rooms typically found in public baths during the era: a frigidarium (cool room), hepidarium (warm room), and calderium (hot room). Ongoing excavations revealed a swimming pool and dressing room adjoining the frigidarium, as well as a sudatorium (sudorific room) in the calderium section. An underground heating system, courtyards, fireplaces, and areas for attendants and storage were all amenities this complex once boasted.

Kurtuluş Savaşı Müzesi (Museum of the War of Independence)

Hard to believe that the rather small, two-storied Kurtuluş Savaşı Müzesi (Cumhuriyet Bul. 14, Ulus, 0312/310-7140, 9 A.M.–5 P.M. daily, 2TL) was the first seat of the Turkish National Grand Assembly from April 23, 1920 until 1924. It reopened on April 23, 1961 as the Museum of Turkish Parliament and as the Museum of the War of Independence on April 23, 1981. Inside, exhibits consist of documents, pictures, weapons, and objects from the War of Independence to the establishment of the Turkish republic. The original parliament hall is anything but modest, with an array of desks and wax figures of all of the presidents á la Madame Tussaud.

Cumhürriyet Müzesi (Museum of the Republic)

The building housing Cumhürriyet Müzesi (Cumhuriyet Bul. 22, Ulus, 0312/310-5361, 9 A.M.–5 P.M. daily, 2TL) was the second seat of the Grand National Assembly of Turkey, 1924–1960. It opened to the public in its current incarnation as display space on October 20, 1980. Inside, the Assembly Hall in the center of the building is built entirely of wood and is girded by corridors that connect to outside rooms. The senate's interior decoration bears homage to both the modesty of Selçukian design and the intricacies of Ottoman style. There are also documents relating Atatürk's visions for his new republic, but understanding the legends affixed to them will be hard unless you speak Turkish. Designed in Turkey's First National Architecture style, the building's exterior deserves a look.

ENTERTAINMENT AND EVENTS
Performing Arts

As the capital of a quickly emerging country, Ankara is ripe with a performing arts scene that rivals those of its European counterparts. The **Presidential Symphony Orchestra** (Talatpaşa Ave. 38, Opera, 0312/309-1343, cso.gov.tr, tickets 15TL) features classical music from renowned Turkish and foreign composers on Fridays and Saturdays October–May. The **State Opera and Ballet** (Opera Sahnesi, Atatürk Bulv. 50, Opera, 0312/324-2210, www.dobgm.gov.tr, tickets 10TL) showcases its talented performers nightly through classical operas and ballets. The **Devlet Tiyatroları** (Turkish State Theaters, www.devtiyatro.gov.tr tickets 6TL) runs Ankara's 16 theaters and their respective programs, which feature the works of international and Turkish playwrights.

To find out what's playing where and read reviews of ongoing shows, log on to the independent website www.tiyatrokeyfi.com. Or, check the Sunday edition of the *Turkish Daily News* for a rundown of all events.

Nightlife

Central Ankara's night scene caters heavily to politicos and diplomats, with highbrow English pubs, jazz clubs, cafés, and a string of coffee shops open till the wee hours of the morning. Arjantin Caddesi in the Gaziosmanpasa quarter has a group of irresistible cafés nicknamed the "Ankara SoHo." For a, dare I say, more youthful—and cheaper—affair head out to Kızılay's Sakarya Caddesi, where Bilkent University's student body hangs out. The restaurants peppering the historic Kale district

The Presidential Symphony Orchestra performs weekly classical music concerts at the Ankara Opera House.

offer atmosphere, late hours, views, and even music on the weekends; a mix that's unbeatable anywhere else in town.

Biber Café and Pub (İnkılap Sok. 3/D, Kızılay, 0312/430-0717, 6 P.M.–late) is lauded as Ankara's best bar for locals. This cavernous joint brings in artists and university students nightly with a variety of shows that vacillate from pop Turkish music to Jazz. At 5TL, beer is priced reasonably enough to get your fill.

The Lord Kinross (Cemal Nadir Sok. 18, Çankaya, 0312/439-5252, 6 P.M.–midnight Mon.–Sat., 10 A.M.–10 P.M. Sun.), named for the late English author and journalist, caters to a British expat clientele. A great place to play darts, have a lager, and nosh on pork bangers, that is, if the highbrow ambience doesn't deter you from placing an order.

The North Shield Pub (Güvenlik Cad. 111, Güven, 0312/466-1266, www.thenorth-shield.com, noon–12:30 A.M. daily) is known for its selections of whiskeys (more than 40) and international beers, as well as its meat grills and pizzas. The Ankara location of this now reputed brand opened in 1997 and it may have the only heated outdoor terrace in town. Locations countrywide are packed on weekends; some come to watch sporting events on large screen TVs, listen to live music on Wednesdays and Fridays, or to meet other singles. The pub is open for brunch on Sundays, 10:30 A.M.–1:30 P.M.

Murphy's Dance Bar (Tahran Cad. 12, Kavalıdere, 0312/466-0054, 9 P.M.–3 A.M., cover charge 15–20TL) is located at the top of the Hilton Hotel. Each night the theme changes, from 100 percent Turkish pop and Latin to rap–hip hop and karaoke. Friday nights, however, are earmarked for University party, one of the most happening affairs in town. The best thing about Murphy's is its clientele, which ranges seamlessly in ages 18–58. You can even learn tango or waltz by joining a one-hour lesson that runs 6:30 P.M.–9:30 P.M. Monday–Thursday.

Festivals

All year-long Ankara's abuzz with festivities,

the largest one being **Victory Day** on August 30, when the capital pulls out all the stops to commemorate the day the Turks quelled a Greek invasion in 1922. The month of April marks Ankara's **International Music Festival** (0312/427-0855, www.ankarafestival. com), when Turkey's top musicians and dancers unite with their international peers for a month-long program of events. The capital's **International Film Festival** (0312/468-3892, ww.filmfestankara.org.tr) occurs in mid-March during a 10-day-long showcase of Europe's best indie films. On April 23, galas and televised concerts featuring children from all over the world mark the celebration of **International Children's Festival**. Atatürk dedicated the day on which Turkey's Grand National Assembly was established to the childred of the world. Activities are sponsored by the state radio and television network (Turkish Radio & Television, 0312/463-2956).

ACCOMMODATIONS

It's all about the battle of the titans in Ankara: the bigger the hotel, the better; the more the amenities, the sweeter it is. That's why trying to find the best accommodations among the five-star hotels is akin to finding the proverbial needle in the haystack. With a plethora of spa treatments, gyms, business centers fit for the discerning executive, and onsite gourmet restaurants, the hotels' hefty price tag is worth it.

Under €100

C Dedeman Ankara (Akay Cad., Buklum Sok.1, Kızılay, 0312/416-8800, www.dedeman. com, €89) is the only moderately-priced five-star hotel in Ankara. Just a 15-minute walk from the Atatürk Mausoleum, the Dedeman boasts 299 units, 18 of which are superior rooms. Standards come with the expected amenities, like 24-hour room service, Internet connection, and interactive satellite TV; while the hotel amenities run the traditional gamut of Turkish Bath, sauna, massage, and fitness center. The top-floor terrace restaurant, Sevilla, actually revolves 360 degrees in an hour, so you

can multitask a romantic dinner and sightseeing the town from above.

Sürmeli Ankara (Cihan Sok. 6, Sıhhiye, 0312/231-7660, www.surmelihotels.com, Internet rate s. €79, d. €89, rack rate s. €199, d. €259) is surprisingly inexpensive for the type of accommodations and amenities it offers. Keep in mind that their rack rates are more than twice those found on their website, so good deals are only available when booking online. The interior decor throughout the public spaces and 200 rooms is minimalist in style. Onsite amenities include swimming pool, sauna and gym, bar, and restaurant. Amenities in the guest rooms include aquabaths, light-sensitive curtains and opulent textiles, interactive flat screen TVs, and cable-free Internet connections.

Best Hotel (Ataturk Bulv. 195, Kavaklidere, 0312/467-0880, www.besthotel.com, US$100) is both small and affordable. Located in the center of town, the hotel's decor is Liberace-esque and the fully-equipped rooms mirror the same ornate style in varying color palettes.

€100 and Up

C Swissôtel (Yildizevler Mahallesi, Jose Marti Cad. 2, Cankaya, 0312/409-3000, www. swissotel.com, d. €131–375, presidential suites from €1600) has endowed its Ankara location with every bit of its reputed impeccability for service and luxurious amenities. The hotel beckons the harried traveler with appealing, restful spaces, and a slew of opulent facilities, like a health club that overlooks the indoor topaz swimming pool; a sauna; and hammam. The rooms boast LCD satellite TVs and personal CD players, dual electrical currents (120v and 220v), espresso machines, and luxurious baths with rain showers. Kiddie rooms even come outfitted with Disney bedcovers and rugs, as well as plushy, almost life-size teddy bears, games, and yummy treats.

Ankara Hilton (Tahran Cad. 12, Kavaklıdere, 0312/455-0000, www.ankara. hilton.com, d. €140–244, suites €375–399) is nothing but upscale, particularly since its last renovation in 2009. Its stark, steely facade is unappealing, but a look inside reveals designer touches that manage to invigorate the bland decor the chain is known for. Of the 315 guest rooms, eight are 55-square-meter apartments (€339), ideal for families, and can accommodate up to four, with two bedrooms, small kitchenette, and living room, plus a balcony with unstopping views of the capital. The rooms and suites offer plush terrycloth robes, large armchair with ottoman opposite 21-inch LCD TV, larger marble bathrooms, and daily delivery of the *Turkish Daily News;* some rooms even have a partial garden. The onsite Greenhouse Restaurant serves a mean Mongolian Barbecue in its covered terrace in the summer; the themed buffet changes daily.

Sheraton Hotel & Convention Center Ankara (Noktali Sok., Kavaklidere, 0312/457-6000, www.sheratonankara.com, d. €172, suites €480) boasts a giant white tower next to a giant white main building, but that's where the starkness ends. Inside, the lobby oozes style with massive glass ball chandeliers, chocolate-hued furniture, and a grand piano, all against a backdrop of floor-to-ceiling glass walls. The deluxe rooms at 35 square meters are ample, with bonuses like designer beds, plasma satellite TVs, and 110v and 220v sockets. Some units are even designed for lefties, while the Smart Rooms provide the workspace and connectivity required for the modern business traveler.

FOOD

If you're a foodie overnighting in Ankara, then you're in luck because this increasingly hip capital is receiving quite a bit of attention from national gourmets. The touristy thing to do for an evening meal is to head to one of the Ottoman mansions converted into swanky terrace diners at the Citadel. Those snubbing casual for pricey duds should aim their fork towards the *in* restaurants in Kavaklidere or Cankaya. Cheap eats and snack-on-the-go options are ubiquitous, try *simit* (Turkish bagel) filled with cream cheese and olive paste, or corn boiled fresh and *döner* (tender slices of roasted lamb) sandwiches, from carts and

stands. Reservations are not necessary during the week, but are recommended on the weekends.

International

Paper Moon (Tahran Cad. 2, Kavaklidere, 0312/428-7474, www.papermoon.com.tr, noon–midnight daily, 28TL) is my—and the Turkish media's—"best of" in both design and cuisine. This über-popular Italian venture into refined-yet-no-frill Italian cuisine launched by Pio Galligani Magrini for Milan's glitterati in 1977 arrived in Ankara in 2006, and since then the nation's jet-set crowd has been raving about its sumptuous, highly innovative fare. One item to try is the octopus carpaccio or the *branzino al limone* (sea bass with a lemon sauce). For dessert, break the bank and order the truly out-of-this-world mille-feuille Napoleon (15TL).

Café de Paris (Abdullah Cevdet Sok. 30/A, Çankaya, 0312/440-5123, www.cafedeparis.com.tr, 25TL) is a modernized bohemian bistro whose decor oozes with nostalgia for the City of Lights' artistic past. Quite chic, but far from pompous, the rather small dining room is romantic with the traditional banquet running down one wall. But unlike the typical French bistro, this one is missing the white tablecloths and the haughty servers. Actually, you'll find nothing but friendly hospitality here. Come on weekends for the signature Café de Paris filet served with crispy French fries, perfect when enjoyed over live French ditties. The international menu also includes fresh pastas, salads, and even children-friendly meals.

Divan Çengelhan Brasserie (Necatibey Mahallesi, Depo Sok. 1, Kale, 0312/309-6800, www.divan.com.tr, noon–2 A.M. Tues.–Sun., 25TL) oozes atmosphere thanks to its location inside the 16th-century caravansary it occupies. Part of the mega-conglomerate Koç Holding, whose current owner dished out millions for the renovation of this historic building, the Divan hotel and restaurant chain replicated the quality and culinary innovation that's earned it a coveted membership in the acclaimed International gastronomic society, la

Chaîne des Rotisseurs. Specialties not to miss are *Ballı Dana Kaburga* (veal rib with honey) or the Wiener Classic Schnitzel. Live music on weekends starts at 8:30 P.M.

Ottoman and Turkish

Boğazıcı Lokantası (Vedat Dalokay Cad. 59, Çankaya, 0312/436-2220, www.bogazicilokantasi.com, 7 A.M.–10 P.M. daily, 15TL) is so synonymous with Ankara and great food that lovers of Anatolian cuisine never visit Ankara without eating here. Original owner Mehmet Recai Boyacıoğlun has run the kitchen over the 57 years since this blue-collar restaurant opened. His secret for longevity is providing consistently excellent quality; and to achieve that he's got to be superhuman, considering his menu includes about 45 new dishes every day and the dining room is typically bursting at the seams with diners. Try the seasonal *zeytinyağlı* (veggies cooked in olive oil and served cool).

Kale Washington (Doyran Sok. 5/7, Hisar, 0312/311-4344, www.washingtonrestaurant.com.tr, 9:30 A.M.–midnight daily, 18TL) is Ankara's landmark haunt for top national politicians and foreign diplomats. Its no-nonsense dedication to quality and service is as steady as it was in 1955 when two brothers from Rize returned from a stint as Turkish diplomats in Washington D.C. The menu reflects exactly what these world policy-makers are after: delectable entrées, a superior wine list, and an ambience that's classy but not over the top. Located in the citadel, the restaurant sprawls over two 400-year-old Ottoman houses and balconies that offer unbeatable views of the capital. The tender filet mignon with mushrooms (20TL) is a house specialty and so are the popular *zeytinyağlıs,* such as pepper or grapevine dolmas.

Uludağ Kebapçısı (Denizciler Cad. 54, Ulus, 0312/309-0400, www.uludagkebapcisi.com, 17TL) expanded its operations with six locations nationwide. But it was here that it all started in 1956 with two simple *döner* (tender slices of roasted lamb) dishes appearing next to a couple of farm-fresh salads and a handful of desserts. Today, meat still dominates the menu, but the options have grown to over 20, of which *pirzola* (lamb chops) remains my all-time favorite.

Seafood

No Turk in his right mind would think about eating fish in the nation's capital; after all, Ankara's at least three hours away from the nearest sea. But that all changed when a highly creative food-loving couple—the Üzmez's—introduced seafood to traditional Turkish recipes and began showcasing the results in 2002 at their Trilye Restaurant in swanky Çankaya, resulting in a frenzy of applause from Turkish food writers. Since then, other restaurateurs have followed suit, leaving absolutely no culinary stone unturned, even this far away from the shore.

Trilye (Reşit Galip Cad., Hafta Sok. 11, GOP, Çankaya, 0312/447-1200, www.trilye.com.tr, 8:30 A.M.–2:30 A.M. daily, 22TL) is tucked in a backstreet of Çankaya's Gaziosmanpaşa quarter. Its reputation lives up to its slogan: "The freshest fish from any of Turkey's coasts can be found here." From Ayvalık's suppler octopus, İğneada's fleshy turbot, Karataş's jumbo shrimps, Antioch's famed grouper, or even Istanbul's revered bluefish, fresh seafood is on offer. Decorated by hospitable owner Süreyya Üzmez in the new Turkish bistro style, the room is elegant and typically packed full of international foodies, but the terrace is infinitely more inviting. House signature dishes, like langoustes on a bed of eggplant purée, accompany all-time favorites, like Belgium's *moules marinières* (mussels), Spain's paella, and even Maine clam chowder.

INFORMATION AND SERVICES

Ankara's **Tourist Office** (Gazi Mustafa Kemal Bulv. 121, Tandoğan, 0312/488-7007, 9 A.M.–5 P.M. Mon.–Fri., 10 A.M.–5 P.M. Sat.) is located across the Maltepe subway entrance. Maps, travel brochures, books, and English-speaking attendants are available. Another, smaller office serves the airport (0312/398-0348). Banks and ATMs are centered in Çankaya's Kavaklıdere and

Altındağ's Ulus quarters. The are over 60 **PTT** (Atatürk Bulv. 95/1, Kızılay, 0312/418-9409, 8:30 A.M.–5:30 P.M. Mon.–Fri.) offices in Ankara, but the one in Kızılay, along with the location just down the street in Ulus, are the most centrally located to the sights. At these offices you can exchange currency and make and receive phone calls.

For emergency services, **Bayındır Hospital** (Atatürk Bulv. 201, Kavaklıdere, 0312/428-0600, www.bayindirhastanesi.com.tr) is centrally located and offers the most technologically and medically advanced services in town. Other private facilities include **Çankaya Hospital** (Bülten Sok. 44, Kavaklidere, 0312/426-1450, www.cankaya-hastanesi.com.tr) and the research facilities and training **Baskent University Hospital** (Fevzi Çakmak Cad., 10th Sok. 45, Bahçelievler, 0312/212-6868, www.baskent-ank.edu.tr).

GETTING THERE
By Air
The new terminal at the award-winning Ankara's **Esenboğa International Airport** (0312/590-4000, www.esenbogaairport.com) was added in 2006 to accommodate the increasing number of domestic flights. National airlines like **Turkish Airlines** (THY, toll free 444-0849, www.thy.com) and **Pegasus Airlines** (toll free 444–0737, www.flypgs.com) provide both domestic and international flights. International carriers Lufthansa, Swiss Air, and United Airlines connect to European hubs.

Esenboğa airport is located 28 kilometers northeast of the city center. THY's national shuttle service **Havaş Shuttles** (toll free 444-0487, www.havas.net, 10TL) runs a shuttle between the airport and the Havaş City Center Office (19 Mayıs Stadyumu, B Gate, Ulus, 0312/310-3555). The trip takes about 25 minutes, and departs every half hour in either direction 3 A.M.–9:30 P.M. Service outside of these times is provided according to flight schedules. An extra 25 percent is added for service midnight–6 A.M. Esenboğa's **taxi coop** (0312/398-0897, www.esenbogataxi.com) charges the going rate of 2.20TL on boarding

and the same amount for every kilometer traveled, so a trip to town runs about 65TL.

By Train
The **Ankara Ekspresi** (toll free 444-8233, www.tcdd.gov.tr) run by Turkish State Railways (TCDD) is the most modern and comfortable of all lines through the country and it is wired for Internet access. The night train departs Istanbul's Haydarpaşa station at 10:30 P.M. and takes about 9.5 hours to complete the 576 kilometers to Ankara's train station. A one-way fare costs 85TL, which includes a bunk for one in a one-person sleeping compartment, and 120TL for two in a double compartment. Tickets for this train are on a reservation basis only. Heed the signs posted by the TCDD in stations throughout the country to keep valuables close.

A traditional train now connects to the high-speed train linking Eskişehir to Ankara in 5.5 hours, shaving 4 hours from the trip. A new system of tracks will connect to Istanbul by 2012; the only way to board this service is by boarding the regular train from Haydarpaşa's train station (departs at 7:10 A.M. daily) to Eskişehir (arrives 10:56 A.M.). From there, the high-speed connection departs at 11:15 A.M. to arrive in Ankara at 12:38 P.M. The return fast train departs every morning at 7 A.M. from Ankara and arrives in Eskişehir at 8:27 P.M.; the connection there is scheduled for Istanbul at 8:42 A.M., pulling in to Haydarpaşa at 12:32 P.M. TCDD offers passengers a 20 percent discount on the purchase of a round-trip ticket; the Sleeping Car Train tour pass costs 500TL and allows unlimited nationwide travel for one month. For other routes and schedules linking Ankara to the rest of Turkey, as well as ticket purchases and reservations, check out their informative website (www.tcdd.gov.tr).

By Bus
Ankara is served by all nine national bus companies, as well as 233 regional carriers. The largest, **Varan** (toll free 444-8999, www.varan.com.tr), **Ulusoy** (toll free 444-1888, www.ulu-soy.com.tr), and **Metro** (toll free 444-3455,

www.metroturizm.com.tr), connect the most cities on their respective grids. There are, for example, 46 buses traveling daily from Istanbul to Ankara. A one-way fare ranges 30–47TL. Metro offers the best deal: a nonstop service (6hr), 10 times throughout the day, every day, for as low as 28TL (Internet purchase only). Travel from Ankara to other Turkish cities is best achieved by checking schedules and fares online and booking ahead to ensure ticket availability and lowest prices.

Ankara's **AŞTI Otogar** (bus station, 0312/207-1000) lies three kilometers west of Ulus, and just two kilometers from Kavaklidere. While a taxi (10–13TL) is the fastest way to reach the center of town, there's also a metro station in front of the *otogar* on Mevlâna Caddesi. Stops include Anıtkabir and Ulus.

GETTING AROUND
Taxis
Since Ankara's sites are located close together, hopping in a taxi won't break the bank. The boarding rate is currently set at 2.20TL, with an additional 2.20TL for every kilometer thereafter. Expect to pay at most a 15TL fare for short trips in the city, even if the streets are clogged. Taxi rates increase by 50 percent nationwide midnight–6 A.M.

Public Transportation
Ankara's grid is quite adequately served by public transportation: *dolmuş* (communal taxi) co-ops, and EGO's (Ankara's transportation supervisory board) bus and metro services. As anywhere else in Turkey, these vehicles are marked with their destination on the front windshield and the passenger boarding side. The signage is pretty self-explanatory: Ulus, AŞTI (bus station), and *gar* (train station). Bus and metro fare is 1.70TL and is sold at kiosks displaying the EGO sign. A *dolmuş* ride ranges in cost, 1.50–2.50TL.

Ankara's two main metro lines include the Ankaray, which runs southwest to northeast from AŞTI to just beyond Kızılay; and, the east-west line connecting Kızılay to Batıkent, via Ulus.

Hattuşaş (Boğazkale)

A most unique archaeological side trip from Ankara, the site of Hattuşaş (0364/452-2006, 9 A.M.–5 P.M., until 7 P.M. in summer) is worth the three-hour trip by car. For more than five centuries, Hattuşaş was the capital of the Hittite Empire. Its archaeological significance cannot be adequately underscored. A massive trove of tablets bearing cuneiform scripts was uncovered. These early Anatolians recorded just about every minute of their daily lives, from birth and wedding announcements to trade and politics. They adopted the cuneiform script of the Assyrians, who, lured by the wealth and resources of these early Anatolians, arrived in droves, bearing textiles and metals from the east. These records were stored in cavern-like libraries for posterity. And thanks to them we have an understanding of every facet of these Bronze Age people.

HISTORY
As natural a citadel as any paranoid ruler might hope for, Hattuşaş was one of the earlier settlements in history. It may in fact have been settled four millennia before what was once thought to be the original landlords, the Hatti civilization (2500–2000 B.C.). By the 19th B.C., Assyrian traders from Assur—who are credited for introducing writing in the form of cuneiform script to the region—founded a trading post and living quarters here. A carbonized layer deep in the earth around the archaeological site suggests a sweeping fire ravaged through the settlement around 1700 B.C. King Anitta from Kussara (a settlement in southeastern Anatolia) claimed responsibility for the act and even put a curse on the city: "At night I took the city by force; I have sown weeds in its place. Should any king after me attempt

© JESSICA TAMTÜRK

a 3,000-year-old Hittite carving in Hattuşaş

titanic clash is the landmark peace treaty that followed, marking the first in mankind's history. One of the original copies of the Kadesh Peace Treaty, which is inscribed in stone, was discovered in the Hattuşaş Palace Archives and moved to the Archaeological Museum in Istanbul. Incidentally, an enlarged replica also exists at the lobby of the United Nations headquarters in New York.

Despite two unsuccessful yet bloody and fiery attempts by the Kaskas—a Black Sea people who girded the Hittites expansion to the north—to gain Hattuşaş and topple its landlords, the Hittites ruled over central and eastern Anatolia, as well as into northern Mesopotamia at the height of their power. But that all changed in 1160 B.C. when the empire burst at the seams under the stress of raging internal pressures and opportune invasions from the Thracians, Phrygians, and Assyrians. The eight centuries that followed are characterized as Hattuşaş's Dark Ages, when the city was all but abandoned, only to be resettled by the Phrygians around 800 B.C. and the Persians two centuries later.

Hattuşaş is strategically located atop a rocky terrain overlooking a vast and fertile valley. At its peak the city sprawled just under two square kilometers, with inner and outer sections girded by a massive eight-meter-high crenelated fortification system built by Great King Shupiluliuma I. The walls had two 12-meter-tall watchtowers, all in various states of erosion. There were several access gates flanked by impressive lions and sphinxes carved in stone. The best remaining examples of these impressive statues can be found at the Museum of Anatolian Civilizations in Ankara.

to resettle Hattush, may the Weathergod of Heaven strike him down."

Ironically, Labarna I—one of Anitta of Kussara's steadfast progeny—returned two centuries later to rebuild a city among the ashes. He named it Hattuşaş, meaning "Land of the Hatti." Labarna even changed his name to Hattusili—or the one from Hattuşaş—in honor of his new capital. His descendants, more than 30 in all, expanded the city over four centuries to include most of Anatolia. This expansion didn't go unnoticed by their Egyptian neighbors, whose growing dominion had come to abut that of the Hittite realm in modern Syria. And by 1279 B.C., time had come to put an end to the contest between the two empires. At the historic Battle of Kadesh, Egyptian Pharaoh Ramses II marched into Hittite territory and confronted the troops of Hittite King Muwatalli II and the battalions sent by his regional allies. The outcome is still a mystery; both rulers returned home claiming victory. But the importance of this

SIGHTS
Büyük Tapınak (Great Temple)

A single entrance to the city remains today; it leads straight to the Lower City and its walled Büyük Tapınak. At 15,000 square meters—or twice the size of an American football field—this temple was Hattuşaş's largest building. It was dedicated to the Weather God of

Hatti and the Sun Goddess of Arinna; only the king and queen, as the high priests of the land, and their personally handpicked temple priests could reach the innermost sanctuary. The inner court was open, surrounded by high walls, and paved with sizable flat stones. Some of these stones can still be seen in the rear (eastern) right corner. While its completion date is uncertain, foundation ruins show over 80 storerooms and dressing rooms believed to have been utilized by priests. The remains of hundreds of 2,000-liter vessels used to store foodstuff attest that the temple was not only used for ritual purposes, but also as a central part of daily life.

Büyükkale
(Great Fortress)
From the Great Temple, walk up the road and turn left at the fork for Büyükkale. This royal citadel dominates the entire ancient city from a rocky pinnacle. Comprised of 16 buildings enclosed by another set of fortifications, the palace housed the king, his court, and palace officials, as well as provided shelter for the "Bearers of the Golden Lances" (the palace guard). The citadel's center offers fantastic views of the city and the valley to the north. The bulk of clay tablets found in Hattuşaş were discovered in the three buildings located on the southern side of the palace. Original contracts, official documents, oracular prophecies, cult practices, folklore, legal decisions, and historical texts were all stored on wooden shelves here.

Nişantaş
(Marked Rock)
Nişantaş—or the Northern Complex—located just above the Great Fortress, is another rock outcropping that once held a grand edifice adorned with massive sphinxes. There's a 8.5-meter-long inscription in which the name of the site appears in Luvian hieroglyphics. The 11 vertical lines chiseled onto the smoothed rock have become so eroded that the text remains indecipherable. It dates from the reign of Shupiluliuma II, the last of the well-known

Great Kings of Hattuşaş. It's highly plausible that the inscription refers to the construction of a monument the Great King commissioned for his father, or details his long list of accomplishments, like a bloody battle at sea followed by a landing on Cyprus.

Hieroglyphic Chamber 2
Across the road from Nişantaş, a footpath leads to Hieroglyphic Chamber 2, where Hattuşaş's best and recently discovered collection of reliefs are on display. These have weathered the test of time exceptionally well thanks to a mound of earth that kept them buried for centuries. A relief of a cloaked sun-god wearing slippers curled at the toe graces the rear wall. The double-winged sun at the top of his head reveals his identity; his left hand holds a curved rod, while his right holds a slightly modified version of an Egyptian ankh (the emblem of life). The relief to the left represents Shupiluliuma II, who commissioned the construction of this chamber. Ever the warrior, he holds a sword in his belt and a lance in his right hand, with a bow over his shoulder. It's interesting that he chose to be portrayed wearing a pointed hat on his head, which was typically ascribed to divinities during the era, even though he was still alive when the building was created. And just across are six lines chiseled in Luvian pictograms, explaining that through the blessings of the gods, Great King Shupiluliuma conquered several lands, including Tarhuntassa (an ancient city whose location is still unknown); established new cities; and made the appropriate sacrifices to the gods. The last sentence speaks of "a divine earth-road," which states that beneath the chamber is a symbolic passage into the underworld.

Kral Kapı
(King's Gate)
Lying on the city's southeastern-most point is Kral Kapı. It is the best preserved of Hattuşaş's five gates, and is a mirror image to the Lion's Gate to the west. This gate is flanked by two towers, each measuring a whopping 10 by 15 meters and bearing its own arched entrance.

The relief of a warrior on this gate faces the city, as opposed to decorating the exterior. The horns appearing on the helmet tell us that the warrior may well be Sharrumma (son of the weather-god Teshub and the sun-goddess Hepat); the deity was the patron and protector of the Great King Tudhaliya IV (1237–1209 B.C.), so the latter may have commissioned this gate.

Ramparts and More Gates

Moving south along the 250-meter-long ramparts at **Yerkapi** (Earth Gate), one enters Hittite Temple District, where 30 temples have been found to date. The artificial ridge of Yerkapı is the southernmost and highest point of the city; it arches along the summit from the Lion's Gate in the west and the King's Gate in the east, connecting through the Sphinx Gate in the center. To get to the latter, you can either take the 70-meter-long postern (tunnel) or climb the narrow stone staircase. The **Sphinx Gate** is not flanked by towers, as opposed to those of great cities of antiquity, but passes unceremoniously through a single tower. It's named for the four sculpted sphinxes that once flanked the city's southernmost entrance. Bearing a human head and the body of a lion, sphinxes are heterogeneous and traditionally ascribed to the Egyptians, who used them to represent their kings. The Hittites adopted their symbol, and softened the facial contours to represent the female. All that remains today is a chipped representation on the western wall. Moving westward, the **Lion's Gate** is still fairly intact, with its well-preserved figures. These beastly felines were popular ornaments used on gates and temple entrances in the Near East and to protect the structures against evil.

Yazılıkaya (Inscribed Rock)

About two kilometers to the northeast of Hattuşaş, the shrine of Yazılıkaya is the most famous Hittite rock sanctuary. Two chambers, preceded by an impressive procession of gods of the Hittite pantheon, are edged by natural 12-meter-high rock faces. While both

Chambers A and B were used for ritual purposes as early as the 15th century B.C., the ornate reliefs of gods were commissioned by Hittite Kings Tudhaliya IV and Shupiluliuma II. This holy site was used to celebrate the new year and the beginning of spring, and has been aptly called the House of the New Year's Celebration. **Chamber A** is by far the most impressive, not only for the prowess of Hittite architects, but also for the sheer beauty of the rock-carved impressions and the amount of data collected about the mythical hierarchy of the ancient Anatolians. The left wall details a procession of male gods, donning traditional kilts, curly slippers, and horned hats; while the right wall depicts a parade of female deities wearing crowns and long skirts. Interestingly, the goddess of love and war Shaushka (Mesopotamian goddess Ishtar) is shown on the male side with her two chambermaids. These lower deities are marching toward a central tableau, which depicts the pantheon's supreme deities: the weather-god Teshub and the sun-goddess Hebat, with their son Sharruma, daughter Alanzu, and their granddaughter bringing up the rear. The wife of Hattusili III, Puduhepa, who was the daughter of a Hurrian priestess, was crucial in integrating Hurrian gods into the Hittite belief system. Such was the case with the Hurrian weather-god Teshub. But other culture's deities were assimilated as well, like the Mesopotamian god of wisdom Ea (Enki) that appears in the main procession. And dominating the main relief is a 3.5-meter-high representation of King Tudhaliya IV, son of Hattusili III and Puduhepa.

Chamber B's reliefs are in a better state of preservation than those in Chamber A because the open-air room remained partly buried with earth until the end of the 19th century. On the wall to the right is a procession of the gods of the underworld; while on the left stands a depiction of Sharruma, the patron god of Tudhaliya IV. Flanking the relief is an unexpected iconography of a large upright sword formed by two lions with the head of a god for a handle. It's attributed to Nergal, the god of the underworld. The last relief, a cartouche inscribed with the name and title of Tudhaliya IV, tells us that this chamber may have been a memorial to the Great King and may have been erected by his son Shupiluliuma II.

ACCOMMODATIONS AND FOOD

Stopping for a bite before the long way back to Ankara or Cappadocia is usually in order, and one of the best places to do just that is the recently restored **Hattuşaş Restaurant** (300m south of Hattuşaş's entrance, 0364/452-2013, www.hattusha.com, 15TL). The fare is typically Anatolian, with vegetables cooked in olive oil, meat grills, and stews. English-speaking owners Ahmet and Mustafa also run the 14 clean and spacious en suite rooms at **Hotel Baykal** (300m south of Hattuşaş's entrance, 0364/452-2013, www.hattusha.com, s. €20, d. €30, breakfast included).

For an overnight, the folks at **Hotel Aşıkoğlu** (Çarşı Mahallesi 25, 0364/452-2004, www.hattusas.com, s. €25, d. €35, breakfast included) offer 33 en suite rooms, each boasting a balcony, TV, and free Wi-Fi. There's also an onsite restaurant with an á la carte menu and an open buffet.

Also, these hotels go a long way as a tourist information center, providing maps, books, and historical anecdotes if you're lucky.

GETTING THERE

Conquering the 210-kilometer distance from Ankara to Boğazkale (the site of Hattuşaş) by bus or *dolmuş* (communal taxi) can take up to five hours. Doing it by car slashes the time spent sputtering the often-serpentine road by at least half. Plus the road up northeast is both scenic and easy to navigate. Out of Ankara, take Highway D200/E80, heading east toward Samsun. Take the Çorum turnoff (D190) past Süngürlü, and continue another six kilometers east until Boğazkale (formerly Boğazköy) signage will take you toward the Tokat road heading south. Another 20 kilometers of spectacular scenery will lead you straight to the archaeological site. Make sure to fill up the tank before departure, or at least before leaving the intercontinental highway (D200/E80), to avoid disasters along the way.

Those adamant on not springing for a car rental can still travel by public transportation. From Ankara, a bus heads to Süngürlü (25TL), where a transfer by *dolmuş* covers the remaining 23 kilometers to Boğazkale.

BACKGROUND

The Land

Straddling easternmost Europe and western Asia, Turkey's western coast extends south from the country's northern borders it shares with Greece and Bulgaria to the province of Anatolia. The coastline hugs the Aegean Sea, the Mediterranean Sea's largest bays, on its journey southward. To the north is Thrace, Turkey's European portion, which is delineated by the Black Sea to the east, the Bosphorus Straits, the Dardanelles and the Sea of Marmara to the south, the Aegean to the west, and Greece and Bulgaria to the north. Thrace's southeastern-most point is Istanbul, Turkey's—as well as Europe's—most populous metropolis. Istanbul straddles the natural Bosphorus Straits, which link the Black Sea to the Sea of Marmara and also mark the continental divide between Europe and Asia. The city sprawls north of the Bosphorus as European Istanbul, and southward as its Asian counterpart.

This book's coverage extends east to the major tourist destination of Cappadocia, at the center of Turkey and the arid Anatolian steppe the country stretches over, and south to the Mediterranean Sea.

GEOGRAPHY

Turkey's western and central regions covered in this book encompass roughly 375,400 square

© JESSICA TAMTÜRK

kilometers and can be divided into four distinct regions: the Marmara region, which spans 67,300 square kilometers; parts of the Mediterranean region, which covers some 61,100 square kilometers; the Aegean region, which covers for 85,000 square kilometers; and Central Anatolia, which measures about 151,000 square kilometers.

Marmara

The Marmara region extends over Europe and Asia and is bisected by three bodies of water, the Bosphorus and Dardanelles Strait as well as the Sea of Marmara, which link to form a natural continental divide. The Thracian Peninsula extends over its northern section, which is girded by the Black Sea to the east, the Aegean to the west, and Greece and Bulgaria to the north.

Exotically magnificent Istanbul is at the point of continental convergence. It has an unmatched architectural legacy that illustrates its highly sought-after strategic location. The city's coasts sprawl along the Bosphorus, whose flanks boast luxuriant green groves pocked by centuries-old firs and colorful Judas trees. Turkey's largest city and one of the world's most expansive and populated metropolises, Istanbul extends over 1,830.93 square kilometers. Its western and southern peripheries are delineated by the Sea of Marmara and even include an archipelago of dainty islands. Marmara's highest peak is Mount Uludağ (2543 meters), a favorite winter destination for snow enthusiasts. At its foot lies "Green" Bursa, whose densely forested mountains and verdant grasslands give the city its moniker. Dotting the region's southern quadrant are wide lakes and sinuous rivers used annually by hundreds of showy migratory bird colonies.

Turkey's Western Mediterranean Region

This region earns its moniker from the adjacent Mediterranean Sea. Turkey's western coast occupies roughly 7 percent of the country's total area. Running parallel to the coast are the lofty Western Taurus mountains—a.k.a.

the Beydağları range; the chain's highest peaks loom at altitudes above 3,000 meters. These crags, which sometime jut dramatically into the Med's limpid waters or form narrow valleys before reaching the coast, start disgorging their snow pack beginning in April, transforming tranquil streams into gushing rivers that give even the best white-water rafters a run for their money. Their remote mountain plateaus boast serene lakes surrounded by the plushest woods. This abundant mountain runoff, compounded with Anatolia's highly fertile soil and the warm and humid Mediterranean climate, makes this region's plains agricultural powerhouses.

Aegean

The Aegean region is one of Turkey's most splendid destinations, thanks to its superb coastline. Bounded by the Marmara region on the north, the Mediterranean region on the south and southwest, and the Central Anatolia region on the east, Turkey's Aegean territory takes its name from the sea that borders on it. Crystal-clear waters lined with unspoiled beaches to the west and hundreds of kilometers of olive groves on rolling hills describe the northernmost territory, while the south gives way to a craggy coastline blanketed in pine forests. Its continuity of plains coupled with its unusually mild climate, highly fecund soil, and constant sea breeze make it a haven for vintners and farmers alike. No wonder every civilization that encountered it was enrapt by this sublime coast, where the Greek language and mythology were born.

Central Anatolia

Geographically speaking, Central Anatolia is a plateau. But what the name lacks in excitement the landscape certainly compensates with a wide variety of terrain. Central Anatolia extends inland from the Aegean Sea between two mountains chains to the point where these ranges meet further east. Accounting for 19 percent of Turkey's land area, it is the largest of the five regions. Its arid highlands comprise the heartland of the country. Ankara, Turkey's remote capital, sits protected in the middle of this elevated plateau. Similar to the steppe in the Russian Federation, Central Anatolia is situated at altitudes of about 600 meters in the west and climbs to about 1,200 meters in the east. Its two largest basins are Konya Ovası and Tuz Gölü (Salt Lake). The north is mostly wooded while the south is rather bland; the eastern area, however, is characterized by the eerie Cappadocian landscape. The distinct and unique tufa cones that pepper this area's wide dusty bowls were formed 50 million years ago during the Tertiary Period, when the surrounding volcanoes spewed out massive amounts of volcanic pediment over the chimneys and craters that dot the terrain. Wind played a big part in the erosion of the chimneys to create the phallic-looking landscape of today.

CLIMATE

Turkey's four western and central regions all boast different climates. The Marmara Region to the northwest, with its former Ottoman capitals of Edirne, Bursa, and Istanbul, enjoys a moderate climate. Average temperatures in winter and summer are 4°C and 27°C, respectively. But expect frost and even snow during the winter season, the wet months of December through March. Summer's humid heat waves last for days, with temperatures closer to 35°C and higher, particularly in the crowded cities. The buffer seasons of spring and autumn are typically mild but can change quickly, moving from showers to sunshine from one day or one hour to the next. The geography is a victim of the wrath of its prevailing winds. Lodos, a southwesterly wind that affects the Sea of Marmara, wreaks havoc on marine transport year-round, and the northeasterly wind known as Poyraz brings the Black Sea's freezing temperatures to the Marmara Region in winter.

Turkey's western Mediterranean region enjoys a characteristically Mediterranean climate with hot dry summers and moderately warm and rainy winters. The summer season lasts nine months, but apart from midsummer the coast is quite bearable. Sunny weather prevails 300 days of the year, and sea temperature never dips below 15°C nor exceeds 28°C.

© JESSICA TAMTÜRK

Istanbul experiences occasional snowfalls in the winter months.

July and August temperatures can hover above the 40°C mark, making those heavily traveled months horrendous on unsuspecting tourists. In Antalya, the region's largest city, winter temperatures rarely dip below 15°C. On the other hand, in 2009 late July afternoon temperatures reached 42°C with humidity at almost 85 percent, demonstrating that the climate can be unexpected even with the best-laid travel plans. The entire Mediterranean coast is protected from cold northerly winds by the Taurus Mountain range.

The climate of the Aegean is superbly mild. Summers are hot but rarely exceed 40°C even during July and August. Both spring and autumn are sunny, with blue skies the norm and daily temperatures averaging in the high teens. Winters are mild with occasional precipitation. What makes this region's climate so ideal for agriculture are the many mountains that stretch both perpendicular and parallel to the coast to allow the sea breeze to be contained within the numerous wide valleys created by the chain. The Aegean cities beyond these hills, like Balıkesir and Manisa, enjoy a more Continental climate. For fun in the sun, like sunbathing and water sports, as well as mountain sports, the Aegean region's summer months can't be beat. If traipsing through ancient ruins is more what you plan to do, more temperate spring and autumn are ideal.

Central Anatolia shows characteristics of a continental climate due to its elevation, but as you move south and east it becomes a cold, semiarid climate. Averaging less than 25 centimeters per year, rainfall is sparse and typically occurs during the fall and spring; water conservation in cities like Konya and Ankara often becomes an issue, particularly during the summer months. Wheat crops, Anatolia's main agricultural staple, fail during years of drought. Summers are bone dry and torrid, with day temperatures averaging 29°C, falling to the mid-teens at night. Winters are cold and snowy, with daytime temperatures generally around 5°C and evenings at -2°C. The rule of thumb for visiting Central Anatolia

is that summers can heat up intensely, while the amount of winter snowfall is directly proportional to altitude. Most folks traveling to Cappadocia for the first time assume that it enjoys the same climate as coastal regions; that couldn't be further from the truth. Cappadocia's summers are dry and sizzling, while the winters can bring snowfall.

ENVIRONMENTAL ISSUES
While Turkey's main environmental angst relates to the lack of water, its economic boom, which began in the early 1990s and has peaked since 2005, coupled with steady population growth have brought increased levels of pollution and have put the country's environment at risk. From marine and noise problems to land and air pollution, Turkey's government has joined its peers worldwide to squarely address sustainable development.

Turkey's coastal resort towns and tourist centers are rich in indigenous flora and fauna and lack the once notorious high level of pollution. Rampant chemical dumping, heavy air pollution in urban areas, and oil spills from ships have been reduced but still happen.

The Turkish public, in tune with the government, is becoming more conscious of the environment, protecting it, and the direct impact of their behavior. The turnaround is attributed to efforts by Greenpeace, who launched nationwide environmentalist activities in the mid-1990s. Local organizations took note and became more active in not only protecting the flora and fauna in Turkey but also propagating it. Municipalities even got on the bandwagon by providing free trees to residents to promote planting, and the Ministry of Forests changed its name to the Ministry of Forests and Environment. In addition to protecting woodlands, the ministry has enacted legislation to safeguard the environment that has included tougher fines for poachers and a zero-tolerance policy on chemical dumping.

Recently, changes in indoor and environmental pollution at the municipal and national levels have seen two big advances. Heavy smoking indoors was one of the big issues, often a negative memory for tourists, until late 2008, when a national ban on smoking in airports, hospitals, and state offices took effect. And in late 2009 smoking was finally banned in all public places, including restaurants and bars. The second advance was the ban on plastic bags proffered at grocery stores.

But Turkey still has a way to go on protecting its environment. The lack of waste and sewage treatment systems is one issue, as is air pollution from heating with coal and rising vehicle emissions. One of the biggest issues remains oil spillage along Turkey's coastline, particularly along the Bosphorus and Dardanelles Strait, where the more than 5,000 ships that pass through annually are strictly monitored for spillage and waste dumping.

Now that Turkey is a formal candidate for membership in the European Union, its environmental and power-generating efforts will be scrutinized even more, so it is taking steps to relieve its dependence on oil and gas imports, including building a large network of hydroelectric plants in the southeastern provinces. It is also seeking cleaner-burning natural gas to replace coal in power generation. What makes these positive changes toward sustainable development so stunning is that Turkey, now a nation of 80 million, is effecting change swiftly at both the national and individual level.

Flora and Fauna

FLORA

Tulips originate from Turkey, not from Holland. People often find this surprising, along with learning about other indigenous plants that grow ubiquitously in specific parts of the country. These include pulses like chickpeas and lentils, nuts such as almonds and hazelnuts, and fruits that include figs, apricots, cherries, and sour cherries. In fact, the Latin names of some of these species even include their point of origin, as with the plump and ever-so-sweet Carian figs, named in Latin as *Ficus caria* after the ancient Anatolian civilization who cultivated them in the southern Aegean region. Turkey is the original home of other showy blooms including crocuses, snowdrops, lilies, and fritillaries.

Anatolia is one of the world's pantries, with plants that have been cultivated here for human and animal sustenance since prehistory; it is no surprise that bipeds and quadrupeds have sought this land's bounty for eons. Two of those crops are wheat and barley, for which Turkey, along with its neighbors to the east, has become one of only four of the world's gene centers for the cultivated foodstuff used agriculturally. More than 30 species of disease- and weather-resistant wheat, for instance, still grow wild on the Anatolian plateau. In the long run, this translates into the transfer of ideal genes from the gene centers to various cultivars around the globe, as well as billions saved for the recipient's economies and a product that retains its taste. Aside from its indigenous crops, Anatolia's climate enables the cultivation of virtually any plant on earth, as is the case in Antalya, where the cultivation of kiwifruit, a native of northeast Asia, now thrives.

While 27 percent of Turkey's territory is forested, the remainder is home to seven species of trees, none more important that the olive tree, which accounts for huge tracts of deliciously green orchards and a billion-dollar industry. The olive leaf, which has been a symbol of abundance, glory, and peace around the world since it appeared in the crowns of the victors of war and sporting events in ancient Greece, comes from a tree that's allegedly indigenous to Anatolia. The wild maple, sycamore, bay laurel, pistachio, Turkish hazel, Cretan date palm, lime, and showy Judas trees are all indigenous to the Anatolian plateau.

Turkey's coasts are lush with vegetation. The Aegean and Mediterranean coasts host tens of thousands of species that thrive in the Mediterranean climate. The more popular

OLIVES AND OLIVE OIL

The ancient Mediterranean people believed olive oil to have magical and medicinal characteristics, and some believed it to be the source of the fountain of youth and beauty. Homer referred to it as liquid gold. The ancient Egyptian pharaohs were ritually buried with flasks of it, as evidenced in Tutankhamen's tomb. Olympians in Ancient Greece anointed their bodies with it, and olive branches, believed to parlay its power onto the beholder, were the original Olympics medal. The olive tree's leafy branch, while still considered the symbol of peace and abundance, once crowned triumphant conquerors after bloody battles. And ultimately, three major organized religions – Islam, Christianity and Judaism – ritually use the golden liquid and olive tree branches to bless and purify.

Turkey is one of the largest suppliers of olive oil to the United States, coming in third after Italy and Spain. As much as 70 percent of Turkish olive oil is exported is blended with lesser quality oils – from Tunisia, for example – to produce a less expensive oil. The bulk of Turkish olive oil makes its way to Italy, where the mixing process takes place, before being re-imported to the United States. This trade between western Europe and Asia Minor, according to fossilized remains found in Spain, North Africa and Italy, dates back to the 6th millennium B.C.

What makes Turkish olives different than those cultivated by its European counterparts is the sandy quality of the soil in which their tree's grow, the prevalence of a sea breeze along the coast, and the sheer variety of the fruits. The whole adds up to a much fruitier, lighter taste than most olive oils. The growing environment is organic, and the fruit itself is generally harvested by hand. This is what the Turks believe, while Italians, on the other hand, staunchly argue that sun, stone, drought, silence and solitude all add up to an ideal growing medium for the olive.

The end user, however, cares more about its health and nutritional values. We know that extra virgin is much better than regular olive oil. In fact, the former is the most digestible of all edible fats. Nutritionists even boast that it assists in the assimilation of vitamins A, D and K; that contains powerful essential acids that the human body does not produce; that it slows down aging; and, that it boosts liver and intestinal functions. But what we truly care about is its unique taste, and its organoleptic properties: flavor, bouquet, and color. By standards applied by the European Community, E.V.O.O. (extra virgin olive oil) only achieves the highest quality when its taste is perfect. That means the oil must have a minimum organoleptic rating of 6.5 out of 10, an acidity of 1 percent or less, and must be untreated.

Olives and olive oil are produced throughout Anatolia, but the water-lapped west is king. The Northwest area around the Sea of Marmara is noted for its black olives – the kind that end up on the Turkish breakfast table. The Aegean and Mediterranean coasts, however, produce the olives that make the best oil. The land surrounding the Gulf of Edremit, particularly around Ayvalık, is reputed to be those who produce some of the best oil in the world.

---

plants include showy oleanders, fuchsias, hydrangeas, jasmines, wisterias, and magnolias; fragrant bushes like rosemary, thyme, oregano, lavender, and juniper; imposing forests of oaks, pines, and cypresses; and fruit trees like lemon, orange, and bergamot.

FAUNA

Turkey is a natural habitat for one of the world's widest varieties of animals. To prove that point, Europe in its entirety boasts 60,000 species, while Turkey has 80,000—and that's without counting subspecies.

Migratory birds have exploited Turkey's strategic position as a bridge linking Europe to Asia and Africa for millennia. In spring, avian migrators fly northwards from Africa to Asia and Europe, and they return in autumn. But what has to be the world's most spectacular migration is that of the showy stork, which

© JESSICA TAMTÜRK

The tulip bulb's origins lay deep within Anatolia.

flies above Istanbul's Bosphorus Straits in spring and autumn. More than 250,000 have been counted as they glide through the clouds over the course of a few weeks. Birds of prey also have opted for this transcontinental route for eons as a migratory course, perhaps for the bounty in the variety of fish species that choose this route to move from the Black Sea to the warmer waters of the Sea of Marmara. The unspoiled wetlands peppering the country's Aegean and Mediterranean regions are ideal habitats for colonies of rare and endangered species of birds like the showy Dalmatian pelican, lustrous pygmy cormorant, the slender-billed curlew, fancy flamingoes, and chatty wild ducks and geese.

While migratory birds retreat inland, the shores of the Aegean and Mediterranean are a refuge for two altogether different near-extinct species. The shy Mediterranean monk seal, whose numbers have dipped to under 400 worldwide, prefers the finned bounty found near the tiny islands off the shore of Foça in the Aegean region. So far, 50 are known to

live in Turkey's waters. The gracious loggerhead sea turtle chooses the warm sands found at specific sites along the coast of southwestern Turkey as ideal nesting grounds. Two species of sea turtles known as *Caretta caretta* breed in Turkey. The species and their breeding grounds are being strictly protected, and efforts by teams of volunteers have been highly effective. İztuzu Beach and neighboring Köyceğiz along the Mediterranean have both been declared off-limits to development and have even been designated as Specially Protected Zones. Consequently there are more than a dozen new sea turtle breeding grounds along the Mediterranean coast.

Indigenous to Central Anatolia are a slew of quadrupeds that used to roam wild in the steppe and along the Taurus Mountains. The fallow deer, which was introduced to Europe in the late 1st century A.D. by the Romans, originates from the foothills of the Taurus Mountains just east of Antalya. This speckled ruminant was the preferred game of Paleolithic hunters more than 10,000 years ago, according to bones found at archeological sites. Another native is the domesticated sheep, a direct descendant of the wild sheep *Ovis musimon anatolica*. The Anatolian leopard was the feline of choice used in gladiator battles during the Roman era; in fact, 2,000-year-old tiger traps can still be seen scattered throughout the Taurus Mountains. The tiger is also from the central and eastern regions of Anatolia, and its modern name is a derivative coined from the Tigris River. The lion was also a native of the Asian plain, as evidenced by Hittite statues found in modern Boğazkale.

The breeds of cats, goats, and rabbits that bear the name Angora are all indigenous to the Turkish capital, Ankara, and its surrounding region in central Anatolia. The rabbit is bred for its long silky hair. The deep-piled fleece harvested once a year from the Angora goat is commercially referred to as mohair, a luxury fiber that is highly sought after for its warmth, sheen, and durability.

History

Linking the Black and Mediterranean Seas, Asia, and Europe, Anatolia has been a crossroads since ancient times. Numerous civilizations have marched across and fought for this expansive peninsula for more than 5,000 years. The Greeks once called it Asia Minor, but today the Anatolian plateau is home to present-day Turkey, whose realm extends northwest into the historically highly coveted Thrace. During the seven millennia since the earliest people set foot on its expanse, more than 20 Eastern and Western civilizations have followed suit. From the early Hittites to the Assyrians, Persians, Greeks, Romans, Selçuks, Ottomans, and finally modern-day Turks, the land has witnessed the rise of numerous cultures, languages, art forms, and religions. This historical legacy, divided among eight distinct eras, is responsible for much of mankind's modern beliefs, indoctrination, and spirituality.

EARLY ANTIQUITY

While a variety of groups inhabited the regions of modern-day Turkey well before the first civilization ever congealed, Asia Minor's history officially begins with the Hittites in 2000 B.C. These warriors, who had migrated to Anatolia from the Pontic Steppe, present-day Ukraine, were a fierce people who rivaled the Egyptians and Babylonians. For 800 years they annotated the minutiae of their daily lives on tablets with a Hurrian cuneiform writing system inherited from the Assyrians. These precious stone relics, which only survive as copies, detail Bronze Age life and relate the major military campaigns of the era. The first to successfully smelt iron, the Hittites also thrived on agriculture, carpentry, and pottery. Silver, then found in massive deposits along the Taurus Mountains, was their currency of trade. They worshipped local deities that appeared in sets of local pantheons, headed by a fertility god responsible for the weather. The sun goddess, Hebat, ruled supreme as the mother of all living things, which suggests that a matrilineal system was alive in Anatolia. A Hittite king served as high priest as well as supreme ruler, military commander, and high judge, but the opinion of his wife was also valued; the signatures of queens Puduhepa and Suppiluliuma I appeared on peace treaties along with those of their husbands.

The great Hittite Empire began its short and dramatic decline at the beginning of the 12th century B.C. As the rise of seafaring peoples from mainland Greece threatened the coast, the Hittites moved troops en masse west to protect their supremacy over the Aegean coast, and the Egyptians attacked Kadesh (now western Syria) in the hope of obtaining another coveted route across Mesopotamia. With troops guarding the western and southeastern fronts, the Assyrians took control of Mitani (now northern Syria). But in the west, the seafaring peoples proved too numerous for the Hittites, and the entire Mediterranean and Aegean coasts fell just as the Assyrians and Egyptians were gaining on Hittite turf 1,000 kilometers to the east. The Hittites found themselves landlocked and vulnerable to attacks from all four directions. By 1180 B.C. their capital, Hattuşaş, was burned to the ground in a collaborative assault not from the empire's known enemies in the west and the east but from a coalition from the north of the Kaskians of the eastern Black Sea region and the Briges from the Balkans.

As the Hittites disappeared from history, several sovereign Neo-Hittite states sprang up in central Asia Minor. Most notable among them were the Urartu, the Carchemish, and the Milid, but they were absorbed by the Assyrians in the 8th century B.C. By that time the Greeks were continuing their onslaught of the Aegean coast, forming small coastal states. According to the *Iliad,* the 8th century B.C. tome written by the legendary poet Homer, an Ionian from the city of Smyrna, the first Greek victory was at Troy when they cunningly overtook the city-state with their mythological wooden horse. thanks to *The Histories* of Herodotus (484–425 B.C.), regarded as the Father of History, we have a record of Persian supremacy and consequent defeat by the Greeks in the first-ever systematic collection of research that has not only been verified for accuracy but also reads like a thriller.

LATE ANTIQUITY

During the mid-first millennium B.C., a variety of neighboring indigenous sovereign states flourished in Anatolia. Phrygia, Galatia, Lycaonia, and Cappadocia composed the inner lands; Thrace, Troya, Mysia, and Bithynia were the northeast; Lydia and Caria the west; Lycia, Pisidia, and Pamphylia made up the southwest; and, Paphlagonia and Cilicia the southeast. While all have left their mark on history, none reached the level of Lydia. Its famous king and later emperor Croesus was *the* celebrity of the ancient world for being, as the saying goes, "as rich as Croesus." He lavished his capital, Sardis, with extravagant monuments and public buildings. His subjects, the Lydians, were the first to mint coins, using the precious metals that abounded in the mines and silt of the nearby Pactolus River. But as good a ruler as Croesus may have been, he was vain, and word of the lavish parties attended by the era's most celebrated dignitaries reached the ear of the Persian emperor Cyrus the Great, founder of the powerful Achaemid Empire. The appeal of Lydia's riches was so great that he launched an assault west toward Croesus's capital, conquering the whole of Asia Minor in the process in 546 B.C. Lydia became a Persian province, and its neighboring sovereign states in Asia Minor, except for Lycia, became Persian satrapies.

This lasted until Macedonian king Alexander the Great accepted the surrender of the Persian provincial capital and treasury of Sardis just weeks after conquering the Persian emperor Darius III's troops at the Battle of the Granicus near the Sea of Marmara in 334 B.C. He went on to lay siege to the Ionians, first at Halicarnassus (modern-day Bodrum) and then all along the coast, forcing his enemies—the pirate Memnon of Rhodes and the satrap of Caria, Orontobates—to escape by sea. And so went his conquests all along the coast: First Lycia's inner realm fell, followed by Pamphylia's and their coastal towns.

But in 323 B.C., Alexander's untimely death, at the age of 32 from a fever brought on by either poisoning or natural causes, forced the breakup of his immense empire. Asia Minor folded into a series of four Hellenistic kingdoms that would be ruled by his successors, known as the Diadochi. Among them, the kingdom of Pergamum was allotted to Alexander's former general Lysimachus. Being a commander by nature, Lysimachus put his officer Philetaerus in charge of both the populace and the treasury in order to embark on military campaigns. After the death of Lysimachus, the impotent yet cunning Philetaerus, by then the sole ruler of Pergamum, went on to reinforce the city and name his nephew Eumenes as his successor. Eumenes I became the first king of the Attalid Dynasty, which lasted for 130 years. During that time, there was constant warfare among the Syrians, the Achaean Greeks, and the Seleucids of Antioch—a dynasty descended from another of Alexander's generals, Seleucus. The kingdom of Pergamum found itself surrounded on all sides by enemies hungry to expand their empires, so Pergamum allied with Rome, which was slowly engulfing the Balkans. By 190 B.C., Eumenes's fears were realized as the Syrians, after suffering an embarrassing loss to the Greeks the year before in east-central Greece, laid siege to the capital of his kingdom. The Romans, who had plowed effortlessly through western Asia Minor, fulfilled their part of the agreement by impressively defeating the Syrians at Magnesia. For their efforts, the Romans absorbed the entire territory of Asia Minor in 188 B.C. but allowed Pergamum sovereignty—until 133 B.C. when the last Attalid king, the heirless Attalus III, bequeathed his kingdom to Rome. The city of Pergamum remained the administrative capital of Asia Minor under the Romans until Ephesus replaced it in 29 B.C.

ROMAN ERA AND CHRISTIANIZATION

Around the time of the birth of Christ, trade and culture flourished in Roman Asia Minor. Roman emperors Augustus (63 B.C.–A.D. 14), Tiberius Julius Caesar (A.D. 14–37), Trajan (A.D. 53–117), and Hadrian (A.D. 117–138) all traveled east from the empire's capital at Rome to assist in the development of the province of Asia Minor. Their ports of call, the great cities of Ephesus, Aphrodisias, Perge, and Aspendos, were all drastically improved. The first action was to lay down a complex road system to connect these early metropolises to the rest of the empire. Next, exquisite monuments and temples were erected throughout. Public facilities like libraries, fountains, and sewage systems were also added. Among the few structures to have survived the many earthquakes that have hit this seismically active region in the two millennia since, the almost-intact Library of Celsus in Ephesus stands as evidence of the mastery of early Roman architecture. Culture was impacted as well; some of antiquity's important scientific and literary authorities originated in Asia Minor during this period. The geographer Strabo (64 B.C.–A.D. 24), who wrote the decisive tome *Geographica,* not only detailed the geography of his era but also its peoples.

The greatest change to sweep through Asia Minor under the Romans was the advent of Christianity. Immediately after the crucifixion of Christ circa A.D. 30, early Christians escaped Roman persecution in Jerusalem and fled to Asia Minor. They settled en masse throughout the plain in cities like Ephesus, Hierapolis, and Cappadocia, practicing their faith underground while the other residents still worshipped the Greek goddess Artemis. Some two decades later, missionaries like Paul the Apostle, who settled for a while in Ephesus to preach, as well as John the Evangelist, who reportedly wrote his Gospel there and brought the Virgin Mary to the city, propagated the Gospels and were key to the conversion of countless early Anatolians. By 380, Theodosius I had declared Christianity the official religion of Asia Minor and legalized the destruction of pagan temples. This development came just 55 years after the First Ecumenical Council, held in Nicae (Iznik), in which 300 church elders under the direction of Roman emperor Constantine the Great defined the religion's basic tenets.

Meanwhile, the metropolises along the coast had been eclipsed by the city on the Bosphorus. Either following the prediction of an oracle or just understanding its strategic appeal, Constantine arrived in the colony of Byzantium and renamed it Constantinopolis. The new capital of the Eastern Roman Empire—or the Byzantine Empire—became a center of learning, prosperity, and cultural preservation. The rest of this eastern empire prospered as well, albeit with less pomp, for the next few centuries. But while prosperity and expansion were constant, the Byzantines were no stranger to internal religious divisions—like the bloody Nika Riots of 532—and experienced recurring conflicts with their Arab neighbors to the east.

MEDIEVAL ERA

By the seventh century, Arab caliphates had launched the first of a series of wars challenging the Byzantines for control of Anatolia. These events, commonly referred as the Muslim Conquests, launched a chain of Christian counterattacks known as the Crusades. Between 634 and 718 the Arabs had twice tried unsuccessfully to capture Constantinople. But they were gaining elsewhere, securing—albeit momentarily—Roman Syria and Africa. After the impressive defeat of the Byzantines at Manzikert in 1071, the Selçuks swept across Anatolia and formed the first Turkic Empire.

The Selçuks, like other Turcoman peoples, had been pressured out of their homeland on the Asian steppes by the Mongols as early as 200 B.C. By the 800s these able shepherds had migrated south to the watershed of Transoxania—today's Central Asian states, where contact with Arabs gradually led them to convert to Islam. Adept farmers and livestock breeders, some Turkish tribes came under central administration following the tenets of Islamic orthodoxy, which even included taxation. Others, like the Oğhuz Turks, remained nomadic, pursuing the *gazı* tradition that sought to expand territory in the name of Islam while amassing huge riches in the process. Put simply, they had become Islamic mercenaries.

By 1080 the whole of Anatolia had fallen to the Selçuks. Along with the new rule came the gradual introduction of the Turkish language and Islamic religion. A century later, the Byzantines reasserted some of their rule in both western and northern Anatolia. The rest remained squarely in the hands of the Selçuk Sultanate of Rûm. In June 1243 the Mongols vanquished the Selçuks in the infamous Battle of Köse Dağ in northeastern Anatolia and proceeded west to conquer the Selçukian capital of Konya. This resulted in turmoil for the whole of Anatolia, and the Selçuk state soon disintegrated. The Mongols, allied with Turcoman chieftains, bloodily engulfed central and eastern Anatolia in 1255 and retained their stranglehold from their garrison near Ankara until 1335.

By the early 14th century, the majority of Anatolia was controlled by a number of Turkish Beyliks—or *ghazı* emirates. These somewhat autonomous states that had evolved from Turcoman tribes remained under the brooding watch of the Mongols. In 1330, two key events occurred: Smyrna, the last Byzantine stronghold, fell to the Turks; and Ottoman ruler Osman I emancipated his emirate by minting his own coins from his capital. The latter may not have been a great feat, but in that era, according to Islamic convention, manufacturing currency was the exclusive right of sovereigns. So with Anatolia entirely under Turkish control, the Ottomans began to systematically acquire Anatolian Turkish Beyliks from their capital in Bursa.

OTTOMAN ERA
A Budding Empire

Among the many Oğhuz leaders, the legendary Ertuğrul started a chain of events at the beginning of the 13th century throughout eastern and central Anatolia that prepared the stage for the birth of the mighty Ottomans. Founded in 1299, this empire developed in the ensuing seven centuries into a military powerhouse that drove though the entire Mediterranean region to absorb southeastern Europe and the Middle East, creating a rich cultural and spiritual legacy and changing the landscape of history. But with the easy expansion of the empire, Western Europe feared that the wrath of the "barbaric Turks" would forever destroy the social and political fabric of the West, and with it, Christianity.

In 1220, Ertuğrul, flanked by his 400 horsemen, joined the Selçuks in their quest westward. His military accomplishments against the Byzantines and other enemies so impressed Selçukian sultan Ala ad-Din Kay Qubadh I that the latter ceded rule of the Kayı clan and Karaca Dağ, a mountainous region near modern Ankara, in 1227. From there, Ertuğrul fulfilled yet another mission and conquered the village of Söğüt near the western Anatolian city of Bursa. By 1299 his eldest son, Osman, declared Söğüt the capital of his newly formed Ottoman emirate.

Osman I then pushed westward toward Bursa, which marked the southeastern frontier of the Byzantine Empire. In 1326, Bursa became the new Ottoman seat from which the protocol and tenets of this nascent political entity were founded. But his hopes were much greater, as he believed in a prophetic vision of an empire in the shape of a big tree whose roots spread through three continents and whose branches covered the sky.

The Ottoman expansion continued at the expense of the Byzantine Empire. With their eyes on Constantinople but not yet feeling ready to take on the heavily defended Byzantine capital, they moved north into the Thracian Peninsula. In 1361 they swept and conquered Adrianople (Edirne). Administratively centralized, fervent in their mission, and militarily unchallenged, the Ottomans gained quick and sweeping support from great numbers of people who had until then lived through decades of conflict and uncertainty. While devoutly Muslim, Ottomans accepted and even welcomed Anatolia's various creeds and religions, as the Selçuks and even the Hittites had done centuries earlier. This new domain became a cultural hodgepodge of Greeks, Turks, and other minorities practicing either Islam or Christianity. In fact, the Sultan Murad I even established a private corps of Janissary Guards—males culled from mostly Christian conquests.

Expansion

By the 1370s this nascent world power had plowed through the Eastern Mediterranean and the Balkans, and in 1389 they vanquished Kosovo, effectively quashing Serbian rule in the Balkans and paving for the way for further expansion through the European continent. But the integration of the fervently Christian Balkans demanded an entirely new system of governance. That's when the *millet* system was established, allowing the various minorities within the empire recognition and granting them autonomy. The last and largest European attempt to defeat the Ottomans occurred at the Battle of Nicopolis in Bulgaria in 1396. This final massive crusade failed miserably and even

served to galvanize the victorious Ottomans. By the beginning of the 15th century, the invincible Sultan Beyazit had grown arrogant. While in Ankara in 1402, his public derision of Tatar commander Tamerlane led to his capture, the defeat of his troops, and the end of the Ottomans' early eastward campaigns.

Recovering from this damaging embarrassment and waiting for the Mongols' retreat eastward took about 10 years. To make matters worse, inner turmoil over who should take the throne raged among Beyazit's nine sons. Mehmet I came out victorious. Swiftly regrouping, he focused on enlarging the empire by first occupying the lands just vacated by the Mongols throughout Anatolia, sweeping through Greece, and launching a first attack on Constantinople.

The ascension of born warrior Mehmet II to the throne in 1451 regalvanized the empire's mission. Aged just 19, Mehmet remained untried, and he equated the conquest of Constantinople as a rite of passage. For the next two years he schemed a strategy that first dealt with strengthening the Ottoman Navy. Then he set out to systematically encroach on and starve the city, the last Byzantine stronghold. He cut all sea access, including constructing the Rumelihisar fortress on the city's European flank to face the existing one on the opposite coast that had been built by his grandfather, Beyazit I. From there, he blocked land access on either side of the straits and halted westbound sea traffic through the cunning use of a massive chain connecting both fortresses. In 1453 the siege of Constantinople began with an army of more than 200,000 troops backed by a navy of over 300 vessels. Legend has it that he directed his fleet to line up side-by-side in the shape of a crescent at the western entrance of the Bosphorus, thus blocking eastbound supply lines from the sea. The Byzantines desperately pled for assistance from Europe, but their appeals went unheeded. The fall of Constantinople came on May 29, 1453, after a seven-week siege. This marked the end of the Byzantine Empire, and in an ironic twist, Mehmet even claimed the title of Roman emperor. His lineage included Byzantine imperials, since his great-grandfather Orhan had married a Byzantine princess. His claim was never recognized by Rome.

After this brilliant success, Mehmet renamed the city Istanbul and established it as the center of the Ottoman Caliphate. An erudite diplomat who spoke seven languages, he established universities throughout the city—many of which are still functioning; integrated Byzantine laws into the Islamic sharia system; erected grand mosques, mostly from the ruins of ancient ornate basilicas; and provided the template for the Ottoman *padishah*—harem—that would be emulated by his successors for more than 400 years.

But as culture flourished in the new capital, the Ottomans continued with the business at hand, that of expansion. Mehmet, by then known as "the Conqueror," launched campaigns annually, alternating between lands on the eastern and western fronts. From 1454 to 1463 he pushed to install a firm military defense line along the Danube River and the Adriatic coast against Hungary and Venice. First Serbia, along with its substantial silver and gold mines of Novo Brdo, fell. Greece's northern regions followed in 1458, along with Athens months later, and the whole of Serbia within a year. In the summer of 1461 another successful campaign engulfed the Candaroğlu Beylik in Sinope, and the Orthodox Christian lands of Armenia under Uzun Hasan and the Empire of Trebizond. Meanwhile, the Ottoman navy saw various successes as well. Competition raged for strongly contested seagoing trade routes with the Italian city-states in the Black Sea, Aegean, and Mediterranean as well as the Portuguese in the Red Sea and Indian Ocean.

As the boundaries of the Ottoman Empire expanded, the Janissary also grew in influence. Young Christian recruits of various cultures flocked from every corner of the growing realm in the hope of securing a lucrative career. With that, the Ottomans created the largest military corps in Europe from highly trained and highly resolved legions of volunteers.

With the ascension of Selim the Grim in 1512, the Ottomans hastened their expansion to the east and south. During one of his first military campaigns, Selim I crushed Shah Ismail of Persia in the Battle of Chaldiran in August 1514. He went on to establish Ottoman rule in Egypt and along the Red Sea, competing for dominance in the region with the Portuguese Empire.

Selim's son, Suleyman I, became known as "the Magnificent" throughout Europe; his acute competence as a strategist and commander was as esteemed as it was feared by his greatest adversaries. But at home, Suleyman gained the moniker of *kanûni*—the law-giver—for ordering the systematic codification of sharia law. He took Belgrade in 1521, and a year later he forced the Knights of Saint John to abandon Rhodes. Five years later, an Ottoman victory at the Battle of Mohács resulted in the conquest of Buda on the Danube. Suleyman tried to capture Vienna in 1529 but failed. This marked the end of Ottoman expansion to the west. After regrouping the troops, North Africa was next on the agenda. Lands up to the Moroccan border came under Ottoman rule during the early 1530s. For the first time, governors personally appointed by the sultan were installed in Algiers, Tunis, and Tripoli. The conquest of Mesopotamia ensued, forcing the Persians to retreat to their capital, Ardabil, in modern Azerbaijan. This victory yielded convenient access to the Persian Gulf.

The Fall of a World Power

During his reign, Suleyman diverted from the ancestral tradition of maintaining and enjoying the sensual comforts of a bevy of exotic beauties by marrying. Until his passing in 1566, he remained faithful to his beloved Hürrem Sultan. This manipulative Ukrainian concubine, who became known in the West as Roxelana, rose in the ranks of the sultan by sheer determination. She was a master plotter and conspired with Suleyman's greedy political aides to have two of her husband's eldest sons assassinated to ensure the ascension of her own son, Selim.

Ironically enough, Selim's competence was nowhere near his father's. Some historians believe that his ascension to the throne may have caused the decline of the Ottoman Empire. Unlike any other sultan who had come before him, he was untrained in the arts of war and politics. In fact, Selim was so utterly disinterested in all things political that he earned the moniker "Selim the Sot" in the west, and Muslims referred to him as "Selim the Drunkard" for his unbridled addictions to sex and alcohol. He relinquished all administrative duties and the rule of the empire to indulge in his other passions. But blaming him for the beginning of the Ottoman demise may be a bit unfair, as his father, Suleyman, may have been the cause. In the 1560s Suleyman attempted military campaigns that failed—the unsuccessful conquest of Malta and a naval ploy at bypassing the Portuguese domination of the Indian Ocean. Suleyman, weary from defeat and brokenhearted at the execution of his two beloved sons, relinquished rule to his chief vizier and withdrew deep inside Topkapı Palace's harem. So while Selim's rule may have lasted just eight years, his legacy of extreme indulgence established a precedent that would last until the empire's last days.

By the early 1600s the Ottoman Empire was still the most powerful state in the world, both financially and militarily. But the hands-on sultans of the past had been completely replaced by a sultanic government. Power shifted for a short time among four major players: the grand Vizier, the *Diwan* (Islamic treasury), the supreme court, and the ever-encroaching Janissaries. By the early 1700s the Janissaries had claimed the upper hand, and for the next century slowly absorbed all military and administrative positions within the administration and, as the sultans had done before them, bequeathed these offices to their sons. Eventually the Ottoman government decentralized into a military feudal class. But politics also ruled the affairs inside Topkapı Palace: Beginning with Roxelana, the first courtesan to participate hands-on in political affairs, the harem's leader—typically the

sultan's mother—brokered power to further the interests of her male progeny, sometimes at the empire's expense. Rebellion, assassination, confinement, and fratricide were common occurrences.

By the 1680s the majority of the Balkans was ceded to Austria, and while cartographers still claimed Egypt and Algeria as Ottoman territories, they had all but claimed temporary independence and would subsequently come under British and Napoleonic French rule. To the north the Austrian Hapsburgs and the Russians were pushing their eastern and southern boundaries just as aggressively. All the while, Western Europeans had regrouped as military powerhouses thanks to the riches flowing from their colonies in the Americas. Ottoman culture, which had grown dramatically during the empire's expansion, had all but faded. To make matters worse, Europeans had become leaders in industry and architecture. Their goods and craftsmanship became the envy of the culturally and scientifically stagnant Ottomans. Advances in engineering, including electricity technology and railway systems, all had to be imported.

At the beginning of the 19th century, sultan Selim III launched a series of military reform efforts to modernize the army along European standards. But the empire's religious leaders and the Janissary corps, who had both become disorganized and rather ineffective, opposed the changes. The Janissaries successfully revolted, bringing an end to Selim's reign and his life. But his successor, Mahmud II, resolutely took the throne, bloodily enacted his father's wishes, and avenged his father's murder by massacring the Janissary corps in 1826.

Meanwhile, the rise of nationalism that had swept through Europe also percolated into the Ottoman territories. With the birth of a national identity came an increasing sentiment for ethnic nationalism. This monumental shift in thought, the most significant of all imports from the West, forced the Ottomans—of all ethnicities and cultural backgrounds—to deal with nationalism both domestically and beyond the empire's frontiers throughout the 19th and early 20th century. Revolutionary political groups took hold; tempers flared; and rebellions ensued, rippling through the beleaguered empire. To deal with the encroaching pressures of ethnicization, a series of constitutional reforms assured equality for all Ottoman citizens regardless of their ethnicity and faith. Christian *millets* gained special rights. In 1863 the Armenian National Constitution, approved by the empire's Islamic leadership, provided a set of 150 articles drafted by the leading Armenian academicians. And as European nations were being created along ethnic and cultural borders from the sweeping empires of the past, the Ottoman amalgam too sought independence from subjugation. Serbia gained its independence in two rebellions in 1804 and 1815. By the end of the 19th century, Greece, the whole of Serbia, Bulgaria, Romania, and Montenegro had gained independence.

Rising Nationalism

By this time, the strategic challenges in defending itself against foreign invasion and occupation had proved too great for the empire. Its leadership chose to ally itself with Western European countries—the Netherlands, France, Germany, and Great Britain—and Russia instead of persisting on its own. In the Crimean War of 1853, the Ottomans allied their efforts with those of Great Britain and Ireland, France, and the Kingdom of Sardinia against the Russian Empire.

Pressured by a group of Western-oriented Turks known as the Young Ottomans who deemed that a constitutional monarchy would solve the empire's mounting social turmoil, Sultan Abdul Hamid was allowed to reign on the sole condition that an Ottoman constitution be enacted. The charter created a representative parliament and guaranteed freedom of expression and religious freedom. With his eyes squarely on the throne, Abdul Hamid created the first Ottoman parliament in 1877. A year later the increasingly dictatorial sultan asked for the parliament's dissolution, the

incarceration of the Young Ottomans' leader, Midhat, and his eventual execution.

Abdül Hamid II's tyrannical rule not only created unrest among the ethnic masses but also among the Western-oriented young Turks. Military cadets as well as students plotted against the sultan's despotic regime in small like-minded groups in cities outside Istanbul, where the Sultan had sworn to quell dissent in any form. A young officer named Mustafa Kemal, who later assumed the surname of Atatürk, set up an underground circle with fellow officers in Damascus. This society soon joined forces with other nationalist reform groups to form the Committee of Union and Progress (CUP). Also known as the Young Turks, this organization aimed to reinstate the 1876 constitution and fuse the empire's various factions into a uniform state. In 1908, as army units in Macedonia revolted and demanded reinstatement of constitutional government, Abdül Hamid II granted parliamentary elections, and the CUP secured all but one of the Turkish seats under a system that allowed proportional representation of all *millets*. Despite this success, the Young Turks' momentum was weakened by rifts among its nationalist and liberal reformers and threatened by traditionalist Muslims and by increasing demands for greater autonomy from non-Turkish communities. Abdül was left with no choice but to abdicate under the pressure.

As European powers in the mid-1800s through the 1950s began jostling among themselves for territory, the once-feared Ottoman Empire, already in dramatic decline, was swept up in these conflicts with ill-chosen alliances. Czar Nicholas I of Russia aptly labeled the Ottomans the "sick man of Europe" in 1853 when discussing his neighbor's increasing financial reliance on European powers and its massive territorial losses.

World War I and Its Repercussions

With political turmoil rife in Istanbul, foreign powers saw the opportunity to attack the empire's peripheral suzerains. Austria annexed

Bosnia and Herzegovina shortly after the 1908 revolution, and Bulgaria declared its independence. Fearing the French would pounce first, Italy heeded a campaign started by its national press and invaded mineral-rich Libya in 1911. A peace treaty signed by the Ottomans yielded the Dodecanese Islands and Libya to Italy. Allied Greece, Serbia, Montenegro, and Bulgaria secured Ottoman-controlled Macedonia and Thrace in October 1912 in the First Balkan Wars. The Ottomans retreated to Europe's easternmost periphery.

With the tumultuous state affairs abroad, political change occurred swiftly in Istanbul. The liberal parliament, which had been reinstated in 1912, was overthrown a year later in a coup plotted by the ambitious nationalistic Enver Paşa. Hardliners among his nationalistic Young Turk organization assumed parliamentary control. At the head of this new administration stood a trio of highly motivated and powerful pashas—Enver, Cemal, and Talat—known as the triumvirate of power. Enver was appointed both general and Minister of War; Talat assumed the role of Minister of the Interior, and Cemal served as the Guardian of Istanbul.

Secretly plotting to regain the former capital of Edirne, Enver allied with Greece, Serbia, and Montenegro in the Second Balkan War when the bloc objected to Bulgaria's territorial greed. The campaign was a success, and Edirne reverted to Ottoman rule. This was the last victory for the empire, but ironically the tumultuous land gains by the Europeans in the Balkans and in the Mediterranean started the malaise among Western powers that would lead to World War I.

As Europe marched toward war, the leadership in Istanbul was torn as to what to do next. Enver, who as a military attaché in Berlin had grown to admire German culture and politics alongside the country's most notable academics, made no qualms about his sentiments for aligning with the German kaiser. He successfully lobbied the bureaucracy and the military by using fear tactics that involved the empire's penultimate enemy, Russia, who by then had joined Britain and France in the war. Despite the fact that Germany had been an ally of the empire during the Balkan conflicts, Talat and Cemal Pashas as well as the Porte (the Ottoman Court) were adamant on neutrality. On August 2, 1914, Enver secretly allied the Ottomans with Germany. The next day mobilization commenced, and the empire found itself embroiled in World War I. To make matters worse, the Allies opened a Middle Eastern flank in an otherwise European conflict.

The first incident to rile the Allies occurred on August 16, 1914, when two German naval vessels that had escaped to a neutral Ottoman port at the time war had been declared in Europe were turned over to the Ottoman navy. The following October, the same two vessels, flanked by an Ottoman armada, bombarded strategic Russian naval bases, including Odessa, while flying the Ottoman flag. Russia declared war on the Ottoman Empire on November 5; Britain and France followed the next day. Eight hundred thousand Ottoman ground troops were fighting on four fronts by April 1915: Russia in northeastern Anatolia, Greece in Thrace, Britain in Arabia, and an Allied front at Gallipoli.

Toward the end of 1914, Enver launched an assault on the Russians in the Caucasus region, hoping a win would shore up support among Russia's Turkish factions against the czar's encroachment of eastern Anatolia. But this ill-prepared campaign resulted in the loss of thousands of troops and territory for the Ottomans, who had by then retreated to the Armenian-dominated Lake Van. The Armenians, seeing Russia as their liberator, conspired against the Ottomans. Convinced that an Armenian revolt was imminent and that the conspiracy extended well beyond eastern Anatolia into the empire, Enver ordered the systematic detainment and deportation of Armenians on April 24, 1915.

The Ottomans appeared to be losing on all fronts of the war, except at Gallipoli. In early 1915 the Allies launched naval and land campaigns in the Dardanelles. Their intent was to take the Ottomans out of the war swiftly and blast their way through the straits to create an open supply route to Russia. But the strategic planning of the campaign's British command was no match for the genius of Ottoman commander Mustafa Kemal. He galvanized the frontline and ordered his men to hold the front and march to their deaths. The invading British and ANZAC forces suffered shocking losses and failed to broaden their beachhead.

By early October 1918 the Ottomans had been defeated. In Istanbul the administration resigned, and the Young Turk triumvirate fled to Germany. Mehmet VI, who had just ascended the throne, petitioned for peace to the liberal-minded administration. An armistice engineered by the Allies was signed at Mudros on October 30, 1918. The peace agreement dictated the surrender of garrisons outside Anatolia and allowed the Allies control of the Dardanelles and Bosphorus Straits, with an addendum granting them the right to occupy the country "in case of disorder."

The greater Treaty of Versailles of 1919 officially reallocated the Ottoman territories of Syria to the French; Mesopotamia, Iraq, and Palestine went to the British; and Arabia to the Europeans. Anatolia's dismantling was contentious. Southwestern Anatolia went to Italy; the British took Istanbul and control of Marmara's straits; the French took the Hatay and various ports in Thrace and along the Black Sea; the Greeks took northwestern Anatolia and Izmir; and the Armenians, supported by a large Russian detachment, took most of northern Anatolia along the Black Sea. According to a secret prewar agreement with Great Britain and France, the Russians were to receive a variety of lands and ports in Thrace and Anatolia for their role in the Armenian revolt against the Ottomans. But the ill-timed Russian Revolution took the Russians out of the running to acquire these territories.

A year later, the Treaty of Sèvres settled all territorial disputes in Anatolia among the Europeans, officially created a kernel of land for the Ottoman Turks, and ensured Woodrow Wilson's plan for a Wilsonian Armenia. This final pact never came into force, as the Turks

soon stood up to the arrogance of the European powers by fighting for their independence.

The Fight for Independence

With an impeccable military reputation despite the defeat of the empire, Mustafa Kemal returned to Istanbul a hero. A Turkish nationalist movement was slowly taking root in the Allied-occupied city, and Mustafa Kemal soon assumed control of it. Considered a threat by the Allies for his expressed opposition to the Allied occupation and his growing political popularity, Mustafa Kemal was sent to eastern Anatolia, supposedly to oversee the demobilization of Ottoman forces. As soon as he arrived in Samsun in May 1919, he marshaled not only public support for the nationalist movement but also volunteers for a nationalist army. Once the congresses in Erzurum and Sivas were held in the summer of 1919, the objectives of the national protocol were set forth, and the insurgence against the occupying forces progressed from guerrilla warfare to a massive offensive against the Greek army.

On April 23, 1920, Mustafa Kemal inaugurated the Turkish Grand National Assembly and established a new interim government in Ankara. Meanwhile, the Greeks proceeded to pursue their dream of recapturing the former territorial grandeur of the Byzantines. They had solidified their foothold along the Aegean, and they aimed for Ankara. Confident from the ease with which they were quelling bands of Turkish freedom fighters, the Greeks launched two massive campaigns, one in Eskişehir and Bursa and the other in Sakarya, but they were bloodily crushed by an organized Turkish army under the command of Colonel Ismet İnönü. The Turks caught up with them at Dumlupınar as they were retreating to the coast. Surrounded, they were killed and captured; the Greeks who survived quickly retreated to Izmir. There too a revolt against Greek occupation—and against Greco-Turks—was underway. On September 9, 1922, the city forced out the enemy forces and the majority of its Greek element. Months later, Anatolia's Greeks were "repatriated" to Greece, and Greco-Turks were sent "home" in the massive population exchange of 1923.

Once more, Mustafa Kemal emerged as the hero of the Turks. He eradicated the sultanate on November 1, 1922, and in its place established a parliamentary government. The international ratification of the Treaty of Lausanne in 1923 legally recognized the independence of the new Turkish nation. More importantly, the pact gave credibility to a people who had been humiliated just three years previously at Sèvres.

BUILDING A NEW REPUBLIC FROM THE GROUND UP

With its existence ratified internationally and still high on the success of the War of Independence, Turkey was in desperate need of a leader, which it found in the charismatic Mustafa Kemal. He parlayed the remarkable strategic and leadership skills he had demonstrated on the front to lead the newly established Grand National Assembly in Ankara, the nation's de facto capital. In turn, he was elected its president. A new constitution was drawn up that promised unequivocal civil rights to all and, most importantly, set up a new protocol for the government. Mustafa formed his cabinet, selecting the national military hero responsible for ousting the Greeks from Anatolia, Ismet Pasha, as his prime minister. His goals of Westernization, modernization, and secularization were swiftly pursued.

Rallying a multiethnic and multicultural population devastated by decades of war proved to be difficult. Mustafa presided over his newly formed democracy with a compassionate iron fist to effect his reform program. Secularization, he deemed, was necessary not only to modernize the country after centuries as an Islamic theocracy but also to align itself with the rest of Europe. In this vein, he ordered the closure of sharia courts and the secularization of all theological schools. This met with opposition from those who wanted an Islamic element in the government and from those Kemal riled with his authoritarian rule and ego. Opponents that included

disillusioned members of his cabinet joined to form Progressive Republican Party. To prove his dedication to free discourse and the democratic process, Mustafa allowed the political party into government, going as far as replacing Ismet Pasha with the PRP's leader, Fethi Bey. This party was short-lived as their acceptance into assembly was concurrent with an insurgency in the Kurdish southeast. The first large-scale Kurdish rebellion, often labeled by modern scholars as "a nationalist rebellion in religious garb," was led by Sheikh Said of the Nakshbendi Order of the Dervishes. And while it is true that he was keen on reinstating the caliphate, the Kurdish sheik and the tribal rebels were first and foremost motivated nationalists. Mustafa Kemal quickly quelled the uprising, issued the Maintenance of Order Act, which outlawed the PRP and returned Ismet Pasha to the post of prime minister. This incident demonstrated Mustafa Kemal's hard-line stance on dissidence and commitment to secularism not only to the bureaucracy but also to the public; the sheik and some 40 others were tried and hanged, and the press was shut down.

The secularization process included a widespread ban on Dervish sects. Other prohibitions included those on tomb-side prayer and the use of honorific titles. Mustafa Kemal considered banning the veil entirely, but decided against it, fearing that such an action would rile his pious opponents; instead head coverings were discouraged. Turkish women in major cities began donning fashionable hats, but the unveiling of the rest of Turkey's women was slow to come. That year, the fez was also outlawed. This blue-tasseled red headdress had signified Orientalism since the days Mahmud II had universalized it in the early 1800s. In its stead, Mustafa Kemal replaced it with the Panama hat, which he donned during a speech in Kastamonu, saying that the ban was a necessary step in Turkey's modernization process, adding that "civilized men wear civilized hats."

In 1926 civil, commercial, and penal codes based on European models were adopted. The new civil law ended Islamic polygamy and

Mustafa Kemal Atatürk in full dress in the early 1930s

divorce by renunciation, and instituted civil marriage. The once-revolutionary *millet* system ended, and the oversight of all provinces—and all ethnic groups—was centralized. More importantly, women received equal rights across the board. The right to education at the secondary and postsecondary level was also granted. That year, growing opposition against Kemal's cultural revolution came to a head, as a wide conspiracy to assassinate the president was uncovered. Some 15 individuals were tried and hanged. A few of them were part of the defunct Republican People's Party. Finally, in 1928, the Republic of Turkey's secularization process was completed with the passage of a constitutional proviso that removed Islam as the national religion.

In 1927 the first official systematic census was undertaken. The results showed that only 10 percent of Turkey's population over the age of seven was literate. Even worse, very few children were attending school; reforms to instate an education system were launched. Language also presented a problem: In the

1920s more than two-thirds of the population spoke Arabic, French, or Persian. Other dialects included Greek, Hebrew, Armenian, and Kurdish. One language was required to unite the Turks, so the Language Revolution of May 1928 began. Numbers that had been written in Ottoman were replaced with their Arabic equivalents—those used in the West. Later that year the Grand National Assembly approved the introduction of a new Latin alphabet, but not without opposition from assembly members who campaigned for a transition period of years rather than the months Mustafa Kemal wanted to shift from the Ottoman system. Once again, Mustafa Kemal's plan for speed won out, and within months the writing system was aligned to Latin letters. To assuage dissent and to prove that his proposal was possible, Mustafa Kemal, armed with chalk and a blackboard, embarked on a weeks-long journey through the republic's villages and schools to educate a people that had suddenly become completely illiterate. Even Islam was forced to abide with the linguistic change when a 1932 law was passed that said the call to prayer had to be broadcast from loudspeakers in Turkish instead of Arabic.

The 1930s brought other sweeping changes. In 1934, Turkish women were given the vote, and the Law of Surnames brought an end to the confusion of identifying people only by their first names. Mustafa Kemal adopted the surname of Atatürk (Father of the Turks), and Izmet adopted the last name of Inönü to commemorate the site where he had vanquished the Greeks. Although the adoption of family names was mandatory, the choice of names was left to the individual. Artisans, craftspeople, and traders were inspired by their profession. Today, entire families are known as the son of the baker or the carpenter. But the titles of old, like *bey* (Mr.) and *hanım* (lady) are still used pervasively after a person's name to denote respect.

Atatürk's legacy still prevails in a set of founding principles known as "Six Arrows." Also commonly referred to as Atatürkism or Kemalism, these fundamental guidelines were the essential building blocks for the establishment of a modern Turkey. The first part, "republicanism," set the bar for the sweeping political revolution that occurred from the multinational Ottoman Empire to the establishment of the state of Turkey and the realization of the national identity of modern Turkey. The scope of the second principle, Kemalist "nationalism," preserved the independence of the budding Republic of Turkey and aimed to aid its political evolution. Not based on race, nationalism honored a nation's right to independence and stood firmly against imperialism and caste systems. With these two firmly in place, Atatürk's "reformism" touchstone cemented the way forward to activate the sweeping changes required to modernize the country from its dated and traditional public institutions and ideologies. The old was eliminated in order to make way for the modern. Since Turkey's modernization hinged on its economic and technological development, Atatürk's "statism" guideline ensured the regulation of the nation's overall economic activity and assumed its management if the private sector was unable to do so, proved inadequate, or was not acting in the best interest of the country. Later on, the state not only emerged as the main regulator of economic activity but also as the de facto owner of the country's main industries. Kemalist "populism" stood against class privilege and distinctions and favored no individual, family, class or organization above another. Although it was somewhat hypocritical, since the government was an elitist group at its inception, the ideology of populism was actually based on the value of Turkish citizenship or national pride. Atatürk believed that indoctrinating the Turkish citizenry in this fashion would elicit the psychological drive necessary make people work harder for the state and unify diverse peoples under a national identity. To that extent, the policy succeeded in revolutionizing the social fabric of Turkey, including suffrage for women and what Atatürk defined as the true rulers of Turkey, its peasants. Finally, "secularism" not only created a division between state and religion but also

separated the latter from educational, cultural, and legal affairs. Only in this manner could independence and individuality of thought be gained. It also did away with the dominance of religious institutions. Kemalist secularism did not endorse atheism nor shun Islam; it is simply anticlerical in nature. It didn't reject Islam in any form but vehemently opposed an Islam that was against modernization.

In hindsight, Atatürk's achievements were many. His five-year plan launched in 1934 to achieve economic independence reversed centuries of virtual nonproductivity that had characterized the Ottoman era. Development packages for industrial and agriculture productivity were inaugurated along with fostering confidence in domestic products. Tariffs on imports were raised and foreign railroad allowances were purchased to protect the domestic market. But in other ways, change was slow to come. The economy still sadly lagged behind European standards, as did living standards. The Labor Act of 1936 addressed some of these issues by providing workers the rights they were seeking. Although strikes were banned, a mediation system was created; a new state insurance program was instituted that guaranteed compensation for unexpected death and accidents on the job, as well as income for seniors.

On the international front, Atatürk aligned his ideal of "peace at home, peace abroad" with a foreign policy of peace. Pacts were signed with all the country's neighbors in the region as well as with larger powers. For the first time in their history, Turks enjoyed peaceful relations with the rest of the world, ending centuries of hostile takeovers. By 1932 Turkey had joined the League of Nations.

At 9:05 A.M. on November 10, 1938, Atatürk's presidency came to an end when he succumbed to cirrhosis of the liver after years of alcohol abuse. He transferred control to Inönü, his partner in war and peace. In his 15 years of presidency, Atatürk had created a modern, relatively democratic republic from the ashes of a defunct dictatorial regime. For this the League of Nations perhaps best characterized his efforts after his death by calling him a "genius international peacemaker." Today, a minute of silence in Atatürk's memory is observed every November 10 at 9:05 A.M.

To understand Atatürk's place in Turkish history, his sweeping achievements must be weighed against the bloody events on the European continent in the first part of the 20th century. His sweeping reforms united a fractured people under one flag and rewarded them with autonomy, national pride, equal rights, and the promise of economic prosperity after one of the most tempestuous periods in world history. To this day, his strength of character, bold reforms, and charismatic persona continue to inspire new generations of Turks.

TROUBLE ABROAD AND AT HOME

Izmet Inönü, Atatürk's partner in war as in peace, was elected president by the Grand National Assembly on November 11, 1938, the day after Atatürk's death. Although the Turkish economy was still lagging far behind those of its European counterparts when he assumed office, an international calamity on a scale never seen before was to rock Eastern Europe and impact Turkey directly.

Once again, allegiances among the World War I blocs were renewed as Soviet Russia and Nazi Germany's zeal for territory threatened not only the Balkans but also the intercontinental Bosphorus Straits. Turkey's geographical position between the two emerging Eastern European powers made the threat even greater if conflict were to arise. Inönü carefully planned amicable and nonaggression treaties with France, Great Britain, and Hitler's Germany. By early 1945, neutral Turkey found itself unscathed by the conflicts that had erupted just outside its borders—until it was required to declare war on Germany in order to join the 50 other nations at the San Francisco Conference, the predecessor to the United Nations. Turkey had become an ally of the United States and a foe of Russia by definition. Availing itself of Turkey's strategic position bordering the Soviet Bloc, the United States lavished Turkey with financial aid. Turkey kept its end of the bargain

by joining the United States in its military campaigns in Korea. For this it was rewarded with an invitation to join the North Atlantic Treaty Organization in 1949.

On the domestic front, democratization of the Turkish government accelerated. The one-party rule that had dominated Turkish politics was brought to an end in 1950, when the Democratic Party swept a majority of the vote and gained control of the assembly. During the next decade the Democrats rolled back some of Atatürk's reforms. First to be reinstated was the call to prayer, which was allowed to be made in Arabic. But as the press of the day joked, power turned the Democrats into despots, and their slogan "rule by the people for the people" was largely ignored. The army stepped in and threw out the Democrats in the coup of 1960. Kemalist by definition, the Turkish army annulled the constitution and began years of insidious tug-of-war between its power and the country's ruling political parties.

The DP's earlier success at gaining a majority of seats in the National Grand Assembly galvanized Turkey's politicians to form a multitude of political parties, ranging from the ultraleft-leaning fascist nationalists to pro-Islamic parties. But while each Turk was represented by a party that mirrored his ideals, the sheer variety of political groups represented in the assembly made the government stagnant at a time when the lagging Turkish economy needed effective governance. A slew of ill-managed economic reforms forced the government to seek out foreign loans. Legions of unemployed Turks with no job prospects chose to look for employment beyond the country's frontiers.

Seeking to return to a one-party system, the then–DP prime minister, Adnan Menderes, launched a censorship campaign by outlawing public political meetings, invoking gag rules on the press, and mandating formal investigations into the political activities of opposing parties. Menderes's rule was widely popular, but Turkey's military machine and its Western-educated academics were opposed to it. Fearing a coup and harassed by spreading student riots, Menderes imposed martial law on April 29,

1960. The Turkish army, headed by commander Cemal Gürsel, seized power in a nonviolent coup d'état on May 27. President Celal Bayar, Menderes, and hundreds of DP sympathizers were arrested and tried. Bayar received a life sentence, dying at the age of 103 in 1986, and Menderes was hanged for treason. The DP was once again dissolved, and the military took power despite commander Gürsel's fierce opposition to permanent military rule. His nationalism compelled him to stay in charge, forming the Committee of National Unity. After his election in 1961 as the fourth president of the republic, Gürsel played an integral part in cementing the way for a new constitution and a return to democracy after the coup. Former president İnönü returned to serve as prime minister. The next five years were characterized by unlikely coalition governments among the Kemalists of the Justice Party, led by Süleyman Demirel; the social democrats of İnönü's RPP; the center-right Turkish Workers Party; and the communist Confederation of Progressive Trade Unions. Opposing ideals made for a stagnant assembly until 1965, when Demirel's JP won a majority of seats. Despite the JP securing a big percentage of the popular vote, the assembly suffered incessant quarrels along party lines as well as party defections. As Turks lost confidence in their government, the turmoil among politicians in Ankara was felt in the streets nationwide. The devaluation rate of the Turkish lira was at an all-time high, and so was unemployment. Civil anarchy raged in the form of student riots, with Leninists and Marxists chanting antigovernment slogans on the streets of Turkey's major metropolises. Political terrorism in the form of political assassinations and kidnappings ensued. The army felt forced to step in once again to depose Demirel's centrist government in the military coup of 1971.

By 1973 power was returned to a newly formed assembly, but difficulties still raged as terrorists from the pro-Islamic National Salvation Party and the ultranationalist neofascist youth organization called the Turkish Nationalist Movement Party, known as the Gray Wolves, wreaked havoc among the populace on the streets. Turning a corner on the street could prove to be fatal if one's political affiliation didn't match that of the terrorists, who were on a mission to eradicate dissenters. This domestic unrest coincided with tensions on the island of Cyprus, following a coup d'état that saw the overthrow of the government in Athens. In July 1974, Ankara, led by then-prime minister Bulent Ecevit, sent 30,000 troops the island to protect its Turkish minority, fearing further attacks from the extremist Greek junta. The West condemned the invasion, which effectively divided the island into two political entities. Incidentally, the north, which accounts for one-third of the island, declared independence in 1983; the Turkish Republic of Northern Cyprus is only recognized by Turkey.

Turkey plunged into a political and economic quagmire. The military, led by army chief of staff General Kenan Evren, once again stepped in and forced a coup on September 12, 1980, which was met by jubilation from Turks and many foreign states. Evren became head of state for the next two years of military rule. Following the adoption of a new constitution by public referendum, Evren became the seventh president of Turkey in 1982. On November 9, 1989, the Motherland Party swept the popular vote; in its pro-Islamic leader, the respected economist and businessman Turgut Özal, the electorate saw the talent necessary to fix the country's ailing economy. And that he did—doing away with Atatürk's dated policy of statism, industry and agriculture were decentralized and subsequently privatized. Aside from Özal's sweeping economic and legal reforms, the 1990s were also characterized by mounting tensions from the Kurdish separatist movement, raging corruption, and the reinstatement of opposing political parties.

AN ISLAM-CENTERED ECONOMIC POWERHOUSE

Paying its dues as a NATO member, Turkey played a major role in the Persian Gulf War of 1990, lending not only its military bases to the Allied effort but also its airspace. In doing so it strengthened its relationship with the United States. One thing Özal's government didn't anticipate was the diaspora of 1.5 million Kurds fleeing the wrath of Saddam Hussein's supporters to northern Iraq. Some made it into southeastern Turkey, fueling the increasing tensions of the Kurdish secession movement there. Another unanticipated turn of events was the creation of a semiautonomous Kurdistan in northern Iraq, where the Kurdistan's Workers Party (PKK) allegedly continues training terrorists. PKK terrorist activities came to a head in the mid-1990s, forcing the Turkish military to take a stand against uprisings in the southeast and imposing martial law until PKK rebel leader and founder Abdullah Öcalan was captured in Kenya after eluding Turkish authorities for more than two years.

While the Kurdish question still remains Turkey's Achilles' heel, its formerly fiercely guarded secularism is slowly eroding. Through the 1990s Özal's notoriously corrupt government was fodder for calls for a return to a morally sound regime, boosting the power of the Islamist movement. Strictly Sunni Saudi Arabia saw an opportunity to provide financial assistance, helping to launch bold social programs and indirectly sowing the seeds of religious fanaticism. By 1996 the Welfare Party, led by Islamic prime minister Necmettin Erbakan, received the majority of seats in the assembly. A year later the Turkish military ousted Erbakan's government for allegedly following an Islamist agenda, an allegation that was corroborated by a court ruling in 1998 that called the party antisecular, banning it and its leader for "violating the principle of secularism in the constitution." Some of the Welfare Party's original members pressed on with their Islamic agenda by regrouping and forming the Justice and Development Party (*Adalet ve Kalkınma Partisi*, AKP) in July 2001. With a much softer message, a more moderate position, and the desire to operate within Turkey's secular framework, AKP swept 34

percent of the vote in the general election of 2002. Turks, unhappy with the previous government's clumsy handling of the 1999 earthquake and its failure to enforce construction laws that allowed not only widespread corruption throughout the construction sector but also for the erection of more than 500,000 buildings that proved structurally unsafe during the earthquake, voiced their outrage at the polls. Their anger wasn't directed only at political profiteers; the message for change extended to the entire assembly for its failure to foresee Turkey's major financial collapse of 2001.

The AKP, led by Bülent Arinç and Abdullah Gül, effected change quickly, even without its ringleader, Recep Tayyip Erdoğan, who in 1997, during a stint as the mayor of Istanbul, had recited Koranic verses in public, which a court ruled was anti-Kemalist. He made the statement, "The mosques are our barracks, the domes our helmets, the minarets our bayonets, and the faithful our soldiers," which got him removed from his mayoral post, banned from participating in politics for a six-year period, and given a jail sentence of four months. Steering the AKP since 2003, Erdoğan got another boost at the polls when 44 percent of Turks rubber-stamped the party's general direction in the 2004 elections. But when Erdoğan nominated Abdullah Gül for the office of president, the Turkish military voiced its disapproval. At issue wasn't Gül, per se, but his wife, Hayrünnisa, who wears a headscarf, at the time forbidden in public buildings, including Ankara's presidential palace. The headscarf remains one of the most contentious issues in mainstream Turkey. Despite the disagreement between the secular social progressives and the Islamic traditionalists, Turkey has finally reached the economic stability and growth Atatürk once dreamed of. In 2010 the country ranks as 17th in the world in terms of gross domestic product and is still awaiting full admittance to the European Union—a process that officially began in the mid-1980s and may take another decade.

Government

Since 2002 Turkey's government has been in the hands of its dominant party, the conservative AKP, which maintains 335 of the 550 seats in the assembly since obtaining 46.6 percent of the general vote during the most recent elections in 2007.

Erdoğan has served as Turkey's prime minister since 2003, roughly a year after the party gained 34 percent of the vote in the general elections of 2002. On the whole pro-European, Erdoğan's government has been successful in introducing national democratic reforms to assuage the country's poor track record on human rights, particularly when its comes to the Kurdish minority. In 2009 the AKP instituted measures to align the rights of the Kurds with those of the rest of the country by lifting a ban on the use of the Kurdish language in public and allowing its broadcast and use during political campaigns. On the financial front, the AKP-led government reversed the deeply stagnant economy it had inherited by introducing bold macroeconomic schemes and successfully luring foreign investment through the removal of most government regulation.

In 2007 Erdoğan may have tilted his agenda a bit too far when he nominated Abdullah Gül for the presidency and tried to lift the ban on headscarves in universities. Both proposals were deemed insolent by the military, the guardian of Turkey's secularism. At issue with Gül's nomination were his past activities in Islamic parties and the fact that his wife, Hayrünnisa, wears a headscarf. The lifting of the headscarf ban at universities was ultimately annulled by the Constitutional Court, leading to a fine and the near closure of the ruling party. But Gül's nomination for the presidency stood and went on to be ratified in the general elections of 2007.

Abroad, Turkey's AKP-ruled government maintains close ties with the United States and Europe. Turkey serves as a nonpermanent member of the United Nations Security Council since being elected to the position by more than two-thirds of the 192 member states in 2008. Along with Austria, Turkey is tasked with protecting Western European interests.

Oriented toward the West since its inception in 1923, Turkey is a founding member of the Council of Europe. Turkey applied for full membership in the European Union in 1987 and was granted associate membership in 1992. Full admission to the bloc may take another 20 years. At issue is Turkey's copious size and population; if accepted, it would become the bloc's second-largest member nation in terms of population, between Germany and Great Britain, and largest in geographic size by far. The EU has remained at odds over Cyprus. Its northern third was declared the de facto Turkish Republic of Northern Cyprus (TRNC) by Turkey after Turkish troops invaded the island in 1974 to protect its Turkish Cypriot minority from militant Greek nationalists. Turkey is the only nation that recognizes the TRNC.

Also determining much of Turkey's foreign relations are its close ties with the United States. Close bilateral relations between the two countries have been continuous since the Soviet threat of the Cold War era. Turkey's military support and allegiance during the Cold War, and especially during the U.S.-led Korean War, galvanized its amity toward Washington. In return Turkey earned full membership in the North Atlantic Treaty Organization in 1952. After the dissolution of the Soviet Union and the end of the Cold War in 1991, Turkey's strategic importance shifted to the Middle East. Turkey houses NATO air bases near the Syrian and Iraqi borders; these have proved crucial to U.S.-led military campaigns in the region. The United States considers Turkey's a primarily Muslim secular democracy, an example for developing Middle Eastern nations to follow, and also supports a crucial allegiance with Turkey's largely positive relations with Israel. Likewise, Turkey continues to benefit from the overall support of the United States, particularly in

Turkey's bid to join the EU. Recent disagreements between the two nations have included tensions over the official definition of the killing of Armenians in 1915. At issue is the massacre of over 1 million Christian Armenians by Ottoman Turks, which is being labeled genocide by an increasing number of states worldwide. Turkey recognizes the atrocities but is steadfast in its assertion that the mass slaying was part of war casualties and not a systematic ethnic cleansing, as the definition of *genocide* entails. But while 20 countries and 44 U.S. states have officially acknowledged the massacre as genocide, the U.S. Congress has yet to follow suit.

ORGANIZATION

The Republic of Turkey is defined as a secular parliamentary representative democratic republic. Since the republic's establishment in 1923, secularism—the idea that government should exist freely of religion or religious belief—has been one of the cornerstones of Turkish politics and its constitution. The prime minister serves as the head of government and of a multiparty system. Power is separated into three branches: executive, judiciary, and legislative. The government follows guidelines established by the constitution.

Ratified on November 7, 1982, after two years of military rule following the nonviolent coup d'état in 1980, Turkey's current constitution maintains that the state is a secular and democratic republic that acquires its authority from the Turkish people. Power is delegated to an elected parliament, known as the Grand National Assembly. The constitution also asserts that Turkey is a unitary nation-state by definition of its attributes: the exclusion of ecclesiastical control, social equality, equality before the law, the republican form of government, and the indivisibility of the republic and of the Turkish Nation.

Supervising the state in a largely ceremonial position is Turkey's president, the head of state. The constitution outlines the president's role as "representing the Republic of Turkey and the unity of the Turkish Nation." Until the controversial nomination of Abdullah Gül in 2007, the president was elected by the assembly. The general public has since received the right to elect its own head of state. Presidents serve five years and can only be reelected once. Both ordinary citizens and members of the assembly can vie for the post. Presidents-elect must break ties with all political parties and resign from any duties within the assembly before assuming the presidency. Once in office, presidential duties include ensuring the implementation of the Turkish constitution and that all parts of the government remain organized and operate smoothly. The current holder of the office, since August 28, 2007, is the country's 11th president, Abdullah Gül.

Executive power is held by the prime minister and his ministerial council. Almost always a member of parliament, the prime minister is elected by members of the assembly in a vote of confidence for the government he or she has presented. The current prime minister is Recep Tayyip Erdoğan, whose conservative Islamic AKP party holds 335 of the 550 seats in the assembly.

The legislative power of the Turkish government is in its parliament, the Grand National Assembly of Turkey. This body of 550 members, who are elected to four-year terms from constituencies, represent 85 districts in Turkey's 81 provinces. Due to the size of their large populations, Istanbul comprises three districts, and Ankara and İzmir have two each. A party must win at least 10 percent of the general vote in a parliamentary election to be represented in the assembly to avoid excessive political fragmentation or hung parliaments. Independents may also run if they've received at least 10 percent of the popular vote in their province. Because of the 10 percent threshold, only three parties ran in the most recent elections in 2007.

As asserted by the Turkish constitution, the judicial branch is free and independent of any private or political organization or institution. The executive and legislative branches of government must submit to the high court's rulings, which must be based on constitutional provisions, existing laws, jurisprudence, and their personal judgment. There are no juries in the Turkish legal system. Rulings are derived directly from judges, who are bound by law to render decisions after all pertaining facts have been presented by legal representation. Justices of the peace are tasked with civil complaints and misdemeanors; one judge oversees each court at this level. Felonies and major civil lawsuits are handled in a three-judge court; convicted criminals automatically win the right of judicial review in a court of appeals. Turkey's High Council of Judges and Public Prosecutors ensures the judicial integrity at all levels nationwide, nominates judges, and oversees court assignments. Incidentally, prime minister Erdoğan currently heads the High Council.

THE ROLE OF THE TURKISH ARMY

Ever since Mustafa Kemal Atatürk founded the Turkish Republic as a modern secular state in 1923, the country's armed forces have taken it upon themselves to maintain the values of its founding father. While Atatürk never envisioned Turkey's military coming head-to-head with its politicians, the reality is that his ideology of a secular state—known as Kemalism—wouldn't have survived if the armed forces hadn't intervened.

Since the latter part of the 20th century, the behavior of civil governments toward Turkey's military has run the gamut from respectful unease to containment, granting the armed forces either too much leeway or divesting it of its authority. On three occasions, in 1960, 1971, and 1980, the Turkish military stepped in, forcing nonviolent coups d'état, where they assumed power for a couple of years before returning the reigns of power to a civilian government. In 1997 the pro-Islamic government of Prime Minister Necmettin Erbakan once again threatened the integrity of Turkey's secularism, but his removal from office and the shutdown of his party prevented this.

More recently, army chief commander General Yaşar Büyükanıt expressed his anger over the ruling conservative Islamic AKP party's politics. At issue were the party's lifting of the headscarf ban at universities and the appointment of a president who had once been a member of a banned Islamic political entity. In a letter, Büyükanıt asserted that these measures ran against Turkey's secular tenets and warned that the Turkish armed forces stood ready to intercede in politics with "absolute" determination. Turkey's high court soon allowed the AKP to continue these policies despite the popular belief that intercession was imminent.

The involvement of the military in Turkish political affairs is seen by the European Union as a deterrent in Turkey's bid for full membership in the bloc. Despite reforms that have created greater civilian control over the direction of the country's National Security Council, which was founded in 1960 to develop national security policy, the EU holds that the power of the Turkish military is still too great.

POLITICAL PARTIES AND ELECTIONS

Turkey's most recent parliamentary elections in July 2007 resulted in a huge victory for the AKP party. Some 46 percent of the general vote went to the Islamist-rooted ruling party. Just five years earlier, AKP had received 34 percent, allowing it to form the government for the first time. The once-popular Republican People's Party (*Cumhuriyet Halk Partisi*, CHP), shepherded by longtime leader Deniz Baykal, came in a dismal second with just 21 percent of the vote. Two new parties—the resurgent far-right Nationalist Movement Party (*Milliyetçi Hareket Partisi*, MHP) and Kurdish Democratic Society Party (*Demokratik Toplum Partisi*, DTP)—broadened the spectrum of the country's politics.

When election results were tallied, the AKP came out on top in the popular vote but lost ground in the number of seats it held in the assembly, losing 7 percent of its 363 seats. The center-left CHP lost a shocking 37 percent of its seats, which was attributed to its supporters' disapproval of leader Baykal's "old guard" rhetoric and his unwillingness to rejuvenate the party with young members. Currently the CHP holds 112 seats, the ultranationalist MHP holds 71, and Independents hold 26. A total of 14 parties contested the elections, but only three received enough votes to gain representation in the assembly.

Reflecting its occasionally turbulent history, the multiparty system in Turkey continues to change. Some parties hardly grow past infancy, as in the case of the Kurdish nationalist DT Party, banned in late 2009 for its alleged ties with Kurdish separatist movements and the terrorist PKK. The near shutdown of the AKP party in 2007 for allegedly trying to compromise Turkey's secular character has led the ruling party to propose constitutional amendments that would create more rigorous procedures to ban political parties.

General elections are held every four years, and presidential elections are organized every five years. A referendum in 2007 shortened the presidential term to five years instead of the previous seven.

As Turkey awaits its next election, due in summer 2011, the outcome of the 2007 election, which saw a huge 84.4 percent turnout at the polls, showed that Turks stood in accord with AKP's conservative leadership, but also that other parties—particularly the CHP—will have to regroup in order to regain lost ground among their secular supporters.

Economy

Like the rest of the world, Turkey has been affected by the global financial crisis of 2008–2009. Modern industry and the service sector are two of its largest income generators, and the country did experience dips in international orders for domestically produced products, business closures, and a reduction in disposable income. That said, Turkey remains the least-affected country in Europe in the recent credit crunch, weathering the global recession better than other emerging economies. Tough regulations, few toxic debts, and limited mortgage schemes have helped the banking sector not only stay afloat but remain profitable. The government didn't have to turn to state coffers to bail out banks, as in most Western nations; instead it launched tax-free incentives on big-ticket items like cars and home appliances to stimulate the domestic economy.

Turkey may be famous for its textiles, but it remains one of the world's largest producers of agricultural products, motor vehicles, ships, construction materials, consumer electronics, and appliances. The private sector, particularly in banking and communications, has also grown by leaps and bounds.

Globally, Turkey ranks 17th in nominal gross domestic product and has been a member of the G-20 since 1999. There is disagreement on the status of Turkey's economy: the CIA defines it as developed, while the World Bank describes it as an emerging economy. Regardless of status, Istanbul, Turkey's financial hub, was ranked by *Forbes* magazine as the city with the fourth largest number of billionaires in the world—35 as of March 2008.

Turkey is now on a path of serious and sustained growth. Exports are increasing annually; in 2009 goods shipped abroad increased by 12.5 percent over the previous year's numbers. The full modernization of the industrial sector is reaching completion and is now competitive with those of Western European nations. The booming tourism sector is slowly surpassing the service industry, enjoying a rank of eighth in the world in the number of international arrivals. Plans to build nuclear power plants demonstrate the growing need for electricity, which in itself is a strong indicator that that the economy is on the rise.

AGRICULTURE

Turkey is the world's largest producer of hazelnuts, cherries, figs, apricots, quinces, and pomegranates. It ranks second in the production of watermelons, cucumbers, and chickpeas, and third in tomatoes, eggplants, green peppers, lentils, and pistachios. Thanks to massive production of onions and olives, Turkey is now the world's fourth largest producer. And while the list is extensive, sugar beets, tobacco, tea, apples, cotton, and barley are also important crops.

When it comes to being agriculturally self-sufficient, Turkey has been able to feed itself and its rapidly increasing population since the mid-1980s. But while the agricultural sector enjoys annual growth, it is not showing the same mobility that other sectors are enjoying.

In 2006 just over 11 percent of the country's labor force toiled in agriculture. A slew of irrigation projects are planned, including the Southeastern Anatolia Project (GAP), an ambitious multisector integrated development project to use the waters of the Euphrates and Tigris Rivers to sustain development for the roughly 10 million people living in Turkey's southeastern Anatolia region. The scope of this US$24 billion project will include 22 dams, 19 hydraulic power plants, and the irrigation of 182 million hectares of land.

The livestock industry remains stagnant, but related products like milk, eggs, and wool account for one-third of Turkey's agriculture. Not to be forgotten, fishing accounts for a large part of the economy, with about 500,000 tons of wild and farmed fish and seafood harvested annually.

INDUSTRY

With China producing ever-cheaper goods, particularly textiles, global clothing manufacturers are slowly losing their interest in producing their brands in Turkey, but the largest industries remain textile and clothing production, accounting for more than 16 percent of industrial output in 2005. Oil refining and the production of food, chemicals, automotive products, and machinery are the main part of the country's manufacturing sector. Clothing and automotive production each account for almost one-fifth of all exports; metals and

© JESSICA TAMTÜRK

Agriculture accounts for 8.9 percent of Turkey's GDP, while its largest sector, the service industry, accounts for almost 60 percent.

home appliances account for 13 and 10 percent of all goods shipped abroad, respectively. In 2006 Turkish clothing manufacturers made almost US$14 billion in exports.

Thanks to the Customs Union agreement adopted by the EU and Turkey in 1995, the lifting of customs restrictions between the two has helped Turkish manufacturers of consumer electronics gain a significant share of the EU market. For example, color TV exports shot up 10-fold in as many years, and by 2005 the Turkish electronics giants Vestel, BEKO, and Profilo-Telra produced 50 percent of the TVs sold in the EU. Likewise, digital device exports surged fivefold, and Turkish-built household appliances now account for 18 percent of the EU market.

The Turkish automotive industry has also grown rapidly, becoming the sixth largest automotive producer in Europe and the 15th worldwide in 2008. More than 1.1 million cars rolled off Turkish assembly lines that year. Turkish automotive giants like TEMSA, Otokar, and BMC are among the world's largest van, bus, and truck manufacturers. Turkey's automotive sector, located around the Marmara Sea region, was founded in the late 1960s. Global exports of automotive goods produced in Turkey accounted for almost US$23 billion in 2008.

Shipbuilding is also one of the country's major industries, ranking third worldwide in the production of leisure yachts and sailboats after Italy, the United States, and Canada. In total orders for oil tankers and cargo ships, Turkish shipbuilders rank fourth worldwide.

In the construction and contracting sector, Turkey ranks third after the United States and China. Twenty-two Turkish construction firms vie for multibillion-dollar international contracts as they expand their domestic development business beyond Turkey's borders into Asia, Eastern Europe, and the Middle East.

COMMUNICATIONS

Turkey ranked 18th in the world in the number of operational telephone lines, with 17.5 million, and 15th in the number of registered cell phones, with almost 66 million. Thanks to the gradual decentralization of telecommunications, which began in 2004 with the establishment of the Telecommunication Authority, private phone companies are able to operate mobile phone, long distance, and Internet services. There are virtually no blackouts on the Turkish communications grid—trust me!—as the remotest areas of the country are covered by a domestic satellite system. In fact, the availability of mobile phone services and inexpensive usage rates are slowly rendering Turkey's land lines redundant. In terms of Internet usage, Turkey ranks 15th in the world, with 24.5 million users whose service is supplied by almost 3 million Internet servers.

TOURISM

Tourism in Turkey has grown rapidly since the late 1990s. Its appeal in the last five years has soared even more as Western travelers discover the country's numerous destinations and multitude of vacation options. Anatolia's historical sites, spanning at least five millennia and some 22 cultures, make Turkey the country with the most archeological sites worldwide. Turkey's sun-kissed coasts and exotic seaside resorts compete with other Mediterranean countries such as Italy and Greece for European travelers.

Tourism is Turkey's fastest-developing sector. According to Thomas Cook, the British-based tour packager, eleven of the world's best hotels are located in Turkey, and *Travel + Leisure* magazine ranks Istanbul the 11th most romantic city in the world in its rankings. But the proof is in the numbers: According to the Turkish Ministry of Culture and Tourism, international arrivals have soared by an impressive 25 percent in just three years, topping 30.9 million in 2008. That year, tourism revenues alone accounted for US$21.9 billion.

Developers have been quick to heed the growing interest from abroad. Luxurious and all-inclusive resorts in Turkey's top two tourism provinces, Antalya and Muğla, on the Turkish Riviera, are providing increasing options not only in the number of facilities but also for the budget-minded. Antalya, for instance, boasts more than 170 luxury resorts.

Revenues since the inauguration of the US$1.4 billion Mardan Palace in 2009 have proved that an over-the-top Las Vegas–style resort in the heart of the Mediterranean region could fill an exclusive niche.

DISTRIBUTION OF WEALTH

Turkey's wealthiest city, Istanbul, ranks fourth on *Forbes* list of cities with the most billionaires; Turkey's rich and upper-middle-class profited dramatically in the late 2000s, when the government offered interest rates on deposits in the high teens to reverse the economic crash of 2001. The ambitious move paid off for the government and also for those with available funds.

The recent introduction of credit-based financial products created a new middle class. Midrange and long-term mortgage and loan schemes has enabled Turks to fulfill dreams of home ownership, while the recent boom in credit-card use allows them to buy now and pay later.

Historically, the distribution of wealth was defined in terms of have and have-not. But the first decade of the 21st century saw the arrival of a growing middle class with a desire to improve its socioeconomic standards and attain a comfortable Western lifestyle. In 2004, just 20 percent of the country's wealthiest people had almost half the total annual household disposable income, and the poorest 20 percent had access to only 6 percent. The per capita nominal gross domestic product, US$5,062, remained low in 2005, meaning Turkey ranked 64th in the world.

People

DEMOGRAPHY

In 2009, Turkey's population stood at 72.5 million. More than 75 percent reside in urban centers. Unlike the aging population of its Western European counterparts, Turkey is a youthful country. More than two-thirds fall in the 15–64 age group, with another 26 percent under the age of 14.

Ethnic Turks comprise 80 percent of the Turkey's population while Kurds account for nearly 20 percent. Since a Turk is constitutionally defined as anyone who maintains Turkish citizenship, regardless of ethnicity, enumerating the other ethnic minorities who became Turkish during centuries of Selçukian and Ottoman rule is virtually impossible, but they include Abkhazians, Adjarians, Albanians, Arabs, Assyrians, Bosnians, Circassians, Hamshenis, Kurds, Laz, Pomaks, Roma, and Zazas. Additionally, Greek, Armenian and Jewish minorities were officially recognized by the 1923 Treaty of Lausanne. A small number of Levantines—Western European minorities of French or Italian descent—have been present in Istanbul and Izmir since the Middle Ages.

Education is compulsory until the completion of eighth grade, or up to the age of 14. Enrollment in 2001 was close to 100 percent nationwide. Schools are free in Turkey, but the quality and the limited scope of the education provided by the state increasingly motivate middle-class parents to seek private schooling. Students can only be admitted to private high schools and universities through rigorous examinations, which require one to three years of serious preparation.

In terms of literacy, 96 percent of Turkish men can read, while women lag behind at 80 percent. According to a 2006 report by the British Broadcasting Corporation, the disparity results from the traditional customs of Arabs and Kurds in southeastern Turkey.

RELIGION

Ninety-eight percent of Turkey's population is Muslim. About 100,000 Turks are registered as non-Muslims; of these, 64,000 are Christians of the Armenian Apostolic, Assyrian Church of the East, and Greek Orthodox sects, and 26,000 are Jews, mainly followers of the Sephardic

TRAVELING DURING SACRIFICE HOLIDAY

Visiting Turkey during *Kurban Bayramı* (sacrifice holiday) may be intense for westerners traveling to a primarily Muslim country for the first time. Known as *Eid el-Adha* or Eid el-Kebir in Arabic, this four or five day observance is by far the most revered Islamic religious festival of the year.

The Sacrifice Holiday is deeply rooted in biblical and Koranic tradition. It commemorates Abraham's will to sacrifice his son on Mount Moriah in order to prove his total submissiveness to God. (God stops Abraham just in time, and instead gives him a ram to sacrifice as He thanks Abraham for his utter obedience.)

On the morning of the first day of the Sacrifice Holiday, each Turkish household sacrifices a sheep. A feast is then prepared for the entire family. Any excess is donated to charity. And if guests happen to be around, be forewarned that they too will take part in the spectrum of "festivities," which may require a strong stomach.

Aside from the ethical issues, traveling during the Sacrifice Holiday will throw a wrench into even the most well-planned itinerary. Since *Kurban Bayramı* coincides with the Haj – the annual pilgrimage to Mecca – travel within and outside Turkey is exceptionally high. During this time, any tickets involving layovers in Europe or the Middle East should be confirmed well in advance, as most flights serving those regions are generally overbooked. The same goes for domestic and international buses and boats.

If you are visiting the area during this time, try to travel a couple of days before the holiday's official first and last days. Confirm rooms, dates, and number of guests after booking your hotels. Banks are closed on those crucial days, so make sure that either your ATM card is valid or that a sufficient amount of cash is on hand. Also, keep in mind that museums and public sites may be closed on the first day of the holiday. Businesses and government offices are closed during the holiday's duration; some villages in remote Turkey may even have gone fishing en masse.

---

liturgy. Atheists and agnostics account for slightly over 3 percent of the population.

Muslim Turks are largely Sunni, with a 15 percent Alevi minority (11 million people) and a small Shiite community. Despite Turkey's staunchly secular stance, one of five Turks considers him- or herself Muslim first and Turkish second. Another 65 percent think religion is crucial but in no way trumps citizenship.

This strong identification with Islam dates back to the Selçuk invasion of Anatolia during the Middle Ages. Centuries later the advent of the Ottoman Caliphate, with Istanbul as the capital of Islam, galvanized the faith. At the time, the empire was a strict theocracy ruled by sharia law. Christian and Jewish minorities enjoyed a healthy amount of autonomy but ultimately answered to the sultan. Until the dissolution of the sultanate and the formation of the modern Republic of Turkey, politics were at least in part ruled by Islamic tenets. Recently, Turkey's ruling pro-Islamist AKP party asserts itself as a strictly secular body but remains staunchly guided by Islamic ethical and moral principals. Their overwhelming approval rate clearly reflects the increasingly conservative convictions of the Turkish people.

Turkey's ministry of religious affairs is tasked with oversight of the 75,000 registered mosques in the country and the employment of imams. Interpreting Islam's Hanafi school of law, this office follows the oldest and most liberal of the four schools of Islam.

Spiritually, Alevi Muslims differ from their Sunni counterparts in several ways. Alevis worship in assembly halls rather than in mosques. Their ceremonies feature music and dance rituals (*semâ*) in which both men and women participate. The liturgy is held in the local language rather than in Arabic. The tenets practiced by Alevis, the majority of whom reside in central and eastern Anatolia, may be construed as somewhat mystical because they approach and interpret

Islam from a more spiritual point of view called Sufism. On the whole they follow the teachings of Ali, the prophet Muhammad's cousin who is said to have been the first Muslim.

The Greek Orthodox Patriarchate, whose oldest centers have been located in Istanbul since the 300s, is currently helmed by Patriarch Bartholomew I. Turkish authorities have never recognized the patriarch as the leader of Orthodox Christianity and continue enforcing strict regulations on the patriarchate. Occasional tensions do arise, particularly in times of political tension with neighboring Greece. The state-forced closure of the Orthodox Theological Seminary on Heybeli in the Princes' Islands and the expropriation of patriarchal property remain contentious issues. The patriarchate also continues to refer to Istanbul by its Greek name of *Kōnstantinoupóleōs* (Constantinople).

Jews are also an integral part of the history of Anatolia. Their presence in limited numbers dates back to the 4th century B.C., but Anatolia's Jewish population swelled when they fled Iberia during the Spanish Inquisition of the late 15th century. Welcomed by Sultan Beyazit II, they settled in the empire's largest cities. By the early 1600s there were 30,000 Sephardic Jews and 44 synagogues in Istanbul. Today, Turkey's Jewish community is estimated at 26,000, primarily in Istanbul and Izmir. The *Hakkam Bashi* (Chief Rabbi) leads the nation's Jewish community as he did under the *millet* governing system decreed by sultan Mehmet II. While anti-Semitism has historically been rare, anti-Jewish attacks by purported Islamic militants have occurred three times since the founding of Israel. There are over three dozen synagogues in Turkey, 20 of which are located in Istanbul. The Zulfaris Synagogue in Istanbul's Karaköy quarter serves as the Jewish Museum of Turkey, which was inaugurated in 2001 to commemorate the 500 years of Jewish history in Turkey.

LANGUAGE

As mandated by the preamble of Turkey's constitution, Turkish is the country's official language. There are no statistics on the distribution of other languages spoken around the country, but the largest ethnic minority—the Kurds—have been allowed to campaign and broadcast in the Kurmanji language since 2009. One of the TV channels operated by national Turkish Radio and Television is solely broadcast in Kurdish, while TRT stations devote a few hours of televised or radio programming in other languages spoken in Turkey, including Arabic, Bosnian, and Kabardian, a North Caucasian language also known as Circassian.

Countless languages and dialects are spoken nationwide. In Istanbul, minorities, including Armenians, Greeks, and Turkic people from the "Stans"—Turkmenistan, Uzbekistan, and so on—communicate in their respective tongues. Turkey's growing expatriate community has propelled the use of English, German, and Russian.

Turkish is an Indo-European language spoken by more than 80 million people worldwide. Its characteristics include vowel harmony, agglutination, and lack of grammatical gender, which is consistent within the Turkic family of Altaic languages spoken throughout Asia. Following Mustafa Kemal Atatürk's linguistic reforms of the 1920s, the Turkish alphabet was romanized from the previous Ottoman system, which is a variant of the Arabic script. And while Turkic words replaced hundreds of loan words from Arabic and Persian in the previously used Ottoman system, a few have remained. Globalization has also had its effect on the Turkish dictionary in recent years, as an increasing number of English loan words are finding their way into its pages, particularly in business and technological fields. The standard dialect of Turkey is called "Istanbul Turkish."

The Arts

The art and architectural scene in Turkey comprises movements spanning the country and Anatolia's vivid history along with the influences that affected its various components. Europe has had a major impact on modern and classical art worldwide, and at one time so did the Middle East and Central Asia. To better appreciate the architectural and artistic nuances of each culture's influence, the whole must be appraised piecemeal beginning with the ancients. For the sake of brevity, this section primarily focuses on the various artistic forms that evolved immediately after the founding of the Republic of Turkey.

Mustafa Kemal Atatürk's 1923 reforms essentially created a national cultural identity for the new state. Thanks to generous government-funded endowments, painters, architects, and musicians helped forge a national artistic movement. Museums, theaters, and opera houses were built, and in the subsequent decades Turkish art evolved to reflect modern and Western influences along with the country's lengthy historical and traditionally religious legacies. Today, a stroll through Istanbul's revived old quarters—or any other metropolis in the country—reveals both the classical and the modern along with every extreme of Eastern and Western culture.

LITERATURE

Postindependence Turkish literature emerged from the heavily Westernized written works created just before the foundation of the republic. The late Ottoman literary scene was deeply rooted in oral folk traditions and the ideology of modernization. With the language and education revolution of 1928, in which the Arabic-based Ottoman script was replaced with an altered Latin alphabet, generated a sweeping literacy movement nationwide. Prose and poetry together with deeply rooted folk traditions would come to constitute Turkey's rich literary scene.

Internationally speaking, one name currently defines modern Turkish prose: Orhan Pamuk. Winner of the 2006 Nobel Prize in Literature, Pamuk is the author of a dozen richly complex novels that analyze Turkish identity through historically based plots. Contentious issues like modernism, secularism, Islamism, Turkic tradition, and the constant pull between East and West are also recurring themes. On the whole, the intrigues and romance of his works are related in a postmodern experimental style of narrative. Pamuk's early thematic inspirations surely flourished from the contemporary Turkish novelists who preceded him. Vivid representations of cultural and societal clashes between East and West in modern-day Turkey were first explored by the renowned essayist, poet, and novelist Ahmet Hamdi Tanpınar in *Huzur* (*A Mind at Peace,* 1949) and *Saatleri Ayarlama Enstitüsü* (*The Time Regulation Institute,* 1961). But the socialist realists also had a voice, boldly discussing society's lower levels and ethnic minorities. No one achieved this as well as short-story writer and poet Sait Faik Abasıyanık (1906-1954). His discussions of Istanbul's destitute and unprivileged classes drew much criticism from nationalistic zealots, forcing him to move to Burgazada in Istanbul's Princes' Islands. But writers of the era didn't only portray life in the city. Works based on village life grew popular among the newly literate generations moving to the nation's largest cities in search of social advancement. The *köy romanı* (village novel) revolves around life in Turkey's small towns and villages. Writers of this now-defunct literary genre were numerous, and the best-known internationally is Yaşar Kemal (born 1923). His *İnci Memed* (*Memed, My Hawk*) made local stories into national epics thanks to the leftist political views he shared with his generation. The various styles of Turkish prose are deeply rooted in the prerepublic era's enchantment with realism and naturalism. This trend peaked in 1932 with the publication of Yakup Kadri Karaosmanoğlu's *Yaban* (*The Wilds*). His narrative is detailed and precise, with a realistic tone that foreshadowed the popular social realism theme and the village novel.

As prose evolved from its roots in the romanticism, realism, and naturalism of the late-19th-century Ottoman era into a complex social commentary, so did poetry. By the 1930s poets like Ahmed Hâşim and Yahyâ Kemâl Beyatlı (1884-1958) were constructing conventional verse in the Ottoman tradition in the newly romanized script. Poems of the time were penned using *Beş Hececiler,* a syllabic metric style that fostered the patriotism of Atatürk's National Literature reform. The arrival of Nâzım Hikmet Ran and his free-verse style not only liberated Turkish poetry from narrow syllabic forms but also applied itself ideally to the richly melodic Turkish language. Although Hikmet's communist-friendly modernist ideology developed over decades of exile in the Soviet Union among that country's intelligentsia, and despite Turkey's political establishment, he attracted many fans among the world's literary giants, including Pablo Neruda and Jean-Paul Sartre. The publication of Hikmet's prose was banned in Turkey, and his controversial ideals caused him to spend much of his adult life in prison, but his free-verse style was adopted by his Turkish contemporaries. To this day, nothing endears the Turkish spirit so deeply as Hikmet's poem *I Love My Country, 1936,* written from a prison in Istanbul. By the early 1940s, the publication of a collection of poems by various writers titled *Garip (Strange)* rocked Turkey's literary scene. This manifesto pleaded for a literary form that would mesh with the tastes and needs of a Turkish readership, more as a conduit to serve the multitudes rather than art. Writers Orhan Veli Kanık (1914-1950), Melih Cevdet Anday (1915-2002), and Oktay Rifat (1914-1988) weren't the first to campaign against the status quo in the literary genres at the time; they were echoing similar ploys first utilized by French poet Jacques Prévert. Their verse was a corruption of Hikmet's free style, but unlike him they used the vernacular of the time to relate everyday themes popular to the commoner. As could be expected in a society defined by haves and have-nots, the reaction was instantaneous and sharply split; the trio was reviled by the literati while the masses rejoiced. This decade-long movement may have proved to be a fad, but the trio's works not only still sell today but have also found an audience in a new generation. Later Turkish poets are synonymous with Turkey's poetry movement, including Can Yücel (1926-1999), who not only wrote colloquially lyrical prose but also played an integral part in the translation of Turkish poetry, and İsmet Özel (born 1944), whose early leftist influence evolved in a powerful spiritual—to some extent Islamist—form of the genre.

DANCE

Much of indigenous Turkish dance revolves around traditionally folk dances. Bar dance is performed by groups outdoors throughout much of Eastern Anatolia. Gender-specific groups line up side-by-side and arm-in-arm, moving to the sounds of the *davul* (leather-lined drum) and *zurna* (shrill pipe). The clarinet enhances women's bar dancing. Another dance form is the Halay, which likewise is performed throughout much of the country's eastern provinces. This dramatic form is structurally rich and is performed to old songs accompanied by the *davul* and *zurna* mixed with the *kaval* (shepherd's pipe), *sipsi* (reed), *çığırtma* (fife), or *bağlama* (an instrument with three double strings played with a plectrum). Native to the Black Sea region, the Horon is a round done in close formation with a rapid tempo and striking rhythms that creates a fast and rigorous pace for spectators, dancers, and musicians alike. It is accompanied by the *davul* and *zurna* as well as a *mey* (bagpipe). Western Anatolia is home to the Zeybek, a slow-paced dance that includes the use of colorful accouterments.

Less formal but just as popular dances include the *karşılama, kolbastı, samah,* and *kaşık oyunları.* Each of these is specific to a region but can still be seen throughout the country. The instruments mentioned above are used for these dances as an ensemble or in combinations. The *karşılama* is a folk wedding dance that is fast in rhythm and movement, while the *kolbastı* is ubiquitous among the nation's male youth. *Kaşık oyunları* (wooden-spoon dances) are performed throughout Turkey's Mediterranean region. The dance's melodic rhythms are accompanied by folk songs played on wooden spoons, the beast bow (violin), the *bağlama,* and the clarinet.

MUSIC

Turkey's musical genres draw inspiration from Central Asian folk music, Arabic, Persian classical music, ancient Greco-Roman music, and modern European and American pop. The country's rich musical legacy evolved into Turkish classical music, which resembles Greek classical music, and into Turkish folk music.

During the 18th century, the exoticism of Ottoman music fascinated Europe's classical composers. The robust sounds of brass and percussion instruments used by the *mehter* (Ottoman Janissary troops), history's original military marching band, impacted them in particular. Joseph Haydn composed his Military Symphony around these Turkish instruments, Beethoven's Symphony No. 9 also featured them, and Turkish motifs inspired Mozart's *Rondo Alla Turca* and various other operas. Although this Oriental influence proved to be a momentary fascination, Turkish cymbals, bass drum, and bells found a permanent place into the symphony orchestra.

On the pop music front, handsome Tarkan is probably the most internationally renowned Turkish artist. The Turkish-Belgian songstress Hadise regularly appears in the Top 10 charts in Western Europe and even placed third in the popular Eurovision Song Contest in 2009. The reigning Turkish diva remains Sezen Aksu, whose trademarked sultry voice and passionate lyrics have enamored generations. Other popular modern singers include the gorgeous—albeit surgically altered—Ajda Pekkan, who has been charming her fans for almost 50 years. Sirens Candan Erçetin and Sertab Erener, the 2003 Eurovision winner, round out Turkey's top pop-music ranks.

Turkish rock, which got its start in the early 1960s, grew from a trio of artists: Cem Karaca, Erkin Koray, and Barış Manço. They were critical in creating the Anatolian rock movement, a genre that mirrored the global lyrical trend of speaking out for peace and democratization while blending traditional Turkish folk and Western-style rock music. The launch of a multiparty politics in Turkey encompassing a variety of ideologies fanned the popularity of outspoken Turkish rockers. The rise of heavy metal and the Seattle sound in the 1980s and 1990s inspired other artists like Şebnem Ferah, Özlem Tekin, and Teoman. Rock genres are thriving in Turkey, not only with domestic performers but also with the biggest international names. Some popular annual gatherings that draw tens of thousands and allow Turkish rock talent to appear onstage with international stars include Barışarock, the H2000 Music Festival, Rock'n Coke, and RockIstanbul.

ESSENTIALS

Getting There

BY AIR

Turkey's main international airport is Istanbul's **Atatürk International Airport** (tel. 0212/465-5555, www.ataturkairport. com). Located 30 kilometers west of Istanbul proper, this hub serves more than 20 million passengers annually through two adjacent terminals: *dış hatlar* (international terminal) and *iç hatlar* (domestic terminal). **Sabiha Gökçen International Airport** (tel. 0216/585-5000, www.sgairport.com) is Istanbul's smaller airport; this hub serves mostly domestic and European charter flights as well as most Turkish airlines. Sabiha Gökçen is located on the Asia side of the city 45 kilometers southeast from Sultanahmet (Istanbul's Old Town).

Turkey's other international airports are located in **Izmir** (Izmir International Adnan Menderes Airport, tel. 0232/455-0000, www. adnanmenderesairport.com), **Antalya** (tel. 0242/444-7423, www.aytport.com), **Dalaman** (tel. 0252/792-5555, www.atmairport.aero), **Bodrum** (tel. 0252/523-0080, www.bodrum-airport.com), and **Ankara** (tel. 0312/590-4000, www.esenbogaairport.com).

Turkey's national air carrier is **Turkish Airlines** (THY, tel. 0212/444-0849, 800/874-8875 in the U.S., www.thy.com), which offers flights to many capitals around

© JESSICA TAMTÜRK

the world, including two stops in the United States, Chicago and New York. Its 2009 inclusion in the global Star Alliance network means that THY now offers more affordable deals worldwide within the airline partner network. **Delta Airlines** (tel. 800/221-1212 in the U.S., www.delta.com) is the only U.S. carrier with direct flights from the United States to Istanbul, from New York's JFK and Atlanta. European carriers such as **Lufthansa** (tel. 800/645-3880 in the U.S., www.lufthansa. com) and **KLM** (tel. 800/255-2525 in the U.S., www.nwa.com) have competitive fares and offer direct flights to hubs in Germany and Holland, requiring a layover from the United States prior to connecting to Istanbul. Airport websites list all carriers and provide their Web links.

BY BOAT

Car and passenger ferries from Italy, Ukraine, and Greece arrive at several Turkish ports; **Ferrylines** (www.ferrylines.com) lists all routes to and from Turkey. Privately run ferry companies organize passenger routes among Turkey's Aegean coast, mainland Greece, and the Greek islands. These in turn are linked by other carriers to Athens's international airport. During the summer daily departures are scheduled, twice a week during spring and fall, and once a week at most in winter, depending on the destination or point of origin.

The port of Çeşme is linked to the Italian ports of Brindisi and Ancona. **Marmara Lines** (tel. 0703/186-6010, www.marmaralines.com, €140–450 one-way) organizes a once-weekly ferry connection between Ancona and Çeşme.

Turkish **Maritime Lines** (www.tdi.com.tr, in Turkish) offers a similar service twice weekly between Brindisi and Çeşme.

Northern Cyprus is linked to Turkey through a daily service offered by **Akgünler Denizcilik** (tel. 0324/741-4033, www.akgunler.com.tr, 114TL one-way) from the northern Cypriot coastal city of Girne to the Turkish port of Taşucu.

UKR Ferry (www.ukrferry.com, €110 one-way) connects the Ukrainian Crimean port city of Odessa to Istanbul once weekly. Other ports of call on the Black Sea include Yalta, Sevastopol, Kherson, and Efpatorya in Ukraine, Novorossisk, and Konstanz. Since schedules and pricing change regularly, check UKR's website.

BY TRAIN

Train service to Istanbul from Europe departs daily from Bucharest (Romania). Run by **Turkish State Railways** (*Türkiye Cumhuriyeti Devlet Demiryolları*, tel. 0212/520-6575 in Istanbul, www.tcdd.gov.tr), this line is called the **Bosphorus Express** and connects to the Trans-Balkan Express to Budapest, Sofia, and Belgrade. Direct transfers to Munich and Vienna are possible. Trains leaves nightly at 10 P.M. from Sirkeci Station for a winding 20-hour journey to Eastern Europe and cost €38.80 second-class, €58.20 first-class.

Border stops allow passengers to purchase visas and clear customs. Those traveling to the easternmost stations in Greece (Alexandropolis or Thessalonika) may choose to continue by bus, but it takes at least six hours to reach Istanbul.

Getting Around

Depending on your destination, the best way to travel within Turkey is by air. Cheap fares—sometimes as low as US$25 one-way across the country—and short 45-minute flight times to almost anywhere in central and western Turkey eliminate the much longer, though highly pleasurable, road trip. Considering the cost of gasoline in Turkey—the highest in the world at US$2.38 per liter—the saving becomes obvious. The most expensive round-trip flight from Istanbul to Antalya for two people in the pricey high season costs about 380TL; add 40TL for airport transfers for a total of about 420TL. Renting an economy car for three days would cost 200TL; add the 140 liters of gas needed to travel the 710 kilometers round-trip to Antalya, about 500TL, and you've got 700TL in expenses for a trip

DOLMUŞ – RIDESHARING THE TURKISH WAY

Literally translated as "filled," the dolmuş – or communal taxi – is one of the main modes of transportation in Turkey. The convenience and reduced price are ideal, if you don't mind sharing a mini-van with six or so perfect strangers. These vehicles circuit the streets between two defined stops, picking up and dropping off fares whenever necessary.

While it's true that its popularity is declining, the dolmuş is still very much in use in the country's metropolitan areas, operating between the city and suburbia, and to and from towns and villages within a province. This type of transportation provides an alternative to costly taxis and the large buses that commute between cities, transporting passengers to popular resorts along a road, important social events, from the railroad or bus station to the city center. Dolmuşes operate from their respective stations in larger cities, while an otogar (bus terminal) serves as the main station for anything from taxis and dolmuşes to all sorts of municipal buses. In Turkish cities such as Istanbul or Ankara, these minibuses often run every few minutes, sometimes even tailing each other from red light to red light.

The fare is rarely more than 3TL from the point of departure to the terminal. Routes linking villages to cities tend to be longer, and are priced accordingly. These higher fares still pale in comparison to a private taxi, but are slightly higher than municipal buses (about 2TL). By law, the fare must be posted in plain view, usually on the lower right side of the windshield. Drivers require only a portion of the fare, which is set by the municipality in which they operate, if the passenger desires to get off, say, a mile from the location where he or she was picked up. Drivers wait for their vehicle to fill prior to departure, and start collecting fares once the vehicle has taken off. They deftly make change while maneuvering through horrendous traffic and sometimes even simultaneously speaking on a cell phone! Fares are passed along between passengers to the driver. Handing along a 5-lira note takes care of most fares, and also does away with having to ask the driver how much the ride costs. But if you must ask, muster your newly-learned Turkish skills and say: Bilet ne kadar? (How much is a ticket?). Who knows, you might just be riding with an English-speaking driver, or at least another passenger may be able to assist. Getting off just requires this little phrase: Ine bilirmiyim? (Can I get off?).

In urban centers, dolmuş stops are generally marked with blue signs displaying a large white D. In some cities, drivers may not be allowed to stop between them, but in Istanbul, for instance, anything goes. A sign displayed on the right side of the vehicle or on its windshield denotes the route.

Get in, take a seat, and get lost in the culture. Although this sounds a little daunting, you won't regret it.

that takes 16 hours. But if road trips are your thing, there's arguably no better place to drive than Turkey. If you really want to go solo by car, avoid the long trips and choose short daily jaunts instead.

Bus travel gives first-time visitors the best of both worlds. It allows scenic views of the countryside without the high cost of driving. Bus travel is more time-consuming than flying, but domestic bus companies have top-of-the-line super-luxurious coaches with pursers to attend to your needs. Bus fares tend to be similar in the high season and the off-season, unlike airline fares, but they are a bit lower during the summer.

BY AIR

Pegasus Airlines (tel. 444-0737 in Turkey, www.flypgs.com) has absorbed many of the national routes offered by other carriers, spreading their network almost nationwide. **Turkish Airlines** (tel. 800/874-8875 in the U.S., tel. 444-0849 in Turkey, www.turkishairlines. com) also provides regular domestic service nationwide. Other Turkish discount airlines include **Onur Air** (tel. 444-6687, www.onurair. com.tr), **Atlas Jet** (tel. 444-3387, www.atlas-jet.com), **Fly Air** (tel. 444-4359, www.fly-air.com.tr), and **SunExpress** (tel. 444-0797, www.sunexpress.com). These carriers offer competitive rates on domestic flights and international flights to Western Europe, and they keep the fares of the two market leaders in check. Choosing a carrier comes down to finding the best flight times. While all of these carriers have last-minute tickets available, flights to and from Istanbul are typically full, so it pays to plan ahead. Domestic flights during the summer season, *semestre tatil* (mid-year school break), and on religious holidays are harder to come by. In terms of safety, service, and reliability, Pegasus and Turkish Airlines are two of Europe's leading airlines.

BY CAR

Nothing beats driving through the Turkish countryside. Formerly shoddy highways and signage have been updated to European standards, and city streets—outside of Istanbul, Izmir, and Ankara—are easy to navigate. Congestion, however, along with one-way traffic infrastructure, manic drivers, and the extreme difficulty of finding parking in the largest cities can make driving in Turkey a memorable experience. Both provincial and municipal police strictly enforce speed limits, so if you have a heavy foot, beware. Driving under the influence, once a common practice nationwide, has been virtually eradicated thanks to ubiquitous sobriety checkpoints.

International car-rental companies are represented in airport terminals and major city centers nationwide. Among them are **Avis** (tel. 800/230-4898 in the U.S., tel. 0212/465-3455 in Istanbul, www.avis.com), **National Car Rental** (tel. 877/222-9058 in the U.S., www. nationalcar.com; tel. 444-4937 in Turkey, www. yesnational.com), and **Hertz** (tel. 800/654-3131 in the U.S., tel. 0216/349-3040 in Turkey, www. hertz.com). **Budget** (tel. 800/527-0700 in the U.S., tel. 444-4722 in Turkey, www.budget. com) has a small presence in Turkey but runs a few offices in the largest cities. German giant **Sixt** (tel. 444-0076, www.sixt.com.tr) has 36 locations nationwide, providing one of the largest

Traffic congestion in Turkey's larger cities is the rule rather than the exception.

fleets available along with budget prices. Keep in mind that promotional rates as well as roadside and medical assistance packages provided by some vendors may come in handy when driving in a foreign country. So will a satellite GPS navigator, provided by all of the companies listed for an extra cost of 15TL per day.

BY BUS

If the idea of traveling cross-country by bus evokes images of chickens running wild in the aisle and 20 strangers in desperate need of a bath, well, that actually was what the experience was like 25 years ago. Today, however, things have changed; strict standards apply to commercial transportation. Domestic long-distance bus companies operate fleets of European-branded, domestically manufactured buses that must be updated every other year. The same rules apply to municipal and local buses and minibuses as well as the ubiquitous shuttles known as the *dolmuş*.

All passenger transport vehicles display their point of origin and destination on the front windshield, either on an electronic display or with more basic signage. In the large cities, this type of transportation is an inexpensive way to get around. In Izmir and Istanbul, fares on public transport vehicles—except the *dolmuş*—can no longer be purchased with cash. A token or electronic debit card is required. Outside the metropolises, however, an onboard cashier sells tickets for cash.

The *dolmuş* is as historical, particularly in Istanbul, as it is wildly popular and convenient. These minivans carry up to up to six passengers and stop at any point along their specified route for a fare set according to the distance traveled. These communal taxis (*dolmuş* translates as "filled") have their route or destination displayed in the windshield and pick up passengers at stops generally marked with a blue sign labeled with a white "D." Fares vary but rarely run more than 4TL (US$2.75). This transport system is ingenious: If a minivan has empty seats, its driver will honk and approach the curb upon seeing a potential fare; if it's full, he'll just keep driving. Fellow passengers

pass cash from those sitting in the rear up to the driver and return the appropriate change. *Dolmuşes* ply their routes daily from 6:30 A.M. to about 8 P.M.

Major long-distance bus companies in Turkey include **Varan** (tel. 444-8999, www.varan.com.tr), **Ulusoy** (tel. 444-1888, www.ulusoy.com.tr), **Kamil Koç** (tel. 444-0562, www.kamilkoc.com.tr, in Turkish only), and **Pamukkale** (tel. 444-3535, www.pamukkale.com.tr, in Turkish only). Varan and Ulusoy have impeccable road safety, service, and reliability records. With considerably fewer stops on their routes, onboard bistros on some itineraries, and individual LCD entertainment screens, their fares are significantly higher than their competitors. All national and intercity bus companies operate from centrally located *otogars* (bus stations), with Varan and Ulusoy offering free shuttle service from specific pickup points.

Traveling by bus is an experience. First, an army of salesmen will greet potential customers at the *otogar*, trying to convince you that, coincidentally, one of their buses just happens to be leaving momentarily for your destination. Since this is rarely true, take time to visit several offices before committing yourself. A note about travel times: The larger carriers post both travel distances and estimated journey times on their websites. Just be aware that the eight-hour driving time from Antalya to Istanbul, for example, increases to a minimum of 10.5 to 14 hours if you are traveling by bus. Beverages and light snacks are provided free of charge on most long-distance runs, which include a 30-minute meal stop at one of the company-run mini-malls.

BY TAXI

Taxis are a great way to get around in Turkey, particularly for short hops. The benefits of this type of travel include door-to-door service and round-the-clock availability. Cab fares in Turkey are inexpensive compared to those in Western Europe and the United States, but there are a lot of shady characters driving these ubiquitous yellow vehicles. To avoid being scammed, follow these important tips.

If traveling from your hotel, ask the front-desk attendant to call you a cab. Restaurants and hotels commit to a single taxi company in exchange for their honesty and timely pickup of guests. If hailing a cab in the street, make sure not to board a *korsan taksi* (pirate taxi). Some 2,000 of these unaffiliated illegal cabs still roam the streets of Istanbul and other major cities. These dubious drivers are almost single-handedly responsible for the bad reputation their trade has earned among tourists. Any taxi that does not display signage on the front doors that indicates the name and phone number of their taxi stand is considered unlawful. Many of these roam tourist-heavy Sultanahmet and Beyoğlu seeking their next fare—or victim.

When boarding a taxi, check that the meter has been activated and displays the proper time of day. The *gündüz* (daytime) fare is the normal transport cost 7 A.M.–midnight; the word flashes just above the posted fare. The *gece* (evening) rate is 50 percent more than the daytime rate. A common scam is using the *gece* rate during the day. If this happens, just let the driver know: say "*gece*" and point to the meter, and get out at the next red light.

Other typical schemes include taking a meandering route that takes twice as long to get to your destination. There isn't much to do except wait until you've arrived. Lastly, the widespread banknote swindle, which has happened to at least half the people I know in Istanbul, involves the cabbie receiving a 20TL or larger bill and claiming that you only gave him a 10TL bill. As a rule, carry 5TL or 10TL banknotes and coins to avoid this type of "misunderstanding."

Visas and Officialdom

Entry visas are required for all foreign nationals entering Turkey. Visas can be acquired painlessly at kiosks just before the immigration desks; it provides a stamp that allows the bearer to stay in the country legally. The fee for a three-month single-entry visa for ordinary passport holders is US$20, €15, or £10; a multiple-entry varies depending on where you're traveling from. Securing a visa from one of the consulates in the United States is far costlier at US$45 for a single-entry visa and US$150 for a multiple-entry visa, but it has the added benefit of online registration through Turkish consular website (www.konsolosluk.gov.tr). If you choose to purchase your visa at your point of entry, make sure to carry enough cash for you and those traveling with you, since no other method of payment is accepted.

All passports requiring visa stamps must be valid for a year from the date of entry into Turkey. Visas are valid from the day they are acquired; the same rule applies if it is issued from a consular office.

STUDENT, WORK, AND RESIDENCY VISAS

Foreign passport holders planning to tour Turkey for a period exceeding 90 days and those seeking to work or study in Turkey must first obtain a special visa from a Turkish embassy or consulate prior to arrival. Residency permits are obtained after the visa holder has arrived in Turkey. Detailed information, instructions, and visa application forms are only available through Turkish embassies and consulates outside Turkey. Foreigners residing in or traveling through Turkey without a work or student visa are not eligible for employment or school enrollment. Keep in mind that the bureaucratic process of acquiring residency in Turkey is an arduous one.

TURKISH EMBASSIES AND CONSULAR OFFICES

The Republic of Turkey maintains an **embassy** in **Washington, D.C.** (2525 Massachusetts Ave. NW, Washington, DC 20008, tel. 202/612-6700, fax

202/612-6744, www.washington.emb.mfa. gov.tr, 9 A.M.–6 P.M. Mon.–Fri., consular services 9:30 A.M.–1 P.M. Mon.–Fri.) and consular offices in **Los Angeles** (6300 Wilshire Blvd., Ste. 2010, Los Angeles, CA 90048, tel. 323/655-8832, fax 323/655-8681, www.losangeles.bk.mfa.gov.tr, 8:30 A.M.–12:30 P.M. and 1:30 P.M.–4 P.M. Mon.–Fri., apply in person 9 A.M.–noon Mon.–Fri.), **New York City** (821 United Nations Plaza, New York, NY 10017, tel. 212/450-9165, fax 212/983-1293, http://newyork.bk.mfa.gov.tr), **Chicago** (360 N. Michigan Ave., Ste. 1405, Chicago, IL 60601, tel. 312/263-0644, fax 312/263-1449, http://sikago.bk.mfa.gov.tr, 9 A.M.–12:30 P.M. and 1:30–4:30 P.M. Mon.–Fri., apply in person 9 A.M.–noon Mon.–Fri.), and **Houston** (1990 Post Oak Blvd., Ste. 1300, Houston, TX 77056, tel. 713/622-5849, fax 713/623-6639, 9 A.M.–4 P.M. Mon.–Fri., apply in person 9 A.M.–2 P.M. Mon.–Fri.). For a full list of embassies maintained by the Republic of Turkey, visit www.konsolosluk.gov.tr.

FOREIGN EMBASSIES IN TURKEY

Embassies and consulates can be of tremendous help to foreign nationals experiencing any kind of serious problem. For emergency medical attention, passport renewal, arrest, or other legal issues, contact the nearest embassy or consulate immediately. In Turkey, many nations maintain embassies in Ankara and consular offices in Istanbul and sometimes in Izmir. You can contact embassies in the capital, Ankara: **U.S. Embassy** (110 Atatürk Blvd., 06100 Kavaklıdere, tel. 0312/455-5555, fax 0312/467-0019, http://turkey.usembassy.gov); **Australian Embassy** (MNG Building, Uğur Mumcu Cad. 88, 7th Floor, 06700 Gaziosmanpaşa, tel. 0312/459-9500, fax 0312/446-4827, www.turkey.embassy.gov.au); **British Embassy** (Şehit Ersan Cad. 46/A, 06690 Çankaya, tel. 0312/455-3344, fax 0312/455-3352, http://ukinturkey.fco.gov.uk); and **Canadian Embassy** (Cinnah Cad. 58, 06690 Çankaya, www.canadainternational.gc.ca).

CUSTOMS

While luggage is rarely checked upon entry, be aware that the Turkish government maintains a list of items that may be brought into the country duty-free. This includes personal effects, such as medical items and clothing, one camera, one laptop, a video recorder, sporting equipment, and gifts not exceeding $500. Carrying, using, or importing drugs considered illegal elsewhere are not only forbidden in Turkey but are also strictly punishable by law. Night-vision binoculars and weapons aren't allowed into the country without obtaining prior permission. Receipts for any valuable item acquired during your stay may be requested at your departure. Large items such as expensive carpets or antiques of any kind require a valid official Certificate of Origin. This is not only necessary to export the item from Turkey but also to import it into other countries. Don't try to avoid this with customs officials in the United States or other countries, as they're well versed in Turkish antiquities and valuables thanks to a worldwide database. Turkish law states that anything older than 100 years—or dating from the late 19th century—needs to be authenticated by a government or museum official before receiving its travel papers. Animal skins of any kind as well as plants aren't exportable, although minerals are, but only with a special permit granted by the General Directorate of Mineral Research and Exploration in Ankara (0312/287-3430, www.mta.gov.tr).

POLICE

Turkey is a relatively safe country. The main worry for tourists is personal theft. Be aware of your surroundings and personal belongings at all times. For immediate police assistance, dial **115;** for emergency medical assistance dial **112.** **Tourist police** headquarters are in **Istanbul** (0212/527-4503), **Izmir** (0232/457-3788), and **Ankara** (0312/384-0606).

In Turkey, law enforcement is the responsibility of the *Emniyet Genel Müdürlüğü* (General Directorate of Security, EGM), which functions under the direction of Turkey's prime minister and the minister of internal affairs. Under the EGM umbrella are five departments and agencies. Only two are vested with general law-enforcement duties.

The **Turkish Police Force** (*Gümrük Muhafaza*) is tasked with enforcing the law in the cities and supporting customs officers at airports and border crossings. Each district also has a district directorate (*İl Emniyet Müdürlüğü*). Police officers wear navy-blue uniforms and caps; patrol vehicles are white with a blue horizontal stripe and the "Polis" logo on both front doors and the front hood. Police officers are required to present their ID when approaching citizens.

The second branch is known as **Jandarma** (Gendarmes). Part of the military law-enforcement force, these officers wear dark green trousers and light green shirts with red-and-blue markings on the collar. Their jurisdiction is in suburban areas and where population is small, as in villages. Tourist resorts also fall under the Jandarma's jurisdiction since their local population is quite small. This branch also maintains a traffic division, known as **Jandarma Trafik,** which patrols country roads.

If you come in contact with any of these officers, respectfully present your passport. In the event of a traffic violation, present your passport, driver's license, and vehicle rental contract. Turkish police are authorized to collect traffic fines on the spot. And while officers generally don't speak English, their command post must provide someone who does.

Accommodations

For hotels in Turkey—as with everything else in the country—buyer beware. Properties are categorized using an archaic system that rates them with stars. A similar scheme is used in other countries, but the amenities and services guaranteed by a five-star hotel in Paris might not be on par with one rated five stars in Istanbul or anywhere else in Turkey. A hotel may receive a fifth star because it offers a pool, but a new seaside construction sans water feature will receive just four. The elusive fifth star applies to properties that provide conference space, pools, night clubs, and so on. It does not take remodeling nor the age of a property into consideration. This ranking also applies to bed-and-breakfasts, which do not receive stars but are listed in an "anything-goes" special category.

If B&Bs are your type of accommodation, the *Little Hotel Book* will be invaluable in your search for ideal lodging. Writers Mujde and Mutlu Tonbekici have reviewed what they consider to be Turkey's 300 best small hotels. The book is available online at www.small-hotels.com.tr. Keep in mind that hoteliers are reviewed in exchange for advertising, so the properties listed may not align with what the text says about them. Likewise, deserving B&Bs not buying ad space are not included.

In the last two years, hotels in Turkey have gone online in an effort to promote their business and undercut travel agents with bargain-basement Web-only rates. Sometimes at 25 percent below rack rates, they may sound too good to be true, but on the whole they're sound, so it pays to prepare and book well ahead of time. Present a copy of the email you received guaranteeing the low rate when you check in to avoid any of the frequent "misunderstandings." There are also a number of travel-oriented websites for Turkey, but in general their reputation with tourists is weak at best; it seems that their income is generated more from advertising than from commissions.

Rates for the properties listed in this book include breakfast and tax (unless otherwise stated). The hot-water shortages and power outages of the recent past are no longer as common. Round-the-clock hot water and air-conditioning are now dependable throughout the country thanks to backup generators. Once in a while, however, an unexpected electricity outage may leave an unsuspecting traveler running for shade in 45-degree weather; here's to hoping that the sea is nearby. Twin beds are the rule rather than the exception, so if you want a "French" (double) bed, verify that the property can honor the request. Other considerations when booking a hotel are its proximity to a mosque, unless a 5 A.M. wake-up call from the sound of a blaring muezzin is part of your holiday plan.

Pensions and other properties rated three stars or below have a couple of issues worth mentioning. First, Turkish beds rarely come with fitted sheets. Even Ikea's dirt-cheap bed-in-a-bag hasn't solved this problem. If you've planned your vacation around this kind of accommodation, consider packing a fitted sheet to ensure a comfortable night's sleep. Another issue may be the bathroom shower, which in some hotels is just a shower head with a shower curtain instead of a shower stall. Add to this the antique sewerage and you've got the makings for a very wet bathroom experience, so bathe with care. This may sound more like camping than a night at a hotel, but overall the savings are worth it. Another advantage of these budget lodgings are the sumptuous rustic meals prepared on-site by grandma.

When shopping for a hotel in Turkey, consider the amenities and luxury before budget. Rates listed here are rarely what the rooms go for. First, asking for a cash discount prior to check-in always pays off, sometimes up to 25 percent of the room rate or more. During the off-season, rates are much lower, and depending on the occupancy rate an owner can even offer additional savings if guests simply ask. Children under age six stay free of charge, and those age 12 and under usually stay at 50 percent of the adult rate.

Food and Drink

FOOD

The bounty of the Turkish table represents the tastes, dishes, and cooking practices accumulated by the Turks over centuries of migrations and conquests. The absorption of minorities into the growing empire led to new culinary customs that colored their early Asian nomadic sustenance traditions into a rich cupboard encompassing the bounty of the Mediterranean, northern Africa, the Middle East, and Eastern Europe.

Early Turks once depended on the animals they herded through the barren steppes of Central Asia for sustenance. Milk derived from livestock was first cultured by these early herdsmen on the plains, producing yogurt for the first time. Incidentally, the word comes from the Turkish *yoğurt,* which itself is a corruption of *yoğurmak* (to knead) and *yoğun* (dense). Livestock and hunted game were cooked on an open fire, a practice that continues today in the form of the ubiquitous grilled kebabs. In time, these nomadic tribes formed the great Selçuk Empire that would sweep through Byzantine Anatolia and expand the affinity of their palates to include the fresh fish and produce utilized by their Greeks subjects. The staples and techniques of Turkish cuisine haven't changed much over the centuries—simple preparation techniques using the freshest produce.

Each region boasts its own specialties, but Istanbul reigns supreme with dishes that were once concocted in the grand kitchens of the Ottoman palaces. The arrival of spices from newly conquered Egypt in the 17th century marked a milestone for the more than 1,000 chefs in the Sultan's employ, and so did the influx of new tastes and techniques from the four corners of the growing empire. The massive Sultan-approved repertory of carefully researched dishes created in the kitchens of Topkapı, Dolmabahçe and Edirne along with official blueprints for the elaborate Ottoman kitchen constituted the official Ottoman culinary bible to be used throughout the empire's provinces. Later on, fierce competition among the guilds of master-chefs required that prized

TURKISH COFFEE: A DISAPPEARING INSTITUTION

Türk Kahvesi, Turkish coffee, is an art and ritual that is slowly entering the history books, leaving in its stead a growing culture based on mass-produced caffeinated beverages. *Real* coffee culture actually got its start in the streets of Istanbul's Tahtakale neighborhood around the mid 1500s. A couple of Syrians had brought coffee to Istanbul – the center of Islam at that time, and began serving it as a brewed beverage to mark an 11 o'clock *pause-café* enjoyed by the harried schedule of palace staff. The custom stuck.

A perfect Turkish coffee is served in a demitasse, with about an eighth-of-an inch of froth. Any bubble appearing along the top of the beverage is considered a *nazar*, or bad omen. Popping any bubbles prior to drinking is a must. The quality of the brew depends on the grade of the coffee, its grind, and the length of time its cooked over a low fire. It takes about one teaspoon of very finely ground coffee mixed in with the amount of water that fills the cup. Together, the grounds and water are gently mixed inside a copper *cezve* – a small rimmed and long-handled pot with a heavy, flat bottom – and slowly brought to a boil over a heat source. When served, the dregs settle at the bottom of the cup.

Ordering a shot of stovetop-made coffee is as simple as stating your sugar preference: *sade* (unsweetened); *az şekerli* (lightly sweetened); *orta* (normally sweetened); and, *şekerli* (with sugar). And knowing how to imbibe it is of utmost importance: the liquid is best sipped, not gulped. If that first taste transforms you from a skeptic to a believer, recapturing that experience at home is as easy as purchasing the best coffee paraphernalia and grounds from the right purveyor. Just head to **Kurukahveci Mehmet Efendi** (Tahmiş SOK. 6; Eminönü; 0212/511-4262; www.mehmetefendi.com) in Tahtakale to grab the necessary items.

Divining coffee grinds is also an art. Some cafés hire fortune tellers, who read the strains left by the wet grounds that have trickled down from the bottom of an inverted cup and have come to rest on the saucer. Who knows? The key to your future might just rest on the bottom of that next cup of Turkish coffee.

---

recipes and techniques in history's first fusion cuisine be kept secret. As a result, most were never passed on. It would take centuries for resolute food anthropologists using ancient Ottoman texts to recreate the exotic and intricate flavors that made Sultans swoon. *Hunkar beğendi*, *Osmanlı humus*, and the saffron-laced rice pudding known as *zerde* are some of the earliest imperial concoctions, dating back to the mid-1400s. Most of these dishes appear on dinner menus nationwide; others can only be sampled in select restaurants in Istanbul.

The backbone of Turkish cuisine is Mediterranean is essence: the use of seasonally fresh vegetables and fruits, rich dairy products, the choicest meats, fish, and seafood. Rare is a woman of marrying age who can't cook, or at least whip up a meal from these simple and luscious ingredients. A traditional Turkish meal at home or in a restaurant is invariably the same:

an array of cold then hot meze platters accompanied with copious amounts of the anise-based aperitif known as *rakı* (though wine is becoming more popular), followed by the main meal, either grilled or stewed fish or kebabs, accompanied by loads of friendly banter and even a ditty or two.

Novices to the Turkish table will find it hard to pace themselves when confronted with such a rich array of starters. Favorites among mezes include *patlican salatası* (pureed eggplant salad), *zeytinyağlıs* (seasonal vegetables cooked in olive oil), *dolmas* (herbed and spiced rice with pine nuts stuffed in grape or cabbage leaves), *sigara böreği* (cheese-filled phyllo wrapped like cigarettes), and *ezme* (the spicy tomato and red pepper salad indigenous to southeast Anatolia). Depending on whether the venue specializes in fish or meat, other starters might include fried calamari rings or mussels served with a

Turkey's cuisine is influenced by both the East and the West.

garlicky walnut sauce for dipping, salted blue-fin tuna, known as *lakerda*, or the meaty appetizers *çiğ köfte* (a fiery raw beef and bulgur meatball) or its close relative *içli köfte* (a boiled or fried bulgur-wrapped lamb meatball with pine nuts, herbs, and spices).

Ordering main courses is simple and involves knowing what the palate craves. The word *kebab* just means roasted meat or fish that hasn't necessarily been skewered. *İzgara* denotes grilling, while *buğlama* specifies the steaming process used in savory fish preparations. Among the most popular kebabs are the *döner kebab* (slices of layered lamb roasted on cooked on a spit), *İskender kebab* (slices of layered lamb stacked on chunks of *pide* bread drizzled with tomato sauce and a generous amount of melted butter and a dollop of yogurt), *Urfa kebab* (roasted ground lamb skewers), and *Adana kebab* (the spicy version of *Urfa kebab*). Another favorite is the blue-collar *köfte*, a popular meatball served with grilled tomatoes, chili peppers, and sometimes onions. Chunks of meat laced with handsome amounts of aromatic spices, root vegetables, tomatoes, and peppers create a perfect synthesis in a stewed dish called *güveç*. The same ingredients roasted tandoori-style is called *saç kavurma*.

But Turks don't live on meat alone. The diet of western and central Anatolians revolves around succulent and very abundant produce, fish, grains, and an insatiable appetite for olive oil. Vegetables find their way into the traditional *mevsim salatası* (seasonal salad) or seared delicately in olive oil. Unlike Westerners, Turks don't fear carbs in the least. The very Turkic dumpling dish of *mantı* doused in garlicky yogurt is a must for pasta lovers. And while rice may be of Asian origin, pilafs are strictly Anatolian. Try the *perde pilavı* (curtain pilaf), a richly spiced, nutty pilaf in a crusty pastry shell. Turkish breads are an institution on their own: the oven-baked *pide*—the Turkish version of pita bread—as well as *lavaş* and the ubiquitous crunchy white bread found in ample volume on breakfast tables or halved and stuffed with tender slices of *döner* or *köfte*. The *lahmacun*—as popular in Turkey as the hot dog is in New York—is a thin clay oven-baked pizza slathered with finely minced onions, peppers, and lamb. Speaking of street food, the *gözleme* (savory crepe filled with spinach, cheese, potato, or meat) and the *simit* (large sesame-crusted tea ring) need to be mentioned.

"Eat sweet, talk sweet" is a popular Turkish idiom, and it's abided with rich desserts. After-dinner sweets fall into two categories: dairy- or flour-based. Dairy-based sweets include the rich oven-baked *sütlaç* (rice pudding topped with hazelnut crumbs) and the simple yet sumptuous *irmik helvası*, which combines semolina, pine nuts, sugar, milk, and loads of butter. Flour-based desserts are crowned by the *baklava*, delicate layers of phyllo dough drenched in syrup covering generous amounts of either walnuts or pistachios. Another sweet tidbit is the *lokum*, known in the West as the Turkish delight. This chewy candy, composed of cornstarch, sugar, and a variety of flavors, including rose and pistachio, has lost the appeal it enjoyed centuries ago among harem concubines.

A couple of soups round out Turkey's food annals. The first is a garlicky tripe soup known as *işkembe*. Generations of Turkish club-goers swear that it's a surefire cure for a hangover. The other is *cacık*—a cold soup made of diluted yogurt, finely diced cucumbers, garlic, mint, and dill.

BEVERAGES

Tea pervades the Turkish lifestyle. Flowing at breakfast, at tea time, and after dinner, the steeped hot drink is enjoyed ritually throughout the day. It is served piping hot and strong in small tulip-shaped glasses with a diminutive spoon to stir in the two sugars that accompany the glass on an equally dainty saucer. Asides from its elegance, the tea glass is constricted in the middle to ensure that the brew retains its temperature. Turkish tea, known as *çay,* is a form of black tea that originates from the Rize region on the Black Sea coast. A perfect serving of tea, which must be brewed in a double kettle known as a*çaydanlık* for at least 15 minutes, is equal parts tea and boiling water. If the brew proves too strong, then request its more diluted version—*acık çay.* For those preferring the decaffeinated version, apple tea (*elma çayı*) is also a favorite.

Sadly, Turkey's traditional coffee culture is slowly being overtaken by Western frappuccinos and doppios; Starbucks, Café Neros, and Kahve Dünyası have replaced the time-honored *kahvehanes* (coffeehouses). At one time, coffee tradition was so pervasive in Turkey that its name made its way into the Turkish word for breakfast (*kahvaltı,* meaning preceding or during coffee time). Officially forbidden in 1511 by orthodox imams for its stimulating effects, coffee was soon so popular among Istanbul's Ottoman hierarchy that the general ban was lifted just a decade later by Sultan Selim I, with Mecca's Grand Mufti Mehmet Ebussuud el-İmadi's enthusiastic approval. A perfect demitasse begins with the finest coffee beans, which are grounded almost to a powder before they are mixed with a cup of purified water. It can be sweetened at this point with sugar. Order it *sade* (unsweetened), *az şekerli* (lightly sweetened), *orta* (sweetened), or *şekerli* (quite sweet). The mixture then cooks slowly over a flame until it comes to a boil, generating a thick foam, before it's tipped into the cup. Begin sipping when it arrives. Once you've finished it, cover the cup with the saucer and flip them over to allow the remaining grounds to coat the inside of the cup. If you're lucky, a waiter may be able to tell your fortune from the shapes and ridges formed by the grounds.

By day Turks enjoy *ayran,* a refreshing, slightly salted yogurt drink. By night, *rakı*—colloquially referred to as lion's milk—reigns supreme. *Ayran* is made by watering down yogurt and adding a pinch of salt. Westerners are almost always reluctant to try it, unaware that yogurt can be just as delicious savory as it is when sweetened with fruit. Once you try it, this rejuvenating drink is an attractive thirst-quencher, particularly during the torrid days of summer. *Rakı* is Turkey's official national drink and hopefully will keep its status through the tenure of the ruling Islamic-leaning AKP party. An alcoholic beverage, it is distilled from grapes and then redistilled with aniseed. It is imbibed neat or diluted with water over ice. A great accompaniment to mezes, the alcohol content of *rakı* is measured at 80 proof, and is best sipped slowly and in moderation.

RESTAURANTS

There are several types of restaurants in Turkey: the family-style *lokanta,* where various prepared dish are displayed behind glass; the Turkish tavern, known as the *meyhane*; and the *restoran,* which typically but not always means a more upscale eatery that either specializes in fish fare or meat, and sometimes both.

Unlike restaurants in the West, Turkish eateries don't always abide by a set menu, and sometimes they don't even have one. Offerings at *meyhanes* are paraded in the variety of fish kept in refrigerated display cases at the entrance and on the meze platters whisked about by enthusiastic waiters. If something is to your liking, simply point to it. Ordering a main course after platters of mezes is not obligatory, nor is accepting all the mezes that are brought to the table. If you do opt for fish, ensure that the price is settled before ordering it. The cost of fish is measured either by its weight in kilograms or per portion. It's perfectly OK to order half a portion, or even to negotiate a lower price for the entire amount if you're paying cash.

BLENDING *RAKI*

Turks refer to *rakı* – the anise-based liqueur – as *aslan sütü* (lion's milk). Although it only reaches its opalescent color when mixed with water, this twice-distilled spirit popular throughout the eastern Greek islands, Turkey and the Balkans does bear its moniker marvelously. *Aslan* is used as a vernacular metaphor in Turkish for a virile, brave man. But the appellation doesn't stop women from drinking, too!

As its name implies, *rakı* is not for the meager; it is a potent potable sipped leisurely to the tune of some 60 million liters annually. While it may be referred to in the West as an apéritif because it's usually consumed alongside *meze*, which Westerners also classify as appetizers, *rakı* is actually served and consumed with meals like wine. It is produced from grapes and raisins, and flavored with pungent anise; its finished form comprises 40–50 percent alcohol.

There are as many brands of *rakı* as there are ways to drink it. While Efe and Tekirdağ typically appearing atop connoisseur's lists, Yeni Rakı is what most people drink. The spirit comes as a shot in a long slender glass. Another identical glass, for icy cold water, is served alongside the first. Mixing *rakı* first with icy water, then adding ice cubes is the the most popular way to drink *rakı*.

So why not give *rakı* a try or two during your escapades through Turkey? Just remember that the more the spirit is diluted with water the less it will affect your own spirits.

Tips for Travelers

ACCESS FOR TRAVELERS WITH DISABILITIES

Although facilities for physically disabled people have improved slightly in the last five years, allowances for those with special needs are almost nonexistent. In all fairness, the government has installed ramps at some national museums to facilitate wheelchair access. Newer buildings are equipped with elevators. Most of the buildings of historical interest, particularly in the big cities, date back to the Middle Ages; a few are even older. Parts of Istanbul, such as Beyoğlu and Sultanahmet, may be particularly difficult for wheelchair users because they're built on steep inclines. Sultanahmet has many cobbled streets. Inside, narrow corridors, uneven flooring, and out-of-the-way facilities make for an arduous outing even for the fittest. Hotels, restaurants, and public transportation aren't much better; few can accommodate guests with special needs. Some of the larger hotel chains have rooms catering to the needs of wheelchair users.

The **Society for Accessible Travel and Hospitality** (347 Fifth Ave., Ste. 605, New York, NY 10016, tel. 212/447-7284, www.sath. org) offers resources for people with all types of disabilities and gives detailed recommendations on destinations, access guides, travel agents, tour operators, vehicle rentals, and companion services. **Moss Rehab** (60 E. Township Line Rd., Elkins Park, PA 19027, tel. 215/663-6000, www.mossresourcenet.org) provides tips and resources on accessible travel.

Some tour operators specialize in tours and hotel bookings for disabled tourists. **Accessible Journeys** (35 W. Sellers Ave., Ridley Park, PA 19078, tel. 800/846-4537, www.disabilitytravel.com, 10 a.m.–6 p.m. Mon.–Fri.) caters specifically to wheelchair travelers and their families and friends.

TRAVELING WITH CHILDREN

Turks are infatuated with children. Families traveling with tots in tow love the extra pervasive gush of attention. Plus it's a great way to see local people at their affable best. Generally, sites of interest are kid-friendly, and it is enjoyable to see them smitten with Turkey's enchanting past: fairy tale–like palaces, creepy underground cisterns, and numerous ancient sites that fill their history textbooks back home. Shopping with kids takes on a whole new dimension in the Grand Bazaar or the Egyptian Bazaar.

All lodging facilities and some transportation options offer some form of discount to children under 13. Children under the age of six stay free in hotels, and those ages 6–12 get a 50 percent discount on the adult rate. Museums admissions and domestic airfares do not typically have child discounts.

Kid-favorite fast food chains such as KFC, Burger King, and McDonald's are pervasive in city centers, but if you want to keep to a local diet, stick with the abundant half-board (breakfast and dinner) options offered at hotels; this will save a lot on food expenses since children get the discount here as well. Restaurants typically don't offer kids menus, smaller portions, or reduced-price dishes. In seaside resorts, opt for park-themed hotels; these provide innumerable athletic and other fun activities for all age groups, as well as themed rooms and children's menus.

Any hotel can accommodate children of any age. Cribs, cots, and rollaway beds can be had for the asking. Affordable self-catering family suites boasting adjoining bedrooms with kitchenettes and separate bathrooms have become the norm in seaside resorts; some can accommodate up to seven people.

Infant needs, such as disposable diapers and jars of baby food, can be purchased in an *eczane* (pharmacy), a *bakkal* (corner grocery store), or a supermarket. On the down side, public facilities are rarely equipped with baby-changing stations, so a little creativity comes in handy. Discretion is advised when nursing in public.

Highly recommended is **Thompson Family Travel** (14 Mount Auburn St., Watertown, MA 02472, tel. 800/262-6255, www.family-adventures.com, 9 A.M.–5:30 P.M. Mon.–Fri.). This outfit specializes in all-out fun learning tours for the entire family that wind through Istanbul, Cappadocia, the Taurus Mountains, and even take travelers on a four-day boat trip on the Mediterranean (from US$4,800 pp, including air fare).

For resources on family travel, visit **Family Travel with Your Kids** (www.alltravelingkids-familyvacations.com). This site is loaded with sensible advice written by parents on how to travel long distances and internationally with kids, and even sells travel games for kids.

WOMEN TRAVELING ALONE

Women touring Turkey solo are treated with the utmost kindness. Turks are unaccustomed to it, as Turkish women tend to enjoy their leisure and social outings in small groups of friends. Women I know who have chosen to tour the country on their own have become the center of attention and have had access to the authentic Turkish warmth and generous hospitality that make this country so memorable.

When dealing with the opposite gender in Turkey, it's hard as a foreigner to draw the line between genuine warmth and covert flirtation. To make matters worse, the amiability naturally displayed by Western women—in particular North Americans and Australians—is regarded by conservative Turks as somewhat unchaste. So toning down the friendliness and closeness is key to saving face.

Despite the relative progress Turkey has made, in rural areas people are still far from accepting the relaxed skin-baring clothing so popular in the West. Short shorts and bikini tops may be OK in resorts along the Aegean and Mediterranean coasts, but such attire is frowned on in seemingly Westernized cities like Istanbul and Izmir. A night out on the town or even a dip in the sea require moderation. Covering your midriff and thighs should keep onlookers at bay. Topless bathing is considered bad taste at best and could even be regarded as offensive.

Istanbullus dress to impress but rarely to shock. Revealing haute couture or tight clothing on the hips may be de rigueur in more liberal neighborhoods such as as Beyoğlu and

THE BANE OF PICKPOCKETS

Pickpockets and purse-snatchers are rampant in most of the world's big cities, and Istanbul's no stranger to minor street crime. Touristy areas like Sultanahmet, Taksim, and Beyolğu, as well as posh shopping malls and strips like Nişantaşı and Bağdat Caddesi are the prime destinations for thieves on the prowl. Being aware of your surroundings and watching out for any unusual behavior is good advice to follow no matter where you travel. Below is a list of typical "cons" pickpockets have been known to use in Turkey.

The staged "fight" or "chase scene": These theatrics are performed on sidewalks to draw the attention of passersby. Once people stop to look at the commotion, thieves sneak up from behind and reach in pockets for wallets or snatch purses. This tactic has become more complex lately, sometimes involving as many as five "actors"; even taxi drivers, whose awaiting vehicles ensure a quick escape, are in on the take. If this happens, it's recommended to immediately step into a shop, doorway, or away from the attack site.

The "spill and snatch": A complete stranger spills his or her beverage on the victim and moves in to snatch wallet or purse, all while pretending to help mop up the mess

The "bump": An individual carrying boxes "bumps" into the victim, while a partner moves in on the wallet or purse. Another con involves a stranger bumping into the victim. He or she then apologizes to no end. . .while snatching the goods.

The ever-present "purse-snatchers": Thieves grab ladies' purses in restaurants, using deceptive tactics, including distraction. Once the deed is done, they just bolt out of the place of business. Another swindle involves ladies and children working the sidewalks in teams. They approach victims, then block their way, distract them, or ask for request medical assistance, while the children reach into the victim's purse for anything of value. The victims generally realize they've been had once they reach into their handbag or for their wallet, sometimes a long time after the thievery occurred.

---

the hip Bosphorus strip but are a no-no in Old Town areas like Fatih and Sultanahmet. Modesty is key when visiting these pious locales, not only in dress but also in behavior. Women are required to cover their heads, legs, and shoulders when entering a mosque, including Sultanahmet's famed Blue Mosque. Bringing along a larger scarf and dressing accordingly will save you from having to don a shawl used by thousands of others.

Women rarely dine alone, and although the practice is becoming more natural in metropolitan areas, a woman enjoying a meal alone at a countryside eatery might find herself the only woman in the place. Avoid smaller eateries and instead opt for the popular restaurants that offer family-friendly dining rooms called *aile salonu*.

Turkey's seaside resorts and tourist meccas have an underground gigolo industry. These crafty businessmen thrive on meeting the needs of foreign women wishing to "fully"

experience the country. Looks don't matter to them as much as bank accounts, age, and nationality; these young men are particularly interested in well-established women aged 35 to 55. Money is always the motive, but so is the prospect of gaining citizenship in a Western country through marriage. Highly adept in the art of attraction and persuasion, they spin tales of woe and financial need that after a while can disarm even the most wary.

Sexual assault is rare, but women traveling in Turkey should take the same precautionary measures they would at home. Be sensitive to local customs and the prevailing attitudes.

SENIOR TRAVELERS

Turkey is an ideal destination for baby boomers, but unfortunately discounts are rarely offered to people over age 55. Healthy rebates of up to 15 percent on tour packages, hotels, airfares, and car rentals can be had through **AARP** (tel. 888/OUR-AARP—888/687-2277 in the U.S., www.aarp.org). Those age 50 or older can join to receive benefits and AARP's monthly magazine. The **American Automobile Association** (AAA, www.aaa.com) offers similar services to its senior members with the added benefit of an online and walk-in travel agency that specializes in deeply discounted cruises and travel packages. Suggested reading includes periodicals like the informative and deal-packed *Travel 50 & Beyond* (tel. 713/974-6903 in the U.S., www.travel50andbeyond.com).

GAY AND LESBIAN TRAVELERS

Turks are paradoxically and simultaneously conservative and liberal. A cursory look around Taksim's İstiklal Caddesi district reveals every permutation of the headscarf and the chador, the miniskirt and the two-piece suit, as well as men walking hand-in-hand chatting with high-heeled transvestites wearing cheek-revealing shorts. This benevolent acceptance stems from the political and social revolutions of the 1960s, when beloved singers like Zeki Müren

and Bülent Ersoy embraced their feminine side by changing gender. But while Ersoy entertains millions of Turks on her weekly reality show, Turks are still conservative, so discretion is prudent.

Pride Travel (İncili Çavuş Sokak, Ateş Pasaji 33, Sultanahmet, tel. 0212/527-0671, www.turkey-gay-travel.com) excels at providing gay-friendly city guides and travel tips as well as bookings for hotels, day-trips, and regional tours. To find travel ideas and travel agents or tour operators in gay and lesbian travel, contact the **International Gay and Lesbian Travel Association** (IGLTA, tel. 800/448-8550 in the U.S., www.iglta.org).

The *OutTraveler* website (www.outtraveler.com) and the monthly magazine *Passport* (www.passportmagazine.com) can assist with hip trip planning options and location guides. **Damron** (tel. 415/255-0404 in the U.S., http://damron.com) offers separate travel guides updated annually that cater to gays and lesbians, as well as a listing of travel agents worldwide specializing in gay and lesbian travel.

Health and Safety

Turkey's medical sector offers up-to-date facilities, technology, treatment, and care. Should you need the immediate assistance of the **police,** call 155, and for **ambulance services,** dial 112. For non-life-threatening medical issues, just hop in a cab and request to be the driven to the nearest *hastane*'s (hospital) *acil servis* (emergency room). To purchase medications of virtually any kind, and for simple nonemergency treatment, visit a local *eczane* (pharmacy). Hotel and restaurant personnel are always glad to assist with any medical emergency, and Turks will drop what they're doing to help even a stranger in dire need.

BEFORE YOU GO

Ensure that all your medical information has been updated before your departure. Carry all prescription medications in their original

packaging, regardless of whether it needs to be packed in a carry-on or in a suitcase. Taking along a copy of the original prescription form is also advised. Loose pills of any kind make customs officers suspicious, but having the packaging on hand makes it easy for Turkish pharmacists to refill the medication with its Turkish or European equivalent. For those with serious illnesses, a copy of your medical records facilitates the task of doctors in case treatment is necessary in Turkey. If you are carrying syringes, be sure to have a doctor's letter specifying their medical necessity. In the case of food allergies, have a translation of the allergen's name to communicate when ordering meals.

Health Insurance

Purchasing health insurance to travel to Turkey is recommended, particularly if you suffer from a chronic medical condition, are traveling with children, or are the intrepid kind. There is a wide spectrum of insurers providing travel health insurance. Check with the **American Automobile Association** (AAA, www.aaa.com); they provide the most extensive travel insurance services at very competitive rates, including insurance for trip cancellations based on medical reasons, trip-interruption insurance, baggage and personal effects coverage, medical and dental expenses coverage, and 24-hour worldwide emergency assistance and evacuation. **Travel Guard** (tel. 800/826-7791 in the U.S., www.travelguard.com) provides the same services at comparable rates, **STA Travel** (tel. 800/495-5498 in the U.S.) specializes in travel insurance for students and teachers, and **World Travel Center** (tel. 866/979-6753 in the U.S., www.worldtravelcenter.com) provides basic through comprehensive travel insurance coverage in the US$60–275 range, depending on the cost and duration of the trip and the age of the traveler.

The assumption that your embassy in foreign countries provides emergency medical evacuation is incorrect. They can assist in making the arrangements, but payment will be the responsibility of the traveler. Also, insured medical services rendered and medications purchased are oftentimes paid for up front by the traveler in the foreign country, and a claim for reimbursement is then submitted to the insurance company after returning home.

Vaccinations

No specific vaccinations are required to enter Turkey. The World Health Organization (www.who.int), however, advises that inoculations be up to date for diphtheria, tetanus, measles, mumps, rubella, and polio as well as hepatitis B. Boosters for tuberculosis and rabies are recommended for individuals traveling to Turkey.

HEALTH CARE
Pharmacies and Medical Necessities

Pharmacies—called *eczanes*—sell almost everything under the sun even without a doctor's order and for a fraction of the prices seen in the United States and even Europe. Some **prescriptions** calling for rare American formulations are not available. For mild illnesses, such as diarrhea and low fevers, pharmacists can provide advice and treatment and deem whether a visit to a physician is required. But don't expect them to do it in English. Toiletries, particularly makeup and sunscreen, are sold in most Turkish department stores and drug stores, but they are much pricier here than anywhere else; it's smart to purchase them before you travel. Stack up on **mosquito repellent,** which is absolutely necessary during the bug-infested days of summer.

Indicated by a square white sign bearing a red "E," pharmacies in Turkey generally operate 9 A.M.–7 P.M. After-hours and Sunday service is available through a designated *nöbetçi eczane* (on-duty pharmacy), whose address and phone number must be posted on the front door of all the pharmacies in the neighborhood.

A travel medical kit always comes in handy. Think about carrying fever and pain reducers, vitamins, antibiotic cream, calamine lotion, bandages, and the like. Foreign over-the-counter medications are rarely as effective as their American equivalents.

Hospitals and Clinics

Private hospitals in Istanbul and Ankara are expensive. For a list of the hospitals available in each city, refer to the *Information* section for that city. A list of English-speaking health care providers and facilities in Turkey that are endorsed by the U.S. Embassy in Ankara (http://turkey.usembassy.gov) can be found on their website's medical information page. For light medical attention, such as minor ailments or moderate cuts and bruises, as well as mom-approved home remedies, *sağlık ocağı* (neighborhood clinics) are a convenient and affordable option.

HEALTH ISSUES
Bug Bites

Insects are a major problem during the summer months in Turkey. Insect-borne diseases do occur in eastern Anatolia but not in the rest of the country. The World Health Organization reports that yellow fever—an acute viral hemorrhagic disease—and malaria, both carried by mosquitoes, are health threats in southeastern Turkey during the warmer months of May–October. If you are planning to travel through Turkey's southeastern provinces, the use of mosquito repellent is advised to prevent bites, along with the use of the antimalarial drug chloroquine in syrup or tablet form.

But mosquitoes (*sivrisinek*) are not the only insects to watch out for; there are bees (*arı*), wasps (*eşek arısı*), and the rarer scorpion (*akrep*) in warmer areas along the coast. If you're allergic to the bites of any of these, carry a syringe of epinephrine—a drug that blocks anaphylactic and allergic reactions. To prevent bites, pack DEET-based mosquito repellent sprays or wrist bands, such as those manufactured by Cutter, Off, or Bug Off. Relieve itching caused by bug bites with calamine lotion, hydrocortisone, or antihistamine creams.

Snakebites

Turkey's humidity, heat, and forest make a perfect habitat for reptiles, and snakes are present. A snakebite claimed the life of an elderly British man in 2006 when he stepped onto his balcony in the Turkish coastal resort of Altınkum. The rare, highly poisonous horned viper, which measures about 60 centimeters long and is easily recognized by the brown patterned horned features on its back, enjoys sunning itself on rocks. To avoid a potential painful encounter, avoid walking barefoot and poking through dense bush, tall grass, under rocks, and in dark crevices. If you're bitten, request emergency medical assistance, do not elevate the limb and keep the affected area below the heart, wash the area with warm water and soap, and wrap an elastic bandage or piece or fabric tightly above the bite. Do not carve or attempt to suck the venom out of the bite. Immediate treatment consists of an antivenin injection.

Dehydration, Heat Exhaustion, and Heatstroke

Traveling through Turkey during the torrid summer, when temperature can soar above 38°C, remaining hydrated becomes an important health issue. Always carry a bottle of water with you, and refill it often. Thirst and dry mouth are often preliminary symptoms of dehydration. Dark urine, sluggishness, and headaches indicate your body's need for fluids. Drink water throughout the day, preferably totaling about 2.5 liters per day, or opt for a tastier sports or energy drinks. Wearing loose-fitting light clothing made of natural fibers allows perspiration to evaporate, and a wide-brimmed light-colored hat protects your head and neck from the effects of the sun.

Hours of traipsing through archeological wonders under the searing sun can leave you physically exhausted, but it can also trigger symptoms of heat exhaustion, including dizziness, headache, disorientation, fever, hot skin with no sweating, and a rapid heartbeat. If this occurs, the primary concern is to reduce the elevated body temperature. Move indoors to a cool, ventilated area. Laying down, taking care to elevate the feet to promote blood circulation, then cooling the skin with wet cloths and ice packs is recommended. This type of exhaustion can easily turn into heatstroke, a potentially life-threatening condition, if left untreated. Hallucinations, seizures, and fainting are symptoms of heatstroke. Seek emergency medical treatment at this point.

No one escapes the extreme heat of the sun, and it's just one of the disadvantages of summer. Children, the elderly, those with heart conditions, and the severely overweight are particularly at risk. Aside from drinking throughout the day and wearing weather-appropriate clothing, another way to avoid heat-related illness is to plan outdoor excursions for the early morning before the sun reaches its peak. Early afternoon can be spent under a beach umbrella sipping iced lemonade by the pool or on the beach, or visiting air-conditioned sites like museums.

Skin Care

The intense summer sun in Turkey, especially along the southern Aegean and Mediterranean coasts, can be brutal on the skin. Wearing a high-SPF facial sunscreen when stepping outdoors every day is recommended; a wide-brimmed hat can provide shade from searing midday rays. Disrobing at the beach means that your body will need protection as well. The farther south along the Turkish coast your travels take you, the more you'll need to increase your sun-protection regimen. Slathering on a high-SPF sunscreen is advisable for the entire body; so is wearing large dark sunglasses. Sunscreen lotions are widely available in pharmacies, beauty supply stores (*parfumeri*) like Sevil, and supermarkets throughout Turkey. German-manufactured Sebamed offers a line of popular high-quality super-high-SPF sunscreens for the entire family. These products, however, tend to be much pricier here than in the United States; Sebamed's SPF 50 costs around US$24 in Turkey, while the U.S. equivalent, Neutrogena Sunblock SPF 45, sells for US$10. The same is true of luxury skin-care brands, designer makeup, and perfumes, so stack up on toiletries before leaving, including those handy travel-sized lotions, sprays, and face products that take up little space in a knapsack.

Traveler's Diarrhea

Diarrhea can be contracted by drinking tap water. According to the World Health Organization, infection arises from ingesting contaminated food or water. Unless it has been satisfactorily filtered or chemically treated, stick to drinking bottled water. Unwashed and unpeeled fruits and vegetables can also cause intestinal or stomach infection that causes loose stools, and at worst, a worm infection. Clean your hands before peeling fruits that have been rinsed with plenty of water. Unpasteurized dairy products and food that has lingered too long on a steam table are also prime candidates for bacterial infections.

Diarrhea is treated with ample fluid intake. Turks also swear by *ayran,* a lightly salted yogurt drink that replaces lost minerals, rehydrates, and soothes upset stomach. Typical diarrhea involves four to five loose or watery

bowel movements each day. Other symptoms include nausea, vomiting, abdominal cramping, bloating, fever, urgency, and overall discomfort. Most cases last 24–48 hours without treatment. If bowel movements prove more intense, more frequent, or the affliction lasts more than three days, a trip to the doctor is necessary. Once diagnosed, treatment for persistent loose stools is antibiotics, fluoroquinolones, and antidiarrheal agents like loperamide.

SAFETY

Turkey is one of the safest countries in the world for travelers. Violent crimes, including crimes involving guns, are rare. Theft, however, is a problem not only for visitors but also for locals. Terrorism is an ongoing issue throughout the country, and so is seismic activity. But the likelihood of either happening during your stay is next to none and should in no way deter you from planning a trip. For more information, read the regularly updated travel warnings issued by the U.S. Embassy in Turkey on their website (http://turkey.usembassy.gov).

Street Crime

Theft and mugging are a concern in most large cities in the world. Maintaining a constant awareness of your surroundings is the single most important factor in preventing this type of assault. You can reduce your chance of being robbed by not attracting attention, remaining low-key, and keeping your belongings on you at all times. Individuals traveling alone are more susceptible to crime, so do your excursions with others if possible. Commuting by taxi is recommended if you're carrying luggage or if you're out at night. Here are a few of the reported tactics used by criminals in larger cities and seaside resorts throughout the country.

Pickpockets thrive in crowded places like bazaars, the metro, tramways, boats, and at the entrance to amusement parks. Watch your handbag, wallet, wristwatch, camera, and jewelry and stand close to others in your group.

Bag slashers and snatchers use scissors and razor blades to slash handbags and travel bags to collect the valuables within. This form of theft is inconspicuous and victims rarely notice that they have been robbed until they need to get an item from their bag and the culprit is long gone. Snatchers are typically spry teenage boys who run past their targets and use their momentum to pry away the purse. Whatever the technique, reduce your vulnerability by carrying your bag in front of you, close to your chest. If this type of attack occurs, don't engage the thief; they typically carry pocket knives. Just scream "*kapkaççi*" (purse snatcher) at the top of your lungs to draw the attention of passersby.

Muggings were typically unheard of until 2005. Thievery by force is on the increase, particularly in tourist areas like Sultanahmet and Beyoğlu. Enclosed quarters like bazaars are being closely monitored by the authorities with high-tech surveillance systems.

Group theft: Families, usually several women wearing long garb with one or several children, target mothers with their tots, doting on the child while a juvenile accomplice pilfers a bag from behind. Once taken, the loot disappears under the voluminous clothing of one of the perpetrators.

Cons

Lone male and 20-something travelers are targets of a variety of scams that ultimately result in robbery. One of these is restricted to the heavily touristed areas of Beyoğlu's Taksim and the bar strip of İstiklal Caddesi, both in Istanbul. The first scenario involves a well-dressed man who strikes up a conversation in impeccable English, then suggests going to a hip bar or nightclub that he knows. The lounge owner or staff are in on the scam, and once seated, several strangers join the party. Once the tab arrives, the traveler is expected to pay the full amount, which always greatly exceeds the amount of cash he is carrying. Unable to pay the exorbitant total, the victim is forcefully coerced to hand over his credit card. Victims of this con have reported the theft of all of their cash, brutal beatings, and even being forced to a nearby ATM to withdraw the daily limit on their credit cards. In 2006 Istanbul police

raided six popular nightclubs, which led to the arrest of more than 100 suspects of the scam and the seizure of firearms and drugs.

Similar attacks can occur at any time in bars or restaurants in tourist areas. Once again, a conversation will be started, then a change of venue will be suggested. The victim who takes the bait is robbed of his wallet and possessions on the way to the "happening" or "scenic" spot and dropped to the nearest curb. Another scam is the "traveling companion," in which a new acquaintance enthusiastically pleads to show you the sights of his beautiful country personally.

To prevent being conned, be aware of the individual sitting across from you. Be in the moment, and use common sense. Order your own drinks, and pay for them on the spot. Adamantly refusing to change location or informing the con artist that a couple of your friends are on the way will most likely deter him. If your new pal doesn't want to accompany you to a bar of your choosing, that's a good indication that he is not to be trusted. If all else fails, just excuse yourself and leave.

Drugging

Drugging isn't as common as it used to be, but it still occurs among young travelers. In this scenario, reported by the victims themselves on Turkish travel-related message boards, the scenario involves groups of Turks pretending to be Middle Eastern or Balkan tourists themselves. Their techniques include spiking alcoholic drinks and then robbing their victims of their personal belongings, even their clothing, after transporting them to a seedy location. This happened to a couple of Germans touring the Grand Bazaar in 2009. Luckily they realized the apple tea handed to them by a store owner had been spiked with the common date-rape drug Nembutal—a fast-acting sedative—before anything worse could occur.

Terrorism and Hostility Campaigns

Terrorism is an ongoing issue in Turkey; the U.S. State Department habitually warns its citizens traveling to the country, particularly Istanbul, to be wary of potential terrorist activity. Sadly, anti-Americanism rears its ugly head sporadically; the U.S. government advises practicing the utmost level of vigilance. That means avoiding demonstrations and large gatherings, as even peaceful protests can turn confrontational and even violent. That said, the risk of harm from any sort of political incident or violence is almost nonexistent.

There are 12 organizations designated as terrorist by the Turkish Directorate General for Security. These militant parties vehemently and violently oppose each other or the state on a variety of political, religious, or ethnic issues. Including Communists, Maoists, Leninists, Marxists, and extreme Zionists, each is active in its cause, but none has been as active as the Kurdish revolutionaries and the PKK (Kurdistan Workers Party). Around 40,000 people have died since the beginning of the PKK's armed struggle in 1984. The PKK's goal is national independence for the Kurds, which has included bomb attacks on tourist and commercial facilities, particularly during the months of March and April and during the busy summer season. In 1999 bombs were detonated in a busy mall and in a residential district in Istanbul, killing 13. In the popular resort of Kuşadası in July 2005, five foreign tourists died when their minibus, headed to the famous Ladies Beach, exploded. Two of Istanbul's synagogues, HSBC Bank, and the British consulate were the targets of separate explosions that killed 57 in November 2003. Islamic militants claimed responsibility for the 2003 attacks.

Have you wondered why there are no garbage bins in Turkey? They've proved to be a convenient drop-off for bombs. Again, vigilance is advised when visiting public areas anywhere in Turkey, and anywhere else in the world.

Information and Services

MONEY

The currency used in Turkey is the *Türk lirası* (Turkish lira; TL). It is broken down into 100 *kuruş*. Coins come in denominations of one, five, 10, 25, and 50 kurus and one and two lira. Bank notes come in five, 10, 20, 50, 100, and 200 lira denominations.

Turkey suffered a massive financial meltdown in 2001 after years of runaway inflation. The then–finance minister, Kemal Derviş, ingeniously stabilized Turkey's economy within just 18 months of taking office, and by January 1, 2005, inflation was hovering in the mid-single digits and the *yeni Türk lirası* (new Turkish lira) was introduced, deleting six zeros from the old currency.

It is wise to travel with a combination of payment options—credit cards and cash. But since there's no currency inspection at customs, and U.S. dollars, euros, and British pounds sterling can be exchanged, wait to buy a small amount of Turkish currency (about 100TL) at the exchange booth near the luggage carousel in the arrivals hall; exchange rates are far more favorable within Turkey than abroad. And unless you are planning a return trip, arrange to spend all your liras during your stay, since no other country uses the currency.

Banks are notorious for handing out large notes to their customers, denominations that shop owners and small restaurateurs are unwilling to break. To avoid the glare of the otherwise friendly cashier at the corner market, try to keep as many smaller-denomination bank notes as possible. Use larger bills for big-item purchases or out on the town.

Keep in mind that the recent global economic meltdown has affected Turkey's tourism and service sector as a whole, leveling off the ever-increasing rates charged previously by hotels and restaurants. To make matters worse, the ebb and flow in currencies and the petroleum market has caused Turkey's emerging economy to fluctuate even more than its

© JESSICA TAMTÜRK

Shopping in Istanbul or in the resort towns to its south and east can be a whole lot of fun; just remember to inspect items prior to purchase, and that shop owners typically inflate their prices by at least 25 percent.

Western European neighbors. A good example is in the recent devaluation of the dollar, which caused hotels throughout Turkey to adopt the euro and drop the U.S. currency when quoting room rates. And despite petroleum's return to more sensible prices, the Turkish government, which has controlled the price of gasoline since 2009, continues to raise the price for consumers. For these reasons, the prices and rates listed in this book may differ from those you'll see during your travels.

ATMs, Banks, Currency Exchange, and Credit Cards

Automatic Teller Machines are widespread in Turkey, except perhaps where tourists need them most: Sultanahmet has only a couple of well-hidden cash dispensers. But on the whole, ATM fees charged by U.S.-based banks, compounded with less-than-friendly exchange rates, can cause unexpected hefty charges. The best solution is to carry cash, in a money belt for added security, and to put pricier purchases

on credit cards. All cities, including airports and major attractions, have ATMs that dispense Turkish liras and accept cards bearing the Cirrus, Maestro, Visa, and MasterCard logos. To serve the growing expatriate community as well as tourists, bank machines now have English menus. The maximum daily withdrawal is 1,000TL, and machines may run out of funds during bank holidays and on weekends, but on the whole their reserves and availability are very reliable. When using ATMs, try to stick to those outside of banks. This not only ensures your safety but also the safety of the cash withdrawal. Use the same common sense you would at home, knowing that scams and thieves are prevalent worldwide.

Banks in Turkey are highly reliable. **Ziraat Bankası, Türkiye İş Bankası, Akbank,** and **Garanti Bankası** are among the country's most reputable banking establishments. Services extended to tourists are currency exchange (rates are typically higher than at exchange kiosks), cashing traveler's checks, and cash withdrawals on credit or debit cards. Most banks are open Monday–Friday from 9 A.M. through 5 or 5:30 P.M., with Türkiye İş Bankası closing 12:20–1:30 P.M. daily.

Owners of currency exchange kiosks at major destinations are in the business of making money. If their rates were higher than at banks, they would not turn a dime. With this in mind, try to deal strictly with exchange offices and post offices (PTTs) to get the best rates. Hotels, and some shops and restaurants do accept U.S. dollars and euros, but they charge a less favorable exchange rate for the convenience.

Credit cards are widely accepted in Turkey. Rare is the *pansiyon* or village diner owner who has not yet added this payment option. While the acceptance of American Express and Diner's Club is limited to industrial hotels, cards with the Visa or MasterCard/Access logos are welcomed by most hotels, shops, bars, and restaurants. Cash can be obtained on these credit cards at ATMs and banks nationwide, and miles or points can be either accrued or redeemed at participating hotels.

Tipping

A 15 percent *servis ücreti* (service charge) is added automatically in the price of menu items in Turkey. That said, leaving an extra lira or two on the table after a quick and inexpensive lunch is in good taste. If you've appreciated the service at better restaurants, use the American custom of leaving 15 percent of the tab. This will ensure regal treatment on your return and a complementary after-dinner tea or demitasse of Turkish coffee.

The etiquette for tipping hotel staff varies. One or two liras per bag is the going rate for bellboys, who not only lug bags but also provide a quick tour of the rooms and their gadgets. A 10 percent extra charge for a meal ordered through room service is standard. The protocol at B&Bs is quite different. No tipping is required, since the owners and their family members typically run their businesses single-handedly; they would more likely be slightly offended by the offer of a tip. But if

housekeeping staff is not part of the family, do tip them for their efforts.

Taxi fares are rounded up to the nearest 50 *kuruş*. When paying, round up to the nearest lira. Turkish cabbies do not accept tips. The little extra not only saves them from making change but also shows goodwill on your part. *Dolmuş* operators don't accept tips. Waitstaff toiling on long-distance bus routes will greatly appreciate a 5TL tip for running up and down the narrow isle of a moving vehicle to answer your calls.

Masseurs and tour guides do expect an additional financial reward over prices quoted for their services. The rule of thumb is no more than 10 percent for more expensive treatments and tours; that can be increased depending on your degree of satisfaction or the cost of the service rendered.

Traveler's Checks

The paperwork involved with accepting traveler's checks is despised by most business owners in Turkey. Who can blame them, when two pieces of identification must be checked, currency exchange rates calculated, and lengthy passport numbers copied down. Still, transporting currency in this way is far safer than touring unknown territory with pockets stuffed with cash. You could plan to carry at least a third of your travel budget in traveler's checks. Once you're in Turkey, redeeming them for cash is easy. Hotels and banks do charge unfavorable commissions for the convenience of on-site exchange; PTT offices take the smallest bite.

Traveler's checks can be purchased at most banks in the United States, or though American Express, Visa, and MasterCard. They're issued in various dominations, from US$20 to US$500, for a commission of up to 4 percent. Retain copies of all the checks at home; these serve as proof of purchase and ensure a refund if they are lost.

COMMUNICATIONS AND MEDIA
Mail

Stamps (*posta pulu*) can be purchased from PTTs (Postal Telephone and Telegraph, tel.

444-1788, www.ptt.gov.tr/en) around the country. These convenient mailing centers are identified by a yellow rectangular sign with the blue "PTT" logo. Visit online or ask your hotel concierge for the nearest location. As of March 2010 the international postage rate was 0.89TL for a 20-gram letter up to 19TL for a 2-kilogram parcel; sending a postcard abroad costs 0.80TL, and cargo up to 30 kilograms can be shipped at a cost calculated when you ship it based on the contents of the package. The Turkish mail system is efficient and quite rapid. If you are shipping important documents, consider sending them by registered mail (*taahhütlü posta*) at an extra charge of 1.35TL per 20-gram letter and 3.50TL for heavier items. Express mail services incur an extra charge of 0.50TL for a 50-gram letter up to 7TL for packages up to 3 kilograms. Other shipping options include **FedEx** (tel. 444-0606, www.fedex.com/tr) and **DHL** (tel. 444-0040, www.dhl.com.tr).

Telephone

Calling internationally from Turkey is inexpensive and easy. Calls (*telefon görüşmesi*) can be made from local PTT offices or using a prepaid phone card (*telefon hazır card*). **Türk Telekom** (tel. 811/212-3636, www.turktelekom.com.tr) phone cards allow you to make calls from any landline in the world using a private password. These can be purchased by phone or online through the company, or at most newspaper stands and corner grocery stores (*bakkals*) displaying the Türk Telekom sign.

To dial Turkey from the United States, dial 011 + 90 + area code + local number; to call the United States from Turkey, dial 001 + area code + number. With as many cell phone lines in Turkey as there are residents, landlines are rarely used. Public phones have become rare, and those that still exist are in a state of disuse. To call within Turkey on a landline, first dial "0," the equivalent of dialing "1" in the United States, then the three-digit area code followed by the seven-digit phone number. Cell phones have the same number of digits, but their numbers all begin with 05. Numbers starting with 444 and 0800 are toll-free within the country. Common area codes in Turkey are Istanbul: 212 and 216; Ankara: 312; Izmir: 232; Antalya: 242; Bodrum: 242; Konya: 332; Cappadocia: 384; Fethiye: 252.

Cell Phones

Some foreign cell phones can be used in Turkey by registering them at any **Avea** (tel. 444-1500, www.avea.com.tr), **TürkCell** (tel. 444-0532, www.turkcell.com), or cstyle:B>Vodafone (tel. 444-0542, www.vodafone.com.tr) shop. To do so, you'll need to present your passport. Once registered, a SIM card will be issued, along with a cell phone number, for about 25TL. Prepaid units (*kontör*) come in denominations of 50 (11TL), 100 (20TL), 150 (30TL), 250 (50TL), 500 (90TL), and 1,000 (170TL) units. As of March 2010 a local cell phone call cost 0.22TL per minute, and from Turkey to the United States cost 12 units or 1.60TL per minute; a 10-minute call would set you back 16TL.

Staff at the TurkCell and Vodafone kiosks located in the lobby of the international arrivals terminal in Istanbul's Atatürk Airport can assist in registering your foreign cell phone, purchasing a starter pack with a SIM card, and buying prepaid units to get you connected right away.

Internet Access

Turkey is online, and in a big way. All cafés and some restaurants have free Wi-Fi access if you have a laptop or a Wi-Fi–capable smart phone like an iPhone or a Blackberry. If you've registered your smart phone for use in Turkey, you can surf the Internet from anywhere by connecting through the cell network using units on a prepaid card.

All hotels in city centers provide free Internet connections or Wi-Fi. The larger ones have in-room wired connections whose use may require a password, and the majority of smaller hotels and B&Bs are equipped with a single line that can be used in the lobby. *Pansiyons* in rural areas may just have a desktop PC for complementary guest use. If you don't have a computer, the use of a terminal may be available in larger hotels for a 3–5TL hourly fee.

Cybercafés dot the heavily-trafficked areas of large city centers, while rural areas and villages may have just one. They charge 2–4TL per hour. While they are safe, most cybercafés in Turkey are used by teenagers and young adults for gaming. Starbucks currently provides free Internet surfing, as do smaller cafés.

English Language Publications

English-language newspapers and magazines are widely available in Izmir, Istanbul, Ankara, and holiday resorts like Antalya and Bodrum. Larger hotels stock daily copies in the lobby for their guests. Most newspaper kiosks and book stores in tourist areas like Sultanahmet and Taksim will have them on hand.

The staunchly secular *Hürriyet Daily News & Economic Review* (www.hurriyetdailynews.com), the AKP party–aligned *Today's Zaman* (www.todayszaman.com), and the *New Anatolian* are three English-based dailies that cover international, national, and local news as well as provide special sections. These newspapers cost 1.50TL. *Hürriyet* and *Zaman* have an online presence, and so do the Turkish-language dailies. International newspapers such as the *International Herald Tribune* (http://global.nytimes.com/?iht), the *Wall Street Journal* (http://europe.wsj.com), and the *New York Times* (www.nytimes.com) are available through bookstores in larger cities for about 5TL.

English-language magazines include the bimonthly *The Guide* (www.apa.com.tr, 7TL), *Time Out Istanbul* (8TL), which appears monthly, and the quarterly connoisseur guide *Cornucopia* (www.cornucopia.net, 20TL). Newsmagazines like *Time* (www.time.com), the *Economist* (www.economist.com), and *Fortune* (www.fortune.com) as well as American lifestyle magazines are readily available at better bookstores throughout Istanbul.

Turkish Press

An assortment of Turkish newspapers can easily be found at kiosks and corner grocery stores. One or two dailies reflect each of the many political sentiments in the country. The dailies with the highest circulation are *Hürriyet*

(www.hurriyet.com.tr), *Zaman* (www.zaman.com.tr), *Haber Türk* (www.haberturk.com), and *Cumhuriyet* (www.cumhuriyet.com.tr). Aside from news, each provides expanded lifestyle sections on weekends.

Turkey-Related Websites

Websites geared for tourists and expatriates residing in Turkey exist online. A Web search on the place you're interested in will provide at least two sites with detailed information about virtually everything there is to know about the destination. One notable website is MyMerhaba (www.mymerhaba.com). It provides a weekly updated calendar of social and public events occurring in Ankara and Istanbul as well as candid articles about the ins and outs of education, work, touring, traveling, and studying in Turkey.

For everything you need to know about culture, history, restaurants and hotels, the arts, and so on, the one-stop website is www.istanbul.com. A website intended for expatriates is www.expatsturkey.com; it boasts dining and entertainment listings for families as well as articles on Turkish cuisine, culture, and trends.

MAPS AND TOURIST INFORMATION
Tourist Offices and Websites

In planning your trip, make sure to visit the website of the **Turkish Culture and Tourism Ministry**'s New York attaché at www.tourismturkey.org. This exhaustive and beautiful resource is geared for the tastes and sensibilities of an American audience. Everything you need to know about Turkey's various destinations, their attractions, and the best times to visit them, along with a trip planner, are included. Similar sites are maintained in English and Turkish by each of Turkey's provinces: Istanbul (www.ibb.gov.tr), Ankara (www.ankara.gov.tr), Izmir (www.Izmir.bel.tr), Bodrum (www.bodrum.bel.tr), and Çeşme (www.cesmebelediyesi.com).

Maps

The coverage of the maps in this guidebook has been limited to ensure user-friendliness.

More detailed maps are available at tourism offices around the country for free or at low cost. Souvenir shops and bookstores also offer commercial maps ranging in coverage from municipal to national levels at a cost of 5–8TL. On the Web, **Google Maps** makes it simple to pinpoint an address or a location, and to familiarize yourself with the lay of the land during your travels; you don't even need to bother folding and unfolding a paper version. Here's a tip: create a personal Google Map before your departure by flagging the sites you want to see, along with the location of hotels and interesting restaurants. Your personal map will be ready to use on the Web during your travels. Other map-generating sites include **Yahoo! Local Maps** (maps.yahoo.com) and **Via Michelin** (www.viamichelin.com).

For a no-nonsense national highway map that lists all turn-offs, distances, and points in Turkey down to the scale of remote villages, get **MepMedya**'s *Türkiye Karayolları Haritası* (12TL). These maps are available at most gas stations and bookstores, including **DK** and **Remzi.** A long list of maps of Turkey, its cities, and its roads exists in paper or downloadable form at **Omnimap** (www.omnimap.com); these can be ordered before your departure or downloaded immediately for a fee.

An exhaustive website covering sites in the country, its history, and much more has been developed by Turkey travel professional Burak Sansal at www.allaboutturkey.com. A veteran tour guide, Sansal relates a wealth of of knowledge he has gathered during 18 years of guiding foreign tourists.

Travel Listings

If you wonder what other visitors really think about Turkey and its destinations, check out **Trip Advisor** (www.tripadvisor.com) and **Virtual Tourist** (www.virtualtourist.com). Thousands of candid reviews of hotels, restaurants, and attractions, and even city guides, are available on their sites. You can post questions or concerns and wait for seasoned travelers to weigh in, or scroll through the message boards to find out the dos and don'ts of a particular region.

WEIGHTS AND MEASURES

Turkey uses the metric system for weights and measures. Distances are calculated in centimeters (1 cm = 0.39 inches), meters (1 m = 3.28 feet or 1.09 yards), and kilometers (1 km = 0.62 miles); weight is measured in grams (100 g = 3.5 ounces) and kilograms (1 kg = 2.2 pounds); land area is in hectares (1 ha = 2.47 acres); volume is in liters (1 L = 2.11 U.S. pints, 33.8 U.S. ounces, and 1.05 quarts); and temperature is in degrees Celsius (20°C = 68°F). Unlike the 12-hour clock with A.M. and P.M. used in English, time in Turkey is stated using the 24-hour clock (17:00 = 5 P.M.).

RESOURCES

Glossary

açık open
açil emergency
ad name
ağız mouth
akşam evening
Amerika Birleşik Devletleri/ABD United States of America/USA
araba car
asla never
Avustralya Australia
ayak foot
ayakabı shoes
ayak parmağı toe
az a little
az şekerli Türk kahvesi lightly sweetened Turkish coffee
bacak leg
bakalım let's see
balık fish
bar bar
baş head
başka another
belediye dairesi town hall
beyaz şarap white wine
bildircin quail
bilgisayar computer
bisiklet bicycle
bitkisel herbal
boyun neck
börek filled pastry
bu/bunlar this/these
bugün today
burun nose
büyük big
café coffee shop
cami mosque

çok a lot/many
çorap socks
çorba soup
dakika minute
deniz sea
deniz mahsulleri shellfish and crustaceans
diğer other
diz knee
dolmuş communal taxi
domuz pork
duble double
dün yesterday
dünya world
el hand
elbise dress
eşarp scarf
et meat
eyalet province/state
feniküler funicular
fıstık nut
gazete newspaper
gece night
geyik deer
gezmek travel
göl lake
gömlek shirt
göz eye
qün day
güveç stew
güzel good
halk public
hamam Turkish bath
harika great
hayat life
hepsi all
her/her biri each

herkes everyone
hükümet government
İngiltere England
insanlar people
ışık light
iyi well
kaburga ribs
kahve coffee
kalça hip
kapalı closed
kara biber black pepper
karanlık dark
keçi goat
kek tea cake
kilise church
kim who
kırmızı şarap red wine
kıtabevi bookstore
kıtap book
kokteyl cocktail, mixed drink
kol arm
küçük small
kulak ear
kuzu lamb
mayo bathing suit
metro subway/metro
meydan square, plaza
meyhane tavern
meyve fruit
mide stomach
ne what
neden why
nehir river
nerede where
ne zaman when
numara number
otel hotel
öğle noon
öğleden sonra afternoon
ördek duck
palto coat
pansiyon inn/pension
pantalon pants
parmak finger

pasaj passage/arcade
paso pass
pasta cake (moist)
patlıcan eggplant
postal kodu postal code
radyo radio
rakı strong Turkish spirit flavored with aniseed
reyhan basil
saat time, hour
sabah morning
sade Türk kahvesi unsweetened Turkish coffee
salata salad
şarap wine
sayfa page
şehir city
şekerli Türk kahve sweetened Turkish coffee
sert hard
seyahat trip
sıcak hot
sığır beef
şimdi now
sinema movie theater
soğuk cold
soyad surname
su milk
şu/şunlar that/those
şu anda right away
süt danası veal
sütlü kahve coffee with milk
telefon telephone
televizyon television
tiyatro theater
tramway tram
Türk kahvesi Turkish coffee
tuz salt
uçak airplane
ülke country
üretilmiş made
yarın tomorrow
yoğurt yoghurt
yumuşak soft
yüz face
zeytin olive
zeytinyağ olive oil

Turkish Phrasebook

Very few people in Turkey speak English. In fact, outside of the big three cities – Istanbul, Izmir, and Ankara – and the popular tourist spots, people are rarely able to understand, let alone communicate, with foreign travelers. Part of the problem is that English didn't find its way into the primary public school curriculum until a few years ago. So while a few kids may be able to use some *Ingilizce* (English), on the whole their elders can't. The lack of foreign-language skills doesn't stop them, however; their unconscious sense of hospitality inevitably coerces them to practice their repertory in an effort to welcome newcomers. Ultimately, to get the most out of your trip it is necessary to learn the basics of the Turkish language, including pronunciation and basic sentence structure. The use of a few well-placed Turkish words will make you popular for taking the troubling to learn the language. The most important phrase to learn is *Pardon, Türkçe konuşmıyorum* (pahr-DOHN Tur-K-che KO-nush-ME-yo-rum), "I'm sorry, but I don't speak Turkish." This tells the listener that you don't speak the language and communicates your humbleness. Refrain from speaking English with strangers without at least breaking the ice by saying *merhaba* (MEHR-hah-bah), meaning "hello," or, *affedersiniz* (af-feh-DEHR-see-neez), "excuse me." These words convey politeness; not using them before speaking English comes across as insensitive.

The Turkish alphabet contains 29 letters, including the 26 familiar letters used in English, without X, Q, and W, plus six modified letters: ç, ğ, ş, ı, ö, and ü.

PRONUNCIATION

The majority of Turkish letters are pronounced as they would sound in English, but there are a few exceptions that are easy to remember. The three golden rules to speaking Turkish are: 1. Each letter is pronounced; 2. each letter has only one sound; and 3. letters are never combined to produce other sounds (like *ph* produces "f" in English). Letters to be emphasized are capitalized.

Vowels

a as 'a' in "tar": *baba* bah-bah (father), *anne* AHN-ne (mother)

e as 'e' in "bed": *sen* (you), *yer* yehr (place)

i as 'ee' in "see": *iyi* ee-yee (good), *sinema* SEE-neh-MAH (movies).

ı as 'i' in "fir": *sıcak* suh-JAHK (hot), *kız* kuhz (girl)

o as 'o' in "often": *kol* kohl (arm), *yok* yohk (no)

ö as 'u' in "urge": *ölüm* UH-luhm (death), *söz* suhz (word)

u as 'ou' in "you": *uzun* oo-ZOON (long), *uçak* oo-CHAHK (airplane)

ü as 'u' in the French "tu": *üzüm* Ü-züm (grapes), *yüksek* yük-sek (high)

Consonants

b, d, f, k, l, m, n, p, r, t, v, and z have almost the same pronunciation as in English.

c as 'j' in "jar": *cam* jahm (glass), *bacak* bah-JAHK (leg)

ç as 'ch' in "chat": *çöp* chuhp (trash), *çim* cheem (grass)

g as 'g' in "golf": *garson* gahr-SOHN (waiter), *göl* guhl (lake)

ğ is not pronounced. This 'g' is crowned by a silencing breve that lengthens the sound of the vowel that precedes it, as is *dağ* daah (mountain) and *değil* DEH-eel (not).

h as 'h' in "hat": *hava* HAH-vah (air or weather), *her* hehr (every)

j as 's' in "treasure": *jandarma* zhan-DAHR-mah (national guard)

ş as 'sh' in "sham": *şair* SHA-eer (poet), *eş* esh (spouse)

Although **w** and **x** are not officially used in the alphabet, they do appear in foreign words that have come into the Turkish vocabulary. Likewise **â,** which dates back to prerepublican Turkish, is used rarely to lengthen the 'a' sound.

BASIC AND COURTEOUS EXPRESSIONS

Turks are polite and use formalities profusely. Use greetings appropriate to the time of the day and the situation, like "good morning," "hello," "pardon me," and so on.

Hello *Merhaba*
Good morning *İyi günler*
Good afternoon *Tünaydın*
Good evening *İyi akşamlar*
Good night *İyi geceler*
How are you? *Nasılsınız?*
Very well, thank you *İyiyim, teşekkür ederim*
Not well *İyi değilim*
So-so *Fenah değilim*
And you? *Siz nasılsnız?*
Thank you *Teşekkürler, Sağ ol* or *Mersi*
Thank you very much *Çok teşekkürler*
You're welcome. *Bir şey değil.*
Good-bye *Allaha ısmarladık*
Pleased to meet you *Memnun oldum*
See you later *Görüşürüz*
Please *Lütfen*
Pardon me *Affedersiniz* or *pardon*
Yes *Evet*
No *Hayır*
I don't know. *Bilmiyorum.*
My name is . . . *Adım . . .*
Just a moment, please. *Bir dakika, lütfen.*
Excuse me (to get attention) *Bakar mısınız*
Excuse me (when you have done something wrong) *Özür dilerim*
Do you speak English? *Siz İngilizce konuşur musunuz?*
Is English spoken here? *İngilizce burada konuşulur mu?*
I want . . . / I don't want . . . *. . . istiyorum / . . . istemiyorum*
I don't speak Turkish. *Türkçe bilmiyorum.*
I don't understand. *Anlamıyorum.*
Would you like . . . *. . . istiyormusunuz?*
Let's go to the restaurant. *Restoran'a gidelim.*
My name is . . . *Adım . . .*

TERMS OF ADDRESS

Strangers should be addressed using the formal pronoun *siz* (you). Once individuals become familiar, using *sen* (you) is appropriate. In general, women are referred to by their first name followed by *hanım efendi* (lady), while *bey efendi* (Mr., sir) is used for men.

I *ben*
you (formal) *siz*
you (familiar) *sen*
he, him; she, her; it *o*
we, us *biz*
they, them *onlar*
Mr., sir *Bey*
Mrs., Miss, Madam *Hanım*
wife *karı*
husband *koca*
friend *arkadaş*
boyfriend; girlfriend *erkek arkadaş; kız arkadaş; sevgili*
son; daughter *oğul; kız*
brother; sister *erkek kardeş; kız kardeş*
older brother *abi*
father; mother *baba; anne*
grandfather; grandmother *dede; büyük anne, babaanne* (father's mother), *anneanne* (mother's mother)

TRANSPORTATION AND DIRECTIONS

Where is . . . ? *. . . nerede?*
How far is it to . . . (Izmir)? *(Izmir) . . . ne kadar uzkta?*
from (Izmir) to (Istanbul) *(Izmir)'den (İstanbul)'a*
Where (how) do I (we) go . . . ? *Nereye (nasıl) giderim (gideriz) . . . ?*
bus; bus station *otobüs; otogar*
bus stop *otobüs durağı*
Where is the bus going? *Otobüs nereye gidiyor?*
taxi; taxi stand *taksi; taksi durağı*
communal taxi; communal taxi stop *dolmuş, dolmuş durağı*
train; train station *tren; tren istasyonu*
boat; steamboat; sailboat *bot, gemi; vapur; tekne*
airport *havalımanı, havaalanı*
plane *uçak*
Can I buy a ticket to . . . ? *. . . bir bilet satın alabilir miyim?*

first (second) class *birinci (ikinci) sınıf*
round-trip *gidiş-dönüş*
reservation *rezervasyon*
baggage *bagaj*
Stop here, please. *buraya durun, lütfen.*
entrance (to enter); exit (to exit) *giriş (girmek); çıkış (çıkmak)*
ticket office; booth *bilet gişesi*
(very) near; far *(çok) yakın; uzak*
to (to Istanbul, to the supermarket); toward *-a (Istanbul'a), -e (market'e); -e doğru, -a do doğru*
by (position, by the door) *yan, kapının yanında*
by (method, by train) *'ile, tren'ile*
through (inside of, among) *içinden, arasından*
from (America) *-den, -dan (Amerika'dan)*
right; left *sağ; sol*
straight ahead *dümdüz*
ahead *ilerde*
front; in front of *ön; önde*
beside *yanında*
in the back of; located behind *arkada*
corner *köşe*
stoplight *trafik ışığı; trafik lambası*
turn; to turn *sapış; sapmak*
right here *tam orada*
somewhere around here *bir yerde burada*
right there *tam orada*
somewhere around there *bir yerde orada*
street; avenue; boulevard *sokak; cadde; bulvar*
highway *otoyol, karayolu, ekspress yol*
bridge *köprü*
toll *geçiş ücreti*
address *adres*
directions; give directions *tarife; tarife vermek*
north; south *kuzey; güney*
east; west *doğu; batı*

ACCOMMODATIONS
hotel *otel*
Is there a room? *Oda var mı?*
May I (we) see it? *Ben (biz) onu görebilir miyim (miyiz)?*

What is the (daily, weekly) rate? *(gündüz, haftalık) tarifesi ne kadar?*
Is that your best rate? *O en iyi tarifeniz mi?*
Can the rate be lowered, if paying by cash? *Nakit ödeyerek, tarife inebilir mi?*
Is there something cheaper? *Daha ucuz bir şey var?*
single room *tek kişilik oda*
double room *iki kişilik oda*
family room *aile odası*
double beds *iki kişilik yatak*
twin bed *tek kişilik yatak*
crib *bebek karyolası*
with private bath *oda içi banyo'ila*
hot water *sıcak su*
air conditioning *klima*
shower *duş*
towel *havlu*
soap *savun*
toilet paper *tuvalet kağıdı*
blanket *battaniye*
bed sheet *yatak çarşafı*
fan *fan, vantilatör*
key *anahtar*
manager *yönetici, manajer*
owner (hotel) *sahip (otel sahibi*
housekeeping *oda hizmeti*

FOOD
I'm (we're) hungry; I'm (we're) thirsty. *acıktım (acıktık); susadım (susadımk)*
menu *menü, yemek listesi*
order; to order *sipariş; sipariş etmek*
glass *bardak*
fork *çatal*
knife *bıcak*
spoon *kaşık*
napkin *peçete*
soft drink *kola, soda*
coffee *kahve*
tea *çay*
bottled water *su şişesi*
tap water *musluk suyu*
bottled carbonated water *soda, gazoz*
beer *bira*
wine *şarap*
milk *süt*
juice *meyve suyu*

cream *krema*
sugar *şeker*
cheese *peynir*
snack *ara öğün, çerez*
breakfast *kahvaltı*
lunch *öğle yemeği*
daily special *günlük yemeği menüsü*
dinner *akşam yemeği*
check, tab *adisyon, hesap*
egg *yumurta*
bread *ekmek*
salad *salata*
fruit *meyve*
vegetables *sebze*
soup *çorba*
dessert *tatlı*
appetizer (hot appetizer) *mezze (ara sıcak)*
main meal *ana yemek*

SHOPPING

money *para*
currency exchange bureau *döviz bürosu*
Can I exchange dollars (traveler's checks)? *Dolar bozdurabilir miyim?*
Can I purchase Turkish liras? *Türk lirası satın alabilir miyim?*
What is the exchange rate? *Döviz kuru ne kadar?*
How much is the commission? *Komisyon ücreti ne kadar?*
Do you accept credit cards? *Kredi kartları kabul ediyor musunuz?*
money order *para havalesi*
How much does it cost? *Bu ne kadar?*
expensive *pahalı*
cheap *uçuz*
more, too much *daha, fazla*
less *az*
a little *biraz*
too much *çok fazla*

HEALTH

Help me please. *Bana yardım edin lütfen.*
I am ill. *Hastayım.*
Call a doctor. *Bir doktor ça ırabilir misiniz?*
Take me to ... (doctor) *Beni ... (doktor'a) götür*
ambulance *ambülans*

hospital *hastane*
pharmacy *eczane*
pain *acı, a rı*
fever *ateş*
headache *baş a rısı*
stomachache *mide a rısı*
burn (sunburn) *yanık (güneş yanığı)*
cramp *kramp*
nausea *bulantı*
vomiting *kusma*
medicine *ilaç*
antibiotic *antibiotik*
pill; syrup *hap; şurup*
aspirin *aspirin*
ointment; cream *melhem; krem*
cotton *pamuk*
sanitary napkin *hijyenik ped*
diaper *bebek bezi*
birth control pills *doğum kontrol hapı*
contraceptive foam *kontraseptif köpük*
condoms *prezervatif*
toothbrush *diş fırçası*
toothpaste *diş macunu*
dentist *diş hekimi*
toothache *diş a rısı*

POST OFFICE AND COMMUNICATIONS

long-distance (international) telephone call *şehirlerarası (uluslararası) telefon konuşması*
May I call ... ? *... ça ırabilir miyim*
collect call *karşı ödemeli*
station-to-station call *santral aracılığıyla konuşma*
person-to-person call *ihbarlı konuşma*
credit card *kredi kartı*
post office *postane*
general delivery *genel dağıtım*
postcard *kartpostal*
stamp *posta pulu*
letter *mektup*
envelope *zarf*
air mail *hava yolu ile*
registered/certified *taahhütlü*
money order *posta havalesi*
package; box *paket; kutu*
string; tape *ip; teyp*

AT THE BORDER

border *sınır*
customs *gümrük*
immigration *göçmen*
immigration booth *göçmen gişesi*
visa *vize*
passport *pasaport*
inspection; control *denetim ,kontrol*
border guard *gümrük görevlisi*
profession *meslek*
marital status *medeni dürümu*
single *bekar*
married; divorced *evli; boşanmış*
widowed *dul*
insurance *sigorta*
title *mülkiyet*
driver's license *ehliyet*

AT THE GAS STATION

gas station *benzin istasyonu*
gasoline *benzin*
unleaded *kurşunsuz*
Fill it up, please. *Depoyu doldur, lütfen.*
car tire *araba lastiği*
air. *hava*
water *su*
oil (change) *yağ değişimi*
grease *makine yağı*
My . . . doesn't work. . . . *çalışmaz.*
battery *akü*
radiator *radyatör*
alternator *alternatör*
generator *dinamo*
windshield *ön cam*
tow truck *çekici*
repair shop *tamirhane*

VERBS

As in any other language, Turkish revolves around verbs. There are two classes of verbs: those that end in -*mak* and others that end in -*mek*. When conjugating, these suffixes disappear to make way for the verb ending for the subject. Note that these endings convey a pronoun, so most Turks opt to do away with the pronoun altogether when speaking. For example, the verb *gelmek* (to come) in first-person singular in the present tense becomes *gelerim* (I come). If you learn to conjugate one verb from each group, you'll have learned Turkish conjugation. It seems daunting, but once you get the hang of it, it becomes fairly easy. Note: Turkish primarily uses the present continuous tense to speak about the now.

to eat *yemek*
I, you eat; he (she, it) eats *ben yerim, sen yersin, o yer*
we, you, they eat *biz yeriz, siz yersiniz; onlar yer*
to climb *tırmanmak*
I, you climb; he (she, it) climbs *ben tırmanarım, sen tırmanarsin, o tırmanar*
we, you, they climb *biz tırmanarız, siz tırmanarsınız, onlar tırmanar*
to do *yapmak*
I, you do; he (she, it) does *ben yapırım, sen yapırsın , o yapır*
we, you, they do *biz yapırız, siz yapırsınız, onlar yapır*
to be *olmak*
I, you are; he (she, it) is *ben olurum, sen olursun, o olur*
we, you, they are *biz oluruz, siz olursunuz, onlar olur*
to buy *satın almak*
I, you buy; he (she, it) buys *ben satın alırım, sen satın alırsın; o satın alır*
we, you, they buy *biz alırız, siz satın alırsınız, onlar satın alır*
To go *gitmek*
I, you go; he (she, it) goes *ben giderim, sen gidersin. o gider*
we, you, they go *biz gideriz, siz gidersiniz, onlar gider*
to walk *yürümek*
to love; to like *sevmek; beğenmek*
to work *calışmak*
to want *istemek*
to eat *yemek*
to swim *yüzmek*
to tour; to travel *dolaşmakgezmek*
to write *yazmak*
to repair *tamir etmek*
to stop *durmak*
to get off (the bus) *inmek*
to get on (the bus); to ride *binmek*

to stay *kalmak*
to drink *içmek*
to leave *ayrılmak*
to look at *bakmak*
to look for *aramak*
to have (own) *sahip olmak*
to give *vermek*
to carry *taşımak*
to come *gelmek*

NUMBERS

zero *sıfır*
1 *bir*
2 *iki*
3 *üç*
4 *dört*
5 *beş*
6 *altı*
7 *yedi*
8 *sekiz*
9 *dokuz*
10 *on*
11 *on bir*
12 *on iki*
13 *on üç*
14 *on dört*
15 *on beş*
16 *on altı*
17 *on yedi*
18 *on sekiz*
19 *on dokuz*
20 *yirmi*
30 *otuz*
40 *kırk*
50 *elli*
60 *altmış*
70 *yetmiş*
80 *seks2n*
90 *doksan*
100 *yüz*
101 *yüz bir*
200 *iki yüz*
500 *beş yüz*
1,000 *bin*
10,000 *on bin*
100,000 *yüz bin*

1,000,000 *bir milyon*
one-half *yarım*
one-third *üçte bir*
one-fourth *dörtte bir*

TIME

What time is it? *Saat kaç?*
It's one o'clock. *Saat bir.*
It's two in the afternoon. *Saat on dört.*
It's one P.M. *Saat one üç.*
five-thirty *saat beş buçuk*
a quarter till 10 *ona çeyrek var*
a quarter past three *üçü çeyrek geçiyor*
an hour *bir saat*

DAYS AND MONTHS

Monday *Pazartesi*
Tuesday *Salı*
Wednesday *Çarşamba*
Thursday *Perşembe*
Friday *Cuma*
Saturday *Cumartesi*
Sunday *Pazar*
today *bugün*
tomorrow *yarın*
yesterday *dün*
a week *bir hafata*
a day *bir gün*
a month *bir ay*
a year (time) *bir sene*
year (age) *bir yaş*
after *sonra*
before *önce*
January *Ocak*
February *Şubat*
March *Mart*
April *Nisan*
May *Mayıs*
June *Haziran*
July *Temmuz*
August *A ustos*
September *Eylul*
October *Ekim*
November *Kasım*
December *Aralık*

Suggested Reading

MODERN TURKEY

Gordon, Philip H. *Winning Turkey: How America, Europe, and Turkey Can Revive a Fading Partnership.* Washington, DC: Brookings Institution Press, 2008. In this short 115-page report, the former director for European Affairs at the National Security Council discusses Turkey's crucial geopolitical importance in the world and its increasing role as a regional economic leader. Gordon also explains that the problems within-surging anti-Americanism, lost hopes for European Union membership, civil-military friction, and PKK threats-have done much to damage an already erratic Turkish political machine. A blueprint to ease the frictions in this pivotal region is proposed. But what would the ultimately cost be if Turkey were to agree to the "grand bargains" Gordon advances to resolve its lingering issues with the Kurds, Armenians, and Greeks?

Kinzer, Stephen. *Crescent and Star: Turkey Between Two Worlds.* New York: Farrar, Straus and Giroux, 2002. Former İstanbul *New York Times* bureau chief and passionate observer of Turkey's path toward Westernization and economic transformation, Kinzer gives a concise introduction to the country: Atatürk's post-World War I foundation of a modern secular Turkish state and the peculiar constitution of contemporary society. He doesn't omit the military's behind-the-scenes role in enforcing Kemalist reforms, and he even expands on the problems plaguing Turkish society today: the rise of Islamic fundamentalism, clashes between the state and the large Kurdish minority, and the continuing lack of democratic freedoms. These insightful examinations are lightened with tongue-in-cheek personal accounts from his four-year stay in the country.

Mango, Andrew. *The Turks Today.* London: Overlook TP, 2006. The fifth of seven titles by this İstanbul-born, United Kingdom-based author, this book presents a concise and kind recap of Turkey's recent history. Mango recounts the decades after Atatürk's death in 1938: or the seeming calm before the storm that succeeded the foundation of the multiparty system, the conflicts with neighboring Greece, and the ensuing departure of İstanbul's Greek minority. The Kurds make a cameo appearance when Mango suggests that this minority's best chance for a peaceful future is to put down their arms and integrate within the state. All around, this information-packed book excels at conveying why this globally unique, Western-looking Muslim country—and its citizens, which Mango knows so well—are so different from its Mohammedan neighbors to the East and South.

Pope, Nicole, and Hugh Pope. *Turkey Unveiled.* London: Overlook TP, 2004. Longtime İstanbul residents, the Popes are a writer-journalist team whose infatuation with Turkey, its people, and its history comes alive on each page. It's at once a successful attempt at demystifying a conflicted country that continues to evade categorization and a historical recital of Turkey's arduous political twists-and-turns since the disintegration of the Ottoman Empire.

HISTORY

Faroqhi, Suraiya. *Subjects of the Sultan: Culture and Daily Life in the Ottoman Empire.* London: I. B. Tauris, 2005. When it comes to learning about the sheer decadence of the sultans and their mysterious harems, this book is indispensable. An Ottoman scholar by trade and an international lecturer, the German-born Faroqhi is a master of Ottoman culture and language. No other book describes the court's day-to-day living practices—even commonplace rituals such as bathing, shopping, loving, and grieving—and its evolution over the six centuries until the sultanate was finally exiled to Western Europe. She also recounts the importance of artisans and artists as well as their crafts, and gives a rare account of the lives of minorities under the Sultans.

Moorhead, Alan. *Gallipoli.* Sydney: Cornstalk, 1992. A movie starring Mel Gibson was adapted from this hard-to-find tome, in which Winston Churchill's catastrophic World War I campaign to gain Istanbul is recounted in sometime tear-jerking detail. Bravery, leadership (heroic and poor), and bad luck combine to rouse and unnerve. Thanks to this magnificent book and the film that ensued, millions worldwide have learned about the Gallipoli tragedy, which had been all but forgotten. Gallipoli today has become a massive national park that welcomes tens of thousands of visitors every April.

Lloyd, Seton. *Ancient Turkey: A Traveler's History.* Berkeley, CA: University of California Press, 1999. If you ever wanted to read up on ancient cultures and the architectural legacy they've left behind, this authoritative book is for you. Neither a textbook nor an archeological guide, this work attempts to bridge the past and the present through a look at the Turks and their ancestors, their land, and the surviving monuments that connect them. You'll meet the Hittites, read about Croesus's violent demise at the hands of Persian king Cyrus, and the conquests of Alexander the Great as Lloyd cross-references his narrative with the ancient sites.

Lord Kinross. *Ottoman Centuries: The Rise and Fall of a Nation.* New York: Harper Perennial, 1979. Kinross is a master writer when it comes to relating lengthy historical accounts into well-paced, succinct, and thought-provoking prose. In *Ottoman Centuries* he packs the more than 600 centuries of grand conquest and ultimate demise of the Ottomans into as many pages. This magnificent book has been considered the bible for Ottoman scholars for the last 30 years. Also greatly recommended is Kinross's *Atatürk: A Biography of Mustafa Kemal* (New York: William

Morrow, 1963), and *Atatürk: The Rebirth of a Nation* (London: Phoenix, 2003).

MEMOIRS AND TRAVELOGUES

Ashman, Anastasia M., and Jennifer Eaton Gökmen. *Tales from the Expat Harem: Foreign Women in Modern Turkey.* Berkeley: Seal Press, 2006. Eaton and Ashman, comrades in quills and Yankee expatriates, ingenuously assembled 30 personal memoirs of women from four different countries living in Turkey. Poignant stories reveal the internal, cultural, and religious intricacies of dealing with the locals in a new, delicious, and aggravating foreign land. Succeeding where so many others have failed, it gloriously, humorously, and sometimes heart-wrenchingly portrays a rich nation and its beautiful people.

Brosnahan, Tom. *Turkey—Bright Sun, Strong Tea: On the Road with a Travel Writer.* Concord, MA: Travel Info Exchange, 2005. Turkey expert Tom Brosnahan humorously relates his travails through the country from his first foray as a bushy-tailed U.S. Peace Corps volunteer and his first Turkish tea almost 50 years ago. He became a prolific travel writer and somewhat of a pseudo-star in his quasi-adopted homeland in the process, penning guidebooks galore, starring in a film, wining and dining in imperial palaces with Istanbul's glitterati, and even escaping wolves on the Iranian border.

Revolinski, Kevin. *The Yogurt Man Cometh: Tales of an American Teacher in Turkey.* Eden, SD: Citlembik/Nettleberry, 2006. Revolinski recounts his yearlong adventures in Turkey while working as a teacher in Ankara. A smidgen of travel, a teaspoon of memories, and a pound of humor all add up to a delectable tale of cultural hopscotch. Follow Revolinski as he learns a new language on the job and ruminates on the difficulties of straightening out Turkish children, while escaping on weekends to explore Turkey's magical backcountry.

Schneider, Dux. *Bolkar: Travels with a Donkey in the Taurus Mountains.* Bloomington, IN: Xlibris, 1978. Enrapt by the southeastern Anatolian range, Schneider took off and rode across the highlands of the Yörük and Tahtacı nomadic peoples, all the while amassing a diary replete with vivid details and amusing anecdotes. His book is a rare window into the daily lives of Turkey's nearly extinct nomadic cultures.

Settle, Mary Lee. *Turkish Reflections.* St. Petersburg, FL: Touchstone, 1992. Settle arrived in Turkey on a whim from the Greek island of Kos long before the country was even on the travel map. She fell in love and traveled the country. Fifteen years later she returned to find that Turkey's tourism industry had encroached on her memories of slumbering coastal villages. She defines the Turk as the ultimate friend whose colorful spirit emerges from an undeniable warmth and honesty. İstanbul, she says, is noisy and frantic, is also "as polite and friendly as a country village."

LITERATURE

Kemal, Yaşar. *Memed, My Hawk.* New York: NYRB Classics, 2005. An epic of grand scale, *Memed* is the story of any small town in Anatolia in the days of the omnipotent *aǧa* (landlord). Seeking a way out of a life of arduous work, young Memed escapes and becomes a bandit in the hope of freeing his people form the clutches of their master. In the process, he becomes as violent as he is kind and as ruthless as he is intrinsically good in his adventurous crusade that spans both history and politics.

Pamuk, Orhan. *Istanbul: Memories of a City.* New York: Knopf, 2005. This sweeping novel offers a glimpse into the soul of one of the world's greatest cities told by its most renowned writer. Recipient of the 2006 Nobel Prize for literature, Pamuk proves he is worthy of the accolade as he attempts to relate the tale of the city in which he lives and his own personal narrative through his fragmented memories. Of the dozen titles penned by Pamuk, these are also highly recommended: *The Black Book* (New York: Vintage, 2006), *My Name Is Red* (New York: Vintage, 2002), *The New Life* (New York: Vintage, 1998), and *Snow* (New York: Vintage, 2005).

Şafak, Elif. *The Bastard of Istanbul.* New York: Penguin, 2008. This is one of award-winning novelist and women's studies professor Elif Şafak's forays into fiction. This tome deals with issues of Turkish national identity and the Armenian "question" through a zany cast of female characters and a plot that extend into North America. For this, Şafak was indicted for "public denigration of Turkishness," charges that were later dropped, but it is brave attempts like this one that beg the question of the lack of democratic freedoms in Turkey. Also by this author: *The Forty Rules of Love: A Novel by Rumi* (New York: Viking, 2010), *The Flea Palace* (London: Marion Boyars, 2007), and *The Saint of Incipient Insanities* (New York: Farrar, Straus & Giroux, 2004).

Internet Resources

Ready, set, go: Get your fingers and your browser ready to collect as much info on Turkey as possible. Thanks to the Internet and the thousands (a conservative estimate) of sites on the country and its tourist goodies, you'll have more than enough resources to plan a most memorable trip. From hotel reviews and personalized maps to candid insight into what sites are really worth seeing, there's a virtual inundation of sometimes conflicting reports. Tastes and requirements are subjective, of course; the food some rave about, others wouldn't touch with a 10-foot pole. My advice is to take it all with a grain of salt and visit as many websites on a topic to find the most impartial information. Searching by hobby or personality type might find you some interesting trip ideas. A hiker planning to visit Turkey, for instance, could search for "hiking" and "Turkey" together, and one of the best hikes in the Mediterranean regions—Kate Clow's Lycian Way (www.lycianway.com)—pops right up. The site not only shows how to trek this 500-kilometer coastal trail but also gives you tons of lodging and eating options along the way. The same kind of search can be done by typing in "gay" and "Turkey," which would bring up a splendid Blue Cruise on the Mediterranean. Lastly, don't discount the written press. Turkey has received increasing coverage both in newspapers and travel magazines. Search article databases in the largest U.S. and British dailies online for the newest trip options in Turkey that have yet to appear in guidebooks. The sections of this book on each region also list travel-specific websites.

TRAVEL INFORMATION
Tourism Turkey
www.tourismturkey.org
This is the official website of the Turkey's Culture and Tourism Ministry. If you've been looking for the loot, this is it, with information on officialdom, region-specific activities, loads of destinations and museums, and

history. There's even a convenient trip planner that lets you peruse massive hotels, holiday resorts, and out-of-the-way B&Bs. Although may be a bit dull, the site is powered in English from New York and is easily navigable. They provide links for cities and provinces, but these may not all be in English.

Turkey Travel Planner
www.turkeytravelplanner.com
Operated by travel writer extraordinaire Tom Brosnahan, Turkey Travel Planner is filled with little-known tips and recommendations that include destination dos and don'ts as well as hotels, restaurants, books, and maps. He even links to a company that sells amazing gizmos that'll simultaneously translate your English phrase and speak its Turkish translation so that you won't have to bother learning the lingo. It's a must-visit site for first-time travelers.

Istanbul
http://english.istanbul.com
One of the oldest sites to cover Istanbul from a tourism perspective, Istanbul.com is jam-packed with lodging and dining options, tour operators and tour ideas, and even articles the city's shopping meccas. Plus their updated events calendar keeps locals and tourists alike abreast of what's going on in the city.

All About Turkey
www.allaboutturkey.com
Passionate Turkey and Europe tour guide Burak Sanal encapsulates 18 years of experience in his field to bring you an award-winning site on his country of origin. Packed with historical details about every civilization that has walked across Anatolia, their religions, and the various regions, the site is exhaustive.

MyMerhaba
www.mymerhaba.com
MyMerhaba is the online bible of tips for expatriates and includes a calendar, cultural articles,

restaurants, and "survival basics" that are a great tool for anyone coming to the city for a few days. MyMerhaba offers extensive links to other sites of interest.

TRIP PRACTICALITIES
U.S. State Department
www.state.gov
The U.S. State Department provides a list of statistics on the country, including economics and demographics. Travel warnings are also posted and updated often, and the legalities of travel, living, studying, and working in Turkey are also discussed.

Turkish Airports
www.tav.aero
Tepe Afken TAV Airports runs Turkey's largest airports—Istanbul, Izmir, and Ankara. Their website briefly discusses each airport and links to the airport websites, where you can find details about the airlines represented, maps of the terminals, and lists of facilities and services.

Index

List of Maps

www.moon.com

DESTINATIONS | ACTIVITIES | BLOGS | MAPS | BOOKS

MOON.COM is ready to help plan your next trip! Filled with fresh trip ideas and strategies, author interviews, informative travel blogs, a detailed map library, and descriptions of all the Moon guidebooks, Moon.com is all you need to get out and explore the world—or even places in your own backyard. While at Moon.com, sign up for our monthly e-newsletter for updates on new releases, travel tips, and expert advice from our on-the-go Moon authors. As always, when you travel with Moon, expect an experience that is uncommon and truly unique.

MOON IS ON FACEBOOK—BECOME A FAN!
JOIN THE MOON PHOTO GROUP ON FLICKR

MAP SYMBOLS

▨▨▨	Expressway	【	Highlight	✗	Airfield	⚲	Golf Course
⋯⋯	Primary Road	○	City/Town	✗	Airport	Ⓟ	Parking Area
⋯⋯	Secondary Road	◉	State Capital	▲	Mountain	◤	Archaeological Site
-------	Unpaved Road	❀	National Capital	✛	Unique Natural Feature	⚱	Church
- - - -	Trail	★	Point of Interest			
⋯⋯⋯	Ferry	•	Accommodation	⋈	Waterfall	⛽	Gas Station
▬▬▬	Railroad	▼	Restaurant/Bar	▲	Park	◌	Glacier
▨▨▨	Pedestrian Walkway	■	Other Location	❶	Trailhead	▨	Mangrove
▥▥▥	Stairs	Λ	Campground	⚡	Skiing Area	▨	Reef
						▨	Swamp

CONVERSION TABLES

°C = (°F - 32) / 1.8
°F = (°C x 1.8) + 32
1 inch = 2.54 centimeters (cm)
1 foot = 0.304 meters (m)
1 yard = 0.914 meters
1 mile = 1.6093 kilometers (km)
1 km = 0.6214 miles
1 fathom = 1.8288 m
1 chain = 20.1168 m
1 furlong = 201.168 m
1 acre = 0.4047 hectares
1 sq km = 100 hectares
1 sq mile = 2.59 square km
1 ounce = 28.35 grams
1 pound = 0.4536 kilograms
1 short ton = 0.90718 metric ton
1 short ton = 2,000 pounds
1 long ton = 1.016 metric tons
1 long ton = 2,240 pounds
1 metric ton = 1,000 kilograms
1 quart = 0.94635 liters
1 US gallon = 3.7854 liters
1 Imperial gallon = 4.5459 liters
1 nautical mile = 1.852 km

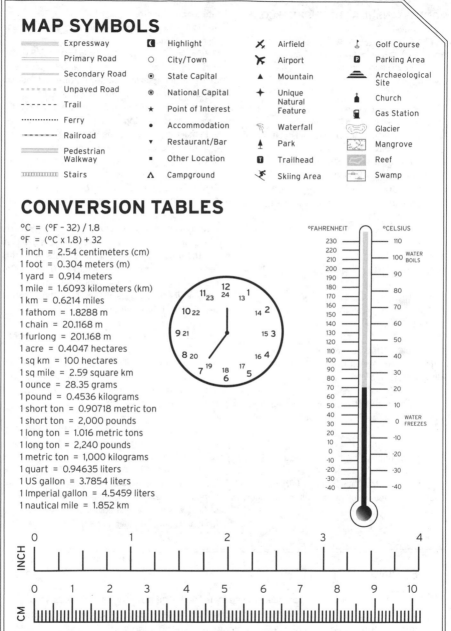

MOON ISTANBUL & THE TURKISH COAST

Avalon Travel
a member of the Perseus Books Group
1700 Fourth Street
Berkeley, CA 94710, USA
www.moon.com

Editor: Shaharazade Husain
Series Manager: Kathryn Ettinger
Copy Editors: Naomi Adler Dancis, Christopher Church
Graphics Coordinator: Tabitha Lahr
Production Coordinator: Tabitha Lahr
Cover Designer: Tabitha Lahr
Map Editor: Brice Ticen
Cartographers: Allison Rawley, Kat Bennett,
   Mike Morgenfeld
Indexer: Rachel Kuhn

ISBN: 978-1-59880-175-0
ISSN: 2155-157X

Printing History
1st Edition – October 2010
5 4 3 2 1

Text © 2010 by Jessica Tamtürk.
Maps © 2010 by Avalon Travel.
All rights reserved.

Front cover photo: Sulymaniye Mosque © Wilfried Krecichwost/Getty Images
Title page photo: Cappadocia's fairy chimneys, Courtesy of Republic of Turkey Culture and Tourism Ministry

Interior color photos:
© **Jessica Tamtürk:** page 6, Leander's Tower; page 12; page 14; page 21; page 22
© **Fuat Tamtürk:** page 7, Galata Tower; page 8 (icon), one of Hagia Sophia's Byzantine mosaics; page 19 **Courtesy of Republic of Turkey Culture and Tourism Ministry:** page 8 (bottom), ferryboat crossing the Bosphorus; page 9 (bottom right), Ascetic Muslim dervishes; page 9 (top left), the surreal travertines of Pamukkale; page 10; page 13; page 24
© **Tom Dempsey/Photoseek.com:** page 9 (bottom left), Library of Celsus; page 9 (top right), the traditional Spoon Dance;
© **Shaharazade Husain:** page 17
Printed in Canada by Friesens

KEEPING CURRENT

If you have a favorite gem you'd like to see included in the next edition, or see anything that needs updating, clarification, or correction, please drop us a line. Send your comments via email to feedback@moon.com, or use the address above.